Law in Action
Understanding Canadian Law

Annice Blair

William Costiniuk

Larry O'Malley

Alan Wasserman

Toronto

National Library of Canada Cataloguing in Publication Data

Blair, Annice, 1948–
    Law in action: understanding Canadian law
Includes index
ISBN 0-13-040592-2

1.   Law – Canada
KE444.L39 2003   349.71   C2002-901185-X

Copyright © 2003 Pearson Education Canada Inc., Toronto, Ontario

ALL RIGHTS RESERVED. This publication is protected by copyright, and permission should be obtained from the publisher prior to any prohibited reproduction, storage in a retrieval system, or transmission in any form or by any means, electronic, mechanical, photocopying, recording, or likewise. For information regarding permission, write to the Permissions Department.

ISBN 0-13-040592-2

Law in Action provides legal information of interest for students studying Canadian law. It is not intended to offer legal advice of any kind. Readers who have personal legal questions should consult a lawyer.

The publisher has taken every care to meet or exceed industry specifications for the manufacturing of textbooks. The spine and endpapers of this sewn book have been reinforced with special fabric for extra binding strength. The cover is a premium polymer-reinforced material designed to provide long life and withstand rugged use. Mylar gloss lamination has been applied for further durability.

Printed and bound in Canada
2 3 4 5 FR 06 05 04 03 02

Publisher: Mark Cobham
Product Manager: Anita Borovilos,
    Melanie Trevelyan
Managing Editor: Elynor Kagan
Project Manager: Geraldine Kikuta
Developmental Editors: Geraldine Kikuta,
    Mary Kirley, Christel Kleitsch,
    Edward O'Connor
Production Editors: Susan Ginsberg,
    Gail Copeland
Proofreader: Lynne Hussey
Editorial Consultant: Craig Jordheim
Production Co-ordinator: Zane Kaneps
Design and Page Layout: Monica Kompter/
    Silver Birch Graphics
Cover Image: VCG/Getty Images/FPG
    (blurry crowd), Heritage Canada
    (*Canadian Charter of Rights and
    Freedoms*), Photodisc/Getty Images
    (scale, handcuffs, wedding bands,
    and handshake)
Cover Design: Monica Kompter/
    Silver Birch Graphics
Illustrations: Anthony de Ridder/
    Silver Birch Graphics
Photo Research/Permissions: Oighrig
    Keogh, Paulee Kestin,
    Michaele Sinko, Karen Taylor

Contents

Table of Cases ix
Table of Statutes xiv
Preface xvii
Acknowledgements xix

Introduction: Studying the Law 1

Getting Started 1
Legal Research 2
Making Notes 2
Studying for Tests and Exams 2

Skills for Understanding Law 3
Learning About Statutes 3
Studying Cases 3

The Importance of Studying Law 6

UNIT 1 OUR LEGAL HERITAGE 7

Chapter 1: Law and Society 8

Law in Our Lives 9
Rules versus Laws 10
What Is Law? 11
The Need for Law 12
Law and Morality 14
Law and Justice 14

Historical Roots of Law 17
The *Code of Hammurabi* 17
Mosaic Law 19
Greek Law 21
Roman Law 21
France and the *Napoleonic Code* 23

Influences on Canadian Law 24
Early British Law 24
The Feudal System 26
Common Law 27
Legal Reforms 27
Aboriginal Law 28

Reflecting on Our Historical Roots 30
■ Looking Back 31

Chapter 2: Classifying Law 34

Sources of Law in Canada 35
Common Law 35
Statute Law 35
Constitutional Law 37

Categories of Law 38
International Law 38
Domestic Law 40
Substantive Law 41
Procedural Law 42
Public Law 43
Private Law 44
■ Looking Back 47

Chapter 3: Government and Statute Law 51

Canada's Constitution 52
British North America Act, 1867 53
A Federal System 53
Division of Powers 54

Patriating the Constitution 57
Problems with the *BNA Act* 57
Constitution Act, 1982 58
Constitutional Conflict 60

Government and Law Making 62
The Executive Branch 62
The Legislative Branch 63
The Judiciary 64
Enacting a Statute 64
The Role of Individuals and Interest Groups 66
■ Looking Back 70

Career Connections 74

UNIT 2 RIGHTS, FREEDOMS, AND RESPONSIBILITIES 75

Chapter 4: *Canadian Charter of Rights and Freedoms* 76

Recognizing Rights and Freedoms 77
Historical Documents 77
Evolution of Rights in Canada 78
Canadian Bill of Rights 79
Entrenching Rights and Freedoms 80

Jurisdiction, Enforcement, and Guarantee 83
Jurisdiction 83
Enforcement 83
Guarantee 84

The Fundamental Freedoms 86
Freedom of Conscience and Religion 86
Freedom of Thought and Expression 87
Freedom of Peaceful Assembly and Association 88

Democratic and Mobility Rights 90
Democratic Rights 91
Mobility Rights 92

Legal and Equality Rights 93
Legal Rights 93
Equality Rights 99

Language and General Rights 100
Language Rights 100
Aboriginal Rights 101
Multicultural Rights 102
Charting the Record 103
■ Looking Back 104

Issue Aboriginal and Treaty Rights 108

Chapter 5: Human Rights 110

Human Rights Legislation 112
Canadian Human Rights Act 112
Provincial Human Rights Codes 113

Administering Human Rights Legislation 115
Filing a Complaint 115
Dismissing a Complaint 117
Role of the Commission 117
Remedies 118

Grounds of Discrimination 120
Employment 120
Accommodation and Facilities 126
Meeting Special Needs 127
Goods and Services 128
■ Looking Back 130

Issue Anti-Terrorist Legislation 134

Career Connections 136

UNIT 3 CRIMINAL LAW 137

Chapter 6: The Nature of Crime 138

Defining Crime and Criminal Offences 139
Criminal Law 140
The *Criminal Code* 141
History of the *Criminal Code* 141
Provincial Jurisdiction 142

The Elements of a Crime 143
Actus Reus 143
Mens Rea 145

Involvement in a Crime 152
The Perpretrator 152
Aiding 152
Abetting 153
Counselling 153
Accessory After the Fact 153
Party to Common Intention 154
Incomplete Crimes 154
■ Looking Back 157

Chapter 7: The Criminal Court System 161

The Criminal Court Structure 162
The Provincial Court System 163
The Federal Court System 165

The Participants 168
The Judge 169
The Defence 169
The Prosecution 170

Other Court Personnel 170
The Witnesses 171
The Jury 171

The Role of the Jury 172
Qualifications 172
Jury Selection 172

The Criminal Trial Process 174
The Crown's Opening Statement 175
Examination of Witnesses 175
The Defence Responds 175
The Rules of Evidence 175
Types of Evidence 177
Voir Dire 179
Summary of the Case 180
Charge to the Jury 180
The Verdict 182
Appeals 182
■ **Looking Back 184**

Chapter 8: Investigation and Arrest 188

Levels of Police in Canada 189
Federal Police 189
Provincial Police 190
Municipal Police 191
Aboriginal Police 191

Starting a Police Investigation 193
Arriving at the Crime Scene 193
Protecting and Preserving the Crime Scene 193
Officers' Roles at a Crime Scene 194

Identifying and Collecting Physical Evidence 195
Tools 196
Impressions 196
Body Elements and DNA 198
Procedures for Labelling Evidence 200

Arrest and Detention 202
Questioning the Accused 202
Arrest and Detention Procedures 203
Searches 207
Procedures After Arrest 210

Pre-trial Release 212
Bail 212
Habeas Corpus 213
■ **Looking Back 214**

Issue National DNA Data Bank 218

Chapter 9: Criminal Offences 220

Levels of Offences 221
Summary Conviction Offences 221
Indictable Offences 221
Hybrid Offences 223

Offences Against the Person 224
Homicide 225
Assault 228
Sexual Assault 230
Suicide 233
Motor Vehicle Offences 233

Offences Against Property 235
Theft 235
Robbery 236
Breaking and Entering 236

Other *Criminal Code* Offences 238
Mischief 238
Fraud 238
Prostitution 239
Gambling 239

Drug Offences 241
Possession 241
Trafficking 243
Money Laundering 244
■ **Looking Back 246**

Chapter 10: Defences for the Accused 250

Mental States 251
Mental Disorder 251
Automatism 255
Intoxication 256

Justifications 258
Self-Defence 258
Battered Woman Syndrome 258

Defence of a Dwelling 259
Necessity 259
Compulstion or Duress 260
Provocaton 262
Aboriginal or Treaty Rights 263

Other Defences 265
Mistakes of Law and Fact 265
Double Jeopardy 266
Alibi 268
Entrapment 268
■ **Looking Back** 270

Chapter 11: Sentencing and the Correctional System 274

Goals of Sentencing 275
Protection of the Public 275
Retribution 276
Deterrence 276
Rehabilitation 276
Restitution 276
Denunciation 277

Sentencing Procedures 278
Perspectives to Consider 278
The Sentencing Hearing 279

Types of Traditional Sentences 281
Discharges 282
Probation 282
Suspended Sentence 283
Intermittent Sentence 283
Conditional Sentence 283
Electronic Monitoring 283
Restitution 284
Binding-Over, Deportation, and Fines 285
Suspension of Privileges 286
Plea Bargaining 287
Incarceration 287

Restorative Justice Programs 290
Victim-Offender Mediation 291
Family Group Conferencing 292
Victim-Offender Panels 293
Aboriginal Sentencing Circles 293

The Correctional System 294
The Provincial Correctionsl System 295
The Federal Correctional System 295

Paroles and Pardons 297
Parole Decisions 297
Conditional Release 298
Pardons 301
■ **Looking Back** 302

Chapter 12: Criminal Law and Young People 306

Youth and Crime 307
Legislative Reform and Young People 308
Young Offenders Act 309
Youth Criminal Justice Act 312
Incapacity of Children 313

Legal Rights of Young People 315
Searches 315
Rights Regarding Evidence 315
Publication of Identities 318

Youth Criminal Justice System 318
Community-based Measures 320
Youth Justice Court 321

Sentencing Options 322
Youth Sentences 323
Adult Sentences 325
Records 326
■ **Looking Back** 328

Issue The Problem of Bullying 332
Career Connections 334

UNIT 4 CIVIL LAW AND DISPUTE RESOLUTION 335

Chapter 13: Understanding Civil Procedures 336

Private Law Procedures 337
Parties Involved in Civil Actions 338
Civil Action 339
Class Action Lawsuits 344

Civil Courts 346
   Small Claims Courts 346
   Superior Courts of the Provinces and Territories 347
   Provincial and Territorial Courts of Appeal 347
   Supreme Court of Canada 348
   Federal Court of Canada 349

Civil Remedies 350
   General Damages 350
   Special Damages 353
   Punitive Damages 354
   Nominal Damages 354
   Specific Performance 354
   Injunctions 354
   Enforcing a Judgment 355
   Alternative Sources of Compensation 356

Alternative Dispute Resolution 358
   Negotiation 358
   Mediation 358
   Arbitration 359
   Advantages and Disadvantages of ADR 360
   ■ Looking Back 361

Chapter 14: Negligence and Unintentional Torts 365
Negligence 366
   Stage One: Duty of Care 367
   Stage Two: Standard of Care 369
   Stage Three: Causation 373
Special Types of Liability 375
   Product Liability 375
   Occupiers' Liability 376
   Hosts 377
   Vicarious Liability 378
   Automobile Negligence 379
   Strict Liability 380
Defences to Negligence 381
   Contributory Negligence 381
   Voluntary Assumption of Risk 381
   Other Defences 383
   Statute of Limitations 383
   ■ Looking Back 385

Chapter 15: Intentional Torts 389
Intentional Torts 390
   Intentional Torts and Criminal Acts 390
Intentional Interference with the Person 391
   Assault 392
   Battery 392
   Sexual Assault 393
   Medical Battery 394
   False Imprisonment 395
   Malicious Prosecution 395
   Nervous Shock and Mental Suffering 396
   Invasion of Privacy 397
Intentional Interference with Property 399
   Trespass to Land 399
   Nuisance 399
   Trespass to Chattels 400
Defences to Intentional Interference 401
   Defences to Interference with the Person 402
   Defences to Interference with Property 403
Defamation of Character 404
   Slander 405
   Libel 405
   Defences to Defamation 406
   ■ Looking Back 409

Chapter 16: Marriage: A Changing Tradition 413
Entering Marriage 414
   Essential Requirements for Marriage 414
   Formal Requirements for Marriage 419
Families Today 423
   Cohabitation 425
   Same-Sex Relationships 426
Ending a Marriage 428
   Divorce 428

Marriage Breakdown 429
■ **Looking Back** 433

Chapter 17: Family Matters 437

Issues in Ending a Marriage 438
Child Custody 438
Access 440
Child Support 443

Other Family Issues 445
Protection of Children 446
Adoption 447

Spousal Support 448
Self-Sufficiency 450
Enforcing Support Payments 450

Family Assets 452
Equal Division of Property 452
Unequal Division of Property 454
Division of Property on Reserve Lands 456
Division of Property in a Common-law Relationship 456
Division of Property on Death 456
■ **Looking Back** 458

Chapter 18: Forming a Contract 462

Classifying Contracts 463
Oral Contracts and Written Contracts 463
Implied Contracts and Express Contracts 464
Contracts Under Seal 465

Elements of a Contract 465
Offer 466
Acceptance 469
Consideration 471

Invalidating Factors 475
Incapacity to Contract 475
Illegality 477
Contrary to Public Policy 478
Mistake 478
Misrepresentation 480
Duress 482
Undue Influence 482
Unconscionability 483
■ **Looking Back** 484

Issue Electronic Copyright Protection 488

Chapter 19: Contract Remedies and Consumer Protection 490

Rights and Obligations 491
Privity of Contract 491
Assignment of Contracts 492

Discharging a Contract 494
Discharge by Performance 494
Discharge by Agreement 495
Discharge by Frustration 496
Discharge by Breach 497

The Sale of Goods 500
Title and Risk 501
Manufacturer's Warranties 503
Implied Conditions and Warranties 505
Remedies for Breach of Sale of Goods 506

Protection for Consumers 508
Federal Consumer Law 508
Provincial Consumer Law 509
Property Situated on a Reserve 510
■ **Looking Back** 512

Issue Protecting Personal Information 516
Career Connections 518

Canadian Charter of Rights and Freedoms 519

Glossary 524

Index 541

Credits 554

Table of Cases

ABBREVIATIONS FOR CITATION REFERENCES

Case-law Reporters

A.R.	Albert Reports
B.C.L.R.	British Columbia Law Reports
C.C.C.	Canadian Criminal Cases
Ch.D	Law Reports, Chancery Division (United Kingdom)
C.H.R.R.	Canadian Human Rights Reporter
D.L.R.	Dominion Law Reports
E.R.	English Reports (United Kingdom)
F.C.R.	Federal Court Reports
Man. R.	Manitoba Reports
N.B.R.	New Brunswick Reports
O.R.	Ontario Reports
S.C.R.	Supreme Court Reports
W.W.R.	Western Weekly Reports

Quicklaw Reporters

A.J.	Alberta Judgments
B.C.J.	British Columbia Judgments
O.J.	Ontario Judgements
P.E.I.J.	Prince Edward Island Judgments
S.J.	Saskatchewan Judgments

Courts

C.A.	Court of Appeal
C.J.	Court of Justice
F.C.A.	Federal Court, Appeal Division
F.C.T.D.	Federal Court, Trial Division
Gen. Div.	General Division
Q.B.	Court of Queen's Bench
S.C.	Supreme Court
S.C.A.D.	Supreme Court, Appellate Division
S.C.C.	Supreme Court of Canada
S.C.T.D.	Supreme Court, Trial Division
Sup. Ct.	Superior Court

CASE CITATIONS

Cases and Guided Cases developed in the text are identified with a "C" and a "GC." Page references for cases are shown in italic at the end of each citation.

C *Al-smadi (father and next friend of Emman Al-smadi),* [1994] M.J. No. 13, *417*

C *Anderson v. YMCA (of Barrie)* (2000), Board of Inquiry (O.H.R.C.), *129*

Andrews v. Grand & Toy Alberta Ltd., [1978] 2 S.C.R. 229, *352*

Andrews v. Law Society of British Columbia, [1989] 1 S.C.R. 143, *99–100*

C *Arsenault-Cameron v. Prince Edward Island,* [2000] 1 S.C.R. 3, *106*

GC *The Attorney General for Alberta v. The Attorney General of Canada,* [2001] 1 S.C.R. 783, *56*

C *Barrett Estate v. Dexter,* [2000] Alta. Q.B. 530, *415*

C *Boston v. Boston,* [2001] S.C.C., *451, 452*

C *Bracklow v. Bracklow,* [1999] 1 S.C.R. 420, *460*

C *British Columbia (P.S.E.R.C.) v. B.C.G.S.E.U.,* [1999] 3 S.C.R. 3, *121*

C *Brushett v. Cowan,* [1990] N.J. No. 145 (Nfld. C.A.), *411*

C *Button v. Jones* (2001), O.J. No. 1976 (Ont. Sup. Ct.), *338, 363*

Canada (A.G.) v. Lavell, [1974] S.C.R. 1349, *80*

C *Carlill v. Carbolic Smoke Ball Company,* [1893] 1 Q.B. 256 (C.A.), *467, 471*

Caron v. Caron, [1987] 1 S.C.R. 892, *450*

C *Cempel v. Harrison Hot Springs Hotel Ltd.,* [1998] 6 W.W.R. 233 (B.C.C.A.), *387*

GC *Central Alberta Dairy Pool* v. *Alberta Human Rights Commission,* [1990] 2 S.C.R. 489, *123*

C *Chartrand* v. *Vanderwell Contractors Limited* (2001), Alta. H.R.C., *124*

GC *Coast Hotels Ltd.* v. *Royal Doulton Canada Ltd.* (2000), B.C.S.C. C956773, *515*

C *Connolly* v. *Woolrich* (1867), 17 R.J.R.Q. (Q.S.C.) aff'd (1869), 17 R.J.R.Q. 266 (Q.Q.B.), *422*

GC *The Copy Cats* v. *Rosney and Rosney (B.D.) Corp.* (1989), 62 Man. R. (2d) 308 (Q.B.), *473*

GC *Crocker* v. *Sundance Northwest Resorts Ltd.,* [1988] 1 S.C.R. 1186, *382, 388*

Cunningham v. *Canada,* [1993] 2 S.C.R. 143, *94*

GC *Dale* v. *Government of Manitoba* (1997), 147 D.L.R. (4th) 605 (Man. C.A.), *487*

C *Debora* v. *Debora,* [1999] Ont. C.A. C23709, *421*

GC *Derrickson* v. *Derrickson,* [1986] 1 S.C.R. 285, *456, 457*

Desjarlais v. *Paipot Band No. 75* [1989] 3 F.C. 605 12 C.H.R.R. D/466 (C.A.) 29, *113*

C *Dickinson* v. *Dodds,* [1876] 2 Ch.D. 463 (C.A.), *468, 471*

GC *Dobson* v. *Dobson,* [1999] 2 S.C.R. 753, *372*

C *Donoghue* v. *Stevenson,* [1932] A.C. 562 (H.L.), *367, 368, 375*

C *Dream Weavers Wedding Consultants* v. *Astley* (2000), P.E.I. S.C.T.D. 32, on-line: CanLII, *486*

C *Dunne* v. *Gauthier* (2000), B.C.S.C. 1603, *397*

C *Empire Co.* v. *Sheppard,* [2001] N.F.C.A. 10, *387*

C *Epp* v. *Town Cobbler* (2000), P.E.I. S.C.T.D. 57, on-line: CanLII, *495*

C *Feiner* v. *Demkowicz,* [1974] 2 O.R. (2d) 121, *435*

C *Felton* v. *Felton,* [1999] B.C.S.C. F970476, *435*

Ford v. *Quebec (Attorney General),* [1988] 2 S.C.R. 712, *81*

C *Francis* v. *Baker,* [1999] 3 S.C.R. 250, *444*

C *F.S.M.* v. *Clarke,* [1999] B.C.J. No. 1973 (B.C.S.C.), *379*

C *Gandy* v. *Robinson* (1990), 108 N.B.R. (2d) 436 (Q.B.), *514*

Gerula v. *Flores* (1995), 126 D.L.R. (4th) 506, *394*

Gordon v. *Goertz,* [1996] 2 S.C.R. 27, *443*

C *Granum* v. *Northwest Territories,* [1992] N.W.T.R. 20 (Terr. Ct.), *500*

C *Groom* v. *MacFarlane* (2000), P.E.I. S.C.T.D. 61, on-line: CanLII, *493*

C *Harry* v. *Kreutziger* (1978), 9 B.C.L.R. 166 (B.C.C.A.), *486*

C *Herman* v. *Graves,* [1998] Alta. Q.B. 471, *403*

C *Iluschnat* v. *Kotyk* (2002), B.C.H.R.T., *132*

International Fund for Animal Welfare v. *The Queen,* [1989] 1 F.C. 335, 45 C.C.C. (3d) 457 (F.C.A.), *87*

Irwin Toy Ltd. v. *Quebec (Attorney General),* [1989] 1 S.C.R. 927, 87, *88*

C *Jeppesen* v. *Ancaster (Town of)* (2001), 39 C.H.R.R., *132*

C *Kadlak* v. *Nunavut (Minister of Sustainable Development)* (2001), Nu.C.J. 1, QL, *44*

C *Kanags Premakumar* v. *Air Canada* (2000), C.H.R.C., *119*

C *Kootenay Ice Hockey Club Ltd.* v. *Slovak Ice Hockey Association,* [2001] B.C.S.C. 51, *477*

Lambert v. *Lastoplex,* [1972] S.C.R. 569, *376*

C *Lavigne* v. *Ontario Public Service Employees Union,* [1991] 2 S.C.R. 211, *89*

C *Laws* v. *Wright,* [2000] A.B.Q.B. 49, *382*

Lovelace v. *Ontario,* [2000] 1 S.C.R. 950, *105*

    Luschnat v. Kotyk (2002), B.C.H.R.T., *132*

GC *M. v. H.,* [1999] 2 S.C.R., *426, 436*

C *MacLean v. Hafford Motors Ltd.* (2000), N.B.R. (2d), *481*

C *Malcolm v. Fleming,* [2000] B.C.J. No. 2400, *398*

    Malette v. Shulman (1990), 72 O.R. (2d) 417, *395*

    Manitoba Language Rights, Re, [1985] 1 S.C.R. 721, *101*

C *Mann v. Cobra Jeans,* [1996] N.B.R. 2d Uned. 3 (Q.B.), *507*

C *Mari v. Mari,* [2001] S.C.B.C., *455*

C *Marinangeli v. Marinangeli,* [1997] 54 O.R. (3d) 179, *454*

GC *Martin v. Mineral Springs Hospital* (2001), A.B.Q.B. 58, *364*

C *Mattern v. Spruce Bay Resort* (2000), Alta. H.R.C., *126*

GC *Mazuelos v. Clark* (2000), B.C.H.R.T. 1, *50*

C *McDonald's Restaurant of Canada Ltd. v. West Edmonton Mall Ltd.,* (1994), A.J. 634 (A.B.Q.B.), *355*

C *Miglin v. Miglin,* [2001] 53 O.R. (3d) 641, *460*

C *Miller v. Devenz* (2001), O.J. 4084 (Ont. Sup. Ct.), *353*

GC *Miller v. Jaguar Canada Inc.* (2000), Man. Q.B. 156, on-line: CanLII, *504*

    Milosevic (IT-99-37-I), *39*

C *Moge v. Moge,* [1992] 3 S.C.R. 813, *450, 451*

    Murdoch v. Murdoch, [1975] 13 R.F.L. 185 (S.C.C.), *453*

    Natural Parents v. Superintendent of Child Welfare, [1976] 2 S.C.R. 751, *448*

GC *Nelles v. Ontario,* [1989] 2 S.C.R. 170, *412*

    Noah Estate, Re (1961), 32 D.L.R. (2nd) 185 (N.W.T. Ct.), *421*

C *Oniel v. Marks* (2001), Ont. C.A. C30682, *396*

C *P. v. R.,* [2000] P.E.S.C.T.D. 22, *330*

    Pelech v. Pelech, [1987] 1 S.C.R. 801, *450*

C *Petersen (guardian ad litem) v. Surrey School District No. 36* (1991), 89 D.L.R. (4th) 517 (B.C.S.C.), *363*

GC *Pettkus v. Becker,* [1980] 19 R.F.L. (2d) 165 (S.C.C.), *424, 456*

C *Pink Panther Beauty Corp. v. United Artists Corp.* (1998), F.C.J. No. 441 (F.C.A.), *349*

C *Prevost v. Vetter,* [2001] B.C.S.C. 312, *378*

C *Purdy v. Purdy,* [2001] A.B.Q.B., *440*

C *R. v. Adey,* [2001] Nfld. P.C. 1300A-01158, *149*

C *R. v. Askov,* [1990] 2 S.C.R. 1199, *97*

C *R. v. Barrow* (2000), Ont. C.A. 305, *240*

C *R. v. Bates* (2000), Ont. C.A. C32619, on-line: CanLII, *280*

C *R. v. Bero* (2000), Ont. C.A. C30048, *216*

    R. v. Big M Drug Mart Ltd., [1985] 1 S.C.R. 295, *86, 102–103*

GC *R. v. Burke* (2001), 153 C.C.C. (3d) 97 (Ont. C.A.), *6, 42*

    R. v. Campbell, [1999] 1 S.C.R. 565, *244*

GC *R. v. Canhoto* (1999), Ont. C.A. C24949, *160*

C *R. v. Cardinal* (2001), Alta. P.C. 92, *260*

    R. v. Carker (No. 2), [1967] 2 C.C.C. 190, *262*

GC *R. v. Crown Zellerbach Canada Ltd.,* [1988] 1 S.C.R. 401, *73*

C *R. v. Cullen* (2000), P.E.S.C.A.D. 16, *237*

    R. v. Daviault, [1994] 3 S.C.R. 63, *256*

    R. v. Dersch, [1993] 3 S.C.R. 768, *105*

C *R. v. Dhillon* (2001), B.C.C.A. 555, *199*

    R. v. D.M.F. (1999), A.J. 1086 (C.A.), *315*

C *R. v. Dudley and Stevens* (1884), 14 Q.B.D. 273, *15*

C	R. v. *Elaschuk* (2000), Alta. P.C. 139, *272*	C	R. v. *Mafi* (2000), B.C.C.A. 135, *226*
GC	R. v. *Ewanchuk*, [1999] 1 S.C.R. 330, *232*		R. v. *Marshall*, [1999] 3 S.C.R. 456, *108*
GC	R. v. *Feeney*, [1997] 2 S.C.R. 13, *217*	C	R. v. *Matthiessen* (1999), Alta. C.A. 31, *245, 269*
C	R. v. *Foisy*, [2000] Que. Mun. Ct., *230*	C	R. v. *McCurrach* (2000), Alta. P.C. 127, *192*
C	R. v. *Ford*, [2000] Ont. C.A. C23709, *154*	GC	R. v. *McSorley*, [2000] B.C.P.C. 0116, *249*
C	R. v. *Germain* (2001), B.C.C.A. 463, *304*	C	R. v. *Menard* (1996), 29 O.R. (3d) 772 (Ont. C.A.), *177*
	R. v. *Glowatski*, [1999] B.C.J. No. 1278, *327*	C	R. v. *Miller* (2000), Alta. P.C. 122, *244*
C	R. v. *Godoy*, [1999] 1 S.C.R. 311, *216*		R. v. *Mills*, [1999] 3 S.C.R. 668, *84*
GC	R. v. *Golden*, [2001] S.C.C. 83, *208, 209*		R. v. *Milne*, [1987] 2 S.C.R. 512, *98*
C	R. v. *Hackett*, [2001] Nfld. P.C. File No. 1300A-1034, *159*	C	R. v. *Morales*, [1992] 3 S.C.R. 711, *213*
C	R. v. *Hébert*, [1989] 1 S.C.R. 233, *148*		R. v. *Morgentaler*, [1988] 1 S.C.R. 30, *94*
C	R. v. *Hibbert*, [1995] 2 S.C.R. 973, *272*		R. v. *Morrisey*, [2000] 1 S.C.R. 39, *105*
C	R. v. *Hovind*, [2000] (Sask. Q.B. QB00257), on-line: CanLII, 279, *285*	C	R. v. *Oakes*, [1986] 1 S.C.R. 103, *84, 85*
GC	R. v. *Hydro-Québec*, [1997] 3 S.C.R. 213, *72*	GC	R. v. *Oickle* (2000), 2 S.C.R. 3, *187*
C	R. v. *J. (J.T.)*, [1990] 2 S.C.R. 755, *317*	C	R. v. *Owens* (2001), B.C.C.A. 0465, *304*
C	R. v. *Johnson*, [2000] B.C.S.C. File 542, *253*	C	R. v. *P. (T.M.)*, [1996] B.C.C.A., *325*
GC	R. v. *Joseyounen* (1995), 6 W.W.R. 38 (Sask. Prov. Ct.), *305*	C	R. v. *Parker* (2000), Ont. C.A. 359, *95*
	R. v. *Keegstra*, [1990] 3 S.C.R. 697, *88*		R. v. *Parks*, [1992] 2 S.C.R. 871, *255*
GC	R. v. *Kerster*, [2001] B.C.S.C. CC000227, *151*	C	R. v. *Pelz*, [2001] Alta. Q.B. 790, *248*
C	R. v. *Koh* (1998), 131 C.C.C. (3d) 257 (Ont. C.A.), *186*	GC	R. v. *Pietrangelo* (2001), 152 C.C.C. (3d) 475 (Ont. C.A.), *173*
	R. v. *Ladouceur*, [1990] 1 S.C.R. 1257, *95–96*	C	R. v. *Polashek* (1999), Ont. C.A. 232, *207*
GC	R. v. *Latimer*, [2001] 1 S.C.R. 3, *289, 301*	GC	R. v. *Proulx* (1998), B.C.C.A. CA023334, *273*
	R. v. *Lavallee*, [1990] 1 S.C.R. 852, *258*	C	R. v. *Quinlan* (1999), 133 C.C.C. (3d) 501 (Nfld. C.A.), *224*
C	R. v. *Lee*, [1991] 3 O.R. (3d) 726 (Gen. Div.), *248*	C	R. v. *Robert*, [2000] Que. Mun. Ct., *230*
C	R. v. *Lemky*, [1996] 1 S.C.R. 757, *257*	C	R. v. *R.S.S.*, [1999] Alta. C.A. 80, *311*
	R. v. *Liew*, [1999] 3 S.C.R. 227, *202*	GC	R. v. *Ruzic*, [2001] 1 S.C.R. 687, *93, 260, 261, 262*
	R. v. *Lyons*, [1987] 2 S.C.R. 309, *98*	C	R. v. *S. (J.)*, [2001] Ont. C.A., *330*
GC	R. v. *M. (M.R.)*, [1998] 3 S.C.R. 393, *316*	C	R. v. *Sharpe*, [2001] 1 S.C.R. 45, *106*
C	R. v. *MacGillivray*, [1995] 1 S.C.R. 890, *144*		

R. v. Smith, [1987] 1 S.C.R. 1987, *97, 98*

R. v. Sparrow, [1990] 1 S.C.R. 1075, *263*

GC *R. v. Stillman,* [1997] 1 S.C.R. 607, *208, 331*

C *R. v. Stone,* [1999] 2 S.C.R. 290, *263*

C *R. v. Taylor* (2000), B.C.S.C. 734, *234*

C *R. v. Turner (S.A.)* (1995), N.B.R. (2d) (N.B.Q.B.), *229*

C *R. v. Tutton,* [1989] 1 S.C.R. 1392, *248*

C *R. v. Van der Peet,* [1996] 2 S.C.R. 507, *264*

C *R. v. Vang,* [1999] Ont. C.A. C29539, *159*

R. v. W. (J.P.) (1993), B.C.J. No. 2891 (YC), *315*

C *R. v. White* (1998), 131 C.C.C. (3d) 463 (Alta. C.A.), *171*

C *R. v. Williams* (1998), 40 O.R. (3d) 301 (Ont. C.A.), *186*

R. v. Zundel, [1992] 2 S.C.R. 731, *88*

Racine v. Woods, [1983] 2 S.C.R. 173, *448*

C *Regina v. Gilling* (1997), 34 O.R. (3d) 392 (Ont. C.A.), *180*

Richardson v. Richardson, [1987] 1 S.C.R. 857, *450*

GC *RJR-MacDonald Inc. v. Canada (A.G.),* [1994] 1 S.C.R. 311, *107*

Robichaud v. Canada (Treasury Board), [1987] 2 S.C.R. 84, *124*

Rodriguez v. British Columbia (A.G.), [1993] 3 S.C.R. 519, 94, *338*

GC *Roncarelli v. Duplessis,* [1959] S.C.R. 121, *13*

GC *Ross v. Beutel,* [2001] N.B.C.A. 62, *407*

C *Runcer v. Gould,* [2000] Alta. Q.B. 25, *411*

C *Saxton v. Aloha Pools Ltd.* (1998), B.C.S.C. A970668, *510*

Smith v. Leech Brain & Co. Ltd., [1962] 2 QB 405, *375*

C *Smith v. McGillivary,* [2001] N.S.S.C. 17, *384*

GC *Spain v. Canada* (1998), Fisheries Jurisdiction (I.C.J.), on-line www.icj-cij.org, *49*

C *Spurr v. Brown,* [1990] N.S.J. No. 441, *431*

Steele v. Mountain Institution, [1990] 2 S.C.R. 1385, *98*

C *Stevenson v. Stevenson,* [1997] B.C.J. No. 1154, *418*

Teno v. Arnold, [1978] 2 S.C.R. 287, *352*

Thibaudeau v. Canada, [1995] 2 S.C.R. 627, *444*

C *Thibault v. Fewer,* [2001] M.B.Q.B. 231, *370*

Thorton v. Board of School Trustees of School District No. 57 (Prince George), [1978] 2 S.C.R. 267, *352*

GC *Toronto Mayor's Committee on Community and Race Relations v. Ernst Zundel* (2002), C.H.R.T., *133*

C *Trizec Equity v. Gallant* (January 1994), W.C.B. Tribunal, *363*

C *Tsaoussis (guardian ad litem) v. Baetz* (1998), Ont. C.A. C27319, *339*

Tweddle v. Atkinson (1861) 121 E.R. 762, *491–492*

C *United States v. Burns,* [2001] 1 S.C.R. 283, *41*

GC *Van de Perre v. Edwards* (2001), S.C.C. 60, *461*

C *Vargek v. Okun* (1997), Man. C.A. AI96-30-02745, on-line: CanLII, *514*

Wilkinson v. Downton, [1897] 2 Q.B. 57, *396–397*

Table of Statutes

ABBREVIATIONS FOR STATUTE CITATIONS

C.C.S.M.   Continuing Consolidation of Statutes of Manitoba
R.S.A.   Revised Statutes of Alberta
R.S.B.C.   Revised Statutes of British Columbia
R.S.C.   Revised Statutes of Canada
R.S.N.   Revised Statutes of Newfoundland
R.S.N.B.   Revised Statutes of New Brunswick
R.S.N.S.   Revised Statutes of Nova Scotia
R.S.O.   Revised Statutes of Ontario
R.S.P.E.I.   Revised Statutes of Prince Edward Island
R.S.Q.   Revised Statutes of Quebec
R.S.S.   Revised Statutes of Saskatchewan
S.O.R.   Statutory Orders and Regulations

STATUTE CITATIONS

British Columbia Fishery (General) Regulations, S.O.R./84-248, *264*

Canada Elections Act, R.S.C. 1985, c. E-2, s. 51(e), *91*

Canadian Bill of Rights, S.C. 1960, c. 44, *75, 77, 79, 80, 85*

Canadian Environmental Protection Act, R.S.C. 1985, c. 16 (4th Supp.) s. 3, *72*

Canadian Human Rights Act, R.S.C. 1985, c. H-6, *112*

Canadian Human Rights Act, R.S.C. 1985, c. H-6 s. 13(1), *113, 133*

Canadian Human Rights Act, R.S.C. 1985, c. H-6 s. 67, *113*

Coastal Fisheries Protection Act, R.S.C. 1985, c. C-33, *49, 159*

Colleges Collective Bargaining Act, R.S.O. 1980, c. 74, s. 53, *89*

Competition Act, R.S.C. 1985, c. C-34, *508–509*

Consumer Product Warranty and Liability Act, S.N.B. 1978, c. C-18.1, *514*

Consumer Product Warranty and Liability Act, S.N.B. 1978, c. C-18.1 s. 12(1), *507*

Consumer Protection Act, C.C.S.M. 1987, c. C200, *514*

Consumer Protection Act, R.S.B.C. 1996, C. 69, *510*

Consumer Protection Act, R.S.Q. c. P-40-1 ss. 248, 249, *87*

Controlled Drugs and Substances Act, S.C., 1996, c. 19, *189, 221, 241, 242, 243*

Controlled Drugs and Substances Act, S.C., 1996, c. 19 ss.9, 9(3), *245*

Controlled Drugs and Substances Act, S.C., 1996, c. 19 s.11(8), *245*

Copyright Act, R.S.C., 1985, c. C-42, *488, 489*

Criminal Code of Canada, R.S.C. 1985, c. C-46 s. 2, *259*

Criminal Code of Canada, R.S.C. 1985, c. C-46 s. 9(3), *245*

Criminal Code of Canada, R.S.C. 1985, c. C-46 s. 11(8), *245*

Criminal Code of Canada, R.S.C. 1985, c. C-46 s. 16, *251, 272*

Criminal Code of Canada, R.S.C. 1985, c. C-46 s. 17, *260, 261, 262*

Criminal Code of Canada, R.S.C. 1985, c. C-46 s. 19, *265*

Criminal Code of Canada, R.S.C. 1985, c. C-46 s. 21(2), *159*

Criminal Code of Canada, R.S.C. 1985, c. C-46 s. 34(1) (2), *258, 273*

Criminal Code of Canada, R.S.C. 1985, c. C-46 s. 40, *259*

Criminal Code of Canada, R.S.C. 1985, c. C-46 s. 41, *259, 260*

Criminal Code of Canada, R.S.C. 1985, c. C-46 s. 140(2), *223*

Criminal Code of Canada, R.S.C. 1985, c. C-46 s. 163.1(3), *106*

Criminal Code of Canada, R.S.C. 1985, c. C-46 s. 163.1(4), *88, 106*

Criminal Code of Canada, R.S.C. 1985, c. C-46 s. 210, *239*

Criminal Code of Canada, R.S.C. 1985, c. C-46 s. 213(1), *239*

Criminal Code of Canada, R.S.C. 1985, c. C-46 s. 215(1), *145*

Criminal Code of Canada, R.S.C. 1985, c. C-46 s. 219(1), *148, 160*

Criminal Code of Canada, R.S.C. 1985, c. C-46 s. 222(1), *225*

Criminal Code of Canada, R.S.C. 1985, c. C-46 s. 231(1), *226*

Criminal Code of Canada, R.S.C. 1985, c. C-46 s. 231(7), *226*

Criminal Code of Canada, R.S.C. 1985, c. C-46 s. 232(1), *228*

Criminal Code of Canada, R.S.C. 1985, c. C-46 s. 234, *227*

Criminal Code of Canada, R.S.C. 1985, c. C-46 s. 241, *94, 233*

Criminal Code of Canada, R.S.C. 1985, c. C-46 s. 249(4), *144*

Criminal Code of Canada, R.S.C. 1985, c. C-46 s. 252(2), *233*

Criminal Code of Canada, R.S.C. 1985, c. C-46 s. 253, *234*

Criminal Code of Canada, R.S.C. 1985, c. C-46 s. 254, *234*

Criminal Code of Canada, R.S.C. 1985, c. C-46 s. 255(1), *234*

Criminal Code of Canada, R.S.C. 1985, c. C-46 s. 265(1), *132, 145, 231*

Criminal Code of Canada, R.S.C. 1985, c. C-46 s. 271(1), *231*

Criminal Code of Canada, R.S.C. 1985, c. C-46 s. 322(1), *235*

Criminal Code of Canada, R.S.C. 1985, c. C-46 s. 343, *145, 237*

Criminal Code of Canada, R.S.C. 1985, c. C-46 s. 354(1), *149*

Criminal Code of Canada, R.S.C. 1985, c. C-46 s. 368(1), *147*

Criminal Code of Canada, R.S.C. 1985, c. C-46 s. 430, *238*

Criminal Code of Canada, R.S.C. 1985, c. C-46 s. 462(31), *245*

Criminal Code of Canada, R.S.C. 1985, c. C-46 s. 469, *165, 166, 222*

Criminal Code of Canada, R.S.C. 1985, c. C-46 s. 494, *206*

Criminal Code of Canada, R.S.C. 1985, c. C-46 s. 495, *205, 315*

Criminal Code of Canada, R.S.C. 1985, c. C-46 s. 529(3), *210*

Criminal Code of Canada, R.S.C. 1985, c. C-46 s. 553, *164, 166, 222*

Criminal Code of Canada, R.S.C. 1985, c. C-46 s. 554, *164, 165, 166, 222*

Criminal Code of Canada, R.S.C. 1985, c. C-46 s. 632, *173*

Criminal Code of Canada, R.S.C. 1985, c. C-46 s. 717, *290*

Criminal Code of Canada, R.S.C. 1985, c. C-46 s. 718, *275*

Criminal Code of Canada, R.S.C. 1985, c. C-46 s. 722, *278*

Criminal Code of Canada, R.S.C. 1985, c. C-46 s. 745, *288*

Criminal Code of Canada, R.S.C. 1985, c. C-46 s. 753, *288*

Divorce Act, R.S.C. 1970, c. D-8, *429*

Divorce Act, R.S.C. 1985, c. 3 (2nd Supp.) *429, 438*

DNA Identification Act, S.C. 1998, c. 37, *218*

Family Law Act, R.S.O. 1990, c. F.3, *426, 436*

Family Relations Act, R.S.B.C. 1996, c. 128, *426, 457*

Fatal Accidents Act, R.S.A. 1994, c. F-5, *364*

Firearms Act, S.C. 1995, C. 39, *56*

Highway Traffic Act, R.S.O. 1990, c. H.8, *286*

Highway Traffic Act, R.S.O. 1990, c. H.8 s. 206(1), *383*

Human Rights Code, R.S.B.C. 1996, s.13, *50*

Human Rights Code, R.S.O. 1990, c. H.19, *114, 127, 132*

Human Rights Code, R.S.O. 1990, c. H.19 s. 19(2), *113*

Human Rights Code, R.S.O. 1990, c. H.19 s. 34(1), *117*

Income Tax Act, R.S.C. 1970-71-72, c. 63 s. 56(1)(b), *444*

Indian Act, R.S.C. 1985, c. I-5, *37, 113*

Indian Act, R.S.C. 1985, c. I-5 s.20, *457*

Indian Act, R.S.C. 1985, c. I-5 s. 89(1), *510*

Indian Act, R.S.C. 1985, c. I-5 s. 89(2), *511*

Lord's Day Act, R.S.C. 1970, c. L-13 s. 4, *86*

Marriage Act, R.S.O. 1990, c. M.3, *421*

Marriage Act, R.S.S. 1995, c. M-4.1 s. 31, *421*

Marriage (Prohibited Degrees) Act, R.S.C. 1990, c. 46 s. 2(2), *416–417*

Narcotic Control Act, R.S.C. 1985, c. N-1, *95*

Narcotic Control Act, R.S.C. 1970, c. N-1 s. 5(2), *98*

Narcotic Control Act, R.S.C. 1970, c. N-1 s. 8, *85*

Ocean Dumping Control Act, S.C. 1974-75-76, c. 55, s. 4(1), *73*

Official Languages Act, R.S.C. 1985, c. 31 (4th Supp.), *101*

Parental Responsibility Act, 2000, S.O. 2000, c. 4, *371*

Parental Responsibility Act, C.C.S.M. 1996, c. P8, *371*

Personal Information Protection and Electronic Documents Act, S.O. 2000, c. 5, *517*

Police Services Act, R.S.O. 1990, c. P.15, *190*

Privacy Act, R.S.B.C. 1996, c. 373, *398, 516*

Safe Street Act, S.O. 1990, c. 8, *205*

Sale of Goods Act, R.S.B.C., 1996, c. 410 s. 17, *515*

Sexual Sterilization Act, S.A. 1928, c. 37, *82*

Tobacco Act, S.C. 1997, c. 13, s.15, *36, 37, 41*

Tobacco Act; Tobacco Products Control Act, S.O.R./89-21, s. 11(1), *107*

Trademarks Act, R.S.C. 1985, c. T-13 s. 6(5), *349*

Young Offenders Act, R.S.C. 1985, c. Y-1, *314*

Youth Criminal Justice Act, S.C. 2002, c. 1, *314*

Youth Criminal Justice Act, S.C. 2002, c. 1 s. 38, *322*

Youth Criminal Justice Act, S.C. 2002, c. 1 s. 38(2), *332*

Youth Criminal Justice Act, S.C. 2002, c. 1 s. 110, *318*

Youth Criminal Justice Act, S.C. 2002, c. 1 s. 146(2), *317, 318*

Preface

Law in Action: Understanding Canadian Law is an exciting new text that offers teachers and students a refreshing introduction to Canadian law. The features of the text are designed to capture interest and to provide information in a clear and comprehensive way.

Each chapter begins with an engaging opener that generates discussion about the topic. Because legal terminology and concepts are sometimes difficult to grasp, they are supported in a variety of ways. Examples from real-life situations have been integrated throughout the text to explain and illustrate applications of the law.

Throughout the text, cases are as up to date as possible. Each case is accompanied by questions, crafted to bring out important points of law for analysis. Landmark cases that established precedent are included where appropriate. Guided cases are introduced with headings to direct the reader through various aspects of the case. Case guidelines include background information about the case, the legal question to be addressed by the courts, the decision, and the significance of that decision for Canadian society.

A feature called Law in Action also helps to illustrate legal concepts. This feature presents legal situations that may never have gone to court but are relevant to the point of law under discussion. Sometimes a Law in Action describes events subsequent to the court decision. Newspaper articles are included as well, demonstrating how points of law relate to daily life.

The Law in the Extreme feature highlights extraordinary and fascinating events in Canadian law. Topics from the *Sexual Sterilization Act* to "Club Fed" prisons are explored with accompanying questions for analysis.

A wide selection of margin notes offers information that introduces interesting facts about the law, relates law to everyday life, and provides opportunities for considering different aspects of controversial questions. Vocabulary terms are also reinforced with clear, concise definitions.

The text is generously enhanced with an assortment of visual material. Cartoons and photographs liven the presentation, and captions communicate concepts with text-related questions. Diagrams, tables, graphs, and timelines clarify information in the text and add variety. Charts are used for comparison, such as distinguishing different types of criminal offences. Flow charts illustrate complex procedures, such as the process for lodging a human rights complaint.

"Lots of excellent, in-body-of-text case examples; really helps to clarify."
— Nanette Levine, reviewer

"Good, recent case illustrations from across the country—nice to see!"
— Carmen Samuda-Lehman, legal consultant

"The evolving figure on Categories of Law is a good idea and works well."
— Dean Castellan, reviewer

Issues covered in the text have been selected for their interest and relevance to student life. Bullying, personal identity theft, and electronic copyright infringement are just three of the topics presented for analysis and discussion.

The Careers feature at the end of each unit provides opportunities to investigate career options with a legal connection, focusing on factors such as education, experience, and skill requirements.

All good things must come to an end, and each chapter concludes with skill development activities that challenge students to check their comprehension of the material, to extend their knowledge through investigation, to communicate their findings in creative ways, and to apply their learning in a culminating activity. A section of cases ends each chapter.

We welcome you to *Law in Action: Understanding Canadian Law*. We invite you to explore its pages, and we welcome any comments you might have regarding its content and presentation. We hope you enjoy the book.

Annice Blair   Larry O'Malley

William Costiniuk   Alan Wasserman

"Communication skills and skills associated with analysis, synthesis, and application are well addressed."
— Ernie Armitage, reviewer

Acknowledgements

Law in Action was a team effort, and the contributions of a number of people deserve to be recognized. The authors and publisher would like to thank the advisers and focus group participants who offered their input at the textbook's initial stages of development and design. Throughout the writing and revision stages, the reviewers and consultants identified below played an instrumental part in shaping the material. We thank them for this contribution. We would also like to thank the students in Ms. Levine's classes for their critical comments, which helped make the text student friendly.

A special thank you to Carmen Samuda-Leman and Mary Jean Rolando for their attention to legal accuracy and Aboriginal concerns. Our thanks to Professor Nicholas Bala of Queen's University for his assistance in interpreting the *Youth Criminal Justice Act* and to Wally Swarchuk, who reviewed and supplemented the questions and activities in the text.

The authors are grateful to the staff at Pearson Education Canada for their support throughout the development of this project. We would particularly like to thank Elynor Kagan for her excellent co-ordination of the project; Geraldine Kikuta for her contributions and commitment to the quality of this text; and Mary Kirley, Ed O'Connor, Christel Kleitsch, Susan Ginsberg, and Lynne Hussey for their insightful and valuable input.

Aboriginal Consultant
Mary Jean Rolando, B.A., LL.B.

Legal Consultants
Nicholas Bala, B.A., LL.B., LL.M.
Kimberly L. Doucett, B.A., LL.B
Feehely, Gastaldi & Hayes
Craig Jordheim, B.A. LL.B.
Nicholas Manning, B.A., B.Ed., LL.B
Mary Jean Rolando, B.A., LL.B.
Carmen Samuda-Lehman, PDP, B.A., LL.B.

Reviewers

George Adams
Dufferin Peel Roman Catholic Separate School Board
President, Canadian Council for History, Social Studies, and Social Sciences

Ernie Armitage
School District 8 Kootenay Lake

James A. Black
Keewatin-Patricia District School Board

Dean Castellan
Halton Catholic District School Board

Bliss Dodd
School District 68 Nanaimo-Lady Smith

Leslie Kruk
Hastings Prince Edward District School Board

Nanette Levine
Toronto District School Board

Jane Ohlke
Halton District School Board

Carmen Samuda-Lehman
School District 23 Coquitlam

Wally Swarchuk
School District 23 Central Okanagan

Anthony Viola
Hamilton-Wentworth District School Board

Douglas Young
Simcoe County School Board

Introduction: Studying the Law

Perhaps you already know a lot about the law. After all, law and legal issues are everywhere. Television programs show every aspect of law, from divorce courts to criminal investigation. Movies about trials and law enforcement are often based on real-life situations. Libraries and stores have shelves full of murder mysteries, detective novels, and books that offer advice on law-related issues. Your daily newspaper and broadcasts on radio and television frequently report on events that involve the law. So, if law is part of your life, why do you need to *study* it?

Studying law will increase your ability to evaluate all of the legal information that surrounds you. Although many legal terms may sound familiar, now you will learn what these terms actually mean. Moreover, you will be able to recognize unfamiliar terms and know when a reported account is accurate or biased. The more you study the law, the more likely you are to make good decisions in your life.

Like many other specialized subjects, law has its own terminology, skills, and strategies. As you work your way through *Law in Action*, you will have the opportunity to increase your legal vocabulary and to build on your analytical skills. In addition to providing you with the basic information you need to know in Canadian law, you will learn how to read case citations; analyze cases; and explain, discuss, and interpret legal issues.

GETTING STARTED

How can *Law in Action* help you excel? First, you must read the text, which may seem obvious. But frequently students fail to answer questions properly because they have a superficial knowledge of the topic. Reading *Law in Action* will help you understand the content thoroughly.

In your law class, you will be introduced to many new concepts and unfamiliar terms. Because listening to unfamiliar material can be difficult, you may hesitate to participate fully in class. Take the time to read assigned sections. Don't just scan the material. Read it; then think about it. Explore the information in the three margin features—Fast Fact, Consider This, and

> **Consider This**
> Which type of activity do you prefer: sharing ideas with a partner, working in small groups, or participating in a class discussion?

Law in Your Life—and plan the arguments you might use if you are called on to interact with your classmates. The better prepared you are before a topic is discussed in class, the more confident you will be in expressing your opinion.

Legal Research

Legal Link
The Web site at **www.pearsoned.ca/law** provides useful links to help you with your legal research. Throughout the text, you will be invited to visit this site. But don't stop there. If a topic interests you, explore the legal links for more information.

Throughout the course, you will be required to prepare essays and presentations. *Law in Action* should be your first reference tool for these assignments. It will provide the basic information you will need to get started. In addition, the Legal Link feature throughout the text will direct you to useful Internet sites for more in-depth research. Although the text is your first source of information, it should not be your last. Your legal research will include a variety of sources, such as interviews, magazines articles, newspaper reports, television documentaries, and other books.

Making Notes

As you read *Law in Action,* make your own notes and pay attention to unfamiliar terminology or to concepts that are not yet clear to you. Important **legal terms** are defined for you in the margins of the text. If you can't remember the meaning of a legal term you studied earlier, you can also refer to the glossary at the back of the book.

legal terms: boldfaced terms that appear in the text and are defined in the margin

Get the most out of the text by familiarizing yourself with the headings and subheadings. This will make it easier for you to find information when you need it. Use the index and glossary to help you locate words and concepts quickly. Similarly, the Table of Cases and Table of Statutes are convenient references for locating information in those areas.

Studying for Tests and Exams

Law in Action is a valuable tool when studying for tests and exams. Reread the sections you will be tested on, concentrating on topics that give you difficulty. To check your comprehension of the material, review the questions in the Building Your Understanding sections. To help you prepare in depth,

consider the quiz, questions, activities, and cases in the Looking Back section of each chapter.

Law in Action also has a Companion Website you can visit to review for tests and exams. There you will find assigned questions for each unit of the text, questions you can use to test yourself either at home on your computer or in your classroom.

SKILLS FOR UNDERSTANDING LAW

Keep in mind that the law does not always provide absolute answers. Straightforward questions such as, "What is the penalty for first-degree murder?" may be answered easily and precisely, but complex legal problems are often open to interpretation of the law. Listening to the summation in a trial, you might find yourself agreeing with one side, only to change your opinion when you hear the summation of the other side. In order to make an informed decision, it is important to know what the law actually says.

Learning About Statutes

As you work through *Law in Action,* you will encounter excerpts from a number of statutes and references to many others. A statute is a law passed by either a provincial Legislature or Parliament. Knowing what a statute means will help you understand why a person was charged with a certain crime or why a particular decision was rendered. When you encounter a statute reference, you will find it helpful to look it up. To do this, it is important to understand the elements of a statute citation.

Reading a Statute Citation

Statutes are revised periodically and bound into volumes. The titles of the volumes are often referred to in abbreviated form. For example, "Revised Statutes" is abbreviated as "R.S." followed by an initial for the province or a "C" for Canada. For example, Revised Statutes of Ontario would be R.S.O., and Revised Statutes of Canada would be R.S.C. Statutes are divided into chapters and sections. When reference is made to a chapter and a section, you will notice a "c." and an "s." followed by the chapter and section designations. The subsection in parenthesis follows the section number.

> Example: *Criminal Code of Canada,* R.S.C. 1985, c. C-46 s. 219(1)

This citation refers to the *Criminal Code,* a Revised Statute of Canada (revised in 1985), chapter C-46, section 219, subsection (1). If you research this example, you will discover that it defines the offence known as criminal negligence. You will learn more about this offence in Chapter 9.

Studying Cases

It may be possible to learn how to drive a car by simply studying a manual, but to truly understand what it means to "press the accelerator" or "yield to oncoming traffic," you need to drive the car on the road. The same applies

Fast Fact
You can find out where a particular statute is discussed in *Law in Action* by referring to the Table of Statutes on page xiv.

Consider This
Explain the particulars of this statute citation: *Pay Equity Act*, R.S.O. 1990, c. P-7

Law in Your Life
A spectator visit to a Canadian courtroom will give you an opportunity to see law in action.

to the study of law. Learning all the rules, statutes, regulations, and precedents is not a substitute for understanding how the rules and regulations apply to people involved in complex legal problems. To help you appreciate the practical aspects, *Law in Action* provides you with examples and cases; by studying actual cases, you will have a better grasp of how the law really works.

Lawyers often study cases to extract important information in order to apply relevant elements to new situations. Many cases in legal reports are extremely long. In *Law in Action,* the cases have been "briefed"; that is, the key components of the case have been summarized to make the cases easier for you to read and understand. Some of these cases have been presented in more detail with these signposts to guide you: Background, Legal Question, Decision, Significance, and Analysis. Studying cases will enhance your legal reasoning and analytical skills.

Reading a Case Citation

citation: the reference heading of a legal case

Cases appearing in national, regional, and provincial reports have a heading or **citation** so that people who are interested in reading the details of a particular case can find the case easily. For this reason it is important to understand the elements of a case citation.

Name of the Case The name of the case identifies the parties involved. The surnames of the parties are always italicized, separated with a "v." in roman type (an abbreviation for "versus"). If the case is a form of public law initiated by the government, or the "Crown," an "R." for Rex (King) or Regina (Queen) will appear as one of the names in the case. In some cases, where a name normally appears, only initials are cited. This usually means that a young person is involved; the law does not permit young offenders to be identified by name. Initials may also protect the names of adult parties.

Fast Fact
You can quickly locate a particular case, such as *R.* v. *Burke* (2001), by checking the Table of Cases on page ix.

Criminal example: ***R.* v. *Burke*** (2001), 153 C.C.C. (3d) 97 (Ont. C.A.)

Civil example: ***Cempel* v. *Harrison Hot Springs Hotel Ltd.,*** [1998] 6 W.W.R. 233 (B.C.C.A.)

Year of the Decision The year of the decision is placed in parenthesis after the name, followed by a comma.

Example: *R.* v. *Burke* **(2001),** 153 C.C.C. (3d) 97 (Ont. C.A.)

Sometimes you will see the year cited in square brackets, preceded by a comma. This usually means the case was referenced in a volume.

Example: *Cempel* v. *Harrison Hot Springs Hotel Ltd.,* **[1998]** 6 W.W.R. 233 (B.C.C.A.)

Report Reference Cases are written up in a number of case-law reporters such as the Supreme Court Reports, which contains only Supreme Court of Canada decisions, or the Nova Scotia Reports, which contains only decisions made by the Nova Scotia courts. In citations, these reports are abbreviated. Supreme Court Reports appears as S.C.R., and Nova Scotia Reports appears as N.S.R. If the case-law reporter is published in volumes, the volume number appears *before* the abbreviation. The page number of the case appears *after* the abbreviation.

Example: *Cempel* v. *Harrison Hot Springs Hotel Ltd.,* [1998] **6 W.W.R. 233** (B.C.C.A.)

This means the case was reported in volume 6 of the Western Weekly Reports starting on page 233.

Often a case-law reporter has been published in a series, in which case the series number (3d) is placed in parenthesis at the end of the abbreviation.

Example: *R.* v. *Burke* (2001), 153 C.C.C. **(3d)** 97 (Ont. C.A.)

Jurisdiction and Court At the end of the citation, the jurisdiction and the court in which the case was heard are identified.

Example: *Cempel* v. *Harrison Hot Springs Hotel Ltd.,* [1998] 6 W.W.R. 233 (**B.C.C.A.**)

This case was heard in the British Columbia Court of Appeal.

If the jurisdiction and court are obvious, as they would be if the case were in the Supreme Court Reports, the name of the court does not appear.

Example: *R.* v. *Stone,* [1999] 2 S.C.R. 290

On-line Reports Some of the cases that appear in *Law in Action* were researched on Internet Web sites for various provincial, federal, and international courts. The citations for these cases show the name of the case, the year of the decision, the jurisdiction, and the applicable court or tribunal.

Example: *Spain* v. *Canada* (1998), Fisheries Jurisdiction (I.C.J.), **on-line: www.icj-cij.org**

This case was heard in 1998 under the Fisheries Jurisdiction at the I.C.J. (the International Court of Justice, located in The Hague).

Considering the Facts

Whether you are reading a short case or one of the more detailed cases in *Law in Action,* make sure you understand the facts of the case. The facts consist of a description of the events and transactions that led one party to initiate legal proceedings against the other party. Ask yourself, "What actually happened?" "Who are the key participants in the case?" "What laws are involved?" and "What is the argument?" Think about the case from different angles and consider the arguments of both sides.

You may be analyzing a case in your textbook, reading about a crime in your local newspaper, or listening to a trial in a courtroom. In each of these

Fast Fact
The case-law reporters with their abbreviations are shown on page ix.

Consider This
Explain the particulars of this citation:
R. v. *Wells* (1998), 127 C.C.C. (3d) 402 (Nfld. C.A.)

Law in Your Life
To assess legal arguments objectively, try not to rely on your moral values; simply focus on what the law has to say about the problem.

situations, the ability to differentiate between fact and opinion is an important legal skill. Suppose a witness, who is asked to describe the weather on a particular day, responds, "It was very hot." Is this statement factual? To some extent it may be; the day in question may have *seemed* hot to the witness, or the witness may have *thought* the weather was hot because she had been exercising that day or is used to colder weather. Heat is a relative concept. On the other hand, what if the witness replies, "It was 35 degrees centigrade"? Although it may not be true, this response would certainly be a fact. What distinguishes the second statement from the first, however, is that the second statement is testable. It is certain and precise, and contains no subjective or emotional adjectives.

Considering the Issue and the Decision

When you are sure of the facts that prompted the action, consider the issue raised in the case. The issue is simply a statement of the legal question that is illustrated and answered in the case. To make it easier to understand, the issue is often stated in the form of a question that allows a "yes" or "no" answer. For example, in R. v. *Burke* (2001), 153 C.C.C. (3d) 97 (Ont. C.A.), the issue was the following: Does a trial judge have the jurisdiction to conduct an inquiry into a verdict after the jury has been discharged?

Most cases in *Law in Action* have already appeared before the courts, and decisions have been rendered. Each case explains why the court made that particular decision. Generally, the decision includes an application of the rules of law to the specific facts of the case. Again, examining R. v. *Burke* (2001), the appeal was dismissed because a majority of the Ontario Court of Appeal felt that the trial judge was only correcting an accidental error.

THE IMPORTANCE OF STUDYING LAW

Law in Your Life
While laws such as the *Youth Criminal Justice Act* are directly related to young people, other aspects of law also have an impact on your life. From purchasing a pizza to testing for a driver's licence, the law affects you. Find out how.

Because the legal system affects almost all aspects of your life, it is important that you understand how the system works and what your rights and responsibilities are as a Canadian citizen. Studying law will provide you with a useful foundation of concepts and information as well as the skills to interpret that information correctly.

As you learn by integrating the information in *Law in Action* with classroom instruction, you will gain a better understanding of the evolution of Canada's legal system, and how the values and beliefs of society shape that evolution. Armed with this knowledge, you will be better prepared to explore avenues you are interested in and to challenge the system when you feel it is appropriate to do so. Although the legal system will no longer be a mystery, it can still be exciting. Let's get started!

Our Legal Heritage

UNIT 1

The laws of a society reflect the values and beliefs of the people in that society. At the same time, law is dynamic and it changes as the values of society change. Unit 1 will examine the structure of the Canadian legal system and some of the historical influences that have helped shape it. You will explore the connections between law, morality, and justice, and you will learn about key concepts in British law and their influences on the development of law in Canada.

Unit 1 discusses constitutional law, common law, and statute law, and it clarifies the complexities of the Canadian legal system by distinguishing the various categories of law and explaining their purposes. Many types of law are briefly introduced in this unit; later in the text you will have an opportunity to study them in greater detail.

Canada's original Constitution, the *British North America Act, 1867*, outlines the division of power for the federal and provincial governments. In this unit, you will find out what those powers are. You will also learn about the different branches of government and the procedure for enacting statute law.

LOOKING AHEAD

Chapter 1 Law and Society

Chapter 2 Classifying Law

Chapter 3 Government and Statute Law

1 Law and Society

CHAPTER OUTLINE

Law in Our Lives

Historical Roots of Law

Influences on Canadian Law

FOCUS YOUR LEARNING

What are the connections between law and morality and between law and justice?

What do the laws of a society tell us about that society?

How does Canadian law reflect the influences of other legal systems?

> "Where law ends, tyranny begins."
> — William Pitt, British prime minister (1759–1806)
>
> "Law is simply the rule of the stronger."
> — Plato, Greek philosopher (427?–347? BCE)
>
> "Law depends on its validity by having a penalty attached."
> — Jane Austen, British author (1775–1817)
>
> "Law is the highest reason."
> — Marcus Tullius Cicero, Roman orator (106–43 BCE)
>
> "The more numerous the laws, the more corrupt the state."
> — Gaius Cornelius Tacitus, Roman advocate at law (56–120 CE)

For centuries, people have been commenting on the subject of law, both positively and negatively. As you will discover, these opinions are important in the study of law because they reflect the values and beliefs held by people in different societies at different times. By examining quotes like these, you can learn about the values people attach to the law.

WHAT DO YOU THINK?

- Choose one of the quotes above and explain what you think the speaker meant.
- Compose a statement of your own that would represent your views of the law.

This chapter will explore the connection between law and morality (accepted standards of right and wrong) and between law and society's concept of justice. It will also guide us back to the past to see how the laws of earlier societies reflected people's values and beliefs at that time. By revisiting the past, we will find out how some of these laws have influenced Canada's legal system.

LAW IN OUR LIVES

We live in a world governed by law. No matter what we do, the legal system and its laws are part of everyday life. As employees or employers at work, we are subject to certain labour laws. We must follow laws to own and drive a car, to rent an apartment, or to purchase a home. There are even laws that restrict our fishing and hunting activities. Law is everywhere.

Figure 1.1 Record all the laws you can think of that might apply to these situations.

"The Rule of Law can be wiped out in one misguided, however well-intentioned, generation."
— William T. Gossett, legal analyst

Consider This
Describe a situation in the news that you feel reflects an injustice in the legal system. Explain why.

Law in Your Life
Sixteen-year-old Canadians cannot vote, but they must obey the laws of the country, even if they may not agree with them.

Canada's legal system strives to represent principles Canadians believe in and value. Each generation influences this system, and the laws that are passed reflect the society of that period. For example, politicians who came to power in Canada in the 1960s and 1970s established the first national divorce law. They also focused on prison reform by emphasizing rehabilitation (helping offenders return to productive lives through training and education). In 1982 the Government of Canada enacted the *Charter of Rights and Freedoms* to guarantee the rights of all Canadians regardless of their age, race, ethnicity, religion, gender, or sexual orientation.

Why is it important to study law? To ensure that the legal system continues to work, Canadians need to become informed, thoughtful citizens capable of effecting meaningful change. Knowing what the law is and how it works in Canada will provide you with the insight and the tools to influence changes that best serve and reflect your generation.

The study of law is the study of people, how they behave, what they value, and how they solve problems. Sometimes you may be angry at what you consider to be the injustices of the legal system. Sometimes you may be bored with the detail of the law, and you may wonder how anything can work in such a complicated system. Despite these obstacles, learning about the law will make you a better citizen. And studying law can be interesting, exciting, and fun!

Rules versus Laws

As you know, sports such as basketball and hockey have certain rules, and there are penalties for breaking these rules. Similarly, your family may have rules regarding curfews or chores. Your school may implement rules that range from wearing uniforms to not bringing a cellphone to class. If you disobey any of these rules, you are penalized.

Rules resemble laws, but unlike laws, rules are not enforced by the courts. If you fail to empty the dishwasher, the police will not come to your house and charge you. Nor will they arrest you on the basketball court for travelling more than two steps with the ball. You can also opt out of rules: if you do not want to play basketball, you do not have to follow the rules; or, in a private game of your own, you can change the rules. Laws are different—you cannot opt out of the law or change laws on your own. As members of society, you recognize and accept that laws are necessary. If you break a law, whether you agree with it or not, you will be punished. Punishment may involve going to prison, paying a fine, or compensating someone for damages you caused.

Remember, rules are not laws, but all laws are rules!

Figure 1.2 How do the rules of this game differ from the laws that apply to the community?

Rules and Laws

1. Not smoking on school property.
2. Getting your homework in on time.
3. Wearing your seat belt in your car.
4. Not buying cigarettes under the age of 19.
5. Not wearing your hat in class.
6. Turning off your cellphone in the movie theatre.
7. Not hunting for deer without a licence.
8. Putting your garbage in the container at the bus stop.
9. Not telling fortunes for money.
10. Not swearing at your teachers.

Figure 1.3 In your opinion, which of these are rules and which are laws? Explain your answers.

What Is Law?

So what is law? There is no simple answer to this question. Philosophers, lawmakers, and ordinary citizens have struggled with this question for many years. When you hear the word *law*, you probably think of crime, police, and courts. However, law involves much more than that. In our complex society, laws regulate our social, political, and economic activities from birth to death. Laws restrict whom we marry, who gets our money when we die, whether we can put a swimming pool in our backyard, at what age we can purchase certain products, and even what ingredients should be in our soft drinks. Laws can differ from nation to nation, province to province, and even city to city. For example, in some Canadian cities, you can make a right-hand turn when the traffic light is red. The same practice in other cities is illegal.

"Law is like time. I know what it is, but if someone asks me, I know not."
— Saint Augustine of Canterbury, fifth century

Figure 1.4 Identify any laws you recognize in this photograph. What rules are reflected in this scene?

Some people argue that there are many examples to show that law is whatever the political party in power says it is. For example, until 1994 the government in South Africa enforced the laws of apartheid, a policy of segregation and discrimination against non-whites. As of 2002, in communist China, forming other political parties was forbidden, and freedom of speech was limited by law.

Other people argue that law is merely a social necessity. If there were no laws stopping individuals from physically assaulting each other or from stealing each other's belongings, everyday life would be chaotic. They might define law as "a civilized people's attempt to regulate life in society by the principles of reason and fairness as opposed to brute force."

Laws tend to change with time and according to location. For example, laws passed today might be quite different from laws passed in 1867, especially with respect to women's rights and equal opportunity. Laws governing snow removal in a city like Sudbury, Ontario, would not be necessary in Victoria, British Columbia. Because laws reflect values as well as practical concerns, they often vary widely among provinces, states, countries, and cultures.

The Need for Law

If you lived alone on a deserted island, you would probably not require laws. However, since most of us live near other people, we must find a way to live together peacefully. To some extent, laws permit us to do that by giving us a certain amount of predictability and a structure for creating a safe and peaceful society. For instance, laws against criminal conduct safeguard our property and protect us from violence. Disputes and disagreements are settled in the courts, not in the streets. If two people claim ownership of the same car,

Fast Fact

The word *law* comes from the Latin word *ligare,* meaning "to bind" or force someone to act or not act; it was also influenced by the Old Norse word *lag,* meaning "laid down or fixed."

CASE

Roncarelli v. Duplessis, [1959] S.C.R. 121

BACKGROUND In the mid-1950s, religious tension arose in Quebec between Jehovah's Witnesses, who were spreading their beliefs by distributing their publication, and Roman Catholics. In an attempt to stop what it considered an insult to the Catholic population, the Quebec government arrested almost 1000 Jehovah's Witnesses for selling their publication without a licence.

Roncarelli, a restaurateur and a Jehovah's Witness, provided bail for almost 400 of those arrested. In response, the Quebec premier Maurice Duplessis ordered the Liquor Commission to cancel Roncarelli's liquor licence, which the restaurant had held for 34 years. Roncarelli sued Duplessis for loss of business resulting from cancellation of the licence.

LEGAL QUESTION Was the premier's action an abuse of power?

DECISION The majority of the Supreme Court of Canada found in favour of Roncarelli and awarded him $25 000 plus damages. The Court held that Duplessis's actions were "a gross abuse of legal power." He had used his personal power to punish Roncarelli and to send a message to others who might be inclined to assist Jehovah's Witnesses.

LEGAL SIGNIFICANCE This case demonstrates an attempt to violate the Rule of Law.

Maurice Duplessis

ANALYSIS

1. Explain which aspect of the Rule of Law Duplessis violated.
2. If the Court had found in favour of Duplessis, what consequences do you think this decision would have had for Canadian society?

---

they do not settle the matter by duelling. Instead, the court decides on the rightful owner.

Some societies enforce law through intimidation, and citizens can be arrested and imprisoned without trial. In Canada, we expect law to protect the rights of individual citizens. We also follow the **Rule of Law**, a three-part principle of justice. Firstly, Rule of Law means that individuals must recognize and accept that the law is necessary to regulate society. Secondly, it means that the law applies equally to everyone, including people in power, such as heads of state, police officers, judges, and politicians. Finally, Rule of Law means that no one in our society has the authority to exercise unrestricted power to take away our rights except in accordance with the law.

Rule of Law: a principle of justice stating that the law is necessary to regulate society, that law applies equally to everyone, and that people are not governed by arbitrary power

Law and Morality

Some laws serve a practical purpose, such as governing property rights or regulating traffic. Other laws reflect the moral values of the majority of society. However, the relationship of laws to moral codes and standards can be controversial. For example, should it be against the law to help a loved one die when this individual is suffering from a terminal illness? Is capital punishment a just punishment or an uncivilized penalty in a civilized society? Should abortion be a criminal or medical matter? Is it acceptable for parents to physically discipline their children? Why does society regulate tobacco and alcohol but consider other drug use criminal? Do laws forbidding the possession of child pornography violate an individual's freedom of expression? Because views on these issues reflect moral values and beliefs, there may be a wide variety of opinions among your classmates.

In a multicultural, democratic society, tension may exist between the law and personal or community standards of right and wrong. Sometimes lawmakers apply standards to society that go beyond what some communities want. For example, although Canadians have always been divided in their support for capital punishment, in 1976 the government abolished the death penalty. At other times, the democratic will of the people challenges Parliament to change laws to represent the moral values of society. For example, in recent years, society has become less tolerant of individuals who drink and drive, resulting in increasing penalties and a wider range of charges.

For the most part, however, laws reflect our collective community standards. Laws based on morality suggest the values, attitudes, and beliefs that Canadian citizens hold in common. Individuals and groups who do not share these moral values are free to speak out publicly and try to change the law.

Law and Justice

The idea of law has always been associated with the idea of justice. Most people would agree that the ultimate goal of law is to ensure justice for all. But what exactly is justice? What do we mean when we say we want to live in a "just" society? The concept of justice has varied from age to age. Ancient Greek society, for example, did not consider inequality an injustice; it was just the way society was structured. Today, most Canadians would place equality at the very heart of justice.

While the law is supposed to be applied equally to all, regardless of position or financial status, ensuring equality in *all* situations may actually be unjust. Consider the person who breaks into an unoccupied cottage and takes a rope to save a drowning friend. Should that person be charged with break and enter and be given the same punishment as someone who breaks in to steal the television? Most of us would say, "No, the law should take the circumstances into consideration." On the other hand, we expect equal treatment in other cases. We expect that all citizens, regardless of gender or race, will have the opportunity to vote and that all children will have the same access to education.

Law in Your Life
Many Canadians hold strong opinions about certain issues and express their views through activities such as letter writing. Identify an issue you feel strongly about and list the ways you might express yourself on this issue.

"An individual who breaks a law that conscience tells him is unjust and who willingly accepts the penalty of imprisonment in order to arouse the conscience of the community over its injustice, is, in reality, expressing the highest respect for the law."

— Martin Luther King, Jr.,
civil rights leader

R. v. *Dudley and Stevens* (1884), 14 Q.B.D. 273

CASE

In the summer of 1883, Tom Dudley and his crew of two, Stevens and Brooks, set sail from England to Australia. Richard Parker, a 17-year-old cabin boy, was also on board. The *Mignonette* sank on July 3, and the four took refuge in the yacht's dinghy with only a few rations.

After 18 days, Dudley and Stevens suggested to Brooks that one of the four should be sacrificed to save the rest. Brooks did not agree, and Parker was not consulted. On the 20th day, Parker became quite weak, and Dudley, with Stevens' approval, killed Parker. The three lived on Parker's flesh and drank his blood over the next four days until they were rescued.

At that time, it was accepted practice for sailors in peril to resort to cannibalism in order to survive. This practice at sea, however, was in conflict with the law of the land. Consequently, on their return to England, Dudley and Stevens were charged with murder. Brooks testified against them. The jury could not reach a verdict, and the case was sent to a panel of five judges. The judges rejected the idea of "necessity"—that it was necessary to kill and eat Parker for survival. They found Dudley and Stevens guilty and sentenced them to hang. Public sympathy was on the side of the sailors, and later the Crown commuted the sentence to six months' imprisonment.

1. What does this case tell you about law and morality in England during this period?
2. What would your verdict be in this case?

The concept of justice is open to debate because our ideas of justice originate from our moral convictions and our values, attitudes, and beliefs, all of which may change over time. Nevertheless, as a society, we agree on certain characteristics of justice. First, underlying the concept of justice is the idea that we should "treat like cases alike and different cases differently." For example, a charge of causing a disturbance against a person who suffers from Tourette's Syndrome (TS), a neurological disorder characterized by uncontrollable tics, vocal sounds, and compulsive uttering of obscenities, might be dismissed once the judge is informed of the person's condition. The fact that this person is treated differently from a person who does not have TS is not regarded as unfair, given the circumstances.

Second, we consider a law unjust if it discriminates on the basis of irrelevant characteristics. For example, you might consider it reasonably fair to be denied admittance to a restricted movie because you did not have proof of legal age. However, if you were denied admission because of the colour of your eyes, you would almost certainly consider this action unjust.

Third, justice should be impartial; that is, laws should be applied regardless of a person's position or financial status. Celebrities who beat their spouses should be charged with assault just as other Canadians would be if they committed the same offence. Being a celebrity should not offer any special protection or privileges.

Finally, we expect the law itself to be just in that it conforms to society's values and beliefs. For example, if the federal government wanted to strengthen

Consider This
All Canadians are supposed to be treated equally under the law. Make a list of situations in which *equal* treatment might not be *just* treatment. For each situation, explain your rationale.

law enforcement by requiring all Canadians to have a sample of their DNA taken at birth and placed in a national registry, some people might oppose such legislation as unfair because they would view it as a violation of their right to privacy. Therefore, passage of this legislation might depend on whether society valued protection over privacy.

Finding a definitive meaning for the concept of justice may seem like an impossible task. What *is* possible is to accept our responsibility as informed citizens to participate in the debate and to continue refining what we mean by justice.

MacIsaac Discharged for Fiddling with Pot

REGINA — Fiddling sensation Ashley MacIsaac was given an absolute discharge and no fine for possessing marijuana in Regina provincial court on Tuesday.

MacIsaac, 26, wasn't in court, so his lawyer Jayme Day entered MacIsaac's guilty plea for him. The award-winning musician was charged July 27 after police stopped him en route to a concert in Saskatoon.

Crown prosecutor Paul Malone said RCMP pulled over a speeding car near Aylesbury, about 100 kilometres northwest of Regina. When the driver rolled down the window, there was "a strong smell of cannabis," Malone said. Inside the car, police found 12 grams of marijuana and a hash pipe. MacIsaac admitted the drugs were his and was charged with possession of marijuana under the *Controlled Drugs and Substances Act*.

The mention of the world-famous fiddler from Cape Breton sent a ripple of excitement through the courtroom.

"Is that *the* Ashley MacIsaac?" asked Judge Linton Smith.

"The same," replied Day.

In granting MacIsaac an absolute discharge, Smith joked that he had only one condition. "The only condition I'd like to attach is if you could get my wife an autograph," Smith told Day.

SOURCE: "MacIsaac Discharged for Fiddling with Pot," *The Globe and Mail*, August 23, 2001, p. R2.

1. What was the charge against Ashley MacIsaac and what was his punishment?
2. In your opinion, was the decision in this case an example of impartial justice? Explain why or why not.

Building Your Understanding

1. Why do you think it is important to study the laws of your country?
2. How do rules differ from laws?
3. Why do we need laws in society?
4. Identify the three aspects of Rule of Law.
5. What is the relationship between law and morality in Canadian society?
6. Use your own examples to explain each of the four agreed-upon characteristics of justice.

HISTORICAL ROOTS OF LAW

Laws in the form of community-enforced rules have existed from the time people started to interact. Early communities created laws related to hunting, ownership of property, family relationships, and responsibilities. Most of these laws were based on common sense or practicality and were passed on by word of mouth to future generations. As populations grew and people began trading, not just within their own villages but also with other nations, laws became more complex. Eventually, it became necessary to put these laws in writing.

Laws were written in many languages. Between 1280 and 880 BCE, lawmakers in India recorded the **Great Laws of Manu.** This document compiled laws that had been passed from generation to generation in an oral tradition. China also had a set of written laws. The Chinese **Code of Li k'vei,** written in approximately 350 BCE, included laws dealing with theft, robbery, prison, and arrest.

Written laws existed in early civilizations all over the world, and they had much in common. Laws concerning property rights, slavery, and the treatment of women and children were similar even in civilizations separated by great distances. Many of the early laws discussed in this chapter have, to some extent, influenced Canada's present legal system.

The *Code of Hammurabi*

The year was 1901. French archeologists working in Susa, Iran, discovered an amazing find—one of the earliest-known sets of written laws called the ***Code of Hammurabi.*** Hammurabi (1792–1750 BCE) was the king of Babylon. During his reign, he **codified,** or recorded, the rules and penalties for every aspect of Babylonian life, from the ownership of property to the rights of adopted children. The king encouraged compliance by attributing his laws to the gods, whom the people feared and respected. Consider these excerpts from the *Code of Hammurabi*:

- If anyone is committing a robbery and is caught, then he shall be put to death.
- If anyone opens his ditches to water his crops, but is careless, and the water floods the fields of his neighbour, then he shall pay for the loss.
- If a man takes a wife and she is seized by disease, and if he then desires to take a second wife, he shall not put away his [first] wife. But he shall keep her in the house and support her as long as she lives.

The laws reflected a patriarchal (male-dominated) society in which the wealthy were given more protection in law than the

> **Consider This**
> Fingerprinting for identification was first used in China in the year 700 CE. What kinds of identification methods are used today? Speculate on possible methods for the future.

Great Laws of Manu: Indian laws compiled between 1280 and 880 BCE, previously transferred through oral tradition

Code of Li k'vei: a set of Chinese laws written around 350 BCE

Code of Hammurabi: one of the earliest-known sets of recorded laws, written by King Hammurabi of Babylon

codified: arranged and recorded systematically

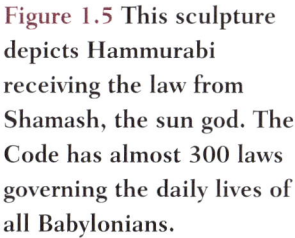

Figure 1.5 This sculpture depicts Hammurabi receiving the law from Shamash, the sun god. The Code has almost 300 laws governing the daily lives of all Babylonians.

"To bring about the rule of righteousness in the land and to destroy the wicked and the evil doers, so that the strong shall not harm the weak."

— Code of Hammurabi

retribution: justice based on vengeance and punishment

poor. Slavery was legal, and women and children were considered the property of men. There also existed a clear hierarchy of power (order of dominance): gods at the top, followed by the king, then male nobles, and then their wives and children, with the poor and slaves at the bottom.

Many of Hammurabi's laws were based on **retribution**, an eye-for-an-eye type of justice, and distinction was not made between an accident and a deliberate action. For example, "If a physician operates and kills the patient, the physician's hands shall be cut off." A law like this might deter a physician from operating at all! Also, because of the hierarchy of power, those who committed crimes often went unpunished. Instead, their female relatives or slaves were expected to accept retribution: "If a man strikes a woman and she dies, the man's daughter shall be put to death."

restitution: payment made by the offender to the victim of a crime

Some penalties may seem excessive and cruel; for instance, "If a slave says to his master, 'You are not my master,' his master can cut off his ear." However, many of Hammurabi's laws were reasonable and just. Consider these examples: **Restitution,** the concept of making payment to the victim of the crime, was common in the event of damage to property or theft. It was recognized that people should not lie, especially at a trial. It was also expected that the strong should protect the weak. If we compare some of our laws with those of Hammurabi, we may find we are not that different from people of 4000 years ago.

Figure 1.6 What do the laws from the *Code of Hammurabi* tell you about morality and justice in Babylonian society?

Laws from the *Code of Hammurabi*

- If anyone brings an accusation of any crime before the elders and does not prove what he has charged, he shall, if it be a capital offence charged, be put to death.
- If a judge shall try a case, reach a decision, and present his judgment in writing, and if later, error shall appear in his decision and it be through his own fault, then he shall be publicly removed from the judge's bench, and never again shall he sit there to render judgment.
- If anyone steals the property of a temple or a court, he shall be put to death, and also the one who receives the stolen thing from him shall be put to death.
- If anyone steals cattle or sheep, a pig or a goat, the thief shall pay tenfold; if the thief has nothing with which to pay he shall be put to death.
- If anyone is committing a robbery and is caught, then he shall be put to death. But if the robber is not caught then shall he who was robbed claim under oath the amount of his loss, then shall the community … compensate him for the goods stolen.

Mosaic Law

One of the greatest influences on our law is biblical law, also known as Hebrew law or **Mosaic Law.** In the Bible, we are told that Moses climbed a mountain called Mount Sinai, where God gave him laws to be followed by the Hebrew people. These laws, now commonly called the Ten Commandments, can be found in the Book of Exodus in the Old Testament. Although the **Ten Commandments** and other Mosaic laws were written some 500 years after the death of Hammurabi, the basic principles are similar. Under Mosaic Law, it was forbidden to commit murder, adultery, and theft, and to worship other gods.

Comparing the *Code of Hammurabi* with Mosaic Law shows how laws evolved from the time of Hammurabi. Mosaic Law was more concerned with punishing a deliberate action than an accidental act of harm. Mosaic Law was also more likely to punish the guilty party than permit a person of high status to shift punishment to a person of lesser status. Care for the poor was another concern expressed in Mosaic Law. Landowners were commanded to leave a small portion of their crops in the field for the poor to harvest.

Mosaic Law: Biblical or Hebrew law found in the Book of Exodus

Ten Commandments: laws given to Moses to guide the Hebrew people

Non Sequitur

NON SEQUITUR © 2001 Wiley Miller. Distributed by UNIVERSAL PRESS SYNDICATE. Reprinted with permission. All rights reserved.

Laws from the Book of Exodus

- Thou shalt not kill.
- Thou shalt not steal.
- If a man steals an ox or a sheep and kills it or sells it, he shall restore five oxen for an ox and four sheep for a sheep.
- If a thief is found breaking in and be smitten that he die, there shall be no blood shed for him.
- Thou shalt not raise a false report, or put thine hand with the wicked to be an unrighteous witness.

Figure 1.7 Based on this excerpt from Mosaic Law, what conclusions can you draw about the concept of justice in Hebrew society at this time?

The *Code of Hammurabi* and the Ten Commandments both emphasized the importance of showing respect for parents. But they differed in how these laws were expressed. While Hammurabi's Code spoke of punishing a son for striking his father, Mosaic Law was less gender specific: "Whosoever strikes his father or his mother shall be put to death." (Perhaps this difference reflects a different attitude toward women within the two societies.) Figure 1.8 compares three aspects of both sets of laws.

Figure 1.8 **Comparison of Laws**

Administration of Justice	Protection of Property	Protection of the Person
Code of Hammurabi If a man has borne false witness in a trial, or has not established the statement that he has made, if that case be a capital trial, that man shall be put to death.	If a man has stolen goods from a temple or a house, he shall be put to death and he that has received the stolen property shall be put to death.	If a son has struck his father, his hands shall be cut off. If a man strikes a man's daughter and brings about a miscarriage, he shall pay for the miscarriage. If that woman dies, his daughter shall be killed.
Mosaic Law You shall not utter a false report. You shall not join hands with the wicked, to be a malicious witness.	If a man steals an ox or a sheep, and kills it or sells it, he shall pay five oxen for an ox, and four sheep for a sheep.	Whoever strikes his father or his mother shall be put to death ... whoever curses his father or his mother shall be put to death.

Figure 1.9 **Sunrise from Mount Sinai where, according to the Bible, Moses received the Ten Commandments, the basis of Mosaic Law**

20   UNIT 1 ◆ Our Legal Heritage

Greek Law

The first form of democracy was born in Greece, although it was not democracy as we know it today. Only a small percentage of the Athenian people, known as "citizens," actually had political rights. Athenian citizenship excluded women, children, aliens, and slaves.

One important principle of Greek democracy was citizen involvement. Athenian citizens were expected to participate in major decisions affecting the running of their country. For example, voting was a major responsibility. Another responsibility was jury duty. The jury system can be traced to Athens, Greece, in approximately 400 BCE. Athenians employed enormous juries, with the largest recorded jury at over 6000 members. Later, their juries were limited to 101, 501, or 1001 citizens. Women who were on trial were not allowed to speak on their own behalf; citizens had to speak for them.

The Greeks also used democracy to decide on the sentence of an accused. If a person were found guilty, both the accused and the accuser would suggest a sentence. The jury then voted on the most appropriate sentence. One of the best-known examples of this democratic process was the trial of Socrates. Socrates was arrested in 399 BCE. His accusers claimed that his ideas misled Athenian youth and undermined Athenian democracy. After a lengthy trial, the 501 jurors found him guilty (the vote was 281 to 220). His accusers recommended the death penalty. Socrates argued that the law under which he was charged was unfair but acknowledged that he had been tried fairly by his peers. As instructed by the court, he drank a cup of poisonous hemlock.

Roman Law

There were two basic principles of Roman law: 1) the law must be recorded and 2) justice could not be left in the hands of judges alone to interpret. Like some of the earlier laws discussed in this chapter, Roman laws were codified, which meant that they were set out in an orderly written arrangement that could be revised as new laws were needed. The Twelve Tablets, among the earliest Roman codes, were written on wood and bronze in 450 BCE. Compiled by a committee of 10 men, this code determined the law of England during the Roman occupation, and is now considered the foundation of modern law. The Tablets promoted the public prosecution of crimes, enacted a system of victim compensation, and protected the lower class (known as plebeians) from being abused by the ruling class (known as patricians). In spite of its advances, Roman law reflected a patriarchal society similar to that of Hammurabi. "Sons shall be under the jurisdiction [legal authority] of the father." Women were not even mentioned since they had no status as "persons."

As we know today, a person accused of a crime should seek legal advice. This practice of having an adviser who specializes in the law first became prevalent during Roman times. By 100 CE, the Romans had a sophisticated and complex society, and the Roman Empire had spread throughout most of

> **Fast Fact**
> The word *democracy* comes from the Greek word *demos* meaning "people."

Figure 1.10 Socrates (470?–399 BCE) was a Greek philosopher known for teaching students by asking them questions. Do you know anyone who uses a Socratic method to teach?

> **Fast Fact**
> Around the year 1088, Irnerius, an Italian jurist who taught Roman law, set up the first law school in Bologna, Italy. By 1150 the school had 10 000 students.

Figure 1.11 At the height of its power, the Roman Empire extended from Britain to Africa and from the Atlantic Ocean to the Caspian Sea. This huge area had one government, one monetary system, and one set of laws.

Europe. Society became even more complex, and more laws were devised to decide such matters as what constituted criminal behaviour, how contracts should be regulated, and how everyday disputes between citizens should be resolved. As the number of laws increased, it became necessary to ask people who had expertise in the law to advise those who did not. These legal advisers were the forerunners of present-day lawyers.

Justinian's Code

After 395 CE, the Roman Empire was split into the Byzantine Empire and the Western Roman Empire. To strengthen his efforts to restore the declining empire to its former glory, Byzantine Emperor Justinian I (527–565 CE) commissioned 10 men to study and clarify the 1600 books of Roman law. By 529 CE the task was complete, and Justinian had a new body of law known as **Justinian's Code.** This code inspired the modern concept of justice and served as an important basis for law in contemporary society. In fact, the word *justice* is derived from the emperor's name. *Justinian's Code* formed the basis of civil law (laws governing personal relationships), which, along with criminal law, became one of the main legal systems to govern Western civilization. (Civil and criminal law will be discussed in greater detail later in the text.) Elements of *Justinian's Code* can be found in the laws of many European countries, especially France.

Justinian's Code: the clarification and organization of Roman law commissioned by Justinian I

France and the *Napoleonic Code*

The French Revolution took place about 1200 years after Justinian's rule (1789–1799). Once the Revolution was over, Napoleon Bonaparte gained firm political control of the government of France. In order to unify French law, he commissioned a new code of laws called the **Napoleonic Code,** also known as the *French Civil Code*. It went into effect in 1804 and spread throughout much of Europe as Emperor Napoleon brought other countries under his domination. These laws represented a compromise between the influences of the Germanic law of northern France and the *Justinian Code* of southern France. The *Napoleonic Code* became popular because its non-technical style made the law accessible to the public. The Code regulated civil matters such as property, wills, contracts, and family law. An excerpt on family law from the *Napoleonic Code* is shown in Figure 1.12.

Napoleonic Code: the civil law of France completed in 1804 (also called the *French Civil Code*)

Fast Fact
More than 20 nations have used the *Civil Code* as a model for their legal systems.

Of the Rights and Respective Duties of Husband and Wife

212. Husband and wife mutually owe to each other fidelity, succour, and assistance.
213. The husband owes protection to his wife, the wife obedience to her husband.
214. The wife is obliged to live with her husband, and to follow him wherever he may think proper to dwell; the husband is bound to receive her, and to furnish her with everything necessary for the purposes of life, according to his means and condition.
215. The wife can do no act in law without the authority of her husband …

Of Causes of Divorce

229. The husband may demand divorce for cause of adultery on the part of his wife.
230. The wife may demand divorce for cause of adultery on the part of her husband, where he shall have kept his concubine in their common house.

Figure 1.12 What do these laws from the *Napoleonic Code* tell you about the status of women in French society at that time?

Building Your Understanding

1. What were the Great Laws of Manu?
2. Identify one of the earliest-known written legal codes.
3. Name the set of laws found in the Book of Exodus in the Bible.
4. What role did the people known as citizens play in Greek society?
5. Which society had the first paid legal advisers?
6. How did the *Justinian* and *Napoleonic Codes* contribute to the development of modern law?

INFLUENCES ON CANADIAN LAW

Although Canadian law reflects aspects of Mosaic, Greek, Roman, and French law, it is British law that has had the most influence in Canada. A visit to any Canadian courtroom in session demonstrates how much of the past is present in today's legal system. For example, in a place of prominence, you will find a photograph of Queen Elizabeth II, the Canadian head of state. The judge, lawyers, and parties involved sit in an area separate from members of the public. Court judges and lawyers wear long, black robes; justices in the Supreme Court of Canada wear scarlet robes trimmed with ermine. All of these traditions come from Canada's roots as a colony of Great Britain.

Figure 1.13 Sketches of courtroom activity appear in local newspapers because photographers are not allowed to take pictures inside a Canadian courtroom while court is in session.

Early British Law

When the Romans conquered Great Britain in 43 CE, they imposed their laws on the inhabitants. Their rule lasted until about 410 CE, when the remaining Roman legions left Britain to deal with threats on the continent against the empire. Roman laws soon gave way to practices that followed local customs and traditions.

Trial by Ordeal

When a lord sitting in judgment was unable to reach a verdict of guilt or innocence based on facts and witnesses, he used a method known as **trial by ordeal.** The accused was required to undergo torture, and guilt or innocence was determined by the outcome of the ordeal. God was said to be the judge in such situations since, it was believed, evil could never triumph over good. Trial by ordeal was only used when the sentence for guilt was the death penalty.

There were several different ordeals, such as "trial by hot iron," "trial by hot water," and "trial by cold water" (called "swimming a witch" when used to

trial by ordeal: requiring a person to undergo torture to determine guilt or innocence judge a case of witchcraft). In a trial by hot iron, the accused was forced to hold a hot piece of iron. The burn was then bound for a number of days. If the wound healed by the time the bandage was removed, the person was declared innocent. Of course, the wound rarely healed because the bandages were not sterile and the wound would become infected.

Using such methods seems like a barbaric, not to mention inefficient, way to determine guilt or innocence. Keep in mind, though, that the accused and the victim were usually well known in the village where the alleged wrongs took place; guilt or innocence had probably been decided before the ordeal had even begun.

Purging by Water

Consider this case, which took place in a village in Cornwall, England, in 1201.

> Denise, wife of Anthony, charges Nicholas Kam of the death of Anthony, her husband, for that he wickedly slew her husband, and this she offers to prove against him under award of the court. Nicholas defends all of it. It is considered that Denise's appeal is null, for she did not see the deed. But everyone who knows him knows that Nicholas is guilty; so let him purge himself by water.

In this case, the community believed in Nicholas's guilt, and the purging by water was merely a formality. Nonetheless, the ordeal gave Nicholas a chance to prove his innocence. After all, it was assumed that God would save Nicholas if he were truly innocent! Unfortunately, many innocent people ended up either confessing or dying because of the ordeal.

Trial by Oath Helping

Another method was used for less serious charges—**trial by oath helping** (sometimes known as compurgation, from the Latin meaning "to purify with"). This method required people who knew the accused to swear an oath on the Bible that he or she was innocent. If they complied, the accused was freed. Would it have been easy for the accused to persuade friends to swear on his or her behalf, regardless of the truth? Perhaps ... but at the time most people feared retribution from God if they bore false witness (lied under oath).

Trial by Combat

After the Norman invasion in 1066, **trial by combat** was introduced to determine guilt or innocence. The two parties involved in a dispute engaged in a duel. Again, it was presumed that God would be on the side of the innocent and that the innocent man would win. Needless to say, many weaker and possibly blameless people were killed.

LAW IN ACTION

1. What aspects of this case explain why trial by ordeal was used to determine guilt or innocence?

trial by oath helping: requiring friends of the accused to swear on the Bible that he or she was innocent

trial by combat: determining guilt or innocence by having the parties fight a duel

Fast Fact
In Canada, extending or accepting a challenge to fight a duel is a criminal offence that carries a penalty of imprisonment for up to two years.

adversarial system: the judicial process whereby evidence is presented by two opposing parties to an impartial judge or jury

Fast Fact
In many parts of Europe, the judicial process is called the inquisitorial system, where the judge participates in assembling evidence and in selecting and questioning witnesses. This model is in sharp contrast to the less active role that judges play in the adversarial system.

While some of the men engaged in these disputes may have been physically weaker than their opponents, they were not necessarily intellectually weaker. Some people recognized that they could hire stronger individuals to fight on their behalf. Sound familiar? The present-day **adversarial system** of justice is based on the same principles. Both sides, represented by lawyers, battle in an arena called "the court" to determine guilt or innocence. Today, of course, the battle is not based on physical strength but on mental ability, where lawyers use their knowledge and skills to argue their cases.

The Feudal System

The arena for most legal battles today is the courtroom. It is assumed that the judge who tries the case will be knowledgeable and impartial, and will uphold the law for everyone. Today, it is taken for granted that "no one is above the law." But this was not always the case.

Up until 1066, there had been no unified system of law since the end of the Roman occupation, so law had become a haphazard affair based on the customs and traditions of independent villages. In 1066, William the Conqueror, Duke of Normandy, invaded England. Although the fighting lasted only 10 hours, the Battle of Hastings became known as the battle that changed European history. William the Conqueror won and quickly established his power as king of England. King William, and later his son Henry I and grandson Henry II, instituted changes in the law by unifying the system and assuming overall authority.

divine right: the concept that monarchs and their successors derived their power to rule from God and were accountable only to God

Figure 1.14 The Battle of Hastings as depicted in a scene from the *Bayeux Tapestry*, designed by Queen Mathilda, wife of William the Conqueror

Like many kings and emperors before him, William *was* the law, and his law prevailed throughout England. This absolute power came from the concept of **divine right,** the belief that monarchs derived their power to rule from God, and that this power was passed to their successors, placing them "above the law," accountable only to God.

William instituted a system of land ownership known as the feudal system, which divided Britain into parcels of land. Each parcel was controlled by a nobleman, and everything within that parcel—the land, the animals, and even the peasants who farmed the land—belonged to the nobleman. This system of ownership resulted in great discrepancies. Because English law was inconsistent, each nobleman judged and sentenced only those under his direct authority. Some noblemen were fair and reasonable, while others were harsh and unjust, so penalties for similar offences differed from village to village. There were no rules of evidence and certainly no thought of the rights of the accused.

By the twelfth century, people rose up against this harsh, unfair treatment. Complaints made their way to the king, who at that time was William's grandson Henry II (1154–1189). Henry's solution to the problem would ultimately change the course of history, reduce the power of the monarchy, and eventually lead to the present-day system of British and Canadian law.

> **Fast Fact**
> Canadian coins bear the inscription "D.G. Regina" from the Latin *Dei Gratia Regina*, meaning "Queen by the Grace of God," referring to the right of inheritance.

Common Law

As the number of disputes in the country increased, King Henry II sought to bring some consistency and fairness to the law. He authorized a number of judges to travel to the various villages and towns and hold court to resolve local disputes. These courts were known as **assizes** and the judges were called **circuit judges.**

assizes: travelling courts

circuit judges: judges of travelling courts

Without a set of rules or a body of codified law, the circuit judges had to rely on their own common sense and principles of justice. They were also guided by existing local customs and traditions that reflected the community's sense of what was just and fair. It could be said that the judges were applying laws that already existed, but in an oral form. Over time, the judges began to notice similarities among various legal problems. Eventually they agreed that similar cases should be decided in the same way, so they began to record both their cases and their decisions. These records helped to establish a common method of dealing with similar legal issues. Such documents formed the basis of what became known as **case law** or **common law** because the information they contained was "common to all."

case law: a method of deciding cases based on recorded decisions of similar cases

common law: law that developed in English courts; relies on case law and is common to all people

Of course, the facts in one case were not always the same as the facts in another, and sometimes the judges could not find a case to follow. However, each time a decision was made, it created a precedent, or an example, which could be followed in future, similar cases. As accurate written reports were made available, it became easier for judges to follow the precedent. This practice led to the principle known as ***stare decisis,*** a Latin phrase meaning "to stand by the decision" or to abide by decisions already made. In other words, the judge of one court would apply the same decision made by the judge of another court, provided the facts of the cases were similar. The process of applying *stare decisis* developed into the **rule of precedent** used today.

stare decisis: a Latin phrase meaning "to stand by the decision"

rule of precedent: applying a previous decision to a case that has similar circumstances

Legal Reforms

Henry's next step was to set up a jury system. The first British juries were used only in land disputes and consisted of 12 elderly men. Because these men had lived in the area for most of their lives, they knew the land in question and could testify as to the ownership or boundaries of the property in dispute. However, they did not decide on a verdict; that was left to the judge. Eventually, King Henry's system of travelling judges evolved into a complex maze of courts. These courts heard disputes about everything from tax collecting and inheritance to serious criminal offences.

Henry II was probably unaware that his great legal reforms would ultimately lead to the downfall of the monarchy's power. By establishing a system of courts that could function independently, he had undermined the power of the king. People began to speculate ... if the king was no longer the maker of the law, perhaps he did not rule by divine right; if the king did not derive his power from God, then perhaps he was not above the law!

After Henry died in 1189, his son John came to power. In June 1215, King John signed the **Magna Carta** and was finally forced to face the reality of limited power.

Magna Carta: a charter of political and civil rights signed in 1215 at Runnymede in England

Legal Link
The original text of the Magna Carta was written in Latin. To view a translation of the text, visit **www.pearsoned.ca/law**.

Rule of Law

The Magna Carta, also called the Great Charter, was the first step in establishing individual basic rights for the people of England. It recognized the principle known as the Rule of Law, which was discussed earlier in this chapter. Rule of Law gave everyone equality before the law. In other words, no one, not even the king or anyone else who made or enforced laws, was above the law.

Habeas Corpus

habeas corpus: a court order designed to prevent unlawful arrest by ensuring that anyone detained is charged before a court within a reasonable amount of time

Another component of the Magna Carta was the writ (legal order) of **habeas corpus,** which is Latin for "you must have the body." A writ of habeas corpus is a court order that commands the custodial authority to present an arrested or detained person before a judge or court to determine the validity of the arrest. The purpose of the order is to secure the release of people who are unlawfully imprisoned. Anyone arrested or detained without explanation is entitled to a court appearance within a reasonable amount of time. This historic right is so fundamental to our legal system that it is now entrenched in the *Canadian Charter of Rights and Freedoms*.

Fast Fact
The Magna Carta was one of the first constitutions in history.

Aboriginal Law

When British and European settlers came to North America, they encountered well-established Aboriginal communities across the continent. The Aboriginal peoples had beliefs that acknowledged a creator in heaven and a strong sense of family and leadership. The people, like the Haida on the west coast and the Mi'kmaq on the east coast, had established governments, religions, social structures, and legal systems. The rules governing the various Aboriginal groups were passed from generation to generation in an oral tradition of storytelling and myths.

Around 1450, five Aboriginal nations—the Mohawk, Onondaga, Seneca, Oneida, and Cayuga—came together to form a League of Nations or Iroquois Confederacy. In 1720, the Tuscarora joined the Iroquois Confederacy, and the Confederacy became more commonly known as the Six Nations. At its height, the influence of the Six Nations extended from Quebec in the east to as far west as Illinois in the United States. The Constitution of the Iroquois Confederacy was eventually recorded in **The Great Binding Law,** or Gayanashagowa.

The Great Binding Law: the Constitution of the Iroquois Confederacy

The Great Binding Law outlined the rights, duties, and responsibilities of the people and included laws covering adoption, emigration, treason, and secession. The Constitution outlined many of the same principles of justice and fairness that are found in modern civil rights documents. An excerpt from The Great Binding Law, shown in Figure 1.16, deals with laws of descent and ownership through clans and consanguity (genetic or blood relationships).

Figure 1.15 This painting shows the interior of a home in Nootka Sound. What do the images in this scene reveal about life in the Nootka community?

On Clans and Consanguity

44. The lineal descent of the people ... shall run in the female line. Women shall be considered the progenitors of the Nation. They shall own the land and the soil. Men and women shall follow the status of the mother.

45. The women heirs of the Confederated Lordship titles shall be called Royaneh [or Nobles] for all time to come.

47. If the female heirs of a Confederate Lord's title become extinct, the title right shall be given by the Lords of the Confederacy to the sister family whom they shall elect and that family shall hold the name and transmit it to their [female] heirs, but they shall not appoint any of their sons as a candidate for a title until all the eligible men of the former family shall have died or otherwise have become ineligible.

Source: Excerpted with permission from "The Constitution of the Iroquois Nations: The Great Binding Law, Gayanashagowa." Prepared by Gerald Murphy (The Cleveland Free-Net - aa300). Distributed by the Cybercasting Services Division of the National Public Telecomputing Network (NPTN).

Figure 1.16 What beliefs and values are revealed by these excerpts from The Great Binding Law of the Iroquois Confederacy?

Legal Link
You will find The Great Binding Law by visiting **www.pearsoned.ca/law**. Select one section of this document and discuss it with a partner.

Reflecting on Our Historical Roots

The Canadian legal system today has been influenced by all of the earlier legal systems discussed in this chapter. Although our laws may not always agree with what the Babylonians or the Hebrews considered wrong, evidence shows that our legal system was deeply affected by many of their laws of custom and religion. We, too, have laws that express our belief that murder, theft, assault, and lying in court are wrong and should be punished.

Mosaic Law is the root of three modern religions: Judaism, Christianity, and Islam. Also, many modern concepts of law and justice come from Christian writers and philosophers who wrote about the role of the Church in creating a moral framework for law and government. For instance, St. Augustine (354–430 CE), a Roman citizen, believed it was the duty of the Church to impose a sense of morality on the government of the state. Other writers suggested that citizens should not obey a state law that went against the laws of God, and that they actually had a moral obligation to disobey an unjust law. Today Western democracies attempt to separate Church and State. However, there is no doubt that religion played an important role in shaping the heritage, values, and beliefs on which the law is based.

To summarize the historical roots of our legal system since the influence of biblical law, we should recall that the Canadian jury process is a modern version of the ancient Greek juries. The Greek concept that an accused has the right to be tried by an impartial jury of his or her peers remains a cornerstone of our own legal system. And we have the Romans to thank for establishing the role of the lawyer and for contributing to the development of the *French Civil Code,* which forms the basis of the **Quebec Civil Code.** Finally, we acknowledge a great debt to the British legal system and its Rule of Law and rule of precedent. These two traditional systems—French and English—are reflected in Canadian law today.

With increasing frequency, Canadian courts are recognizing Aboriginal interpretations of early land claims and treaty rights. Also, Aboriginal systems of justice that emphasize community involvement and rehabilitation are enjoying an increasing measure of respect and consideration among Canadian lawmakers. For example, one alternative to imprisonment is compliance with the decisions of a sentencing circle. The sentencing circle gathers the offender, the victim, law enforcers, and other members of the community together to determine how to assist both the offender and the victim in the healing process.

Legal Link
To learn more about the history of law, visit **www.pearsoned.ca/law** and tour the Law Museum.

Quebec Civil Code: the system of law used in Quebec for resolving private matters

Building Your Understanding

1. How was trial by oath helping similar to the jury system of Greek law? How was it different?
2. Explain the meaning of "case law" and how it has evolved since the reign of King Henry II.
3. Define "rule of precedent," using an example.
4. Describe the importance of the Magna Carta for the people of Britain.
5. In the Iroquois Confederacy, how does the right of ownership pass from one generation to another?

LOOKING BACK

Reviewing Your Vocabulary

adversarial system *p. 26*
assizes *p. 27*
case law *p. 27*
circuit judges *p. 27*
Code of Hammurabi p. 17
Code of Li k'vei p. 17
codified *p. 17*
common law *p. 27*
divine right *p. 26*

Great Laws of Manu *p. 17*
habeas corpus p. 28
Justinian's Code p. 22
Magna Carta *p. 28*
Mosaic Law *p. 19*
Napoleonic Code p. 23
Quebec Civil Code p. 30
restitution *p. 18*
retribution *p. 18*

Rule of Law *p. 13*
rule of precedent *p. 27*
stare decisis p. 27
Ten Commandments *p. 19*
The Great Binding Law *p. 28*
trial by combat *p. 25*
trial by oath helping *p. 25*
trial by ordeal *p. 24*

Quick Quiz

1. Match the vocabulary terms above with these clues:
    a) one of the earliest known written codes
    b) based on case law, it was developed by circuit judges in England
    c) laws given to Moses, which became the foundation of Judeo-Christian legal systems
    d) a battle between two people to determine guilt
    e) known as the Great Charter, it became the forerunner of many civil rights documents
    f) a legal system based on two lawyers arguing the case in court before an impartial judge
    g) a peace agreement among six Aboriginal tribes in what is now Canada and the United States
    h) an early code of law from China
    i) a Roman code of law written by an emperor whose name is synonymous with the concept of justice
    j) the term that literally means "to stand by the decision"
    k) the basis for the *Quebec Civil Code*
    l) a historic right to a court appearance within a reasonable amount of time

Checking Your Knowledge

2. Adil breaks into a neighbour's home and steals some goblets and jewellery. Adil blames a friend for the crime. The friend has now been charged with a crime for which he may be put to death.

    a) If Adil is caught telling lies about his friend, what, according to Babylonian law, will happen to him? Would this behaviour be an offence in Mosaic Law?
    b) The judge who hears the case against Adil's friend finds him guilty. Later he changes his mind about his verdict. What would happen to this judge according to the *Code of Hammurabi*? Would the judge be punished in Mosaic Law?

3. How does democracy today differ from democracy in early Greece?
4. Why was the codification of laws so important to the Roman Empire?
5. Explain why legal advisers were required during Roman times.
6. Explain why Rule of Law is an essential concept of justice in Canada's legal system.

Developing Your Thinking and Inquiry Skills

7. Examine the following cases. Indicate whether you believe the outcomes are 1) somewhat just, 2) just, 3) somewhat unjust, or 4) unjust. Explain your answers.
   a) James had been robbed five times. The sixth time, he pulled out a shotgun and fired as the robbers were running away, hitting one of them in the buttocks. James was convicted of assault causing bodily harm and sentenced to 10 months in jail.
   b) Yvan Turcotte was charged with child abuse after severe bruises caused by the cord of an iron were detected on the legs of his 10-year-old son. Turcotte claimed he was exercising his right as a father to discipline his child and that his religious beliefs sanction physical discipline when a child misbehaves. The judge agreed that Turcotte's freedom of religion was paramount and that the discipline was not excessive. Turcotte was acquitted.
   c) A man convicted of causing the death of a high-school student during a road rage incident is given permission to leave the country to visit his ailing mother before being sentenced.
   d) A court authorizes a blood transfusion to a minor even though his life was not endangered. Blood transfusion is a practice forbidden by the family's religion.

8. Prepare a chart that includes a column for each of the societies identified in the section called Historical Roots of Law. Include a column for Canadian society. Organize the aspects of the law highlighted for each of these historical societies. Identify the similarities and differences between the laws in these societies and laws covering similar situations in Canada.

9. Many European countries use the inquisitorial system of justice rather than the adversarial approach. Research the two systems to find out how they differ. Then outline the merits of each system.

10. Find out more about trial by ordeal. Identify the types of offences that would have been tried in this manner, and explain the process involved. Present your findings in a visual display.

11. Using the Internet and other resources, research laws practised by an Aboriginal nation of your choice. Consider such nations as Haida, Salish, Cree, Blackfoot, Mi'kmaq, and Beothuk. Describe which of the nation's values and beliefs you believe inspired these laws.

Communicating Your Ideas

12. Starting with the *Code of Hammurabi*, complete a Legal History Timeline for display in class. Illustrate your timeline with drawings or photographs.

13. Interview a judge, a lawyer, or another member of the court system to find out his or her views on the concept of justice in the Canadian legal system. Use a camcorder or an audiotape to record your interview and present it to the class.

Putting It All Together

14. Investigate laws that appear to discriminate against a particular group on the grounds of age, race, ethnicity, religion, gender, or sexual orientation. The examples you choose may be laws in Canada or in other parts of the world. Record these laws, identify the country in which they exist, and discuss the punishments imposed for breaking the law. Present your findings in the form of a newspaper or magazine article.

Law and Morality—Ethics Exercise

Most people consider it the first duty of a citizen not only to obey the law but also to uphold it. Sometimes, upholding a law may bring you into conflict with your conscience, a moral principle, your own self-interest, personal loyalties, values, or beliefs.

Choose one of the problems in the opposite column and analyze your choice according to the following guideline:

1. State the legal issue (if there is one) that underlies the situation.
2. State what you believe would be the ideal or moral thing to do.
3. Give the possible consequences of performing such an action.
4. Outline what you would do if faced with a similar situation.

PROBLEMS

a) While browsing through a department store, you see a woman stuff some articles of clothing inside her coat while she continues her regular shopping.

b) You are expecting a tax refund of $90 and are surprised to find a cheque made out to you for $9000.

c) Walking through a park, you observe a mother hitting a small child with her fists.

d) You are a bartender, and a woman who is obviously pregnant comes in and orders a vodka martini.

e) On the way out of the parking lot, while driving your dad's car, you accidentally back into another car, denting its fender. Your dad's car is not damaged.

f) You have been offered $10 000 if you would sell one of your kidneys to the parents of a child who is dying of kidney failure.

g) Your best friend, who is a computer whiz, has managed to break into the school computer and increase the marks you have both earned to apply to university. High marks will automatically guarantee you a place and a scholarship.

h) A law is passed that makes it a crime for anyone to speak out against the government and requires those who hear people doing so to report them to the authorities. Your father frequently speaks out against the government in your presence.

i) You are a lawyer, and your client has just instructed you to remove certain videotapes from the scene of a horrible crime. When you view the videotapes, you discover that they implicate not only your client, but also an accomplice who claimed that she did not participate in the crime. Failure to provide the Crown with the tapes may result in your being charged with "obstruction of justice." Turning over the tapes may violate your client's rights to absolute privilege, and you may be disbarred.

2 Classifying Law

CHAPTER OUTLINE

Sources of Law in Canada

Categories of Law

FOCUS YOUR LEARNING

What are the sources of law in Canada?

Which sources of law override others?

What aspect of society does each category of law regulate?

WHAT DO YOU THINK?

- Which of these situations involve the law?
- Explain how the law is involved in the situations you have chosen.

On close examination, you will discover that all of the situations shown in the photographs opposite involve the law. Because the law is such an important part of our lives and affects almost everything we do, we should, as responsible citizens, understand where laws come from and how they are made. The purpose of this chapter is to discuss the sources of law in Canada and to clarify how the law is organized into different categories.

SOURCES OF LAW IN CANADA

In Canada laws originate from three sources: from the Canadian Constitution (constitutional law), from elected government representatives (statute law), and from previous legal decisions (common law). As Figure 2.1 shows, each source of law has a different level of authority: constitutional law can override (prevail over or counteract) statute law, and statute law can override common law. To get a good sense of how laws originate, we will start at the bottom of the pyramid with common law and review some of the principles discussed in Chapter 1.

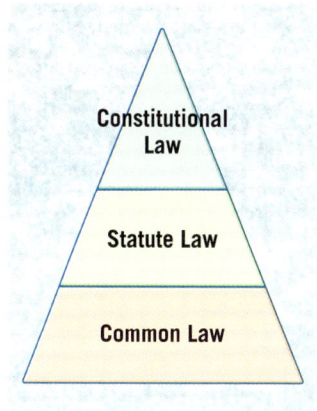

Figure 2.1 Sources of Law. Constitutional law appears at the top of the pyramid because it overrides all other laws.

Common Law

As you read in Chapter 1, common law can be traced to the ancient, unwritten laws of England. It is called "common law" because it is common to all and has a general and universal application. Common law is also called "case law" because its sources include the decisions made by judges in previous cases. Case law, or common law, is sometimes referred to as **English common law** or judge-made laws.

Common law is constantly evolving as judges decide new cases based on previous judicial decisions. Today, Canadian courts continue to follow the legal principle known as *stare decisis,* relying on the decisions made by other courts when determining the outcome of similar cases. Following this legal maxim, lawyers look for favourable precedents to argue the outcome of their cases.

The rule of precedent is not the only way Canadian courts judge cases. What would happen if the judge disagreed with the decision made by another judge, or the precedent was set some time ago and is no longer applicable in today's society? Or suppose the current case involves new technology and is so unique that no previous case law exists. In all of these situations, the presiding judge may reject previous decisions and create a new precedent. This process is called **distinguishing a case.**

English common law: law that originates from decisions made by judges in previous cases

distinguishing a case: identifying a case as being sufficiently different from previous cases as to warrant a different decision

statute law: a law or act passed by government

Statute Law

Another source of Canadian law is **statute law,** which consists of laws that are passed by elected representatives in the form of acts. Acts become law when they pass through a formal procedure in Parliament or provincial legislatures. Many of our laws today are actually statutes—common law decisions that have been codified. Statutes generally override previous common law,

Figure 2.2 Canada's Parliament in session in the House of Commons, Ottawa

as shown in Figure 2.1. Where no statute exists to deal with a particular situation, the common law will prevail.

In practice, statutes and common law co-exist in Canadian law. When a judge interprets and applies a statute, that decision then sets a precedent. From that point on, similar cases must be interpreted in the same way by all lower courts. A defence counsel would refer to this body of precedent law to find a precedent that might be used to interpret a statute in favour of his or her client. If you look at cases in law reports or on the Internet, you will find references to previous cases that both sides have cited to show that precedent has been set.

Each level of government—federal, provincial, and municipal—has the power to enact legislation in its own area of political **jurisdiction** (authority and control). Indian Bands and Aboriginal groups with self-government agreements also have the authority to enact legislation. Statute law will be explained more extensively in Chapter 3, Government and Statute Law.

jurisdiction: the political or legal authority to pass and enforce laws, or the judicial authority to decide a case

Federal Government

The federal government enacts laws within its own jurisdiction, which includes criminal law, federal penitentiaries, employment insurance, banking and currency, marriage and divorce, and postal services. Everyone in Canada is subject to these laws.

The federal government passes legislation in other areas as well. Have you ever wondered why a package of cigarettes carries messages like "Cigarettes cause fatal lung disease" or "Smoking can kill you"? By law, cigarette manufacturers must label their packages in this way according to s. 15 (section 15) of the *Tobacco Act,* S.C. 1997, c. 13, which states the following:

15. (1) No manufacturer or retailer shall sell a tobacco product unless the package containing it displays, in the prescribed form and manner, the information required by the regulations about the product and its emissions, and about the health hazards and health effects arising from the use of the product or from its emissions.

The federal government enacted this statute to protect the public by regulating what it considered to be a dangerous product.

Provincial Governments

Provincial governments have authority to make laws within their provincial jurisdictions, such as laws affecting hospitals, police forces, property rights, highways and roads, and provincial jails. You will learn more about the division of jurisdictional powers in the next chapter.

Local Governments

Municipal or local governments make laws called **bylaws,** which are regulations that deal with local issues, such as how high the backyard fence should be, who should clear the snow from the sidewalk, or how often the garbage should be collected.

Aboriginal Governing Structures

Indian bands established under the federal *Indian Act* are like local governments. Each Indian band has some authority to make bylaws that apply to each band's reserve lands. These bylaws include the regulation of road and bridge construction and other public works located on reserves.

Another form of Aboriginal government can be established under a self-government agreement between the Aboriginal group and the government. A self-governing Aboriginal group has wider law-making powers than an Indian band. For example, the Nisga'a Nation in British Columbia has the power to make laws with respect to marriage, adoption, education, and the provision of social and health services. These law-making powers are generally exercised by provinces.

Constitutional Law

The third source of Canadian law is the Constitution, a document that determines the structure of the federal government and divides law-making powers between the federal and provincial governments. **Constitutional law** also limits the powers of government by setting out certain basic laws, principles, and standards that all other law must adhere to. As Figure 2.1 illustrates, constitutional law is at the top of the pyramid because it overrides all other laws; that is, the courts will interpret other laws to ensure that they are consistent with the Constitution. If a law is found to be in violation of the Constitution, it may be struck down by the courts on the grounds that it is "unconstitutional." You will learn more about this source of Canadian law in Unit 2.

> **Consider This**
> Discuss whether governments should be allowed to pass legislation that regulates the advertising and labelling of products in the private sector.

bylaws: laws that deal with local issues and are passed by municipal governments

constitutional law: body of law dealing with the distribution and exercise of government powers

Building Your Understanding

1. Identify the three sources of Canadian law. Design your own diagram or chart to show how one source has priority over the other.
2. Explain the process known as "distinguishing a case."
3. Look for a newspaper article that includes information about a federal or provincial statute. Find out when this statute was passed into law.
4. Name three bylaws that have been made by the local government of your community. Suggest a new bylaw that you think should be passed.

CATEGORIES OF LAW

Legal disputes rarely fit neatly into one category or another without overlapping at some point. However, categories provide distinctions that help to clarify and organize a complex body of laws. Broad categories of law include international and domestic law, substantive and procedural law, and public and private law. Later in the chapter, public and private law will be further subdivided to deal with specific aspects of society.

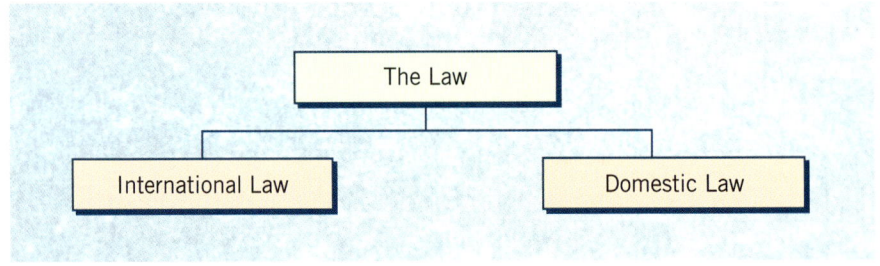

Figure 2.3 Categories of Law. The broadest categories are international law and domestic law. Throughout this chapter, new categories will be added to the chart.

International Law

international law: law that governs relations between independent nations

International law includes laws that govern the conduct of independent nations in their relationships with one another. Without any one global, law-making authority, international law is generally created by custom. Custom means consistent and general practice among states and the acceptance of this practice as law by the international community.

Nations that sign treaties, or international agreements, consider these treaties as binding as any law. Treaties can also contain provisions that codify customary international law. For example, Canada has entered into many agreements with other countries: extradition treaties (agreements that arrange to send persons to other countries to be tried for crimes committed there); free-trade agreements that reduce or remove trade barriers; and defence treaties that govern organizations such as NATO (North Atlantic Treaty Organization). There are even agreements among nations on such matters as ownership of the moon and outer space, responsibility for space debris, and the control of satellites.

Fast Fact

Canada was instrumental in negotiating a treaty to ban anti-personnel landmines. In 1997, 122 countries signed the Ottawa Convention, which went into force on March 1, 1999.

Milosevic on Trial

LAW IN ACTION

The International Criminal Tribunal for the Former Yugoslavia (ICTY) was established by the United Nations Security Council to prosecute persons responsible for serious violations of international humanitarian law committed by various parties during the breakup of former Yugoslavia since 1991.

Between January 1 and June 20, 1999, the Armed Forces of the Federal Republic of Yugoslavia (FRY), the police forces of the FRY, the police forces of Serbia, and paramilitary units executed a campaign of terror and violence against the people of Kosovo, a province of Serbia. Approximately 740 000 Kosovo civilians of Albanian descent were forced to flee the province. Their homes were looted and their villages shelled. Many were abused or killed as they fled, and massacres were reported in a number of areas.

On April 1, 2001, Slobodan Milosevic was arrested in Belgrade by local authorities. He was transferred to the ICTY on June 29, 2001, for trial. He was charged as President of the FRY, Supreme Commander of the Armed Forces, and President of the Supreme Defence Council with violations of the customs of war and with crimes against humanity.

The accused refused to recognize the authority of the ICTY or to enter a plea. Consequently, the Trial Chamber entered a not-guilty plea on his behalf. In the interests of securing a fair trial, the Trial Chamber also invited the Registrar to designate counsel to appear as *amicus curiae* (a friend of the court). The role of *amicus curiae* is to act, not as defence counsel, but as an impartial party who represents the interests of the accused. This person may make submissions or objections to evidence and act in appropriate ways to prevent injustice.

In October, 2001, at his third appearance since his extradition from Yugoslavia, Milosevic refused to enter pleas to a new indictment accusing him of atrocities and murder in Croatia in 1991, and to additional charges implicating his forces in Kosovo in 1999. Once again, he rejected the court's jurisdiction and claimed that the Croatia indictment was illegitimate (which was also his position regarding the Kosovo indictment). By now, the accused had three *amici curiae*—British, Dutch and Yugoslav. But Milosevic still refused to co-operate, so counsel entered not-guilty pleas on his behalf.

At trial, Slobodan Milosevic presented his own defence. He faced 66 counts of war crimes, including the charge of genocide.

1. Explain why Milosevic was charged.
2. On what authority did the ICTY prosecute Milosevic?
3. Why were *amici curiae* designated at trial?

> "Those who commit war crimes, genocide or other crimes against humanity will no longer be beyond the reach of justice. Humanity will be able to defend itself—responding to the worst of human nature with one of the greatest human achievements: the rule of law."
>
> — UN Secretary-General Kofi Annan on the International Criminal Court

Figure 2.4 Canada played a major role in creating the International Criminal Court, which was approved by over 60 countries on April 11, 2002. The mandate of this court is to try individuals accused of crimes against humanity, eliminating the need for temporary tribunals such as the one set up to try Slobodan Milosevic.

Figure 2.5 Louise Arbour served as the International War Crimes Tribunal's chief prosecutor during the investigations into the massacres in Rwanda and the former Yugoslavia. Today, she is a Justice on the Supreme Court of Canada.

domestic law: law that governs activity within a nation's borders

Not only countries, but also a number of organizations have international legal status. These organizations can help develop laws and, in some cases, adjudicate, or act as a court to settle disputes. Two examples include the United Nations (UN), whose member states signed a Universal Declaration of Human Rights in 1948, and the International Court of Justice (ICJ), based at The Hague in the Netherlands. The ICJ hears disputes between member nations and even adjudicates disputes between individuals and their governments.

A major difference between international law and laws made within nations is enforcement. Although UN peacekeepers, known as "blue helmets," can be sent to warring nations to help restore and maintain peace, their power is limited. Similarly, while law enforcement agencies co-operate to combat crimes such as terrorism or international drug trafficking, no international police force exists with the authority to enforce an international system of law. As worldwide communication, travel, and access to information accelerate due to advances in technology, an international police force may become necessary. But how such a body would be granted its authority or carry out its responsibilities remains unclear.

Domestic Law

Within its defined boundaries, a nation's law-making authority comes from the power to govern—usually from a monarchy or a constitution. Law made and enforced within a nation's borders is known as **domestic law,** and it includes both case law and statute law. When you cross the border of another country, you enter a sovereign nation that has its own laws and legal system, which may be very different from the laws familiar to you. In fact, you may break a law in another country without even knowing it. For example, laws in some Middle Eastern countries prohibit certain types of dress or forbid the drinking of alcohol. When you travel outside Canada, you do not have the protection of Canadian law. If you break a law in another country, there is very little that the Canadian government can do to help you.

Figure 2.6 Categories of Law. Domestic Law is divided into substantive and procedural law.

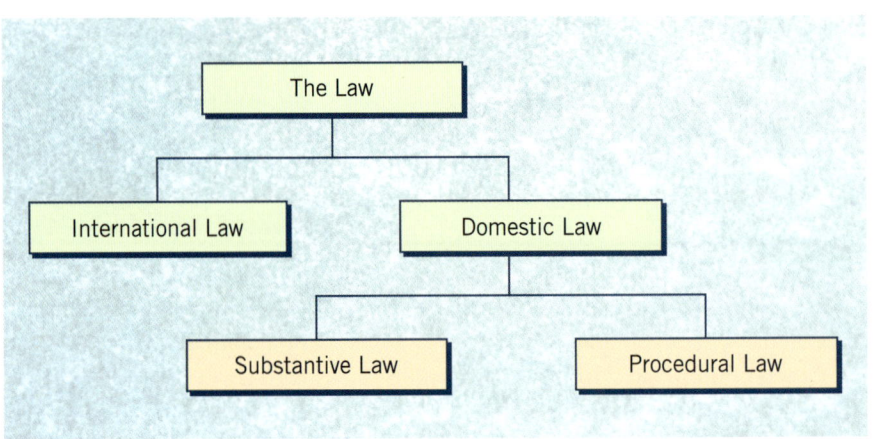

United States v. Burns, [2001] 1 S.C.R. 283

CASE

In July 1994, the Rafay family was found beaten to death with a baseball bat in their Bellevue, Washington, home. The suspects in the slayings, Glen Sebastian Burns and Atif Rafay, fled to Canada. When they were arrested a year later in Vancouver, the accused, both Canadian citizens, confessed to undercover RCMP officers in statements they later contested. Rafay and Burns were charged in Washington with the murders and were held in Vancouver jails.

Canada's minister of justice ordered their extradition without seeking assurances from the United States that the death penalty would not be imposed or carried out. Under Canadian law, this was considered a violation of the rights of the accused, and the British Columbia Court of Appeal directed the minister to seek assurances as a condition of surrender. The minister appealed this ruling to the Supreme Court of Canada.

On February 15, 2001, the Supreme Court of Canada unanimously ruled that, in all but exceptional cases, no one facing the death penalty in another country should be extradited from Canada without assurance against execution. In March 2001, Norm Maleng, the prosecutor for Washington, gave assurances to the Canadian minister of justice that Burns and Rafay would not face the death penalty. However, he indicated that he was not pleased with the situation:

> While I take issue with the notion that an offender can commit murder in Washington State, and then flee to Canada to seek the protection of Canadian laws for crimes committed in the United States, I also have an interest in seeing these men brought to justice and achieving finality in this tragic case. It's unfortunate that one country dictated to another how to implement justice or how they can try somebody.

1. How does this case illustrate differences in the domestic law of Canada and the United States?
2. Explain the Supreme Court ruling in your own words.
3. Critics of the Court's ruling suggest that Canada could become a safe haven for criminal fugitives. Explain why you agree or disagree with this suggestion.

Substantive Law

One category of domestic law is **substantive law,** which defines the rights, duties, and obligations of citizens and levels of government. Examples include the right to own and protect property, to enter into a legal contract, and to seek remedies if that contract is broken. Section 15 of the *Tobacco Act*, which you read earlier in this chapter, is another example of a substantive law, as is the definition of careless driving found in the *Highway Traffic Act*. When you examine the definition of a charge such as "failing to remain at the scene of an accident" or "careless driving," you are examining substantive law.

As a citizen, your conduct is governed by substantive law. Should you be accused of an offence, your lawyer will examine the law to determine if your actions did, in fact, fall within the meaning of the substantive law.

substantive law: law that defines the rights, duties, and obligations of citizens and government

CASE

R. v. Burke (2001), 153 C.C.C. (3d) 97 (Ont. C.A.)

Howard Burke

BACKGROUND Mr. Burke was charged with attempted murder. At trial, when the verdict was read, the trial judge mistakenly thought the foreperson had said "not guilty." As a result, the judge recorded a verdict of not guilty, discharged the jury, and released the accused. Minutes later, a court officer informed the judge of the error. The next day, the judge conducted an inquiry into the verdict. He determined he had misheard the verdict, entered a conviction, and sentenced Burke to twelve-and-a-half years' imprisonment. Burke's lawyer appealed this conviction to the Ontario Court of Appeal.

LEGAL QUESTION Does a trial judge have the jurisdiction to make this kind of correction after the jury has been discharged?

DECISION The appeal was heard by a panel of judges and dismissed. The majority of the court considered the matter as merely a clerical mistake or an error arising from an accidental slip or omission that could be corrected. Mr. Burke's conviction was reinstated.

Mr. Justice Stephen Goudge gave a dissenting point of view; that is, he did not agree with the majority. He said that he would restore Burke's acquittal because the law is clear. A discharged jury cannot be recalled for questioning about the true nature of their verdict—which is what the trial judge had to do to determine if a mistake had been made. Justice Goudge said that forbidding such questioning respects the importance of having finality in criminal cases and not letting an accused person's liberty hang under a cloud.

HISTORICAL SIGNIFICANCE The Burke case prompted the province to reconsider procedures for recording jury verdicts to avoid future errors of this type.

ANALYSIS

1. Explain why Justice Goudge disagreed with the majority and why he would have allowed the acquittal to stand.
2. Assume you are one of the judges who supported reinstating the conviction. What reasons would you give to support your position?

Procedural Law

procedural law: law that prescribes the methods of enforcing the rights and obligations of substantive law

Fast Fact
One example of procedural law is the process that governs how a case can be appealed to a higher court.

While substantive law is the content of the law, **procedural law** is the law that prescribes methods of enforcing the rights, duties, and responsibilities found in substantive law. For example, procedural law refers to gathering evidence properly, following the legal requirements for a lawful arrest, and adhering to correct trial procedures. Police officers cannot simply arrest people on made-up charges and put them in jail because they do not approve of their actions. All persons with lawful authority must follow certain procedures, a requirement that creates a level of predictability. Procedural law helps ensure that all citizens are treated fairly and that neither the police nor the courts act arbitrarily.

Public Law

Substantive law can be divided into the categories of public law and private law. **Public law** regulates the relationship between the government and its citizens. In addition to constitutional law, which you read about earlier, public law includes administrative law and criminal law. All public laws are ultimately subject to the *Canadian Charter of Rights and Freedoms,* which is part of the Canadian Constitution.

public law: law related to relationships between individuals and the state

Administrative Law The everyday lives of Canadians are probably more affected by administrative law than by any other branch of law. Victims of violent crimes seeking reparation for injuries or expenses, injured workers seeking compensation, and people concerned about a subdivision being built near a conservation area all find themselves involved in the legal branch known as administrative law. **Administrative law** refers to the many government departments, boards, and tribunals that play a role in regulating the relationship between people and government agencies. Examples include the Liquor Control Board, the Labour Board, Workers' Compensation Board, and Victims' Compensation Board.

administrative law: law related to the relationship between people and government departments, boards, and agencies

Public administrators make legal decisions every day, ranging from who receives welfare to who gets access to medical services. If citizens disagree with any of these decisions, their recourse through administrative law is to approach administrative tribunals and then, ultimately, the courts.

Criminal Law This is the category that attracts the most media attention, both on the news and on television programs that focus on law enforcement and criminal court cases. **Criminal law** prohibits and punishes behaviour that causes harm to others, such as murder, robbery, or assault. All crimes are described in the *Criminal Code of Canada* and related federal statutes, such as the *Controlled Drugs and Substances Act* or the *Youth Criminal Justice Act.*

criminal law: law that identifies crimes and prescribes punishment

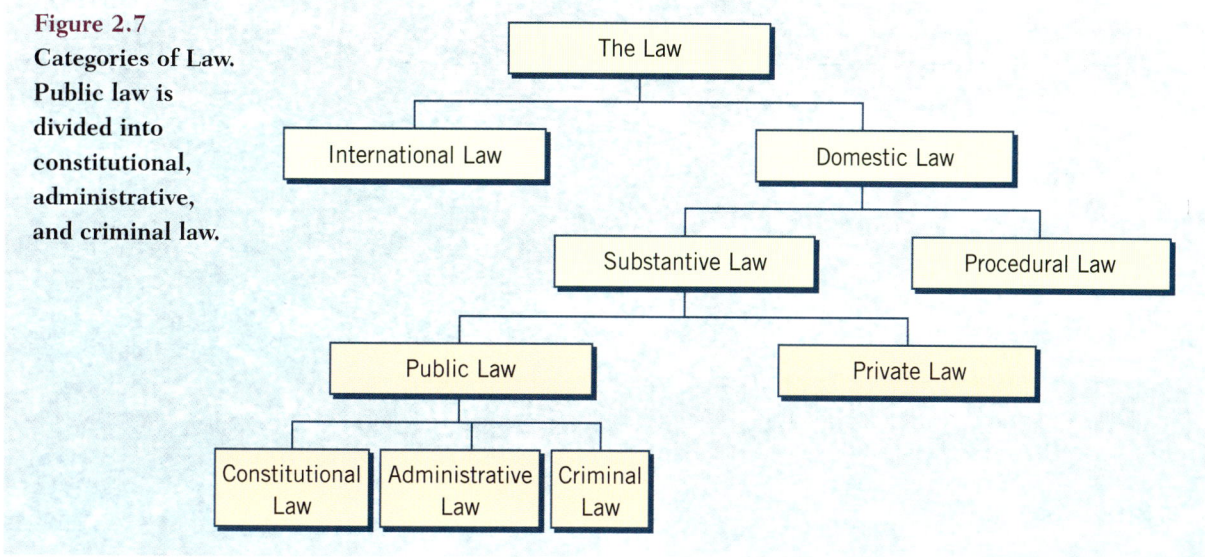

Figure 2.7 Categories of Law. Public law is divided into constitutional, administrative, and criminal law.

CASE

Kadlak v. Nunavut (Minister of Sustainable Development)
(2001), Nu.C.J. 1, QL

1. What is the function of government-appointed boards and tribunals such as the board mentioned in this case?
2. What conditions do you think could have been devised to address the concern for public safety?

Kadlak, a member of the Inuit community, was granted permission by the Nunavut Wildlife Management Board to hunt bear, using a spear or harpoon. However, the Minister of Sustainable Development for Nunavut overturned the Board's decision, on the basis that hunting bear with a spear or harpoon was contrary to public safety. Kadlak appealed this ruling.

Judge Kilpatrick, speaking for the Nunavut Court of Justice, found for Kadlak. He said the Inuit right of harvest contained in the Nunavut Land Claims Agreement was constitutionally protected by virtue of the agreement's incorporation into s. 35 of the *Constitution Act*. The Minister's decision to restrict the harvesting right was based on a valid legislative objective—public safety. Nonetheless, Judge Kilpatrick held that reasonable conditions could have been devised to address the Minister's concerns.

In Canadian law, a crime is carried out not only against the individual, but against society as a whole, which is represented by the Crown. This is why case citations follow the format *R. v. Accused*, with "R" standing for *Regina* or *Rex*, the Latin terms for Queen or King (the Canadian head of state).

In Canada, only the Crown attorney can lay a criminal charge, and the crime must be one that can be found in the *Criminal Code* or a related statute. For example, before 1993, a person could be stalked (pursued or harassed), and the police could do nothing about it because stalking was not an offence in the *Criminal Code*.

Only the federal government has the authority to pass criminal legislation. For example, British Columbia cannot pass an act called the *British Columbia Criminal Code*. (Law making will be covered in greater detail in Chapter 3.) However, all provinces and territories have the authority to administer, or implement, criminal law. In this capacity, they appoint provincial trial court judges, employ Crown attorneys, and manage the running of the criminal courts.

Private Law

private (or civil) law: law governing the relationships between private individuals and between individuals and organizations

Private law, more commonly known as **civil law,** covers all the areas of law that deal with legal relationships between individuals and between individuals and organizations (excluding the government). The main purpose of private law is to regulate conduct and compensate individuals who have been harmed by the wrongful actions of others. Private law refers to torts (civil injuries), contracts, and family law, which you will learn more about in later chapters. Private law also includes wills and estates, property law, and employment law. The following section will serve as a brief introduction to each of these branches of law.

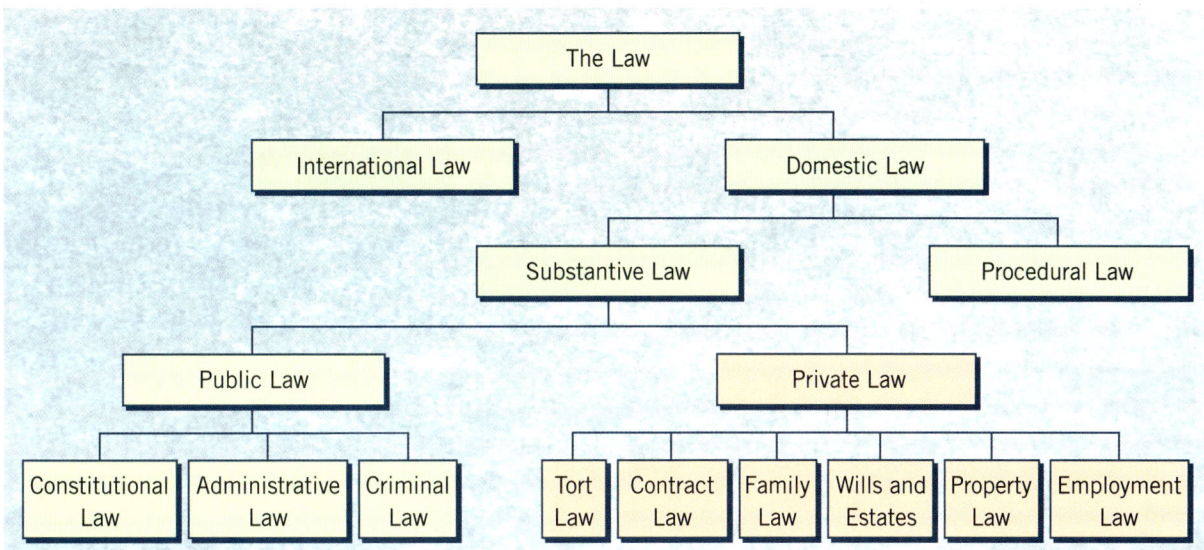

Figure 2.8 Categories of Law. Private law is divided into tort law, contract law, family law, wills and estates law, property law, and employment law.

Tort Law "Woman seeks $1.5 million for damages after finding the head of a rat in her burger." You are probably familiar with headlines like this one—perhaps not as gruesome—that proclaim demands for large amounts of money to compensate for harm, pain, suffering, or financial loss caused by the careless actions of others. Most of these claims are based on laws in the legal branch known as the law of torts. When someone is injured or harmed as a result of the negligent or deliberate action of others, and the injured party seeks compensation from the wrongdoer, the action will be decided under the principles of **tort law.**

People generally do what they can to avoid being held responsible for accidental injuries. For example, store owners or employers will often place notices (such as "slippery when wet" signs) warning people of possible danger. However, when a lawsuit does occur, the person who has been harmed (the plaintiff) brings an action against the person who has caused the harm (the defendant). The onus is on the plaintiff to prove to the court that the defendant's actions caused the damage. You will learn more about this process in Unit 4.

tort law: the branch of civil law that holds persons or private organizations responsible for damage they cause another person as a result of accidental or deliberate action

Contract Law Whether you purchase a burger and fries in your school cafeteria, hire a DJ for your party, or buy a new car, you are entering into a contractual agreement. **Contract law** deals with everyday transactions in which people purchase or provide goods and services. If people are satisfied with their purchases or the level of service provided, and they pay what is owed, disputes do not arise. However, if one party fails to uphold the terms of the agreement, the other may seek the court's assistance to have the terms enforced.

contract law: the branch of civil law that provides rules regarding agreements between people and businesses

Family Law **Family law** covers such matters as marriage, property division upon separation, custody and support of children, and divorce. This branch of

family law: the branch of civil law that deals with various aspects of family life

CHAPTER 2 ◆ Classifying Law

Figure 2.9 Which branches of private law do you think these photographs represent?

 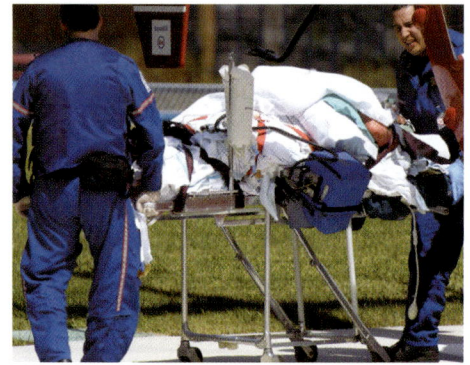

law also specifies the requirements for obtaining a divorce and may determine how often a separated parent can have access to his or her children.

estate law: the branch of civil law concerned with the division and distribution of property after death

Wills and Estates Law governs life from birth to death. **Estate law,** or succession law, deals with the division of property after death. Estate lawyers make sure that their clients have legally binding wills that properly reflect how they want their property to be divided when they die. Estate law also resolves disputes if someone challenges the terms of the will after the person dies; or, it governs what will happen to the property if that person dies without a will.

property law: the branch of civil law that governs ownership rights in property

Property Law **Property law** regulates ownership rights in all property, including the ownership and transfer of real estate. Originally, most Canadian laws dealing with property came from British case law. Today much of our property law can be found in statutes.

employment law: the branch of civil law that governs employer-employee relationships

Employment Law **Employment law** covers relationships between employers and employees. Federal and provincial governments have enacted laws that regulate the workplace and balance the rights of employer and employee. In Canada, laws protect children under a certain age from being forced to work, restrict the number of hours employees are obliged to work, and specify the minimum wage employers must pay. Employment law also governs hiring and firing practices; protection from discrimination and harassment (unwelcome conduct or attention); safety rules and procedures for protection in the workplace; and laws regulating unions and their activities.

Building Your Understanding

1. a) Explain the difference between statute law and common law; international law and domestic law; substantive and procedural law; and public and private law.
   b) Draw a diagram or an illustration to show how these categories of law are interconnected.

2. Provide an example of procedural law not described in this chapter.

3. Describe an important function of administrative law.

4. What branches of law are covered under the category of private law?

LOOKING BACK

Reviewing Your Vocabulary

administrative law *p. 43*
bylaws *p. 37*
civil law *p. 44*
constitutional law *p. 37*
contract law *p. 45*
criminal law *p. 43*
distinguishing a case *p. 35*
domestic law *p. 40*
employment law *p. 46*
English common law *p. 35*
estate law *p. 46*
family law *p. 45*
international law *p. 38*
jurisdiction *p. 36*
private law *p. 44*
procedural law *p. 42*
property law *p. 46*
public law *p. 43*
statute law *p. 35*
substantive law *p. 41*
tort law *p. 45*

Quick Quiz

1. Match the vocabulary terms above with these clues:
   a) the term for municipal laws
   b) a category of law requiring the involvement of a police officer
   c) two terms, one covering law within a country and one covering law between nations
   d) a category of law that involves the Ontario Human Rights Commission and the Wildlife Management Board
   e) the term describing acts passed by Parliament
   f) a category of law under which a person can sue for injuries
   g) the type of law the family of a man who dies without a will must rely on to distribute his property
   h) the category of law that covers divorce, custody, and separation
   i) two categories of substantive law

Checking Your Knowledge

2. What is meant by judge-made law?
3. Provide two examples of statutes (or acts) enacted by the federal government.
4. What is the role of constitutional law in the Canadian legal system?
5. Explain why criminal law falls under the category of public law.
6. Define tort law.
7. Tax law and environmental law were not discussed in this chapter. Would you categorize these branches as public or private law? Why?

Developing Your Thinking and Inquiry Skills

8. What categories of law would apply to the following situations?
   a) A skier steals your snowboard.
   b) A parent pays you less for babysitting than the agreed-upon hourly rate.
   c) Your parents buy a cottage and register a deed.
   d) Your wages are below the minimum specified by provincial law.
   e) You are arrested for drinking under age.
   f) Although you are underage, you want to get married.
   g) Your grandmother had promised you her engagement ring, but she failed to prepare a will before she died.
   h) You purchased a DVD player that stopped working after one month.
   i) As a student, you feel you should not have to pay income tax.
   j) At a noisy party, the police arrest you and refuse to tell you why.

k) Even though you see the "No Trespassing" sign, you hop the fence for a swim in a privately owned pool.
l) Canada enters a free-trade agreement with Cuba.

9. Keep a log of all your activities for one full day. In a three-column chart, identify the activity or situation, the law involved, and the category of law it falls under.

10. Choose one European and one Asian country. Research the domestic laws of those countries as they relate to punishment for the possession of illegal drugs. Prepare a report on your findings. If possible, include examples of people who have been prosecuted in the countries you chose.

11. Choose an Indian band in your province. Contact a spokesperson for the band or conduct research to find out what bylaws the band has enacted during the last five years. Present your findings in a report.

Communicating Your Ideas

12. Locate newspaper or magazine articles that describe a legal situation for each of the private law categories shown in Figure 2.8. Write a paragraph summarizing each article and identifying the category of law it represents.

13. Debate this topic: There should be a uniform set of international laws and an international court to deal with countries, organizations, and people who violate those laws.

14. A person interviewing you for a job cannot ask whether you have any physical disabilities. This question is considered discriminatory and is prohibited by law. Conduct research to discover other employment restrictions prohibiting practices that are considered discriminatory. Present your findings in a pamphlet or a poster.

15. Your municipality has drafted a pet bylaw that requires owners to register all cats and dogs. The proposed bylaw will limit the combined number of pets in one residence to no more than six. Should government have the authority to restrict pet ownership? Take a position on this question and compose a letter to the editor of a local newspaper expressing your views with supporting arguments.

Putting It All Together

16. In January 2001, the Ontario Film Review Board, a government-appointed tribunal, announced a change to its movie rating system—the first rating change in 15 years. The Adult Accompaniment (AA) rating was replaced with a two-tier classification called 14A (children under 14 must be accompanied by an adult) and 18A (children under 18 must be accompanied by an adult). This change aligns the movie classification system with the one used in the video market. Movies that tend to spark controversy over content may be affected.
    a) Under what category of law do the Film Board's activities fall?
    b) With a partner, list the possible advantages and disadvantages of the new rating system. After weighing the pros and cons, decide whether the new system will be an improvement on the previous system.
    c) Research a provincial board or tribunal and explain its role to the class.

CASES

Spain v. Canada (1998), Fisheries Jurisdiction (I.C.J.), on-line <www.icj-cij.org>

BACKGROUND On March 9, 1995, Canadian authorities boarded the *Estai,* a Spanish fishing trawler, in the Grand Banks area off the Canadian coast. The vessel was seized, and its master and crew were arrested and charged with the illegal fishing of Greenland halibut, a violation of the Canadian *Coastal Fisheries Protection Act.* Part of their catch was confiscated. On April 18, 1995, the Attorney-General of Canada discontinued proceedings against the *Estai* and its master. Bail was repaid and a portion of the catch was returned.

Spain instituted proceedings against Canada with regard to this incident, claiming in part that "the subject matter of the dispute is Canada's lack of title to act on the high seas against vessels flying the Spanish flag." Spain was also seeking reparation for damages and injuries. On June 15, 1998, Spain asked the International Court of Justice to adjudge (decide) and declare that it had jurisdiction in this case.

Earlier, on May 12, 1994, Canada had amended the *Coastal Fisheries Protection Act* to extend its authority to include the Regulatory Area of the Northwest Atlantic Fisheries Organization (NAFO). It also included a declaration, known as "subparagraph (d) to paragraph 2" that excluded the International Court's jurisdiction in "disputes arising out of or concerning conservation and management measures taken by Canada with respect to vessels fishing in the NAFO Regulatory Area …" In Canada's view, the *Estai* dispute concerned the conservation and management of fisheries stocks in the NAFO Regulatory Area. On June 17, 1998, Canada asked the Court to adjudge and declare that it had no jurisdiction to adjudicate upon the application filed by Spain.

LEGAL QUESTION Does the International Court of Justice have jurisdiction to hear this case?

DECISION According to the Court, the "measures" taken by Canada to amend its coastal fisheries legislation constituted "conservation and management measures" as they are understood in international law. The Court also noted that Spain's dispute with Canada arose because of the conservation and management measures taken by Canada with respect to the *Estai* in the NAFO Regulatory Area. This being the case and given paragraph 2(d) of the Canadian declaration of May 10, 1994, the Court ruled, by twelve votes to five, that the Court had no jurisdiction to adjudicate upon the dispute.

The *Estai*

POLITICAL SIGNIFICANCE According to Article 36 of the statute of the International Court of Justice, it is up to each state to decide what limits it will place on accepting the jurisdiction of the Court. In its declaration of May 10, 1994, Canada chose to exclude the Court's jurisdiction in disputes involving conservation and management measures.

ANALYSIS

1. What did Spain and Canada ask the International Court of Justice to do?
2. Explain why the Court ruled as it did.
3. Based on the information you have read in this case, assess the effectiveness of the International Court of Justice in settling disputes.

CASES

Mazuelos v. Clark (2000), B.C.H.R.T. 1

BACKGROUND In July 1995, Mary Jo Clark hired Maria Mazuelos as a live-in nanny. Ms. Clark favoured Ms. Mazuelos over other candidates she had interviewed because she had a "settled personal life." Employment would begin on September 5 for a 24-month period. Mazuelos' hours would be from 7:30 a.m. to 4:00 p.m., for which she would receive a monthly salary of $1380. From this salary, $300 would be deducted for room and board. Clark paid $125 for a work permit for Mazuelos.

When Clark arrived to pick up Mazuelos on September 4 to move her into the family home, Mazuelos was distraught. In tears, she revealed that she was 14 weeks pregnant and had begun suffering from nausea. She said that she still wanted the job. She explained that she would arrange for her sister to come to Canada to substitute for her until she could resume her duties following the birth. Clark told Mazuelos that she would have to discuss the situation with her husband and she left. The next day, Clark phoned Mazuelos and discontinued her employment. She asked Mazuelos to repay the $125 immigration fee, which she did.

Mazuelos complained to the British Columbia Human Rights Commission, alleging that Clark discriminated against her by refusing to continue her employment because of her sex, contrary to s. 13 of the *Human Rights Code*, R.S.B.C. 1996. The complainant sought compensation from the respondent for the $125 immigration fee, lost wages of $10 620 from September to the baby's birth in April, and compensation of $3500 for injury to dignity, feelings, and self-respect.

LEGAL QUESTION Was Mazuelos' pregnancy a factor in Clark's decision not to continue to employ her?

DECISION In testimony, the respondent had admitted that Mazuelos' physical and emotional state, which Clark believed were caused by her pregnancy, were key considerations in her decision to discontinue employment. Also, Clark had determined that Mazuelos would be unable to perform her duties on the basis of a single conversation. She had made no effort to find out whether Mazuelos' nausea could be controlled with medication so that she could perform the job for which she had been hired. However, the complainant had not convinced the tribunal that she had actively looked for work throughout the period for which she was claiming lost wages.

The tribunal found the complaint justified and ordered Clark to pay Mazuelos one month's lost wages ($1380) plus the immigration fee ($125). She was also ordered to pay Mazuelos $1500 to compensate her for injury to her dignity, feelings, and self-respect.

LEGAL SIGNIFICANCE The evaluation of the testimony described in the decision reflects the fair and equitable treatment tribunals are intended to exercise.

ANALYSIS

1. What category of law is being described in this case?
2. Discuss how different circumstances might have changed the decision.

Government and Statute Law

3

CHAPTER OUTLINE

Canada's Constitution

Patriating the Constitution

Government and Law Making

FOCUS YOUR LEARNING

How is power divided in Canada's federal system of government?

Why was it necessary to patriate the Constitution?

What is involved in making statute laws?

This sign publicizes a law that appears to be quite simple. It is easily understood, the penalty is clear, and most people would agree that spitting is unhealthy and unattractive. The question is, should there be a law against spitting?

Consider the following questions plus three of your own that a law like this might encounter. Then reword the law, making sure you cover all the exceptions and possible problems you have identified.

- Does the law apply to all people in all situations?
- Would there be any exceptions, and if so, what would they be?
- How would this law be enforced?

WHAT DO YOU THINK?

- On a scale of one to five, with one being easy, how would you rate the task of making a law?
- Should the task of law making be assigned to one person or a group of people? Why?

Whether it is a municipal bylaw banning skateboarding on city property, a provincial law enforcing a zero-tolerance policy toward violence in schools, or a federal law dealing with divorce proceedings, making laws is a difficult task. Laws must be able to meet both the legal challenges and the approval of most citizens. They must be enforceable, and they should balance frequently competing interests. For instance, a law enforcing non-smoking in restaurants may be criticized as discriminating against smokers.

In this chapter, you will learn how the powers for law making are allocated and how government, its agencies, and you, the ordinary citizen, play a role in making Canada's laws.

CANADA'S CONSTITUTION

With the Royal Proclamation of 1763, British North America was subject to English law and governed by Great Britain in the interests of Great Britain. Many people living in the Atlantic provinces of New Brunswick, Nova Scotia, Prince Edward Island, and Newfoundland were content to remain colonies of Great Britain. However, men like John A. Macdonald, George Brown, and George-Étienne Cartier supported the idea of a more independent country with control over its political and economic systems while still retaining strong ties to Britain.

The 1860s brought opportunities for change. The United States was engaged in a bloody civil war, and there were those in Canada who feared that once the war was over, the States would attempt to take over the rest of North America. In 1864, a group of 36 men met in Prince Edward Island and Quebec to discuss unification. Eventually, New Brunswick, Nova Scotia, Quebec, and Ontario agreed to a framework for union. The proposal was taken to Britain for approval.

Figure 3.1 At the Charlottetown Conference in Charlottetown, Prince Edward Island, discussions began that would ultimately result in a new Dominion of Canada and a Constitution—a system of laws and rules to govern the new country.

Remarkably, there was little debate in England regarding this significant change to the political structure of one of its colonies. The *British North America Act (BNA Act)* was passed by the British Parliament in 1867 and was proclaimed into law on July 1 of that year. The Act established Canada as a country, and John A. Macdonald became the first prime minister of the new Dominion.

> "We are laying the foundation for a great state. Perhaps one which at a future day may even overshadow this country."
> — Lord Carnarvon, the colonial secretary of Great Britain

British North America Act, 1867

The *BNA Act,* passed in 1867 by the British Parliament, still forms a major part of Canada's Constitution. In 1867, the Act set out the rules for how Canada should be governed and what kind of country it would be. Significantly, it was not meant to be a Constitution for a totally independent country—it was a Constitution for a colony. Canada could not make its own laws independently of Great Britain until much later. For example, the Dominion could not enter into international trade agreements without British approval, nor could it make any amendments (changes or additions) to the Constitution without first asking permission from the British Parliament. Nonetheless, on March 29, 1867, the *British North America Act* recognized that Canada was a separate political entity within the British Empire, and it prepared the way for the Canada we live in today.

Fast Fact
Not everyone agreed with Confederation. Headlines in a Nova Scotia newspaper on July 1, 1867, read "Died! Last night at twelve o'clock, the free and enlightened Province of Nova Scotia." Flags in the province were flown at half-mast.

A Federal System

In choosing a system of government for the new country, the framers of the Constitution looked at systems used in other countries. The United States, for instance, had a beautifully written Constitution and Bill of Rights, and yet the Americans were engaged in a destructive civil war. John A. Macdonald believed that one of the problems with the American system of government was that it gave too little power to the central government and too much to the states, resulting in a struggle for power between the northern and southern states.

Another obvious model to consider was the **unitary system** of Great Britain, where power was centralized in one parliament led by a prime minister. Because of the difference in geographic size between Canada and Great Britain, this system did not seem practical for a country as large and diverse as Canada.

unitary system: a one-level system of governing

A compromise was suggested. Canada would have a **federal system** in which the responsibilities for governing would be divided between two levels of government: the central government and the provincial government. Each level would have exclusive control over its own jurisdictions; however, the central government could overrule a provincial law if doing so was considered in the best interests of all Canadians.

federal system: a two-level system of governing

Because the *British North America Act* stated that Canada would have a government similar to that of the United Kingdom, Canada's Constitution also includes all of the unwritten conventions of the British parliamentary system, including the monarch as head of state and the principle of Rule of Law.

Division of Powers

The *BNA Act* outlined the responsibilities of each level of government. It was determined that the federal government's powers should include matters that would be applied uniformly to every province, such as postal service or currency. These powers are set out in s. 91 of the *BNA Act*. Provincial powers would be of a local nature and they could vary from province to province. Section 92 outlines the responsibilities of the provincial government. In s. 93, the responsibility for education was given to the provinces in recognition of special language and religious rights of people in different parts of the country. The division of responsibilities is shown in Figure 3.2.

The *BNA Act* identified powers for two levels of government only, so the provinces delegated their responsibilities for local matters to a third level of government—municipalities and townships. This allocation of power gives communities control and flexibility over issues of local importance. Furthermore, in the negotiation of self-government with Aboriginal peoples, certain federal and provincial powers have been delegated to Aboriginal governments to be exercised within a defined territory.

Legal Link
To learn more about the federal system and the division of powers, visit **www.pearsoned.ca/law** and read the *BNA Act*, now called the *Constitution Act, 1867*.

Conflict of Power

A residual (remaining) category gives the federal government law-making powers in legislative areas that were not specifically assigned to either the federal government or to the provinces. These areas are sometimes referred to as **residual powers** and would include authority over such activities as airports and telecommunications. This general power to legislate is expressed in s. 91 as shown on the following page.

residual powers: federal responsibility to make laws in legislative areas not assigned to the provinces

Figure 3.2 Division of Powers. Not all of these areas of responsibility appear in the original document. Some, like employment insurance, were included through amendments to the Act.

Federal Responsibilities		
Banking	Foreign affairs	Public debt
Bills of exchange	Indian affairs	Residual powers (see
Census and statistics	Marriage and divorce	Conflict of Power)
Citizenship	Navigation and shipping	Seacoast and inland
Criminal law	Old age pensions	fisheries
Currency and coinage	Patents and copyrights	Taxation
Defence	Penitentiaries	Trade and commerce
Employment insurance	Postal service	

Provincial Responsibilities		
Compensation to injured workers	Maintenance of hospitals	Provincial courts and laws
Direct taxation within the province	Municipal institutions	Solemnization of marriage
Education	Natural resources	
Labour and trade unions	Property and civil rights in the province	

Figure 3.3 In the *BNA Act*, responsibility for seacoast and inland fisheries was allocated to the federal government. These federal officers are leaving to patrol the Burnt Church reserve on Miramichi Bay in New Brunswick, where a dispute centres on Aboriginal fishing rights.

91. It shall be lawful for the Queen, by and with the advice and consent of the Senate and House of Commons to make laws for the Peace, Order, and Good Government of Canada.

In the past, this wording in s. 91 has enabled the federal government to justify legislation in areas not specifically covered by the Act. It has also allowed Parliament to intervene in activities that normally fall under provincial jurisdiction but have acquired such importance as to concern the "Peace, Order, and Good Government of Canada." Should the nation be threatened, the federal government might also use this constitutional phrase to justify invoking emergency powers.

Even though federal and provincial responsibilities are generally specified in the *BNA Act*, disputes occasionally arise over conflicts in overlapping legislation or in the clarification of residual areas of responsibilities.

Doctrine of Ultra Vires

As shown in Figure 3.2, each level of government may make laws only in its own jurisdiction. Passing a law *within* a government's jurisdiction is known as ***intra vires***, which is a Latin phrase meaning "within the power." However, suppose the Government of Saskatchewan objects to the federal government's laws dealing with youth offenders and decides to pass a law making it possible to publish the name of a youth accused of an offence, something prohibited by the federal *Youth Criminals Justice Act*. If the province enacts such a law, the federal government could object, arguing that according to the *BNA Act* such a law would not be within the legislative authority of the provincial government. Failing any compromise or negotiation, the Supreme Court of Canada may then be asked to have the provincial law declared ***ultra vires***, which means "beyond the powers." In other words, the provincial government has no responsibility for criminal law and is, therefore, *ultra vires*, or beyond its power to make laws concerning criminal matters.

intra vires: within the power of government to pass laws

ultra vires: beyond the power of government to pass laws

CASE

The Attorney General for Alberta v. The Attorney General of Canada, [2001] 1 S.C.R. 783

BACKGROUND Prior to 1995, the *Criminal Code* restricted access to firearms, mainly automatic weapons and handguns, by classifying some as prohibited and some as restricted. In 1995, Parliament amended (revised) the *Code* by passing the *Firearms Act*. This Act extended the classification to include all other firearms, generally rifles and shotguns or "ordinary firearms." Under this amended statute, owners of all firearms must obtain licences and register their guns.

The Province of Alberta challenged the constitutionality of this legislation in the Court of Appeal, claiming that the law falls under provincial power over property and civil rights. The province argued that guns are private property and cannot be regulated by the federal government. The federal government claimed that gun-control laws fall under its criminal-law authority.

The majority of the Court of Appeal ruled that the Act was *intra vires* Parliament. In other words, it was within the jurisdictional power of the federal government to enact such legislation. Alberta appealed this decision to the Supreme Court of Canada.

LEGAL QUESTION Does Parliament have the constitutional authority to enact the *Firearms Act*?

DECISION In examining the case, the Supreme Court of Canada considered the purpose of the Act—to deter the misuse of firearms, to control those given access to guns, and to control specific types of weapons. The Court also considered the essence of the Act—the promotion of public safety. Moreover, the Act met the criteria for a criminal law, which include a valid criminal-law purpose backed by a prohibition and a penalty.

In its decision, the Court found that the province had not established that the effects of the Act on provincial jurisdiction over property and civil rights are more than incidental. This being the case, the *Firearms Act* does not infringe on provincial powers. In other words, upholding the Act as a criminal law would not upset the balance of federalism.

The Court held that the appeal should be dismissed. The provisions of the *Firearms Act* are constitutional.

SOCIAL SIGNIFICANCE The intent of the *Firearms Act* is not to burden farmers and hunters with red tape. Guns are dangerous and they pose a risk to public safety. Supporters of the Act argue that gun registration will reduce gun misuse, curtail criminals from acquiring firearms, and make stolen guns more traceable—all of which are in the interests of public safety.

ANALYSIS

1. The Alberta government claimed that the federal government was making law outside its jurisdiction. What is the legal term for this argument?
2. The Supreme Court of Canada disagreed with the Alberta government and sided with the federal government. What reasons did the Supreme Court have for its decision?
3. If you were a lawyer for the Government of Alberta, what arguments would you use to show that the federal government could not make such a law?

Building Your Understanding

1. Explain why a unitary system of government would not be practical for Canada.
2. How does Canada's federal system differ from the federal system of the United States?
3. List three responsibilities given to the federal government under the *British North America Act*.
4. Why was responsibility for education given to the provinces in 1867?
5. Use an example to explain the doctrine of *ultra vires*.
6. To which level of government would you assign responsibility for the regulation and use of Internet communication? Explain your answer.

PATRIATING THE CONSTITUTION

Over the years, the *British North America Act* was amended as statutes were added, deleted, or rephrased. Gradually, Canada gained more independence from Great Britain. One important constitutional change was the **Statute of Westminster** passed in 1931. This Act greatly extended the law-making power of Canada. The Statute allowed Canada to make its own laws independently; moreover, these laws could not be overruled by Britain if they contradicted British laws. In other words, Canada was no longer subject to the laws of Great Britain. In addition, Canada could make agreements with other countries, such as trade agreements, without British involvement or approval. However, Canada could still not amend its own Constitution without approval from the British Parliament.

Statute of Westminster: legislation passed in Britain that extended Canada's law-making powers

Problems with the *BNA Act*

As long as the *BNA Act* remained in Britain, Canada did not enjoy total independence. Each time the Canadian government wanted to add laws to the Constitution, it had to ask the British Parliament for permission. For the most part, the British Parliament gave its permission. In fact, Britain would have been happy if Canada had "taken home" the Constitution long ago, thereby ensuring that all legislative authority lay with Canada. Other Commonwealth countries had already done so; Australia and New Zealand, for example, brought their Constitutions home after World War I. However, Canada delayed this process because the federal and provincial governments could never agree on procedures to amend the Constitution.

Another problem associated with the *British North America Act* was confusion regarding the division of powers, such as responsibility for natural resources. According to the *BNA Act*, responsibility for the fishing industry lay with the federal government. Timber and wood, another natural resource, was under provincial jurisdiction. Who, therefore, was responsible for other natural resources such as uranium, oil, water, or natural gas? Because the Act was unclear, both branches of government claimed responsibility for the sale and management of these resources.

Despite the residual category in s. 91, there were still disputes over which level of government should have the power to make laws concerning

Fast Fact
The *BNA Act* does not mention any person or office known as the Prime Minister, nor is there any reference to a Cabinet.

responsibilities that were non-existent in 1867. Whenever this happened, Canada had to ask the British Parliament for permission to include these powers. Sometimes to avoid arguing their case in the British Parliament, the federal and provincial governments simply agreed to share the cost for some programs. These arrangements were called **shared cost agreements.** For example, money for health care would be provided to the provinces by the federal government as long as the provinces agreed to spend the money according to federally established guidelines. However, even these arrangements created problems since many provinces objected to following guidelines set by the federal government.

Finally, some people were concerned that nothing in the Constitution specifically guaranteed **civil liberties.** For all of these reasons, it became increasingly important to bring the Constitution home.

shared cost agreements: arrangements between the two levels of government to share the cost for programs in areas not identified in the *BNA Act*

civil liberties: basic individual rights protected by law, such as freedom of speech

Constitution Act, 1982

Previous attempts to bring the Constitution back to Canada were unsuccessful primarily because neither level of government was prepared to give up any of its powers acquired under the *BNA Act*.

When Pierre Elliott Trudeau was elected prime minister, one of his mandates was to **patriate,** or bring home, the Constitution. After numerous negotiation attempts with the first ministers (the premiers of the provinces), Trudeau threatened to bring back the Constitution without their approval. The provincial premiers argued that such a move would be unconstitutional, so Trudeau took his case to the Supreme Court of Canada and won—sort of! The Court stated that the federal government had the legal authority to patriate the Constitution without provincial approval, but warned that this action would be politically unwise and would be contrary to the unwritten principles of the *British North America Act*.

patriate: to bring legislative power under the authority of the country to which it applies

In 1981, in one last attempt to get their agreement, Trudeau called the first ministers together in Saskatchewan. The provincial premiers engaged in four days of heated debate and bargaining. In particular, the province of Quebec consistently sought more economic and cultural powers. Finally, during the night, in the absence of Quebec Premier René Lévesque, the nine other premiers agreed on a compromise bill. When Lévesque awoke the next morning and found out what had happened, he was furious and refused to sign the proposed bill. Nonetheless, the *Constitution Act, 1982*, which included the *British North America Act, 1867,* came into being. Trudeau finally patriated the Constitution on April 17, 1982.

Figure 3.4 Quebec became the only province to withhold its consent from the *Constitution Act, 1982*. Do you think René Lévesque was justified in refusing to sign the agreement? Why or why not?

The provisions in the *British North America Act, 1867*, did not die with the passing of the new Constitution. The division of power between the federal and provincial governments as set out in the Constitution remains the same, as does the mandate for the federal government to make laws within its jurisdiction for the Peace, Order, and Good Government of Canada. However, the new Canadian *Constitution Act, 1982*, added four key elements:

- a principle regarding the equalizing of services across Canada
- a clearer interpretation of who was responsible for control and management of natural resources
- a formula indicating what terms would be necessary to make future amendments to the Constitution
- a charter guaranteeing individual rights and freedoms

Principle of Equalization

Most Canadians believe that essential services such as health care, education, or access to social services should be available equally to residents in all parts of Canada. However, provinces with small populations, such as Newfoundland or Prince Edward Island, may not be able to collect sufficient provincial tax revenue to make this happen. Traditionally, through their taxes, the richer provinces equalized services for all Canadians. This tradition was affirmed as a constitutional commitment in the **Principle of Equalization:**

> 36. (1) Without altering the legislative authority of Parliament or of the provincial legislatures, or the rights of any of them with respect to the exercise of their legislative authority, Parliament and the legislatures, together with the government of Canada and the provincial governments, are committed to
>
> (a) promoting equal opportunities for the well-being of Canadians;
>
> (b) furthering economic development to reduce disparity in opportunities; and
>
> (c) providing essential public services of reasonable quality to all Canadians.
>
> (2) Parliament and the government of Canada are committed to the principle of making equalization payments to ensure that provincial governments have sufficient revenues to provide reasonably comparable levels of public services at reasonably comparable levels of taxation.

Natural Resources

The new Constitution also granted provincial powers over resources, such as natural gas in Alberta or oil in Newfoundland. There are, however, some restrictions. For example, a province cannot charge higher prices or limit the supply when exporting non-renewable natural resources (such as oil) to another part of Canada.

"Quebec finds itself all alone!"
— René Lévesque, former premier of Quebec

Fast Fact
With the patriation of the Constitution, the *BNA Act* was renamed the *Constitution Act, 1867*.

Principle of Equalization: Section 36 of the *Constitution Act, 1982*, which provides for equal access to essential services for all Canadians

"To define and protect the rights of individuals is a prime purpose of the constitution in a democratic state."
— Frank. R. Scott, professor of law, McGill University

Consider This
Only Alberta, British Columbia, and Ontario have legislation in place to control fresh water exports. In provinces that do not have such legislation, should the federal government intervene to protect this natural resource? Discuss.

amending formula: procedure for changing the Constitution

Canadian Charter of Rights and Freedoms: a section of the *Constitution Act, 1982,* which sets out constitutionally protected rights and freedoms

"I think it was put together with Band-Aids, Krazy Glue, and coat hangers by a bunch of inadequate politicians."

— Mordecai Richler, Canadian author, on the Charlottetown Accord

Amending Formula

One of the major problems in patriating the Constitution had been the lack of agreement on an **amending formula**—a method of making future changes. This problem was addressed in the new Constitution. It was decided that any amendment requires the approval of Parliament plus two-thirds of the provinces representing 50 percent of the population.

Other amending provisions are also included. For example, if a constitutional change affects activity in one province only, then all that is necessary to make the change is the agreement of that province and the federal government. This was the case in 1997 when Newfoundland amended the Constitution to allow publicly funded schools in that province to operate as denominational schools (schools that provide religious education).

Charter of Rights and Freedoms

Finally, despite some opposition, the Constitution now includes a charter of individual rights and freedoms for all Canadians. The **Canadian Charter of Rights and Freedoms** is perhaps the most significant part of the new Constitution. Entrenching the Charter in the Constitution gives these laws constitutional status. Any law or government action violating these constitutional laws may be declared invalid and may be struck down. In Chapter 4, you will learn more about the rights identified in the Charter.

Constitutional Conflict

Even though the Constitution had been patriated, the federal government continued to try to entice Quebec to sign the *Constitution Act*. In 1987, Prime Minister Brian Mulroney thought he had finally made a deal when the provincial premiers signed the Meech Lake Accord. This agreement increased the powers of the provinces and acknowledged Quebec as a "distinct society" with the right to protect its unique culture.

However, opposition to the Accord mounted around the country. In 1990, Elijah Harper, a Cree member of the Manitoba Legislature, used delaying tactics that prevented the province from meeting its deadline. He stopped the Accord from coming to a vote mainly because he opposed any agreement that did not deal with Aboriginal issues. In response, Premier Clyde Wells of Newfoundland refused to take a vote in his Legislature, believing that without Manitoba's participation, Newfoundland's vote would be irrelevant. The deadline passed and the Accord collapsed.

Why was there so much resistance to the Meech Lake Accord? Firstly, in negotiating the agreement, the premiers failed to acknowledge Aboriginal rights; as a result, Aboriginal leaders opposed the Accord. Secondly, strong political opposition came from the newly created Reform Party, which received most of its support from the West. Thirdly, many Canadians objected to conferring any kind of special status on one province. And finally, former prime minister Pierre Trudeau spoke out against the agreement, arguing that it gave too much power to the provinces and weakened the federal government. He also suggested that if one province was given special status, there was nothing to stop other provinces from demanding similar powers.

Nonetheless, Prime Minister Mulroney tried one more time. He established a special committee headed by former prime minister Joe Clark to travel across the country, hold town-hall meetings, and talk to Canadians. The committee's mandate was to draft an amendment to the Constitution that would satisfy all Canadians. In August 1992, a constitutional meeting was held in Charlottetown to consider the new proposal. Although many political and Aboriginal leaders supported what became known as the Charlottetown Accord, others did not.

The Charlottetown Accord had many critics. Among them were the Western-based Reform Party, the separatist Parti Québécois (a Quebec provincial party), and the Bloc Québécois, a federal separatist party formed after the failure of Meech Lake. Some people in Quebec feared that the provision for Aboriginal self-government would affect large portions of their province. Also, while critics in Quebec believed the Accord did not give them enough power, critics in other parts of Canada felt that it gave Quebec too much power. In a referendum on October 26, 1992, about 54 percent of all Canadians voted "no." The Accord was dead.

Figure 3.5 To delay the proceedings, Elijah Harper holds up an eagle feather during the Manitoba debate on the Meech Lake Accord.

Quebec has still not ratified (signed and approved) the *Constitution Act, 1982*. However, according to the Supreme Court of Canada, that province is still subject to the Constitution, and the people of Quebec are protected by the *Charter of Rights and Freedoms*.

Building Your Understanding

1. How did the Statute of Westminster expand Canada's power?
2. Identify three problems associated with the *British North America Act, 1867*.
3. The federal government decided to ask the Supreme Court of Canada to rule on the constitutionality of its decision to patriate the Constitution without provincial approval. What was the decision of the Supreme Court?
4. What were the four key elements added to the *Constitution Act, 1982*? Why was it important that these elements be included in the Constitution?
5. Why do you think the Supreme Court of Canada decided that Quebec is subject to the Constitution even though that province never ratified the agreement?

GOVERNMENT AND LAW MAKING

Earlier we learned how jurisdictional powers are divided between the two levels of government. Before we discuss how legislation for these areas is actually passed, it is important to understand the structure of the various branches of government.

Our federal and provincial governments are made up of three distinct branches: the executive branch, the legislative branch, and the judiciary. Each branch has an important role to play in making, interpreting, and enforcing laws in Canada.

The Executive Branch

executive branch: the administrative branch of government responsible for carrying out the government's plans and policies

At the federal level, the **executive branch** comprises the prime minister, the Cabinet, and the public or civil service (see Figure 3.6). Members of the Cabinet are elected representatives appointed by the prime minister to positions of responsibility. For example, your Member of Parliament (MP) may be appointed to the position of Minister of Justice, responsible for proposing new laws and ensuring that existing federal laws are enforced. Cabinet positions are important appointments because this level of government—the administrative branch—sets policy, administers laws, and has the crucial task of controlling government spending.

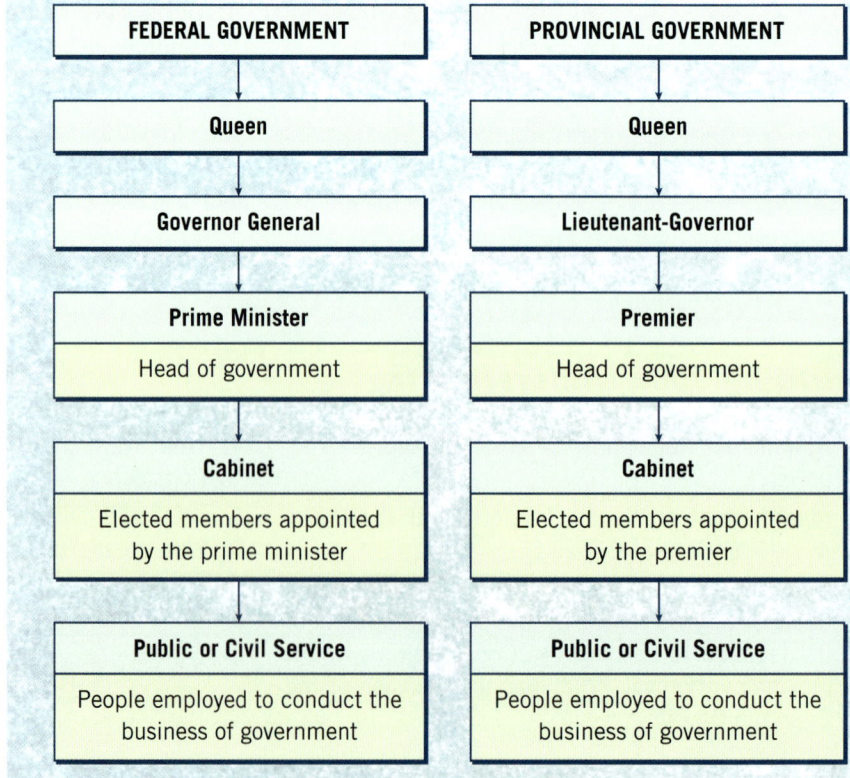

Figure 3.6 The Executive Branch

SOURCE: Adapted from Infosource 4-3 in Mark Evans et al., *Citizenship: Issues and Action*, Toronto: Pearson Education Canada Inc., 2000, p. 108.

Law in Your Life
When you test for your driver's licence or post a letter you have contact with the civil service. In what other ways does the civil service affect you?

The executive branch at the provincial level works much the same way (see Figure 3.6). The premier of the province appoints the elected Members of the Legislative Assembly (MLAs) or, in Ontario, Members of the Provincial Parliament (MPPs), to the Cabinet. Your elected MLA or MPP may be appointed to a Cabinet position for your province (such as Minister of Education) and hold that position in addition to his or her duties as your representative. Of course, the provinces also have a public or civil service to conduct the business of the government.

Legal Link WWW
Visit www.pearsoned.ca/law to find out the name of the Minister of Education for your province.

The Legislative Branch

At the federal level, the **legislative branch,** also called Parliament, consists of both the House of Commons and the Senate (see Figure 3.7). It is the legislative branch that actually passes statute laws.

In the *Constitution Act, 1867,* our federal government was set up to parallel the British system of two houses—the House of Commons and the House of Lords. The House of Lords was referred to as the "upper house of Parliament." Our upper house is the Senate and is made up of members appointed by the Governor General on the advice of Cabinet. Senators retain their seats until they reach the age of 75, unless they resign or die.

legislative branch: the branch of government that has the power to make, change, and repeal laws

The Senate has very wide powers. Even if legislation is passed by an overwhelming majority in the House of Commons, it can be defeated in the Senate or sent back to the House for revisions. Although the Senate rarely defeats an approved bill, this does occur.

"If a Second Chamber dissents from the first, it is mischievous; if it agrees, it is superfluous."
— Abbé Sieyè (1748–1836)

At the provincial level, Parliament is usually called the Legislature or the Legislative Assembly. The Legislature acts in the same way as Parliament at the federal level, except that provinces do not have Senates.

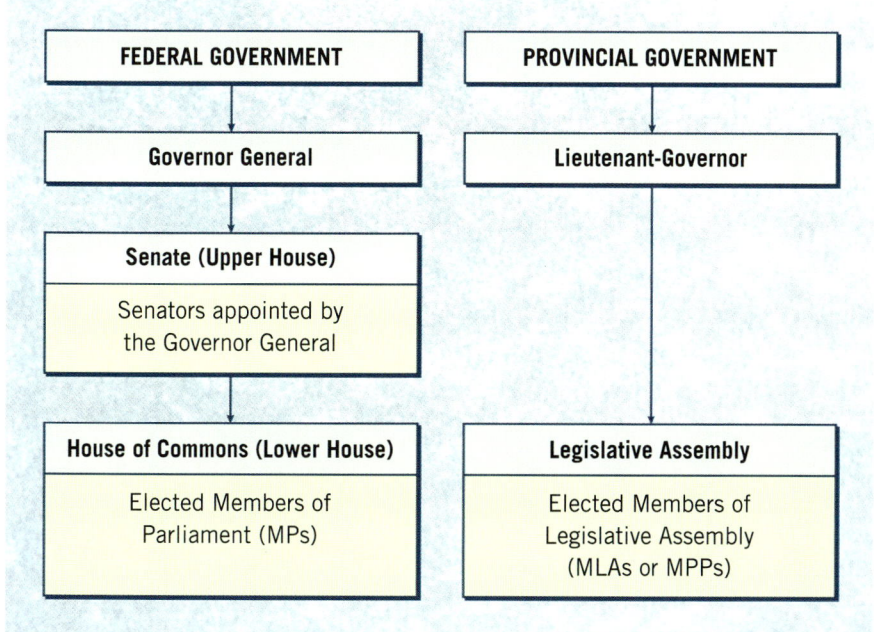

Figure 3.7 The Legislative Branch

SOURCE: Adapted from Infosource 4-5 in Mark Evans et al., *Citizenship: Issues and Action,* Toronto: Pearson Education Canada Inc., 2000, p. 113.

Fast Fact
The Lieutenant-Governors of the provinces are appointed by the Governor General and paid by the federal government.

The Judiciary

judiciary: the branch of government responsible for presiding over Canada's court system

The **judiciary** is part of the government but independent of the other two branches. The judiciary is made up of justices, or judges, who adjudicate disputes, interpret the law, and decide on punishments in Canada's court system. Justices are apolitical and independent. In other words, their appointments are based on merit rather than political motivation or party affiliation. Beneath the Supreme Court of Canada, the nation's highest court, there are three levels of provincial courts: the Provincial Court of Appeal, the Superior Court (for serious offences), and the Provincial Court (for less serious matters). Justices of the higher courts (Court of Appeal and Superior Court) are appointed by federal officials. Trial court judges for the lower courts are usually provincial appointments.

"Elected legislators are important, but so is the judiciary. Both are essential to effective and just government."
— The Right Honourable Beverley McLachlin, Chief Justice of Canada

With the entrenchment of the *Canadian Charter of Rights and Freedoms* in the *Constitution Act, 1982*, the judiciary has gained in importance. Justices must now interpret all laws in light of the Charter; any law that conflicts with the Charter may be struck down.

Enacting a Statute

Legal Link
Access the information available on federal- and provincial-government Web sites by visiting **www.pearsoned/law.ca**.

The power to make or pass laws lies solely in the hands of the government in power. The government may draft legislation that addresses public concerns, reflects its policies, or considers technological advances. If an existing law is found to conflict with the *Canadian Charter of Rights and Freedoms*, the law may be struck down. On those occasions it may be necessary to draft new legislation. For example, suppose the Supreme Court of Canada finds that a section in the *Criminal Code of Canada* conflicts with a person's fundamental right to freedom of expression. It may be necessary to amend this section so that it no longer conflicts with that Charter right.

bill: proposed legislation

government or public bill: legislation proposed by a Cabinet minister

Here is how the law-making process works at the federal level. A proposed law, or **bill,** is introduced in the legislature. When a bill is introduced by a Cabinet minister (usually the minister of the department that will be most affected by the bill), it is called a **government or public bill.** The Minister of the Environment, for example, might introduce a bill that proposes certain legal protections for species at risk. Government bills are rarely defeated if the government holds a majority of seats in the House of Commons.

THE WIZARD OF ID — Brant parker and Johnny hart

A bill may also be introduced by a private member, an elected representative who does not hold a Cabinet post. Although a **private member's bill** may be initiated by citizens, lobby groups, or corporations, the bill is always introduced by an MP. The procedure going through the Legislature is much

private member's bill: legislation proposed by an MP who is not in the Cabinet

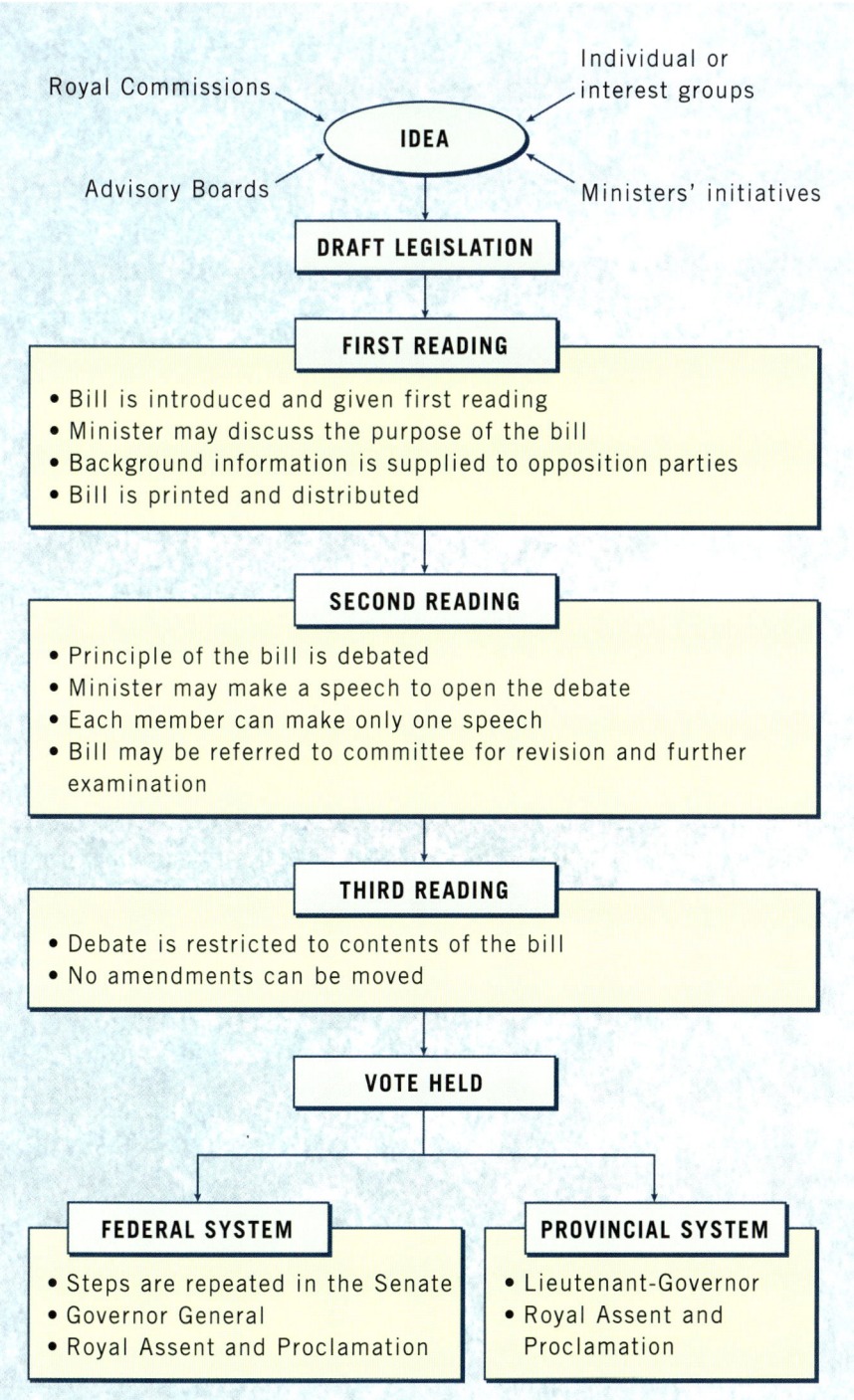

Figure 3.8 Enacting Legislation

Fast Fact
Bills that originate in the House of Commons have a "C" preceding the number of the bill. Bills that are initiated by the Senate begin with an "S."

Legal Link

To find out the progress of a particular bill, visit **www.pearsoned.ca/law**.

the same as for a government bill. However, since a private member's bill does not start out with Cabinet support, it is more difficult to pass than a government bill.

All bills go through the stages shown in Figure 3.8 before they become law. The first reading of a bill is for information. At this point, MPs can talk to their constituents (voters in their ridings) to find out their opinions about the proposed bill. They can also conduct research to prepare for debating the bill in the House of Commons. The second reading is for debate. Each member is allowed to speak once about the contents of the bill. If significant flaws or objections are found or if good suggestions are made, the bill is usually revised accordingly by a committee.

The third reading comes just before the vote in the house in which it was introduced (most commonly the House of Commons, although a bill can be introduced in the Senate first). The purpose of the third reading is to refresh the members' minds regarding details of the bill, including any changes that may have been made by the committee. After the third reading, the final vote is taken. When members of Parliament vote on a bill, they usually support their party's position. However, on controversial issues, the government may hold a free vote to allow MPs to vote according to their conscience or the position held by most of their constituents.

After the bill passes in one house, it goes through a similar process in the other house, usually the Senate. However, if a bill is defeated or if Parliament adjourns before the vote is taken, the bill dies on the floor of the Commons. If the government is still intent on passing this piece of legislation, the bill has to be reintroduced in a new parliamentary session, and the process starts again.

Once a bill is passed into law, it goes to the Governor General, the Crown's representative in Canada. The Governor General assents to the bill in the name of the Queen, thereby declaring it to be in force. The bill then becomes an Act, is given a Statute number, and is reprinted. The Queen, through her representative, could withhold consent and refuse to sign a bill, preventing it from becoming law. However, this has never happened in Canada. Within two years, the Queen could also overrule her representative and withdraw her assent. This has never happened either. The Queen has a limited role in Canada and no longer has any real political power.

At the provincial level, legislation follows a similar process. A bill is introduced into the Legislative Assembly by an MLA or an MPP. It goes through the various readings and the vote is then taken. Since the provincial government does not have a Senate, a bill that is passed by the Legislative Assembly goes directly to the Lieutenant-Governor for royal assent.

Figure 3.9 James Bartleman, a member of the Minjikanig First Nation, became Ontario's first Aboriginal Lieutenant-Governor in March 2002.

The Role of Individuals and Interest Groups

As you know, only governments can enact statute laws. However, the impetus to make new laws or to amend old laws may come from many sources. Sometimes suggestions are made by individuals, legal experts, or lobby groups. Ideas may also come from the government's legal advisers who recognize the need for new laws in particular situations. Occasionally, the findings of a government-appointed advisory board, such as a Royal Commission, may indicate that new laws are necessary.

Over time, as public opinion changes, governments respond by amending existing laws and making new ones. For instance, at one time Canada had laws prohibiting the sale of alcohol; suicide was considered a criminal act; members of First Nations were not permitted to vote. In some cases, laws are amended because ordinary citizens convince legislators that change is necessary. As a citizen you can access the political process to influence the laws that the government introduces.

Lobby Groups

Organizations, or **lobby groups,** such as MADD (Mothers Against Drunk Driving) and the Coalition for Gun Control have not only convinced legislators to change the law regarding drinking drivers and the registration of firearms, they have also succeeded in altering public opinion on these issues. Other organizations such as LEAF (Legal Education Action Fund) challenge existing laws in court and have forced a broad range of changes in law on matters from sexual assault to pay equity. Environmental lobby groups have managed to persuade legislatures to pass laws to protect the environment.

lobby groups: people who try to influence legislators in favour of their cause

Figure 3.10 **Students light candles on an altar at St. Joseph's Oratory in Montreal in memory of 14 women killed by Marc Lepine on December 6, 1989. In response to this tragedy, the Coalition for Gun Control lobbied the government for changes to the law. Their efforts were rewarded in 1995 when the** *Firearms Act* **was passed. What measures might lobby groups take to influence changes to the law?**

Fast Fact

Canadian sprinter Ben Johnson was stripped of his Olympic gold medal in 1988 when he tested positive for drugs. A Royal Commission was later established to investigate the use of drugs in sports.

Royal Commissions

Royal Commissions, or commissions of inquiry, also influence changes in the law. Royal Commissions are appointed by the federal Cabinet, and their role is to conduct impartial investigations of specific national problems. Royal Commissions have ranged from investigations into the proper weighing of butter and cheese to the use of insanity as a legal defence. For example, between 1993 and 1996 a Royal Commission, led by Horace Krever, investigated Canada's blood-supply system. This commission was appointed because individuals had contracted hepatitis C and HIV in the 1980s after receiving blood and blood products screened by the Red Cross.

LAW IN ACTION — *Royal Commission on Aboriginal Peoples, 1996*

1. Why might some Canadians object to the idea of Aboriginal peoples establishing a "third order of government"?

2. Should the federal government consider implementing the findings of a Royal Commission even if its suggestions are unpopular with many Canadians? Why or why not?

In the summer of 1990, the Mohawk people of Kanesatake engaged in an armed struggle with the villagers of Oka, Quebec, over the expansion of a private golf course onto land that the Mohawks claimed as their own. The Mohawk Warriors Society set up a blockade, which was stormed by the Quebec police force, resulting in the death of a police officer. Troops of the Canadian Armed Forces were called in, and a standoff ensued, lasting 78 days. Once the conflict was over, a Royal Commission was set up to investigate and report on the dispute.

The Commission made 440 recommendations, including reforms to Aboriginal health care, housing, training, and land claims. The cost of these reforms was estimated at $30 billion. The Commission also revived the idea that Aboriginal peoples should form a "third order of government," with suggestions for setting up an Aboriginal Parliament, a university, and development banks. Many Canadians questioned the $30 billion price tag, and many objected to the idea of a self-governing nation within Canada. However, George Erasmus, co-chair of the Commission and former chief of the Assembly of First Nations, said that the Royal Commission was the first step in establishing trust between Aboriginal peoples and the federal and provincial governments.

Building Your Understanding

1. Describe the law-making roles of the executive, legislative, and judicial branches of government.
2. Why has the role of the judiciary become more important since 1982?
3. What is the difference between a government bill and a private member's bill?
4. What happens on the second reading of a bill?
5. Distinguish the procedures for passing bills in the federal and provincial governments.
6. Define the Senates role in enacting legislation.
7. Why might an existing law that conflicts with the *Canadian Charter of Rights and Freedoms* be struck down?
8. How does a Royal Commission differ from a lobby group?

law in the extreme

Medical research brings hope and controversy

When John A. Macdonald and his colleagues were deciding on the division of jurisdictional powers, the concept of "reproductive technology" would have been the stuff of science fiction. No doubt, they would have been shocked by the idea that in 1983, for the first time in Canadian history, a baby would be born due to a process called "in vitro fertilization." During this reproductive technique, an egg is removed from the mother's uterus and is fertilized in a Petri dish. The fertilized egg, or embryo, is then transferred back to the mother's body. If the mother is unable to carry the baby to term, the embryo can be implanted in another woman, called a "surrogate mother." In vitro fertilization and surrogacy are only two procedures in a wide range of modern reproductive technologies that raise legal and controversial questions.

One medical technique that brings both hope and controversy is stem-cell research. When cells from an embryo begin to divide, the first few cells are called "stem cells" because they have the capacity to develop specialized cells that eventually become tissues and organs. If stem cells can be extracted from the embryo and implanted in humans, perhaps their capacity to generate new cells will help replace destroyed tissue, leading to a cure for diabetes, Parkinson's disease, leukemia, retinal degeneration, muscular dystrophy, and spinal-cord injuries.

How can research that strives to cure disease be so controversial? Some people argue that extracting stem cells destroys the embryo, thereby destroying life itself. Others are concerned that using existing embryos, frozen and stored due to other procedures, may not be sufficient, and that scientists will create new embryos for the sole purpose of producing a "bank" of stem cells for further research.

Technically, any type of genetic, embryonic, or reproductive research, including cloning human beings, is permitted in Canada because there is nothing to legally prohibit such procedures. Canada is one of the few industrialized countries that do not have laws to cover these rapidly advancing fields of research. This dilemma raises moral and ethical issues.

In 1989, the government established a Royal Commission on New Reproductive Technologies, which issued its report in 1993. A bill was tabled in 1995, but died prior to the 1997 election. During that election, Health Minister Allan Rock promised a revised bill.

On May 3, 2001, Rock tabled another bill on reproductive technology before the Commons committee on health. The committee conducted hearings and delivered its guidelines on March 4, 2002.

The guidelines prohibit

- creating human embryos specifically to obtain stem cells
- creating stem cells through cloning
- combining human or non-human stem cells with a human embryo or fetus
- donating stem cells for use on specific individuals, except for self-donations

The guidelines allow use of

- cells taken from a human fetus or amniotic fluid after an abortion
- cells taken from an umbilical cord or placenta of a newborn (with informed parental consent only)
- adult stem cells taken from other human tissue (with informed consent only)
- cells taken from surplus human embryos created for reproductive use

Health Minister Anne McLellan planned to introduce legislation by May 10, 2002. Opposition parties called for more time, requesting a moratorium.

Analysis Questions

1. Assume you are a Member of Parliament when this legislation is introduced. Make a list of questions you have and concerns or problems that you want clarified. Describe any additions or changes you think should be made along with your reasons for requesting them. Prepare to debate your position at the second reading.

2. The United States passed legislation on reproductive technology in 2001. Using information found on the Internet or in magazine articles, compare U.S. legislation with the guidelines proposed by the Commons committee on health. Organize your information in a chart.

LOOKING BACK

Reviewing Your Vocabulary

amending formula *p. 60*
bill *p. 64*
Canadian Charter of Rights and Freedoms *p. 60*
civil liberties *p. 58*
executive branch *p. 62*
federal system *p. 53*
government or public bill *p. 64*
intra vires *p. 55*
judiciary *p. 64*
legislative branch *p. 63*
lobby groups *p. 67*
patriate *p. 58*
Principle of Equalization *p. 59*
private member's bill *p. 65*
residual powers *p. 54*
shared cost agreements *p. 58*
Statute of Westminster *p. 57*
ultra vires *p. 55*
unitary system *p. 53*

Quick Quiz

1. Indicate whether the following statements are true or false. Be sure to correct any statements you identify as false.
    a) *Ultra vires* means "within the government's jurisdictional power."
    b) The executive branch of the government administers laws.
    c) Residual powers are identified in the *BNA Act, 1867*.
    d) A "bill" is another word for an "act."
    e) Prime Minister Mulroney was instrumental in patriating the Constitution.
    f) The *Canadian Charter of Rights and Freedoms* is considered constitutional law.
    g) A government bill can be introduced by a cabinet member.
    h) The amending formula and the Principle of Equalization are two sections of the *Canadian Charter of Rights and Freedoms*.
    i) In a federal system, the federal government has more power than it would have in a unitary system.
    j) The Statute of Westminster is an amendment to the *BNA Act, 1867*.
    k) The shared cost agreement was one of the four key elements added to the *Constitution Act, 1982*.
    l) Lobby groups represent people who share a common concern.

Checking Your Knowledge

2. Why were the constitutional models of Great Britain and the United States rejected at the time of Confederation?
3. What are residual powers and which level of government has them?
4. Using examples, explain the concepts of *intra vires* and *ultra vires*.
5. Define the Principle of Equalization. Provide an example of how this principle could be applied.
6. Which level of government is responsible for natural resources?
7. Explain the amending formula for changing constitutional law.
8. Why did the Meech Lake and Charlottetown Accords fail?
9. Explain what happens to a bill in the following situations:
    a) the bill is passed by the Senate
    b) Parliament adjourns before the vote is taken
    c) the bill is passed by the House of Commons
    d) the bill is defeated by the House of Commons
10. What is the role of a Royal Commission in making law?

Developing Your Thinking and Inquiry Skills

11. Identify the level of government you would contact in each of these situations:
    a) You have just lost your job and need to find out if you are eligible to collect employment insurance.
    b) You want to register a patent for a chocolate-chip cookie recipe that contains no fat and has few calories.
    c) The roots of your neighbour's willow tree are ruining your swimming pool. You read somewhere that it is against the law to plant willow trees in suburban areas, so you decide to report your neighbour.

12. Identify a federal or provincial law that you think should be enacted or a law that you believe must be changed. Draft your proposed legislation or amendments and outline your plan for getting your draft presented in the House of Commons or the Legislative Assembly.

13. Explain the quote by Abbé Sieyè on page 63 in relation to the Senate's role in enacting legislation. Do you agree with this assessment? Why or why not?

14. In recent years, gambling was legalized in some provinces. Identify an emerging trend—social, political, or workplace—and explain how you think this trend might lead to changes in the law.

Communicating Your Ideas

15. Should the Senate, an appointed body, have the power to defeat legislation passed by elected members of Parliament? Prepare an oral presentation either supporting or opposing this Senatorial power.

16. The Student Council has asked you to invite a member from a lobby group to speak at your school. Prepare a research report on a lobby group of your choice to present to your Council. Consider such groups as MADD, Greenpeace, or CAVEAT (Canadians Against Violence Everywhere Advocating Its Termination). In your report, inform the Council members about the goals of the group, the group's influence on the law, its membership, and why you believe a member of the group should speak at your school.

17. The government has proposed an amendment to your province's education act that will include the following oath of citizenship to be sworn by all students at the start of each school day:

    > I affirm that I will be faithful and bear true allegiance to Her Majesty Queen Elizabeth the Second, Queen of Canada, and to her heirs and successors, and that I will faithfully observe the laws of Canada and fulfill my duties as a Canadian citizen.

    The government intends to present the bill in the Legislature, but it would like some feedback on the "oath" part of the bill. Hold a mock town-hall meeting in the classroom, with each member of the class assuming one of the following roles: student, parent, teacher, principal, and school-board representative. Prior to your meeting, work in groups to prepare the arguments each person will present either for or against the proposed oath.

Putting it All Together

18. Consider the clause of Peace, Order, and Good Government in the light of Canada's federal system of government and the division of powers outlined in the Constitution. Given the growth of Canada since 1867, do you think this clause gives the federal government too much legislative authority today? Explain your position.

CASES

R. v. Hydro-Québec, [1997] 3 S.C.R. 213

BACKGROUND In early 1990, Hydro-Québec allegedly dumped polychlorinated biphenyls (PCBs) into a river. This activity was a violation of provisions in the *Canadian Environmental Protection Act* dealing with toxic substances that pose a risk either to the environment or human life and health. Hydro-Québec was charged with two infractions.

At trial, Hydro-Québec brought a motion seeking to have the provisions of the Act declared *ultra vires* the Parliament of Canada on the grounds that they do not fall within federal jurisdiction as set out in s. 91 of the *Constitution Act, 1867*. The Court of Quebec granted the motion. Appeals by the Crown to the Superior Court and the Provincial Court of Appeal were dismissed. The case was then appealed to the Supreme Court of Canada.

LEGAL QUESTION Do the provisions of the *Canadian Environmental Protection Act* fall within federal jurisdiction to enact criminal law?

DECISION In a 5 to 4 decision, the Supreme Court held that the appeal should be allowed. The provisions of the Act are valid because under s. 91 of the *Constitution Act, 1867,* Parliament was given the power to make criminal law in the widest sense. According to the majority of the Court, protecting the environment by prohibiting toxic substances is a legitimate exercise of this power. Consequently, Parliament may enact prohibitions under its criminal-law power for the purposes of preventing pollution. PCBs are highly toxic, long lasting, and extremely mobile; owing to their properties, they move up the food chain and pose significant risks to both humans and animals.

In the dissenting opinion, the justices pointed out that the provisions do not define any offence. In other words, they are not intended to *prohibit* environmental pollution, but simply to *regulate* it. Therefore, the provisions fail to meet the test of having a legitimate criminal purpose.

LEGAL SIGNIFICANCE As this decision indicates, determining the jurisdictional division of powers about contemporary issues can be complex. Decisions like this one are important because they set precedent for future cases.

ANALYSIS

1. What was the Supreme Court's decision? In your own words, discuss why the majority of the Court made this decision.
2. Explain the dissenting opinion.
3. Speculate on what this decision will mean for Hydro-Québec.

CASES

R. v. Crown Zellerbach Canada Ltd., [1988] 1 S.C.R. 401

BACKGROUND During the course of its logging operations, Crown Zellerbach Canada dumped wood waste into the waters of Beaver Cove, British Columbia. The company had a permit to dump, but it did not cover this site. Crown Zellerbach Canada was charged with contravening s. 4(1) of the *Ocean Dumping Control Act*. This federal statute prohibits the dumping of any substance at sea, the sea being defined as including the internal waters of Canada, other than fresh waters. The waters of Beaver Cove flow into Johnstone Strait, which joins the Pacific Ocean.

At trial, the charges against Crown Zellerbach Canada were dismissed. Both the British Columbia Supreme Court and the British Columbia Court of Appeal held that s. 4(1) of the Act was *ultra vires* Parliament. The case was appealed to the Supreme Court of Canada.

LEGAL QUESTION Is s. 4(1) of the *Ocean Dumping Control Act* constitutional in its application to the dumping of waste in waters, other than fresh waters, within a province?

DECISION According to s. 91(12) of the *Constitution Act, 1867,* seacoast and inland fisheries falls under federal legislative jurisdiction. In addition, s. 4(1) of the *Ocean Dumping Control Act* is constitutionally valid because it falls within the national concern doctrine of the Peace, Order and Good Government power of the Parliament of Canada:

> For a matter to qualify as a matter of national concern ... it must have a singleness, distinctiveness, and indivisibility that clearly distinguishes it from matters of provincial concern.... Marine pollution, because of its predominantly extra-provincial as well as international character and implications, is clearly a matter of concern to Canada as a whole.

In a 4 to 3 decision, the Supreme Court of Canada held that the appeal should be allowed and that the judgments of the Court of Appeal and British Columbia Supreme Court should be set aside.

Speaking for the majority, Justice Gerald Le Dain said that the constitutional question should be answered as follows:

> Is section 4(1) of the *Ocean Dumping Control Act,* S.C. 1974, 75, 76, c.55, *ultra vires* of the Parliament of Canada, and, in particular, is it *ultra vires* of the Parliament of Canada in its application to the dumping of waste in the waters of Beaver Cove, an area within the province of British Columbia?

> Answer: No.

HISTORICAL SIGNIFICANCE An important consideration in this decision was the national concern doctrine called the Peace, Order and Good Government power of the Parliament of Canada found in s. 91 of the *Constitution Act, 1867*. This doctrine applies to new issues that did not exist at Confederation and to issues that have become matters of national concern.

ANALYSIS

1. Why did the Court consider this Act a matter for national concern?
2. Why is the national concern doctrine in s. 91 of the *Constitution Act, 1867,* significant when considering the question of the division of powers?

Career Connections

What is the first occupation most people think of when they hear the word *law*? Usually "lawyer" comes to mind. No doubt choosing a career as a lawyer has advantages. As you learned in Chapter 2, there are a variety of legal areas to specialize in. There are also a number of tangible benefits. The average income for lawyers is among the highest for professional occupations in Canada, and the unemployment rate is well below the national average. The challenges and rewards of a career as a lawyer go hand in hand with many hours of hard work both before and after you begin to practise law.

Imagine investing your time, money, and energy into become a lawyer and then discovering that practising law is not what you had envisioned. In real life, the legal profession may be quite different from what you see portrayed on television or in movies. If you are considering a career as a lawyer, try to spend some time with a lawyer. Find out as much as you can about what a lawyer does. Visit a law library, examine legal documents, visit a courtroom, and watch a lawyer in action. Perhaps your school has a mentoring program that will provide you with an opportunity to do some paralegal work. Make sure that this is the career for you *before* you invest time and money.

Even with preliminary exploration, there are no guarantees that you will choose to practise law once you graduate. The good news is that you will acquire valuable knowledge and skills from your legal training. Rigorous analytical skills will help you think critically, and your verbal and negotiating ability will be greatly enhanced. With your keen understanding of legalese, you will be able to assess legal issues and interpret and structure contracts. Because studying the law provides so many opportunities to learn, both graduates and experienced lawyers sometimes use their legal knowledge in other careers such as business, teaching, or politics.

MAKING CONNECTIONS

1. Using resources in your guidance centre, explore the education, training, and experience you will require to become a lawyer. Create a flow chart that includes the average amount of time each step might take. Include the cost for each stage in your flow chart, based on current tuition fees.

2. Research one of the following careers and explain how the skills you acquire pursuing a law degree would help you in this position:
   - corporate executive
   - real estate broker
   - loans officer in a financial institution
   - newspaper reporter
   - sports or literary agent
   - Member of Parliament

These law students are studying International Law. Find out what other courses are available in a law-school curriculum.

Rights, Freedoms, and Responsibilities

UNIT 2

Since 1992, the United Nations' Human Development Index has ranked Canada as one of the best countries in the world to live in. One reason Canada is so highly rated is that Canadians enjoy rights and freedoms that are guaranteed by law. This was not always the case. Canada did not have any legislation guaranteeing rights and freedoms until the *Canadian Bill of Rights* became law on August 10, 1960. However, the *Bill of Rights* was a statute, which means it could be nullified by new legislation at any time. In other words, these rights were not protected. It was not until the *Canadian Charter of Rights and Freedoms* became part of the Constitution that Canadians were given the protected rights and freedoms they have today.

In Chapter 4, you will learn what those constitutional rights and freedoms are and how they have been used in the courts to protect individuals. As you examine the various sections of the Charter, you will discover just how fortunate you are to be living in Canada.

Canadians also have rights that are *not* contained in the Charter. These rights are found in the various provincial and territorial human rights acts. In Chapter 5, you will examine such concepts as stereotyping and prejudice, and learn about the prohibited grounds for discrimination. You will discover what options are available to anyone who experiences discrimination in a restaurant, in the workplace, or while seeking accommodation.

It is important to know what your rights are and how to exercise them.

LOOKING AHEAD

Chapter 4 *Canadian Charter of Rights and Freedoms*

Chapter 5 *Human Rights*

4 Canadian Charter of Rights and Freedoms

CHAPTER OUTLINE

Recognizing Rights and Freedoms

Jurisdiction, Enforcement, and Guarantee

The Fundamental Freedoms

Democratic and Mobility Rights

Legal and Equality Rights

Language and General Rights

FOCUS YOUR LEARNING

What rights and freedoms are contained in the *Canadian Charter of Rights and Freedoms*?

How are your rights and freedoms limited in the Charter?

What is the role of the Supreme Court in interpreting the Charter?

WHAT DO YOU THINK?

- List five rights that you consider essential and rank them from least to most important. Share your list with the class and compile a class list of the ten most important rights.

- What criteria did you use to reach a consensus?

76

Canadians are willing to go to court and march in the streets with placards, demanding that their rights be recognized. Civil disobedience and even violence have been carried out in the name of rights and freedoms. What are rights and freedoms? Quite simply, a **right** is a legal, moral, or social claim that people are entitled to, primarily from their government. For example, in Canada, a person accused of committing an offence is *entitled* to a fair trial.

Freedom, on the other hand, is a right. It is the right to live your life without interference by the government. For example, you have the right to seek employment in any part of Canada. As you will learn, however, freedoms do have limitations that are necessary to protect public safety and the fundamental rights and freedoms of others.

In this chapter, you will explore the history of the struggle for rights and freedoms in Canada, which culminated in the *Canadian Charter of Rights and Freedoms*. You will also study some of the Charter rights and freedoms in detail and learn how they are interpreted by the Supreme Court of Canada.

right: a legal, moral, or social entitlement that citizens can expect, mainly from the government

freedom: the right to conduct one's affairs without governmental interference

RECOGNIZING RIGHTS AND FREEDOMS

For thousands of years, political thinkers the world over have struggled with the concept of human rights. As ideas about rights evolved and took form in legal codes and proclamations, the same questions came up again and again: What rights should people have? Should some rights be absolute (unrestricted)? Is everyone entitled to the same rights? What is the power of the state in creating and enforcing rights? How can people ensure that governments do not restrict their rights and freedoms?

Historical Documents

As you discovered in Chapter 1, the Magna Carta, which was signed by King John in 1215, was the first step in establishing basic individual rights for the people of England. In 1869, the *Bill of Rights* gave British parliament supremacy over the monarchy and extended certain civil and political rights such as free elections, reasonable bail and fines, and freedom from cruel or unusual punishment.

In the eighteenth century, many human rights questions were addressed by the *Declaration of Independence* signed in the United States in 1776 and the *Declaration of the Rights of Man* signed in France in 1789. These two documents declared that all people have natural rights, and they provided for individuals' **inalienable rights** to equality and liberty.

A more recent document, the *Universal Declaration of Human Rights,* passed by the United Nations in 1948, gives even broader recognition to

Figure 4.1 The rights of children are outlined in the *Declaration of the Rights of the Child,* passed by the United Nations in 1959.

inalienable rights: guaranteed entitlements that cannot be transferred from one person to another

Legal Link
You will find a copy of the *Universal Declaration of Human Rights* at **www.pearsoned.ca/law**.

franchise: the right to vote

Fast Fact
One important UN rights document is the *Declaration on the Elimination of Discrimination Against Women* (ratified in 1979).

human rights. In addition to recognizing the equal and inalienable rights of all members of the human family, it provides for fundamental freedoms of thought, opinion, expression, conscience, religion, and peaceful assembly and association. It also declares the equal rights of men and women, equality before the law, the right to be presumed innocent until proven guilty, education rights, and freedom from torture or inhumane punishment.

Evolution of Rights in Canada

It may be hard to imagine that the rights and freedoms you enjoy today were not always part of life in Canada. Slavery, limited **franchise,** discriminatory laws and practices against non-whites and immigrants, anti-Asian riots, and women being classified as "non-persons" are all part of Canadian human rights history. Figure 4.2 illustrates some of the events in Canada's checkered human rights record.

Figure 4.2 Starting with the *Canadian Bill of Rights*, update this timeline in your notebook to reflect recent human rights events in Canada.

Significant Human Rights Events in Canada

1833 Slavery is abolished under the *British Emancipation Act*

1884 *Indian Act* is amended to outlaw cultural and religious ceremonies such as the potlatch

1900 *Chinese Immigration Act* increases $50 head tax to $100

1900 *Dominion Elections Act* excludes minorities from voting in federal elections

1908 "No stoppage" rule requires immigrants to travel directly to Canada, reducing the number of immigrants from India

1914 *Komagata Maru* incident: officials allow only 20 of the 376 potential immigrants to enter Canada, forcing the rest to return to India

1928 Supreme Court of Canada decides that the word *person* does not apply to women

1928 Alberta passes the *Sexual Sterilization Act*, ordering the sterilization of patients in psychiatric hospitals

1927 *Indian Act* is amended to make it illegal for Aboriginal peoples to hire lawyers to pursue land claims without the consent of the superintendent general of Indian affairs

1921 Quebec court upholds the right of a theatre owner to refuse to allow a black patron to sit in the orchestra seats

1920 Federal government makes the franchise universal, except for some minorities and Status Indians

1919 Women are allowed to stand for Parliament

1918 Women are granted the right to vote in federal elections

1916 Manitoba grants women the right to vote in provincial elections

***Komagata Maru* immigrants**

78 UNIT 2 ◆ Rights, Freedoms, and Responsibilities

Canadian Bill of Rights

Because of the horrendous human rights abuses in Europe during World War II and the subsequent passage of the 1948 *Declaration of Human Rights*, the attention of the world was focused on the issue of rights and freedoms. During the next 15 years, comprehensive human rights codes were enacted along with provincial legislation regarding racial discrimination, fair accommodation and employment practices, and equal pay for women. You will read about many of these laws in Chapter 5, Human Rights.

The first attempt to codify rights and freedoms across Canada was *The Canadian Bill of Rights,* a statute enacted by Parliament in 1960 under the leadership of Prime Minister John G. Diefenbaker. *The Canadian Bill of Rights* recognized

- the rights of individuals to life, liberty, personal security, and enjoyment of property
- freedom of religion, speech, assembly, and association
- freedom of the press
- the right to counsel and the right to a fair hearing

> "I am a Canadian, free to speak without fear, free to worship in my own way, free to stand for what I think right, free to oppose what I believe wrong, or free to choose those who shall govern my country. This heritage of freedom I pledge to uphold for myself and all mankind."
> — Prime Minister John G. Diefenbaker, July 1, 1960

Legal Link WWW
You will find a copy of the *Canadian Bill of Rights* at **www.pearsoned.ca/law**.

1929 "Famous Five"—Emily Murphy, Nellie McClung, Louise McKinney, Henrietta Muir Edwards, and Irene Parlby—appeal "person decision" to the Privy Council in England, which rules that women are persons

1934 People libelled because of race or creed can get a court order to stop the libel

1940 Communist Party is outlawed under the *War Measures Act*

1942 Hutterites, Doukobhors, and enemy aliens are barred from buying land

1942 Japanese Canadians are forcibly removed from their homes and sent to detention camps

1945 Covenant restraining the sale of land to Jews is struck down

1947 *Saskatchewan Bill of Rights Act* is the first broad, human rights statute passed in Canada

1948 People of all races, except for Status Indians, are given federal franchise

1950 Supreme Court of Canada rules that Jehovah's Witnesses can distribute religious pamphlets

1953 *Fair Employment Practices Act*

1956 *Female Employees Equal Pay Act*

1960 Status Indians are granted the right to vote in federal elections

1960 *Candian Bill of Rights*

"Famous Five"

Japanese Canadians

The *Bill of Rights* had its limitations. Firstly, as a federal statute, it applied only to matters under federal jurisdiction. Although Diefenbaker had intended the bill to apply to the provinces, in reality, it did not. In provincial human rights matters, the provinces could legislate as they wished. Secondly, as a statute, the *Bill of Rights* had the same status as other statutes. In other words, it did not take precedence over any other statute. If another statute conflicted with the *Bill of Rights*, it was up to the judge to decide which law to enforce. Finally, as a statute, it could be amended by a majority vote in the House of Commons. This meant that at any time, the protections offered in the bill could be changed or even eliminated.

Entrenching Rights and Freedoms

Because of its limitations, some people believed that the *Bill of Rights* did not offer Canadians sufficient protection. One of these individuals was Pierre Elliott Trudeau. As you learned in Chapter 3, when Trudeau became prime minister, one of his goals was to patriate the Constitution and to **entrench** the *Canadian Charter of Rights and Freedoms*. Having rights and freedoms identified as part of the Constitution ensures that they are protected, regardless of the government in power. It also means that they become constitutional law, which can override all other laws. Any law enacted by federal or provincial governments must be consistent with the terms set out in the Constitution.

Entrenching the *Charter of Rights and Freedoms* was significant because it shifted power from the supremacy of Parliament and Legislatures toward supremacy of the Constitution. But this factor concerned some politicians. Agreement on the terms of patriation between the federal government and nine of the provinces was finally reached on November 5, 1981, but only on condition that a clause be added that would allow the provinces some power to **override** or legislate around the *Charter of Rights and Freedoms*.

The Notwithstanding Clause

Section 33 of the *Charter of Rights and Freedoms*, known as the notwithstanding clause, grants the federal and provincial governments limited power to pass laws that are exempt from s. 2 (the fundamental freedoms) and ss. 7 to 15 (the legal and equality rights) of the Charter. This exemption can only remain in effect for up to five years. At the end of that period, the government must make a renewed declaration. When a government decides to **invoke** the notwithstanding clause to pass legislation that violates one of the protected

Figure 4.3 When Jeannette Lavell married a non-Native, she lost her rights as a Status Indian. In *Canada (A.G.) v. Lavell*, [1974], the Supreme Court ruled that the *Bill of Rights* had no power to override the *Indian Act*.

entrench: to protect and guarantee a right or freedom by ensuring that it can only be changed by an amendment to the Constitution

override: to prevail over

invoke: to put into effect

rights in the Charter, it must identify the particular law and the sections of the Charter that are being overridden.

One of the early uses of the **notwithstanding clause** took place in 1988. In *Ford* v. *Attorney General of Quebec*, [1988], the Supreme Court of Canada ruled that Quebec's Bill 101, which required all public signs to be in French only, was invalid because it infringed s. 2(b) (freedom of expression). In response, the Quebec government introduced another bill (C 178), invoking the notwithstanding clause to allow the "French only" law to stand.

A less successful attempt to invoke s. 33 took place in Alberta in 1998 when the provincial government tried to limit the rights of victims to sue for compensation. (See Law in the Extreme on page 82.)

Many rights advocates believe that the most important Charter provisions are those sections of the Charter affected by the notwithstanding clause. Supporters of the clause argue that it puts final power where it belongs—in the hands of elected representatives who can be voted out if they make poor decisions or deprive minorities of their rights. Critics of the clause argue that rights are too important to be left to politicians whose political strategies are often focused on winning votes. They believe that the courts should protect the rights and freedoms of Canadians.

notwithstanding clause: s. 33 of the *Canadian Charter of Rights and Freedoms*, which allows federal and provincial governments to pass legislation that is exempt from s. 2 and ss. 7 to 15 of the Charter

"The notwithstanding clause will be a red flag for opposition parties and the press. That will make it politically difficult for a government to override the Charter. Political difficulty is a reasonable safeguard for the Charter."

— Allan Borovoy, Canadian Civil Liberties Association

Figure 4.4 In 1993, the United Nations Human Rights Commission ruled that Quebec's "French only" sign law violated the international statute of freedom of expression. Bilingual commercial signs are now allowed, but the French lettering must be twice as large as the English.

law in the extreme

Public Pressure Prevails

Between 1928 and 1972, the Alberta Eugenics Board sterilized 2822 wards under the provincial *Sexual Sterilization Act*. Eugenics is the science of "improving" the human race through parent selection. As residents of provincial psychiatric institutions, men and women were sterilized without their consent to prevent the transmission of their disability to the next generation.

Following World War II, the eugenics theory met with disapproval. Moreover, medical research did not support the claim that disabilities were inheritable. In spite of these factors, the Board continued to order sterilizations.

In 1996, one ward, Leilani Muir, successfully sued the province. Ms. Muir has normal intelligence, so not only was she sterilized, but she was also wrongfully institutionalized at Red Deer's Provincial Training School for Mental Defectives. In acknowledging her claims, an Alberta court awarded Muir $972 800 in damages and legal expenses.

By 1998, about 700 other victims had filed claims for a variety of damages, including
- wrongful sterilization
- wrongful confinement
- inappropriate medicating
- physical and sexual abuse

Their claims totalled $764 million, which represented 6 percent of Alberta's yearly budget, or $300 from every resident in the province, including children.

Ralph Klein and Leilani Muir

Critics felt that the Alberta government panicked. Instead of negotiating with the claimants and quickly settling the claims out of court, on March 10, 1998, the Alberta government introduced Bill 26. The proposed *Institutional Confinement and Sexual Sterilization Act* would limit compensation to $150 000 per claim and protect the government from legal challenges under the *Charter of Rights and Freedoms* by invoking the notwithstanding clause. According to Premier Ralph Klein, it was not fair that his government should have to pay potentially hundreds of millions of taxpayers' dollars in compensation for abuses committed by previous governments.

The announced legislation was met with an overwhelming outburst of protest from the media, civil rights groups, and the general public. Within 24 hours, Bill 26 was dead. But public debate continued.

Editorials and letters to local newspapers condemned the tactics of the premier and his justice minister. Discussion in legal circles again focused on the benefits and shortcomings of the notwithstanding clause. Lawyers argued that if the government had acted quickly in negotiations, it would have spent less than the ceiling stated in the proposed bill.

For Alberta taxpayers, the reality of the situation hit home. Now, their tax dollars would be used to settle the claims. Some Albertans questioned their responsibility for an event that occurred before many of them were born. Wayne Ruston is one taxpayer whose tax dollars will be spent satisfying these claims; he is also one of those who were wrongfully confined and sterilized. When asked why the taxpayers of today should pay for the sins of the past, he replied, "I'm sorry about that, but I'm a taxpayer, and I didn't ask for any of this."

Analysis Questions

1. What legislation did the provincial government propose and why did it invoke the notwithstanding clause?

2. Do you think taxpayers should have to compensate victims for abuses committed by previous governments? Explain your position.

Building Your Understanding

1. What is the difference between a right and a freedom?
2. What distinguishes the *Universal Declaration of Human Rights* from the other historical documents discussed in this section?
   a) Referring to Figure 4.2, identify the various groups that were denied human rights and indicate which rights they were denied.
   b) List the positive human rights developments shown in Figure 4.2.
3. What is the most important difference between the *Charter of Rights and Freedoms* and the *Canadian Bill of Rights*?
4. What power is granted by s. 33? Why was it included in the Charter? Do you agree that it belongs in the Charter? Explain.

JURISDICTION, ENFORCEMENT, AND GUARANTEE

In this section, you will examine three important areas of the Charter: its area of authority, how it is enforced, and the guarantees it affords Canadians.

Jurisdiction

The *Canadian Charter of Rights and Freedoms* has 34 sections that define the relationship between people, organizations, and companies in Canada and the government. Jurisdiction—the area of authority set out in s. 32(1)—includes the legislative, executive, and administrative branches of government as well as Crown corporations, federally incorporated companies, banks, and other organizations regulated by the federal government. The Charter also applies to all provincial governments.

The Charter does not have jurisdiction to protect your rights if discrimination or other injustices occur in situations that do not involve the government. Suppose you notice an "Apartment for Rent" sign, and you apply. The superintendent takes one look at you and slams the door in your face, mumbling that she "doesn't rent to people like you." You cannot rely on your Charter rights in this situation. Does this mean you have no protection? Federal and provincial human rights codes offer protection for individuals wronged by the actions of private individuals and agencies. You will read more about these codes in Chapter 5.

Law in Your Life
You will find a copy of the *Canadian Charter of Rights and Freedoms* on page 519.

Enforcement

The Supreme Court of Canada has often been called the "guardian of the Constitution." The *Charter of Rights and Freedoms* was written in general language, and the nine justices that make up the Supreme Court of Canada are responsible for interpreting and enforcing its terms. Section 24(1) of the Charter gives people who believe that their Charter rights have been infringed or violated by government or its agencies the right to challenge the government in court.

Consider This
The right to "the enjoyment of property and the right not to be deprived thereof except by due process of law" is included in the *Canadian Bill of Rights* but not in the *Charter of Rights and Freedoms*. Why?

Figure 4.5 The Right Honourable Beverley McLachlin is the first woman to be appointed Chief Justice.

Before the Charter was enshrined in the *Constitution Act, 1982*, the role of the Supreme Court of Canada was to interpret existing law rather than uphold the rights of citizens. Today, in many cases appealed to the Supreme Court of Canada, the issue of whether a right has been violated is paramount. To determine whether a rights case has merit and will be heard, the Supreme Court considers these questions:

- **Was the right infringed or violated by government or its agencies?** Remember, the Charter only covers matters involving the government.
- **Is the right in question covered under the Charter?** Some rights are covered by legislation such as labour acts and human rights codes rather than the Charter.
- **Is the violation or infringement within a reasonable limit?** If a violation of the Charter has occurred, the court must decide if the violation can be justified under s. 1.

Once the justices of the Supreme Court have determined that a Charter right or freedom has been infringed or violated, they may strike down the offending legislation, using s. 52 of the *Constitution Act, 1982*. In other cases, the justices may provide a certain length of time for the legislation in question to be changed or amended. In criminal cases, the courts also have a number of options to choose from. They may exclude certain types of evidence, order a new trial, or, depending on the circumstance, dismiss a case completely.

Interveners

interveners: third-party participants in a legal proceeding; also called "friends of the court"

If you examine the court report for certain cases, you might find a list of **interveners** or "friends of the court"—individuals or organizations that have a special interest in the proceedings and are permitted to promote their own views. The court may grant interveners a certain amount of time to present ideas relating to the case at hand. For example, among the interveners in *R. v. Mills*, [1999], a case involving sexual assault of a minor, were the Women's Legal Education and Action Fund (LEAF), a watchdog organization concerned with cases involving equality for women and abuse against women and girls; the Canadian Civil Liberties Association, which focuses on cases where civil rights precedents may be set; the Sexual Assault Centre of Edmonton; and the Canadian Psychiatric Association. All of these organizations had an interest in this case and were prepared to put forward information or viewpoints that might help the court come to a decision.

Consider This
Mothers Against Drunk Driving (MADD) often acts as an intervener to express the view that drunk drivers must be held accountable for their behaviour. Discuss whether interveners should be allowed to promote their views in Supreme Court cases.

Guarantee

Section 1 of the Charter guarantees our rights and freedoms while, at the same time, making it clear that these rights and freedoms are not absolute but are subject to "reasonable limits." For instance, if a province wishes to pass a law that limits a Charter right, it must show that this limitation can be justified in a free and democratic society. The criteria for reasonable limits in s. 1 were established in *R. v. Oakes* in 1986. In fact, the four criteria established in *R. v. Oakes* came to be known as the "Oakes test."

R. v. Oakes, [1986] 1 S.C.R. 103

CASE

Oakes was charged with unlawful possession of a narcotic for the purpose of trafficking. When the judge found him guilty of possession of hashish oil, Oakes brought a motion challenging the constitutional validity of s. 8 of the *Narcotic Control Act,* R.S.C., 1970, which stated:

> … if the court finds that the accused was in possession of the narcotic … he shall be given an opportunity of establishing that he was not in possession … for the purpose of trafficking …

Oakes argued that s. 8 of the *Narcotic Control Act* violated the presumption of innocence contained in s. 11(d) of the Charter:

> Any person charged with an offence has the right …
> (d) to be presumed innocent until proven guilty according to law in a fair and public hearing by an independent and impartial tribunal

Both the trial judge and the Ontario Court of Appeal upheld Oakes's Charter claim. The Court of Appeal wrote that the "reverse onus" (placing the burden of proof on the accused to disprove an essential element of an offence) in s. 8 of the *Narcotic Control Act* was unconstitutional. However, Justice Martin of the Court of Appeal wrote that some reverse onus provisions may be constitutionally valid provided they satisfy two conditions: they constitute "reasonable limitations" on the right to be presumed innocent and are demonstrably justified in a free and democratic society according to s. 1 of the *Charter of Rights and Freedoms.*

The Crown appealed to the Supreme Court of Canada. The Court's decision stressed the importance of the principle of presumption of innocence by noting its inclusion in the *Canadian Bill of Rights*. The Supreme Court agreed that "it may become necessary to limit rights and freedoms in circumstances where their exercise would be inimical [opposed] to the realization of collective goals of fundamental importance [to the people of Canada]." The Court established the following four criteria for "reasonable limits" and then applied them to the case:

1) The reason for limiting the Charter right must be shown to be important enough to justify overriding a constitutionally protected right.
2) The measure carried out to limit the right must be reasonable and logically connected to the objective for which it was enacted.
3) The right must be limited as little as possible.
4) The more severe the rights limitation, the more important the objective must be.

The Court found that the first criterion was satisfied. The second, however, was not; the possession of a small quantity of narcotics does not logically lead to the conclusion that trafficking is the intention. The appeal against Oakes was dismissed.

1. State in your own words the meaning of "reverse onus." Why was the reverse onus in s. 8 of the *Narcotic Control Act* found to be contrary to the Charter?
2. What reason could be considered important enough to satisfy the first criterion used to justify limiting a right?
3. Does the third criterion apply to this case? Is it possible to partially limit the right to be presumed innocent? Explain.

Building Your Understanding

1. a) Identify the three questions used to determine whether a Charter rights case can be heard before the Supreme Court of Canada.
   b) Two of these questions have a jurisdictional focus. Explain why these two questions are important.
2. What are the Supreme Court's responsibilities toward the Charter?
3. What legal problems might occur if rights contained in the Charter were not subject to limitations?
4. State the criteria established in *R. v. Oakes* to judge whether limitations on a Charter right can be justified.
5. Which of the interveners identified in *R. v. Mills* would be most interested in presenting their ideas in the *R. v. Oakes* case? Explain why.

THE FUNDAMENTAL FREEDOMS

Most Canadians would undoubtedly agree that the fundamental freedoms described in s. 2 are an indispensable part of the liberty Canadians enjoy. Yet, even these fundamental freedoms are not absolute; some limitations are necessary. For example, your right of freedom of expression is limited in that you are not allowed to make libelous statements about another person.

Freedom of Conscience and Religion

Section 2(a), freedom of conscience and religion, means that you have a right to entertain the religious beliefs you choose, to declare these beliefs openly without fear, and to express your religious beliefs through practice, worship, teaching, and **dissemination.** According to this section of the Charter, no one can be forced to act in a way contrary to one's beliefs or conscience.

Laws prohibiting certain activities on Sunday have come under scrutiny under s. 2(a). *R. v. Big M Drug Mart Ltd.*, [1985] was a landmark case that tested the *Lord's Day Act*, prohibiting the sale of goods on a Sunday. The Act was struck down as contrary to freedom of conscience and religion because it compelled the observance of Sunday as a day of rest. The courts have also upheld employees' rights to be accommodated in the practice of their religion, for instance, permitting days off for observance of religious holidays.

Like other freedoms, a person's freedom of religion is limited by the rights and freedoms of others. It is in this area of conflicting rights that the Supreme Court of Canada has had to interpret the *intent* as well as the *extent* of the Charter. For example, the Court has found that while parents are free to engage in religious practices, these activities may be curtailed when they interfere with the "best interests of the child." For example, in a case where blood transfusions are against the parents' religion, the courts will order that children be given transfusions if their lives are in danger. The parents may argue that their right to freedom of religion has been violated, but a child's right to survival comes first in the eyes of the law.

dissemination: spreading ideas widely

"When the protected rights of two individuals come into conflict ... Charter principles require a balance to be achieved that fully respects the importance of both sets of rights."

— former chief justice Antonio Lamer

Calgary teen to appeal transfusion ruling

An Alberta court decision forcing blood transfusions on a 16-year-old Jehovah's Witness has renewed debate over when—and under what circumstances—a young person is mature enough to refuse medical treatment.

Jehovah's Witness leaders yesterday bitterly criticized a decision by Justice John Rooke of the Court of Queen's Bench allowing doctors in Calgary to proceed with the transfusions as part of the girl's treatment for leukemia. The youth, who is in the care of the province and cannot be named, had refused the blood based on her religion....

Courts in Ontario, New Brunswick, and Saskatchewan have all ruled in the past two decades in favour of minors who were deemed capable of understanding the information related to their treatments and the consequences of refusing them....

Ontario, among other jurisdictions, has passed legislation granting the power to decide to youngsters who understand the consequences of their actions. Alberta has left the lower courts to make decisions on a case-by-case basis.

In 1995, the Supreme Court found the state has the right to intervene in a parent's decision to stop transfusions. But it has not yet ruled on whether youngsters may be deemed mature enough to make the decision on their own.

SOURCE: Charlie Gillis, "Calgary teen to appeal transfusion ruling," *National Post* online, February 22, 2002.

1. Explain why the Alberta Court of Queen's Bench allowed doctors to proceed with the transfusions.
2. At what age do you think a minor should be granted the power to decide on matters related to their medical treatment?
3. If the 16-year-old in this case challenges the decision as an infringement of her s. 2(a) Charter right, do you think her appeal will be allowed? Why or why not?

Freedom of Thought and Expression

Under s. 2(b) of the Charter, you are free to think and believe what you want and to publicly express your opinions through writing, speech, painting, photography, and other means. Freedom of expression has always been regarded as one of the key freedoms in a democracy, one that the Court has been reluctant to restrict except in the clearest of circumstances. Freedom of the press and other media is included in s. 2(b) because these media are seen as the means for communicating information to the public and as a forum for speaking out on issues.

The right of the public to know and the right of the press to fulfill its mandate to inform the public have both been protected in Charter decisions by the Supreme Court. For example, in *International Fund for Animal Welfare Inc. v. The Queen*, [1989], the Court ruled that restricting members of the press from approaching a commercial seal hunt violated the right of the press to gather information.

A landmark case in the area of freedom of expression was *Irwin Toy Ltd. v. Quebec*, [1989]. The issue in this case was the limitation the *Consumer Protection Act* of Quebec placed on advertising directed at children under

Law in Your Life
In 1976, Alice Munro's *Lives of Girls and Women* and Margaret Laurence's *The Diviners* were removed from some high schools. Discuss whether s. 2(b) of the Charter protects against this type of censorship.

Figure 4.6 Robin Sharpe leaving the B.C. Supreme Court. Do you think he was successful in his constitutional challenge? Why or why not?

the age of 13. In considering this case, the Supreme Court declared that "all activities conveying or attempting to convey meaning are expression for the purposes of s. 2(b)" and, as such, are protected by the Charter. Nonetheless, the Court ruled in this case that the Act did not infringe unreasonably on Irwin's right to freedom of expression.

The definition of "expression" outlined in *Irwin Toy Ltd. v. Quebec,* [1989] has subsequently been cited in many s. 2(b) cases, most significantly those involving hate and obscenity issues. Two of these controversial Charter cases were *R. v. Keegstra,* [1990] and *R. v. Zundel,* [1992].

Section 2(b) has also been used in challenges involving child pornography charges. When Robin Sharpe was charged with possession of child pornography under s. 163.1(4) of the *Criminal Code,* he challenged the constitutionality of the law, claiming it violated his constitutional guarantee of freedom of expression.

Freedom of Peaceful Assembly and Association

Canadians' freedom to assemble for peaceful purposes, such as demonstrating against a government action or marching in support of a cause, has always been part of common law and is now enshrined in the *Charter of Rights and Freedoms* as s. 2(c). You will note that freedom of assembly specifies that the assembly must be "peaceful." The word *peaceful* allows the court to distinguish between a *lawful* assembly, such as an orderly demonstration or a group of picketers, and an *unlawful* assembly or riot. To be classified as a riot, an unlawful assembly must consist of 12 or more persons. Under the *Criminal Code,* an assembly can be dispersed if it disturbs the peace "tumultuously" or causes fear in persons nearby.

Figure 4.7 Many Charter cases regarding freedom of association are concerned with union or collective bargaining issues.

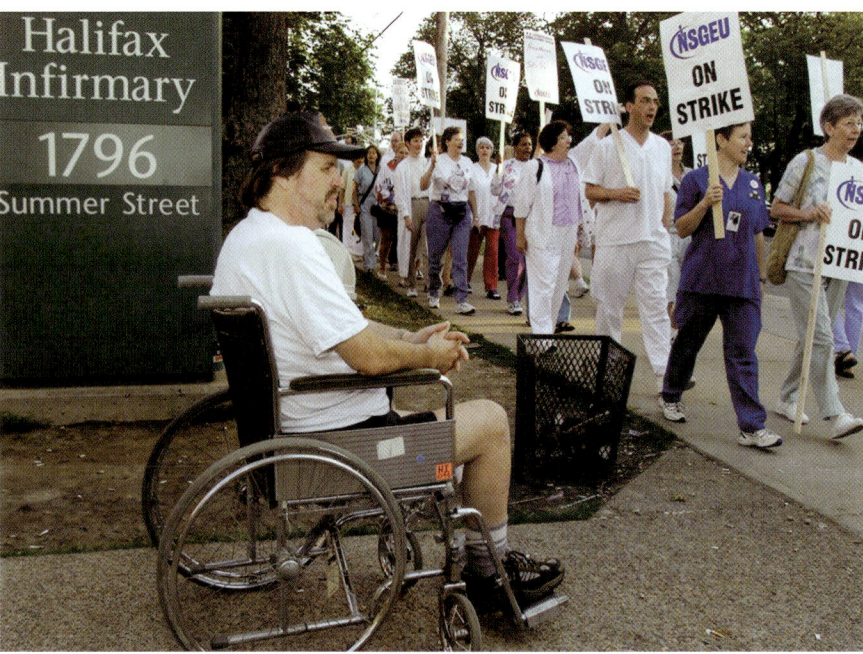

Freedom of association in s. 2(d) is closely linked to freedom of assembly. Freedom of association refers to the ability to connect with other people or groups such as unions, political parties, cultural groups, educational organizations, or sporting clubs. As with other fundamental freedoms, there are limitations on the freedom of association. For example, young offenders may be ordered as part of a probation order not to associate with some of their friends. A prison inmate cannot have unrestricted freedom of assembly or association because such freedom would undermine discipline and security.

The Supreme Court of Canada has ruled that freedom of association does not guarantee trade unions the right to bargain collectively; however, such rights are protected under the *Canada Labour Relations Act* and other trade union acts. Certain groups, such as RCMP officers and federal lawyers, have been specifically barred from forming or joining unions.

> **Fast Fact**
> Freedom to hold parades to celebrate cultural events and the distinctiveness of ethnic groups living in Canada falls under s. 2(c) of the Charter.

CASE

Lavigne v. Ontario Public Service Employees Union, [1991] 2 S.C.R. 211

As a teaching master at the Haileybury School of Mines, Lavigne had never become a member of the Ontario Public Service Employees Union (OPSEU), the bargaining agent for college teachers. However, he was required to pay dues to the Union. The dues were deducted from his paycheque under the terms of the collective agreement between the Council of Regents, acting as a Crown agent, and OPSEU. In addition to collective bargaining expenditures, the dues were used to support the New Democratic Party, disarmament campaigns, and the National Union of Mine Workers in the United Kingdom.

Lavigne took OPSEU to court, arguing that ss. 51, 52, and 53 of the *Colleges Collective Bargaining Act,* which require compulsory payment of dues, violated his Charter rights under ss. 2(b) (freedom of expression) and 2(d) (freedom of association). Lavigne objected to the use of his dues to support causes he did not endorse.

The trial judge found that the *Canadian Charter of Rights and Freedoms* applied, that Lavigne's freedom of association guaranteed by section 2(d) had been infringed, and that the infringement was not justified under s. 1. There was, however, no infringement of Lavigne's freedom of expression. OPSEU appealed the ruling.

The Court of Appeal reversed the judgment. It found that the use of the dues by the Union was a private activity by a private organization and, therefore, beyond the reach of the Charter. There had been no infringement of Lavigne's freedom of association, since he remained free to associate with others and to oppose the Union. Lavigne appealed to the Supreme Court of Canada.

The Supreme Court disallowed the appeal and upheld the judgment of the Court of Appeal. It concluded "that the agreement which compels Lavigne to make payments to the Union does not fall within the concept of compelled association because it does not associate him with the causes to which the Union may devote a portion of its funds."

1. Why did Lavigne take the union to court?
2. In your own words, explain the trial judge's decision.
3. Identify two reasons the Court of Appeal found in favour of the union. Which reason is connected to legal jurisdiction? Explain.
4. Do you agree with the judgments of the Court of Appeal and the Supreme Court of Canada? Why or why not?

Building Your Understanding

1. What conflicting right can limit a person's freedom of religion? Explain.
2. What limits are placed on your right to expression?
3. a) Distinguish between the freedom of peaceful assembly and the freedom of association.
   b) What limitations have been placed on each of these freedoms?
4. Identify individuals and groups that have had their freedom of association limited or barred. Provide reasons for these restrictions.

DEMOCRATIC AND MOBILITY RIGHTS

As you read earlier, women were not allowed to vote until 1918. Chinese Canadians and Japanese Canadians could not vote in federal elections until 1947, and Status Indians were denied voting rights until 1960. You may be surprised to learn that the right to vote or run for public office was not guaranteed in law prior to 1982. These rights were recognized under Canadian law in various election acts, but as mere statutes they had no more force or effect than any other statute; they could be changed or repealed at any time. In other words, theoretically, the government had the power to take away the right to vote or eliminate the election process altogether.

The *Canadian Charter of Rights and Freedoms* protects both democratic and mobility rights for all Canadians. Sections 3, 4, and 5 of the Charter guarantee democratic government, and s. 6 protects the right of Canadians to enter and leave Canada and to move from province to province.

Figure 4.8 Canadian citizens, permanent residents, and, in some cases, refugees and illegal immigrants, are protected by the Charter. However, the right to vote (s. 3) and the right to enter, remain in, and leave Canada (s. 6) are extended only to Canadian citizens.

Democratic Rights

Although s. 3 states that "every citizen" has the right to vote in an election and run for office, there are restrictions. The right to vote is subject to reasonable restrictions such as age, mental capacity, residence, and registration. In addition, certain groups are excluded from the right to vote. Members of the judiciary, for example, do not have the right to vote, presumably to ensure their independence from government. At one time, all inmates in federal or provincial institutions were denied the right to vote. After a series of legal battles, the *Canada Elections Act* was amended so that prisoners serving a sentence of less than two years can now vote in federal elections.

The Charter guarantees not only voting rights, but also the right to exercise these rights on a regular basis. Section 4 provides that Canadians are assured the opportunity to elect a new federal and provincial government every five years except under extraordinary circumstances such as war or national emergency (s. 4). Parliament and provincial legislative assemblies must hold at least one session a year (s. 5). This guarantee provides an opportunity for both elected members and the public to question government actions and policy.

Fast Fact
On November 27, 2000, homeless people were able to vote for the first time in a federal election.

Law in Your Life
In 1970, the *Canada Elections Act* lowered the voting age and the minimum age to run for office from 21 to 18.

Should Inmates Be Allowed to Vote?

LAW IN ACTION

Richard Sauvé was serving a 25-year sentence for first-degree murder. In 1992, he brought an action against the chief electoral officer of Canada to have paragraph 51(e) of the *Canada Elections Act* struck down as being contrary to s. 3 (right to vote) and s. 15 (equality rights) of the Charter. At that time, paragraph 51(e) denied the vote to all inmates serving sentences in any penal institution for the commission of any offence. The Ontario Court of Appeal and the Federal Court of Appeal declared the paragraph unconstitutional. These decisions were upheld by the Supreme Court of Canada.

In response, Parliament amended the offending paragraph so that prisoners serving a sentence of two years or more in a correctional institution were prohibited from voting. Consequently, those prisoners serving less than two years were given voting privileges.

Once again Sauvé challenged the limitation, and in 1995 he was successful. Consequently, all prisoners were entitled to vote in the 1997 federal election. However, the victory was short-lived. In 1999, the Federal Court of Appeal overturned the decision. The amended paragraph 51(e) that denied the vote to prisoners serving more than two years remained in force. In 2000, Sauvé appealed the decision to the Supreme Court of Canada. As of March 2002, the appeal had not been heard, and the issue continued to be the subject of ongoing litigation.

1. Do you think inmates in federal and provincial prisons should retain their democratic rights while incarcerated? Explain your position.

2. Use the four criteria of "reasonable limits" established in *R. v. Oakes* to determine how you think the Supreme Court of Canada will rule on Sauvé's appeal. Provide reasons for your answer.

Mobility Rights

Section 6, which has four subsections, concerns the rights of Canadian citizens to move in and out of the country and between provinces. The majority of Charter cases involving s. 6(1) concern the issue of **extradition** and the federal *Extradition Act*. The Supreme Court of Canada has ruled that accused persons can be sent to other countries to face trial because suppressing crime is of "... sufficient importance to warrant overriding the constitutionally protected right of citizens to remain in Canada...." On the other hand, the Court has ruled against extraditing people accused of **capital offences** to a country where the death penalty is legal. It is the Court's view that sending a suspect to face the possibility of a death penalty would violate that person's right to life.

Why are there limitations to Canadians' rights to move to any province and secure work? When the Charter was being negotiated, provincial governments in wealthier provinces worried about being flooded by unemployed residents from other provinces, seeking work and using services paid for by permanent residents. Governments in poorer provinces were concerned that Canadians outside the province would come and take away already scarce jobs. In order to protect existing residents, publicly funded social services can be restricted to those who have lived in the province for a certain length of time [s. 6 (3)(a) and (3)(b)]. Also, a province with a higher unemployment rate than the rest of Canada can create programs to favour its own permanent residents [s. 6(4)].

extradition: surrendering an accused person to another jurisdiction to stand trial

capital offence: a crime punishable by death in some jurisdictions

Fast Fact
Having children who were born in Canada does not confer any Charter right on parents to remain in Canada.

Figure 4.9 Many Canadian universities charge higher fees to students from other provinces. How might this practice be related to mobility rights?

Building Your Understanding

1. a) Identify restrictions placed on the right to vote.
   b) Name one group that does not have the right to vote. Explain why.
2. a) Why have opposite rulings been made with regard to extraditing suspects to face trial outside Canada?
   b) Identify the factors considered in each ruling.
3. Why do provincial governments want the power to restrict the movement of Canadian citizens from one province to another?
4. Should subsections (3) and (4) of the Mobility Rights section be removed? Why or why not?

LEGAL AND EQUALITY RIGHTS

All Canadians who become involved with the criminal justice system are guaranteed certain basic protections under the *Canadian Charter of Rights and Freedoms*. Sections 7 to 11 of the Charter cover all areas of criminal law—from investigating a crime, ensuring procedural fairness at trial, and deciding about use of evidence right through to sentencing convicted offenders. If any of these rights are infringed on by the police, by the Crown, or by anyone else involved in the justice system, a judge may be compelled to exclude the evidence or dismiss the charges. Sections 12 to 14 cover punishment for crimes and issues related to being a witness at a trial. Section 15 addresses equality rights.

Legal Rights

If the courts find that a criminal law infringes on the rights and freedoms of Canadians, and the Crown fails to justify the need for such a law "in a free and democratic society" (s. 1), the law may be struck down. *R. v. Ruzic*, [2001] (see Chapter 10) is an example of the courts ruling that a law in the *Criminal Code* is unconstitutional. This section explores those parts of the Charter that address criminal law issues concerning arrest and detention.

Life, Liberty, and Security of the Person

Section 7 of the Charter declares that everyone has the right to life, liberty, and security of the person and cannot be deprived of these rights except in accordance with the principles of fundamental justice. At first glance, these rights may seem self-evident or easy to define, but s. 7 has actually been one of the most difficult sections of the Charter for the courts to come to terms with. For instance, in abortion cases, the right to life enshrined in s. 7 has become a controversial issue. The Supreme Court of Canada has ruled that since a fetus is not a "person," it is not afforded the protection of the right to life as stated in s. 7.

A terminally ill person's right to assisted suicide has also been examined under this section. Sue Rodriguez suffered from amyotropic lateral sclerosis (ALS), a debilitating, terminal disease that attacks the central nervous system. Rodriguez wanted to be able to end her life at a time of her choosing but

Consider This
The Supreme Court of Canada has ruled that a fetus is not a "person." Do you agree with this ruling? Why or why not?

Fast Fact
ALS is commonly called Lou Gehrig's disease after the famous New York Yankee who died of the illness in 1941 at the age of 37.

Figure 4.10 Four months after the Supreme Court decision, Sue Rodriguez committed suicide with the assistance of an unidentified doctor. Do you think people with debilitating diseases should have the right to physician-assisted suicide? Why or why not?

"For some, the choice to end one's life with dignity is infinitely preferable to the inevitable pain and the diminishment of a long, slow decline."
— former chief justice Antonio Lamer

knew that she would be physically incapable of killing herself when the time came. Obtaining help was prohibited by s. 241(b) of the *Criminal Code,* which prevented anyone from assisting her suicide. In *Rodriguez v. British Columbia (A.G.),* [1993], she argued that s. 241(b) violated her constitutional rights, particularly s. 7 of the Charter, which guarantees the right to security of the person.

On September 29, 1993, Sue Rodriguez lost her legal battle when the Supreme Court of Canada decided by a vote of 5 to 4 that assisted suicide should not be legalized. In its decision, the Court stated that the purpose of s. 241(b) is to protect life and those who are vulnerable, and that the law "is reflective of the fundamental values at play in our society."

The "right to liberty" is most often associated with criminal cases. A person must not be deprived of this right, or imprisoned, except in accordance with the principles of fundamental justice. In this sense, "fundamental justice" refers to the due process of the law, such as the presumption of innocence, the burden of proof, the right to a fair hearing before an impartial decision-maker, and the right of habeas corpus.

The "right to security" of the person has been interpreted to protect people against certain forms of corporal punishment and physical suffering. In *R. v. Morgentaler,* [1988], the Supreme Court ruled that provisions of the *Criminal Code* relating to abortion violated a woman's right to security of the person.

As noted, fundamental justice can be interpreted in a narrow sense, such as "due process" of the law, or in a broader sense to refer to all the legal rights that are explicitly mentioned in ss. 8 to 11 of the Charter. It is important to note, however, that fundamental justice refers not only to the rights of people who have been arrested or accused of crimes, but also to the rights of society to be protected from criminal activities. In *Cunningham v. Canada* (1993), the Supreme Court of Canada stated that a "fair balance" must be struck between the rights of the individual and those of society as a whole.

Unreasonable Search and Seizure

Section 8 of the Charter guarantees that people will not be subject to unreasonable search and seizure. This means that the police must have a good reason for searching the person, home, or belongings of an accused. The search must also be conducted fairly. For instance, police can search the place where a person is arrested in order to find a weapon or articles relating to the offence, but they cannot use their searches as "fishing expeditions" to see if something else turns up that could be used against the suspect in court. Some laws outside the *Criminal Code* give the police specific search powers. For example, the *Controlled Drugs and Substances Act* grants the police the

R. v. *Parker* (2000), Ont. C.A. 359

CASE

Parker suffered for 40 years from a severe form of epilepsy. He experienced frequent seizures that were sometimes considered life threatening. Parker tried to control his seizures through surgery and conventional medication. The surgery was a failure and the medication only moderately successful. He found that smoking marijuana substantially reduced the number of seizures. Since he had no legal source of marijuana, he began growing it himself. On two occasions, the police searched his home and seized the marijuana, charging him with possession.

Parker decided to fight the charges by showing that the prohibition against possession of marijuana was unconstitutional. He claimed that the legislation infringed his right to fundamental justice as guaranteed by s. 7 of the Charter. Because Parliament made the cultivation and possession of marijuana illegal, Parker faced the threat of imprisonment as the penalty for trying to preserve his health. He argued that a statute having this effect is not consistent with the principle of fundamental justice. At trial, Parker cited evidence of the therapeutic value of marijuana for treating epilepsy, glaucoma, the side effects of cancer treatment, and the symptoms of AIDS.

The trial judge ruled in favour of Parker and found that the prohibition against marijuana infringed his rights under s. 7 of the Charter. The judge stayed (suspended) the proceedings against Parker and read into the legislation an exemption for persons possessing or cultivating marijuana for their "personal, medically approved use."

The Crown appealed this decision. The Ontario Court of Appeal dismissed the appeal. However, the Court of Appeal disagreed with the trial judge's remedy of reading an exemption into the law. Instead, the appeals court declared the law to be "of no force." It suspended its declaration for one year to give Parliament the chance to amend the law to bring it into agreement with s. 7 of the Charter. On July 30, 2001, Canada became the first country in the world to legalize doctor-prescribed marijuana for people suffering from terminal illnesses or severe, chronic pain.

1. What did Parker mean when he argued that the law prohibiting possession of marijuana violated the principle of fundamental justice? Identify the specific Charter right that is most relevant to this situation.
2. Explain why the Court of Appeal suspended its declaration against the marijuana law for one year.
3. How do you think the law to legalize doctor-prescribed marijuana will effect the attitudes of the public and the police toward this drug?

power to search any place (except a residence) where they suspect drugs are concealed without obtaining a warrant beforehand. You will learn about search warrants and how they are obtained in Chapter 8, Investigation and Arrest.

Arbitrary Detention or Imprisonment

Section 9 of the Charter guarantees that "everyone has the right not to be arbitrarily detained or imprisoned." This means that people cannot be held for questioning, arrested, or kept in jail by the police without good reason. Does this also mean that police roadside checks for drivers' sobriety are illegal? This question was answered in *R. v. Ladouceur*, [1990].

Fast Fact
In 1996, the *Narcotic Control Act*, R.S.C. 1985, was amended as the *Controlled Drugs and Substances Act*.

Fast Fact
The Reduce Impaired Driving Everywhere (RIDE) program has been extended to random checks for sobriety of boaters and snowmobilers.

In November 1989, while conducting random traffic checks, police stopped Gerald Ladouceur. At the time, police had no reasonable grounds to suspect Ladouceur of any unlawful conduct. However, as soon as they discovered that his driver's licence was suspended, he was charged with driving while his licence was under suspension. Ladouceur was convicted of the charge. On appeal to the Ontario Court of Appeal, the conviction was upheld. Ladouceur appealed to the Supreme Court of Canada on the basis that the random traffic checks violated ss. 7, 8, and 9 of the Charter.

In its decision, the Supreme Court determined that although random stops by police do violate s. 9, they can be justified under s. 1 of the Charter. Section 1 allows for "reasonable limits prescribed by law" regarding the rights guaranteed in other sections. The appeal was dismissed.

Rights While Under Arrest or Detention

Section 10 of the Charter describes the rights people have while under arrest or detention. The first right is to be promptly and clearly informed of the reason for the arrest or detention. In most cases, the person must be given the reason *while* the arrest or detention is being carried out. The police cannot withhold the information and give it to the accused only at the police station or at a later date. If the police fail to provide a reason promptly, then the arrest or detention is unlawful, and the judge will be compelled to dismiss the charges. (It should be pointed out that "promptly" is a relative term, so its meaning may depend on the circumstances.)

Law in Your Life
Young people who are arrested or detained have additional rights under the *Youth Criminal Justice Act*. You will learn more about these rights in Chapter 12.

The accused also has the right to be informed without delay that he or she may obtain the assistance of a lawyer. The accused is to be provided with a reasonable opportunity to contact a lawyer in order to obtain legal advice as soon as possible. (However, not being able to get in touch with a lawyer after a reasonable period of time will not be construed as a breach of s. 10 rights; in such instances, the accused might simply use this excuse as a delay tactic.) If the accused cannot afford a lawyer, it must be made clear that legal counsel is available at no charge. Once an arrested person decides to talk to a lawyer, the police must stop their questioning until the accused and the lawyer have a chance to talk privately. If the police listen in on the conversation between the accused and the lawyer, the charges may be dismissed in court.

Rights When Charged with a Criminal Offence

Section 11 of the Charter sets out several important rules that protect anyone charged with an offence under federal or provincial law. As stated in s. 11(a), anyone accused of a crime must be told promptly what the offence is. Section 11(b) states that the trial must take place within a reasonable time, and 11(c) states that the accused cannot be forced to testify at his or her own trial.

Anyone accused of breaking the law is presumed innocent until proven guilty. The trial must be conducted fairly and before a court that is unbiased and independent of political or any other influence [s. 11(d)]. An accused person has the right not to be denied reasonable bail without just cause [s. 11(e)] and, for serious charges, has the right to trial by jury [s. 11(f)]. A court cannot convict an accused unless the law under which he or she was charged

R. v. Askov, [1990] 2 S.C.R. 1199

CASE

In November 1983, Elijah Askov, Ralph Hussey, Samuel Gugliotta, and Edward Melo were charged with conspiracy to commit extortion. Counsel agreed to a date in July 1984 for a preliminary hearing, but it could not be held until September of that year. The trial was set for September 7, 1985, but the case could not be heard during that session. The case finally came to trial in September 1986, two years after the preliminary hearing. The judge ruled that the major part of the delay stemmed from institutional problems and granted the accused a stay of proceedings. The Ontario Court of Appeal reversed that decision and directed that the trial proceed.

The accused appealed to the Supreme Court of Canada, which allowed the stay of proceedings. The Court ruled that according to s. 11(b), an accused person's right to be tried within a reasonable period of time was a matter of fundamental justice. A quick resolution of the charges also has important practical benefits because memories fade with time, and witnesses may move, become ill, or die. Victims, too, have an interest in trials taking place within a reasonable time, as does society, since it is important for the community to see that lawbreakers are brought to trial promptly.

1. Why is it important from an accused person's point of view for the trial to be held within a reasonable period of time? Why is it important from society's point of view?

2. Since the Askov case, thousands of cases have been thrown out of court because of long delays before trial. In your opinion, did the Askov decision have a positive or negative outcome for society in general? Explain.

---

was in force at the time of the offence and specifically stated that the actions in question were illegal [s. 11(g)].

If someone is tried for an offence and found not guilty, that person cannot be tried on the same charge again. Moreover, according to s. 11(h), if the person is found guilty and is punished for the offence, he or she cannot be tried or punished for it again (a situation known as "double jeopardy"). If someone commits an offence, and prior to sentencing, a new law alters the fine or term of imprisonment, that person must be sentenced under whichever law is more lenient [s. 11(i)].

Cruel and Unusual Treatment or Punishment

Section 12 means that governments cannot treat or punish individuals in an unnecessarily harsh fashion. Cases continue to be brought before the court in an effort to seek a definition of what may constitute "cruel and unusual treatment or punishment." For example, inmates in federal penitentiaries have tried to argue that being denied cigarettes falls under this category.

In *R. v. Smith*, [1987], a case involving the importation of seven and a half ounces of cocaine, the Supreme Court of Canada explained that in assessing whether a punishment is grossly disproportionate, the Court must consider

- the gravity of the offence,
- the personal characteristics of the offender, and
- the particular circumstances of the case.

Fast Fact

In *R. v. M. (T.)* (1991), the judge found that conditions in the detention centre constituted "cruel and unusual treatment" because the cells were hot, dirty, and overcrowded; the staff was untrained to work with youths; and there were no planned activities for those detained.

The Court must assess the punishment, using the "most innocent possible offender" test. In *R. v. Smith,* Justice Lamer used the example of whether a young person entering Canada with one marijuana cigarette should go to prison for seven years, which was the minimum sentence for importation of narcotics specified in s. 5(2) of the *Narcotic Control Act,* R.S.C. 1970. The Court found that s. 5(2) was contrary to ss. 7, 9, and 12 of the Charter.

The dangerous offender provision of the *Criminal Code* allows for criminals who have committed a certain number of indictable offences to be declared dangerous and subject to an indefinite penalty. This provision was unsuccessfully challenged under s. 12 in *R. v. Lyons,* [1987] and in *R. v. Milne,* [1987]. However, in *Steele v. Mountain Institution,* [1990], the Court held that a parole board's wrong decision to deny a "dangerous offender" parole violated s. 12.

The Robert Latimer sentencing (see Chapter 11) presented a particular challenge for the court in determining whether, in this particular case, the 10-year mandatory minimum sentence for a conviction of second-degree murder constituted "cruel and unusual punishment."

Rights of Witnesses in Court

Section 13 of the Charter guarantees that witnesses giving evidence in court cannot have their testimony used against them. Suppose Malik is giving eyewitness testimony about a hit-and-run accident. He states that he was at the scene of the accident because he was involved in a drug deal. Malik's ad-

Figure 4.11 If someone lies while giving evidence in court, this testimony could be used against that person in a perjury trial. Why is this situation different from an admission of unrelated illegal activity?

mission of selling drugs could not be used as evidence against him if he were tried on drug-related charges.

To ensure that persons charged with a criminal offence are given a full and fair opportunity to understand the case against them, s. 14 of the Charter states that anyone who is hearing impaired or cannot understand or speak the language used in court has the right to an interpreter. This section is intimately related to Canada's claim to be a multicultural society, which is expressed in part through s. 27 of the Charter.

Equality Rights

Section 15 states that every individual is considered equal and that government cannot discriminate in its laws or programs. Section 15(1) can be broken down into three parts:

- every citizen is equal before and under the law
- every citizen has the right to equal protection and benefit of the law
- these rights are to be applied equally and without discrimination

Under s. 15(2), programs set up by governments to **ameliorate,** or improve, the conditions of certain disadvantaged groups or individuals are permissible even if they are seen as discriminatory to the majority. For example, a law that provides for preferential parking for handicapped persons is acceptable.

The wording of s. 15 has been the subject of much debate. Lawyers and constitutional experts have challenged almost every word. For example, s. 15 begins with "every individual" rather than "every citizen," "everyone," or "every person." The intent of this wording is to show that this section does not apply to corporations, unlike some other sections of the Charter. The phrase "in particular" means that the listed prohibited areas of discrimination are merely examples. Areas *not* listed, such as marital status or sexual orientation, may also be considered protected areas of discrimination.

The Supreme Court of Canada took the opportunity to define how it intended to interpret "discrimination" in *Andrews* v. *Law Society of British Columbia,* [1989], one of the first cases that came before the Court to argue discrimination based on s. 15(1). Mark Andrews, a British subject, was denied a licence to practise law in British Columbia because he was not a Canadian citizen. At that time, all lawyers were required to be Canadian citizens before they could receive a licence to practise. Andrews argued that this requirement discriminated against people who were not Canadian citizens. The Supreme Court agreed. In its judgment, the Court set out a clear definition of what it considered discrimination:

> Discrimination is a distinction, whether intentional or not but based on grounds relating to personal characteristics of the individual or group, which has the effect of imposing burdens, obligations, or disadvantages on such individual or group not imposed on others, or which withholds or limits access to opportunities, benefits, and advantages available to other members of society.

Consider This
"Equality does not necessarily mean that everyone should be treated the same." Use examples to explain this statement.

ameliorate: to improve

Fast Fact
If the Supreme Court of Canada strikes down a law based on Charter infringement, Parliament or the Legislature can enact a new law. If the new law is challenged in court and struck down, the process begins again.

The Court suggested that the test of discrimination should have two parts:

1) The complainant must show that he or she has been treated unequally and that the effect of the unequal treatment was discriminatory.
2) The government must then try to demonstrate that the law is "demonstrably justified" under s. 1 of the Charter as a reasonable limit.

For example, although "every individual is equal," a nine-year-old cannot legally drive a car.

Building Your Understanding

1. What is meant by "the right to life, liberty, and security of the person"?
2. Explain one controversial aspect of s. 7 of the Charter.
3. What considerations did the courts weigh in striking a balance between the right to security for those accused of criminal offences and the rights of the public?
4. Why were certain provisions of the *Criminal Code* ruled as a violation of a woman's right to security of the person?
5. Explain why random police spot checks to determine whether motorists have been drinking are legal even though they violate s. 9 of the Charter.
6. Katrina was arrested for possession of marijuana. The police informed her that she had the right to contact a lawyer without delay. Katrina said, "Who can afford a lawyer?" The police laughed and then asked Katrina several questions about who sold her the marijuana and how much she paid for it. Katrina answered all of their questions. Can this evidence be used against her in court? Why or why not?
7. Explain the principle of "double jeopardy."
8. Use the test of discrimination to explain why discrimination based on age can be justly applied to restrict those under 18 years of age from voting.

LANGUAGE AND GENERAL RIGHTS

Sections 16 through 22 of the *Charter of Rights and Freedoms* affirm that Canada is a bilingual country and that French and English have equal status as official languages in Parliament and federal government agencies. Section 23 guarantees the right of English-speaking and French-speaking minorities in any province to have their children educated in their own language, provided sufficient numbers warrant it. What constitutes sufficient numbers is relative and open to judicial interpretation. Section 25 protects the rights of Aboriginal peoples in Canada, including Indians, Inuit, and Métis. The multicultural nature of Canadian society is recognized in s. 27 of the Charter.

Language Rights

Specific provisions of ss. 16 to 22 include the following:

- English or French can be used in Parliament
- statutes, records, and journals of Parliament are to be published in both languages

- members of the public are entitled to communicate with the federal government in both languages
- the federal government must provide services in both languages at central offices and elsewhere if there is sufficient demand
- either language can be used in courts established by Parliament, including the Supreme Court of Canada

The equal status and rights of French- and English-speaking people in New Brunswick are also recognized, making New Brunswick the only official bilingual province in Canada. Section 133 of the Constitution provides that any person may use either English or French in debates in Parliament, before the federal courts, and in the Quebec Legislature and courts.

Section 22 of the Charter allows languages other than English and French to be acquired and enjoyed. In keeping with this Charter right, the *Official Languages Act* of the Northwest Territories provides that the languages used by Aboriginal peoples are among the official languages of the territories, making the Northwest Territories a distinct society within Canada. For example, Inuit or Dene persons have the right to speak in Inuktitut and Slavey, respectively, in all government institutions in the Northwest Territories.

Fast Fact
In *Re Manitoba Language Rights*, [1985], the Supreme Court of Canada held that s. 23 of the *Manitoba Act, 1870*, a constitutional document, required both English and French in the Manitoba Legislature and courts.

Language Education Rights

In the nine provinces and three territories where most people speak English, citizens have the right to have all their children educated in French if any one of the following applies:

- their first language is French,
- they received their own primary education in Canada in French, *or*
- they have a child who is already receiving or did receive education in French.

In Quebec, where most people speak French, citizens have the right to have their children educated in English if they received their own primary instruction in Canada in English, or if they have a child who is receiving or did receive education in English. When in the minority, if schooling in either official language is to be provided anywhere in Canada, there must be a sufficient number of children to justify this service.

Consider This
Only French and English language education rights are addressed in the Charter. If numbers warrant it, do you think that minority language education rights should be extended to people who speak languages other than French or English? Explain.

Aboriginal Rights

The intention of s. 25 is to protect the culture, customs, traditions, languages, and other rights or freedoms pertaining to Aboriginal peoples. Such rights and freedoms include those recognized by the Royal Proclamation of 1763 and those existing or acquired through land-claim agreements. The terms of the Charter must not be seen as a way to either **abrogate** or **derogate** (nullify or diminish) the rights of Aboriginal peoples. The courts have held that s. 25 confers no new rights but rather protects the rights of Aboriginal peoples from the Charter provisions.

abrogate: to abolish or annul
derogate: to take away or detract

Figure 4.12 Mi'kmaq bands from the Gaspé and Maritime provinces protest in front of the Supreme Court of Canada in Ottawa over disputed land and fishing rights.

Fast Fact
The Royal Proclamation of 1763 established the constitutional framework for the negotiation of treaties with the Aboriginal peoples of Canada.

We must have government and legal structures that recognize our diversity and allow us to live together in harmony and in a way that promotes the fullest possible contribution from all of our citizens regardless of our race or background.
— The Right Honourable Beverley McLachlin, Chief Justice of Canada

Multicultural Rights

Canadian society has been called a cultural mosaic of races from all over the world. Our interest in respecting and preserving the cultural differences among Canadians is upheld by s. 27 of the Charter. In *R. v. Big M Drug Mart Ltd.*, [1985], for example, the Supreme Court of Canada drew attention to the fact that neither the Islamic nor Jewish Sabbath observances fell on Sunday. Consequently, imposing restrictions on merchants and shoppers of these faiths was not in keeping with the spirit of s. 27 of the Charter. As mentioned previously, this Act was also struck down as contrary to s. 2(a), freedom of conscience and religion.

Charting the Record

There is no doubt that the *Canadian Charter of Rights and Freedoms* has had a significant impact on Canadian society. Some critics argue that the will of the majority is being subverted by special interest groups, aided and abetted by nine appointed Supreme Court justices who have the power to change law and social policy for every Canadian. In response to this charge, Chief Justice Beverley McLachlin has said, "There is no evidence that the judges of the Supreme Court have used the Charter to increase their own power at the expense of Parliament and the elected legislatures."

The justices who sit on Canada's highest court do, in fact, have immense legal power. Since the Charter came into effect in 1982, the Supreme Court of Canada has overturned some 80 laws passed by democratic parliaments. Many more proposed laws have not been enacted because legislators knew they would not survive a Charter challenge. On the other hand, some feel that s. 33 of the Charter serves to balance the power of the court and the power of elected representatives.

Others point to the number of times the notwithstanding clause has been used by provincial governments and argue that it weakens the power of the Charter to an unacceptable degree. In 1987, for example, the Saskatchewan government used the clause to end strikes by public employees and to impose a legislated contract. The government argued that denying workers the right to strike was justified because of the disruption all Saskatchewan residents would suffer if public employees were permitted to strike.

There is no doubt that since the entrenchment of the Charter, Canadian judges are more powerful than ever. Chief Justice Beverley McLachlin has said that the *Charter of Rights and Freedoms* cannot be all things to all people. She has also stated that the court is being thrust into the "uncertain sea of value judgments."

> "Guilty thugs are walking free because of the Charter of Rights and Freedoms *and nit-picking judges who let them go on technicalities."*
> — Justice Sterling Lyon of the Manitoba Court of Appeal

Consider This
Justice Bertha Wilson has stated, "It is my view that a right or freedom may have different meanings in different contexts." What do you think she means? To what extent is this true of cases you have read in this chapter?

Building Your Understanding

1. Identify the institutions in which the public can obtain services in both French and English.
2. What criteria have been established to ensure that the English minority in Quebec and the French minority in the rest of Canada have equal language education rights?
3. Explain how the purpose of s. 25 is consistent with the principles established in ss. 1 and 15(2) of the Charter.
4. a) Discuss some of the criticisms made against the Charter.
   b) How would you respond to each criticism?

LOOKING BACK

Reviewing Your Vocabulary

abrogate *p. 101*
ameliorate *p. 99*
capital offences *p. 92*
derogate *p. 101*
dissemination *p. 86*

entrench *p. 80*
extradition *p. 92*
franchise *p. 78*
freedom *p. 77*
inalienable rights *p. 77*

interveners *p. 84*
invoke *p. 80*
notwithstanding clause *p. 81*
override *p. 80*
right *p. 77*

Quick Quiz

1. Choose the appropriate term from the vocabulary list above to complete the following statements:
   a) ____ is the right to conduct one's affairs without government interference.
   b) A Charter right cannot abrogate or ____ from any Aboriginal treaty or other rights or freedoms pertaining to Aboriginal peoples.
   c) If Parliament or provincial Legislatures disagree with a decision made by the Supreme Court of Canada, they can use s. 33, the ____ to ____ the decision.
   d) The Equality Section of the Charter permits government to make a law that may discriminate in order to ____ the condition of a disadvantaged group.
   e) One of Trudeau's goals was to ____ a guaranteed *Charter of Rights and Freedoms* within the *Constitution Act, 1982*.
   f) ____, or friends of the court, can present viewpoints during a Charter case.
   g) Status Indians were not given a federal ____ until 1960.
   h) Guaranteed human and political entitlements that cannot be restricted, transferred, or denied are called ____.

Checking Your Knowledge

2. Using your knowledge of the Charter, indicate whether the following statements are true or false. Correct any statements you identify as false.
   a) Section 2(a) of the Charter gives freedom of religion to everyone. A person who belongs to a religious group that allows its members to have more than one spouse is entitled to marry more than one person.
   b) Section 2(b) of the Charter guarantees freedom of the press. Therefore, a newspaper in Canada can print anything it likes.
   c) You cannot be tried for the same crime twice.
   d) If the Supreme Court of Canada determines that prohibiting inmates in a provincial jail from running for public office is a violation of the Charter, the government can still override that decision.
   e) Eric, who is 16, was denied the opportunity to apply for the police force until he turned 18. Eric claims his right of protection from discrimination is infringed because of this age restriction.

3. Consult the Charter to determine which of the following situations would be considered reasonable or unreasonable search or seizure. Explain your answers.
   a) Someone is strip-searched coming through customs into Canada.

b) Visitors to federal penitentiaries are searched for drugs or weapons before being allowed to visit with inmates.

c) During a spot check, police stop a car. The passengers behave strangely, so the police ask to search the car. They find a weapon in the car.

Developing Your Thinking and Inquiry Skills

4. Examine the following situations, which are based on actual cases. In each situation, the defendants argue that one of their fundamental freedoms as defined in the *Canadian Charter of Rights and Freedoms* has been denied. Explain which Charter right each defendant feels has been violated. Using your knowledge of the Charter, write a decision on whether you believe these defendants would be successful in their challenge.

    a) Kristin belongs to a religious group called the Utopians. Some religious ceremonies include dancing naked in the woods at midnight, sacrificing animals (such as goats or chickens), and smoking marijuana. Police have charged Kristin and her fellow Utopians with indecent exposure, cruelty to animals, and possession of marijuana. Kristin claims that her rights under the Charter have been violated.

    b) Garth is a member of an organization opposed to the government of Indonesia. When the Indonesian prime minister came to Canada as the guest of the Canadian government, Garth organized a protest. Garth and 20 of his supporters lay down on the road, blocking the car that was driving the prime minister to Parliament. No one was injured, but Garth and his followers were arrested for causing a disturbance. Garth says his rights under the Charter have been violated.

    c) *The British Columbia Herald* published a cartoon of the prime minister, depicting him as a spider plucking off the heads of members of the public. The cartoon implied that the prime minister had lured British Columbians into his web and was now taking all their money for one of his own enterprises. The prime minister sued. The newspaper is arguing a Charter right.

Communicating Your Ideas

5. Work with a partner to develop an information brochure to inform students of their legal rights under s. 11 of the *Canadian Charter of Rights and Freedoms*. For each right, provide a brief explanation and an example.

6. Choose one of the following cases, or research your own case and present your findings to your class. Outline the facts of the case, the legal question, the decision, and any Charter application or precedent. Use **www.pearsoned.ca/law** to locate the information.
    - *R. v. Dersch*, [1993] 3 S.C.R. 768
    - *R. v. Morrisey*, [2000] 1 S.C.R. 39
    - *Lovelace v. Ontario*, [2000] 1 S.C.R. 950

7. A poll conducted by the Institute for Research on Public Policy showed that two-thirds of Canadians do not know who appoints Supreme Court judges. Create and conduct your own poll to measure Canadians' basic knowledge about the Supreme Court of Canada. Then create an engaging word puzzle or quiz that would help improve general knowledge about the Supreme Court.

Putting It All Together

8. "Dissatisfied minority groups, corporations, criminals, and their lawyers are the only people who have benefited from the Charter." Write an argumentative essay, either agreeing or disagreeing with this quote. In your essay, include information about the Charter, relevant cases, and Supreme Court decisions.

CASES

R. v. Sharpe, [2001] 1. S.C.R. 45

The accused was charged with two counts of possession of child pornography under s. 163.1(4) of the *Criminal Code* and two counts of possession of child pornography for the purposes of distribution or sale under s. 163.1(3). Prior to his trial in the British Columbia court, the accused challenged the constitutionality of s. 163.1(4) of the Code, alleging a violation of his right of freedom of expression.

Both the trial judge and the British Columbia Court of Appeal ruled that the prohibition of child pornography as defined under section 163.1(4) of the *Criminal Code* was not justified in a free and democratic society, and they struck down the law under s. 1 of the Charter. In the decision, Justice Mary Southin stated:

> This has been the century of the Gestapo and the KGB—of a state encouraging betrayal by children of their parents to the authorities, of smashing down doors and burning books, all in the name of the greater good.... Legislation which makes simple possession of expressive materials a crime can never be a reasonable limit in a free and democratic society. Such legislation bears the hallmark of tyranny.

The Crown appealed to the Supreme Court of Canada. Child advocates feared that the Supreme Court would uphold the Court of Appeal's decision, so they called on Parliament to invoke the notwithstanding clause to override the Court's ruling.

However, although the Supreme Court agreed with the British Columbia Court of Appeal that the "public good" defence should be liberally interpretted, it ruled that s. 163.1(4) does *not* go too far in restricting freedom. Freedom is not absolute, and the protection of children is a universally accepted goal. Child pornography, stated the Court, warrants less protection because it is far removed from core values normally protected by freedom of expression. Finally, the Court upheld section 163(4), stating that it is a reasonable and justifiable limit whose main objective is to protect children.

1. Explain the conflict between section 163.1(4) of the *Criminal Code* and s. 2(b) of the Charter.
2. Critics of the Supreme Court decision say that the law, as it stands, allows for parents to be charged with possession of child pornography if they have baby pictures of their children naked. Do you agree? What arguments would you make in this case?
3. If the Supreme Court of Canada had agreed with the British Columbia Court of Appeal, would you have supported the government in invoking the notwithstanding clause? Explain.

Arsenault-Cameron v. Prince Edward Island, [2000] 1 S.C.R. 3

A group of parents asked the French Language Board to establish a French school for grades 1 to 6 in the Summerside area of Prince Edward Island. The number of students met the minimum requirement, and the Board made a conditional offer. The minister of education acknowledged that the children were entitled to educational instruction in the French language, but he refused to approve the Board's offer. Instead, he proposed that the students be bused to an existing French language school in Abram's Village, a 57-minute ride.

The parents took the province to court. At trial, the judge ruled that there were sufficient numbers to start a school in Summerside. The ministry appealed. The Court of Appeal set aside the judgment and reinstated the minister's decision. The parents then appealed to the Supreme Court of Canada.

In a unanimous decision, the justices agreed that s. 23 of the Charter provides for a French school in Summerside if the numbers are sufficient to warrant it. The object of providing minority language education is to provide minority students with high-quality education in their own language. Although the minister could exercise discretion regarding the demand for services, the promotion and preservation of the French culture must also be weighed.

1. Identify two relevant arguments the ministry might have used to defend the option of busing students to Abram's Village.
2. Explain the grounds on which the Supreme Court made its ruling in this case.
3. What was the reasoning behind including s. 23 in the Charter?

CASES

RJR-MacDonald Inc. v. Canada (A.G.), [1994] 1 S.C.R. 311

BACKGROUND The *Tobacco Products Control Act*, which came into force on January 1, 1989, prohibited advertising and activities designed to encourage the sale of tobacco. It also regulated the labelling of tobacco products, indicating that all tobacco packages must carry health warnings and that these messages could no longer be attributed to Health and Welfare Canada. The purpose of the legislation was "to provide a legislative response to a national public health problem of substantial and pressing concern." According to RJR-MacDonald, a cigarette manufacturer, compliance with this new regulation would require the tobacco industry to redesign all of its packaging and to purchase equipment and supplies at a cost to the industry of about $30 million.

RJR-MacDonald Inc. challenged the constitutional validity of this Act. The company claimed that the Act was *ultra vires* the Parliament of Canada, which means the government had gone beyond the powers granted to it by the Constitution. RJR-MacDonald also claimed that the Act violated s. 2(b) (freedom of expression) of the *Charter of Rights and Freedoms*.

At trial, Justice Chabot of the Quebec Superior Court concluded that the regulations enforced on tobacco companies by the Act violated the Charter freedom described in s. 2(b). The government appealed this decision. The Court of Appeal found that the legislation was valid and was enacted for the "peace, order, and good government" of Canada. R.J.R.-MacDonald Inc. appealed this ruling to the Supreme Court of Canada.

LEGAL QUESTION Was the *Tobacco Products Control Act* invalid based on these constitutional challenges?

DECISION In a 5 to 4 ruling, the majority of the Supreme Court of Canada held that it was wholly within the jurisdiction of Parliament to enact the *Tobacco Act* under its criminal-law power. However, it also ruled that certain provisions of the Act were inconsistent with s. 2(b) of the Charter and did not constitute a reasonable limit under s. 1 of the Charter.

These provisions required the manufacturer to put warning labels on tobacco products in such a way that made it look as though the warning was issued by the manufacturer rather than by the government. The Court held that the non-attribution of the warnings and the ban on adding other information on the packages violated the right to say nothing or the right *not* to say certain things. The Court struck down the provisions in question, while upholding the remainder of the Act.

POLITICAL SIGNIFICANCE Under the Charter, Canadian courts have the power to make an order striking out legislation that is found to be unconstitutional. If the Supreme Court of Canada makes such an order, the legislation has no force.

ANALYSIS

1. Identify the three courts involved in this case. What was the ruling of each court?
2. Do you think the Supreme Court of Canada would have struck down the provisions if the warnings added to the package came from the government, or if the manufacturer could add its own information? Explain.
3. Why do you think the parties in this case considered the legislation so important?

issue

Aboriginal and Treaty Rights

The earliest treaties with Aboriginal peoples date back to the seventeenth and eighteenth centuries. Later, as European settlement moved westward, vast tracts of land were freed up in land cession treaties in exchange for benefits such as treaty rights and continued hunting and fishing rights. In 1973, the Supreme Court of Canada recognized that Aboriginal rights still exist in areas where there were no treaties.

Prior to patriation in 1982, Aboriginal peoples vigorously lobbied to have their rights addressed in the Constitution. They were concerned that without constitutional protection, their Aboriginal and treaty rights would continue to be modified or extinguished through federal legislation. Treaties are important to Aboriginal peoples because they recognize certain rights and define the relationship between Aboriginal peoples and government. Moreover, constitutional protection acknowledges an important distinction: Aboriginal peoples were Canada's first occupants.

As a result of lobbying, several constitutional protections were included in the *Constitution Act, 1982*. Section 35 recognizes and affirms existing Aboriginal and treaty rights. It also identifies who is considered an Aboriginal person, confirms that treaty rights include those in existing and future treaties, and guarantees these rights equally to male and female persons. These provisions exist outside the *Charter of Rights and Freedoms,* which means that they are not subject to the limitations found in s. 1 of the Charter. Also, s. 25 of the Charter provides that Charter rights cannot infringe on rights pertaining to Aboriginal peoples.

In the past, government agents made unrecorded promises. Consequently, Aboriginal peoples and government are often at odds over verbal promises and the meaning of treaty provisions. Such differences have led to confrontation in public and in the courts. As a result, the Supreme Court of Canada has enunciated various legal principles regarding the interpretation of treaties. It also established legal tests to determine the existence of treaty and Aboriginal rights and to justify limits on those rights.

THE MARSHALL CASE

In *R.* v. *Marshall,* [1999], Donald Marshall was charged with various offences contrary to fishery regulations. He argued that he was exercising his treaty rights to fish eels and to "trade in fish" according to the Treaty of 1760. This treaty provided that the Mi'kmaq and Maliseet would trade for "necessaries" (food, clothing, etc.) only with traders and in "truckhouses" (trading posts) approved by the British. Marshall claimed that this right to "trade" also included the right to hunt, fish, and gather. The Crown argued that no such treaty rights currently exist and that the truckhouses were temporary restrictions on trade during the war with the French. Also, if there were such rights, they could be regulated. The Crown further argued that a recognized right to trade would result in uncontrolled fishing, putting non-Aboriginal commercial and sports fishers at a disadvantage.

Having reviewed the evidence, the Supreme Court of Canada rejected the Crown's argument. It held that the truckhouses provided considerable financial benefits to the Mi'kmaq and Maliseet and could not be extinguished. It also rejected the notion of "uncontrolled fishing" in light of the limitation in the treaty to trade for necessaries rather than accumulate wealth." On September 17, 1999, the Supreme Court concluded that the fishery regulations infringed on the Mi'kmaq and Maliseet treaty rights. Therefore, the regulations were inoperative, unless they could be justified; however, the issue of justification was not raised.

CONFLICT IN THE MARITIMES

In the Maritimes, different interpretations of the Marshall decision fuelled the tensions between Aboriginal and non-Aboriginal people. Fishers from the 34 communities that benefit from the treaty began to trap lobster, claiming that there were no limits on their rights.

Clashes between the two groups resulted in the destruction of lobster traps, boats, and fish-processing plants. Non-Aboriginal fishers, concerned that stocks would be depleted, called on the government to issue

Community and spiritual leaders organize a rally at Burnt Church, New Brunswick, over government intervention in the fishing dispute.

a ban on lobster fishing. They argued that unregulated fishing would affect their livelihood and that if *they* were regulated, Aboriginal fishers should be, too.

The Aboriginal communities, many of which faced dire financial difficulties, argued that they had been deprived of the commercial fishery for over 200 years, that treaty promises had been violated, and that they were entitled to benefit economically without restriction.

THE MARSHALL CASE REVISITED

The West Nova Fishermen's Coalition applied to the Supreme Court of Canada to rehear the appeal in the Marshall case and to set aside its judgment pending a rehearing. The rehearing was denied, but in an unusual move, the Court clarified its earlier ruling. It reiterated that the treaty rights were always subject to justifiable government regulation for such purposes as conservation. Governments and non-Aboriginal peoples viewed this clarification as a positive step. However, Aboriginal peoples believed that the Court had bowed to public pressure. Moreover, because s. 35 of the Constitution recognized their treaty rights, the treaty beneficiaries considered "justifiable government regulation" a violation of their constitutional rights.

This decision raises the question: Should rights protected under the Constitution be subject to justifiable exceptions?

AN ONGOING ISSUE

Negotiations are continuing in order to determine how Aboriginal and non-Aboriginal communities should share resources. The government is also working with these communities to implement a long-term plan to address the broader treaty rights issue in the Maritimes. Despite these initiatives, tensions continue in Burnt Church, New Brunswick. In April 2002, the government released a report with recommendations to address fishery regulation as well as other community issues in Burnt Church.

LOOKING AT THE ISSUE

1. Find out what recommendations the government proposed in its 2002 report on Burnt Church. Which recommendations have been implemented?

2. Discuss other circumstances where government regulation of Aboriginal and treaty rights might be justified. Argue for or against such regulations.

3. Research another confrontation in Canada involving Aboriginal or treaty rights. Explain the issue and suggest a solution.

4. Examine the Constitution, including the Charter, to determine what other groups possess recognized rights. Identify these rights and explain whether they should be subject to justifiable government regulation.

5 Human Rights

CHAPTER OUTLINE

Human Rights Legislation

Administering Human Rights Legislation

Grounds of Discrimination

FOCUS YOUR LEARNING

Which documents protect human rights?

How is a human rights complaint filed?

What rights are protected under human rights legislation?

Chief Justice Urges Students to Value Diversity

Canada's future will be determined by how successfully it deals with its diverse cultures, the country's top judge told University of Toronto law students yesterday.

"We must have government and legal structures that recognize our diversity and allow us to live together in harmony and in a way that promotes the fullest possible contribution from all of our citizens, regardless of our race or background," said Supreme Court Chief Justice Beverley McLachlin....

McLachlin singled out numerous [past] examples where the law was used against members of minority racial groups including

- confinement by law of Aboriginal peoples to reserves....
- restricting, marginalizing, and subordinating Chinese Canadians....
- subjection of Canadian Jews "to anti-Semitism and legalized discrimination" through racially based, restrictive covenants on properties....

McLachlin described numerous advances over the years, culminating with a strong *Charter of Rights and Freedoms,* the introduction of human rights codes, and the development of affirmative action programs. But she cautioned the students that in spite of progress in dealing with conflicts and tensions in Canada's multiracial society, "the task is not complete."

McLachlin urged the students to use the law to help create a country "in which all peoples may live in dignity and respect."

SOURCE: Adapted from Harold Levy, "Chief justice urges students to value Canada's diversity," *The Toronto Star,* January 30, 2002, A6.

WHAT DO YOU THINK?

- Record your reactions to this article. What do you think Chief Justice McLachlin is referring to when she says, "the task is not complete"?
- As a class, brainstorm a list of circumstances that you consider unjust. Share your ideas for rectifying these injustices.

What are "human rights"? As you learned in Chapter 4, a "right" is a legal, moral, and social claim that people are entitled to, primarily from their government. **Human rights** include the right to receive equal treatment, to be free from prohibited discrimination and harassment, and to have equal access to places, services, and opportunities. **Discrimination** occurs when an individual is treated unfairly because he or she is a member of a certain group.

Even at the dawn of the twenty-first century, Canada's struggle for equal rights continues. In spite of enormous gains and the fact that Canada has one of the strongest human rights records in the world, several groups continue to experience discrimination. Disabled persons are still fighting for accommodation in the workplace; the gay community is striving for equal rights to marry or adopt children; and Aboriginal peoples and ethnic minorities continue to challenge the law to live up to its mandate of a just society.

Canadians' rights are protected at a number of levels. At the federal or national level, Canadians are protected from abuses by government or its agencies through the *Canadian Charter of Rights and Freedoms*. As you learned in Chapter 4, the Charter is Canada's most important rights document; however, it does not provide legal protection for citizens if they are discriminated against by other individuals or by private organizations. Remedies for such acts are found in provincial **human rights codes,** which protect individuals from prohibited discrimination. What is considered "prohibited" differs from province to province; however, it generally includes discrimination based on race, national or ethnic origin, colour, religion, age, sex, sexual orientation, mental or physical disability, and family or marital status.

human rights: the right to receive equal treatment, to be free from prohibited discrimination and harassment, and to have access to places, services, and opportunities

discrimination: making a distinction between people and treating them differently on a basis other than individual merit

human rights codes: legal documents that protect people from prohibited discrimination

Figure 5.1 In 1998, the Raging Grannies, a national social action group, protested in Fredericton, New Brunswick, because the mayor had refused gays and lesbians the right to organize a parade.

HUMAN RIGHTS LEGISLATION

Canadians like to think of themselves as tolerant people. Canada is, after all, a nation of immigrants; immigrants and refugees have arrived from all over the world to be part of Canadian society. Every person has the right to be treated equally, yet discrimination is still a fact of life in Canada.

Discrimination is often based on **stereotyping.** Stereotyping can be defined as creating an oversimplified, false, or generalized portrayal of a group of people. Stereotyping involves taking a characteristic of one member of a group and applying it to all members of that group. Stereotypes are often the basis of many ethnic or gender jokes. The statement "all teenage males are reckless drivers" is an example of stereotyping.

A belief in stereotypes can lead to **prejudice,** which is a preconceived opinion. Someone who is prejudiced judges an individual according to the group to which he or she belongs without taking into account individual qualities or abilities. For example, assuming that an individual is a reckless driver simply because he is a teenage male is a prejudice. There is no way of knowing whether the person is a good or bad driver if opinions are based on the stereotype that all teenage males are reckless drivers.

When someone's behaviour toward another person is based on stereotypes and prejudices, the result is discrimination. In other words, discrimination involves putting prejudice into action. For example, if Angela owned a courier company and refused to hire Taylor simply because she believed that all teenage males are reckless drivers, this behaviour would constitute discrimination. There is little that the law can do to stop people from developing and holding negative opinions based on stereotyping and prejudice; however, the law can prevent someone from acting on these views. Human rights legislation is used to correct and prevent the injustice of discrimination.

stereotyping: having an oversimplified, standardized, or fixed judgment of a group of people

prejudice: a preconceived opinion based on a stereotype or inadequate information

Canadian Human Rights Act

The opening paragraph of the *Canadian Human Rights Act* (CHRA) sums up the purpose of the Act:

> The purpose of this Act is to extend the laws in Canada to give effect, within the purview of matters coming within the legislative authority of Parliament, to the principle that all individuals should have an opportunity equal with other individuals to make for themselves the lives that they are able and wish to have and to have their needs accommodated, consistent with their duties and obligations as members of society, without being hindered in or prevented from doing so by discriminatory practices based on race, national or ethnic origin, colour, religion, age, sex, sexual orientation, marital status, family status, disability or conviction for an offence for which a pardon has been granted.

The *Canadian Human Rights Act* was passed in 1977 and applies to federal government departments, Crown corporations, and business and industries that are under the jurisdiction of the federal government. For example, people

"Human rights are your rights. Seize them. Defend them. Promote them. Understand them and insist on them. Nourish and enrich them.... They are the best in us. Give them life.

— Kofi Annan, secretary general of the United Nations

who work in post offices, chartered banks, or airlines can seek a remedy under the CHRA if they believe they are victims of discrimination.

The *Canadian Human Rights Act* prohibits discrimination on the following grounds:

- race
- colour
- national or ethnic origin
- religion
- age
- sex or gender (including pregnancy and childbearing)
- marital status, family status
- physical or mental disability (including dependence on alcohol or drugs)
- pardoned criminal conviction
- sexual orientation

The CHRA also covers matters such as hate messages and pay equity.

Section 67 of the *Canadian Human Rights Act* provides that nothing in the CHRA affects any provision of the *Indian Act* or any provision made under or pursuant to the *Indian Act*. The purpose of s. 67 is to ensure that the *Canadian Human Rights Act* does not conflict with the application of the *Indian Act*. This means that those who work for Indian bands or those who are discriminated against by Indian bands may not be able to seek a remedy under the CHRA if the discrimination is a result of a provision in the *Indian Act*.

Rose Desjarlais, a Band Council employee who was subject to discrimination by the Piapot Band on the basis of her age, challenged this umbrella protection afforded to Indian bands by s. 67. In *Desjarlais v. Piapot Band* (1989), the Canadian Human Rights Commission held that s. 67 did not prevent it from ruling on the matter. Since the Piapot Band did not have a registered band bylaw dealing with employment, and because there was no policy section of the *Indian Act* that gave implied authority to the band to dismiss Desjarlais, the band did not fall within the protection of s. 67.

Provincial Human Rights Codes

All provinces have enacted human rights codes. As acts of provincial Legislatures, the codes are amended periodically and are also subject to the *Canadian Charter of Rights and Freedoms*. In other words, if the courts find that a provision of a provincial human rights code violates the Charter, the provision could be struck down. For example, in 1986, the Ontario Court of Appeal struck down s. 19(2) of the Ontario *Human Rights Code,* which permitted athletic organizations to deny membership based on gender. Justine Blainey had been denied the right to play on a boys' hockey team, but the court found that this policy violated her equality rights under s. 15(1) of the Charter. Other examples have arisen in recent years. For instance, most provinces have been forced to amend their human rights codes so that they do not violate the rights provided to gays and lesbians under the Charter.

Fast Fact
In 2001, anti-terrorist legislation replaced s. 13(2) of the *Canadian Human Rights Act.* The new legislation makes the communication of hate messages by means of a computer, a group of interconnected computers, or the Internet a prohibited ground of discrimination.

Legal Link
You will find all provincial human rights codes at **www.pearsoned.ca/law**.

Law in Your Life
Identify some facilities that you are restricted from because of your age or gender. Do you think these restrictions would be supported by human rights codes? Why or why not?

Figure 5.2 Justine Blainey raises her hockey skates in victory after the Supreme Court of Canada rejected an Ontario Hockey Association (OHA) bid to keep her from playing on a boys' team. How do you think the OHA justified its position?

Is Forced Retirement Discriminatory?

Forcing Ontario residents to retire at 65 is wrong and the human rights code should be changed to reflect that, Chief Commissioner Keith Norton says.

"It is discriminatory, just as discriminatory to require people at 35 to retire arbitrarily," Norton said yesterday after handing down his annual report. "If they want to continue to work, why shouldn't they have a choice as opposed to being arbitrarily dismissed at 65?"

Both employer and seniors groups agreed yesterday [that] it's time to make a change.

Norton said the way the Ontario *Human Rights Code* is worded, any individual older than 65 who is still working can be discriminated against on the basis of age and they simply have no recourse....

The province needs to amend its human rights code to target age discrimination, which is cited in 7 percent of complaints to the commission, Norton said.

Norton said [that] often mandatory retirement has a disproportionate impact on women, particularly those who get back into the work force after raising a family. He cited a case where a woman who went back to teaching was the victim of a new retirement policy.

"She was then hired back on a contract by the same college to teach except she had no benefits ... and she was paid less than half of what she had been previously making for performing the same job. Those kinds of things because somebody happens to turn 65 ... [are] clearly discriminatory," he said....

The federal government allows employees to work until they turn 70 and four other provinces have eliminated a legal retirement age altogether.

Doug Robson, president of the Ontario Chamber of Commerce, said the time is right to revisit the mandatory retirement age.

SOURCE: Adapted from Richard Brennan, "Put an end to retirement at 65, rights chief says," *The Toronto Star*, May 18, 2001, A1.

1. Why does Norton believe that forcing people to retire at age 65 is wrong?
2. According to this article, how has this policy had a "disproportionate impact on women"?
3. a) Do you agree that retirement at age 65 is discriminatory and should be eliminated? Why or why not?
   b) What are the pros and cons of eliminating mandatory retirement altogether?

Building Your Understanding

1. Distinguish between the protection provided by the *Charter of Rights and Freedoms* and provincial human rights codes.
2. Define these terms and provide an example of each: discrimination, stereotyping, and prejudice.
3. What is the purpose of the *Canadian Human Rights Act*?
4. What happens when there is an inconsistency between the *Charter of Rights and Freedoms* and federal or provincial human rights legislation?
5. Explain the ripple effect of the precedent-making decision in the Justine Blainey case.

ADMINISTERING HUMAN RIGHTS LEGISLATION

To administer and enforce various human rights codes, provincial governments have appointed commissions. Most complaints are settled by commissions, but the 4 percent that cannot be resolved at this point must go on to boards of inquiry or tribunals, which have the power to make the ultimate decision about a complaint.

Filing a Complaint

Those who feel they have been victims of discrimination must follow the procedures established by their province's human rights code. Some provinces have a Commission's Inquiry Services Unit; in other provinces, individuals can contact a complaints analyst at the provincial Human Rights Commission. Individuals do not need a lawyer to file a complaint, and they can choose to withdraw their complaints at any time after the file is opened. All inquiries made to the Human Rights Commission are completely confidential. Using the province of Alberta as an example, Figure 5.3 shows a chart outlining the stages of a complaint process.

If you are the **complainant**—the person making the allegation of discrimination—you will be provided with a package of information to assist you in filing your complaint. You will probably be asked to fill out a "complaints form" describing the events and circumstances you considered discriminatory. As the accuser, it is up to you to prove your case.

Using employment discrimination as an example, in order to establish a **prima facie** case (a case whose first impression is legally convincing), you must prove that

1) you were qualified for the particular employment;
2) you were not hired; and
3) someone no better qualified subsequently obtained that position—someone who lacked the distinguishing feature that represents the **gravamen** (significant part) of the human rights complaint (e.g., race, colour, etc.).

Legal Link
To find out how to file a human rights complaint in your province go to www.pearsoned.ca/law. Click on the link for your province's Human Rights Commission.

complainant: the person making an allegation of discrimination

prima facie: legally convincing unless disproved by contrary evidence

gravamen: the most serious part of an accusation

Fast Facts
The words *prima facie* are Latin, meaning "at first sight"; the word *gravamen* comes from the Latin word *gravis,* meaning "heavy"—the part that bears most heavily on the accused.

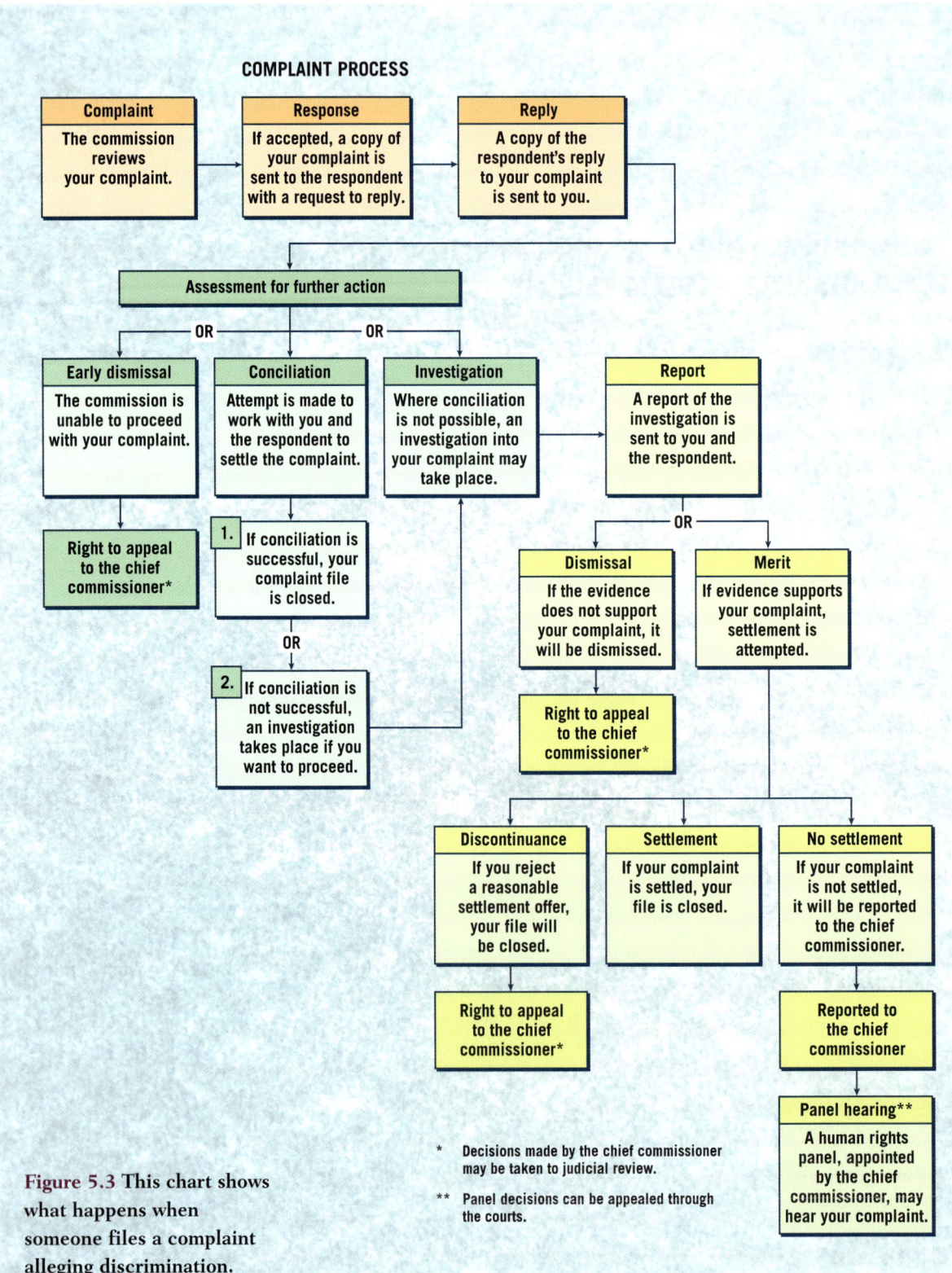

Figure 5.3 This chart shows what happens when someone files a complaint alleging discrimination.

Dismissing a Complaint

At this stage, the Human Rights Commission may dismiss the complaint for a variety of reasons (see Figure 5.3). For instance, in the Ontario *Human Rights Code,* the reasons for dismissal are set out in s. 34:

> 34. (1)(a) where there is another legislative act that can more appropriately deal with the issues raised in the complaint;
> (b) where the complaint is trivial, frivolous, vexatious, or made in bad faith;
> (c) where the complaint is not within the jurisdiction of the Commission; and
> (d) where the complaint was filed more than six months from the last incident of discrimination, and it appears the delay was not incurred in good faith, and there is evidence of substantial prejudice to the parties because of the delay.

Figure 5.4 Why is discrimination sometimes difficult to prove?

The final section dealing with time limits varies from province to province, and in some jurisdictions the time period is one year. Check your province's human rights code to determine the time limit for filing a complaint.

The response to your inquiry will inform you whether your complaint is covered by your provincial code. If so, the Commission will serve your complaint upon the **respondent** (the organization or persons you are alleging discriminated against you). The respondent is asked to formally respond to the allegations of discrimination (see Figure 5.3).

respondent: the person or organization that the complainant alleges committed discrimination

Role of the Commission

If your complaint is not dismissed, you move on to the next step. The Commission will ask you and the respondent to enter into **mediation.** A mediation process was introduced as a means of settling disputes prior to a formal investigation. The parties are assisted by a mediation officer in an attempt to resolve the problem themselves.

If the parties do not agree to mediation, or if no settlement is reached in mediation, the complaint is referred to investigation services for a formal investigation by a human rights officer (see Figure 5.3). This process involves gathering evidence relevant to the complaint; inspecting documents, records, and correspondence related to the case; examining the facilities; and interviewing witnesses.

After the investigation, the human rights officer writes a report to inform the parties of the results of the investigation. The officer may also try to resolve the complaint through **conciliation**—bringing the parties to a

mediation: intervention between conflicting parties that promotes compromise or settlement of the dispute

Fast Fact
Mediation occurs in about 70% of the complaints filed, and almost 75% of these complaints end with a settlement at this point.

conciliation: bringing conflicting parties to a resolution of their differences

resolution of their differences. If no resolution is reached, the case is referred to the commissioners. The commissioners are a group of people who oversee the Human Rights Commission and make decisions about cases.

If the commissioners do not believe that there is enough evidence to prove discrimination, they will dismiss the complaint. The complainant has 15 days to appeal this decision by formally requesting a review in writing. If the commissioners turn down the review, then the decision is final (see Figure 5.3).

However, if the commissioners believe that there is evidence of discrimination, the complaint is referred to a board of inquiry or human rights tribunal—formal bodies that will hear the case and make a decision based on the evidence. The hearing is similar to a trial in that witnesses are called to testify under oath and are cross-examined by lawyers for both the Commission and the respondent. The decision of a board of inquiry may be appealed and sent for judicial review. In Ontario, for example, a decision can be appealed to the Divisional Court of the Ontario Court of Justice and, ultimately, to the Supreme Court of Ontario.

> **Fast Fact**
> The Ontario Human Rights Commission receives about 2000 complaints each year; of these, approximately 4% are sent to a board of inquiry for resolution.

Remedies

A number of remedies are available when discrimination has occurred. Generally, the remedies are intended to put complainants in the same position they would have been in had the discrimination not occurred. For this reason, the remedy will depend on the circumstances of the case. Possible remedies include the following:

- ordering the person or organization who contravened the human rights code to stop the practice
- compelling the respondent to issue a letter of apology
- ordering the respondent to pay the complainant for mental anguish or for any losses suffered in pay or benefits
- compelling an employer to give the complainant back his or her job or to grant the promotion that was denied
- ordering an organization to adopt programs designed to relieve hardship or economic disadvantage, or to assist disadvantaged groups in achieving equal opportunity in the organization
- requiring an organization to provide human rights and anti-discrimination training for all employees, to develop comprehensive policies to eliminate discrimination and prevent harassment, or to undertake other similar remedies

"The courts ruled that we had to open it up to all stuffed animals."

Kanags Premakumar v. Air Canada
(2000), C.H.R.C.

CASE

Kanags Premakumar, originally from Sri Lanka, applied for a baggage-handler position with Canadian Airlines at Pearson Airport in March 1998. Although Premakumar had worked at other airlines in Canada and Sri Lanka, he was not successful in obtaining a job (despite the fact that people with no experience in the airline industry were hired).

Premakumar filed his complaint with the Canadian Human Rights Commission, alleging that he had not been hired because of his race, colour, and national or ethnic origin. He was able to show evidence of a prima facie case of discrimination. Since Canadian Airlines and the employees who conducted the interview were not able to provide a reasonable explanation for their actions, the Canadian Human Rights Commission found that discrimination had occurred. The Commission ordered the following remedies:

- Premakumar was awarded compensation for lost wages and employment benefits.
- Air Canada (the company that had subsequently taken over Canadian Airlines) had to pay Premakumar an additional amount to cover the income-tax liability that he incurred as a result of the monetary award.
- Air Canada was to provide a written apology to Premakumar, signed by one of the two employees who conducted the interview.
- Air Canada had to pay an additional $4000 to Premakumar for the pain and suffering he endured after being refused a position.

1. Why was this case heard by the Canadian Human Rights Commission?
2. Define the term "prima facie." How does it apply in this case?
3. Do you think these remedies were adequate? If not, what other remedies would have been appropriate?

Building Your Understanding

1. Who are the complainant and the respondent in a human rights case? Give an example to illustrate your answer.
2. List the governmental bodies involved in a human rights complaint and define their roles.
3. What must be proven to establish a prima facie case of discrimination?
4. Under what circumstances can a complaint be dismissed?
5. Which remedies do you think would be appropriate in each of the following human rights cases?
   a) A new alcohol- and drug-testing program came into effect in Avi's company. Avi disclosed that a few years ago he had had an alcohol problem. As a result, he was moved to another job and subjected to rigorous management supervision. The Commission ruled that the program discriminated against persons on the basis of their disabilities or "perceived disabilities."
   b) Fowzia claimed discrimination at work based on her race and colour. She was subjected to racial slurs, held up to ridicule, and deprived of a scheduled salary increase. The Commission found that Fowzia had been discriminated against because of her race and colour. However, evidence showed that her job performance did not meet expectations.
   c) Sam Nang was dismissed from her position as counter help at a coffee bar. She said her employer, Roger, claimed that her hearing impairment interfered with her ability to carry out her job. Roger denied this statement and claimed that Sam Nang was fired for poor job performance. The Commission found that the evidence did not support the respondent's claim.

GROUNDS OF DISCRIMINATION

Now that you have seen how the complaint process works, you will examine the activities protected by human rights legislation. You will also learn that although certain actions may *appear* discriminatory, they are actually considered exceptions under the law.

Where grounds do exist, the cases that follow will clarify how human rights codes can assist Canadians who face discrimination.

Employment

Legal Link
According to the *Employment Equity Act,* women, Aboriginal peoples, members of visible minorities, and people with disabilities must have fair access to jobs and promotions. To learn the details of this legislation, visit **www.pearsoned.ca/law**.

Everyone has a right to "equal treatment with respect to employment" in the job application process as well as in training, transfers, promotions, apprenticeship, dismissal, and layoffs. Those who feel they have been discriminated against in these areas of employment may file a human rights complaint.

Exceptions Under the Law

Before exploring the various grounds of discrimination, it is important to note that certain actions are not considered discriminatory if they are "reasonable and justifiable" under the circumstances. One example of a reasonable and justifiable action would be the higher insurance fees charged for young drivers. Statistics show that young drivers tend to file more claims than older drivers do; since insurance premiums are based on claim rates, fees for young drivers are higher.

In some cases, specific skills are necessary to do the job. For instance, a transport company would require all persons hired as drivers to have a valid driver's licence. Because such a requirement is essential to the job, it is a **bona fide occupational requirement** and is, therefore, not considered discriminatory. (The words *bona fide* come from the Latin, meaning "in good faith.")

bona fide occupational requirement: a qualification that would normally be considered discriminatory but is necessary for proper or efficient job performance

affirmative action: giving advantages to groups who have been discriminated against in the past

Affirmative action is also allowed under human rights legislation. **Affirmative action** gives advantages to groups who have been discriminated against in the past. For instance, where there are two equally qualified candidates applying for a job, priority *will* or *may* be given to the applicant who is a member of a historically disadvantaged group. Affirmative action is often practised in organizations that serve a particular community and may wish to limit employment to that community. For example, a female candidate might be chosen over a male candidate for the position of security guard at a women's shelter, even though his work experience might be more extensive than hers.

Law in Your Life
In a job interview, you cannot be asked discriminatory questions. However, for some positions, such as security guard, not having a criminal record may be a bona fide job requirement.

Constructive and Direct Discrimination

Sometimes seemingly neutral requirements for employment might lead to what is called **constructive discrimination**—employment policies that inadvertently exclude certain individuals. For example, in the past, police departments had a minimum height requirement that effectively excluded most women and many minority groups. This type of constructive discrimination has been struck down by the court.

constructive discrimination: employment policies that inadvertently exclude certain individuals, resulting in discrimination

British Columbia (P.S.E.R.C.) v. B.C.G.S.E.U., [1999] 3 S.C.R. 3

CASE

The British Columbia government established minimum physical fitness standards for its forest firefighters, which were measured by a series of four standardized tests. One of the tests was an aerobic standard that required the firefighter to run 2.5 km in 11 minutes. Tawney Meiorin, a female firefighter who had in the past performed her work satisfactorily, failed to meet the aerobic standard. After four attempts, her best time was 49.4 seconds over the minimum allowed. She was laid off as a result of failing to meet the physical fitness standard.

An arbitrator found that Meiorin had established that she was a victim of constructive discrimination. This ruling was based on the fact that because of physiological differences, in general, women have a lower aerobic capacity than men. Also, unlike most men, most women cannot sufficiently increase their aerobic capacity through training to meet the aerobic standard. Furthermore, the government had failed to demonstrate that achieving this standard was necessary to perform the work of a forest firefighter safely and efficiently. In other words, the government had not demonstrated that passing this test was a bona fide occupational requirement.

The arbitrator ordered that Meiorin be reinstated and that she receive compensation for lost wages and benefits. This decision was appealed to the Court of Appeal for British Columbia. The Court overturned the arbitrator's decision because it held that provided the standard was necessary to ensure safe and efficient performance, and as long as it was applied throughout *all* individual testing, no discrimination existed. This ruling was appealed to the Supreme Court of Canada.

The Supreme Court of Canada allowed the appeal and restored the arbitrator's ruling. The Court found, as the arbitrator had, that passing the physical fitness test was not a bona fide occupational requirement.

1. Explain how the terms "constructive discrimination" and "bona fide occupational requirement" apply in this case.
2. The Supreme Court's ruling contradicted a claim made in the Court of Appeal's decision. What was this claim?
3. Why is the Supreme Court's decision significant? Discuss whether you agree with this ruling.

Figure 5.5 It took Tawney Meiorin five years to get back her job as a forest firefighter.

Constructive discrimination may be more difficult to detect than direct discrimination. **Direct discrimination** refers to discrimination that is practised openly, such as refusing service or employment to someone simply because of his or her membership in a particular group.

direct discrimination: an overt act of discrimination

Figure 5.6 Suppose you are meeting a group of friends in a shopping mall. A security guard approaches your group and tells you to "stop loitering." This occurs regularly at the mall, but only with teens. Would this practice be considered discriminatory by a human rights tribunal? Why or why not?

Duty to Accommodate

The Supreme Court of Canada has ruled that an employer has a legal duty to **accommodate** an employee's individual needs. This means that the employer must take reasonable measures to implement policies or working conditions to meet the special needs of an employee. For example, if an employee is unable to work on a particular day because of religious beliefs, the employer must try to resolve this conflict in a way that satisfies both parties.

The employer would not, however, be expected to suffer undue hardship in order to accommodate the employee. **Undue hardship** is the result of a change that would affect the economic viability of the enterprise or produce a substantial health and safety risk that outweighs the benefit of accommodating a particular group or individual worker. For example, suppose Emiko has a physical disability and is required to carry boxes up a flight of stairs. It would be considered an undue hardship to expect the employer to install an elevator just to accommodate Emiko. A reasonable solution might be to have someone else carry the boxes up the steps and have Emiko assume some of that employee's duties in exchange. This arrangement accommodates Emiko, and her employer suffers no undue hardship. In such cases, the employer has the burden of proving that accommodating an employee would cause undue hardship for the business.

accommodate: eliminate or adjust requirements or conditions to enable a person to carry out the essential duties of an activity or job

undue hardship: the result of a change that would affect the economic viability of an enterprise or produce a substantial health and safety risk that outweighs the benefit of the accommodation

Harassment in the Workplace

Everyone has the right to be free from experiencing humiliating or annoying behaviour. Such behaviour, or **harassment,** can be based on one or more of the grounds found in provincial human rights codes. For example, racial, sexual, or religious slurs can be considered harassment if they are repeated or ongoing. Similarly, sexual harassment is not permitted. **Sexual harassment** includes unwelcome sexual contact, remarks, leering, demands for dates, requests for sexual favours, and displays of sexually offensive pictures or graffiti.

harassment: persistent behaviour that violates the human rights of the victim

sexual harassment: unwelcome sexual contact, remarks, leering, demands for dates, requests for sexual favours, and displays of sexually offensive pictures or graffiti

CASE

Central Alberta Dairy Pool v. Alberta Human Rights Commission, [1990] 2 S.C.R. 489

BACKGROUND Jim Christie was employed by the Central Alberta Dairy Pool. After he joined the World Wide Church of God, Christie worked the early shift on Friday to avoid a conflict with his observance of the Saturday Sabbath of his new faith. He also requested permission to take two unpaid leaves for religious reasons. Christie received approval to take the first day off, but was denied permission for Easter Monday. Mondays were extremely busy because all the milk that arrived on the weekend had to be canned to prevent spoilage. He was told that his employment would be terminated if he failed to report for work on Monday. Christie did not report for work on that day, and his employment was terminated.

The Board of Inquiry found that Christie had been discriminated against, but the Alberta Court of Queen's Bench overturned the decision. After the Alberta Court of Appeal upheld this ruling, the decision was appealed to the Supreme Court of Canada.

LEGAL QUESTION Did the employer attempt to accommodate the employee to the point of undue hardship?

DECISION The Supreme Court of Canada ruled against Central Alberta Dairy Pool. The Court found that the employer had not made a reasonable attempt to accommodate the employee. In the written ruling, the Court noted: "If the employer fails to provide an explanation as to why individual accommodation cannot be accomplished without undue hardship, the duty to accommodate has not been discharged...." Central Alberta Dairy Pool had not shown that it had encountered undue hardship because of Christie's request and, in fact, provided no suitable explanation for the refusal.

SOCIAL SIGNIFICANCE This case has become an important precedent in establishing an employer's duty to accommodate the individual needs of its staff. Unless an employer can demonstrate that a substantial financial loss would result from accommodating the special needs of an employee, the employer has a duty to accommodate those needs.

ANALYSIS

1. How might the Central Alberta Dairy Pool have dealt adequately with Christie's request for the day off?
2. What circumstances might have resulted in the employer suffering "undue hardship"?
3. Do you agree with the decision in this case? Why or why not?

| CASE | ***Chartrand v. Vanderwell Contractors Limited***
(2001), Alta. H.R.C. |

1. Complete a flow chart to outline the steps in this case, starting with March 1998. Use symbols or illustrations if you wish.
2. What could the respondent have done to prevent such incidents from happening?
3. It is fair to hold an employer liable for the actions of an employee? Why or why not?

Jean Chartrand, a 38-year-old mother of two, was employed at Vanderwell Contractors Limited at Mitsue Lake Industrial Park near Slave Lake, Alberta, from 1995 to 1998. On August 4, 1998, Chartrand terminated her employment because she felt that her shift supervisor, Maurice Conrad, was sexually harassing her. Chartrand brought a complaint to the Alberta Human Rights Commission and sought compensation for monetary losses and other damages.

Chartrand testified that Conrad had, on various occasions, used sexually inviting language and had physically touched her and rubbed his body against hers. Furthermore, she had brought these allegations to Ken Vanderwell, one of the owners, in March 1998, and had asked to be transferred to a different shift. In response to her complaint, Vanderwell spoke to Conrad and told him that the "horseplay" had to end. At this time, Chartrand sought advice from the Human Rights Commission and was advised to keep a record of any future incidents. She recorded further incidents until she finally quit her job in August 1998.

Conrad denied that he sexually harassed Chartrand but did admit that he grabbed her "around the wrist more that once, that he had grabbed her around the chest, that her necklace was torn off her neck in one of these encounters, and that he had promised to get it fixed." There was testimony from other Vanderwell employees that supported Chartrand's allegations that she was being sexually harassed by Conrad.

So far, the complainant had established a prima facie case of discrimination. The onus then shifted to the respondent to establish a justification for the discrimination. Vanderwell Contractors was not able to justify such inappropriate behaviour by one of its employees. The Commission found that Chartrand had been sexually harassed and that she had quit her job because of this harassment. The remedy imposed was financial compensation—six months' wages, damages for humiliation and hurt feelings ($5000), and the reimbursement of legal fees—all to be paid to Chartrand jointly by Vanderwell Contracting and Maurice Conrad.

Consider This
A friend confides in you that he is constantly the butt of insulting jokes and comments from his co-workers. He is clearly upset but does not want to leave his part-time job. What advice would you give him?

Employers are responsible for ensuring that the conduct of their employees does not constitute harassment. This principle was established by the Supreme Court of Canada in the case of *Robichaud* v. *Canada (Treasury Board)*, [1987]: "An employer can be held responsible for the unauthorized discriminatory acts of its employees, in the course of their employment."

Poisoned Environment

The case of Jean Chartrand is clearly one of sexual harassment. However, such harassment is not the only type of disturbing or difficult situation peo-

Figure 5.7 Under the law, no one should have to put up with sexual harassment in the workplace. Do you think that a pin-up of a scantily clad model, posted in a conspicuous location, constitutes sexual harassment? Explain.

ple face. When a person or group of people is continually subjected to actions or comments that create an uncomfortable atmosphere, this atmosphere is called a **poisoned environment.** A poisoned environment can occur when comments or actions create real or perceived inequality. For instance, a female employee might be subjected to a poisoned environment if she constantly hears disparaging comments from her male co-workers such as, "Women just aren't as capable as men." As with harassment, it is the responsibility of the employer to ensure that a poisoned environment does not exist in the workplace.

poisoned environment: an uncomfortable or disturbing atmosphere created by the negative comments or behaviour of others

A Poisoned Environment Causes Pain

Joe was excited about getting his first job as a mechanic after he had served his apprenticeship. He had been rated at the top of his class and was confident of his abilities. On the first day of work, Joe was met with some hostility from his co-workers. Comments about his race, his lunch, and the colour of his skin were frequent and hurtful. Still Joe said nothing, thinking that his co-workers would soon recognize he was a hard worker and a nice guy.

However, the atmosphere did not change over time. Although some colleagues did warm up to him and were friendlier, the hurtful comments and not-so-funny practical jokes continued. Joe finally spoke to his boss, who told him not to be so sensitive since everyone in an all-male workplace is usually subjected to this kind of treatment. Joe became depressed, and his work began to suffer. Finally, in frustration, he quit his job and filed a complaint for harassment.

LAW IN ACTION

1. Why does this situation constitute a poisoned environment?
2. Other workers also experienced the same kind of behaviour. Does this fact make any difference to Joe's claim or the employer's defence? Explain.

Accommodation and Facilities

accommodation: the place where people live or want to live

In this context, **accommodation** refers to the place where people live or want to live. Accommodation may be long term (e.g., purchasing or renting a home) or temporary (e.g., staying at a hotel or college residence). In her speech at the beginning of this chapter, Chief Justice Beverley McLachlin referred to the restrictive covenants that once prohibited the sale of property to certain groups, such as Jews. Quite clearly, such discrimination would not be allowed under today's human rights laws.

Fast Fact
In Ontario, teenagers under the age of 18 have the right to equal treatment with respect to occupancy and contracting for accommodation.

All people have the right to equal treatment in accommodation, and this right is protected by provincial human rights codes. For example, in a 2001 settlement, a Saskatchewan woman of Aboriginal ancestry complained to the Human Rights Commission that the manager of an apartment building refused to rent an apartment to her because of her race. When she asked the superintendent about the vacancy, she was told that the suite was no longer available, but when she asked a friend to inquire, the friend was told that the suite was available. The woman was awarded $550 in compensation, and the owner of the apartment building agreed to post an anti-discrimination policy in the building.

Protection in this area includes the right to be free from discrimination based on age, marital status, or source of income. Many cases have been documented regarding unmarried women with children who are on social

CASE

Mattern v. Spruce Bay Resort (2000), Alta. H.R.C.

1. Explain how Mattern and Russell were able to establish a prima facie case of discrimination.

2. The panel ruled that the resort's actions were "reasonable and justifiable based on sound business practices." Explain what this means and how it affected the outcome of this case.

3. Do you agree with the Court's ruling to uphold the panel's decision? Why or why not?

Mattern and Russell each filed a complaint with the Alberta Human Rights Commission, alleging discrimination on the basis of family status. Mattern and Russell attempted to rent a campsite at Spruce Bay Resort, which advertises itself as a family campground. They were to be joined by some friends and their brothers later that night. The resort manager testified that it was unclear whether Mattern and Russell wanted to have the spot for one night or two and that the resort had a policy of booking sites for a minimum of two nights on weekends. It was also unclear how many people would actually be staying at the campsite. The manager explained that he was concerned that the group would stay up late and make noise that would bother other campers.

Mattern and Russell claimed that Spruce Bay Resort refused to rent them a campsite because of their single status. The human rights panel hearing this case did find a prima facie case of discrimination. However, the panel decided that the decision of Spruce Bay Resort not to rent a campsite to the complainants was reasonable and justifiable based on sound business practices. Therefore, the complaint was dismissed. This decision was appealed to the Alberta Court of Queen's Bench, where the decision of the panel was upheld.

assistance and have been refused rental accommodation. A property manager who has a policy of not renting to "welfare moms" is, in fact, guilty of discrimination.

Facilities refer to areas or buildings designated for public use. Examples include parks, concert halls, or hockey rinks. Discrimination can sometimes occur in the provision of facilities. Suppose a rink attendant jeers at a women's hockey team and gives the team less than its allotted ice time. The players complain to the manager, who does nothing. In this case, the rink attendant and the manger have violated the women's rights. Human rights legislation states that "every person has a right to equal treatment with respect to services, goods and facilities without discrimination because of ... sex." First of all, by not receiving allotted ice time, the women's team is not being treated equally. Secondly, the attendant's jeering and the manager's refusal to act, taken as a whole, has created a poisoned environment that is threatening and demeaning to women. This environment robs the women of their rights to use the facility without discrimination.

facilities: areas or buildings designated for public use

After 25 years of struggle, people with disabilities are still a long way from the 'equal benefit and protection of the law' guaranteed in our ... Charter."

— Laurie Beachell,
national co-ordinator, Council of
Canadians with Disabilities

Meeting Special Needs

Most provincial human rights codes prohibit discrimination on the basis of disability and require employers to accommodate the needs of workers with psychological, emotional, or physical disabilities. Suffering from an addiction to drugs or alcohol is also likely to be considered a disability protected under human rights legislation.

Under the Ontario *Human Rights Code,* for example, persons with disabilities have the right to full integration and participation in society. Employers, landlords, service providers, and others have a duty to consider special needs. Buildings, programs, procedures, and services must be designed to include all persons equally and fully. Where it is impossible to remove barriers without undue hardship, special arrangements must be made so that persons with disabilities can participate.

As mentioned previously, any limits to the duty to accommodate fall under the category of undue hardship. To prove undue hardship, three factors are considered: cost, outside sources of funding, and health and safety. Depending on the nature of the job or activity and the extent of the disability, an employer, landlord, or service provider may be able to plead undue hardship.

Figure 5.8 This automated bank machine in Ottawa, Ontario, equipped with a Braille keypad and headphones, issues instructions by voice to assist customers who are visually impaired. What other obstacles face people with visual disabilities?

LAW IN ACTION

The Final Curtain

1. Apply the consideration of undue hardship in this situation.
2. Do you think the outcome of these events was a triumph or a defeat for people who use wheelchairs? Explain your position.

Barbara Turnbull

In 2001, five complainants—Barbara Turnbull, Marilyn Chapman, Domenic Fragale, Ing Wong-Ward, and Steven Macaulay—brought a case to the Ontario Human Rights Commission against Famous Players Theatres. Their complaint alleged discrimination on the basis of disability. Three of the movie chain's Toronto threatres—the Uptown (which was a prime venue for the Toronto International Film Festival), the Backstage, and the Eglinton—were inaccessible to people in wheelchairs. A fourth theatre was included but was dropped from the case since Famous Players was not renewing its lease on this property.

The Board of Inquiry ruled that Famous Players had to make the theatres accessible to people who use wheelchairs. The decision stated: "Persons using wheelchairs [have] just as much right to be granted admittance to a Famous Players theatre and watch a movie as able-bodied patrons." Famous Players was also ordered to pay damages of $8000 each to Turnbull and Chapman, $10 000 each to Wong-Ward and Macaulay, and $12 000 to Fragale, who suffered mental anguish over the ordeal. The movie chain was given one year to comply with this order for the Backstage theatre and two years for the Uptown and Eglinton theatres.

During the public hearing into this complaint, Famous Players refused to provide any financial data. The company argued that its ability to pay for the renovations was not an issue. Yet, in January 2002, Famous Players announced that it would close the three theatres before the deadlines imposed by the Board of Inquiry.

Keith Norton, chief commissioner of the Ontario Human Rights Commission said, "I am disappointed by this decision as it deprives local moviegoers from accessing services at these theatres. Clearly the closings are based on economic reasons and [are] not related to the decision of the Board."

In response to Famous Player's announcement, Barbara Turnbull commented: "I find it unfortunate that they [Famous Players] are trying to blame the closings of historical and popular theatres on us simply because we want the same options as people who don't use wheelchairs. That's all this has been about—giving us equal access."

Goods and Services

goods: merchandise that can be purchased

services: ways of meeting consumer needs that do not involve the purchase of tangible goods

The term "goods and services" applies to a wide area of activities. **Goods** generally refer to merchandise that can be purchased, such as books, clothing, CDs, or computer equipment. **Services** provide a way to meet consumer needs that do not involve the purchase of tangible goods, such as banking, dry cleaning, taking a bus, staying in a hotel, or using club memberships. Under human rights legislation, everyone has a right to equal access to goods and services.

Anderson v. YMCA (of Barrie) (2000), Board of Inquiry (O.H.R.C.)

CASE

Anderson and O'Neill brought a complaint to the Ontario Human Rights Commission because women were unable to buy premium memberships at the Barrie YMCA (Young Men's Christian Association). Men who belonged to the premium membership category were entitled to use a separate change facility that had many amenities not available to regular members. No comparable facility with similar amenities were available to women.

After examining the evidence, the Board of Inquiry found that the facilities at the Barrie YMCA constituted an infringement of the complainant's rights to be free from discrimination on the basis of sex for provision of services. The Board ordered the Barrie YMCA to build a women's premium facility comparable in size and amenities to its men's premium membership facilities. In addition, the Barrie YMCA was required to post copies of the Board's decision around the facility and place a synopsis of the decision in the women's change room.

1. Suppose services had been available for an extra fee to women but not to men. Would this constitute discrimination on the basis of sex? Discuss.
2. If some self-defence courses were offered to women only, would this be considered discriminatory? Why or why not?

Building Your Understanding

1. a) Define "bona fide occupational requirement," providing an example from three different professions.
   b) Why is a bona fide occupational requirement not considered discriminatory?
2. How would you justify hiring someone with equal or fewer qualifications on the basis of affirmative action?
3. Using examples, distinguish between constructive discrimination and direct discrimination.
4. Explain the term "accommodate" as it applies to employers and employees.
5. What can an employer do to ensure that the conduct of employees does not constitute harassment of a co-worker?
6. What three factors are considered when trying to determine if undue hardship exists in accommodating the needs of persons with disabilities?
7. How does undue hardship affect the employer's duty to accommodate?
8. Provide examples of facilities or programs that are available in public schools to help accommodate the needs of students with physical or learning disabilities.

LOOKING BACK

Reviewing Your Vocabulary

accommodate *p. 122*
accommodation *p. 126*
affirmative action *p. 120*
bona fide occupational requirement *p. 120*
complainant *p. 115*
conciliation *p. 117*
constructive discrimination *p. 120*
direct discrimination *p. 121*

discrimination *p. 111*
facilities *p. 127*
goods *p. 128*
gravamen *p. 115*
harassment *p. 122*
human rights *p. 111*
human rights codes *p. 111*
mediation *p. 117*

poisoned environment *p. 125*
prejudice *p. 112*
prima facie *p. 115*
respondent *p. 117*
services *p. 128*
sexual harassment *p. 122*
stereotyping *p. 112*
undue hardship *p. 122*

Quick Quiz

1. Match the vocabulary terms above with these clues:
   a) humiliating or annoying behaviour that violates a person's human rights
   b) gives priority to members of groups who have been historically disadvantaged
   c) occurs when comments or actions of others create an uncomfortable atmosphere
   d) limits the employer's legal duty to accommodate an employee's individual needs
   e) legally convincing unless disproved by contrary evidence
   f) the qualification deemed necessary to ensure safe, efficient job performance
   g) policies that set job requirements that inadvertently result in discrimination
   h) intervention between conflicting parties, promoting compromise and settlement
   i) prejudging an individual based on an oversimplified characterization of a particular group
   j) unfair treatment of an individual because he or she is a member of a certain group

Checking Your Knowledge

2. Discuss how the following laws protect the human rights of Canadians: *Canadian Charter of Rights and Freedoms, Canadian Human Rights Act,* and provincial human rights codes.

3. Use examples to explain how stereotyping and prejudice can lead to discrimination.

4. Outline the procedure for lodging and resolving human rights complaints.

5. What duty do employers and landlords have to accommodate persons with disabilities?

6. Explain how the concept of "undue hardship" applies to human rights cases.

Developing Your Thinking and Inquiry Skills

7. a) Complete a comparison organizer for **two** of the following documents: the *Universal Declaration of Human Rights,* the *Canadian Charter of Rights and Freedoms,* the *Canadian Human Rights Act,* and your provincial human rights code.
   b) Referring to your organizer, write a paragraph summarizing the documents' similarities and differences.

8. a) Lionel Rhany came before the Canadian Human Rights Commission, arguing that his religious rights were being denied. Lionel is a Muslim and wears a Kufi, a traditional Muslim head covering. He was wearing his Kufi when he entered a Canadian courtroom to observe a trial. Before the trial, the judge said that no hats were permitted in the courtroom, and anyone wearing a hat should remove it or leave the courtroom. Lionel pointed out that he was wearing religious apparel, not a hat. The judge issued the dress protocol required in his courtroom stipulating that male heads must be bare as a sign of respect. Lionel was ordered to leave the courtroom.
   - Was this a case of discrimination? Explain.
   - What factors would you consider if you were deciding this case?

   b) Lynn Taylor, 17, was having problems at home since her mother re-married; she did not get along with her stepfather. Lynn decided to leave home and apply for social assistance. She was awarded social assistance and, along with some money saved from a part-time job, applied to rent an apartment close to her school. However, when Lynn arrived with a post-dated cheque for the first and last month's rent, the landlord looked at her and said he would not rent the apartment to someone so young.
   - Would Lynn have a case against the landlord for discrimination on the basis of age?
   - Explain, using your knowledge of the human rights code in your province.

9. Review the *Canadian Human Rights Act* and apply your knowledge to the following case:

   Jane Bear, a member of the Chill Lake First Nation, applied to the Housing Authority for on-reserve housing. The Housing Authority, which was established by the Band Council, rejected Jane's application on the basis that she did not meet the two-year residency requirement prior to making her application. The residency requirement was set out in the Authority's housing policy, but there was no evidence that the policy was made pursuant to any provision of the *Indian Act*.

   a) Can Jane seek a remedy under the *Canadian Human Rights Act*?
   b) Would Jane be able to seek a remedy under the CHRA if the residency requirement was made pursuant to a provision of the *Indian Act*?

Communicating Your Ideas

10. Write a letter to the editor outlining your reaction to the Famous Players decision to close its theatres.

11. Participate in a debate on one of the following resolutions:
    - Affirmative action is unjust and should not be included in rights legislation.
    - Human rights legislation is biased against employers.

    Express your opinion by making an initial list of arguments. Conduct research to support your position, using resources such as libraries, newspaper and magazine databases, and the Internet. Make note of your sources in case you are challenged during the debate.

Putting It All Together

12. Locate a newspaper or magazine article about a recent human rights case. Formulate a list of questions about the background and issues involved in the case and conduct research to find the answers. Organize your data into an oral report.

CASES

Luschnat v. Kotyk (2002),
B.C.H.R.T.

Ms. Luschnat began working for Mr. Koytk in August 1995 but left in October 1998 for a job at a restaurant. About one month later, she approached Koytk about employment, and he rehired her to work at one of his stores, called the PoCo Vitamin Centre. Luschnat worked 28 hours per week—full shifts on Friday and Saturday and six-hour shifts on Thursday and Sunday.

In May 1999, Luschnat learned she was pregnant. In June, she began to experience morning sickness, which, in July, became so severe that she had to be placed on medication by her doctor and was forced to take time off work. During her absence, she did not receive sick benefits from her employer, but she did receive employment insurance benefits. In August, she was well enough to return to work but was informed by her supervisor that her hours would be reduced to four hours on Saturday and six hours on Sunday.

Luschnat also had a doctor's note explaining that due to her pregnancy, she fatigued easily and would have to sit down periodically. Kotyk told her that if she could not stand at work then she should not come back until she was feeling better. Luschnat did not return to work for Kotyk and brought an action before the British Columbia Human Rights Commission, claiming discrimination on the basis of sex and disability. Luschnat was awarded $2352 for compensation for lost wages caused by Kotyk's discrimination and $2500 as compensation for injury to her dignity, feelings, and self-respect.

1. Explain how Luschnat could claim discrimination on the basis of sex and disability.
2. Outline the steps that would be involved in resolving this case.

Jeppesen v. Ancaster (Town of)
(2001), 39 C.H.R.R.

Mark Jeppesen began to serve as a part-time firefighter with the Ancaster Fire and Emergency Services in 1988. Jeppesen had the requisite Class A licence that permitted him to drive a fire truck and was well regarded as a firefighter. In fact, he performed his duties with distinction for almost a decade.

At that time, the Ancaster Fire and Emergency Services provided ambulance as well as firefighting services. Full-time firefighters were required to have a Class A or D licence for driving a fire truck and a Class F licence for driving an ambulance.

In December 1995, Jeppesen contracted histoplasmosis, an airborne fungal disease that affected his left eye. He lost central vision in that eye but retained his peripheral vision and, for all practical purposes, could see well with both eyes open. Due to his visual impairment, he no longer met the visual acuity standards for a Class F licence, but he was able to retain his Class A licence.

Twice Jeppesen applied for a position as a full-time firefighter but was denied the job on both occasions because of his inability to obtain a Class F licence. The chief took the position that a Class F licence was a bona fide requirement for all firefighters and that no exceptions could be made. Jeppesen formally requested accommodation; that is, he asked to be hired to perform firefighting duties only.

The Board of Inquiry ruled that Jeppesen had a disability under the Human Rights Code. The Board also held that requiring all full-time firefighters to obtain a Class F licence constituted prima facie discrimination because it excluded those with visual disabilities from becoming full-time firefighters; after all, the fire departments was hiring firefighters, not ambulance operators. The Board also held that Ancaster Fire and Emergency Services could have accommodated Jeppesen without undue hardship by allowing him to perform firefighting duties only. A sufficient number of available ambulance operators meant that not every firefighter needed to be capable of driving an ambulance.

1. If you were one of the judges on the Board, what factors would you consider in determining the outcome?
2. What remedy do you think should be applied in this case?

CASES

Toronto Mayor's Committee on Community and Race Relations v. Ernst Zundel (2002), C.H.R.T.

BACKGROUND In July 1996, the Mayor's Committee on Community and Race Relations filed a complaint with the Canadian Human Rights Commission. The Committee alleged that from October 10, 1996, onward, Ernst Zundel was posting messages on his Web site, offering to provide pamphlets and publications that were likely to expose Jewish persons to hatred and contempt. These messages included the following: "66 Questions and Answers on the Holocaust," "Jewish Soap," and "Did Six Million Really Die?" Section 13(1) of the *Canadian Human Rights Act* prohibits the use of federally regulated telecommunications systems to spread hate messages. Sabina Citron, who identifies herself as a Jew and a survivor of the Holocaust, lodged a parallel complaint against Zundel on September 25, 1996.

LEGAL QUESTION The tribunal had to consider four important questions:
1. Did Zundel actually control the Web site?
2. Was the material on the Zundel site transmitted by a telecommunications system covered by the legislative authority of Parliament?
3. Was this material likely to expose persons to hatred or contempt because those persons are identifiable on the basis of a prohibited ground of discrimination?
4. If s. 13(1) of the CHRA applies to the Internet, does it violate s. 2(a), s. 2(b), or s. 7 of the *Canadian Charter of Rights and Freedoms*?

DECISION Although Zundel claimed not to control the Web site, the tribunal found that he did. The tribunal also ruled that since transmission of data on the Internet operates via the telephone, the Web site did fall under Parliament's jurisdiction. The materials posted on the Web site were found to promote hatred toward an identifiable group and were, therefore, discriminatory. The tribunal also ruled that s. 13(1) of the *Canadian Human Rights Act* was a "reasonable limit" of Zundel's rights under ss. 2(a), 2(b), and 7 of the Charter. The tribunal ordered Zundel to remove his hate messages from the site and to stop sending such material over the Web.

HISTORICAL AND SOCIAL SIGNIFICANCE The ruling in the Zundel case will have wide-reaching implications in Canada. This decision means that material published on the Internet is subject to the prohibited grounds of discrimination set out in the *Canadian Human Rights Act* and that the Canadian Human Rights Commission has the power to shut down sites that do not conform to federal human rights law.

The case also brought up a new issue: How can the ruling be enforced if Zundel does not comply? Catherine Barratt, a spokesperson for the Canadian Human Rights Commission, was not able to state what would be done if Zundel failed to comply with the order. "We have no experience with enforcing compliance in cases involving the Internet. We are hoping Zundel will voluntarily stop what he is doing."

ANALYSIS
1. Why was it important to determine whether Internet communications operate telephonically?
2. How does this case demonstrate the relationship between the *Charter of Rights and Freedoms* and human rights law?
3. Do you agree that s. 13(1) of the *Canadian Human Rights Act* should be considered a reasonable limit on Zundel's Charter rights? Write a legal argument to support your position.
4. What do you think the Commission could do to enforce orders involving the Internet?

issue

Anti-Terrorist Legislation

Sometimes it seems that terrorism is, unfortunately, a feature of modern life. It is not new, however. It has existed as a tactic to achieve political goals since the development of organized political activity. Terrorism is the deliberate use of intimidation to create a climate of fear that extends beyond the immediate act. The use of terrorism knows no ethnic, political, or religious boundaries.

One of the most outrageous terrorist acts occurred on September 11, 2001. The magnitude of the attacks on the World Trade Center in New York City and the Pentagon in Washington, D.C., shocked people around the world. Individuals from many countries lost their lives, including 24 Canadians.

Many observers noted that the people who had carried out the attacks took advantage of the democratic principles of freedom and individual liberty, which meant that strict security measures were not in place. Was it possible that the protection of individual rights and freedoms may have put the collective security of society at risk? In the aftermath of September 11 amidst the fear of future attacks, security, not freedom, became the fundamental concern of many citizens and their governments.

Both the Canadian and American governments responded to appeals for increased security and state protection by introducing far-reaching anti-terrorism laws. In both countries, this legislation raised the question, "Are individual freedoms being jeopardized in the effort to combat terrorism?"

INTRODUCING BILL C-36

The Canadian government introduced Bill C-36, a 170-page anti-terrorism bill praised by law enforcement officials but condemned by many civil liberties groups. Justice Minister Anne McLellan, who introduced the bill, said, "People who live in daily fear of their personal security and safety cannot live in a free and democratic society." She believed the bill had the support of the Canadian public and that the bill was a fair balance between civil rights and the right to state protection. As a measure of civil rights protection, the legislation would be reviewed every three years, and the Supreme Court of Canada would be the final arbiter of the bill's lawfulness.

With the passage of Bill C-36, terrorism would be defined in Canadian law for the first time. In the proposed legislation, "terrorist activity" was defined as "an act or omission for a political, religious, or ideological cause that is intended to intimidate the public, a government, or a domestic or international organization." Terrorist acts include killing, endangering life, risking health or public safety, damage to property, and any serious interference or disruption of an essential service or facility, whether private or public.

The law would also define new criminal offences, such as "knowingly harbouring a terrorist" and "participating in, facilitating, or instructing a terrorist act." Police would be allowed to arrest without a warrant and detain suspects for up to 72 hours. Anyone with information relevant to an ongoing investigation could be summoned to a hearing and compelled to testify. Knowingly collecting or giving funds to terrorist groups would also be considered a crime, and governments could freeze and seize the assets of any person or group engaged in terrorist activities.

Under the proposed legislation, police and authorities would have more power to use electronic surveillance against suspected terrorist groups. Courts would be able to order the deletion of publicly available hate propaganda on the Internet. The government would also be allowed to block the release of information concerning suspects but only if the information collected was for reasons of security, international relations, or defence.

CRITICISM OF BILL C-36

Critics of the legislation raised concerns about the scope of the bill. Opponents claimed that its powers were too broad and that it was a serious threat to the rights of the accused. Furthermore, it would suppress information and erode the right to privacy in Canada.

Michelle Farlardeau-Ramsay, chief commissioner of the Canadian Human Rights Commission, claimed that the anti-terrorism bill could have a serious impact on fundamental human rights because aspects of the bill were open to interpretation. Opponents of Bill C-36 were particularly concerned about the absence of a "sunset" clause limiting the time period these powers could be used.

AMENDMENTS TO BILL C-36

On November 20, 2001, in response to public criticisms and concerns, Justice Minister McLellan announced proposed amendments, including a sunset provision limiting powers to five years. However, the sunset clause would only apply to selected provisions rather than the entire bill. Moreover, the powers could be extended for another five years, simply through votes in the House of Commons and the Senate.

Another proposed amendment was a narrow definition of terrorist activity to better protect protesters, dissenters, and trade union activity. The tighter definition would focus on harmful conduct. In addition, federal and provincial attorneys-general would be required to produce public, annual reports on how the law is being applied, with a parliamentary review of C-36 in three years' time.

CONTINUED CONTROVERSY

Bill C-36 was passed in the House of Commons on November 28, 2001. Nonetheless, the controversy continued. Those who fiercely protect the legal and civil rights of Canadians regarded these amendments as cosmetic. An open letter issued by a nationwide coalition of religious, ethnic, and legal organizations urged the federal government to redraft the anti-terrorist measures. The letter stated, "While it is necessary to implement measures to ensure the safety of Canadians in these uncertain times, we are concerned that Bill C-36—the Anti-Terrorism Act—is itself a threat to the legal and civil rights that Canadians now enjoy."

In response, Deputy Minister Herb Gray said, "This bill is not an attack on civil liberties. It's there to provide a foundation for protection of civil liberties."

Bill C-36 received Royal Assent on December 18, 2001. Whether the anti-terrorism law will prove to be a measured response to an extraordinary threat or an unprecedented trampling of civil rights remains open for debate. The Canadian government is asking its citizens to trust that it will not abuse these powers and that the laws will target those capable of killing thousands of innocent people and not those who engage in legitimate political protest.

If erosion of civil liberties is the legacy of the terrorist acts of September 11, then the terrorists will have achieved their goal.

LOOKING AT THE ISSUE

1. Do you think the amended provisions for a sunset clause are adequate to protect legal and civil rights? Explain your position.

2. Research the key points of anti-terrorist laws in either the United States or Great Britain. Create a chart comparing U.S. or British laws with the Canadian anti-terrorism law. You will find a copy of Bill C-36 at **www.pearsoned.ca/law**.

3. Minister of Justice Anne McLellan said that freedoms mean nothing if people live in "daily fear of their personal security and safety." Write an editorial either supporting or opposing this point of view.

Career Connections

For many people, work is a four-letter word. They spend their workday wishing they were somewhere else, doing something they enjoy. A person who likes to be outside, for example, probably wouldn't be happy sitting in a law library searching for precedents.

Imagine how rewarding it would be to work at something you enjoy doing. That's not as difficult as you might think. With some investigation and planning, you can find the right career for you.

EDUCATION AND TRAINING

Different careers require different investments in time and resources. This is an important consideration when deciding which career path to follow. If you are eager to complete your education and enter the workforce, then a career that requires several years of post-secondary education and training may not be the choice for you. For example, you might prefer to enroll in a two-year course in law security to become a correctional officer, security guard, or customs or immigration officer.

ENVIRONMENTAL CONDITIONS

What type of circumstances and surroundings do you enjoy? Do you prefer to work inside or outdoors, in an office or on the road, with others or independently? Would you consider a career that involves hazards or discomforts? What about travel? Police officers, for example, may experience any or all of these environmental conditions.

APTITUDES AND SKILLS

Careers require a variety of aptitudes and skills. An aptitude is the ability to acquire information and apply it. For instance, a person with spatial acuity may excel at designing diagrams or sketches, while a person with verbal ability may be capable of conveying complex information simply and clearly. As an example, consider the aptitude and skills required by forensic scientists to decipher the evidence obtained at a crime scene.

AREAS OF INTEREST

What type of personality are you? Are you a directive person who likes to assume responsibility for projects and coordinate the work of others? Perhaps you a methodical person who prefers to be guided by established policies and procedures. If you are, then you might consider a career as a court reporter. Possibly you are an innovative person who likes to initiate creative ways to solve problems. Do you enjoy dealing with people, identifying their needs and providing support, or would you prefer to work with data, instruments, or equipment?

As you can see, you have a lot to consider before you can decide on the right career—a career that will use your talents and meet your needs.

MAKING CONNECTIONS

1. Using the categories described above, create an organizer that identifies your profile.
2. Conduct research to select three law-related careers that might match your profile. Create a PMI chart to evaluate these three choices.

While salary expectations and opportunities for career advancement are important, there is so much more to consider when choosing your career.

Criminal Law

UNIT 3

Unfortunately, crime is a common occurrence. In this unit, you will learn about the nature of crime and how Canada's criminal law system reflects the values of society. The unit will take you through the process of criminal law and the criminal court system from police investigation and arrest to sentencing and incarceration. You will be introduced to the various principles that are involved in each stage of the criminal law process.

While you may have heard such terms as manslaughter, assault, and first-degree murder, you may not know what these terms actually mean. Not only will you discover their meaning, but you will also find out what defences are available to someone who is accused of such crimes.

The last chapter in this unit examines the law as it applies to young people like you. You will discover how the law has evolved to protect you. The most recent stage in this evolution was the passage of the *Youth Criminal Justice Act*. Why was this new legislation considered necessary? How does it differ from the *Young Offenders Act* of 1984? This chapter gives you the opportunity to explore the answers to these questions.

LOOKING AHEAD

Chapter 6 The Nature of Crime

Chapter 7 The Criminal Court System

Chapter 8 Investigation and Arrest

Chapter 9 Criminal Offences

Chapter 10 Defences for the Accused

Chapter 11 Sentencing and the Correctional System

Chapter 12 Criminal Law and Young People

6 The Nature of Crime

CHAPTER OUTLINE

Defining Crime and Criminal Offences

The Elements of a Crime

Involvement in a Crime

FOCUS YOUR LEARNING

How is crime defined in Canada?

What must a person do to be convicted of a crime?

Who is involved in committing a crime?

What is an incomplete crime?

SURVIVOR ISLAND

You and your classmates are travelling to a mock trial competition in Sydney, Australia. Somewhere over the South Pacific, the pilot is forced to crash land just off the coast of a deserted island. All the adults on board are killed, but you and your classmates manage to get out of the plane and swim to the island. There you find breadfruit and coconut palms, and the surrounding waters are teeming with fish. This discovery is fortunate because all your communications equipment has gone down with the plane, and the chances of rescue any time soon are slim. All you have managed to salvage are a few pens, a waterproof package of paper, some clothing, and a small supply of medicine.

WHAT DO YOU THINK?

Develop a set of criminal laws to follow while you are stranded on the island. Be sure to answer the following questions:

a) How will you define a criminal offence?
b) What categories will you use to classify different types of crime?
c) How will you enforce your laws?
d) What process will you use to change a particular law?

Crime happens everywhere; it has an impact on every community in Canada and on every community around the world. For many people, crime also holds an element of intrigue. Mystery novels that deal with criminal behaviour are perennial bestsellers, courtroom dramas capture high ratings on TV, and newspaper editors feed their readers a steady diet of lurid and sensational criminal cases. However, there is nothing glamorous about crime in real life. Criminals cause immeasurable grief and suffering to their victims and cost our country billions of dollars in damages every year. Understanding criminal law—why it is necessary and how it functions in society—is a serious and important matter for all Canadians.

After completing this chapter, you will be able to describe the elements that must exist for a person to be charged with and convicted of a crime under Canadian law. You will learn how to differentiate between the people or "parties" involved in the commission of a crime. You will also be able to explain why some serious crimes are called "incomplete" crimes.

"It is deliberate purpose that constitutes wickedness and criminal guilt."

— Aristotle (384–322 BCE), Rhetoric, 1.13.

DEFINING CRIME AND CRIMINAL OFFENCES

A **crime** is any act or omission of an act that is prohibited and punishable by federal statute. "Omission of an act" means that some crimes are not acts in the strict sense, but rather the *failure* to act in certain situations. For instance, if you failed to stop at the scene of an accident in which you were involved, you could be charged with an offence under s. 252(1) of the *Criminal Code of Canada*.

The Law Reform Commission of Canada has said that, in general, four conditions must exist for an act or omission to be considered a crime:

1. The act is considered wrong by society.
2. The act causes harm to society in general or to those (such as minors) who need protection.
3. The harm must be serious.
4. The remedy must be handled by the criminal justice system.

crime: an act or omission of an act that is prohibited and punishable by federal statute

Fast Fact
One in five Canadians fears being a victim of crime in his or her own community.

As you will discover, what society considers wrong can vary over time and from place to place. Prostitution is legal in some European countries, such as the Netherlands, but it is illegal in Canada. Adultery used to be a criminal offence in Canada, but it no longer is. Similarly, crimes that were once regarded as serious offences, such as possession of marijuana, are now considered less serious. Penalties have also changed. In 1795, a dozen people were hanged in Halifax for the crime of theft, one for stealing a few potatoes. Today, capital punishment is no longer a sentencing option even for the most serious of crimes. Over the years, criminal law in Canada has evolved to reflect society's changing standards.

Figure 6.1 **How does crime affect people in your community? Make a list of the crimes that are committed in your community, and beside each crime indicate the impact it might have on its victims.**

Criminal Law

A crime is considered to be an offence not just against the direct victim of the crime, but against the public, or society as a whole. When a thief steals a portable CD player from an electronics store, it is not just the owner of the store who is affected. The owner will increase prices to compensate for lost merchandise, which means that customers who have to pay those higher prices will have less money to spend on other things. The repercussions of the theft will carry through the rest of society.

Because crime has an impact on society as a whole, it is the government's responsibility to investigate and act against people who commit crimes. **Criminal law** is the body of laws that prohibit and punish acts that injure individual people, property, and the entire community. The main purposes of criminal laws are to

- protect people and property
- maintain order
- preserve standards of public decency

As citizens of Canada and members of society, we all have the responsibility to act in a law-abiding manner. In addition to not committing crimes ourselves, we have an opportunity to participate in crime-prevention programs that have been developed over the years. These programs include Crime Stoppers, Neighbourhood Watch, and Block Parent. Figure 6.2 provides statistics for a British Columbia Crime Stoppers program over a 14-year period. By examining these statistics, you can see that citizen support of such programs can help protect the community and save a substantial amount of money over time.

criminal law: the body of laws that prohibit and punish acts that injure people, property, and society as a whole

"The only thing necessary for the triumph of evil is for good men to do nothing."
— Edmund Burke (1729–1797),
British Parliamentary
orator and political thinker

Statistics of Central Okanagan Crime Stoppers from September 1987 to April 2001	
Topic	**Number or Dollar Value**
Tips files started	7873
Cases cleared	2208
Suspects charged	1595
Property recovered	$2 546 444
Drugs seized	$19 442 580

SOURCE: www.BCCrimeStoppers.com

Figure 6.2 Make a list of any crime prevention programs or strategies used in your community. Do you think they work? Why or why not?

The *Criminal Code*

The *Criminal Code of Canada* is a federal statute that contains the majority of the criminal laws passed by Parliament. The *Criminal Code* lists not only the offences, but also the sentences to be imposed and the procedures to follow when trying those accused of crimes. The Code is meant to reflect the social values of the majority of Canadians. When a new issue becomes important for society, or when national security and public safety are at risk, Parliament amends the Code to reflect this change in values or to ensure the protection of Canadian society.

One issue that has become increasingly important to Canadians is that of protecting children from sexual abuse. The federal government has responded by making changes to the *Criminal Code*. On October 18, 1999, Parliament passed Bill C-7, making the criminal records of pardoned sex offenders available for background checks. This law allows the police to explore the criminal background of anyone wishing to work with children. Such investigation includes examining an applicant's criminal record for designated sex offences even when this person has been pardoned by the National Parole Board.

In some cases, technology may create the need for developing new laws. Airplane hijacking, credit card fraud, and the unauthorized use of computers are three examples of crimes where revisions to the *Criminal Code* were made necessary by technological advances. Also, outdated laws can be revised or repealed. For instance, in 1976 the sentencing option of capital punishment was removed from the *Criminal Code*.

Law in Your Life
Did you know that s. 43 of the *Criminal Code* allows schoolteachers, parents, or guardians to use "reasonable force" in disciplining children under their care? What would you consider "reasonable force"? Do you think this section of the Code should be amended? Explain.

History of the *Criminal Code*

Before Confederation in 1867, each province was responsible for creating its own criminal laws. Canada's criminal law system (except in Quebec) was inherited from Great Britain. Before Confederation, Canadian courts relied entirely on British statutes and precedents. John A. Macdonald, Canada's first prime minister, believed that a single, uniform set of criminal laws for the

Figure 6.3 Prime Minister John A. Macdonald strongly advocated having one set of criminal laws for the whole country. What are the advantages to this type of system?

entire country would eliminate some of the confusion and unfairness that existed at that time. A criminal act would be considered an offence regardless of where the act was committed, and the sentence (or range of sentences) for this offence would no longer vary from province to province.

Section 91(27) of the *Constitution Act, 1867* granted the federal government the power to exercise the legal authority to make criminal laws for Canada. In July 1892, the Canadian Parliament passed a statute called the *Criminal Code of Canada*. It was called a "code" because it combined a description of crimes and criminal-law procedure into a single statute. Since its initial passage, the Code has been amended almost every year. Efforts to reform the Code in 1955 reduced it from 1100 sections to 753. In 1986, the Law Reform Commission of Canada produced a revised draft of the entire *Criminal Code* to make it less complicated, better organized, and easier to understand. Parliament, however, failed to implement the Commission's recommendations, with the result that there has never been a complete revision of the Code since its passage in 1892.

In spite of the original intentions of Canadian lawmakers to include *all* crimes in the Code, several other federal laws now contain criminal offences. These laws include the *Controlled Drug and Substances Act,* the *Customs Act,* the *Competition Act,* the *Youth Criminal Justice Act,* the *Food and Drug Act,* and the *Income Tax Act.*

Provincial Jurisdiction

Although the Parliament of Canada has exclusive jurisdiction to establish and revise criminal law for the whole country, legal authority for administering the criminal justice system is shared between the federal and provincial governments. Each provincial government appoints its own judges and pays for and administers its own provincial court system. These courts handle the bulk of criminal law in each province. You will learn more about the provincial court system in Chapter 7.

Legal Link WWW
For on-line access to the full text of the *Criminal Code*, visit **www.pearsoned.ca/law**.

The provinces have the power to pass laws on matters that fall under their jurisdiction, such as traffic and liquor regulations. When they choose, the provinces may transfer jurisdiction to municipalities within their boundaries. Technically, laws passed by provinces or municipalities are not considered criminal laws but **quasi-criminal laws.** These laws generally cover less serious offences, and the usual punishment for breaking them is paying a fine. In a few cases, offenders can be sentenced to jail. In Ontario, for instance, quasi-criminal laws may be found in the *Liquor Control Act,* the *Highway Traffic Act,* and the *Wildlife Act.* Such laws may not be the same in every province; they differ according to the needs of each province.

quasi-criminal laws: laws covering less serious offences at the provincial or municipal level; most often punishable by fines

Building Your Understanding

1. What are the four conditions that must exist for an act or omission to be considered a crime?
2. Why is crime an offence against society as a whole, not just against the direct victims of crime?
3. Identify three purposes of criminal law.
4. What is the main source of criminal laws in Canada?
5. Why are laws in the *Criminal Code* added, revised, or repealed?
6. Use examples to explain the responsibilities of the federal and provincial governments in the area of criminal law. How were these jurisdictions established?
7. Every province in Canada has passed laws that prohibit the sale of tobacco to people under a certain age. Are these criminal laws or quasi-criminal laws? Explain your answer.

THE ELEMENTS OF A CRIME

To convict a person of a criminal offence in Canada, the Crown must usually prove that two elements existed at the time the offence was committed: the act itself and the intention to commit the act. In law, these two elements are identified by the Latin terms *actus reus* and *mens rea*.

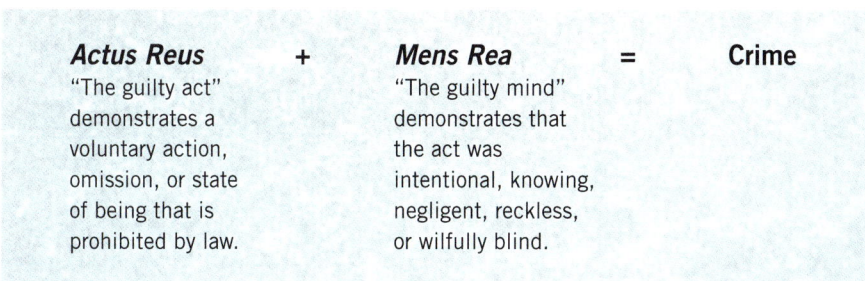

Figure 6.4 This criminal equation shows which elements must be present for a crime to occur.

Actus Reus

Most criminal offences involve an action that causes a) harm or loss to a person or group of people or b) damage to property. In Latin, the words ***actus reus*** mean "the guilty action," referring to the physical act involved in committing the offence described by the criminal law. For instance, if you argue with another person and then strike that person in the face, you have committed the criminal act of assault. Section 265(1)(a) of the *Criminal Code* clearly states that a person commits the wrongful act (*actus reus*) of assault when "without the consent of another person, he applies force intentionally to that person, directly or indirectly." Note that the *Criminal Code* defines the wrongful act in a clear and precise fashion so that we understand exactly what is prohibited by law. Note, too, that in most cases a criminal act must be completed to qualify as an offence. If you only *thought* of striking someone, but the person saw you were angry and ran away before you could hit or threaten this individual, you would not be guilty of assault.

actus reus: "the guilty act"—the voluntary action, omission, or state of being that is forbidden by the *Criminal Code*

Figure 6.5 If you strike another person in anger, you could be charged with the crime of assault. According to the *Criminal Code*, what is the *actus reus* of assault?

CASE

R. v. MacGillivray, [1995] 1 S.C.R. 890

1. How did the defendant's actions conform to the *actus reus* for dangerous driving as defined by the Supreme Court?

2. Check s. 249(4) of the *Criminal Code* to find the maximum sentence for dangerous operation of a motor vehicle causing death. Do you think this offence should have a longer prison sentence? Explain.

On a clear summer day, MacGillivray drove his boat at considerable speed toward a known swimming area off Cribbons Point in Nova Scotia. As he approached, a group of swimmers waved their arms and shouted to alert the accused of a dangerous situation. The bow of the boat was up at such an angle that MacGillivray could not see in front of the boat. It was possible to have some visibility ahead by leaning over the side and looking forward. The trial judge specifically found that this was not done. The boat ploughed through the group of seven teenagers, and one of them was struck and fatally injured by the propeller.

The accused was charged with dangerous operation of a motor vehicle causing death, contrary to s. 249(4) of the *Criminal Code*. The trial judge considered the circumstances and all the evidence, and convicted the accused. The conviction was upheld by the Court of Appeal of Nova Scotia, and the Supreme Court of Canada also dismissed MacGillivray's appeal. In its majority decision, the Supreme Court identified the *actus reus* for dangerous operation of a motor vehicle as "the creation of a significant risk of danger to others by a significant departure from the standard of a reasonably prudent person."

In some cases, *failing* to do something can be considered a wrongful act under the *Criminal Code*. This is called an "omission." For example, consider the case of parents who do not give their infant child enough food to eat.

As a result, the child dies of malnutrition. Under s. 215(1) of the *Criminal Code*, those parents can be charged with failing to provide a child with the necessities of life.

The *Criminal Code* also contains offences for which the *actus reus* is neither an act nor an omission but a "state of being." Being in possession of stolen goods, being in possession of break-in tools, and being found in a gaming or betting house are three offences for which the wrongful act is a state of being.

Note that the *actus reus* must be voluntary, not forced by another person. If Robert puts a knife to Ahmed's back and forces him to rob a variety store, Ahmed cannot be found guilty of committing a criminal act. Similarly, if Jeanette did something illegal while sleepwalking, *actus reus* would not apply. Neither can a reflex reaction be considered a wrongful action in law. If Naima has an epileptic seizure and her arm jerks back, striking Emily in the face, this is not a voluntary act. The law would not hold Naima criminally responsible for assaulting Emily.

> **Law in Your Life**
> Describe a situation involving teens in which the element of *actus reus* is uncertain. Explain why.

Mens Rea

Mens rea is the second element that, in most cases, must be present with *actus reus* for a criminal offence to be committed. In Latin, the words **mens rea** mean "the guilty mind"; the term implies moral guilt—that the accused person deliberately did something he or she knew to be wrong, with reckless disregard for the consequences. The Crown can establish *mens rea* by showing that the accused had the *intent* to commit an offence or *knowledge* that what he or she did was against the law.

mens rea: a deliberate intention to commit a wrongful act, with reckless disregard for the consequences

Intent

To say that a person had the **intent** to commit a criminal act means that he or she *meant* to do something wrong, was reckless regarding the consequences, and knew or should have foreseen the results of the wrongful act. In describing offences, the *Criminal Code* often uses words such as *wilfully* or *intentionally* to signify intent. Recall that in describing the act of assault, s. 265(1)(a) reads "applies force intentionally." Here the word *intentionally* signifies the *mens rea* of the criminal offence of assault.

In Canadian criminal law there are two kinds of intent. **General intent** means that a person commits a wrongful act for its own sake, with no ulterior motive or purpose. For example, if Guy strikes Curtis because he is angry with him and wants to vent his anger physically, then he has a general intent to commit assault. To establish *mens rea,* the Crown must simply prove that Guy did in fact strike Curtis. **Specific intent** applies when someone commits one wrongful act for the sake of accomplishing another. According to s. 343(c) of the *Criminal Code,* "Every one commits robbery who assaults any person with intent to steal from him." If Guy strikes Curtis with the intention of taking something valuable from him, then he has committed an assault for the sake of accomplishing a theft. To prove that Guy had the *mens*

intent: a state of mind in which someone desires to carry out a wrongful action, knows what the results will be, and is reckless regarding the consequences

general intent: the desire to commit a wrongful act, with no ulterior motive or purpose

specific intent: the desire to commit one wrongful act for the sake of accomplishing another

Father Jailed in Death of Son Left Unsupervised

Mother also sentenced after van ran over boy

EDMONTON—The father of a five-year-old boy, killed when he was run over by a van while riding his bike unsupervised, was sentenced yesterday to a year in jail. Robert Shaw, 44, and Starlene Gibson, 35, were sentenced for failing to provide the necessities of life for their son Leslie. Gibson was given a conditional sentence of seven months to be served in the community. Maximum sentence for the offence is two years in jail.

"I find it particularly bothersome because they had been previously warned," Justice Del Perras said of the parents.

Denise Nelson, Shaw's sister, was upset that her brother was jailed. "Robert wasn't driving that van. He did not send his child out in traffic to play. He did not want to kill his son and that's how they made it look," she said outside the court.

Leslie Shaw was riding his bike alone near his inner-city home when a cable-TV company van backed over him in August 1999. Police determined that the driver was not at fault. The jury at his parents' trial was told that Leslie and his three-year-old brother were often seen unsupervised and that Shaw and Gibson were told by social workers that their children would be seized if they were not monitored properly. The neighborhood is known for heavy traffic and is frequented by drug dealers and sex offenders.

A child welfare worker visited the couple's home on July 6, 1999, to investigate an allegation that one of the children had almost been run over by an ambulance. The worker found Gibson "extremely impaired" from drugs. At that time, Shaw promised the social worker he would supervise the children when they were outside. Perras said Shaw's failure to keep that promise, and a long criminal record, were factors in his decision to jail the father.

Perras also said a comment Shaw made to police the day Leslie died—about how he hoped child welfare officials wouldn't come after them—was self-centred and showed "no remorse for Leslie's death."

His sister said that's not true. "Robert has a soul, he has a heart, it's broken, he's paid, his son is dead. He has feelings. He loved his boys and he loves them now."

SOURCE: Mary Jo Laforest, "Father jailed in death of son left unsupervised," *Canadian Press*, May 2000.

---

1. According to the law, what omission was Robert Shaw guilty of (that is, what did he *not* do that he should have done)?
2. What evidence did the Crown produce to prove *actus reus* in this case?
3. Should the driver of the van or the child welfare worker who visited the couple share some of the blame for Leslie Shaw's death? Why or why not?
4. Do you think Robert Shaw should have been sentenced to a year in jail? Why or why not?

Consider This

Under current Canadian law, children under 12 are not considered capable of forming *mens rea*; therefore, they are not held responsible for the crimes they commit. Should they be held criminally responsible? Discuss.

rea to commit robbery, the Crown has to show not only that he assaulted Curtis, but that he did so with the specific intent of stealing from him.

What is the significance of this distinction between general and specific intent? For the most part, general intent offences are easier to prove. This may explain why, in certain cases, the Crown decides to prosecute someone for manslaughter (unplanned or unintended homicide), which is a general intent offence, rather than for murder (planned and deliberate homicide), which is a specific intent offence. Also, as we will see in Chapter 10, certain defences such as intoxication are more likely to succeed against specific intent offences. Consider the case of Marcel, who broke into a computer warehouse and knocked out the security guard. When Marcel was charged with break and enter with intent to commit robbery, he pleaded not guilty by reason of intoxication. The judge acquitted Marcel, ruling that he was too impaired to be able to form the specific intent to commit robbery.

Note that intent is not the same as motive. A **motive** is the *reason* a person commits a crime, while intent refers to that person's state of mind and willingness to break the law. If Alicia kills her mother to receive an inheritance, the inheritance is her motive, but it does not establish her state of mind or her intent to commit murder. The Crown must establish intent by showing that the killing was "planned and deliberate." While a motive may be useful evidence in a murder trial, it is not one of the elements of the offence that the Crown must prove to convict the accused.

motive: the reason a person commits a crime

Knowledge

In some cases, the Crown can establish *mens rea* by showing that the accused had **knowledge** of certain facts. For example, s. 368(1)(a) of the *Criminal Code* states: "Every one who, knowing that a document is forged, uses, deals, or acts upon it," is guilty of the offence of circulating a forged document. The word *knowing* indicates the *mens rea* of this offence. To establish guilt, the Crown only has to establish that the accused knew the document he or she used was forged. In this case, the Crown does not need to demonstrate the defendant's intent to do something either general or specific.

knowledge: an awareness of certain facts that can be used to establish *mens rea*

Figure 6.6 The legal term *mens rea* is usually translated as "the guilty mind." It implies that the offender knew a particular act was wrong but did it anyway.

"Can you keep a huge secret? I was guilty."

CASE

R. v. Hébert, [1989] 1 S.C.R. 233

1. In this case, what did the Supreme Court identify as the *mens rea* for perjury?
2. Does the criminal offence of perjury show a general or specific intent? Explain.
3. Suppose you were the judge in Hébert's new trial on one count of perjury. How would you decide whether he was telling the truth about his reasons for giving false testimony? If he was telling the truth, should he be acquitted? Explain.

Hébert gave false evidence at a preliminary hearing and was charged with perjury (giving false evidence with the intent to mislead) and obstructing justice (interfering with the course of justice). At trial, Hébert relied on s.17 of the *Criminal Code* and said he was compelled to give false evidence because of death threats made against him. The trial judge acquitted Hébert on the charge of perjury. The Crown appealed, and the acquittal was reversed. Hébert then appealed to the Supreme Court of Canada.

The Supreme Court ruled that s. 17 did not apply in this case but found there were legitimate grounds for appeal based on Hébert's argument that he had no *mens rea* to commit perjury. While Hébert admitted to deliberately lying, he said he had no intent to mislead in doing so. On the contrary, he intended that his testimony would be so obviously false that it would attract the judge's attention, and he could then tell the judge about the threats made against him.

The Supreme Court ordered a new trial on the charge of perjury. In its decision, the Court stated, "For there to be perjury, there has to be more than a deliberate false statement. The statement must also have been made with intent to mislead. While it is true that someone who lies generally does so with the intent of being believed, it is not impossible, though it may be exceptional, for a person to deliberately lie without intending to mislead."

Criminal Negligence

In some cases, the Crown can establish that *mens rea* existed by proving that the accused showed negligence. This means that the accused failed, under certain circumstances, to take precautions that any reasonable person would take to avoid causing harm to another person. In s. 219(1) of the *Criminal Code*, **criminal negligence** is defined in the following manner:

> Every one is criminally negligent who
> (a) in doing anything, or
> (b) in omitting to do anything that it is his duty to do, shows wanton or reckless disregard for the lives or safety of other persons.

criminal negligence: wanton or reckless disregard for the lives and safety of others, sometimes causing serious injury or death

Suppose Victor leaves a loaded .22-calibre target pistol on top of the night table beside his bed. One day his 10-year-old daughter, Sandy, takes the pistol and accidentally shoots her friend Celeste. Victor's *mens rea* for criminal negligence is the "wanton or reckless disregard" he showed by leaving a loaded firearm in a place where his young daughter could easily find it.

Recklessness

recklessness: consciously taking an unjustifiable risk that a reasonable person would not take

The Crown can also establish *mens rea* by proving that the accused demonstrated recklessness. **Recklessness** involves consciously taking an unjustifiable risk that a reasonable person would not take. Assume you know that you require prescription glasses to operate an automobile safely. You have misplaced your glasses at a friend's house, but instead of getting someone else to drive you home, you decide to drive without your glasses. As a result, you cannot see properly, and you fail to negotiate a curve in the road. You veer into oncoming traffic and cause a major accident. In these circumstances, you had the necessary intent to commit a crime because you behaved recklessly. The police could charge you with the dangerous operation of a motor vehicle.

Wilful Blindness

Finally, *mens rea* can be the result of **wilful blindness,** which involves deliberately closing your mind to the possible consequences of your actions. You are considered wilfully blind when you are aware of the need to make an inquiry but fail to do so because you do not wish to know the truth. For example, suppose a fellow student offers to sell you a TV for a really good price. Oddly enough, the name of your school board is spray painted on the side of the TV. You know you should ask why this student is selling a television set that obviously belongs to the school board, but the price is too good to pass up, so you buy the TV. In this case you could be charged with possession of stolen goods. You have the necessary *mens rea* because you have been wilfully blind to the fact that the television has likely been stolen.

wilful blindness: a deliberate closing of one's mind to the possible consequences of one's actions

CASE

R. v. Adey, [2001] Nfld. P.C. 1300A-01158

Adey bought a stolen satellite dish from a stranger at the Viking Mall in St. Anthony, Newfoundland. He paid $175 for the dish and had it set up at his house. The dish had originally been purchased by a Mr. Russell in St. John's. He had paid $349 (plus tax). The dish was stolen from him on a flight through St. Anthony.

Adey was arrested and charged with possession of stolen property contrary to s. 354(1) of the *Criminal Code*. The Crown argued that the *mens rea* for the offence was established in this case by the defendant's wilful blindness—Adey had ignored a number of "red flags" and proceeded in his purchase despite knowing that he should inquire further into the dish's origin. Counsel for the accused argued that the price paid for the dish was not so outrageously low that it should have caused the accused to be suspicious; therefore, the Crown had not established that wilful blindness applied.

In his decision, the trial judge noted that wilful blindness "requires suspicion, combined with a conscious decision to refrain from making inquiries. This is why our law equates it with having actual knowledge. An accused cannot deliberately remain ignorant and escape criminal liability as a result."

The judge found Adey not guilty, stating that the Crown had not proven that the accused had the necessary *mens rea*. The judge accepted Adey's argument that the price of the satellite dish was not low enough to raise his suspicion that the dish was stolen. To establish wilful blindness, it is not enough for the Crown to prove that the accused "ought to have known"; the Crown must show that suspicion actually existed on the part of the accused.

1. Look up the offence called the possession of stolen property in s. 354(1) of the *Criminal Code*. Which word indicates the *mens rea* of the offence?
2. Explain why, in Canadian law, wilful blindness is equated with having the knowledge necessary to demonstrate *mens rea*.

Strict and Absolute Liability

regulatory laws: federal or provincial statutes meant to protect the public welfare

liability: legal responsibility for a wrongful action

strict liability offences: offences that do not require *mens rea* but to which the accused can offer the defence of due diligence

due diligence: the defence that the accused took every reasonable precaution to avoid committing a particular offence

For some less serious offences, the Crown does not have to establish *mens rea* to win a conviction. Such offences are often against **regulatory laws,** which are federal and provincial statutes meant to protect the public welfare. Examples of regulatory laws are those dealing with environmental protection, workplace safety, hunting and fishing regulations, and traffic offences such as speeding. In writing these laws, legislators must include words such as *wilfully* or *with intent* if they wish to show that the Crown must establish *mens rea*. When such words have not been included, it is assumed that the offences do not require *mens rea*.

Offences that do not require *mens rea* can be grouped into two **liability** categories: strict liability offences and absolute liability offences. For **strict liability offences,** the accused may acknowledge that the offence took place but then offer the defence of **due diligence,** which means that he or she took every reasonable precaution to avoid committing the offence in question.

Figure 6.7 Do you think companies like this one should be charged with strict liability for contributing to smog? Why or why not? What precautions should they take to curb environmental pollution?

absolute liability offences: offences that do not require *mens rea* and to which the accused can offer no defence

Many offences dealing with environmental pollution are strict liability offences. Consider the case of the Acme Waste Disposal Company, charged with polluting a river that runs close to its treatment facility. Lawyers for the defence showed that the company spent several million dollars over the last five years in the installation of monitoring devices and special training for staff precisely to avoid the kind of runoff that occurred from its containment ponds. Further, the defence proved that the runoff occurred as a direct result of three days of torrential rains that exceeded anything recorded in the last 100 years. In this case, the judge ruled that the company had shown due diligence. Acme was acquitted of the charges.

For **absolute liability offences,** there is no defence possible. Once the Crown has established that the offence took place and the accused was responsible for it, the court must find the accused guilty. Driving without a license or exceeding the speed limit are examples of absolute liability offences. Because offenders can offer no defence to such a charge once the facts have been established, the Supreme Court has ruled that they cannot be imprisoned for these offences. The usual penalty is a fine.

CASE

R. v. Kerster, [2001] B.C. S.C. CC000227

BACKGROUND Kerster, using a false name, exchanged several e-mails with Detective Constable Headridge, a member of the Vancouver Police, who was also using a false name. The accused said he was willing to pay for the sexual services of a person under 18 years of age. Headridge said his wife would meet with the accused to make final arrangements for him to have sex with her 11-year-old daughter.

Daryl Heatherington posed as Headridge's wife. She and Kerster met in a Vancouver restaurant, where Kerster described the kind of sex he wanted to have with the girl. Heatherington told the accused that her daughter's name was Leez. When she asked if he had brought the money, Kerster showed her several $100 Canadian bills.

Kerster accompanied Heatherington to a hotel. Outside room 326, Heatherington called, "Leez, open the door." A detective from the Vice Squad opened the door and arrested the accused. The 11-year-old girl, Leez, did not exist. Kerster was charged with attempting to obtain the sexual services of a person he believed was under 18.

LEGAL QUESTION Should the accused be convicted of an attempt to commit the offence if the person under the age of 18 did not exist?

DECISION The Court found the accused guilty. On the question of whether a crime could have been committed when the victim did not exist, the Court referred to legal precedents to establish that an attempt is by its nature an incomplete offence and its *actus reus* will always be deficient. In this case, the absence of an 11-year-old girl in the hotel room is a deficiency in the *actus reus* that makes the *completion* of the offence impossible. The accused can still be convicted of the *attempt* to obtain a child's sexual services. The Crown can establish *mens rea* in such a case by proving that the accused had the necessary intent to commit the offence. *Actus reus* can be established by showing that the accused took steps beyond mere preparation for carrying out his intent. The actual performance of the sexual act is irrelevant to the *actus reus* of attempt.

Figure 6.8 The use of the Internet to obtain illicit sexual services has become an increasing social problem in Canada and around the world.

LEGAL SIGNIFICANCE The Court's decision affirmed earlier rulings involving "sting" operations where it was found that the actual existence of illicit goods or persons is not necessary to convict the accused of criminal attempt.

ANALYSIS

1. Describe the steps the accused took to fulfill the *actus reus* for criminal attempt. If necessary, consult the description of attempt at s. 24(1) of the *Criminal Code*.
2. Describe how the accused showed the necessary intent or *mens rea* for attempting to obtain the sexual services of a person under 18.
3. Which do you think was more important for the Crown to establish in this case, *mens rea* or *actus reus*? Explain.
4. Do you think it is right for the police to organize this kind of "sting" operation? Debate this issue in class; defend your point of view.

Building Your Understanding

1. Name the legal terms for the two elements that must be present in most cases for an action to be considered a criminal offence under Canadian law. Define both terms in your own words.
2. Must these two elements occur at the same time for a crime to occur? Explain.
3. In the following excerpt from the *Criminal Code*, indicate which word or words establish the *mens rea* for the offence in question:

    342(1) Every person who ...
       (d) uses a credit card, knowing that it has been revoked or cancelled, is guilty of ...
       (e) an indictable offence ...
4. What is the main difference between a strict liability offence and an absolute liability offence?
5. One night, in a municipal parking lot in downtown Winnipeg, someone throws a rock and breaks a window in one of the parked cars. The vandal flees, and when the police officer arrives, she finds that Maria is the only person on the street. She questions her, but Maria is evasive. The officer asks her to open her knapsack. When Maria refuses, she threatens to arrest her for public mischief. Maria opens her knapsack, and the officer finds two small crowbars known as jimmies—tools used by burglars to open locked windows and doors. Even though Maria has done nothing wrong, can she be charged with committing a crime? Explain.

INVOLVEMENT IN A CRIME

Many crimes are not the work of a single person. A successful bank robbery, for instance, usually requires careful planning and co-operation among several people. Violent crimes, such as assaults and murder, are sometimes perpetrated by two or more people against a single victim. Vandalism and muggings are often the result of gang behaviour. How does the law divide blame among the various offenders in a single criminal case? In this section, we will discuss the legal terms for different participants, some of the charges that can be brought against them, and some of the sentences they might receive.

The Perpetrator

perpetrator: the person who actually commits the crime

The **perpetrator** is the person who actually commits the criminal offence. When more than one person is directly involved in committing a crime, they are called "co-perpetrators." For example, if a lone robber walks into a bank, points a gun at the teller, collects the cash, and then escapes, that person is the perpetrator. If two people rob a bank, one holding the gun and the other collecting the cash, they are known as co-perpetrators. In every case, the person actually has to be present at the scene of the offence to be identified as either a perpetrator or a co-perpetrator.

Aiding

parties to an offence: those people who are indirectly involved in committing a crime

In some situations, people are not directly involved in committing a crime but may be considered partly responsible for it. Such individuals are **parties** to an offence. They are linked to the crime because they have somehow assisted the perpetrator, the person who actually committed the crime.

In criminal law, **aiding** means helping a perpetrator commit a crime. To aid the perpetrator, one does not have to be present when the offence is committed. For example, a pharmacy clerk named Lisa supplies the store key to her boyfriend, Bob. He uses the key to break into the pharmacy and steals prescription drugs. Lisa aids Bob in breaking the law even though she is not present at the break-in.

aiding: a criminal offence that involves helping a perpetrator commit a crime

Abetting

Abetting means encouraging the perpetrator of a crime without actually providing physical assistance. When Bill assaults Raj in the school parking lot, Carlos eggs Bill on, urging him to hit Raj repeatedly. Carlos has not touched Raj himself and is quite surprised when the police arrest him that evening. He demands to know what he is being charged with, and the police say, "You are charged with abetting an assault."

abetting: the crime of encouraging the perpetrator to commit an offence

Note that a person is not guilty of aiding or abetting just because he or she has knowledge of a crime or is present at the scene. The party must be aware that a criminal action was intended and must have committed some action that assisted the perpetrator. Presence at the time of the offence, however, *can* be used as evidence of aiding and abetting if it is accompanied by other factors such as prior knowledge of the perpetrator's intention to commit the offence.

Counselling

The crime of **counselling** involves advising, recommending, or persuading another person to commit an offence. As with aiding, a person who counsels does *not* have to be at the scene of the crime to be guilty. When Natasha persuades Melinda to steal goods from the store where Natasha works and advises her of the best way to accomplish this act, Natasha commits the criminal offence of counselling Melinda to steal.

counselling: a crime that involves advising, recommending, or persuading another person to commit a criminal offence

Accessory After the Fact

Even after a crime takes place, it is possible for someone who did not participate in it or help plan it to be held responsible for that crime. A person is considered to be an **accessory after the fact** if he or she knew that someone was involved in an offence and received, comforted, or assisted that person in escaping from the police. Consider the case of Nirmala, who is injured in a fight with store security officers after being caught shoplifting. She manages to escape and make it to her friend Simone's apartment. After hearing what happened, Simone offers to let Nirmala stay with her and provides her with food, clothing, and medical assistance. When the police finally track Nirmala down, they arrest Simone, too, and charge her as an accessory after the fact.

accessory after the fact: someone who knowingly receives, comforts, or assists a perpetrator in escaping from the police

CASE

R. v. Ford, [2000] Ont. C.A. C23709

1. List the actions that Ford performed that would constitute the *actus reus* of counselling murder.

2. According to evidence at the trial, Ford took a very active role in planning the murder. Could he have been charged as a co-perpetrator? Explain.

3. Do you think Ford should have received a longer sentence, given that he was the instigator of the crime? Give reasons for your view.

John Doe (a pseudonym) was a member of a break-and-enter gang headed by Ford. According to Doe, Ford said he had a problem with another member of the group, Martin Bidwell. During a meeting in a bar, Ford brought up the topic of killing Bidwell and said that he wanted Doe to do it.

According to Doe, Ford offered him $1000 in cash and about $500 for lawyer's fees, and supplied him with a handgun, ammunition, a police scanner, and a balaclava. Doe testified that Ford took him to downtown Toronto to show him where Bidwell lived and the places he frequented. Ford photographed Bidwell's apartment and showed Doe possible escape routes. Ford also suggested various scenarios of how to carry out the killing but left the final decision up to Doe.

On May 13, 1991, after "constant goading" by Ford, Doe loaded up his equipment and proceeded to Bidwell's apartment. He gained entry by breaking a window in the front door. When Bidwell arrived at 6:10 p.m., Doe jumped out and shot him in the face. Bidwell managed to stumble down the stairs and asked the building superintendent to call an ambulance. He survived, but the gunshot wound caused trauma to his head and, according to expert testimony, could have proved fatal.

At Ford's trial, the jury returned verdicts of not guilty on counts of attempted murder and conspiracy (making an agreement) to commit murder, but convicted Ford on a charge of counselling murder. Ford appealed on grounds that his conviction for counselling murder was inconsistent with his acquittal on the other charges. The Ontario Court of Appeal dismissed his appeal, affirming his conviction on the single charge of counselling murder.

Ford was sentenced to 18 months in prison. John Doe, however, was sentenced to 12 years in prison for attempted murder and related offences.

Party to Common Intention

Consider a situation in which two or more people set out to commit a crime and, in the process, end up committing several additional crimes. All the participants in the original crime will be held responsible for any other offences they committed in the process. This shared responsibility is known as **party to common intention,** which means that the participants can be charged with all of these additional crimes even though they were not directly involved in them. For instance, if six people hijack a security truck and one of them shoots and kills the driver, all six can be charged with murder.

party to common intention: the shared responsibility among criminals for any additional offences that are committed in the course of the crime they originally intended to commit

Incomplete Crimes

When we discussed *actus reus* and *mens rea* earlier in this chapter, we noted that a criminal act must be completed for a crime to exist. In other words,

Judge Fired for Lying

LAW IN ACTION

In June 2001, the Supreme Court of Canada ruled that Richard Therrien should be removed from his position as a judge of the Court of Quebec. In applying for the judgeship, Therrien had lied about his conviction for a crime committed 30 years earlier. In 1971, Therrien was sentenced to one year in jail for allowing four terrorists from the Front de Libération du Québec (FLQ) to hide in his Montreal apartment during the October Crisis of 1970. The terrorists had just kidnapped and murdered Quebec labour minister Pierre Laporte. Therrien also helped the four men by obtaining materials to build a hideout for them, and he mailed three letters to newspapers containing articles supporting the outlawed FLQ.

The Supreme Court heard evidence that after being released from custody, Therrien went on to become a highly respected lawyer, and in 1987 received a pardon for the earlier offence. He applied several times for an appointment as a judge. On at least two occasions, he was turned down after revealing his conviction and pardon in interviews. In 1996, he applied again and answered, "No," after being asked if he had ever "been in trouble with the law." This time he got the appointment.

The Supreme Court said it was Therrien's lie, not the criminal conviction that was sufficient reason for Quebec's judicial council and the Court of Appeal to recommend that he be fired. "The public will demand virtually irreproachable conduct from anyone performing a judicial function," wrote Mr. Justice Charles Gonthier in the unanimous decision. "What is demanded of them is something far above what is demanded from their fellow citizens."

Richard Therrien

1. What three things did Richard Therrien do to assist the FLQ members after they kidnapped and murdered Pierre Laporte?
2. What party to an offence did Therrien qualify as by helping the FLQ terrorists?
3. Therrien's offence was 30 years old at the time of the Supreme Court ruling. He had received a full pardon and had proven himself to be a respected and productive member of society. In light of all this, was it right to fire him as a judge? Give reasons for your position.

---

there can be no theft where property is not actually taken. However, there are some exceptions to this rule, covered by the laws governing incomplete crimes. There are two major types of incomplete crimes: criminal attempt and conspiracy.

Attempt

Even when a person is unsuccessful in the commission of a crime, that person can be charged with criminal **attempt.** This means that he or she had the intent to commit the crime but, for some reason, failed to carry it through. An attempt does require *actus reus,* but technically the guilty act begins the mo-

attempt: the intention to commit a crime, even when the crime is not completed

ment mere preparation turns into an action required to commit the offence. *Mens rea* can also be established as occurring at the beginning of an illegal act.

To prove someone guilty of a criminal attempt, all the Crown has to show is that the accused had the necessary intent and took some obvious steps toward committing the crime. In the case of a terrorist bombing, for example, such a step might be the construction of the bomb itself or getting in a car to transport the bomb to the target site. Either of these actions could indicate a realistic threat, and either would make the participants liable to charges of criminal attempt.

Conspiracy

conspiracy: an agreement between two or more people to carry out an illegal act, even if that act does not actually occur

Conspiracy is an agreement between two or more people to perform an illegal act. It does not matter whether the act is actually carried out. Even if the conspirators change their minds or do not get a chance to commit the offence, they are still guilty of conspiracy because they once agreed to commit the crime. For example, Ted and Tracey plan to murder Mario. They hire a hit man who turns out to be an undercover police officer, and Ted and Tracey are arrested. Although they cannot be charged with murder because Mario was not killed, they are charged with conspiracy for *planning* to kill him.

Building Your Understanding

1. Explain the difference between aiding and abetting a crime.
2. Organize a two-column chart. In the first column list the following participants in a bank robbery. In the second column identify which party to an offence each of these participants is.
   - "lookout" person
   - driver of the getaway car
   - "mapper," the person who draws up the bank's floor plan
   - "insider" who works at the bank and advises the robbers on the best time of day to strike
   - two robbers, one to carry a gun, the other to grab the cash
   - person who owns the "crash pad" where the robbers go after the holdup
3. What are the similarities and difference between attempt and conspiracy?
4. Gilbert and Jamal work for a high-powered accounting firm in Halifax. They devise a plan to embezzle $500 000 from the firm. They are sure their plan will succeed until Dahlia, another employee, learns of it and threatens to tell the police unless Gilbert and Jamal give her $250 000. At Gilbert's urging, Jamal strangles Dahlia and dumps her body into the Halifax harbour. Can both Gilbert and Jamal be charged with a crime? Explain.
5. Nicole is a professional pickpocket who works the Montreal subway system during rush hour. One morning in a crowded subway car, she puts her hand in Michel's jacket pocket to lift his wallet but discovers the pocket is empty. She withdraws her hand a little too slowly, and Michel grabs her by the wrist. Can Michel have Nicole charged with criminal attempt? Explain.

LOOKING BACK

Reviewing Your Vocabulary

abetting *p. 153*
absolute liability offences *p. 150*
accessory after the fact *p. 153*
actus reus p. 143
aiding *p. 153*
attempt *p. 155*
conspiracy *p. 156*
counselling *p. 153*
crime *p. 139*

criminal law *p. 140*
criminal negligence *p. 148*
due diligence *p. 150*
general intent *p. 145*
intent *p. 145*
knowledge *p. 147*
liability *p. 150*
mens rea p. 145
motive *p. 147*

parties to an offence *p. 152*
party to common intention *p. 154*
perpetrator *p. 152*
quasi-criminal laws *p. 142*
recklessness *p. 148*
regulatory laws *p. 150*
specific intent *p. 145*
strict liability offences *p. 150*
wilful blindness *p. 149*

Quick Quiz

1. Indicate whether the following statements are true or false. Be sure to correct any statements you identify as false.
   a) A person accused of an absolute liability offence can use the defence of due diligence.
   b) A quasi-criminal offence is usually punishable by a lengthy prison sentence.
   c) *Actus reus* is defined as a guilty act.
   d) Recklessness is a legal term that refers only to motor vehicle offences.
   e) With respect to *mens rea,* motive is the same as intent.
   f) The perpetrator is the person who actually commits a particular crime.
   g) Aiding and abetting are basically the same.
   h) To prove a person guilty of conspiracy, the Crown must show that the person agreed to commit a particular crime.
   i) To find someone guilty of counselling to commit a crime, that person must be present when the crime is committed.
   j) Quasi-criminal laws fall under federal jurisdiction.
   k) A regulatory law is usually one that has been passed to protect the public welfare.

Checking Your Knowledge

2. Which two levels of government share jurisdiction for administering the criminal justice system?
3. Does the *actus reu*s of a crime always involve a physical action? Explain.
4. What is the difference between general and specific intent?
5. Explain in your own words the *mens rea* of wilful blindness.
6. How does the criminal offence of counselling differ from that of aiding?
7. Which one of the following offenders has to be present at the scene of a crime?
   a) aider
   b) abettor
   c) accessory after the fact
   d) co-perpetrator
8. Abigail decides to intimidate Barney, her competitor in the canning industry, by having a biker break his legs. She meets the biker in a bar to discuss the plan. The biker sets his fee at $800. Abigail asks for 24 hours to think it over. She never calls the biker back. Meanwhile, the biker tells several regulars at the bar about Abigail's plan, and word gets back to Barney. Can Abigail be charged with conspiracy? Explain.

Developing Your Thinking and Inquiry Skills

9. In 2001, Health Canada reported that smoking was the leading cause of preventable death and injury in Canada and killed more than 45 000 Canadians a year. Do you think Parliament should amend the *Criminal Code* to outlaw the sale of tobacco in this country? Give at least three reasons to support your position.

10. Using issues of your local newspaper, find three examples of recent court cases, each one dealing with a different criminal offence. For each case, identify the
    a) specific offence as listed in the *Criminal Code*;
    b) *actus reus* for each offence and tell whether it involves an action, an omission, or a state of being; and
    c) *mens rea* for each offence and tell whether it shows intent, knowledge, recklessness, criminal negligence, or wilful blindness.

Communicating Your Ideas

11. Choose one of the following crimes and write a brief, three-paragraph essay explaining why it is a crime against Canadian society as a whole and not just against the direct victim.
    a) Keith is held up at gunpoint on his way to class. Even though he hands over his wallet without a struggle, the robber shoots and kills him.
    b) Sheila walks home every day after work. One day while walking through a park, she is accosted by a man with a knife and is sexually assaulted.
    c) Benito is paid to analyze some ore samples from a new gold mine. He suspects that the samples have been "salted," that is, they contain gold deposits that could only have come from another mine. Benito says nothing and releases a favourable report. The mining company's share price soars, and the owners pay Benito a tidy bonus under the table.

Putting It All Together

12. You are a new judge and have been assigned the following case:

    > Walter lives on a residential block with shared driveways where overnight parking is not allowed. He works the night shift at a local laboratory, and by the time he gets home, his neighbour has parked in the driveway. For parking on the street, a traffic officer has given Walter several parking tickets over the past three months. Walter feels that the officer is picking on him. After the sixth ticket, he is so angry that when he sees the officer, he calls him a "bloodsucker" and threatens to "get him."
    >
    > Finally, Walter offers to pay Cecil, an acquaintance of his, $500 to beat the officer with a baseball bat. Cecil takes the $500 in cash and then tells the officer what Walter has asked him to do. The officer arrests both Walter and Cecil and charges them with criminal conspiracy. The Crown brings the case to court.

    As judge you must produce a written decision that includes the following:
    - a summary of the crime in your own words
    - your opinion of whether the proper charge has been filed against both men; if you think another charge should have been filed in either case, identify it and explain why
    - the *mens rea* and *actus reus* for each of the accused
    - the role each of the accused played in committing the offence, that is, the legal terms describing their participation in the crime
    - the sentence each of the accused should receive under the provisions of the *Criminal Code* for the crime committed

    Your written decision should be about three pages long and should deal with each of these matters in some detail.

CASES

R. v. Hackett, [2001] Nfld. P.C. File No. 1300A-1034

Fisheries officers found seven lobster traps in an area of the Humber Arm in Newfoundland. Attached to the traps were year-2000 lobster tags issued to Mr. Michael Hackett, Sr., father of the accused. The accused was the "designated fisher" under Mr. Hackett, Sr.'s licence. The lobster-fishing season had closed three days before, and these traps were outside the area in which the licence allowed the accused to fish for lobster.

Hackett admitted the traps belonged to him, but said they had been stolen and put there by someone else. He said that s. 25(2) of the *Fisheries Act*, under which he was charged, was a "strict liability" offence. He argued that he should be acquitted on the basis of due diligence. He pointed to his regular checking of his lines, his steps to maintain the security of his traps, his manner of only attaching his tags to the traps when they were placed in the water, his removing the traps from the water over time rather than on the last day of the season, and his attempts to prevent poaching.

The Crown argued that Hackett failed to show that he had acted with sufficient care to establish the defence of due diligence. He should have contacted fisheries officers as soon as he realized some of his traps had been stolen.

The Court found that failure to report the theft would not have prevented the commission of the offence that took place. The accused was found not guilty of the offence charged.

1. Does the Crown have to establish *mens rea* in this case? Why or why not?
2. What steps did the accused take to guard against the theft and misuse of his lobster traps? Do you think these steps establish due diligence in this case? Explain your answer.

R. v. Vang, [1999] Ont. C.A. C29539

On the evening of March 10, 1996, a party at the Star Café in Kitchener, Ontario, progressed in an uneventful fashion until closing time. At that point, Bobby Rampersaud verbally abused several guests by using racial slurs. In retaliation, Rampersaud was attacked by three people, beaten, kicked, hit over the head with a beer bottle, and stabbed in the back seven times. He survived, but his lung was punctured and his kidney was lacerated, causing potentially fatal bleeding.

At trial, Nguyen was found to be the perpetrator, the person who stabbed Rampersaud. He was sentenced to 15 months in prison. Vang and Thangsavath were convicted as parties to common intention under s. 21(2) of the *Criminal Code*. They were each sentenced to 11 months in prison. Their appeal was dismissed by the Ontario Court of Appeal.

The Court of Appeal accepted the Crown's submission that Vang and Thangsavath assisted Nguyen, the stabber, so that three were fighting against one. The Court stated: "Parties to the offence are bound by the consequences in the same manner as the perpetrator."

1. What is the *actus reus* of aggravated assault? (See s. 268[1] of the *Criminal Code*.) What did Vang and Thangsavath do to make themselves parties to the offence of aggravated assault?
2. Compare the perpetrator's sentence (15 months) with the sentences received by the parties to the offence (11 months each). Do you believe that Vang and Thangsavath should have received the same sentence as the perpetrator? Explain your answer.
3. Considering that Rampersaud could have died from his injuries, some people may feel that the punishment did not "fit the crime." Do you agree with the severity of the sentences imposed? Why or why not? What sentences would you impose if you were the judge in this case?

CASES

R. v. Canhoto (1999), Ont. C.A. C24949

BACKGROUND This tragic and bizarre case involves the death of two-year-old Kira Canhoto. Kira's grandmother believed that Kira was possessed by evil spirits transmitted to her by her mother's boyfriend. The grandmother also believed that she could exorcize those spirits.

On the day she died, Kira, her mother Maria, and her grandmother were at the home of the Aguiars, friends who shared the grandmother's beliefs that she could communicate with angels and exorcise evil spirits. The grandmother decided to expel Kira's spirits. The exorcism involved a combination of prayer and forced ingestion of water until the child vomited thereby "expelling" the evil spirits. Kira was taken into the kitchen and water was forced down her throat. She resisted strenuously, screaming and kicking. In response, Daniel Aguiar held her legs until she eventually fell silent and died. Her inability to breathe combined with aspiration of the water caused Kira's death.

Maria Canhoto, who was present during part of the attempted exorcism and in the adjacent room for the rest of the time, was charged with manslaughter on the basis of criminal negligence. The Crown argued that Maria was under a legal obligation to come to her daughter's aid and that her failure to do so demonstrated a wanton and reckless disregard for her life and safety. The trial judge found that Maria knew or ought to have known that the child's life or security was at risk and that Maria was capable of distinguishing between cries of discomfort and cries of a child fighting for her life. The trial judge added:

> What is clear to me on the evidence is that Maria was so convinced that her child was possessed by evil spirits, of her mother's ability to rid the child's body of those spirits by forced feeding and of the critical importance of doing so that her concern for Kira's health or safety was secondary.

Maria was convicted of manslaughter. After serving a one-year sentence, she appealed the conviction. The legal argument offered by the appellant was that the Court should distinguish between crimes of criminal negligence arising out of acts and crimes of criminal negligence based on a failure to act where there is a duty to do so.

LEGAL QUESTION Is a person who fails to act to avert harm less culpable than the person whose actions cause the risk of harm?

DECISION On the basis of facts, the trial judge found that Maria had participated to some degree in the activity that caused Kira's death, so her liability was not limited to her failure to act. On this basis, the Court of Appeal found that this legal argument failed.

Moreover, the language of s. 219 of the *Criminal Code* denies the distinction between acts and omissions. It provides that *either* actions *or* omissions constitute criminal negligence where they show a wanton or reckless disregard for the lives or safety of others. The appeal was dismissed.

LEGAL SIGNIFICANCE In Canada, statute law and common law co-exist, but statute law always overrides common law; therefore, the *Criminal Code* is the primary source to examine in determining the elements of a crime. The *Criminal Code* shows no distinction between the fault element of criminally negligent conduct and the fault element of a criminally negligent failure to act where there is a duty to do so.

ANALYSIS

1. What was Maria Canhoto's *actus reus*?
2. What was her *mens rea*?
3. Do you think the appeal would have been allowed if Maria had stayed in the adjacent room throughout the attempted exorcism? Explain.

The Criminal Court System

7

CHAPTER OUTLINE

The Criminal Court Structure

The Participants

The Role of the Jury

The Criminal Trial Process

FOCUS YOUR LEARNING

How is Canada's criminal court system structured?

Who is involved in the system and what are their roles?

What are the key aspects of the criminal trial process?

What are the rules of evidence?

WHAT DO YOU THINK?

As the cartoon above demonstrates, sometimes a defendant under cross-examination will be more concerned with establishing an alibi than telling the truth.

- Define the term "perjury" in your own words.

- What do you think would happen if the dialogue from the cartoon were given as testimony in a Canadian court?

- Should defendants have to provide testimony that could be used against them or make them appear guilty of a crime? Explain.

161

As you discovered in Chapter 1, the framework of the Canadian court system is derived from English common law dating back to the days of William the Conqueror, who came to the throne in 1066. The original meaning of "court" referred to an enclosed place, as it still does in words such as *courtyard* and *tennis court*. Initially, judicial tribunals were enclosures where judges sat at the head of the chamber. Other participants such as the Crown, the defence attorneys, the jury, and the public had to remain on the other side of a bar, which led to the expression "called to the bar." A lawyer who is called to the bar has passed all the exams, is deemed qualified to practise law, and is formally admitted into the legal profession.

Today, criminal courts are complex administrative organizations. They oversee the entire process of prosecuting criminal offences and ensuring that the trial is conducted in accordance with the principle of fairness. The rules of procedure, rules of evidence, statutory laws, and constitutional laws have shaped the Canadian trial process into its present form. This chapter will discuss the criminal court structure and its jurisdiction, the roles played by different parties in the court process, the rules of evidence, and the various stages of a criminal trial.

THE CRIMINAL COURT STRUCTURE

When discussing the division of powers in Chapter 3, you learned how the *Constitution Act, 1867,* divided the responsibility for Canada's criminal courts between the federal and provincial governments. The federal Parliament is responsible for formulating criminal law and procedure, and it can establish courts for administering various federal laws. Parliament has used this authority to create the Supreme Court of Canada, the Federal Court of Canada, and the Tax Court of Canada. Provincial legislatures are responsible for organizing,

Figure 7.1 Artist's sketch of a criminal court in session

administering, and maintaining the criminal court system. Each provincial legislature appoints judges to the lowest level in the hierarchy of courts, simply known as the Provincial Court. The federal government appoints judges to the superior courts and to the provincial courts of appeal.

The chart in Figure 7.2 is intended to apply to all of the provinces of Canada, but there are, in reality, significant differences from province to province. For instance, in British Columbia, the highest trial court is called the British Columbia Supreme Court, which has two divisions: trial and appeal. The highest court in the province is the British Columbia Court of Appeal. In some provinces, two or more of these courts are combined into a single court with various divisions. For example, in Alberta, a judge of the Provincial Court has jurisdiction to sit in either, some, or all of the criminal, small claims, family, or youth divisions. In Ontario, the Provincial Court is divided into family, criminal, and youth divisions; the small claims court is a division of the Superior Court.

The Provincial Court System

The provincial court system consists of the provincial courts and the superior courts of the province. The provincial courts have trial divisions, while the superior courts have both trial and appeal divisions.

The Provincial Court, Criminal Division

The **Provincial Court** is at the bottom of the hierarchy of Canadian courts. These courts are constituted under provincial statutes with judges appointed by the provincial government. Cases are tried by a judge alone, not a jury. Each province divides this court into separate divisions such as criminal, civil (small claims), and family. This chapter will examine only the criminal division of the Provincial Court. The other divisions will be discussed in Unit 4.

Provincial Court: the lowest level in the hierarchy of Canadian courts

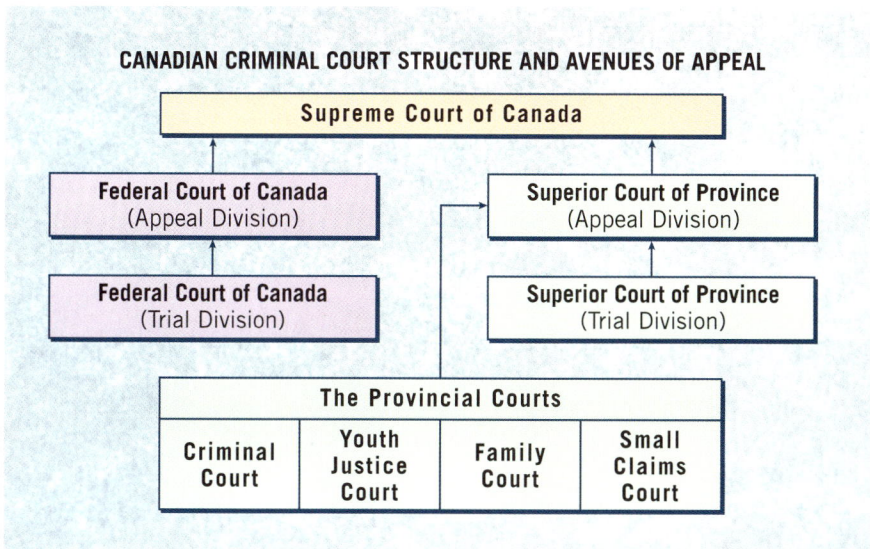

Figure 7.2 The Canadian criminal court structure and avenues of appeal. What are the courts at the bottom of the hierarchy called? What are the avenues of appeal?

Fast Fact

About 90% of all criminal cases in Canada are handled by the provincial courts.

preliminary hearing: a judicial inquiry to determine whether there is sufficient evidence to put the accused person on trial

Consider This

Some people believe that preliminary hearings should be eliminated and the accused person should go directly to trial. Do you agree or disagree? Why?

appeal: an application to a higher court to review the decision made by a lower court

Provincial Court judges in the criminal division have the jurisdiction to hear summary conviction offences and certain indictable offences. (See Figure 7.5.) Summary conviction offences are less serious crimes that carry a lighter penalty, such as public nudity or causing a disturbance. Indictable offences are more serious crimes that carry a heavier penalty, such as offences in s. 553 of the *Criminal Code* (e.g., mischief or theft under $5000) or offences in s. 554 (e.g., theft or fraud over $5000). For offences tried in Provincial Court, the accused cannot choose a trial by jury but must be tried by a judge alone. Both summary conviction and indictable offences will be discussed in detail in Chapter 9.

The Provincial Court also tries violations of provincial statutes or municipal bylaws. For example, persons charged with careless driving (a provincial statute violation) or parking in a no-parking zone (a municipal bylaw violation) would have their cases tried in the Provincial Court.

An accused person's first contact with the criminal court system usually begins in the Provincial Court, Criminal Division, because this court also conducts all **preliminary hearings** to determine whether there is sufficient evidence to put the accused on trial by a higher court. The preliminary hearing serves as a screening process and protects the accused person from an unnecessary trial; it also protects the Crown and the public from the expense of a trial that may not be required. In the words of the Supreme Court of Canada, "The purpose of a preliminary inquiry is clearly defined by the *Criminal Code*—to determine whether there is sufficient evidence to put the accused on trial."

An **appeal** from the Provincial Court regarding a summary conviction offence is heard by a single judge of the Superior Court of the province. An appeal regarding an indictable offence is heard by the appeal division of the Superior Court, which comprises a panel of three or five judges.

Figure 7.3 Parking in a no-parking zone violates a municipal bylaw. If the driver wishes to contest the ticket for this offence, in which level of court will the case be heard?

Superior Courts of the Province

The **Superior Court of the province** is the highest level of the provincial criminal and civil court system. It consists of a trial division and an appeal division. This court has jurisdiction in both civil and criminal matters that go beyond the jurisdiction of the lower courts. The superior court system is similar across Canada, although the names of the courts are not the same for all provinces. (For the proper name of each court, see the list in Figure 7.4.) The Superior Court has jurisdiction to hear all offences in s. 469 of the Code. These offences must be tried by a judge *and* a jury unless the accused person and the provincial Attorney General consent to a trial by judge alone. Section 469 offences are the most serious crimes, such as murder and treason. (See Figure 7.5.)

Superior Court of the province: the highest criminal and civil court, consisting of a trial division and an appeal division

Fast Fact
The *Canadian Charter of Rights and Freedoms* guarantees that any person charged with an offence punishable by imprisonment of five years or more has the right to trial by jury.

Figure 7.4 The name of the Superior Court in each province or territory

Province or Territory	Provincial Superior Court
Alberta	Court of Queen's Bench
British Columbia	Supreme Court of British Columbia
Manitoba	Court of Queen's Bench
New Brunswick	Court of Queen's Bench
Newfoundland and Labrador	Supreme Court of Newfoundland and Labrador
Northwest Territories	Supreme Court of the Northwest Territories
Nova Scotia	Supreme Court of Nova Scotia
Nunavut	Nunavut Court of Justice
Ontario	Superior Court of Justice
Prince Edward Island	Supreme Court of Prince Edward Island
Quebec	Superior Court of Quebec
Saskatchewan	Court of Queen's Bench
Yukon Territory	Supreme Court of the Yukon Territory

As Figure 7.5 indicates, the Superior Court may also try indictable offences in s. 554 of the Code in which the accused may choose (or elect) the mode of trial. For these offences, the accused may elect to be tried by a judge alone in Provincial or Superior Court, or by a judge and jury in Superior Court. Such offences include breaking and entering, robbery, and attempted murder.

Appeals from the Superior Court, Trial Division, are heard in the Superior Court, Appeal Division of the province. Three or five judges hear the cases brought to this court, and the appeal is won or lost based on the majority decision of the judges.

Consider This
Put yourself in the place of someone accused of a s. 554 offence. Who do you think would be more sympathetic—a judge alone or a judge and jury? State the reasons for your choice.

The Federal Court System

The federal court system consists of the Federal Court of Canada, which has a trial division and an appeal division, and the Supreme Court of Canada—the country's highest **court of appeal.**

court of appeal: a court with the authority to review decisions made by lower courts

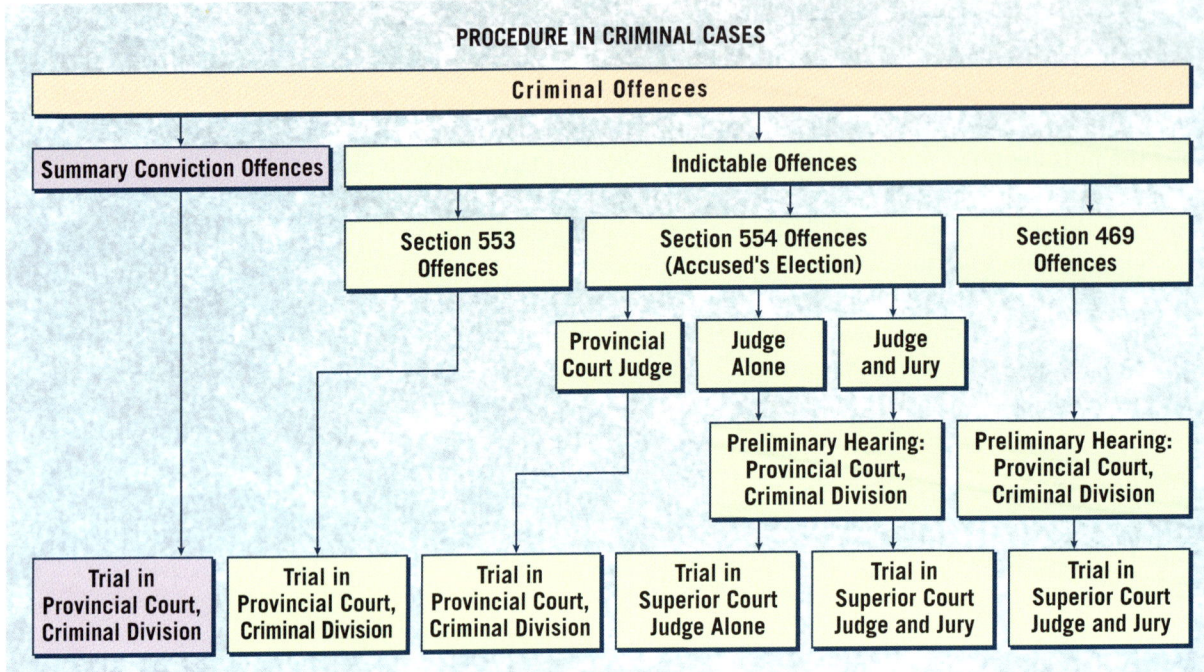

Figure 7.5 This chart outlines the court procedure for criminal cases. What types of offences require a preliminary hearing?

Federal Court of Canada

Federal Court of Canada: a court that hears cases involving the federal government; consists of a trial and an appeal division

The **Federal Court of Canada** has a trial division and an appeal division. In its trial division, the court has jurisdiction to try civil claims involving the federal government. The Federal Court also has jurisdiction to hear appeals from federally appointed boards, commissions, and administrative tribunals, such as the Immigration Appeal Board and the National Parole Board. You will learn more about the Federal Court of Canada in Chapter 13.

Supreme Court of Canada

Supreme Court of Canada: the highest appeals court in Canada; also deals with constitutional questions referred to it by the federal government

The **Supreme Court of Canada** is the highest court in the country. It consists of a chief justice and eight justices (judges), all of whom are appointed by the federal government. By law, three of the justices must come from Quebec. By tradition, three come from Ontario, two from Western Canada and one from the Atlantic Provinces. The Court sits in Ottawa for three sessions a year: winter, spring, and fall. Cases are heard by a panel of five, seven, or nine justices, depending on the type of appeal. Sometimes the Court uses teleconferencing to hear presentations from other parts of Canada.

The Supreme Court of Canada is strictly an appeals court; it has no trial division. It can hear appeals of decisions made by different provincial courts of appeal and by the Federal Court of Appeal. However, it can be difficult to move a case to the Supreme Court of Canada because of the high volume of cases in the system. Generally, the Supreme Court grants **leave,** or permission to appeal,

Fast Fact
Automatic appeals to the Supreme Court when acquittals were overturned on appeal were eliminated in 1997.

Figure 7.6 The Supreme Court of Canada building in Ottawa. What kinds of cases are heard here?

Consider This

Some people argue that the court structure should be simplified to help the public understand and access the criminal justice system. To this end, should each province and territory create a single court to try all *Criminal Code* offences? Discuss.

only for matters of national significance or when decisions conflict in the provincial appeals courts.

The federal government may ask the Supreme Court of Canada to provide advice or to rule on specific questions relating to constitutional issues or other federal matters. For example, in 1996, after the close results of the 1995 referendum in Quebec, the federal government asked the Supreme Court to rule on whether Quebec could legally secede from Canada. In 1998, the Court unanimously decided that secession is legal but only after negotiations take place with the rest of Canada to amend the Constitution.

Other Courts

In 1983, the Tax Court of Canada was established to replace the Tax Review Board, an administrative tribunal. The Tax Court of Canada is primarily responsible for hearing cases dealing with income tax matters. Appeals of decisions made by the Tax Court are heard by the Federal Court of Canada.

Another specialized federal court is the Court Martial Appeal Court. This court hears appeals from courts martial in the Armed Forces. The judges who sit on the Court Martial Appeal Court are not members of the military but are usually appointed from provincial superior courts or from the Federal Court of Canada.

Under its treaty on lands and self-government, the Nisga'a Nation in British Columbia has the jurisdiction to establish a Nisga'a Court. This court will function in the same way as a Provincial Court. An appeal from a decision of the Nisga'a Court will be taken to the British Columbia Supreme Court. Note that the Nisga'a Nation does not have the power to write criminal laws because

leave: permission to appeal a case from a lower court to a higher court

"Through thousands of decisions, the Supreme Court of Canada has woven the tissue of Canadian justice."

— The Right Honourable Beverley McLachlin, Chief Justice of Canada

Legal Link WWW

For on-line access to decisions from the Supreme Court of Canada and from other courts across the country, visit
www.pearsoned.ca/law.

that would interfere with the federal government's exclusive jurisdiction in this area. As with provincial governments, however, the Nisga'a Nation can write laws that set out quasi-criminal or regulatory offences.

In some places across Canada, judges have been taking part in Aboriginal sentencing circles, which are not actually courts but rather judicial procedures equivalent to sentencing hearings. However, the physical set-up for a sentencing circle is completely different from the seating arrangement in the traditional courtroom—the judge, police officers, social workers, band officials, victims, and convicted person sit in a circle to consider an appropriate sentence. This practice is most often used when the punishment for an offence does not exceed two years in prison. See Chapter 11, Sentencing and the Correctional System, for a further discussion of Aboriginal sentencing circles.

Building Your Understanding

1. a) Outline the responsibilities given to the provincial governments for Canada's criminal court system under the *Constitution Act, 1867.*
   b) Identify three responsibilities over criminal law that were given to the federal government.
2. What are the lowest and highest criminal courts of your province?
3. Provide an example of an offence tried by the criminal division of a Provincial Court for each of the following:
   a) a federal statute
   b) a provincial statute
   c) a municipal bylaw
4. What is the purpose of preliminary hearings, and what court is responsible for conducting them?
5. List the choices of trials available to a person accused of committing an electable offence under s. 554 of the Code.
6. Name the court of your province that has jurisdiction in the following cases:
   a) a murder charge
   b) a violation of a provincial statute
   c) a preliminary hearing
   d) perjury (an electable offence)
7. What is the highest court of appeal in Canada? Explain what it does.
8. Generally, cases may be appealed to the Supreme Court of Canada only with leave. Why do you think this is so?

THE PARTICIPANTS

beyond a reasonable doubt: a standard of proof whereby a defendant's guilt must be proven to the extent that a reasonable person would have no choice but to conclude that the defendant did indeed commit the offence

Canada's criminal justice system has two fundamental principles: an accused person is innocent until proven guilty, and guilt must be proven **beyond a reasonable doubt.** These principles mean that a judge or jurors cannot convict an accused person unless they are satisfied that the Crown has proven the defendant's guilt to the extent that a reasonable person would conclude that this individual did indeed commit the offence in question. If there is any doubt about the defendant's guilt, the person must be acquitted. Therefore, the evidence introduced by the Crown and defence attorneys, the testimony of the witnesses, and the roles played by the judge, jury, and other court personnel are all critical in maintaining the integrity of the trial system. This section discusses the people involved in a typical criminal trial and the role that each person plays.

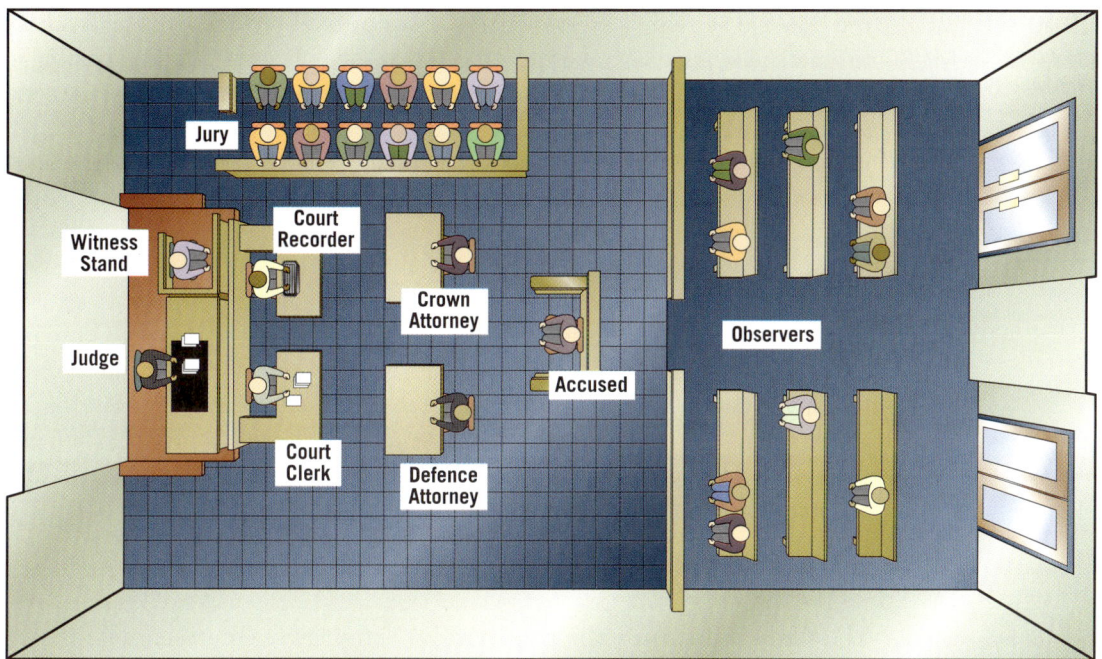

Figure 7.7 This diagram shows the seating arrangement of key participants in a traditional courtroom.

The Judge

The **judge** makes decisions on the admissibility of evidence, controls the events in the courtroom, and interprets the law pertaining to the case. In a jury trial, the judge is known as the "trier of law" and the jury as the "trier of fact." The judge instructs the jury on points of law, the jury decides the verdict based on the judge's instructions and on the evidence or facts presented, and the judge sentences the convicted person. In a non-jury trial, it is the judge who decides on the guilt or innocence of the accused and then passes sentence.

A **justice of the peace** has less authority than a judge but can perform a number of judicial functions, especially in the preliminary stages of a case. A justice of the peace can issue arrest or search warrants and hear bail applications. In some jurisdictions, this court official can hear cases involving infractions of municipal bylaws and certain provincial statutes, such as the *Highway Traffic Act*.

judge: the court official appointed to try cases in a court of law and to sentence convicted persons

justice of the peace: a court official who has less authority than a judge but can issue warrants and perform other judicial functions

The Defence

The person charged with a crime is called the **accused (or defendant).** Defendants may represent themselves at trial, but since the law is so complex, it is usually advisable for defendants to seek trained legal assistance. Duty counsel, "on duty" in a police station or courtroom, is a lawyer hired through

accused (or defendant): in criminal court, the person charged with committing a criminal offence

duty counsel: a lawyer on duty in a courtroom or police station to give free legal advice to persons just arrested or brought before the court

defence counsel: the lawyer who defends an accused person on trial

the legal aid system of the province. **Duty counsel** provides free legal advice to a person being charged or interrogated at the police station or appearing in Provincial Court for the first time. This lawyer can advise clients of the right to plead guilty or not guilty and can help them apply for bail or seek an adjournment (a postponement). Sometimes a duty counsel can represent clients when they plead guilty or appear at a sentencing hearing.

The **defence counsel** is the lawyer who represents the interests of the accused. If the accused pleads not guilty, the defence counsel will try to show that there exists a reasonable doubt of the defendant's guilt. If the accused pleads guilty or is found guilty after trial, the defence counsel will recommend an appropriate sentence to the judge. The Crown will also make a sentencing recommendation, one that often differs substantially from that of the defence. If both attorneys agree on an appropriate sentence, they will present a joint submission to the judge. After hearing the recommendations, the judge will make the decision.

The Prosecution

Crown attorney (or prosecutor): the lawyer representing the government, responsible for instituting legal proceedings against the accused

evidence: information that tends to prove or disprove the elements of an offence

The **Crown attorney (or prosecutor)** is the lawyer representing the government's interests in investigating and punishing criminal offences to ensure society's safety. The prosecutor must prepare the government's case by researching the law, assembling the evidence for trial, reviewing exhibits, and taking statements from witnesses. In 1955, the Supreme Court of Canada emphasized that the role of the prosecutor is not necessarily to obtain a conviction but to bring forward credible evidence of a crime. **Evidence** is information that tends to prove or disprove the elements of an offence. An important source of the Crown's evidence is the testimony of the arresting officer and other witnesses. Often the prosecutor submits physical evidence, which might include fingerprints, a weapon, or articles of clothing belonging to the victim or the accused.

Other Court Personnel

court clerk: the court official who assists the judge

court reporter: the court official who records everything said in court during a trial

transcript: a typed record of everything said in court during a trial

court security officer: the court official who maintains security in the courtroom

sheriff: the court official responsible for jury management

bailiff: the court official who assists the sheriff

The **court clerk** assists the judge by keeping a record of the trial exhibits, administering oaths, and announcing the beginning or end of the court session. Using an electronic monitoring system, the **court reporter** records verbatim everything that has been said during the trial. After the trial, the court reporter can produce a transcript of the trial if one is required. A **transcript** is a typed record of everything that was said in court. In British Columbia, the positions of court clerk and court reporter are combined.

The **court security officer** handles accused persons who are in custody and helps maintain security in the courtroom. The **sheriff** is usually responsible for jury management; that is, the sheriff will summon, pay, seclude, and guard jurors as required. A **bailiff** is the court official who assists a sheriff. In British Columbia, the sheriff also performs the duties of the court security officer and the bailiff.

R. v. White (1998), 131 C.C.C. (3d) 463 (Alta. C.A.)

CASE

After a jury found White guilty of fraud in 1983, he fled prior to sentencing. In 1994, White was discovered living illegally in the United States. He went to court to stop his extradition from the U.S. and was not returned to Canada until 1996. White then raised a series of objections to being sentenced and did not launch an appeal until approximately 14 years after his conviction. He appealed on the basis that the court reporter's shorthand and the tape recording from his trial were no longer available, so a transcript of the trial could not be produced. (Court reporters are permitted to discard their shorthand notes and tapes after 10 years if no appeal has been filed.)

In 1998, the Alberta Court of Appeal dismissed White's appeal of his conviction. The Court noted that the loss of the tapes from the earlier trial were not the result of any misconduct on the part of the Crown. Rather, White was the author of his own misfortune by fleeing the country before sentencing and by waiting 14 years to file his appeal.

1. What was the basis of the defendant's appeal?
2. Why did the Court of Appeal dismiss the defendant's appeal?

The Witnesses

Witnesses give evidence, under oath, concerning their knowledge of the circumstances surrounding a crime. The prosecutor or defence counsel may compel a witness to appear in court by issuing a **subpoena,** a court order requiring the witness to appear on a certain date to give evidence. If the witness fails to appear on the specified date, he or she can be held in contempt of court for obstructing the course of justice. If found guilty of contempt (disobeying the court's authority), a witness may be fined a maximum of $100 and/or imprisoned for up to 90 days.

During the trial, witnesses called to testify must take an oath on the Bible or make a solemn affirmation to tell the truth. Witnesses commit **perjury** if they knowingly make false statements in court while giving evidence under oath or affirmation. Perjury is a serious crime. The *Criminal Code* treats it as an indictable offence with a maximum penalty of 14 years' imprisonment.

witnesses: persons who give evidence while under oath in a court of law

subpoena: a court order requiring the witness to appear in court on a certain date to give evidence

perjury: knowingly making false statements in court while giving evidence under oath or affirmation

The Jury

In a criminal trial, a **jury** is a group of 12 men and women, chosen by the Crown and defence counsel from a pool of ordinary citizens in the community the court is located in. The jurors listen to the trial, examine the evidence, and follow the judge's instructions about the law. At the end of the trial, they withdraw to the jury room to deliberate, considering all the evidence and deciding together whether the accused is guilty or not guilty. As mentioned previously, to convict in a criminal trial, the jurors must find the defendant guilty beyond a reasonable doubt. Their decision must be unanimous.

jury: in a criminal trial, a group of 12 people who decide whether the accused is guilty or not guilty

Building Your Understanding

1. List three judicial functions performed by the justice of the peace.
2. Explain the connection between the role of duty counsel and the principles of fundamental justice. Be specific.
3. Whom do Crown attorneys represent? Describe three activities they perform to prepare their cases.
4. What are the functions of the court clerk and court reporter?
5. List what you believe are three characteristics of a good witness.
6. What is required for a conviction in a criminal trial?

THE ROLE OF THE JURY

Fast Fact
The word *jury* is derived from the French word *jurer,* which means "to swear an oath."

Juries are a fundamental part of the Canadian justice system. For a criminal trial, 12 people are chosen at random to decide the fate of a human being. These people are then placed in the unfamiliar setting of a courtroom, where they are required to listen to and observe the unfolding of a real-life drama. Afterward, they deliberate in secret and return a verdict for which they are not required to give any reasons—not an easy task and one laden with awesome responsibility.

This section will describe jury members' qualifications for this crucial role as well as the process of selecting a jury.

Qualifications

"Trial by jury is the most transcendent privilege which any subject can enjoy."

— Sir William Blackstone, famous English jurist

Each province passes its own legislation to establish the qualifications of potential jurors. Usually, to be eligible for jury duty the individual must be a Canadian citizen 18 years of age or older and a resident of the province for at least one year. In most cases, publicly elected politicians and people working in the justice system, such as lawyers, prison guards, police officers, and probation officers, cannot serve as jurors.

Sometimes people called to serve as jurors want to be exempted from jury duty due to religious or health issues. Some people may fear serious financial hardship since jurors are unable to work during a trial. Exemptions are usually available to those who have served on a jury within the past two years. Anyone wishing to be excused from jury duty may apply to the sheriff.

Jury Selection

jury panel: the large group of randomly selected citizens from which jury members are chosen

arraignment: the first stage of a criminal trial in which the court clerk reads the charge and the defendant enters a plea

Potential jurors are selected randomly from electoral polling lists; these lists represent a wide cross-section of citizens in the community. A group of potential jurors is called a **jury panel.** The accused is brought in front of the judge and jury panel for **arraignment** to enter a plea of guilty or not guilty. If the plea is not guilty, the Crown and defence attorneys will select jurors from the jury panel under the judge's supervision. The selection process includes the six steps listed on the following pages:

R. v. Pietrangelo (2001), 152 C.C.C. (3d) 475 (Ont. C.A.)

BACKGROUND Pietrangelo was charged with attempted murder and assault with a weapon. The accused represented himself at trial. At the outset of the trial, Pietrangelo indicated that he wished to challenge potential jurors for cause—for partiality due to pre-trial publicity, which had been substantial because the victim was the local mayor. At the suggestion of the Crown, instead of allowing the accused to challenge for cause, the trial judge addressed the entire jury panel under s. 632(c) of the *Criminal Code* and asked whether any potential jurors might have been influenced by pre-trial publicity. A number of jurors came forward and were excused on this basis. Pietrangelo was not allowed to challenge for cause those remaining on the panel regarding the question of bias.

LEGAL QUESTION Did the trial judge err in refusing Pietrangelo the opportunity to challenge prospective jurors for cause?

DECISION The Court of Appeal ruled that the trial judge did make a mistake in law by refusing the defendant's request to challenge potential jurors for cause. The trial judge's statutory power under s. 632(c) cannot prevent the accused from making his or her own challenge for cause where proper grounds exist, as they did in this case. This type of error warranted a new trial.

LEGAL SIGNIFICANCE The ruling by the Court of Appeal confirmed that when there is sufficient basis in law for a challenge for cause, the defendant must be allowed to make such a challenge to potential jurors.

ANALYSIS

1. Why did Pietrangelo want to challenge for cause instead of making peremptory challenges?
2. Given the pre-trial publicity associated with this case, do you think it was possible to find 12 impartial jurors in the community where the alleged offence took place? Why or why not?

1. The names of the people on the jury panel are written on cards that are put into a box and selected at random. Selected names are read aloud to the court.
2. The person whose name has been chosen goes to the front of the court and faces the accused.
3. Both the Crown and defence may object to a potential juror by challenging this individual.
4. Either counsel may make a **challenge for cause** if they believe that the prospective juror a) has already formed an opinion on the case; b) is physically unable to perform the duties of a juror; or c) has been convicted of a serious offence. Each side is allowed to make an unlimited number of challenges for cause.

challenge for cause: the right of the Crown or defence to exclude someone from a jury for a particular reason

peremptory challenge: the right of the Crown or the defence to exclude someone from a jury without providing a reason

Consider This
The peremptory challenge is one way for the accused to exert some control over the make-up of the jury. Should the number of peremptory challenges for all criminal offences be increased? Should the defence be allowed more peremptory challenges than the Crown? Explain.

5. After a potential juror is accepted as suitable and impartial, the Crown and defence still have the chance to reject this person through the use of peremptory challenges. A **peremptory challenge** is one that requires no reason for eliminating a potential juror from jury duty. A criminal trial is an adversarial process, with the accused on one side and the state or government on the other. Clearly, the state is the more powerful party. Peremptory challenges were developed as a way of granting the accused some control over the adversarial process and against the powers of the state. In effect, a peremptory challenge allows the accused to say, "I don't want that person deciding my case." In serious cases, such as first-degree murder or treason, each side may use 20 of these challenges. In less serious cases in which the accused may be sentenced to more than five years in prison, 12 peremptory challenges are permitted; where the sentence is less than five years, 4 such challenges are allowed.

6. When the selection process is completed, the 12 jurors take the juror's oath: "I swear to well and truly try and true Deliverance make between our sovereign lady the Queen and the accused at the bar, whom I have in charge, and a true verdict give, according to the evidence, so help me God."

Building Your Understanding

1. What qualifications must a juror have? Do you think that any other qualifications should be required? Explain.
2. List three reasons a person may be exempted from jury duty.
3. What does it mean when a prospective juror is challenged for cause? What principle of fundamental justice is involved?
4. What is a peremptory challenge, and why is it an important right?

THE CRIMINAL TRIAL PROCESS

As mentioned earlier, a criminal trial is an adversarial process that pits the Crown against the accused. Section 11(d) of the *Charter of Rights and Freedoms* states that each person charged with an offence is to be "presumed innocent until proven guilty according to law." This presumption of innocence is one of Canada's most fundamental legal principles, and it places the burden of proof squarely on the Crown. The **burden of proof** means that the Crown has the obligation to prove the guilt of the accused; it is not up to the accused to demonstrate innocence. According to a long-standing tradition of common law, proof of guilt must be beyond a reasonable doubt.

burden of proof: the Crown's obligation to prove the guilt of the accused beyond a reasonable doubt

The trial begins with the judge explaining the jury's role as the trier of facts. Then the judge asks the 12 jurors to select a foreperson who will represent them and communicate with the judge. The foreperson will also lead the other jurors through their deliberations and, at the trial's conclusion, will inform the court of their verdict.

The Crown's Opening Statement

The Crown presents its case before the defence because it has the burden of proof, so the trial always begins with an opening statement by the Crown. This statement identifies the offence committed, summarizes the evidence against the accused, and outlines the way the Crown will present its case. The jury is not meant to consider the opening statement as evidence; the Crown will introduce evidence only after its opening statement is complete. Most of the evidence in a criminal trial is presented through witnesses.

Examination of Witnesses

The first examination of a witness is called a **direct examination,** or an examination-in-chief. The Crown will ask each witness to tell what he or she observed about the crime. After the direct examination, defence counsel may cross-examine the witness. The purpose of a **cross-examination** is to test the accuracy of the evidence or to convince the jury that there are contradictions in the witness's testimony that weaken the Crown's case.

direct examination: the first questioning of a witness to determine what he or she observed about the crime

cross-examination: the second questioning of a witness to test the accuracy of the testimony; performed by the opposing attorney

The Defence Responds

When the Crown has finished calling its witnesses, the defence may bring a **motion for dismissal** if counsel believes that the Crown has failed to prove guilt beyond a reasonable doubt. As trier of the law, the judge may agree with the defence and will withdraw the case from the jury to enter a **directed verdict** of not guilty.

If the judge does not dismiss the charges, and the accused pleads not guilty, the trial must continue. The defence begins by summarizing its case in an opening statement. The defence may choose to call witnesses to refute testimony provided by the Crown's witnesses or to show reasonable doubt. The procedure of direct examination (this time by the defence) and cross-examination (this time by the Crown) is repeated. The defendant may choose to testify on his or her own behalf but, according to s. 11(c) of the *Charter of Rights and Freedoms,* "cannot be compelled to be a witness."

After the defence has presented all its evidence, the Crown has the opportunity to **rebut,** or contradict, any new evidence the defence has introduced. Defence counsel can then present further evidence for a **surrebuttal,** a contradiction of the Crown's rebuttal.

motion for dismissal: a request by defence counsel that the judge dismiss the charges against the defendant

directed verdict: a decision by the judge to withdraw the case from the jury and enter a verdict of not guilty

rebut: to contradict evidence introduced by the opposing side

surrebuttal: a reply to the opposing side's rebuttal

The Rules of Evidence

During the trial, either the Crown or the defence may object to questions asked by the opposing attorney or to answers provided by witnesses. When an objection is made, the judge rules on whether the evidence in question is "admissible," that is, whether it may be accepted by the court. Following are some of the most common grounds for objection in a criminal trial.

Leading Questions

A leading question suggests to the witness a particular answer. During direct examination, it is generally not permitted to ask a witness a leading question unless it involves a fairly unobjectionable matter, such as establishing the age of a witness (e.g., "You are 21 years old, aren't you?"). But concerning the more contentious issues of a direct examination, Crown or defence counsel would not be allowed to ask a question such as, "Wasn't it Tom you saw holding the knife and stabbing Al?" The question would have to be reworded; for instance, "What did you see Tom do to Al?" This question does not suggest an answer but asks for an explanation of what occurred.

In cross-examination, counsel would be allowed to ask a leading question as long as it pertained to previous testimony: "You want this court to believe you saw Tom stabbing Al?" This question refers to a fact—the witness saw Tom stabbing Al—a fact that was already established in the direct examination.

Hearsay Statements

An attorney may ask a witness only about what the witness saw or experienced first-hand, not about something he or she heard from a third party. For example, if a witness said, "Ann told me that she saw Tom stab Al with a knife," this statement would be **hearsay evidence**, and it would not be admissible in court.

hearsay evidence: evidence given by a witness based on information received from someone else rather than personal knowledge

Opinion Statements

Defence counsel or the Crown cannot ask a witness to give an opinion about a matter that goes beyond common knowledge unless the witness is a recognized expert in the field. For example, any eyewitness can give an opinion about the car at the crime scene. But only an expert—for instance, a car mechanic who was allowed to examine the car—could give an opinion about the condition of the car's brakes.

Immaterial or Irrelevant Questions

Consider This

Immaterial questions are usually considered inadmissible. Why do you think an attorney might ask such a question during a trial?

An immaterial or irrelevant question has no connection with the matter at hand; as a result, it is considered inadmissible. For example, in a murder trial, if defence counsel asks the investigating officer a question about his personal life, the question may be dismissed as irrelevant if it has no bearing on the case.

Non-Responsive Answers

Sometimes the Crown or defence counsel will question a witness and receive a reply that does not really answer the question. This is called a non-responsive answer. When this happens, counsel may ask the judge to direct the witness to answer the question properly.

Types of Evidence

As noted previously, evidence is the information that will prove or disprove disputed facts presented in a court of law. All evidence must be "material"—it must be important and relevant to the case in question. Evidence is considered relevant if it has probative value, that is, if it tends to make more or less probable a certain fact pertaining to the guilt or innocence of the accused.

Direct Evidence

Direct evidence is the testimony given by a witness to prove an alleged fact. The most common type is an eyewitness account of a crime. For example, in a robbery case, Beatrice's testimony that she saw Samir assault Dawn and steal her purse would constitute direct evidence. But even direct evidence can be challenged. Samir's lawyer might rebut the evidence by proving that Beatrice has poor vision and left her glasses home on the day in question.

direct evidence: testimony given by a witness to prove an alleged fact

---

CASE

R. v. Menard (1996), 29 O.R. (3d) 772 (Ont. C.A.)

The victim was a part-time taxi driver in Montreal. On April 12, 1991, his taxi was discovered submerged in the Madawaska River, near Arnprior, Ontario. His body was not found until June 9, 1991, when it was discovered off the side of a road just outside Arnprior. An autopsy revealed that he had been killed by multiple stab wounds to the back. Wounds to several ribs indicated a substantial use of force.

On the same day the victim disappeared, a man noticed a taxi being driven toward the Madawaska River. When he ran to the river, he saw the taxi sinking into the water. He turned and saw Menard with a duffle bag and some clothing. He called the police, and Constable Nicholas of the Ontario Provincial Police arrived at the scene. Nicholas asked Menard what had happened. Menard replied that he had been hitchhiking and was picked up by a man named Phil who stopped the car and told him to get out. Phil then drove the car into the river and ran away toward the highway.

More police arrived and examined the area where the car had entered the water. They found only one set of footprints. On top of the hill they discovered a bundle of wet clothing with stains of blood. After the victim was found and the car was removed from the water, the bloodstains on the driver's seat and on the floor plus the blood on the wet clothes were matched to the victim's blood. All the blood samples were consistent with the victim's blood type, which is shared by less than 1 percent of the population. Contact staining consistent with the victim's blood type was also found on Menard's jeans. A forensic geologist testified that soil samples taken from the area where the victim's body was found were consistent with samples found on Menard's boots.

A jury convicted Menard of second-degree murder. His appeals to the Ontario Court of Appeal and the Supreme Court of Canada were dismissed.

1. Categorize the Crown's evidence under the headings Eyewitness Evidence, Physical Evidence, and Expert Witness Evidence.
2. Given that the victim suffered multiple stab wounds, what valuable piece of evidence is missing from the case summary?
3. Put yourself in the position of Menard's lawyer. How would you challenge the type of evidence presented?

Circumstantial Evidence

circumstantial evidence: indirect evidence that leads to a reasonable inference of the defendant's guilt

If there is no one to provide eyewitness testimony, the offence may be proven by **circumstantial evidence.** Suppose no one saw Samir assault Dawn and take her purse, but the investigating officer found the purse in a nearby trash can and it was covered with Samir's fingerprints. Also, a witness testifies that he saw Samir in the area at the approximate time the crime took place. This testimony might allow the judge or jury to infer, or conclude from the evidence, that Samir robbed Dawn.

Circumstantial evidence is generally admissible in court unless the connection between the evidence and the inference is too weak to help decide the case. In determining the admissibility of a piece of evidence, the judge must be convinced that the defendant's guilt is one of the conclusions that could be drawn from the evidence.

Character Evidence

character evidence: evidence used to establish the likelihood that the defendant is the type of person who either would or would not commit a certain offence

Character evidence establishes the likelihood that the defendant is the type of person who either would or would not commit a certain offence. Generally, the Crown is not allowed to attack the defendant's character. This rule guards against the jury's tendency to infer that because the defendant has a "bad character," he or she must be guilty. Defence counsel, on the other hand, is permitted to introduce evidence of the defendant's *good* character to convince the jury that he or she is *not* the type of person who would have committed the offence. Once defence counsel introduces this type of evidence, however, the Crown is allowed to rebut it by presenting contradictory evidence.

The Crown *is* allowed to introduce evidence of the defendant's past convictions. Such evidence is not to be used for the sake of attacking the defendant's character but only for testing the defendant's credibility, that is, the likelihood of whether he or she is telling the truth.

Electronic Surveillance

electronic surveillance: the use of any electronic device to overhear or record communications between two or more people

wiretapping: the interception of telephone communications

bugging: recording a speaker's oral communication by using an electronic device

Technological advances have allowed the police and other law enforcement agencies to benefit from highly sophisticated surveillance devices. **Electronic surveillance** is the use of any electronic device to overhear or record communications between two or more people. Wiretapping and bugging are two of the most common methods of electronic surveillance.

Wiretapping is the interception of telephone communications, generally at a point some distance away from the target premises. **Bugging** is the recording of a speaker's oral communication by means of an electronic device that overhears, broadcasts, or records that communication. Bugging devices may be installed in cars or buildings and are very effective in recording conversations that take place within range of the device. Generally, any evidence obtained by wiretapping or bugging is admissible in court only if the interception is authorized beforehand by a judge. Exceptions occur in cases where a police officer believes the situation is an emergency or where the interception is necessary to prevent a violent act.

Polygraph Tests

A polygraph or "lie detector" is a machine that allows a skilled examiner to detect physical signs that indicate deception on the part of the person being tested. The machine measures changes in pulse, respiration, and blood pressure. The examiner begins the test by asking the person control questions that have been designed to elicit answers that the examiner knows are untrue. The examiner carefully observes the person's physical reaction when making these untruthful responses and then observes whether the same reactions take place when this person is asked about the criminal charges in question.

The main weakness of a polygraph test is that its accuracy depends on the competence of the examiner. Over time, even a highly skilled examiner will have an accuracy rate of less than 100 percent. For this reason, the *results* of a polygraph test are not admissible evidence for determining whether a defendant is lying or telling the truth about a particular crime. However, the Crown may introduce as evidence anything the defendant *says* during the course of the exam.

Fast Fact
An average polygraph test lasts 2–3 hours. This period includes a 45–90 minute pretest interview, during which all the questions that will be asked during the actual test are reviewed.

Voir Dire

A **voir dire** is a mini-trial that takes place during the trial. The jurors are escorted from the courtroom and asked to wait in the jury room. Then the judge, the Crown, and the defence discuss the issue that is keeping the trial from moving forward, such as whether a particular piece of evidence is admissible. One of the most common reasons for a *voir dire* is to determine whether a defendant's confession was given voluntarily. In this situation, the

voir dire: a mini-trial in which jurors are excluded while the admissibility of evidence is discussed

Figure 7.8 **From the point of view of the accused, what are some of the pros and cons for taking a polygraph test?**

Fast Fact
The term *voir dire* comes from Old French, meaning "to speak the truth."

defendant or other witnesses may be called to testify. After hearing arguments from both sides, the judge will decide whether the evidence is admissible in whole, in part, or not at all. Then the jurors are summoned back into the courtroom, and the trial resumes.

CASE: *Regina v. Gilling* (1997), 34 O.R. (3d) 392 (Ont. C.A.)

1. Explain why the judge found it necessary to hold a *voir dire* during the trial.
2. Why was the father's videotaped statement considered hearsay evidence?
3. Why did the Court of Appeal overturn the judge's verdict?

Gilling was charged with second-degree murder for slashing the victim's throat. Gilling's father took him to the police station where the father gave a videotaped statement that told of a conversation he had had with his son. He said his son told him that he had slashed the victim to ward off a sexual assault. The father also said that he was not sure when the accused arrived at his house. At trial, the father recanted his earlier statement, denying that Gilling had admitted committing the murder. He also stated that he was certain his son had arrived at his house the day before the murder.

The trial judge held a *voir dire* to determine the admissibility of the father's earlier, videotaped statement. The defence objected to the statement on the grounds that it was hearsay evidence. After ruling the statement admissible, the judge informed the jury that he had carefully considered the admissibility of the statement according to a Supreme Court ruling. He said he had found the videotaped statement sufficiently reliable to allow it to be entered as evidence.

The accused was convicted and appealed to the Ontario Court of Appeal. The higher court overturned the conviction, stating that the judge's remarks on the reliability of the father's videotaped statement may have led the jury to believe that the judge thought the statement should be regarded as true.

Summary of the Case

After all the testimony has been given, each counsel presents a summary of the case in the form of closing arguments. If the defence called witnesses during the trial, then defence counsel closes first. If not, the Crown closes first.

The Crown will attempt to show that the defendant's guilt has been proven beyond a reasonable doubt. The defence will try to show that the Crown has failed to establish *mens rea* or *actus reus*, thereby demonstrating that a reasonable doubt does exist. The closing arguments are not to be considered as evidence, but are intended to help the jurors better understand the issues involved in the case.

Charge to the Jury

charge to the jury: the judge's explanation to the jurors of how the law applies to the case before them

After the summaries by opposing counsel, the judge gives a **charge to the jury**—an explanation of the law and instructions on how the law applies to the case before them. The judge will also advise the jurors on how to consider the evidence and how to return a verdict in accordance with the law. The judge must be very careful in making the charge to the jury. If the charge is deficient in any way, it may form the basis for an appeal of the verdict. In fact, a deficient charge is the most common basis for a successful appeal. After the charge has been given, the sheriff escorts the jurors to the jury room. There the jury members will deliberate on their verdict.

As explained earlier, it is the judge's role to decide on matters of law and the jury's task to decide on matters of fact. While the judge rules on what evidence is admissible, the jury decides on what evidence is believable. If the jurors believe the accused, or if they do not know whom to believe, they must acquit. If they do not believe the accused but are left with a reasonable doubt regarding the defendant's guilt, the jury is obliged by law to return a verdict of not guilty.

Judges to receive plain-language guidelines

SASKATOON — Judges across Canada will soon be given standard templates in plain, understandable language to use when giving instructions to juries about how to reach verdicts on everything from rape to murder.

Supreme Court of Canada Chief Justice Beverley McLachlin, who outlined the national initiative yesterday, described it as "one of the most far-reaching law reform projects ever completed in this country."

The templates, which will include hundreds of prefabricated charges to juries, are being created to ensure common, user-friendly standards across the country and reduce appeals by losing lawyers who want to challenge a judge's explanation to a jury.

The Canadian Judicial Council, the body that oversees the country's federally appointed judges, has spent the past two years crafting the manual. It is expected to be dispersed across the country to all trial judges, along with accompanying training, in the next year or so.

Madam Justice McLachlin, who is chairwoman of the council, said the national standards will probably be tested on the public before they come into force. "It crystallizes those legal principles in an understandable, clear form that we hope members of the jury could understand," she told reporters at the annual meeting of the Canadian Bar Association.

Although some U.S. states have uniform standards, the Canadian initiative is believed to be one of the first national programs in the world. Madam Justice McLachlin, however, stressed that the instructions will serve as guidelines and will not be binding on judges.

"This does not eliminate the need for a judge to very carefully consider his or her comments and tailor them to the facts and legal issues of a particular case, but what it does is say on certain types of offences, 'This is a summary of the legal principles that you have to tell a jury,'" she said.

The Supreme Court has dealt in recent years with numerous appeals challenging judges' instructions to juries. Some of the templates will be modelled on the high court's guidelines governing such legal tenets as reasonable doubt.

SOURCE: Janice Tibbets, *The National Post/Southam News*, August 13, 2001, A6.

1. Why did the Canadian Judicial Council think that templates for charges to juries would be useful?
2. List three advantages these templates would offer a criminal court judge.
3. When using templates, what should judges do to overcome the pitfall that "one size fits all"?

Figure 7.9 This courtroom sketch shows a judge charging a jury before they leave to deliberate. How might a deficient charge form the basis of an appeal?

Fast Fact
As early as 1367, a recorded case in England noted that unanimity was necessary for a jury's verdict to be valid.

hung jury: a jury that cannot reach a unanimous verdict and is consequently dismissed from the case

The Verdict

Once the verdict has been reached, it is read in open court. Both the Crown and the defence have the right to ask that the jury be polled—each jury member must stand and confirm his or her agreement with the verdict. A jury's verdict must be unanimous. A jury that cannot reach a unanimous decision is called a **hung jury.** In this situation, the jury is discharged, and a new jury is selected to try the case again.

Appeals

No legal system is free from error. For this reason, the right to appeal is an important safeguard in Canada's adversarial system. Usually, a notice of appeal must be filed within a short period of time, in most cases within 30 days. The appeal is then heard in an appeals court, which has the authority to review the decision and make one of the following rulings: a) to affirm the lower court's decision; b) to reverse the lower court's decision; or c) to order a new trial.

In a criminal case, either the defence or the Crown can appeal a decision it considers improper. Either side can also appeal the sentence given to a defendant found guilty. For example, an accused may ask the appeals court to reduce the sentence, or the prosecution may ask to have the sentence increased. The side that files the appeal is called the **appellant;** the side that responds to the appeal is called the **respondent.**

appellant: the party that files an appeal

respondent: the party that responds to an appeal

An appeal is generally heard by a panel of three or five judges. Witnesses do not usually testify again. Instead, the attorneys use the trial transcript, exhibits from the trial, and legal arguments prepared for the appeal. The appeals court

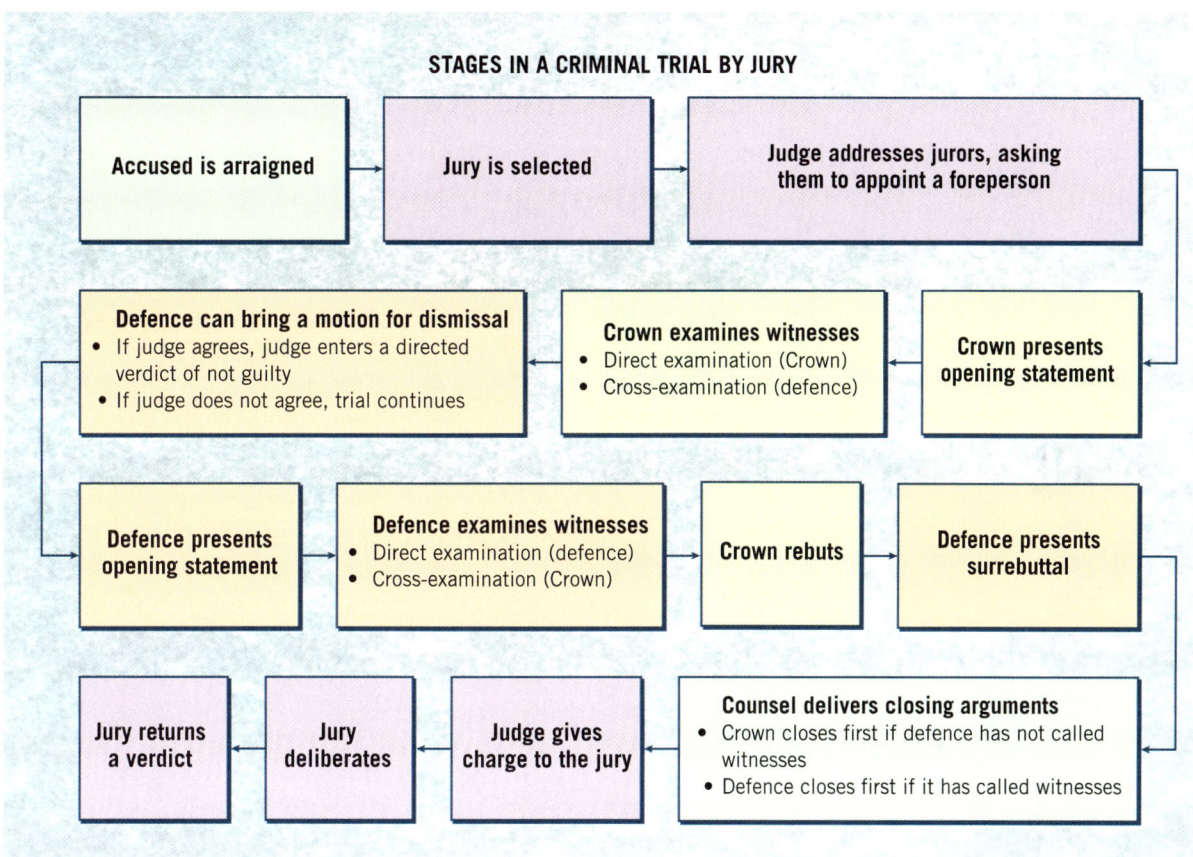

Figure 7.10 This flow chart refers to a trial by jury. What would it look like for a case tried by a judge alone?

then decides whether any errors in law have been made. The court's verdict does not have to be unanimous; a majority decision is sufficient. The majority usually explains its decision in writing. Dissenting judges can also issue written opinions explaining why they did not hold with the majority.

Building Your Understanding

1. Distinguish between a direct examination and a cross-examination.
2. List three grounds for objection and briefly explain each.
3. Under what circumstances may leading questions be asked?
4. When may a witness offer an opinion?
5. Explain the difference between direct and circumstantial evidence, and provide an example of each.
6. When is circumstantial evidence admissible?
7. Define character evidence. When is it admissible? Why might counsel use character evidence as testimony for the defence?
8. Why is it necessary to obtain a judge's authorization for electronic interception or surveillance?
9. What is the main weakness of a polygraph test?
10. List three possible decisions the higher court may make after hearing an appeal.

LOOKING BACK

Reviewing Your Vocabulary

accused (or defendant) *p. 169*
appeal *p. 164*
appellant *p. 182*
arraignment *p. 172*
bailiff *p. 170*
beyond a reasonable doubt *p. 168*
bugging *p. 178*
burden of proof *p. 174*
challenge for cause *p. 173*
character evidence *p. 178*
charge to the jury *p. 180*
circumstantial evidence *p. 178*
court clerk *p. 170*
court of appeal *p. 165*
court reporter *p. 170*
court security officer *p. 170*
cross-examination *p. 175*

Crown attorney (or prosecutor) *p. 170*
defence counsel *p. 170*
direct evidence *p. 177*
direct examination *p. 175*
directed verdict *p. 175*
duty counsel *p. 170*
electronic surveillance *p. 178*
evidence *p. 170*
Federal Court of Canada *p. 166*
hearsay evidence *p. 176*
hung jury *p. 182*
judge *p. 169*
jury *p. 171*
jury panel *p. 172*
justice of the peace *p. 169*
leave *p. 167*

motion for dismissal *p. 175*
peremptory challenge *p. 174*
perjury *p. 171*
preliminary hearing *p. 164*
Provincial Court *p. 163*
rebut *p. 175*
respondent *p. 182*
sheriff *p. 170*
subpoena *p. 171*
Superior Court of the province *p. 165*
Supreme Court of Canada *p. 166*
surrebuttal *p. 175*
transcript *p. 170*
voir dire *p. 179*
wiretapping *p. 178*
witnesses *p. 171*

Quick Quiz

1. Choose the appropriate term from the vocabulary list above to complete the following statements:
   a) A _____ is the exclusion of a prospective juror from jury duty for no reason.
   b) The concept of _____ means that the Crown must prove the offence beyond a reasonable doubt.
   c) _____ occurs when the witness lies in court under oath.
   d) A _____ is a court order requiring the witness to give evidence in court.
   e) A _____ occurs when the Crown or defence attorneys question their own witnesses for the first time.
   f) A _____ is held to determine whether there is sufficient evidence to put the accused on trial.
   g) The _____ is the person responsible for managing the jury.
   h) The _____ hears disputes regarding trademarks and patents.
   i) The _____ is the highest trial and appeals court of the province.
   j) A _____ records verbatim everything said during a trial.
   k) _____ is the permission required to appeal a case from a lower court to a higher court.

Checking Your Knowledge

2. Create a diagram of your own to illustrate the Canadian court structure and avenues of appeal, using symbols or illustrations if you wish.
3. List any five participants in the criminal trial process and briefly explain the role of each.
4. Summarize the steps in selecting a jury for a criminal trial.

5. When is the Crown allowed to introduce evidence of the defendant's past convictions?
6. Who returns a directed verdict, the judge or the jury?

Developing Your Thinking and Inquiry Skills

7. By tradition, the justices appointed by the federal government represent different regions of Canada. Would it be better to appoint justices based on merit regardless of region? Discuss.
8. What is the chief advantage to having an odd number of judges on an appeal panel?
9. Do you think that Canadian jurors should be allowed to interrupt a trial and ask for clarification of the evidence at any stage of the trial? Discuss.

Communicating Your Ideas

10. Select a case that appears in your local newspaper, and keep a daily log of events as they occur. Prepare a display, showing dates and using newspaper articles and photos to illustrate the various stages of the trial.
11. As a class, choose any case from Chapter 6 or 7, and role-play a mock jury selection for that trial. Pick your roles—judge, defendant, Crown attorney, defence counsel, and members of the jury panel. Each potential juror will create a fictional profile by completing a form with the following information: name, age, occupation, and type of dwelling. These forms will be arranged alphabetically and will be made available to counsel. Follow the procedure for jury selection as outlined in the chapter and apply the guidelines for peremptory challenges. After the jurors have been selected, both sides will share their reasons for accepting or rejecting various members of the panel.

Putting It All Together

12. Imagine that you have been selected as a potential juror in a murder trial. Answer the following questions pertaining to the case:
    a) What is the name of the court that would hear the murder case?
    b) Both the Crown and defence counsel decide to challenge you as a potential juror. Explain the two types of challenges they may use.
    c) You are accepted on the jury. Soon after the trial begins, you are escorted to the jury room while the admissibility of a piece of evidence is being debated in the courtroom. What is this process called? Why do you think you are not allowed to listen to the debate?
    d) During the trial, you may hear some objections stating that certain evidence or testimony violates the rules of evidence and is, therefore, inadmissible. List some objections you may hear during the trial, and provide an example of each.
    e) Because the defence has called witnesses to the stand, the Crown is the last to give closing arguments. Do you think it matters if the defence or Crown closes last? Discuss.
    f) What would happen if, during deliberation, you could not reach a unanimous decision?
    g) If the murder trial is appealed, what court will hear the appeal? Identify reasons for appealing the verdict in a murder trial.
    h) Under what circumstances might this case be granted leave to appeal to the Supreme Court of Canada?

CASES

R. v. *Williams* (1998), 40 O.R. (3d) 301 (Ont. C.A.)

Williams was the passenger in a car driven by a Mr. Snieg who was stopped by Canada Customs officials while seeking entry into Canada from Niagara Falls, New York. Snieg told the customs officer that both he and Williams lived in Bowmanville, Ontario, and had been away for a day and a half in Athens, Georgia. Williams simply nodded his head to indicate he had nothing to declare.

Customs officers found seven bags of cocaine concealed inside the car's rear speaker and under the front dashboard. The customs officer testified that the screws for the speaker box and the dashboard were all loose and easily removed. Officers also found a receipt from New York in Williams's wallet dated one day before the seizure of the cocaine.

Both Snieg and Williams were charged with importing a narcotic, and Snieg alone was charged with possession for the purposes of trafficking. Neither defendant testified, and the defence did not call any witnesses. Williams's counsel submitted to the jury that the Crown had not proven that Williams knew there was cocaine in the vehicle. The jury returned a verdict of guilty on the one count against Williams and on both counts against Snieg.

Williams appealed his verdict on the grounds that the trial judge erred in his charge to the jury by failing to instruct them that "mere passive acquiescence" on the part of the accused to transportation of drugs was not sufficient to support a conviction. The Court of Appeal accepted this argument, set aside the conviction, and ordered a new trial for Williams.

1. Why do you think the jury convicted Williams of importing a narcotic? What was the *actus reus* for this offence? What was the *mens rea*?
2. Explain the grounds for Williams's successful appeal. Discuss whether his grounds for appeal refer to the *actus reus* or the *mens rea* of the crime.

R. v. *Koh* (1998), 131 C.C.C. (3d) 257 (Ont. C.A.)

Koh, Lu, and Lim were charged with conspiracy to import heroin, conspiracy to traffic in a narcotic, and possession of a narcotic for the purposes of trafficking. The defence wished to challenge potential jurors by asking, "Would the fact that the accused were persons of Chinese origin and visitors from Singapore affect your ability to judge the evidence fairly and without prejudice?" The trial judge refused to permit a challenge for cause on these grounds. The three were convicted on September 26, 1996, and received life sentences for one or more of the counts. They appealed their conviction and the sentences.

The Court of Appeal found that the trial judge made an error in law by drawing a distinction between racial prejudice in a social setting and prejudice in a judicial setting. The threshold test is whether there exists a realistic potential or possibility of partiality. The Court of Appeal noted that the fact of racism against visible minorities is a notorious fact that has repeatedly received judicial notice. Consequently, all defendants who are members of a visible racial minority should have the right to challenge prospective jurors for cause. However, challenge for cause only relates to race and should not incorporate other features. The question that would be permitted should not include reference to Singapore. Prejudice is racial, not geographical. The appeal was allowed, the convictions were set aside, and a new trial was ordered.

1. On what grounds did the accused wish to challenge for cause?
2. According to the Court of Appeal, does a defendant who is a member of a visible racial minority have to establish that there is a reasonable possibility of prejudice before challenging for cause? Explain.

CASES

R. v. Oickle (2000), 2 S.C.R. 3

BACKGROUND During the police investigation of eight fires in Waterville, Nova Scotia, Oickle agreed to submit to a polygraph. The test took place in a motel, and the police audiotaped the events. The accused was informed of his rights to silence and to counsel, and was told he could leave at any time. The police also told him that the polygraph results were not admissible in court but anything he said during the test was admissible. At around 5:00 p.m. when the test was finished, a police officer told Oickle he had "failed" the test.

Oickle was reminded of his rights and interrogated for about an hour. At 6:30 p.m., a second officer began questioning Oickle, and after about 40 minutes, the accused confessed to setting fire to his fiancée's car and provided the police with a statement. At this point, he appeared emotionally distraught. Oickle was arrested, informed of his rights, and then taken to the police station, where he was placed in an interview room. Here he was videotaped while answering questions about the other fires. Twice he complained of being tired and said he wanted to go home. The police informed him that he was under arrest and was not allowed to leave. A third officer took over the interrogation, and at about 11:00 p.m., the accused confessed to setting seven of the eight fires. He put his head in his hands and began to cry. At 2:45 a.m., after taking a written statement from the accused, the police put him in a cell to sleep.

At 6:00 a.m., an officer asked the accused if he would agree to a re-enactment. On the videotape of the re-enactment, Oickle was informed of his rights and advised that he could stop the process at any time. The police drove him to the fire scenes where he described how he had set each fire. He was charged with seven counts of arson. The trial judge ruled in a *voir dire* that Oickle's statements, including the videotaped re-enactment, were voluntary and admissible, and subsequently convicted him on all counts. The Court of Appeal excluded the confessions and entered an acquittal. The Crown then appealed the acquittal to the Supreme Court of Canada.

LEGAL QUESTION Was the voluntary nature of the defendant's confession violated by the police telling him beforehand that he had "failed" the polygraph test?

DECISION In a majority decision, the Supreme Court of Canada ruled that even though trickery was used in obtaining the defendant's confession, the confession was still given voluntarily. Citing earlier decisions, the Supreme Court noted that confronting a suspect with the results of a polygraph test is not substantially different from showing the suspect a signed confession from a co-accused, or from saying that the suspect's fingerprints were found at a crime scene, even when this was not the case.

"On this view," wrote the Court, "police trickery or use of inadmissible evidence is not necessarily grounds for exclusion.... In short, merely confronting a suspect with adverse evidence—even exaggerating its accuracy and reliability—will not, standing alone, render a confession involuntary."

LEGAL SIGNIFICANCE The decision made it clear that although the results of a polygraph test are not admissible as evidence in court, the police may use the test as an investigative tool, even to the point of obtaining a confession.

ANALYSIS

1. Do you think the police were abusive to the accused in any way, or did they simply conduct a skilful interrogation? Explain your answer.
2. If polygraph results are not admissible in court, should the police be allowed to use the test as an investigative tool? Why or why not?
3. In this case, do you agree with the Court of Appeal's decision to acquit the defendant, or do you agree with the Supreme Court's decision to reinstate his conviction? Support your position.

8 Investigation and Arrest

CHAPTER OUTLINE

Levels of Police in Canada

Starting a Police Investigation

Identifying and Collecting Physical Evidence

Arrest and Detention

Pre-trial Release

FOCUS YOUR LEARNING

What are the different levels of policing in Canada?

How do the police investigate crime?

How is physical evidence collected?

What are the elements of a legal arrest?

Which release procedures are available to defendants awaiting trial?

These cases made headlines …

Figure 8.1 Donald Marshall was found guilty of murdering Sandy Seale. He served 11 years in prison before he was exonerated in a new trial.

Figure 8.2 Guy Paul Morin was convicted of murdering Christine Jessop. He spent 18 months in prison before DNA testing proved he could not have committed the crime.

Figure 8.3 David Milgaard, convicted in 1970 of the rape and murder of Gail Miller, spent 22 years in prison before his conviction was overturned by the Supreme Court of Canada.

WHAT DO YOU THINK?

These people were wrongfully convicted of committing a crime in Canada.

- What factors do you think might lead to the arrest and conviction of innocent people?

- For the factors you identified, what safeguards would you recommend to prevent wrongful convictions?

Have you ever wondered what steps the police take to investigate a crime? Did you know that specific procedures govern the careful collection of evidence and that the police must follow strict rules when arresting and questioning a suspect?

This chapter will discuss the different levels of police forces in Canada. You will learn how the police investigate crimes by collecting evidence and questioning suspects. You will also examine the elements of a legal arrest and explore different types of pre-trial releases that are available to defendants awaiting trial.

LEVELS OF POLICE IN CANADA

Although Canada has an intricate network of courts and costly prisons that house thousands of criminals, the most expensive component of the criminal justice system is policing. Canada's police forces cost about $6 billion annually and include almost 60 000 police officers at three different levels: federal, provincial, and municipal. Since the 1970s, arrangements have also been made for Aboriginal police forces to service many of the Aboriginal communities in Canada.

Federal Police

The Royal Canadian Mounted Police (RCMP) was formed in 1873 as the North-West Mounted Police. The RCMP or "Mounties," as they are popularly known, make up the federal police force of Canada. They provide investigative and protective services to the federal government and serve as the provincial police (as well as the municipal police in some communities) in all provinces and territories except Ontario and Quebec. In Nunavut, the Yukon, and the Northwest Territories, the RCMP is the only operating police force, although this arrangement may change if Aboriginal forces are established in these territories.

At the federal level, most of the RCMP's work focuses on the following eight areas.

1) **Customs and Excise** investigates cases of international smuggling and enforces the *Customs Act* in isolated areas of the country where there are no other federal customs officers. Excise duties are taxes collected on goods produced within Canada, such as cigarettes and alcohol. The Canada Customs and Revenue Agency imposes these taxes, and the RCMP investigates violations of the *Excise Act*.

2) **Drug Enforcement** enforces the laws identified in the *Controlled Drugs and Substances Act*. This branch of the RCMP consists of about 1000 officers who give the highest priority to cases involving international and interprovincial drug smuggling.

3) **Economic Crime** focuses on commercial fraud, organized crime, technological crime, and securities fraud. This branch also works with the

Figure 8.4 Applicants to the RCMP must be Canadian citizens who are at least 19 years old.

Fast Fact
Experts estimate there are as many as 3 million illegal handguns in Canada. Most of them have been smuggled into the country from the United States and China.

Bank of Canada to deliver early warnings to local police of currency counterfeiting activity.

4) **Federal Policing** enforces 286 federal laws and 17 sets of regulations that cover such areas as hazardous waste transportation, environmental law, explosives, vehicle odometer tampering, student loans, and other public safety and consumer protection issues.

5) **Immigration** gathers information on the smuggling of aliens into Canada and the counterfeiting of passports and visas. This branch also works with Immigration Canada to screen out immigration applicants who are members of criminal organizations or perpetrators of war crimes and acts of terrorism.

6) **Proceeds of Crime** division identifies and confiscates money or property that has been acquired through criminal activities.

7) **Criminal Intelligence** specializes in gathering **intelligence,** or information, on organized crime and terrorist groups.

8) **International Liaison and Protective Services** provides security for federal officials and visiting heads of state. This division also co-operates with foreign police agencies such as Interpol (International Criminal Police Organization).

intelligence: the collecting, evaluating, analyzing, and reporting of information, especially of a military, criminal, or political nature

It is important to note that policing in these eight areas is not done exclusively by the RCMP. Provincial and municipal police forces and other provincial and federal agencies often work together to enforce the law in these areas.

Provincial Police

Provincial police forces have jurisdiction in rural areas and in unincorporated regions around cities. The largest of these forces is the Ontario Provincial Police (OPP), followed by the Sureté du Québec and the Royal Newfoundland Constabulary. As noted previously, in all other provinces and in some parts of Newfoundland and Labrador, the RCMP operates as the provincial police.

Using the Ontario Provincial Police as an example of a provincial police force, consider these responsibilities as outlined in the *Police Services Act*:

- policing municipalities that are not required by law to maintain their own police force;
- responding to municipal police requests for special assistance in emergencies;
- providing traffic control on all 400-series and major highways, including those sections that are in the jurisdiction of municipal police forces;
- providing investigative services, on request, to the coroner's office and to other provincial ministries; and
- performing other assigned duties, such as maintaining the provincial firearms registry, providing security at Queen's Park, and protecting Ontario government officials and dignitaries.

Law in Your Life

Would you like to find out first-hand what it feels like to be a police officer? At the OPP Museum in Orillia, Ontario, you can examine specialized police equipment, try on a uniform, or even participate in police work at the interactive computer station.

Figure 8.5 This constable is operating a spot check near Gravenhurst, Ontario. Alcohol is a major contributor to snowmobile accidents.

Municipal Police

Municipal police forces have jurisdiction over policing in towns and cities throughout Canada. Each municipality funds its own police force. Smaller towns or cities that do not have municipal funds for their own forces use the services of the provincial police or the RCMP.

A municipal police force is usually organized into numbered divisions that service the local community. The divisions, in turn, are divided into squads that specialize in certain types of crimes. Examples of these squads or units include the Gang Crime Unit, the Robbery Squad, the Homicide Squad, and the Explosives Disposal Unit.

A municipal police officer's duties may include any or all of the following:

- preserving the peace
- preventing crimes from occurring
- assisting victims of crime
- apprehending criminals
- laying charges and participating in prosecutions
- executing warrants
- enforcing municipal bylaws

Fast Fact
In 2002, there were 300 municipalities in Canada.

Aboriginal Police

The First Nations Policing Policy is administered by the Department of the Solicitor General and provides for a partnership among the federal government, provincial/territorial governments, and Aboriginal peoples to develop police services for Aboriginal communities. Each First Nation can enter into an agreement with the federal and provincial governments to establish stand-

CASE

R. v. McCurrach (2000), Alta. P.C. 127

1. Referring to the co-ordinated effort in this case, name one police force from each of the three levels of police forces in Canada.

2. At trial, the Court noted that the Hell's Angels have an "unsavoury reputation." Do you think the police were justified in adopting the measures they used against such an organization? Explain.

3. Acting as counsel for the Hell's Angels, outline how you would convince the Court that the police violated your clients' rights under ss. 7, 8, and 9 of the Charter.

On June 23, 1997, the Hell's Angels Motorcycle Club officially came to Alberta when two Hell's Angels chapters were formed through a charter-granting ceremony held in Red Deer, Alberta. On June 24, many of those who had attended the ceremony drove from Red Deer to Calgary and were stopped by police just inside Calgary's city limits.

The check stop was a co-ordinated effort involving more than 20 police departments from across Canada as well as the federal Department of Immigration. Participating police forces included the Edmonton Police, the Halifax Police, the Sureté du Québec, and RCMP detachments from Red Deer, Nanaimo, and Ottawa. The Calgary Police, in co-ordination with the Criminal Intelligence Service of Alberta and the RCMP, had developed a "zero tolerance" policy toward the Hell's Angels.

It was a hot day, but the motorcyclists were not allowed to remove their helmets, and waiting times varied from one to four hours. Although they had not been arrested, gang members were videotaped and photographed. Anyone who refused to be photographed was threatened with criminal charges for obstruction of justice. The police issued tickets for "causing unnecessary noise from a motor vehicle," "chin strap not done up on helmet," "failing to ride single file" on the way to the check area, and "littering." Many motorcyclists had their helmets confiscated even though they had been approved for use by the provincial Department of Transportation and bore official stickers testifying to that effect.

The Hell's Angels applied to the Provincial Court of Alberta, alleging breaches of the *Canadian Charter of Rights and Freedoms*. The Crown argued that no Charter breaches had occurred, but if they had, those breaches were the result of reasonable limits prescribed by law on the applicants' rights and freedoms. The judge found the police had violated the gang members' Charter rights under s. 7 (security of the person), s. 8 (unreasonable search and seizure), and s. 9 (arbitrary detention). No breaches of Charter rights were found under s. 2(d) (freedom of association) or s. 6 (mobility rights).

Legal Link www

Visit www.pearsoned.ca/law to browse the Web site for the Dakota-Ojibway Police Service. Check the window that lists qualifications for people who want to join the Police Service.

alone Aboriginal police forces or to develop First Nations contingents within existing forces. The goal of such police forces is to offer services that are both professional and sensitive to the needs of the community.

The Dakota-Ojibway Police Service was one of the first stand-alone Aboriginal police services in Canada. It was established in 1977 in southwestern Manitoba and has 21 officers serving six Aboriginal communities. In New Brunswick, the first RCMP detachment consisting of Aboriginal officers who serve an Aboriginal community was established in 2000 for the Maliseet First Nation in Tobique. The detachment has offices in the Community Wellness Centre and consists of four Aboriginal officers and a receptionist.

Building Your Understanding

1. Using a three-column chart, identify each level of the police force and describe their jurisdictions and responsibilities.
2. Conrad murdered Leo. Which police force would investigate this crime in the city of Vancouver? In a remote region of British Columbia? In a remote area of northern Ontario?
3. Locate the Web site of your municipal or provincial police force. Research the qualifications necessary to become a police officer, and report on your findings.
4. Discuss reasons for having Aboriginal police forces service Aboriginal communities.

STARTING A POLICE INVESTIGATION

What happens when the police first arrive at the scene of a crime? What roles do different officers play? What preliminary steps do they have to take to carry out their investigation? These questions will be answered in the following sections.

Arriving at the Crime Scene

The location or site where an offence takes place is referred to as the **crime scene.** When officers arrive, they have three tasks to perform. Their first task is to call an ambulance and assist injured people at the scene. They must also call in reinforcements to help eliminate any hazards that still pose a risk, such as fires or unexploded bombs. Finally, officers must continue to search the crime scene even if witnesses say the perpetrators have left. To protect people at the crime scene, the officers must assume that the perpetrators are present and armed; once police have thoroughly searched the scene, they can assume it is safe.

crime scene: the site where the offence took place

Protecting and Preserving the Crime Scene

The Crown's success in prosecuting offenders often depends on the condition of the physical evidence taken from the scene of the crime. To protect the crime scene, the officers must accurately establish two boundaries: the **centre** and the **perimeter.** The centre of the crime scene is the area in which the offence was actually committed. The perimeter consists of the surrounding areas where the offender may have been present or may have left evidence. These areas include any entry or escape routes used by the offender.

Crime scenes are preserved for three reasons: to allow for a thorough search of the scene, to seize and collect physical evidence, and to ensure that the physical evidence seized is admissible in court. If evidence obtained at the crime scene is not managed properly, it can become contaminated. **Contamination** is the loss, destruction, or alteration of physical evidence. Contaminated evidence may not be admissible in court, and it may lead the police to draw inaccurate conclusions.

One way to protect and preserve evidence is to document the scene carefully and accurately. Investigators keep a **police log,** which is a written

centre: the area in which the offence was actually committed

perimeter: the areas surrounding the centre, where the offender may have been present or may have left evidence

contamination: the loss, destruction, or alteration of physical evidence

police log: a written record of what an officer has witnessed

Figure 8.6 Which of these police officers do you think has the most interesting role in criminal investigation? Why?

record of what each officer has witnessed at a crime scene or has learned from questioning witnesses or suspects. Officers use their logs to document their daily activities. Later, these logs will help officers recall events, particularly when they testify at a trial. Investigators also use photographs, sketches, and other recording techniques to document the evidence found at a crime scene.

Officers' Roles at a Crime Scene

Four types of police officers investigate a crime scene, and each officer has a separate and well-defined role to play. For example, a "patrol officer" has a "beat" or an area that he or she checks regularly. Usually the patrol officer is the first member of the police department to arrive at a crime scene. The officer's primary duty is to secure the crime scene and ensure that no evidence is lost or tampered with. The officer will usually wrap yellow police tape around the perimeters of the crime scene and conduct the initial interviews with witnesses to the crime. Patrol officers may also arrest suspects if they come upon a crime in progress.

A "scenes of crime officer" is trained in evidence collection and preservation techniques. These officers are usually skilled photographers, trained in lifting fingerprints and foot and tire impressions. They also collect blood and hair evidence. Scenes of crime officers tend to work on less serious offences such as break and enters and car thefts.

A "criminal identification officer" is responsible for searching the crime scene, examining the scene for physical evidence, gathering and analyzing evidence, and sending certain types of evidence to a laboratory for analysis.

Figure 8.7 Criminal identification officers, experts in collecting evidence from a crime scene, are primarily involved in serious crimes such as homicides and robberies.

For instance, if a murder victim has struggled with the murderer, a criminal identification officer may collect bits of the murderer's skin from under the fingernails of the victim and send them to a lab to be analyzed.

A "criminal investigations bureau officer" is a plainclothes detective with experience in a particular area of crime, such as homicide, robbery, or sexual offences. These officers are trained to supervise the investigation, interview witnesses, interrogate suspects, draw conclusions from the physical evidence, and arrest suspects.

Building Your Understanding

1. What three tasks must the police complete when they first arrive at a crime scene?
2. What two boundaries must the police establish at a crime scene? How do these boundaries help their investigation?
3. Provide an example of a piece of contaminated evidence and explain why it would have an adverse impact on the Crown's case against an accused.
4. Briefly explain why the police keep a log of their activities at a crime scene.
5. Compare the roles played by a patrol officer and a criminal identification officer.

IDENTIFYING AND COLLECTING PHYSICAL EVIDENCE

In many criminal trials, the Crown must be able to prove beyond a reasonable doubt that the accused was present at the crime scene when the offence was committed. For this reason, the collection, preservation, and analysis of physical evidence is a crucial aspect of police work. **Physical evidence** may be defined as any object, impression, or body element that can be used to prove or disprove facts relating to an offence. This type of evidence is especially valuable because it often carries greater weight in court than evidence obtained through witnesses' statements.

Forensic science is the application of biochemical and other scientific techniques to criminal investigation. Forensic scientists examine and analyze the physical evidence found at a crime scene. They do most of their work in laboratories, but they also spend considerable time giving expert testimony at trials and inquests. Perhaps the best-known type of forensic scientist is the medical doctor who performs autopsies to determine a murder victim's cause and time of death. Some scientists specialize in firearms and are able to analyze bullet fragments or gunshot residue to identify the type of gun used in a crime. Forensic chemists can also determine the type of vehicle driven by the offender by examining a paint chip left at a crime scene, and entomologists (insect specialists) can determine a murder victim's time of death by identifying the life stages of insects found on the corpse.

physical evidence: any object, impression, or body element that can be used to prove or disprove facts relating to an offence

forensic science: the use of biochemical and other scientific techniques to analyze evidence in a criminal investigation

Legal Link WWW
To find out what it's like to investigate a murder as a forensic scientist, try the computer simulation at **www.pearsoned.ca/law**.

Mother Goose and Grimm

Tools

The most frequently used tools in the commission of a crime are hammers, screwdrivers, and crowbars. Often these tools will have individual characteristics on their surfaces or edges that can be detected in crime laboratories. These marks can be made either in the manufacturing of the tool or by normal wear and tear.

Impressions

impressions: patterns or marks found on surfaces and caused by various objects

Impressions are patterns or marks found on various surfaces, caused by different objects such as fingers, gloves, shoes, tires, or tools. Collecting impression evidence is done in two stages. First the impression is recorded by photographing or scanning it, or taking a mould. Then the police try to match the impression with the object that made it, such as matching a fingerprint lifted at the scene with a print taken from a suspect at the police station.

class characteristics: the general attributes of an object

Impressions have two characteristics: class characteristics and individual characteristics. **Class characteristics** are the general attributes of an object, such as type, make, model, style, and size. For instance, a tire's class characteristics might be described as a 12-inch, steel-belted radial, manufactured by the B.F. Goodrich Company in the year 2000. Because these characteristics are shared by thousands of other tires, they lack specific details that might narrow down the range of possibilities to one particular tire on one particular car. On the other hand, **individual characteristics** refer to specific and unique features of an object. Regarding the tire, these features might include the specific wear and tear it showed as the left rear tire on a Ford Taurus. Such characteristics could narrow the range of possibilities considerably and help investigators make a positive identification of a hit-and-run driver.

individual characteristics: the specific and unique features of an object

Fingerprints

fingerprint: a mark left behind after a fingertip touches an object

A **fingerprint** is a patterned mark left on a surface by a fingertip. Prints can also be taken of a person's hands, feet, or toes, but fingerprints are easier to work with and classify. Because fingerprint patterns never change and are unique to each individual, a fingerprint is the best type of impression to use to identify an offender. No two people have ever been found to have the same fingerprint pattern. Even identical twins have different patterns.

There are two types of prints. A **visible fingerprint** can be observed by the naked eye and is usually formed when the fingertip is coated in dirt, blood, grease, or some other substance. This type of print can be photographed immediately. A **latent fingerprint,** made by the perspiration and oils that naturally form on the skin surface, cannot be seen by the naked eye. This print has to be "developed" before it is photographed. Three methods are used to develop latent prints:

- Prints on non-absorbent surfaces, such as metal or plastic, can be dusted by using a graphite powder that sticks to the ridges of the print. The print is then lifted using adhesive tape and placed on a white cardboard surface, where it is photographed. The cardboard is initialled by the police officer who lifted the print, and the print is safely stored so it can be used later as evidence in court.
- The technique called "iodine fuming" is used to lift prints from absorbent surfaces such as paper and cloth. The area being investigated is placed under iodine fumes; any existing fingerprints absorb the iodine and become visible.
- A laser beam can be used to illuminate the print. Sweat compounds deposited on the surface absorb the laser, and the print turns yellow and can be photographed.

visible fingerprint: the print formed when a fingertip is coated in blood, grease, or some other substance; it is visible to the naked eye

latent fingerprint: the print formed by natural oils and perspiration on the fingertip; it is invisible to the naked eye

Fast Fact
Fingerprint patterns never change and are usually the last surface to decompose after death.

Gloves

Criminals who use gloves to conceal their fingerprints may be in for an unpleasant surprise. Police can use glove impressions to identify a suspect in almost the same way they use fingerprints. To make a positive identification, they compare the impression's class characteristics (such as the overall pattern of the glove and the spacing of its stitches) and the individual characteristics (such as worn or torn areas) with the gloves of a suspect.

Shoe Prints and Tire Tracks

Shoeprints and tire tracks can be matched to the suspect's shoes or tires to help place the suspect at the scene of the crime. If the police can find four shoe prints—two of the left foot and two of the right—they can learn an amazing amount about a suspect. These prints can help them determine the suspect's approximate height and weight, any injuries he or she might have sustained in committing the crime,

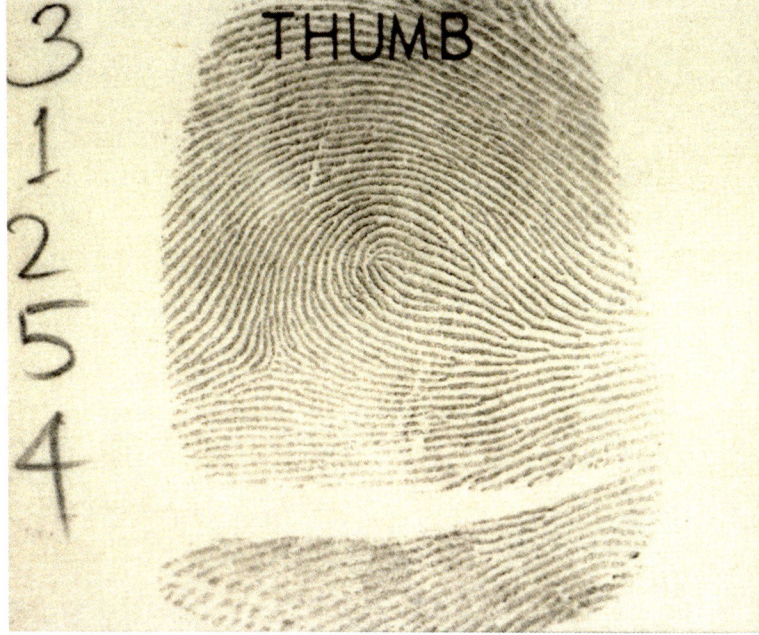

Figure 8.8 Fingerprints are also used to identify people who have died or those injured beyond recognition.

Figure 8.9 Before collecting tire impressions, scenes of crime officers take photographs and make sketches of the tracks. Next, they use dental stone to make casts of the impressions; once hardened, the casts are packaged and submitted to the lab.

Law in Your Life
Take a look at the bottom of your shoes. Do you notice any distinctive patterns? Most shoe manufacturers, such as Nike and Reebok, have their own patterns, which are some of the class characteristics that help police identify shoes that leave impressions at a crime scene.

whether the suspect was carrying anything, and whether he or she was walking or running. Tire impressions can help investigators determine the type of tires, the make of car, and the direction in which the car was travelling as it entered or left the crime scene.

Body Elements and DNA

Crimes against people often result in the transfer of bodily fluids or other bodily elements from the suspect to the victim. Such elements include blood, semen, mucus, sputum, hair, and skin. The police can use any of these substances for DNA testing and other laboratory tests in order to match the elements with a particular suspect.

Blood is the most common body substance found at a crime scene. Investigators send blood samples for laboratory analysis to determine whether the sample is, in fact, human blood. If it is human blood, then the sample is further analyzed to see whether it matches the blood type of the victim or suspect. Because blood types are like class characteristics, they cannot be used for purposes of positive identification without DNA testing.

Hair and clothing fibres can be easily transferred from an offender to a victim during the commission of a crime. The police can use these fibres to

R. v. Dhillon (2001), B.C.C.A. 555

CASE

On April 14, 1977, Carolyn Lee, aged 12, disappeared while walking the four blocks between her afternoon dance class and her family's restaurant in Port Alberni, British Columbia. Her family began looking for her immediately, and at about 8:30 p.m. her father called the RCMP to report her missing. Her body was found the next day by a local farmer on his property near Cox Lake. Forensic evidence established that Carolyn had been sexually assaulted and bludgeoned to death.

The farmer said that his attention was drawn to the area when he noticed tire tracks not normally seen at a fork in the road about 100 metres from where the body was found. The terrain at the fork was muddy, but there was no slippage or backing up evident from the tire tracks, which led the farmer to believe the tracks had been made by a light-duty, four-wheel-drive vehicle. The front and rear tire tracks were clearly visible, and they continued sporadically all the way from the fork to where the body was found. Photographs and drawings were made of one clear impression. A local storeowner compared the tread pattern and size of the markings with actual tire stock in his store. He concluded the impressions had been made by Seiberling 700/15 heavy lug tires.

Ten days after Carolyn's body was found, the RCMP discovered that Dhillon, a local foundry worker, owned a 1977 Blazer with four Seiberling lug tires. Dhillon and his wife both admitted to police that he had washed and vacuumed his vehicle as soon as he arrived home the night Carolyn disappeared. On the victim's jacket, the police had found a partial shoe print made by a boot that could have been similar to the type Dhillon wore at the foundry.

When police interrogated Dhillon, he produced an alibi. He said he was at a bar at the time the girl disappeared and then went home for dinner. A lie detector test seemed to substantiate his alibi. Witnesses gave conflicting statements about Dhillon's whereabouts on the evening in question. The police felt there was insufficient evidence to lay a criminal charge against him.

Semen taken from the victim's body in 1977 remained available, and thanks to advances in scientific technology, it was used for DNA testing. Forensic scientists matched the DNA in the seminal fluid to DNA in Dhillon's blood. On March 13, 1997, 20 years after Carolyn Lee's body was found, the police charged Dhillon with first-degree murder. After a month-long trial, a jury convicted him, and the judge sentenced him to life imprisonment with no eligibility for parole for 25 years. In 2001, Dhillon's appeal to the British Columbia Court of Appeal was dismissed.

1. Were the tire and shoe impressions representative of class or individual characteristics? Explain.
2. List the other types of evidence collected.
3. Why were the tire impressions and the shoe print so useful in the investigation?
4. Why was the evidence insufficient to lay charges until the DNA match was made 20 years later?

match those found in a suspect's clothes, car, or home. Investigators can then take representative fibres from the suspect's belongings and submit them to a forensic laboratory for comparison.

DNA Testing

What is DNA? DNA (deoxyribonucleic acid) is the building block of a person's genetic make-up. It is found in every cell in the human body and determines a person's physical characteristics, such as height, weight, and hair colour. The DNA of every cell in a person's body is identical. However, the *pattern* of the DNA is different for each person, with the exception of identical twins.

A forensic scientist can extract a person's DNA from as small a sample as a few drops of blood or a couple of hair fibres. This sample is then analyzed, creating a DNA profile that can be used in much the same way that fingerprints are used to identify a person. A suspect's DNA "print" can be compared with the DNA profile of a sample from the crime scene. If the profiles match, investigators will conclude that the two samples came from the same person. If the profiles do not match, then the samples must have come from different people, and the investigators will have to find another suspect. Therefore, DNA analysis can be used to either link suspects with physical evidence or free them from suspicion.

Fast Fact

One important advantage to DNA testing is that DNA molecules are stable. If properly preserved, they can be used in an investigation decades after the crime occurred.

Procedures for Labelling Evidence

One primary task of scenes of crime officers is to label items of evidence so they can be easily identified at a later date. Proper labelling also ensures that the evidence has not been contaminated or tampered with in any way. For these reasons, the officers take pains to establish a proper chain of custody for the evidence. A **chain of custody** is the witnessed, written record of all of the people who had control over the items of evidence. This chain remains unbroken from the time the evidence is discovered at the crime scene to the time it is produced in court. It must show

- who had contact with the evidence;
- the date and time the evidence was handled;
- the circumstances under which the evidence was handled; and
- what changes, if any, were made to the evidence.

chain of custody: the witnessed, written record of the people who maintained unbroken control over an item of evidence

All evidence collected at the scene of the crime is tagged and placed in an "evidence package." The following information usually appears on both the tag and the exterior of the package:

- brief description of the item
- police case number
- date when the evidence was collected
- location of collection
- brand name of the item, if any
- serial number or clothing information
- name and badge number of the officer who collected the evidence
- destination of the item for analysis or storage

Consider This

An error in labelling does not necessarily exclude the evidence. If the defendant's rights have not been violated, the judge can include the evidence on the basis that a "reasonable person" would not be shocked by any misconduct in evidence handling. Discuss whether judges should have this discretion.

Forensic Test Dashes Hopes

A damning DNA test result has exploded the hopes of a murderer many believed would be declared Canada's most recent victim of a wrongful conviction, Roy Kenshin Lee.

Using a sophisticated DNA-analysis technique, England's Forensic Science Service determined that two hairs on the body of murder victim Robert Borden quite possibly came from Mr. Lee. Mr. Borden, a blustery nightclub bouncer in Niagara Falls, Ontario, was murdered on April 27, 1987. A shadowy figure burst into his bedroom and plunged a sword into Mr. Borden's head and midriff.

"My position is that we are now left at a dead end in terms of proving Mr. Lee's innocence," James Lockyer, a Toronto lawyer and a key figure in the Association in Defence of the Wrongly Convicted, said. "Unless something fresh comes up, there is nothing further that can be done on this case."

The English laboratory determined one person in a hundred possesses hair matching the DNA profile of the hairs found near the victim. Mr. Lee is among them. Mr. Lockyer said the result doesn't prove the hairs belong to Mr. Lee, only that he is among the 1 percent whose hair matches the two sample hairs.

The $13 000 price tag for the tests was financed by Ontario's Ministry of the Attorney-General, the first time it has paid for this sort of testing abroad to determine the soundness of a conviction. Crown prosecutors Carol Brewer and Shawn Porter said yesterday that if the results had favoured Mr. Lee, they would have allowed him to revive his defunct appeal to have the Supreme Court of Canada hear his case.

Ms. Brewer said Mr. Lee's conviction was based largely on testimony of a controversial witness who claimed to have heard him confess, which made it especially important that the hairs—the only physical evidence in the case—be properly tested. Mr. Porter stated that should Mr. Lee take any further action to overturn his conviction, the Crown will be at liberty to use the DNA results against him.

SOURCE: Kirk Makin, "Forensic test dashes hopes of prisoner," *The Globe and Mail*, July 21, 2001, p. A9.

1. Briefly describe the two types of evidence in Lee's case. Which is the more important of the two? Why?
2. Explain the role that forensic scientists played in this case.
3. Lee is among the 1 percent whose hair matches the sample. Do you think this fact is sufficient to confirm his guilt? Why or why not?

Building Your Understanding

1. Which type of evidence carries more weight in a court of law: physical evidence or a witness's testimony? Explain why.
2. Using examples, distinguish between the class and individual characteristics of impressions.
3. Explain how latent fingerprints can be lifted from a crime scene and entered as evidence.
4. What is the most common body substance found at a crime scene?
5. Briefly explain how the use of DNA profiling helps the police solve crimes.
6. Why is the chain of custody for physical evidence so important to a police investigation?

ARREST AND DETENTION

Once the police have collected physical evidence, they usually begin to question the suspects. Depending on the amount of evidence collected, the police may make an arrest either before or after questioning. Procedures for dealing with suspects have been codified in the *Criminal Code,* developed through case law, and enshrined in the *Charter of Rights and Freedoms.* If the police do not conduct their investigation according to established procedures, they run the risk of watching the case fall apart later in court because evidence obtained improperly may be considered inadmissible.

Questioning the Accused

Police officers are required to ask suspects questions as they investigate a crime. They cannot, however, *force* a suspect to answer their questions. Section 7 of the Charter has been interpreted to grant a detained or arrested person the right to remain silent. According to *R.* v. *Liew,* [1999], the police must give the suspect a chance to "make a free and meaningful choice about whether to speak or remain silent." The police are required by law to promptly inform arrested persons of the reason for their arrest and of their right to counsel. The procedure is standard; the arresting officer must say the following:

> You have the right to retain and instruct legal counsel without delay. You have the right to telephone any lawyer that you wish. You also have the right to free legal advice from a legal aid lawyer. If you are charged with an offence, you can contact the Legal Aid Plan for legal assistance. Do you understand? Do you wish to telephone a lawyer now?

Once an arrested person has been informed of his or her rights, anything he or she says to the police or puts in writing can be used against that person in court.

Young people are given special rights and protection under the *Youth Criminal Justice Act,* which will be examined in detail in Chapter 12, Criminal Law and Young People.

Interrogation Techniques

When police officers interview a suspect, their primary goal is to obtain the truth. The best way to accomplish this goal is to develop a trusting relationship with the suspect. At the beginning of the questioning process, the police tend to use open-ended, non-threatening questions, such as, "Tell me what happened." These questions are designed to encourage the suspect to talk about the incident and provide answers with lots of information. Later, investigators ask closed questions such as, "What time did you leave your house?" These questions are designed to elicit specific answers.

Most of the time, police use a four-stage approach in the interrogation process. They ask the suspect to describe

1) the entire incident
2) the period before the offence took place

Consider This

While being interrogated in September 2000, Stuart McKellar Cameron told police seven times that he didn't want to talk. Nonetheless, officers continued their interrogation until Cameron finally confessed to the murder of one sister and the attempted murder of the other. Should Cameron's confession be allowed in this circumstance? Explain.

Fast Fact

Interrogation techniques must be persuasive enough to convince a guilty person to admit guilt, but not so powerful that they cause an innocent person to confess.

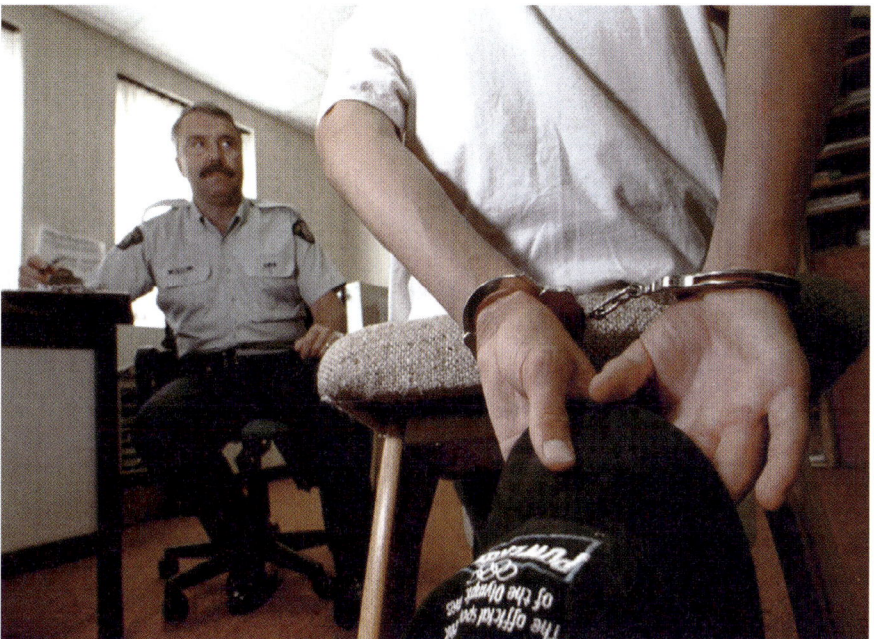

Figure 8.10 How would the four-stage approach of interrogation help the police learn the truth of what actually occurred?

3) the details of the actual offence
4) the period following the offence

Arrest and Detention Procedures

A criminal case usually begins when the police formally charge a person with committing an offence. The police may either arrest or detain the suspect. A person placed under **arrest** is deprived of his or her liberty by legal authority. In order for an arrest to be lawful, the arresting officer must follow these four steps:

1) identify himself or herself as a police officer
2) advise the accused that he or she is under arrest
3) inform the accused promptly of the charge and show the arrest warrant if one has been obtained
4) touch the accused to indicate that he or she is in legal custody

Once the accused is in custody, the police must inform the person of the right to counsel.

In certain circumstances, instead of arresting the suspect, the police will "detain" the person. **Detention** involves stopping someone and asking the individual to answer a few questions. When the police place someone under detention, they are depriving that person of liberty, with or without physical restraint. People detained by police must be promptly informed of the reasons for the detention and of their right to retain counsel.

The following example illustrates the distinction between arrest and detention. Suppose the police are called to the scene of a serious assault. The

arrest: legally depriving someone of liberty by seizing or touching the person to indicate that he or she is in custody

detention: legally depriving a person of liberty for the purpose of asking questions, with or without physical restraint

victim is conscious and able to give the police a description of the person who assaulted him. The police comb the neighbourhood and find Francis, who fits the description in every respect. They stop Francis and ask him to accompany them to division headquarters to answer a few questions. He asks if he has a choice in the matter, and the police say no—he fits the description they were given by an assault victim. He is obliged to go with them but may call a lawyer when they get to the station. At this point, Francis has been detained by the police. If he refuses to accompany them, the police may place Francis under arrest and take him to the station against his will.

The police cannot arrest just anyone they suspect of committing a criminal offence. They must have some proof that an offence has been committed, and they must have reasonable grounds for suspecting that the person they wish to arrest was the offender. **Reasonable grounds** means that based on the information available, a reasonable person would conclude that the suspect had committed a criminal offence. For example, if the police find Wendy sitting in a car with bags of money in the vicinity of a bank that has just been robbed, they would have reasonable grounds to arrest her.

Responsible citizens usually co-operate with the police when stopped or questioned. If the questioning persists beyond an appropriate point, the individual may demand to speak to a lawyer and be given the officer's name and badge number. If someone is detained or arrested in an arbitrary or improper manner, that person may sue the police for unlawful arrest.

reasonable grounds: information that would lead a reasonable person to conclude that the suspect had committed a criminal offence

Appearance Notice

The police have three methods of apprehending an offender. They can issue an appearance notice, arrest the suspect with a warrant, or arrest the suspect without a warrant.

For most summary conviction offences and for those indictable offences that are less serious, the police will not arrest the accused person but will issue an **appearance notice,** a legal document compelling the accused to appear in court on a certain date at a specific time. The accused must sign the appearance notice and be given a copy. If the accused fails to attend court on the date shown, the police may ask a judge to issue a **bench warrant.** Then the accused will be arrested for the original offence and charged with another offence called "failure to appear." In this case, the accused may find it more difficult to be released from custody before the court date.

appearance notice: a legal document, usually issued for less serious offences, compelling an accused person to appear in court

bench warrant: an arrest warrant issued directly by the judge when an accused person fails to appear in court

Arrest with a Warrant

When a person is suspected of committing a serious indictable offence, the police may ask a judge or justice of the peace to issue a **summons.** This usually happens when the police have reason to believe that the suspect will appear in court voluntarily. Delivered by a sheriff or deputy, the summons informs the accused of the charges and when to appear in court. Usually, the accused is directed to go to the police station for fingerprinting. Failure to do so may lead to the issuing of a bench warrant.

summons: a legal document issued for an indictable offence, ordering an accused person to appear in court

If the police have reasonable grounds to think that someone accused of a serious indictable offence will *not* appear in court willingly, they can obtain an arrest warrant, which involves providing a sworn "information" before a judge or a justice of the peace. An **information** is a statement given under oath, telling the court the details of an offence. Once the police "lay an information," the judge or justice decides if it is in the public interest to issue a warrant for the person's arrest. An **arrest warrant** is a written court order directing the police to arrest the suspect. The warrant provides the name of the accused, the offence the person is charged with, and the reason for the warrant.

information: a statement given under oath, informing the court of the details of the offence

arrest warrant: a written court order, directing the arrest of the suspect

Arrest Without a Warrant

Section 495 of the *Criminal Code* lists three circumstances under which the police may arrest suspects without a warrant:

- They have reasonable grounds to suspect a person has either committed an indictable offence or is about to commit one.
- They find a person in the act of committing a criminal offence.
- They find a person who they believe is named on an arrest warrant.

Note that the provisions in s. 495 are extended not just to the police, but to all peace officers. The status of **peace officer** is granted to many officials, including mayors, prison guards, customs officers, aircraft pilots, and fisheries officers.

Consider This
Ontario's *Safe Street Act* (1999) gives police the authority to arrest aggressive panhandlers and "squeegee kids" without a warrant. Does this law violate the right of Canadians *not* to be arbitrarily detained or arrested? Explain.

peace officer: a person responsible for preserving the public peace, such as a police officer, a mayor, or a customs officer

Figure 8.11 This suspect has been arrested at his home without a warrant. Under what circumstances may such an arrest take place?

citizen's arrest: an arrest without a warrant by any person other than a peace officer

Fast Fact

Passengers and crew who come to the aid of the pilot to help subdue a violent passenger are protected by s. 25 of the *Criminal Code,* which states that they are "in aid of a peace officer."

Citizen's Arrest

The most common form of citizen's arrest involves incidents of shoplifting. Instead of being arrested by a peace officer, the suspect is arrested by a store detective or a salesperson. Immediately after a **citizen's arrest** is made, however, the suspect must be turned over to a peace officer. Generally, citizen's arrests are rare—many people are afraid they may be sued for false arrest or injured in a fight with a desperate or violent suspect.

Section 494 of the *Criminal Code* outlines the circumstances where a citizen's arrest can be made:

(1) Anyone may arrest without a warrant
    (a) a person whom he finds committing an indictable offence; or
    (b) a person who, on reasonable grounds, he believes
        (i) has committed a criminal offence, and
        (ii) is escaping from and freshly pursued by persons who have lawful authority to arrest that person.
(2) Anyone who is
    (a) the owner or a person in lawful possession of property, or
    (b) a person authorized by the owner or by a person in lawful possession of property may arrest without warrant a person whom he finds committing a criminal offence on or in relation to that property.

Figure 8.12 Physically restraining or touching someone under arrest indicates that the suspect is in legal custody. Clermont Thomassin, left, was arrested along with 13 other members of the Rock Machine motorcycle gang.

R. v. Polashek (1999), Ont. C.A. 232

CASE

On July 5, 1996, at about 1:00 a.m., Constable Ross stopped Polashek for a *Highway Traffic Act* violation. A conversation took place with Polashek sitting in his car and Ross standing beside the car. During this conversation, Ross detected a "strong odour" of marijuana. He saw no smoke, however, and could not tell whether the smell came from burned or unburned marijuana. When Ross said he smelled marijuana, Polashek looked slowly around the inside of the vehicle and said, "No, you don't." Based on the smell, on Polashek's response, on the neighbourhood where he had stopped Polashek, and on the time of night, Ross believed he had reasonable grounds to arrest him for possession of narcotics.

Ross asked Polashek to step out of the car and searched him. In the pockets of the suspect's shorts, Ross found some cannabis resin. He placed Polashek under arrest for possession of marijuana and continued the search, finding more than $4000 in cash. He handcuffed Polashek and placed him in the cruiser. Ross and another officer then searched the car. In the trunk they found shoeboxes containing wrapped bags of marijuana, a small quantity of LSD, some rolling tobacco, and a set of scales. Polashek was arrested for possession for the purpose of trafficking and, for the first time, was informed of his right to contact a lawyer. This was about 13 minutes after the original arrest. Asked about the drugs, Polashek said, "What can I say? You caught me; I'm busted."

Polashek was convicted of possession of narcotics for the purpose of trafficking and possession of LSD. He appealed to the Ontario Court of Appeal, arguing that the mere smell of marijuana did not provide Ross with a lawful basis to search and arrest him without a warrant. He also argued that there was an unjustifiable delay in informing him of his right to contact a lawyer.

The Court of Appeal ruled that if Ross had based his search and arrest solely on the smell of marijuana, there would have been no reasonable grounds, but since the smell was only one of four factors on which Ross based his decision, the Court found his grounds reasonable. The Court did find, however, that Polashek's right to counsel had been violated by the more than 10-minute delay in informing him of this right. The suspect should have been informed as soon as he was placed under arrest the first time. The Court overturned Polashek's convictions and ordered a new trial.

1. Constable Ross did not have a warrant to arrest or search the suspect. Explain why he was legally entitled to take both of these steps anyway.
2. What circumstances indicated that Polashek possessed drugs for the purpose of trafficking?
3. Why did the Court of Appeal overturn the conviction and order a new trial?
4. Why is it important to inform a suspect of the right to counsel immediately? Explain how a suspect is harmed when this procedure is delayed.

Searches

Because the law seeks to balance the individual's right to privacy with the state's need to conduct a thorough investigation, both statute and common law carefully explain at what point the police may conduct searches during a criminal investigation and what kind of evidence they may collect. As you learned in Chapter 4, s. 8 of the Charter protects people in Canada from unreasonable search and seizure. Generally, the police have to obtain a warrant before conducting a search, but as the following sections show, there are important exceptions to this rule.

Searching a Person

The police do *not* have to obtain a warrant to search a person they have just arrested. According to the Supreme Court decision in *R. v. Stillman,* [1997], the police have to satisfy three conditions for this exception to be legal:

- the arrest must be lawful
- the search must be connected to the lawful arrest
- the manner in which the search is carried out must be reasonable

Except in the case of someone suspected of impaired driving, an arrested person does not have to supply the police with a breath, blood, or urine sample, unless compelled to do so by a warrant. Even with a warrant, the arrested person is usually allowed to confer with a lawyer before providing the sample. For certain "designated offences," such as murder or aggravated sexual assault, the police may obtain a warrant that forces a person to provide a sample for DNA profiling.

In most cases, to ensure that the arrested person is not carrying weapons or concealing evidence, the police will do a cursory search or "pat-down" immediately after the arrest. A more thorough search may take place at the police station. The practice of strip searching suspects, even those arrested for non-violent crimes, has been relatively common in Canada. In *R. v. Golden,* [2001] on page 209, the Supreme Court placed limits on strip searches by laying down strict guidelines for when and how they may be conducted.

Searching a Place

In most cases, the police must obtain a warrant before searching places such as a residence, an office, or a storage area. A **search warrant** is a court document that gives police the right to search a specific location. When preparing a search warrant, the police must ensure that the warrant is correctly obtained and properly filled out. Any irregularities may result in the court throwing out evidence obtained through the warrant.

To obtain a search warrant, a police officer must deliver a sworn information to a judge or justice of the peace. The information will specify the crime, the items the police are looking for, and the reasonable grounds they have for believing that those items will be found in a specific location. If the court grants the warrant, this document will list all these details as well as the date and time the police are allowed to conduct their search. For searching a residence, the warrant usually specifies one day during which the search may be carried out. Unless otherwise noted, the search must take place during daylight hours, that is, between 6:00 a.m. and 9:00 p.m.

Before conducting their search, the police must identify themselves and show the warrant to the person living or working in the place to be searched. During the course of the search, the police may confiscate other items that are not listed in the search warrant, as long as these items are related to the crime and are in plain view. Any objects to be used as evidence in court will

Fast Fact
The case *R. v. Stillman* appears in Chapter 12 on page 331.

search warrant: a court document that gives the police the right to search a specific location

Law in Your Life
Police officers who do not have a warrant can search a residence with the homeowner's permission. Discuss whether police officers should have the right to search your room without your permission, even if they have your parents' permission to search the residence.

CASE

R. v. Golden, [2001] S.C.C. 83

BACKGROUND In January 1997, Metropolitan Toronto Police officers set up an observation post in a building across from a sandwich shop. They were trying to detect illegal drug activity in an area where trafficking was known to occur. Using a telescope, one of the officers observed Golden twice accepting money in exchange for packets containing a white substance, which the officer assumed to be cocaine. Four officers entered the shop and arrested Golden and two other suspects.

One officer frisked Golden and did not find any weapons or narcotics. He then took Golden into the stairwell leading to the washrooms. On the stair landing, the officer peeled back Golden's pants and underwear and observed a clear plastic package protruding from his buttocks. When the officer tried to remove the package, Golden almost knocked him down the stairs. The officer took Golden back into the restaurant and forced him to bend over a table, lowering his pants to remove the package. Golden ended up on the floor with several officers restraining him, and the package was finally removed. It contained more than 10 grams of crack cocaine worth about $1000. While Golden was being strip-searched, the two other suspects, the shop employee, and five police officers were present.

A jury found Golden guilty of possession for the purpose of trafficking, and he was sentenced to 14 months in prison. When the Court of Appeal for Ontario dismissed his appeal, Golden appealed to the Supreme Court of Canada.

LEGAL QUESTION Common law gives the police the power to search people they have just arrested, but is this power broad enough to allow them to do strip searches?

DECISION In a majority decision of 5 to 4, the Supreme Court of Canada threw out Golden's conviction and entered an acquittal. The Court ruled that the strip search was not conducted in a "reasonable fashion." Although the Court found that police do have the power to strip search people they have just arrested, this power is subject to strict limitations; searches cannot be done in every situation or with the purpose of punishing the accused.

LEGAL SIGNIFICANCE Emphasizing that strip searches are "inherently humiliating and degrading," the Court ruled that such searches cannot be "carried out as a matter of routine police department policy applicable to all arrestees." In the future, strip searches should only be conducted when

- the police have reason to believe the accused is concealing a weapon, drugs, or other evidence;
- the search is authorized by a senior officer;
- the search is done by an officer of the same sex; and
- searches of body cavities are done only by medical personnel.

Strip searches should be conducted at the police station and not in the field except under the most pressing circumstances, e.g., when there is good reason to believe the suspect is concealing a weapon. The Court urged that Parliament pass legislation defining precisely "when and how strip searches should be conducted."

ANALYSIS

1. Why did the Supreme Court of Canada enter an acquittal? What was the significance of this decision?
2. Golden was strip-searched twice: first in the stairwell and then in the restaurant. Under the Supreme Court's new guidelines, would either of these searches be legal? Explain.
3. Instead of strip searching Golden in a public place, what alternatives did the police have? What would you have done if you were the officer in charge? Why?

telewarrant: a search warrant obtained by phone or fax

Fast Fact

The *Criminal Code* grants police the authority to search any place except a residence for illegal firearms without first obtaining a warrant.

be kept in police custody until the trial. Other items must be returned to the owner within three months.

In cases where the police believe they must act quickly to preserve evidence, they may obtain a telewarrant to search the premises. A **telewarrant** is a search warrant obtained over the telephone or by fax. The officer gives the judge or justice of the peace all the required information over the phone, and the judge makes a record of the information and files it with the court. The officer then makes a facsimile warrant and shows this warrant at the scene of the search.

A search warrant is almost always required if the police wish to search a private home. However, under s. 529(3) of the *Criminal Code,* two exceptions apply where pressing circumstances make it difficult to obtain a warrant in time. Police must have reasonable grounds to believe that entering the dwelling is necessary to prevent 1) imminent injury or death to any person or 2) the destruction of evidence relating to an indictable offence.

The *Controlled Drugs and Substances Act* gives the police the authority to search any premises *except* a person's residence for illegal drugs without first obtaining a warrant. Anyone found within the premises can also be searched if the police have reason to believe they are carrying illegal drugs. Also, provincial liquor laws give police the right to search automobiles for illegal alcohol without first obtaining a warrant. A warrant is still necessary, however, to search a residence for illegal alcohol.

Procedures After Arrest

Once a person has been arrested, a number of procedures may follow, such as taking photographs and fingerprints or placing the person in a line-up.

Figure 8.13 If this officer searches the suspect's home without a proper search warrant, what might happen to the evidence he obtains. Why?

The only suspect the police have the right to photograph and fingerprint is someone who has been arrested for an indictable offence. If the police do not charge the person, or if the person is charged but acquitted in court, the police will usually retain the arrest record (including the fingerprints and photographs) for 10 years before destroying them.

The police do not have the right to force an arrested person to participate in a line-up. A **line-up** is a grouping of suspects shown to a victim or a witness for the purpose of identifying the perpetrator. Usually the people in a line-up are all of the same gender and share the same general characteristics of age, height, and build. Depending on the lawyer's advice and the circumstances of the case, the defendant may either participate in the line-up or refuse to do so. Sometimes co-operating with the police may help the defendant's case.

line-up: a grouping of people shown to a victim or a witness for the purpose of identifying the perpetrator

Legal Link
Not all crimes are solved. To find out about unsolved crimes and rewards for information leading to arrest and conviction, visit **www.pearsoned.ca/law**.

"You look like this sketch of someone who's thinking about committing a crime."

Building Your Understanding

1. When questioning suspects, can the police force them to answer? Explain.
2. In your own words, describe the steps a police officer must take in making a legal arrest.
3. Identify the similarities and differences between arrest and detention.
4. Can a police officer arrest a suspect on the mere suspicion that he or she has committed a crime? Explain.
5. Give two reasons citizen's arrests are seldom made.
6. What three conditions must be satisfied for the police to search someone without a warrant?
7. Under what circumstances can the police compel a person to supply a breath, blood, or urine sample?
8. For what type of offences must a person *not* be fingerprinted and photographed?

PRE-TRIAL RELEASE

Once a person has been arrested, fingerprinted, and photographed, the police will often release the accused until the trial. Release is usually automatic for people accused of a summary or indictable offence that carries a fine of $5000 or less. If the police believe the accused will appear in court voluntarily and will not commit any offences while awaiting trial, the accused will sign a **promise to appear.** If the accused does *not* appear on the assigned date, the court will usually issue a bench warrant for his or her arrest.

In some cases, the accused may be required to sign a **recognizance**—a guarantee to appear in court when required. A fine of up to $500 may be levied if the accused fails to appear. Unless the accused comes from another province or lives more than 200 kilometres away, a deposit is not usually required. The police may also request a **surety,** someone who is willing to pay a certain sum of money if the accused fails to appear at trial. The surety also has to sign the recognizance form.

promise to appear: a signed agreement that an accused person will appear in court at the time of the trial

recognizance: a guarantee that the accused will appear in court when required, under penalty of a fine of up to $500

surety: a person who agrees to make a payment if the accused does not appear at trial

Bail

Usually the police will try to keep suspects accused of a serious indictable offence in custody after arrest. In such cases, the accused has the right to make a bail application. **Bail** is the temporary release of a prisoner who posts a sum of money or other security to guarantee his or her appearance in court. A bail hearing must be held within 24 hours of arrest, or, if a magistrate is unavailable, as soon as possible thereafter.

Section 11(e) of the *Charter of Rights and Freedoms* guarantees that no one is to be denied reasonable bail without just cause. If the Crown does not want the accused released before trial, a **show-cause hearing** is held to "show cause" and convince the judge that the prisoner should stay in jail until the trial date. "Cause" includes reason to suspect that the accused may flee, concern that the accused's release may be a threat to the safety and protection of the public, or any other just cause. If the Crown is successful, the judge will issue a detention order to keep the accused in jail.

Some circumstances may justify a **reverse onus,** which means that the burden of proof shifts; rather than the Crown having to show cause that the accused should be imprisoned, it is up to the defence to show cause why bail should be granted. This happens when

- the accused is charged with committing an indictable offence while already out on bail;
- the offence is indictable and the accused is not a Canadian resident;
- the charge involves failure to appear or breach of a bail condition; or
- the accused is charged with importing, trafficking, or possession for the purpose of trafficking narcotics (or conspiracy to commit any of these crimes).

If an accused falls into one of these categories, bail will be denied unless the accused convinces the judge that he or she will attend court as required, not commit a crime while out on bail, and not interfere with the administration of justice in any way.

bail: the temporary release of an accused who posts money or some other security

show-cause hearing: a judicial hearing in which the Crown or the accused has to convince the judge either to detain or release the accused before trial

reverse onus: the burden of proof shifts to the defence

Fast Fact

Sometimes an accused can be released from custody by posting a "property bond" instead of money. If the accused fails to appear in court on the scheduled date, the court can sell the property to collect the bail money.

Habeas Corpus

In our criminal justice system, a writ of habeas corpus is an extraordinary remedy that has historical roots. It is not a solution that is commonly used when bail is denied by a competent court. However, if an accused person who has been arrested and denied bail believes that he or she has been illegally detained, that person can file a writ of habeas corpus to appeal the court's refusal to a higher court.

As you learned in Chapter 1, a writ of habeas corpus requires the Crown to produce the detained person in court and then give reasons to justify keeping this person in custody until trial. It also requires the Crown to show that the prisoner is not being mistreated in any way. If the Crown cannot justify the continued detention of the prisoner to the higher court's satisfaction, the court may order that the prisoner be released until trial.

R. v. Morales, [1992] 3 S.C.R. 711

CASE

Morales was charged with narcotics offences and was alleged to have conspired with a major smuggling network to import cocaine into Canada. At the time of his arrest, he was awaiting trial for assault with a weapon, an indictable offence. The court denied Morales bail and ordered him detained in custody until trial.

Morales filed a writ of habeas corpus with a Quebec Superior Court judge, arguing that the reverse onus clause violated his right to reasonable bail under s. 11(e) of the Charter. He was released by the judge, who held that pre-trial detention is only justified when the Crown has established that the accused will not appear for trial or would represent a danger to public safety if released. The Crown appealed to the Supreme Court of Canada, which ruled in favour of the Crown and held that the reverse onus provision did not infringe on a defendant's Charter rights. The Supreme Court then returned the case to the Superior Court for a new bail hearing in which the onus would be clearly placed on Morales to show why he should be granted bail.

1. In this case, why was the Crown justified in applying the reverse onus clause?
2. Explain why a writ of habeas corpus would be a direct challenge to a reverse onus clause.

Building Your Understanding

1. Describe three types of pre-trial releases and identify the situations in which they apply.
2. In most cases, will a person charged with a summary offence be kept in jail before trial? Why or why not?
3. Explain the concept of "reverse onus." Provide one instance where reverse onus applies in a show-cause hearing.
4. What does a writ of habeas corpus compel the Crown to do?

LOOKING BACK

Reviewing Your Vocabulary

appearance notice *p. 204*
arrest *p. 203*
arrest warrant *p. 205*
bail *p. 212*
bench warrant *p. 204*
centre *p. 193*
chain of custody *p. 200*
citizen's arrest *p. 206*
class characteristics *p. 196*
contamination *p. 193*
crime scene *p. 193*
detention *p. 203*

fingerprint *p. 196*
forensic science *p. 195*
impressions *p. 196*
individual characteristics *p. 196*
information *p. 205*
intelligence *p. 190*
latent fingerprint *p. 197*
line-up *p. 211*
peace officer *p. 205*
perimeter *p. 193*
physical evidence *p. 195*

police log *p. 193*
promise to appear *p. 212*
reasonable grounds *p. 204*
recognizance *p. 212*
reverse onus *p. 212*
search warrant *p. 208*
show-cause hearing *p. 212*
summons *p. 204*
surety *p. 212*
telewarrant *p. 210*
visible fingerprint *p. 197*

Quick Quiz

1. Complete the following sentences by selecting the appropriate term from the vocabulary list above.
   a) In handling physical evidence, it is important to keep the ___ unbroken.
   b) A(n) ___ must be developed before it can be seen with the naked eye.
   c) The ___ of a crime scene is where the offence actually took place.
   d) An accused person is entitled to a(n) ___ if the Crown does not want the judge to grant bail.
   e) A(n) ___ gives police the right to examine a particular place, such as a suspect's apartment.
   f) Evidence that is exposed to ___ may prove worthless in court.
   g) Anyone who sees another person commit a crime may conduct a(n) ___.
   h) A fingerprint is an example of the ___ an offender may leave at a crime scene.
   i) The outer area of a crime scene is known as the ___.
   j) A(n) ___ is a guarantee that the accused will appear in court under penalty of a fine.
   k) The general attributes of an object, such as size or model, are called ___.

Checking Your Knowledge

2. Using the four-stage approach to interogation, develop a list of questions a police officer might ask someone suspected of committing a break and enter.
3. For which types of offences will police issue an appearance notice?
4. Explain the difference between a bench warrant and an arrest warrant.
5. What is a telewarrant and when is it used?
6. Describe two situations in which the police may search a residence without first obtaining a search warrant.
7. Describe the circumstances under which an arrested person is entitled to a show-cause hearing.

Developing Your Thinking and Inquiry Skills

8. Conduct research on bail hearings, and write a one-page letter to a friend in another country describing when and how bail hearings are conducted in Canada.
9. You are a police officer on patrol. Over your radio, you receive an order to respond to a 911 call. The

caller reported an emergency but did not identify the problem. Upon your arrival, a man answers the door, informs you that there is no problem, and refuses to allow you to inspect the premises. This situation presents some obvious problems:
- An injured person may be inside.
- The person who answered the door may be the offender.
- No consent is given to enter.
- The radio message was vague and did not specifically state whether an offence had been committed.

a) Explain the legal position for you (as the police officer) and for the occupant of the home.
b) As the first police officer to reach the scene, what will you do?
c) Justify your action in this situation.

Communicating Your Ideas

10. In small groups, debate *one* of the following statements:
    a) Bail should never be granted to people who are accused of violent crimes.
    b) Police should be able to search any premises, vehicle, or other location without a search warrant.
    c) Anyone accused of a crime should have to answer any questions the police ask.

11. Work with a partner to research *one* of the branches of forensic science listed below. Describe your selected topic, the education the scientists in this branch must have, the type of instruments they use, and how they aid the police in investigating and solving crimes. Also, provide one example of a case they helped to solve. Discuss your research findings in a brief presentation to the class.
    - alcohol analysis
    - anthropology
    - biology
    - chemistry
    - document identification and forgery
    - fingerprints
    - firearms
    - odontology
    - pathology
    - toxicology
    - entomology
    - trace evidence

Putting It All Together

12. You are employed as a scenes of crime officer working for your local police department. A break and enter has been committed in your community, and you have been assigned to investigate the case. After your investigation, you must complete a report for use in a criminal trial. You are given the following clues:
    - Footprints were found in the snow outside the house, leading to a broken patio door in the backyard.
    - Pieces of broken glass were found on the floor inside the living room.
    - Bloodstains were found on the floor of the living room.
    - A computer and a small quantity of cash were stolen.
    - The books and materials in the home office were destroyed.
    - Tire prints were found in the driveway.
    - A leather glove was found in the backyard.
    - The front door of the house was left open.
    - The phone was off the hook.

    a) To help you discover as much as possible about the crime, complete a four-column chart using these headings: Clue Observed, Tests to be Conducted, Assumptions About the Suspect, Assumptions About the Crime.
    b) Write a one-page report for the trial.

13. Watch a television series or movie that explores one or more of the following themes:
    - police investigations
    - the collection of forensic evidence
    - questioning a suspect

    Record the sequence of events that take place and compare them with the real-life activities of investigators as described in this chapter. Did the show or film present an accurate account of what really happens? Write a brief summary of your observations, explaining what aspects were realistic and what aspects were not.

CASES

R. v. Godoy, [1999] 1 S.C.R. 311

Two police officers received a call from radio dispatch about a 911 call from Godoy's apartment. This was an "unknown trouble call" in which the line had been disconnected before the caller could be identified. Along with two back-up officers, the police arrived at the apartment and knocked on the door. Godoy opened the door part way and, when asked if things were all right inside, responded, "Sure, there is no problem." One of the officers asked if they could enter to investigate, but Godoy tried to close the door. The officer prevented him, and all four officers entered the dwelling. They could hear a woman crying.

They found Godoy's wife in their bedroom, sobbing. She said Godoy had hit her. The accused resisted arrest and was charged with assaulting a police officer. The trial judge dismissed the charge, holding that the officers' entry into Godoy's apartment was unauthorized; therefore, all their subsequent actions were illegal. The Ontario Court (General Division) allowed the Crown's appeal and ordered a new trial. The Court of Appeal upheld that decision, and Godoy appealed to the Supreme Court of Canada.

The Supreme Court dismissed his appeal. The Court recognized that residents have a right to privacy within the sanctity of their home, but held that that right must be balanced with the public interest in maintaining an effective emergency response system. In an emergency, the police are permitted to intrude on a resident's right to privacy. The intrusion must be limited to the protection of life and safety. The police do not have further permission to search the premises or otherwise intrude on a resident's privacy or property.

1. Explain why the Supreme Court held that the police were justified in entering the defendant's apartment without first obtaining a search warrant.
2. Why do you think the police give a high priority to an "unknown trouble" call?

R. v. Bero (2000), Ont. C.A. C30048

Bero met Mills in a bar, and they left together in Mills' truck. A short time later, the vehicle ran off an expressway ramp, rolled over, and came to rest on its roof in a grassy area dividing the expressway. Bero and Mills were thrown from the truck and seriously injured. Mills told police that Bero was driving at the time of the accident. The police charged Bero with impaired driving causing bodily harm and driving with a blood-alcohol content over the legal limit. In court, Bero denied driving. He said he had struck his face on the passenger-side of the dashboard and hit his head on the windshield before being thrown from the truck. He was convicted on both counts and sentenced to 30 months in prison.

Bero appealed his conviction, arguing that the prosecution had allowed the truck to be destroyed before the defence could have it examined by a forensic expert. He argued that a proper forensic examination would have proved that Mills was the driver. The prosecution's failure to maintain custody of the truck denied Bero his constitutional right to make full answer to the charges. The Ontario Court of Appeal accepted Bero's argument, set aside his convictions, and ordered a new trial.

1. The Crown allowed an important piece of physical evidence to be destroyed before the defence could examine it. Explain how this weakened the Crown's case against the defendant.
2. Mills was the owner of the truck, not Bero. What effect would this fact have had on the Crown's case against Bero?
3. Bero wanted a forensic expert to examine the truck. What evidence might the expert have found to back up Bero's claim that he was not driving?

CASES

R. v. Feeney, [1997] 2 S.C.R. 13

BACKGROUND Police found the body of Frank Boyle, 85, in his blood-spattered home in Likely, British Columbia. He had been struck five times in the head with an iron bar. Bystanders said they had seen Boyle's truck in a ditch earlier that day and Feeney walking down the road nearby with a beer in his hand. The police went to Feeney's house, where his sister told them Feeney was asleep in the trailer behind the house. Without obtaining a warrant, an officer went to the trailer. When no one answered the door, he entered and woke Feeney by touching him on the leg. He brought Feeney outside where the light was better. There he noticed blood on his shirt and arrested him.

The police told Feeney of his right to counsel and then asked him questions, which he agreed to answer. The police seized his shirt and took him to the detachment, where, before Feeney could consult a lawyer, they took further statements and fingerprints. Then the police obtained a warrant and returned to the trailer, where they seized Feeney's shoes and other evidence.

At trial, the jury convicted Feeney of second-degree murder. His appeal to the British Columbia Court of Appeal was unanimously dismissed. He then appealed to the Supreme Court of Canada.

LEGAL QUESTION Did the police violate the defendant's right to privacy by entering his home without a warrant?

DECISION In a majority decision of 5 to 4, the Supreme Court of Canada allowed Feeney's appeal and ordered a new trial, excluding the evidence obtained without a warrant. Since the police did not have a warrant when they entered Feeney's dwelling, the arrest was illegal, regardless of whether they had reasonable grounds for the arrest. There were no exceptional circumstances to justify not obtaining a warrant; the police were not in "hot pursuit," nor were they in an emergency situation that required immediate action to protect the public or to keep evidence from being destroyed.

LEGAL SIGNIFICANCE This decision affirmed that a person's right to privacy in one's home is a matter of fundamental justice protected under s. 8 of the Charter. In most cases, this right will take precedence over the right of the police to collect evidence.

Figure 8.14 Only in exceptional circumstances may the police enter a person's home without a warrant. What circumstance do you think would be considered exceptional?

ANALYSIS

1. Based on the evidence, what grounds did police have for arresting Feeney?
2. If you were the officer investigating this case, what factors would you consider in deciding between entering the suspect's home immediately or waiting to get a search warrant?
3. In your opinion, did the Supreme Court strike a proper balance between a person's right to privacy and society's right to protection from violent offenders? Explain why you agree or disagree with the Court's decision.

issue

National DNA Data Bank

Once a controversial issue, fingerprint collection of convicted offenders is now commonly recognized as an effective crime-solving tool. Recently, a more sophisticated tool for matching a suspect to a crime has become available. Deoxyribonucleic acid, known as DNA, contains the genetic make-up found in human cells. If even a small trace of DNA is left behind—a strand of hair, a drop of blood, a piece of skin tissue—it can be used to identify a suspect.

However, DNA evidence is useful only if DNA found at the scene can be matched to a suspect. To assist in the search for a possible match, Canada has enacted legislation called the *DNA Identification Act*. This Act permits the state to collect DNA evidence from convicted criminals and to store the evidence in a DNA data bank.

THE NATIONAL DNA DATA BANK

On June 30, 2000, the National DNA Data Bank of Canada was created in Ottawa. This new data bank includes DNA profiles from youths and adults convicted of serious offences. The data bank also includes a crime-scene index of DNA profiles from unsolved crimes. Legislation allows this information to be cross-referenced with other law enforcement data banks.

A CONTROVERSIAL QUESTION

While the RCMP and other law enforcement agencies see the introduction of the data bank as an important tool in solving crimes, others see it as a gross violation of civil liberties. This difference of opinion raises the following question: Is the collection and storage of DNA samples from arrested suspects a justifiable infringement of civil liberties?

According to Canada's Solicitor-General Lawrence MacAulay, the data bank will "help ensure that those guilty of a serious crime will be apprehended more quickly, while excluding the innocent from suspicion." Those who support the data bank point to the fact that fingerprints, criminal profiles, DNA taken from crimes scenes, and other information involving criminal activity are already available on computer data banks. They see the National DNA Data Bank as just one more tool available to law enforcement agencies to help fight crime and protect the public.

Crown prosecutors argue that the creation of a DNA data bank does not violate rights under the *Charter of Rights and Freedoms* any more than taking and storing the fingerprints of convicted criminals. Defence lawyers disagree. They have challenged the collection of DNA as a violation of ss. 7 and 8 of the Charter. In response, the Supreme Court of Canada has concluded that while collecting DNA samples may infringe on a person's rights, it is a minor and justifiable intrusion that may be used to exonerate the accused. Such was the case in the wrongful convictions of David Milgaard and Guy Paul Morin, who were both finally released when DNA testing proved they could not have committed the crimes.

Supporters of the data bank believe that the benefits outweigh the concerns. They argue that using a data bank does not mean a suspect will be convicted purely on the basis of DNA evidence; the standard of reasonable grounds to obtain a conviction will remain. Opponents reject these assurances, claiming it is the prosecutor's responsibility to prove guilt beyond a reasonable doubt, without invading the privacy of the accused. They equate a DNA data bank with a warrantless search and seizure. Aside from the issue of privacy rights, they ask, what about the risks of human error or the potential for planting evidence?

Opponents to the creation of the National DNA Data Bank also claim that collecting DNA evidence is more intrusive than collecting fingerprints. They point out that the amount of information gleaned from the two investigative tools is vastly different. Fingerprint evidence merely identifies a suspect, but DNA is a biological blueprint, providing information that could be misused. Although the purpose of the National DNA Data Bank is law enforcement, in an age where information is often sold to the highest bidder, such information might be used for other purposes. Some people believe that providing any government access to such a large body of personal information could be dangerous.

Forensic DNA Analysis

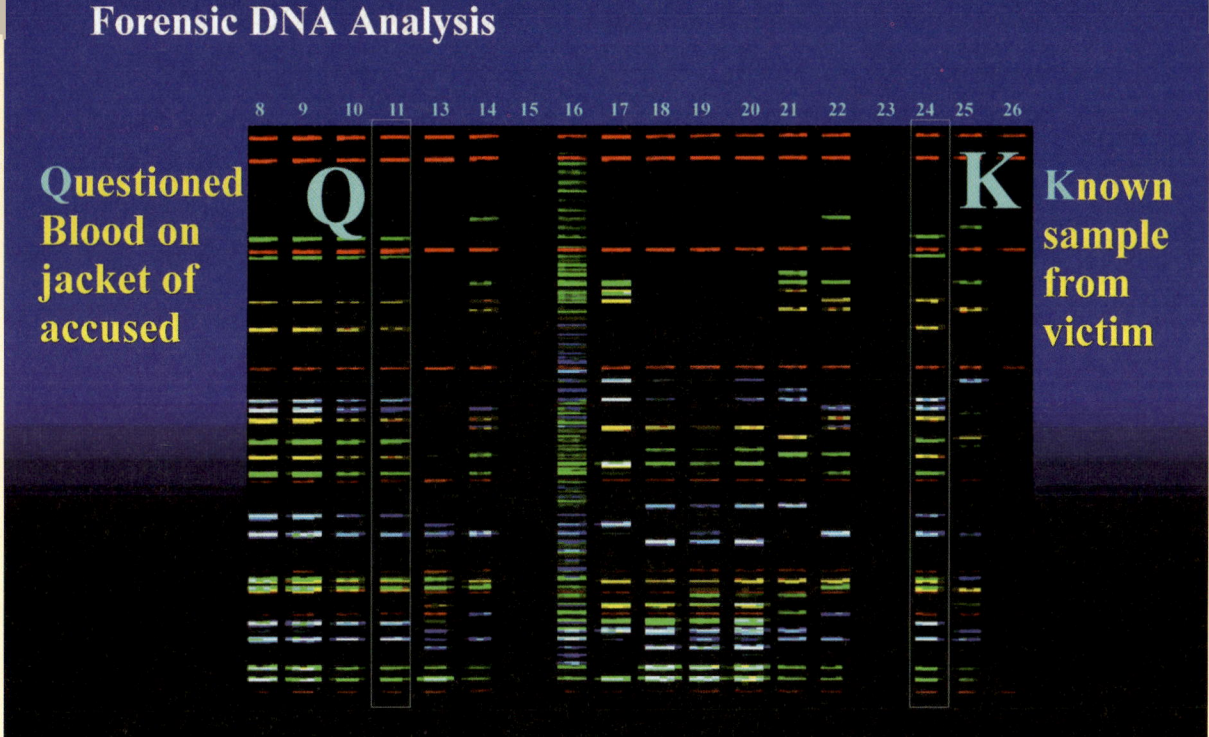

In this illustration of forensic DNA analysis, a blood sample from the defendant's jacket is compared with a blood sample from the victim. Each vertical "lane" contains one profile of DNA, and only possible matches are shown. As you can see, lanes 11 and 24 match each other.

SOURCE: National DNA Data Bank of Canada

Not only do critics consider the data bank a violation of civil liberties, they also consider it discriminatory. DNA is collected without consent from a specified segment of the population on the basis that these individuals may commit crimes in the future. Any citizen *might* break the law, yet only the DNA of those who have *committed* a crime is stored. In addition, critics worry that vulnerable members of society may be singled out for DNA collection. If the government can justify testing convicted criminals in the interest of crime detection, what will prevent it from introducing legislation to test welfare recipients, individuals in psychiatric institutions, AIDS patients, or any other target group? Some have suggested that this data bank could be the forerunner of a DNA national registry for all Canadians.

LOOKING AT THE ISSUE

1. Supporters of the data bank claim that the fears of those opposed to the collection and storage of DNA are unjustified and exaggerated. Create a pro and con organizational chart on this issue, using information found here, interviews with experts on the topic, and additional research. Refer to the information in your chart to write an opinion paper explaining which side of the issue you support.

2. Suppose your province has proposed the following bill:

   > DNA samples will be collected from all newborns and all children in elementary and secondary schools in the province. The DNA samples will be stored in Ottawa and will be available to law enforcement agencies throughout Canada for the purpose of crime investigation only.

   The government claims that this information will help solve cases of missing children, assist police in solving crimes, and prevent future criminal activity. Take a position on the bill, prepare your arguments to support your position, and participate in a debate on the bill.

Criminal Offences

CHAPTER OUTLINE

Levels of Offences

Offences Against the Person

Offences Against Property

Other *Criminal Code* Offences

Drug Offences

FOCUS YOUR LEARNING

What are the different types of criminal offences?

How does the *Criminal Code* classify crimes?

What are the most common violent crimes in Canada?

What are the most common crimes against property?

Which federal statute deals with drug offences?

Voyeurism Laws to Get a Fresh Look

OTTAWA — At a federal-provincial meeting in Nova Scotia next week, the country's justice ministers will consider filling a gaping hole in the *Criminal Code* by making voyeurism an offence.

Justice officials across Canada have complained that the old laws against peeping Toms have not kept up with technological advances, which allow voyeurs (people who take pleasure in watching others undress or engage in sex) to place tiny cameras in places such as washrooms and locker rooms. In some cases, these images are then placed on the Internet.

Currently, prosecutors can charge suspected voyeurs only with offences such as trespassing at night or mischief, which many feel are inadequate. At next week's meeting, justice ministers will be asked to say whether they want to create a specific offence of surreptitious viewing and photographing of individuals in a sexual context.

Government officials say they're waiting for the green light from federal and provincial ministers to start working on legislation, which would then be between one and two years away. Since Ottawa is in charge of amendments to the *Criminal Code,* it would take the lead on the issue.

SOURCE: Daniel LeBlanc, "Voyeurism laws to get fresh look at meeting," *The Globe and Mail,* September 5, 2001, A4.

WHAT DO YOU THINK?

- What is meant by the statement, "the old laws against peeping Toms have not kept up with technological advances"?

- Should the *Criminal Code* be amended to make electronic voyeurism a separate offence? Explain.

- If the federal government makes voyeurism a separate offence, what do you think the maximum penalty should be?

We saw in Chapter 6 that the *Criminal Code* has been revised many times. Often legislators propose adding new offences that the Code's original framers could not have foreseen. Through such amendments, the Code is revised to meet the needs of changing times. Such was the case in October 2001, when the federal government introduced legislation to curb terrorist activity in Canada. This move came as a direct result of the terrorist attacks on the United States on September 11, 2001.

This chapter will examine how the *Criminal Code* classifies and defines various offences. We will also consider some of the criminal offences listed in another federal statute, the *Controlled Drugs and Substances Act*.

> *"Our Criminal Code is largely the product of nineteenth-century thought."*
> — Law Reform Commission of Canada

LEVELS OF OFFENCES

Canada's justice system handles various criminal offences differently depending on the seriousness of the crime. The type of offence has a bearing on custody issues, bail requirements, trial procedures, and sentencing. The three levels of crimes include summary conviction offences, indictable offences, and hybrid offences. Summary conviction and indictable offences were mentioned briefly in Chapter 7 but are discussed in greater detail in the following sections.

Summary Conviction Offences

A **summary conviction offence** is a minor offence that carries a relatively light penalty. Generally speaking, a person convicted of such a crime will be fined up to $2000 and/or imprisoned for up to six months. Treating a matter in a "summary fashion" means dealing with it quickly and simply, so as the term implies, these cases usually proceed through the court system fairly rapidly. As indicated in Chapter 7, summary conviction offences are tried in Provincial Court before a judge (or a justice of the peace) without a jury. With the permission of the judge, the accused does not have to appear in court but can be represented by a lawyer. The *Criminal Code* states whether a crime is classified as a summary conviction offence.

summary conviction offence: a crime that is considered less serious and carries a lighter penalty

Fast Fact
Examples of summary conviction offences include public nudity in s. 174(1), causing a disturbance in s. 175(1), and joyriding in s. 335(1).

Indictable Offences

An **indictable offence** is a serious crime and carries a heavier penalty than a summary conviction offence. The *Criminal Code* establishes maximum penalties for indictable offences, ranging anywhere from two years' imprisonment for committing a common nuisance up to life imprisonment for aggravated sexual assault. Sometimes the Code sets a minimum penalty for an indictable offence, such as four years for robbery where a firearm is used or life in prison for murder.

The method for trying an indictable offence differs according to the severity of the sentence that the offence carries. For an offence with a maximum penalty of less than five years' imprisonment, the trial will be heard in Provincial Court or the Superior Court of the province before a judge

indictable offence: a crime that is more serious than a summary conviction offence and carries a heavier penalty without a jury. If the maximum penalty is more than five years, the accused can opt for trial in Superior Court, either with a judge alone or with a judge and jury. The most serious indictable offences, such as murder and treason (listed in s. 469 of the Code), must be tried in Superior Court. Figure 9.1 provides a summary of criminal trial jurisdictions. Figure 9.2 compares summary conviction offences with indictable offences.

Figure 9.1 **Criminal trial jurisdictions**

	Provincial Court	**Superior Court of the Province**
Tries	• summary conviction offences • indictable offences from s. 553 • electable offences from s. 554 of the Code for which the accused elects to be tried in Provincial Court	• indictable offences from s. 469 • indictable offences from s. 554 of the Code for which the accused elects to be tried by a judge alone • indictable offences from s. 554 for which the accused elects to be tried by a judge and jury
Conducts	• all preliminary hearings or inquiries	
Hears Appeals		• from the Provincial Court • from the Superior Court, Trial Division

Figure 9.2 **If all offences were tried as indictable, what effect would this have on the criminal court system?**

	Summary Conviction Offences	**Indictable Offences**
Limitation periods	Offence must be prosecuted within six months of the date it occurred	No limitation on time when the offence may be prosecuted
Prosecution	Private person may prosecute if Crown refuses to lay charges	Private person may prosecute with the permission of the Crown, but it is almost always the Crown that prosecutes
Pre-trial procedures	No preliminary hearings	Preliminary hearings may be held
Type of court	Tried in Provincial Court	Tried in Provincial Court or Superior Court
Method of trial	No jury trials	Accused may choose to be tried by a judge or jury
Presence of accused	Not required (may be represented by a lawyer)	Required
Penalties	Limited to fines of up to $2000 and/or up to six months in prison	Heavier penalties allowed, up to life in prison
Criminal record	No criminal record results from a conviction on a summary offence	A criminal record results from a conviction on an indictable offence

Hybrid Offences

A **hybrid or dual procedure offence** is one that the Crown can decide to try either as a summary conviction or indictable offence. The *Criminal Code* always makes it clear when an offence is hybrid by stating explicitly that it can be treated either on a summary or indictable basis. For example, under the offence of public mischief, the Code states:

> 140. (2) Every one who commits public mischief
> (a) is guilty of an indictable offence and liable to imprisonment for a term not exceeding five years; or
> (b) is guilty of an offence punishable on summary conviction.

Hybrid offences are always treated as indictable until charges are laid in court. At that point, the Crown must decide how to treat the offence. The Crown's decision often depends on the circumstances of the particular case. Suppose Connie has been charged with theft of CDs worth $100. She has never been arrested before and has a steady job. In this case, the Crown may decide to proceed on a summary basis, and Connie will receive a light penalty, perhaps a fine. If Connie had a long record of arrests for theft, and if she had stolen several thousand dollars worth of CDs, the Crown might decide to proceed with the offence as indictable. In that case, Connie could face a jail term.

hybrid or dual procedure offence: an offence that the Crown can try either as a summary or indictable offence

Fast Fact
Theft under $5000 in s. 334(b), impaired driving in s. 255(1), and sexual assault in s. 271(1) are examples of hybrid offences.

Legal Link
If you do not have a copy of the *Criminal Code* in class, find it on the Internet at **www.pearsoned.ca/law**.

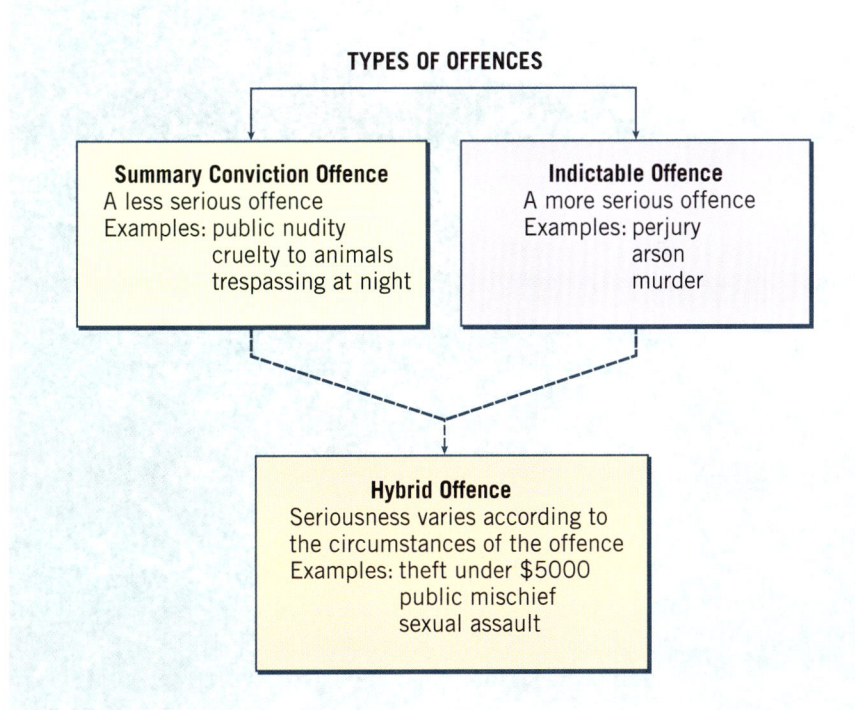

Figure 9.3 It is up to the Crown to decide whether to try a hybrid offence on a summary or indictable basis.

CASE

R. v. Quinlan (1999), 133 C.C.C. (3d) 501 (Nfld. C.A.)

1. Did Quinlan commit a summary, indictable, or hybrid offence? Explain.
2. If the payment had been less than $5000, what type of offence would Quinlan have committed?

Leo Quinlan was employed by Bluewater Newfoundland Ltd., a shipping supply firm with its head office in Halifax, Nova Scotia. Quinlan was manager of the company's Newfoundland operations. On July 26, 1996, the captain of an Icelandic ship paid Quinlan more than $6700 for supplies provided by Bluewater while the vessel was in port at Harbour Grace. Quinlan never gave this money to his employer. He was subsequently arrested and charged with theft over $5000, to which he pleaded guilty.

Building Your Understanding

1. Explain in your own words the differences between a summary, an indictable, and a hybrid offence.
2. Why are trials for some offences heard by a judge alone?
3. If the accused is charged with a hybrid offence, who decides whether the charge proceeds as summary or indictable?
4. a) With a partner, categorize the offences listed below according to the severity of the crime. Organize the offences on a chart, using the headings Indictable, Summary Conviction, and Hybrid.
   b) Now use a copy of the *Criminal Code* to check whether you and your partner were correct in the way you organized the offences listed. Use the section numbers to locate each offence in the Code.

Section	Offence
334	Theft Under $5000
434	Arson
174	Appearing Nude in a Public Place
356	Theft from Mail
231(7)	Second-Degree Murder
380(1)	Fraud Under $5000
177	Trespassing at Night
372(3)	Making Harassing Phone Calls
342.1(1)	Unauthorized Use of a Computer
446	Causing Unnecessary Suffering to Animals
255(3)	Impaired Driving Causing Death

OFFENCES AGAINST THE PERSON

Crimes in the *Criminal Code* are classified under different categories according to the type of offence. For example, all gambling offences are found in Part VII, Disorderly Houses, Gaming, and Betting. Figure 9.4 lists the 11 classifications of criminal offences found in the *Criminal Code*.

Part VIII, Offences Against the Person and Reputation, includes violent crimes in which the victim is threatened, injured, or killed. Across Canada, police reported 291 000 incidents of violent crime in 1999. This may seem like a lot, but it is worth noting that violent crime declined in Canada between 1993 and 1999 after 15 years of increases.

Fast Fact

In 1999, Saskatchewan and Manitoba reported the highest violent crime rates in Canada; Quebec and Prince Edward Island had the lowest.

Part II	Offences Against Public Order
Part III	Firearms and Other Weapons
Part IV	Offences Against the Administration of Law and Justice
Part V	Sexual Offences, Public Morals, and Disorderly Conduct
Part VI	Invasion of Privacy
Part VII	Disorderly Houses, Gaming, and Betting
Part VIII	Offences Against the Person and Reputation
Part IX	Offences Against Rights of Property
Part X	Fraudulent Transactions Relating to Contracts and Trade
Part XI	Wilful and Forbidden Acts in Respect of Certain Property
Part XII	Offences Relating to Currency

Figure 9.4 The classification of criminal offences in the *Criminal Code of Canada*

"Overall, homicides are committed primarily by someone known to the victim. In 1998, of the 431 homicides solved by the police, 45% of victims were killed by an acquaintance, 40% by a family member, and 15% by a stranger."
— Statistics Canada, *The Daily,* October 7, 1999

Homicide

The *Criminal Code* defines homicide in the following way:

222. (1) A person commits **homicide** when directly or indirectly, by any means, he causes the death of a human being.

Technically speaking, an execution is a form of homicide; so is a planned murder or an unplanned killing resulting from a jealous rage.

There are two main types of homicide: culpable and non-culpable (the word *culpable* means "blameable"). A **culpable homicide** is a killing for which the accused can be held legally responsible. That is, someone intentionally causes the death of another person or shows such recklessness that these actions are likely to cause death. Examples include murder, infanticide, and manslaughter (which will be discussed in the following sections). A **non-culpable homicide** is a killing for which the accused cannot be held legally responsible, such as a death caused by an unforeseeable accident. In

homicide: the killing of another human being, directly or indirectly

culpable homicide: a killing for which the accused can be held legally responsible

non-culpable homicide: a killing for which a person cannot be held legally responsible

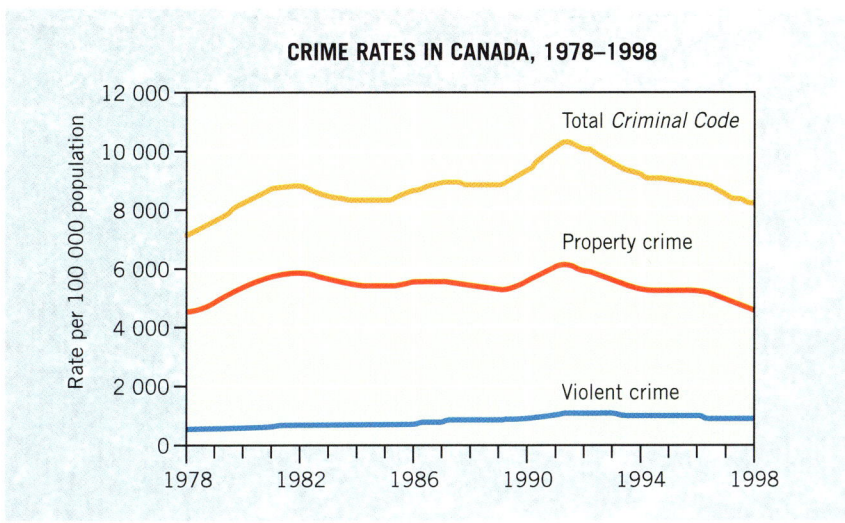

Figure 9.5 This graph focuses on a 20-year period and shows how crime rates in Canada have decreased since 1992. What factors might explain this trend?

SOURCE: Statistics Canada, Catalogue No. 85-205-XPE.

Canada, there are other cases in which homicide is considered non-culpable—a soldier acting under orders in times of war, or an individual defending oneself or another person. In countries that sanction capital punishment, executions are considered a form of non-culpable homicide.

Murder

murder: the intentional killing of another human being

first-degree murder: a killing that is planned and deliberate, is the result of a contract, causes the death of a peace officer, or is committed during another serious crime

Murder, the intentional killing of another human being, is a form of culpable homicide. Section 231(1) of the *Criminal Code* classifies murder into two categories: first degree and second degree. A killing qualifies as **first-degree murder** in any one of the following situations:

- It is planned and deliberate.
- One person hires another to commit murder.
- The victim is a police officer, prison employee, or other person employed for the preservation and maintenance of the public peace.
- The murder is caused while committing or attempting to commit another serious offence, such as hijacking, sexual assault, sexual assault with a weapon or causing bodily harm, aggravated sexual assault, kidnapping and forcible confinement, and hostage taking. In these situations, murder does not have to be planned and deliberate to qualify as first degree.

second-degree murder: any murder not classified as first-degree murder

Section 231(7) of the *Criminal Code* defines **second-degree murder** as any murder that does not fit into one of the four situations listed in the category of first-degree murder.

The mandatory minimum sentence for both first- and second-degree murder is life imprisonment. The only difference is the date at which the offender can apply for parole. Generally, anyone convicted of first-degree murder has to serve 25 years in prison before qualifying for parole. An offender convicted of second-degree murder can usually apply for parole after serving 10 years.

CASE

R. v. Mafi (2000), B.C.C.A. 135

1. Why was Mafi charged with second-degree rather than first-degree murder?
2. Why do you think Mafi's parole eligibility was set at 20 years instead of the usual period of 10 years?

Mafi worked as a waiter in a Vancouver restaurant. At about 10:30 p.m., the restaurant closed. Mafi was either found removing money from the till or accused of doing so. He took a 12-inch butcher knife from the kitchen and stabbed the owner 15 times and another employee 12 times. The owner was still able to make a 911 call, and the first police officer arrived one minute later. Mafi's arms and shirtfront were covered in blood. In his pocket he had several hundred dollars, and these bills were also soaked in blood. Both stabbing victims died.

Mafi was convicted of two counts of second-degree murder and sentenced to life imprisonment with no parole eligibility for 20 years. He appealed his conviction, and when that appeal was dismissed, he appealed his sentence. That appeal was also dismissed.

Infanticide

Infanticide occurs when a mother kills her newborn child. Cases of infanticide are very rare in Canada. All three of the following circumstances must be present for the crime to be considered infanticide:

- the accused must be the natural mother of the victim;
- the victim must be less than 12 months old; and
- at the time of the killing, the accused must have been suffering from a mental disturbance caused by not being able to recover from giving birth to the victim.

The maximum punishment for infanticide is five years' imprisonment. This sentence was placed in the *Criminal Code* in 1948, when juries were reluctant to convict mothers of murder. The five-year maximum sentence for infanticide is considerably less than the minimum sentence for second-degree murder (i.e., life imprisonment). If the mother can show that when she killed her child she was still suffering from an affliction such as post-partum depression (depression after the birth of a child), then she can plead to the lesser charge of infanticide.

infanticide: the killing of a newborn infant by the child's mother

"The children who are killed by women are killed in a circumstance where women are quite young—almost like children having children—and are overwhelmed by their circumstances."
— Neil Boyd, criminologist at Simon Fraser University

Manslaughter

Section 234 of the *Criminal Code* defines **manslaughter** as any culpable homicide that is not murder or infanticide. The *actus reus* of manslaughter consists of killing someone through a wrongful act, even if the killing was not intentional. The classic example of manslaughter is a killing that happens during a barroom brawl. Nelson and Angelo started fighting in the Flaming Onion Tavern. Nelson knocked Angelo backward with a blow to the jaw, and Angelo hit his head on a corner of the pool table. He died later that night

manslaughter: any culpable homicide not classified as murder or infanticide

Figure 9.6 If you kill a pedestrian by accident while driving a car in a dangerous fashion, you could be charged with manslaughter. Why would you not be charged with murder?

from internal bleeding caused by a severe concussion. Nelson had wanted to hurt Angelo, but he did not mean to kill him. Nevertheless, Angelo died as a direct result of Nelson's wrongful act. The police arrested Nelson and charged him with manslaughter.

The *mens rea* for this offence is that any reasonable person could have foreseen that the wrongful act would pose a risk of bodily harm that was "neither trivial nor transitory" (neither insignificant nor temporary). To be found guilty of manslaughter, the offender did not have to foresee that the wrongful act could result in death. Note, too, that a charge of manslaughter can be brought in the event of criminal negligence that results in death. The accused can be charged with either manslaughter or criminal negligence causing death, but cannot be charged with both for the same offence.

A charge of murder can be reduced to manslaughter if the accused can show **provocation** on the part of the victim; in other words, the victim did something so insulting or outrageous that it caused the accused to lose self-control. Consider the following example. Derrick and Li are arguing in Li's kitchen. As the argument grows more heated, Derrick gets frustrated and spits in Li's face. Li is so enraged that he grabs a knife from the counter and plunges it into Derrick's chest, killing him instantly. Since Li acted "in the heat of passion caused by sudden provocation" (s. 232[1]), it is likely he will be allowed to plead to manslaughter rather than murder. Note that in a case of manslaughter there is no cooling-off period; if Li goes home after Derrick spits on him and broods on the matter before killing Derrick two days later, then something "planned and deliberate" has occurred. Li will be charged with murder.

Assault

In Canada, the most common form of violent crime is assault, which in 1999 accounted for approximately 76 percent of all reported violent crime. The *Criminal Code* classifies assault according to three levels of severity:

Level 1: The first level of assault is a hybrid offence and carries a maximum penalty of five years' imprisonment. Examples include pushing someone or threatening a person with violence. Words by themselves, however, cannot be considered an assault; they must be accompanied by an act or a gesture. **Assault** comprises any *one* of the following actions:

- intentionally applying force to another person, either directly or indirectly, without that person's consent;
- attempting or threatening, by an act or gesture, to apply force;
- accosting or impeding another person, or begging, while openly wearing or carrying a weapon or an imitation of a weapon.

Level 2: The second level of assault is **assault with a weapon or causing bodily harm.** This type of assault is defined as injuring a person in a way that has serious consequences for the victim's health or comfort. It may also involve carrying, using, or threatening to use a weapon. This is a hybrid offence and carries a maximum penalty of 10 years' imprisonment.

Fast Fact
In Canada about 1 in 10 people have a criminal record.

provocation: words or actions that could cause a reasonable person to behave irrationally or lose self-control

assault: threatened or actual physical contact without consent

assault with a weapon or causing bodily harm: injuring a person in a way that has serious consequences for the victim's health or comfort

R. v. Turner (S.A.) (1995), N.B.R. (2d) (N.B.Q.B.)

CASE

John Ryan Turner was three months short of his fourth birthday when he died of starvation in 1994. The examining physician at the New Brunswick hospital testified that John Ryan's body looked like nothing he had seen before, either in Canada or in Zimbabwe, where he had observed several cases of malnutrition in children. The body was emaciated, with wasting muscle tissue and protruding bones, especially in the hip and rib areas. Sores around the mouth indicated the child had been gagged, and other sores on the neck and back indicated the use of a leather restraining harness of a type later found in John Ryan's bedroom. The child had sustained four fractures to his arms, none of which had been medically treated, and at least one of which appeared to be a year old. Expert testimony indicated that the fractures would have been extremely painful. The body weighed slightly more than nine kilograms, which was two-thirds of what a child of John Ryan's height should have weighed. The autopsy confirmed that the child had been "grossly underfed over a long period of time." The judge trying the case said that pictures taken of the body resembled those of "severely undernourished children in concentration camps."

Police arrested John Ryan's parents and charged them with manslaughter. Testimony at trial revealed that the mother had suffered from severe and prolonged depression after the birth of her son and received a series of medical and psychiatric treatments over the course of three years. Testimony also indicated the boy's father had a very passive personality and had withdrawn from his son in a misguided attempt to improve the emotional bonding between John Ryan and his mother.

The judge found both parents guilty of manslaughter and sentenced them both to 16 years in prison. In the written decision on the case, the judge noted that, "*Mens rea* for manslaughter ... was shown since the risk of bodily harm was neither trivial nor transitory, and a reasonable person in the circumstances of the accused would have known that."

1. Explain why John Ryan's mother was charged with manslaughter rather than infanticide.
2. In your own words, rephrase the judge's explanation of the *mens rea*. Identify the *actus reus*.
3. Do you think the Turners should have been charged with murder rather than manslaughter? Explain.

Figure 9.7 Rainbow Park in Saint John, New Brunswick, built in memory of John Ryan Turner

CASE

R. v. Robert, R. v. Foisy, [2000] Que. Mun. Ct.

1. According to the judge, what was the *actus reus* in this case?
2. What led the judge to conclude that these actions were criminal acts rather than a form of creative protest?
3. Do you agree with the judge's decision and sentence in this case? Explain why or why not.

In May 1999, Patrick Robert and Benoit Foisy threw cream pies into the face of federal Intergovernmental Affairs Minister Stéphane Dion. At the time of the incident, the minister was giving out soup to the poor in Montreal. The accused claimed that their act was not criminal but a form of creative protest.

Intergovernmental Affairs Minister Stéphane Dion

The judge of the Quebec Municipal Court found both men guilty of assault and sentenced them to six-month suspended sentences and 50 hours of community service each. Robert and Foisy said that they may appeal the ruling, adding, "Cream pies are one of the last means we have to get ourselves heard; otherwise, we'd have to resort to violence, lobbying, or joining a political party."

The judge, however, clearly thought they *had* resorted to violence, saying, "There is no doubt in my mind that force was used. … It wasn't insignificant. It can't be set aside because it was a joke. I conclude that criminal acts were committed and the two are guilty."

---

aggravated assault: wounding, maiming, disfiguring, or endangering the life of the victim

Level 3: The most violent level of assault is **aggravated assault**, which is defined as wounding, maiming, disfiguring, or endangering the life of the victim. This is an indictable offence and carries a maximum sentence of 14 years in prison.

Sexual Assault

Before 1983, only two types of sexual assault were identified in the *Criminal Code*: rape and indecent assault. In 1983, new legislation was introduced to reclassify sexual assault into three categories or levels. The changes were made for several reasons. Firstly, the Justice Department wished to emphasize that "sexual assault involves physical violence against another person." It also wanted to recognize that spouses can be charged with sexual assault and that victims can be either male or female. The three levels of sexual assault resemble those of regular assault.

sexual assault: touching of a sexual nature that is not invited or consensual

Level 1: The first level is **sexual assault**—the most common offence and the one where the victim suffers the least physical injury. Sexual assault is not defined in s. 271(1) of the *Criminal Code*. Generally speaking, it may be defined under s. 265(1) as an assault that violates the victim's sexual integrity. It usually involves touching of a sexual nature that is not invited or consensual. According to Statistics Canada, almost 97 percent of reported sexual assaults fall into this first level. Since Level 1 sexual assault is a hybrid offence, the Crown can proceed by way of indictment or summary conviction. The maximum penalty for the first level of sexual assault is 10 years in prison.

Level 2: The second level is **sexual assault with a weapon, threats to a third party, or causing bodily harm** and involves sexual assault in combination with threats or the use of weapons, or that results in bodily harm. This carries a maximum sentence of 14 years' imprisonment.

Level 3: The third level of sexual assault is **aggravated sexual assault,** which is defined as wounding, maiming, disfiguring, or endangering the life of the victim of a sexual assault. Because this is the most violent level of sexual assault, an offender can receive a maximum sentence of life imprisonment.

Consent is a valid defence to a charge of sexual assault if the accused person had an honest and reasonable, even if mistaken belief that the victim was consenting to sexual contact. However, consent cannot be used as a defence in three instances: 1) when a victim says no, either by words or conduct, such as directly repulsing physical advances or struggling to escape an embrace; 2) when the accused is intoxicated and not able to determine if consent has been given; or 3) when the accused person was reckless or deliberately blind to the victim's responses, or failed to take reasonable steps to find out if the victim was consenting.

sexual assault with a weapon, threats to a third party, or causing bodily harm: a form of sexual assault that involves the use of weapons, threats, or physical injury

aggravated sexual assault: sexual assault that involves wounding, maiming, disfiguring, or endangering the life of the victim

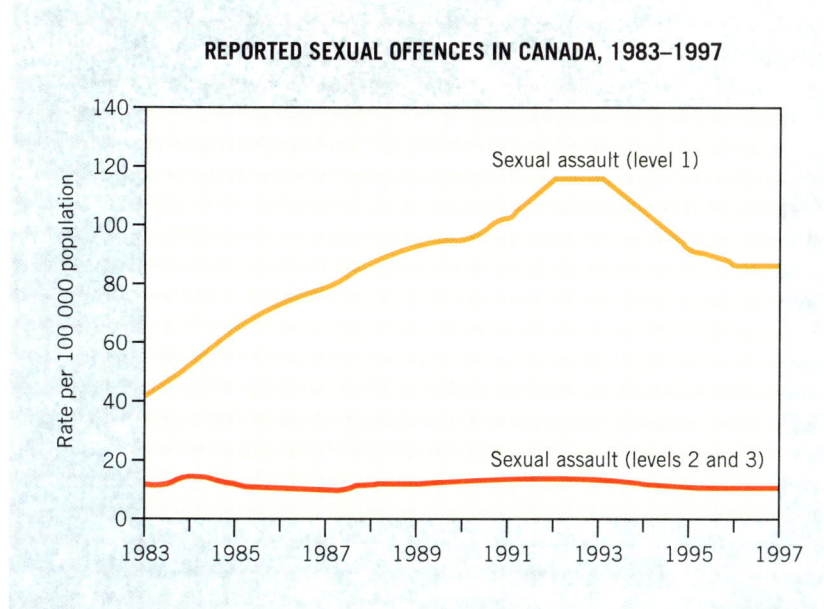

Figure 9.8 Reported sexual offences in Canada, 1983 to 1997

Source: Statistics Canada, Catalogue No. 85-002-XPE.

CASE

R. v. *Ewanchuk,* [1999] 1 S.C.R. 330

BACKGROUND Ewanchuk interviewed a 17-year-old woman in his van. She left the van door open because she was hesitant about discussing a job offer in his vehicle. The interview was conducted in a polite, business-like fashion. After the interview, the accused invited the woman to see some of his work, which was in the trailer behind the van. The woman purposely left the trailer door open, but the accused closed it in a way that made her think he had locked it. At this point she became frightened.

Ewanchuk suggested a mutual massage and the young woman complied. She told him "no," however, when his hands approached her breasts and when he began to touch her sexually. He stopped every time she said "no," but persisted again with more serious advances. She then left the trailer.

The woman was very upset, and on arriving home, she called the police. Ewanchuk was arrested and charged with sexual assault. He was tried by a judge without a jury, and the judge found him not guilty based on the defence of "implied consent." When the Court of Appeal of Alberta upheld the verdict, the Crown appealed to the Supreme Court of Canada.

LEGAL QUESTION Was the trial judge correct in allowing the defence of "implied consent?"

DECISION The Supreme Court of Canada held that there is no basis in Canadian law for a defence of "implied consent." The Court overturned the defendant's acquittal, entered a conviction on the charge of sexual assault, and returned the case to the trial judge for sentencing.

LEGAL SIGNIFICANCE This case established the requirements for *actus reus* and *mens rea* in sexual assault offences. The Supreme Court established that the *actus reus* of sexual assault is proven by three elements: touching, the sexual nature of the contact, and the absence of consent. It determined that the *mens rea* in sexual assault has two components: intending to touch, and knowing about or being recklessly or wilfully blind to the lack of consent.

The Supreme Court also stated that a person can only consent or not consent. It is wrong to hold that

Figure 9.9 Is it right to assume that a woman implies consent to sexual touching by visiting a man she has recently met in his trailer?

a person can deny consent verbally but "imply" consent through conduct. In addition, consent must be freely given.

ANALYSIS

1. How did the young woman in this case indicate her absence of consent to sexual touching?
2. How did the accused show evidence of *mens rea* for sexual assault?
3. The trial judge and the Court of Appeal both found the defendant not guilty, while the Supreme Court of Canada entered a conviction. With which court do you agree? Explain why.

Suicide

Suicide or attempted suicide has not been a crime in Canada since 1972. However, anyone who counsels a person to commit suicide or aids or abets a person to commit suicide is guilty of an indictable offence according to s. 241 of the *Criminal Code*. As you learned in Chapter 4, one of the most difficult cases the Supreme Court of Canada has ever had to judge involved Sue Rodriguez's petition for assisted suicide.

Fast Fact
The maximum sentence for an offence under s. 241 is imprisonment for a term not exceeding 14 years.

Motor Vehicle Offences

Most motor vehicle offences, such as speeding or failing to stop at a red light are under provincial jurisdiction. As a result, they are not addressed in the *Criminal Code*. However, because of their seriousness, the following offences are contained in the Code.

Dangerous Operation of a Motor Vehicle

A "motor vehicle" is defined in s. 2 of the *Criminal Code* as a vehicle that is drawn, propelled, or driven by any means other than muscular power. Such vehicles include cars, snowmobiles, motorcycles, motor boats, and all-terrain vehicles. To convict an accused of dangerous operation of a motor vehicle, the Crown must prove that the safety or lives of others were endangered because the driver failed to exercise the same care a prudent driver would have exercised under the same conditions. This offence can be committed in a number of ways, depending on the manner and circumstances in which the vehicle is operated. For example, René is late for work. On his way, he drives over the speed limit and passes another motorist on a double line, forcing an on-coming car off the road.

Dangerous operation of a motor vehicle is a hybrid offence punishable for a term of up to 5 years. Dangerous operation causing bodily harm is an indictable offence with a maximum punishment of 10 years. If someone driving in a dangerous fashion causes a death, the maximum penalty is 14 years in prison.

Consider This
From April to September, rickshaws, or pedicabs, are a common sight on downtown streets in Ottawa and Toronto. Motorists often consider these vehicles a traffic hazard. Discuss whether these vehicles should be included in s. 2 of the *Criminal Code*.

Failure to Stop at the Scene of an Accident

According to s. 252(2) of the *Criminal Code*, anyone who is involved in a motor vehicle accident and does not stop, offer assistance, and give his or her name and address is presumed to show intent to escape civil or criminal liability. This person may be charged with failure to stop at the scene of an accident. Commonly known as "hit and run," this is a hybrid offence punishable by a term of up to 5 years. The maximum punishment for a hit-and-run accident causing bodily injury is 10 years. If the accident causes a death, the offender can be sentenced to a maximum of life in prison.

Impaired Driving

The proof that a driver is impaired, either by drugs or alcohol, can come from a number of sources. A person's erratic driving, slurred speech, or inability to walk a straight line, or the smell of alcohol on his or her breath can serve as proof of the driver's impairment. Another source of proof is a breath or blood

Law in Your Life
If you are convicted of impaired driving in Alberta, Ontario, or Quebec, you must install a Breathalyzer ignition interlock in your vehicle once your driving privileges are restored. This device records the number of times you start your car with alcohol on your breath. Depending on the results, you may face another licence suspension.

> **Consider This**
>
> An Environics poll commissioned by the Canada Safety Council in 2000 found that 65% of Canadians think that Canada's impaired-driving laws are not strict enough. Review the penalties under s. 255(1) of the *Criminal Code* and explain why you think these penalties are too heavy, too light, or exactly right.

test, both of which measure the amount of alcohol in the person's bloodstream. Section 253(b) of the *Criminal Code* makes it an offence to drive or to have "care or control" of a motor vehicle while the amount of alcohol in the bloodstream exceeds 80 milligrams in 100 millilitres of blood.

Under s. 254, if the police have reasonable and probable grounds to believe that an impaired person is or has been operating a motor vehicle within the last three hours, they may demand that this person take a Breathalyzer test. Any individual who cannot take the test because of an existing medical problem may be asked to give a blood sample instead. The blood sample may only be taken by a qualified medical practitioner who is satisfied that doing so will not endanger the subject's health.

Operating a motor vehicle while impaired and refusing to provide a breath or blood sample are both hybrid offences under s. 255(1) of the *Criminal Code*. The severity of the punishment increases for subsequent offences. Impaired driving causing bodily harm is an indictable offence with a maximum penalty of 10 years in prison. If an impaired driver kills someone, the maximum penalty is life in prison.

CASE

R. v. *Taylor* (2000), B.C.S.C. 734

1. How far over the legal limit was the defendant's alcohol level?
2. What is the maximum penalty if an impaired driver kills someone?
3. What factors may have prompted the judge to double the prison sentence recommended by counsel? Explain why you agree or disagree with the judge's sentence.

Taylor, 25, failed to stop at a stop sign and collided with the passenger's side of a vehicle driven by Ms. Gregg. The Gregg vehicle was proceeding lawfully through the intersection after stopping at the stop sign that governed traffic in its lane. A passenger sitting in the rear of the vehicle was killed, and the other three passengers and the driver were injured. Taylor's vehicle was damaged but still drivable. He put his car into reverse and fled the scene of the collision, leaving the occupants of the other vehicle to fend for themselves.

The accident took place shortly after midnight. About one hour later, a member of Crime Watch reported seeing a car without headlights driving west on Broadway Street in Vancouver. Police arrested Taylor as he was making a telephone call from a booth. A Breathalyzer test administered shortly after 3:00 a.m. showed readings of 160 and 170 milligrams of alcohol in 100 millilitres of blood.

Taylor was arrested and pleaded guilty to impaired driving causing death, impaired driving causing bodily harm, and failure to stop at the scene of an accident. Evidence submitted to the Court indicated he had been an alcoholic since his teenage years. Two weeks before colliding with the Gregg vehicle, he was charged with impaired driving and refusing to provide a breath sample. In the two years between the collision and his sentencing hearing, he continued to drink heavily.

The Crown and defence presented a joint submission recommending that Taylor receive a total sentence for all three offences of two years less a day in prison, followed by a period of probation. The judge rejected this recommendation and imposed a total sentence of four years in prison. In addition, he suspended Taylor's driving privileges for a period of eight years.

Building Your Understanding

1. Distinguish between culpable and non-culpable homicide.
2. What is the difference in sentencing between first- and second-degree murder?
3. Compare the *mens rea* for manslaughter with the *mens rea* for murder or infanticide.
4. Fatima is charged with first-degree murder and pleads provocation. What advantage does Fatima have if the court accepts her plea?
5. While Bruno is being questioned on a minor offence, he jumps up and runs down the hallway. When a detective tries to grab him, Bruno pushes him down the stairs. The detective breaks his neck and dies. What offence will Bruno be charged with now? Explain why.
6. Identify one similarity between each level of sexual assault and regular assault. Why did the Justice Department revise the law on sexual assault?
7. What two factors must the Crown prove to convict someone accused of the dangerous operation of a motor vehicle?
8. Provide three examples of motor vehicle offences.

OFFENCES AGAINST PROPERTY

The protection of private property is an important function of the *Criminal Code*. There are many different kinds of offences against property, but the most common are theft, robbery, and breaking and entering.

Theft

Theft, the taking of property, permanently or temporarily, without the owner's permission, is the most commonly reported criminal offence in Canada. The *Criminal Code* defines theft in an elaborate but precise fashion:

> 322. (1) Every one commits theft who fraudulently and without colour of right takes, or fraudulently and without colour of right converts to his use or to the use of another person, anything, whether animate or inanimate, with intent
> (a) to deprive, temporarily or absolutely, the owner of it, or a person who has a special property or interest in it, of the thing or of his property or interest in it;
> (b) to pledge it or deposit it as security;
> (c) to part with it under a condition with respect to its return that the person who parts with it may be unable to perform; or
> (d) to deal with it in such a manner that it cannot be restored in the condition in which it was at the time it was taken or converted.

Suppose Sally borrows a car from her friend Mohammed. She tells Mohammed she is going to the mall and will return the car in three hours. At the mall, Sally meets another friend, Naya, who lives out of town. Sally gives Naya a ride home in Mohammed's car and then stays with her for a couple of days. On the third day, she tries to return Mohammed's car but is stopped by a police officer who charges her with theft. Although Sally had permission to use Mohammed's car, it was for a stated period of time—three hours. When she kept it for two days without asking the owner's permission, she committed an act of theft.

theft: taking property permanently or temporarily, without the owner's permission

Fast Fact
Auto theft in Canada costs the Canadian insurance industry over $600 million each year. When the additional costs to the medical, law enforcement, and judicial systems are factored in, auto theft costs the Canadian economy over $1 billion annually.

Figure 9.10 If this woman is caught, what will she be charged with? Is this an indictable, summary, or hybrid offence? In what court will her case be heard? Indicate the maximum penalty for this offence.

colour of right: the honest belief that a person owns or has permission to use an item

Note the use of the term "colour of right" in the *Criminal Code* definition of theft. **Colour of right** is the honest belief that a person owns or has permission to use the article in question. To continue the example above, suppose Sally states in court that Mohammed told her, "Keep the car as long as you like." She is claiming colour of right; she took Mohammed at his word and honestly believed she had permission to use the car for as long as she wanted it.

Sentencing for theft depends on the value of the goods stolen. Theft of goods worth over $5000, commonly known as **theft over,** is an indictable offence with a maximum punishment of 10 years in prison. Theft of goods worth under $5000, commonly known as **theft under,** is a hybrid offence with a maximum punishment of 2 years in prison.

theft over: the indictable offence of stealing goods worth over $5000

theft under: the hybrid offence of stealing goods worth under $5000

Robbery

robbery: the theft of personal property through violence or the threat of violence

Robbery may be defined as theft involving violence or the threat of violence. The seriousness of this offence is reflected in its maximum sentence—life imprisonment. According to Statistics Canada, in 1997 approximately 52 percent of robberies involved the use of a weapon.

Breaking and Entering

breaking and entering: breaking or opening something in order to enter the premises without permission with the intent to commit an indictable offence

Committing the crime of **breaking and entering** involves not only breaking into a place but also having the intent to commit an indictable offence once inside. The "place" is usually a "dwelling house" (a home), a commercial building, or some other structure; the intention is usually to commit robbery. Just breaking in *without* the intent to commit an indictable offence is not considered breaking and entering.

Consider the case of Mario. While deer hunting with several companions in northern Ontario, it begins to snow. Mario becomes separated from the others and loses all sense of direction as the wind picks up and creates a whiteout. He stumbles upon a vacant cottage, kicks open the door, and takes

R. v. Cullen (2000), P.E.S.C.A.D. 16

CASE

On August 23, 1999, at about 6:00 p.m., Cullen, 37, walked into the Island Food Centre Co-op and entered a small office at the back where the head cashier was preparing a bank deposit. Cullen was dressed in black, wore a blue nylon stocking over his face, and carried a sawed-off .12-gauge shotgun. He wore two belts full of shotgun shells, one around his neck and one around his waist. He said to the cashier, "Give me all your money." The cashier filled the bag with cash and cheques totalling over $13 000.

At 8:30 p.m., the RCMP stopped Cullen and an accomplice in a taxi on their way to Moncton, New Brunswick. Both men were arrested, and the officers found over $9000 in cash in their possession. The cheques were never recovered. Cullen was charged with robbery under s. 343(d) of the *Criminal Code*. He was held in custody for four months until his trial and pleaded guilty to the robbery charge.

The Court was aware that Cullen had a long history of personal problems—drug addiction, attempted suicide, the inability to retain employment, and a lengthy criminal record including a previous conviction for armed robbery. The judge sentenced him to five years in prison and prohibited him from possessing firearms for ten years. When the Crown appealed the sentence as too lenient, the Appeal Court overturned it and sentenced Cullen to seven and a half years in prison. He was also prohibited from possessing firearms for the rest of his life.

1. Why was Cullen charged with robbery instead of theft?
2. Check s. 343(d) of the *Criminal Code*. Explain how Cullen's crime conformed to the *actus reus* of robbery as described.
3. How did Cullen demonstrate the *mens rea* for robbery?
4. What is the maximum sentence for armed robbery? Do you think Cullen should have received the maximum sentence? Why or why not?

---

shelter until the storm blows over. Mario is not guilty of breaking and entering because he had no intent to commit an indictable offence once inside the house.

The *Criminal Code* treats breaking and entering as a serious crime, and the penalties can be correspondingly heavy. This offence is punishable by a maximum sentence of 10 years in prison if the place broken into is a commercial building rather than a dwelling house. If it is a dwelling house, the maximum penalty increases to life in prison. The severity of this sentence reflects society's belief that people have a right to security in their own homes.

Fast Fact
Breaking and entering is commonly known as "B & E" or burglary.

Building Your Understanding

1. What is the most commonly reported criminal offence in Canada?
2. What type of offence is theft under $5000? Over $5000?
3. Define the term "colour of right."
4. Distinguish between theft and robbery. How is this difference reflected in the sentences for these offences?
5. Why is the intent to commit an indictable offence an important element in the offence of breaking and entering?
6. What is the maximum sentence for breaking and entering a home? A warehouse? Provide reasons for this difference.

OTHER *CRIMINAL CODE* OFFENCES

Mischief, fraud, prostitution, and gambling are some of the more common *Criminal Code* offences that are not listed under Crimes Against the Person or Crimes Against Property.

Mischief

Mischief is listed under Part XI of the *Criminal Code,* Wilful and Forbidden Acts. According to s. 430, mischief may be committed in various ways, but mainly in relation to property and data ("data" being defined in the Code as any information prepared in a suitable form to use in a computer system). One common form of mischief is vandalism, which involves destroying or defacing property. According to the Code, **mischief** is committed by wilfully destroying property or data, rendering property or data useless, interfering with the lawful use of property or data, or interfering with any person in the lawful use of property or data. Both types of mischief (property and data) are hybrid offences.

According to s. 430(2), anyone found guilty of mischief that endangers another person's life can be sentenced to life in prison. It is not necessary for the actual harm to materialize as long as the act has been committed. Suppose Pierre and Matthew were drinking at a local restaurant. On their way home, they rolled a tree trunk onto the railroad tracks. The next morning, the train engineer spotted the tree and was able to stop the train before it could hit the obstruction. Even though no one was killed or injured, Pierre and Matthew could be sentenced to life in prison for their thoughtless, and potentially fatal, act.

Public mischief is a completely different crime, listed under Part IV of the Code. Classified as a hybrid offence, **public mischief** occurs when someone provides false information that either misleads the police in their investigation or tricks them into thinking that a crime has been committed when no crime has actually taken place. One of the most common examples of public mischief is falsely reporting a stolen car.

mischief: wilfully destroying or damaging property or data, interfering with the lawful use of property or data, or interfering with any person in the lawful use of property or data

public mischief: providing false information that causes the police to start or continue an investigation without cause

Fraud

Listed in the *Criminal Code* under Part X, Fraudulent Transactions, **fraud** is defined as intentionally deceiving someone in order to cause a loss of property, money, or service. To convict a person of fraud, the Crown must prove that the accused purposely intended to deceive. There are many types of fraud, including falsifying employment records, failing to collect fares, manipulating the stock market, forging trademarks, and adding precious minerals to a mine to increase its value.

As with theft, the penalties for fraud are determined by the value of the fraudulent transaction. When the fraud is valued at less than $5000, the Crown can charge the accused with either a summary offence punishable by a fine or an indictable offence with a maximum punishment of two years in prison. When the fraud is valued at more than $5000, it is an indictable offence with a maximum punishment of ten years in prison.

fraud: intentionally deceiving someone in order to cause a loss of property, money, or service

Figure 9.11 Morel D'Amour, who fraudulently collected almost $15 000 in welfare benefits, was ordered to repay the money at $100 a month, serve a 90-day jail sentence on weekends, and perform 200 hours of community service. Was D'Amour charged with a summary or indictable offence? Explain.

Prostitution

In Canada, the act of prostitution itself is not a criminal offence; what is criminal is the act of soliciting (communicating for the purpose of prostitution). Although not defined in the *Criminal Code,* **prostitution** (either male or female) usually refers to the act of engaging in sexual services for money. Section 213(1) makes it clear that either the prostitute or the client can be charged with soliciting if, in a place open to public view, he or she

(a) stops or attempts to stop any motor vehicle,
(b) impedes the free flow of pedestrian or vehicular traffic or ingress [entry] to or egress [exit] from premises adjacent to that place, or
(c) stops or attempts to stop any person, or in any manner communicates or attempts to communicate with any person, for the purpose of engaging in prostitution or of obtaining the sexual services of a prostitute.

prostitution: the act of engaging in sexual services for money

For instance, if a man in a tavern offered a plainclothes police officer money for sex, he could be charged with soliciting because the communication occurred in a public place. Soliciting is a summary conviction offence; fingerprints or photographs are not taken, and the offender will not acquire a criminal record.

Keeping a common bawdy house (s. 210) is also a summary offence. A common bawdy house is a place kept, occupied, or used by a person for the purpose of prostitution or the practice of indecent acts. Procuring and living off the avails of prostitution (income from prostitution) are indictable offences with a maximum penalty of 10 years in prison, 14 years if the prostitute is under 18. Currently, this law is most commonly enforced against procurers living off the income of street prostitutes.

Fast Fact
Substance abuse is cited as one factor that leads young people to engage in prostitution.

Gambling

As with prostitution, in Canada gambling itself is not a criminal offence; but offences can be committed in relation to gambling. These offences are primarily divided into those involving "disorderly houses" and those involving illegal forms of betting.

CASE

R. v. Barrow (2000), Ont. C.A. 305

Barrow ran an escort agency in the city of Sault Ste. Marie, Ontario. In 1996, a police investigation revealed that Barrow arranged "dates" between male clients who called the agency and female escorts who were employed by the agency. For her services, Barrow kept one-third of a fee that ranged between $150 and $180. On occasion, the escorts had sex with the clients, and Barrow was aware of this. Evidence showed that Barrow did not coerce the escorts; in fact, she was supportive of them.

Barrow was charged with a number of prostitution-related offences. These charges were based on the evidence of two female undercover officers who posed as potential employees, and on the testimony of four of the escorts. At trial, Barrow was convicted on two counts of attempting to procure women to become prostitutes, two counts of attempting to procure illicit sexual intercourse, three counts of living off the avails of prostitution, and one count of breach of probation. She was sentenced to a total of 12 months in prison.

Barrow appealed the convictions and the sentence, particularly regarding the offence of living off the income from prostitution. Barrow argued that according to case law this offence requires proof of a "parasitic relationship" between the accused and the escorts; she claimed that there was no such evidence. She said that her relationship with the escorts was supportive rather than exploitative. She provided services that allowed the women to remain off the streets in relative safety. No escort was forced to take a particular job or perform any particular act. She provided advice, and in some cases, friendship.

The Court of Appeal dismissed Barrow's appeal on this charge, ruling that her actions did indeed fall within the scope of the offence. Her occupation was "parasitic" in that she took a portion of the money the women made as prostitutes and used it for her own benefit. The fact that on some occasions the escorts did not provide sexual services simply meant that Barrow did not live wholly off the income from prostitution.

1. What is the maximum sentence for someone convicted of living off the income from prostitution?
2. Explain the meaning of a "parasitic relationship." Do you agree that Barrow had such a relationship with her escorts? Why or why not?

---

disorderly house: a common bawdy, betting, or gaming house

Fast Fact
In 1999 to 2000, charity-run gambling in Canada generated $712 million in net revenues.

The *Criminal Code* contains a general definition of a **disorderly house** as a common bawdy house (discussed under prostitution), common betting house, or common gaming house. A common betting house is a place where people bet among themselves (e.g., on a horse race or a football game) and where the keeper of the house receives a portion of the winning bet. A common gaming house is a place kept for gain or profit where people play games, such as poker, and where the keeper of the house keeps a portion of the winnings from the game. It is a criminal offence to keep a disorderly house, to be found in a disorderly house, or to permit a place to be used as a disorderly house. Anyone who keeps a common betting or gaming house is guilty of an indictable offence and can be sentenced to a prison term of up to two years.

There are exceptions to these laws. A bona fide social club, for instance, is exempted from the definition of a common betting or gaming house. Such a club is formed by a group of people who get together for a social purpose, such as playing cards, and not for the purpose of making a profit. The system of betting at horse races is also legal, as long as the track has government approval. In this case, the operators pay the government a percentage of the money their customers bet on the races.

> **Consider This**
> Should governments benefit from racetrack betting even though it is a criminal offence for an individual to benefit from keeping a common betting house? Discuss.

Building Your Understanding

1. List four ways mischief could be committed in relation to data.
2. Regarding the offence of "mischief endangering life," is it necessary for actual harm to materialize? Discuss.
3. Provide an example of public mischief not found in this chapter.
4. What must the Crown prove to convict a person of fraud?
5. Give three examples of different types of fraud.
6. List three criminal offences related to prostitution.
7. Vladimir owns a convenience store with a small room that he rents out for card games. Five percent of each winning hand goes into a "pot," which is given to Vladimir at the end of the evening. Acting on a tip from a disgruntled gambler, the police raid Vladimir's store and arrest him. What offence will he be charged with?

DRUG OFFENCES

The *Controlled Drugs and Substances Act* is the federal statute that deals with narcotics and other controlled drugs such as heroin, cocaine, and marijuana. This Act was passed on May 14, 1997, replacing the *Narcotic Control Act* and those parts of the *Food and Drugs Act* that dealt with controlled and restricted drugs. Some of the more common drug-related offences discussed in this section are possession, trafficking, and money laundering.

The *Controlled Drugs and Substances Act* refers to narcotics and other controlled drugs as "controlled substances" and lists them in a series of schedules. For the purposes of the Act, therefore, a **controlled substance** is defined as any drug included in Schedule I, II, III, IV, or V. Some controlled substances are shown in Figure 9.12.

controlled substance: any drug listed in Schedules I to V of the *Controlled Drugs and Substances Act*

Possession

Under the *Controlled Drugs and Substances Act*, it is unlawful to be in unauthorized possession of any of the drugs listed in Schedules I to III only. (Some of these drugs may be prescribed for medical purposes.) Figure 9.12 indicates the maximum penalties for possession of these substances. Note that penalties vary according to type of substance and prior convictions.

Quite simply, **possession** is the state of having knowledge of and control over something. The term is defined the same way in the Act as it is in s. 4(3) of the *Criminal Code*. Within this more complex definition of possession, there are three important points to remember:

possession: the state of having knowledge of and control over something

Figure 9.12 These drugs are only some of the items listed in the *Controlled Drugs and Substances Act.* The penalties for unauthorized possession of substances listed in Schedules I to III can vary. Why are the penalties highest for Schedule I substances?

Schedule	Controlled Substances	Maximum Penalty for Possession

Schedule I	Opium and its derivatives, including codeine, morphine, and heroin
	Cocaine
	Methadone
		Indictable 7 years
		Summary
		  First offence
		    $1000 and/or 6 months
		  Subsequent offence
		    $2000 and/or 1 year

Schedule II	Cannabis and its derivatives, including cannabis resin (hashish) and marijuana	Indictable 5 years
		Summary
		  First offence
		    $1000 and/or 6 months
		  Subsequent offence
		    $2000 and/or 1 year

Schedule III	Amphetamines and their derivatives, including methamphetamine (speed) and MDA (ecstasy)
	LSD
	DMT
	Psilocybin
	Mescaline
		Indictable 3 years
		Summary
		  First offence
		    $1000 and/or 6 months
		  Subsequent offence
		    $2000 and/or 1 year

Schedule IV	Barbiturates Diazepam (Valium) Anabolic steroids	(Not an offence)
Schedule V	Phenylpropanolamine Propylhexedrine Pyrovalerone	(Not an offence)

Firstly, the person in possession must know what the item is and have some measure of control over it. Jiri held a grudge against Charles. He gave Charles a package of white powder and told him it was foot powder, when it was actually low-grade heroin. After Charles left, Jiri called Crime Stoppers with a "tip" that Charles was carrying drugs. Charles was arrested, but the judge dismissed the charges when Charles was able to prove that he never knew the powder was a controlled substance.

Secondly, a person may be found in possession even if he or she gave the item in question to another person. Jenny placed an ounce of marijuana in Celeste's gym bag. School authorities searched the bag, found the drug, and called the police. Jenny was charged with possession of a controlled substance, even though the marijuana was found in the other girl's bag.

Thirdly, a person can be charged with possession even if the person does not own the controlled substance or have it in his or her possession, as long as the person knows about it and consents to

its possession by someone else. Deirdre and Consuela were going to a party when Deirdre stopped to pick up several capsules of ecstasy. She told Consuela what she was doing, and Consuela offered no objection. Even though the drugs did not belong to Consuela and she was not taking them herself, she still could have been charged with possession on the basis of consent. Keep in mind that "consent" can be broadly interpreted. It could mean that Consuela gave "express consent" by saying out loud that Deirdre's possession of the drugs was all right with her. It could also mean that she gave "implied consent" because although she knew about the drugs, she did nothing to remove herself from the situation.

Trafficking

According to the *Controlled Drugs and Substances Act*, **trafficking** means to sell, give, administer, transport, send, deliver, or distribute a controlled substance; to sell an authorization for a controlled substance (e.g., a doctor's prescription); or to offer to do any of the above.

As discussed, possession is an offence for substances in Schedules I to III only, but as indicated by Figure 9.12, trafficking and possession for the purpose of trafficking apply to Schedule IV substances as well. Note, too, that although trafficking and possession for the purpose of trafficking are separate offences under the Act, they have identical penalties.

trafficking: a criminal offence that involves selling, giving, transporting, or distributing a controlled substance or an authorization for a controlled substance

Trafficking or Possession for the Purpose of Trafficking

Substances	Type of Offence	Maximum Penalty
Schedule I or II	Indictable	Life imprisonment
Schedule III	Indictable Summary	10 years 18 months
Schedule IV	Indictable Summary	3 years 1 year

Figure 9.13 Do you agree that the penalties for trafficking and possession for the purpose of trafficking should be identical? Why or why not?

CASE

R. v. Miller (2000), Alta. P.C. 122

1. Under the *Controlled Drugs and Substances Act,* what was the maximum sentence Miller could have received?
2. Explain why the Court concluded that Miller meant to traffic in cocaine.
3. If Miller had been previously convicted for trafficking, what effect do you think this prior conviction would have had on his sentence?

In 1996, in an effort to control the flow of drugs into Edmonton, the RCMP instituted the Jetway Program. Trained officers observed the behaviour of travellers as they arrived at airports, bus terminals, and railroad stations. If the police noticed people behaving suspiciously, they would approach them.

On April 13, 2000, the Jetway Program was in operation at Edmonton International Airport. Police observed passengers who had just deplaned from a Vancouver flight, and they noticed Miller, 25, pacing up and down. He appeared nervous and seemed to be waiting for someone. Then the police saw him reach for a bag on the carousel, stop, and walk out of the airport.

The officers followed Miller outside and asked if they could speak with him, adding that he was under no obligation to comply. Miller agreed to speak with the police and told them he had just returned from spending one day in Vancouver. The police and Miller went back into the terminal. Except for a duffel bag, tagged with his name, Miller had no other luggage. He gave the police permission to look in the bag.

The police found over a kilogram of cocaine, 76 percent pure. If sold by the gram, the value of the drug would be between $80 000 and $100 000. This quantity would supply a heavy user with half a gram a day for 2000 days. Miller stated that he did not use cocaine himself. He also said that he had one previous conviction, an assault for which he received probation. At trial, he pleaded guilty to possession of a controlled substance for the purpose of trafficking and was sentenced to four and a half years in prison.

To obtain a conviction for possession for the purpose of trafficking, the Crown must prove beyond a reasonable doubt that the accused possessed the controlled substance with the *intention* of trafficking. Intention can be established in a number of ways. For example, the Crown could show that the quantity of drugs the accused had was much greater than what is required for personal use. However, even when the accused is found with only a small amount, there may be other evidence of intent to traffic, such as scales, bags, lists of names, or a large amount of cash.

Note that to convict someone for trafficking, proving the mere *offer* to sell a controlled substance may be sufficient. For instance, according to *R. v. Campbell,* [1999], the Crown only has to prove intent to make the offer, not intent to carry it out.

Money Laundering

money laundering: transferring cash or other property to conceal its illegal origin

Money laundering is the practice of transferring cash or other property to conceal its illegal origin. To prevent criminals from being able to transfer and conceal the source of money they earn from criminal activity, money laundering has been made a criminal offence. Provisions against this offence appear in

s. 462(31) of the *Criminal Code* and in s. 9 of the *Controlled Drugs and Substances Act*.

Money laundering is a hybrid offence. To win a conviction, the Crown must prove the following elements:

a) *Actus reus,* which is extremely broad for money laundering. Any use, transfer, or possession of, sending or delivering, transporting, transmitting, altering, disposing of, or otherwise dealing with any proceeds of crime can be a criminal offence.
b) *Mens rea,* which is divided into two parts: the *intention* to conceal or convert the illegally obtained money or property, and the *knowledge* that all or part of the money or property was illegally obtained.
c) "Subject matter of the offence," meaning the existence of the money or property obtained by committing a criminal offence, participating in a conspiracy or an attempt to commit an offence, counselling or being an accessory after the fact, or committing any act or omission related to an offence.

The penalty for money laundering is a maximum prison sentence of 10 years if tried as an indictable offence. As a summary offence, the penalty is a $2000 fine and/or six months in prison. Note that under s. 11(8) of the Act, the police are allowed to seize anything they believe, on reasonable grounds, has been obtained by committing a criminal offence. Also, under s. 9(3), it is legal for the police themselves to set up a money laundering operation as part of a criminal investigation. See *R. v. Matthiessen* (1999), in Chapter 10, for an example of such a case.

Building Your Understanding

1. Identify the three important elements in the definition of possession.
2. What is the difference between express and implied consent?
3. Ten people are at a party. Two of them, with the knowledge and consent of the other eight, have marijuana with them. The police raid the party. What offence will all ten people be charged with?
4. What evidence can be used to help prove intent to traffic?
5. What factors determine the penalty for trafficking?
6. Define "money laundering." Explain the three elements the Crown must prove beyond a reasonable doubt to convict someone of money laundering.

LOOKING BACK

Reviewing Your Vocabulary

aggravated assault *p. 230*
aggravated sexual assault *p. 231*
assault *p. 228*
assault with a weapon or causing bodily harm *p. 228*
breaking and entering *p. 236*
colour of right *p. 236*
controlled substance *p. 241*
culpable homicide *p. 225*
disorderly house *p. 240*
first-degree murder *p. 226*
fraud *p. 238*
homicide *p. 225*
hybrid or dual procedure offence *p. 223*
indictable offence *p. 221*
infanticide *p. 227*
manslaughter *p. 227*
mischief *p. 238*
money laundering *p. 244*
murder *p. 226*
non-culpable homicide *p. 225*
possession *p. 241*
prostitution *p. 239*
provocation *p. 228*
public mischief *p. 238*
robbery *p. 236*
second-degree murder *p. 226*
sexual assault *p. 230*
sexual assault with a weapon, threats to a third party, or causing bodily harm *p. 231*
summary conviction offence *p. 221*
theft *p. 235*
theft over *p. 236*
theft under *p. 236*
trafficking *p. 243*

Quick Quiz

1. Match the vocabulary terms above with these clues:
   a) intentionally deceiving someone in order to cause a loss of property, money or service
   b) wounding, maiming, disfiguring, or endangering the life of a victim
   c) theft of a radio that has a value of $187
   d) reporting a crime to the police when such a crime has not really occurred
   e) theft of an automobile that has a value of $9800
   f) taking property permanently or temporarily without the owner's permission
   g) touching of a sexual nature that is not invited or consensual
   h) culpable homicide that is not murder or infanticide
   i) a person's honest belief that he or she owns or has permission to use the article in question
   j) theft of personal property through the use of violence
   k) threatening or actual physical contact of a person without consent

Checking Your Knowledge

2. Discuss three differences between indictable and summary conviction offences.
3. Name three types of culpable homicide, and briefly explain each.
4. If one function of the law is to protect the most vulnerable in society, then why does infanticide carry a lighter sentence than murder? Explain why you agree or disagree with the maximum penalty for infanticide.
5. Name two ways the amount of alcohol in the bloodstream may be determined.
6. Distinguish between theft, robbery, and breaking and entering. Provide an example of each.
7. List the three types of houses contained in the definition of a "disorderly house," and briefly describe each.
8. Identify the federal statute that deals with narcotic offences, and describe one type of offence.

Developing Your Thinking and Inquiry Skills

9. In pairs, create a chart to classify the following cases as First-Degree Murder, Second-Degree Murder, Manslaughter, or No Offence. Provide reasons for each classification.
   a) To get even with the management of a theatre that ejected her, Gwyneth decides to set off a bomb that will destroy the theatre. One evening shortly before closing time, she puts a package containing a bomb in the washroom. A patron discovers the package and starts to open it. The bomb detonates, killing her instantly.
   b) Virgil and Parker get into a furious argument over Parker's flirtation with Virgil's wife. Virgil loses his temper and strikes Parker. Parker strikes back to protect himself. Both men punch each other several times. The next day at the hospital, Parker learns that he suffered a serious kidney injury during the fight. Six weeks later he dies as a result of the injury.
   c) Melody has bought her boyfriend, Haron, many expensive gifts including a sports car and a gold watch. One day Haron tells her that he no longer wants to go out with her. Melody becomes very angry. Several days later she visits Haron, pulls out a gun, and kills him.
   d) Marc is in the process of robbing a bank. He is very nervous. To frighten the bank employees, he fires a shot at the ceiling. The bullet strikes a concrete pillar and deflects, striking the manager in the head. The manager dies instantly.

Communicating Your Ideas

10. After giving birth, 19-year-old Diana begins to suffer a severe case of post-partum depression. When the baby is four months old, Diana tries to asphyxiate herself and her son by sitting in a closed garage with the car engine idling. The baby dies, but Diana is rescued. The police charge Diana with infanticide, and the judge gives her the maximum sentence of five years in a federal penitentiary. Write a one- or two-page position paper arguing your stand on the following resolution: The penalty for infanticide as it is defined in the *Criminal Code* is too severe.

Putting It All Together

11. For each of the situations described below, identify the offence committed and whether it is summary, indictable, or hybrid.
    a) While walking down a quiet street, Al is approached by Bill, who forces him at gunpoint to hand over his wallet.
    b) Simon goes to a supermarket to buy meat for his dinner. He replaces a $6.99 price sticker with a $3.49 sticker and pays the cashier $3.49.
    c) Lenore has the brakes of her car repaired at a local garage. She writes a cheque for $297 and picks up her car. When the mechanic attempts to cash the cheque, the teller tells him that Lenore has no account at that bank.
    d) Sasha befriends a man at a local bar, not realizing that he is an undercover police officer. Later that evening, Sasha sells the officer some cocaine for $125.
    e) At a RIDE stop, an officer smells alcohol on Enrico's breath The officer suspects that he has been drinking and asks him to take a Breathalyzer test. Enrico refuses to take the test.
    f) Phillipa arrives home to find the back door of her house forced open. She discovers that a sum of money and her jewellery are missing. A suspect is apprehended by the police and charged.
    g) Curran and Meg are working at a hiking camp. One evening, Curran touches Meg's breasts without her consent. The next day, a police investigation is underway and Curran is charged.
    h) Jim, the local bootlegger, sells alcohol to Solomon. Jim thought he was selling grain alcohol, when in fact it was wood alcohol. Solomon dies and Jim is arrested.

CASES

R. v. Lee, [1991] 3 O.R. (3d) 726

Although he had previously tested negative for HIV, Lee suspected he might be infected. In 1990, he had unprotected sex with a woman. She was aware that Lee often had sex and shared needles with a mutual friend who was gay. After having sex with Lee, the woman tested HIV-negative for over a year. Lee was charged with aggravated assault, but the Court acquitted him.

1. Why was Lee charged with aggravated assault?
2. Do you agree that Lee should be acquitted? Why or why not?

R. v. Tutton, [1989] 1 S.C.R. 1392

Arthur and Carol Tutton were parents of a five-year-old diabetic. They believed in faith healing, but their religious convictions did not prevent them from seeking and following medical advice or taking medication. At some point they believed that their child was miraculously cured of diabetes, so they withheld the child's prescribed insulin. The child subsequently died, and the Tuttons were both charged with manslaughter. They raised the defence that they had honestly believed their daughter was cured and that this mistaken belief would render their conduct non-culpable.

The Tuttons were convicted of manslaughter. They appealed to the Ontario Court of Appeal, which overturned their convictions and ordered a new trial. The Crown appealed this ruling to the Supreme Court of Canada. The Supreme Court dismissed the Crown's appeal and ordered the new trial to proceed.

1. In your own words, explain the Tuttons' defence and the meaning of the phrase "render their conduct non-culpable."
2. Why did the Crown charge them with manslaughter instead of first- or second-degree murder?
3. Why do you think the Supreme Court of Canada dismissed the Crown's appeal?

R. v. Pelz, [2001] Alta. Q.B. 790

In May 2001, 18-year-old Pelz was caught taking a bag of potato chips worth $1.89 from the Zellers store in the West Edmonton Mall. He attempted to flee, a commotion broke out, and he was caught and forcibly taken back to the store. Pelz was charged with theft under.

Pelz failed to show up for fingerprinting and missed his first two court dates. In addition, he was on probation at the time of his arrest for another theft-under conviction for which he had been fined $55, a fine he never paid. When Pelz did appear in Court, he pleaded guilty to the second theft-under charge and was sentenced to 60 days in jail. Pelz applied for bail and appealed his sentence on the grounds that it was excessively harsh. His bail application was heard after he had served 19 days of his jail sentence.

At the bail hearing, Pelz acknowledged that he should not have taken the potato chips or missed his fingerprinting and court dates. He advised the Court that he had lived in Edmonton all his life, had many family members in the city, and could pay his current and next month's rent.

The judge concluded that continued incarceration was not required for such a trivial crime as stealing a $1.89 bag of potato chips. He released Pelz on a $500 bond for which he had to pay a deposit. The judge also prohibited Pelz from entering the Zellers store until after his sentencing appeal was concluded.

1. Why was Pelz given a relatively heavy sentence for such a minor theft?
2. List the factors that likely convinced the judge at the bail hearing to release Pelz after serving less than a third of his sentence.

CASES

R. v. McSorley, [2000] B.C.P.C. 0116

BACKGROUND On February 21, 2000, the Vancouver Canucks and Boston Bruins were struggling to make the playoffs. In their game that night, Vancouver jumped to an early lead. In the first period, following the first Canuck goal, Marty McSorley of the Bruins and Donald Brashear of the Canucks engaged in a fight. Brashear landed several heavy blows and wrestled McSorley to the ice. McSorley was in considerable pain. After the players were separated, Brashear skated by the Boston bench dusting his hands, as if to show that he had made short work of McSorley.

In the same period, with Vancouver ahead 4 to 0, McSorley cross-checked Brashear from behind and used his glove to swat Brashear's head several times. Brashear did not respond, and McSorley was given a 10-minute penalty for inciting a fight. During McSorley's penalty, Brashear was penalized for interfering with the Boston goalie.

Midway through the third period, another Boston player slashed Brashear and was given a penalty. As Brashear returned to the Vancouver bench, he assumed a "Hulk Hogan pose," antagonizing the Boston players. With 20 seconds left in the game, the Boston coach sent McSorley onto the ice. McSorley felt that he was being implicitly ordered to engage Brashear in a fight to salvage Boston's pride. With 3 seconds left, McSorley slashed Brashear in the head from behind, knocking off his helmet and sending him to the ice with a third-grade concussion.

LEGAL QUESTION Did McSorley's slashing of Brashear constitute criminal assault, or did it fall within the norms and unwritten rules of the game?

DECISION The judge found McSorley guilty of assault with a weapon, concluding that the blow to Brashear's head was intentional, even if it was the result of an "instantaneous reaction." A deliberate and forceful blow to the head with a player's stick contravenes the written rules of hockey, the unwritten code of conduct agreed to by the players, and the informal guidelines laid down by officials. McSorley was subsequently granted a discharge, conditional on good behaviour for 18 months.

Marty McSorley

SOCIAL SIGNIFICANCE The judge's decision confirmed that even in contact sports, where the players and general public accept a certain level of violence, there is a point at which a violent act becomes a criminal offence.

ANALYSIS

1. In the trial judge's eyes, what was the *mens rea* of assault in this case?
2. Do you think that Brashear was guilty of provoking McSorley to slash him? If so, would this provocation provide a legal excuse for McSorley's action? Explain.
3. Suppose this incident happened on the street instead of a hockey rink. One man attacks another with a stick and hits him hard enough to cause a severe concussion. With what level of assault would the attacker be charged? Would he likely be granted a discharge if found guilty? Why or why not?
4. Do you agree with the judge's decision? What impact do you think this decision will have on the sport of hockey? Give reasons for your answers.

10 Defences for the Accused

CHAPTER OUTLINE

Mental States

Justifications

Other Defences

FOCUS YOUR LEARNING

How is a defence defined in law?

What defences are available to an accused person?

How are different defences applied to specific criminal cases?

Battered-child defence raised in teen's sentencing

A 16-year-old who repeatedly stabbed his mother a day after she tried to strangle him should not be jailed because he is a battered child, his lawyers say. It is believed to be the first time a Canadian court has been asked to accept a battered-child defence for either trial or sentencing purposes.

Forensic psychologist Dr. Charles Ewing testified that there are parallels between battered women who kill their abusers and children who kill abusive parents. They have both had long-standing abusive relationships with family members, they are depressed, and they feel trapped in the relationship....

The youth, originally charged with first-degree murder, was transferred to the young offenders jurisdiction, where he pleaded guilty to manslaughter and faces a sentence ranging from probation to three years in jail.

An agreed statement of facts filed with the Court says that on January 23, 1997, the youth, now 18, was unable to stop his mother from bad-mouthing him and "picked up a knife that was on a table in the living room and began stabbing [her]." He stabbed her 10 times, also using knives from the kitchen.

Ewing characterized the repeated stabbing as typical "overkill" in such situations, "an unleashing of rage built up for years and years ... that results in a torrent of homicidal frenzy."

Ewing identified years of physical and emotional abuse, including being beaten by his mother almost daily, and years of being called "stupid," dumb," and "ignorant."

SOURCE: Harold Levy, *The Toronto Star*, September 4, 1998, B7.

WHAT DO YOU THINK?

- Give reasons to explain why the charge against the youth may have been reduced from first-degree murder to manslaughter.
- If the Court had accepted the battered-child defence during the trial, what effect would this defence have had on the youth's *mens rea* for manslaughter? Discuss.

The most common defence to a criminal charge is denial. If accepted, this defence represents the absence of *actus reus,* and the accused will be acquitted. In some situations, however, the accused may admit to the crime in question but may still advance a defence to excuse or justify his or her actions. If such a defence is accepted, the court may acquit the accused or, in some cases, find the accused guilty of a less serious offence. A **defence,** therefore, is either a denial of having committed a wrongful act or a justification for what would otherwise be regarded as criminal behaviour.

defence: a denial of, or a justification for, criminal behaviour

For a defence to succeed, the accused must produce evidence that supports it. Consider the case of Genevieve, charged with assault for hitting Daniel with a two-by-four. The Crown is able to prove at trial that Genevieve committed the wrongful act intentionally. Unless Genevieve raises a defence, she will be convicted. Suppose her lawyer presents eye-witness evidence that Genevieve was defending herself. If the jury accepts that she acted in self-defence and acquits her, she will succeed in justifying behaviour that would otherwise be classified as criminal conduct.

Consider This
The importance of the presumption of innocence is reflected in this saying: "It is better for a guilty person to go free than for an innocent person to be convicted." Do you agree with this saying? Explain.

This chapter will present the various defences an accused person may use at trial to justify his or her behaviour.

MENTAL STATES

The mental state of the accused at the time the alleged offence was committed has an impact on whether the accused can be held criminally responsible for the offence. Also, before a trial can proceed, the court has to determine whether the accused is mentally fit to understand the proceedings and to participate in his or her defence. This section will explore the defences of mental disorder, automatism, and intoxication.

Mental Disorder

Mental disorder (formerly called the insanity defence) is defined in the *Criminal Code* as a "disease of the mind." An accused person who suffered from a mental disorder at the time the offence was committed cannot be held criminally responsible because he or she would have been unable to form the *mens rea* of the offence. In other words, the accused may have committed the offence but is not criminally responsible because of a mental disorder.

mental disorder: defined in the *Criminal Code* as a "disease of the mind"

The defence of mental disorder is found in s. 16 of the *Criminal Code,* where it states that a person is presumed *not* to suffer from a mental disorder until the contrary is proven "on the balance of probabilities" (a greater likelihood). The balance of probabilities is somewhat less than "beyond a reasonable doubt." The burden of proof is on the party that first raises the issue, which is usually the defence. The defence would have to prove that there is a greater likelihood that the accused did suffer from a mental disorder than that he or she did not.

Fast Fact
The term "insanity" was changed to "mental disorder" in the *Criminal Code* in 1994, partly to avoid the use of outdated and degrading terms such as "lunatics" and "insane asylums."

The defence of mental disorder can be used by fulfilling *one* of the following two requirements:

- The mental disorder left the accused incapable of appreciating the nature and quality of the act. Suppose the accused repeatedly stabbed another person, not realizing that this act could lead to severe injury or death. Due to a mental disorder, the accused would not have been able to foresee the consequences of the act.
- The mental disorder left the accused incapable of knowing that the act or omission was wrong. For example, Phillip had a mental disorder that led him to believe that Aaron was a dictator bent on destroying democracy. A psychiatrist testified that Phillip thought that by killing Aaron he was protecting his country. The court concluded that Philip did not know that his actions were wrong.

If the court finds that the accused is not criminally responsible, the judge may either "make an order" concerning the accused, or refer the case to a provincially appointed Criminal Code Review Board. If the judge makes an order, there are three choices available: an absolute discharge, a conditional discharge, or a term in a psychiatric hospital. The judge may grant an absolute discharge if the mentally ill person is not a threat to society. If the judge orders that the person be kept in a psychiatric unit, the judge's order lasts for a maximum of 90 days. After 90 days, the provincially appointed Criminal Code Review Board reviews the case.

If the judge does not make an order and refers the case to the Review Board, the Board holds a hearing and decides on a course of action for the accused. The Board then has the same three choices that are available to the judge. However, if the Board commits the accused to a psychiatric hospital, it will be for an indefinite period of time, with regular reviews of the person's status. If the Board is convinced, on evidence provided by qualified professionals, that the accused has been cured, then the Board will order that the accused be released.

For the most part, the defence of mental disorder is only used for the most serious offences because the period of confinement in a mental institution could last longer than a prison sentence for a less serious offence.

Figure 10.1 Rockwood Asylum in Kingston, Ontario, was built as a permanent asylum for the criminally insane in 1850. By 1900, when this photo was taken, it had been converted to a hospital for people suffering from mental illness.

R. v. Johnson, [2000] B.C.S.C. File 542

CASE

Just before midnight on December 20, 1998, the New Westminster police received a telephone call. The caller identified himself as Richard Johnson and gave the address of an apartment building but not the apartment number. He said he was holding a hostage at knifepoint and would stab him unless the police responded immediately. The police sent several officers to the building, but they left without knocking on any doors or conducting more than a cursory investigation.

Between 4 and 5 a.m., Mr. Tront staggered out of his apartment, stabbed through the heart. He proceeded downstairs to the lobby, where he collapsed and died. The police returned and took Johnson into custody when he came out of Tront's apartment. Despite being told not to say anything, Johnson stated, "I stabbed him. He had a knife and I stabbed him." Johnson's Charter rights were explained to him, and the police took a videotaped statement from him.

Johnson was allowed to contact a lawyer. He gave another videotaped statement in which he described the events as follows: "It was like Star Wars, believe me. You know, laser eyes comin' through, infrared, comin' through at me, and ah um tryin' to pick me out, to take me out in the room, in the dark, in the whole apartment."

The videotaped interviews provided more information about Johnson's mental condition than a written statement would have done. The tapes clearly showed the excited manner in which he responded to questions both verbally and physically. Evidence from the videotapes showed that Johnson was candid and straightforward about the events of the previous night.

Johnson was charged with the first-degree murder of his friend Tront, with whom he was staying at the time of the killing. The Crown maintained that the killing was planned and deliberate. Two psychiatrists testified on behalf of the defence.

Johnson was found not criminally responsible by reason of a mental disorder. The Court ruled that at the time of the killing he was suffering from a major mental illness that resulted in severely disordered thinking. He lacked the capacity to measure and foresee the consequences of his acts, and he lacked the capacity to decide rationally whether his acts were right or wrong.

1. Why would psychiatrists testify on Johnson's behalf?
2. Use evidence from this case to explain the Court's reasons for finding Johnson not criminally responsible by reason of a mental disorder.

Fitness to Stand Trial

An accused person is presumed fit to stand trial unless the court is convinced that the accused is suffering from a mental disorder at the time the trial is scheduled to take place. Such a disorder may mean that the accused is unable to understand the nature of the trial proceedings, to understand the consequences of the proceedings, or to instruct counsel. If at any time during the trial there are reasonable grounds to suspect that the accused is mentally unfit, the judge can issue an assessment order and then decide on an appropriate course of action based on the assessment report.

Consider This

Discuss the advantages and disadvantages of videotaped interviews for both the Crown and the defence.

law in the extreme

The Brian Smith Murder Case

The Brian Smith murder case illustrates many of the problems that exist in the way mental illness is dealt with in the criminal justice system. Brian Smith, an Ottawa sportscaster and former hockey player, was killed by a gunshot to the head on August 1, 1995. Smith was shot by Jeffrey Arenburg, a man afflicted with schizophrenia so severe that he heard voices in his head that he believed were broadcast by the media. Under this delusion, Arenburg decided to kill someone in the media. Brian Smith happened to be the first media figure he encountered.

Arenburg admitted to murdering Smith but used the defence of mental disorder. A hearing was held to determine whether he was mentally fit to stand trial, and the jury found he was not. The Court ordered Arenburg to undergo a form of treatment in which he was forcibly injected with anti-psychotic drugs that eventually caused his schizophrenia to go into remission. He was then tried and found not criminally responsible for the murder by reason of a mental disorder.

At issue in this case is the improper treatment of mentally ill persons—or the failure to treat them at all. Brian Smith's widow cited many examples in Court to point out that mental health systems in both Ontario and Nova Scotia had completely failed to treat her husband's killer. For instance, Arenburg had been allowed to refuse psychiatric treatment in Ottawa, Ontario, and in Bridgewater, Nova Scotia, even though at a previous trial in Bridgewater, his conduct had suggested he was suffering from serious mental problems. (At one point, he broke every window in the Bridgewater court house.) Arenburg was eventually treated with medications in a Bridgewater hospital, but he soon checked himself out and stopped taking the medications. After he threatened workers at an Ottawa radio station in 1991, the Ontario Review Board ruled that the Royal Ottawa Hospital could not force him to stay for treatment.

Brian Smith's widow believes that if Arenburg had been properly treated, her husband would still be alive.

SOURCE: Based on Dave Rogers, "Killer not responsible for Smith's death," *Ottawa Citizen*, April 30, 1997; Dave Rogers, "Smith killing avoidable, irate widow insists," *Ottawa Citizen*, May 1, 1997.

Brian Smith, sportscaster

Analysis Questions

1. On what evidence did the jury find that Arenburg was unfit to stand trial? Was he judged mentally unfit because he did not understand the nature of his act in shooting Smith, or because he did not understand that this act was wrong?

2. Assume that you are a member of the Ontario Review Board. What recommendations would you make in order to prevent such a tragedy from happening again? Consider such issues as the defendant's capacity to make decisions, the rights and freedoms of the individual, and protection of the public.

Automatism

Automatism refers to a condition in which a person acts without being aware of what he or she is doing. For instance, a sleepwalker gets out of bed, goes to the kitchen, and prepares a sandwich. The sleepwalker eats the sandwich but does not remember what happened. This person is in a state of automatism because his or her actions were not guided by a conscious state of mind. Examples of other situations that may result in automatism include suffering a severe concussion or taking the wrong medication. Automatism negates the *actus reus* of a crime because someone in such a state does not act voluntarily.

Current case law recognizes two types of automatism: insane automatism and non-insane automatism. **Insane automatism** is caused by a mental disorder. A person suffering from insane automatism will be found not criminally responsible due to a mental disorder. The *Criminal Code* allows for

automatism: a condition in which a person acts without being aware of what he or she is doing

insane automatism: a form of automatism caused by a mental disorder

Figure 10.2 Kenneth James Parks, shown here with his wife and lawyer (left), was acquitted of first-degree murder. Five medical experts testified that Parks was sleepwalking at the time he killed his mother-in-law with a kitchen knife. The Crown appealed to the Ontario Court of Appeal and to the Supreme Court of Canada. Both courts dismissed the appeal.

Consider This
The *Criminal Code* does not define the word *automatism*. Should the Code define the term or should the courts continue to rely on case law to determine what "automatism" means? Discuss.

Legal Link
You can read more about *R. v. Parks*, [1992] 2 S.C.R. by visiting the Pearson site at **www.pearsoned.ca/law** and clicking on the link for the Supreme Court of Canada.

non-insane automatism: a form of automatism caused by an external factor

intoxication: the condition of being overpowered by alcohol or drugs to the point of losing self-control

Law in Your Life
Intoxication is never a defence to a drunk driving charge. If you were driving while intoxicated, had an accident, and unintentionally killed a friend, you could be charged with impaired driving causing death. The maximum penalty is life in prison.

a range of results, including sending the individual to a psychiatric hospital. **Non-insane automatism** is caused not by a mental disorder, but by an external factor, such as a concussion or medication. If proven, the accused will be acquitted.

Intoxication

Intoxication is the condition of being overpowered by alcohol or drugs to the point of losing self-control. Generally, intoxication is not a defence to a crime. A person who gets drunk and commits a criminal offence is still responsible for his or her actions. However, there are exceptions. Firstly, according to case law, intoxication may be a defence to crimes of *specific* intent, but not to those of *general* intent. As you saw in Chapter 6, a general intent offence occurs when a person commits a wrongful act for its own sake, with no ulterior motive. A specific intent offence occurs when a person commits one wrongful act for the sake of accomplishing another. For example, the offence of robbery is a specific intent offence, requiring that the accused person commit assault with the intention of stealing something from the victim.

If a person lacks the ability to form the specific intent to commit the offence because of intoxication, then the mental element cannot be proven, and the accused person cannot be found guilty of the specific intent offence. In such a case, however, the accused person may still be found guilty of a general intent offence. For example, a person acquitted of the specific intent to commit robbery may still be found guilty of the general intent to commit assault. In the same way, a person not guilty of murder, a specific intent offence, may be found guilty of manslaughter, a general intent offence.

The second exception to the rule is if a person's intoxication is so extreme that it almost amounts to a mental disorder. This defence, sometimes used for general intent offences, was established by the Supreme Court of Canada's 1994 decision in the case of *R. v. Daviault*. The defendant had consumed a large amount of alcohol and then sexually assaulted a 65-year-old, partially paralyzed woman. The Court ruled that Daviault's intoxication was so severe that he was incapable of forming even the most basic or simple intent to commit the wrongful act. The Court said that in such cases of extreme intoxication, convicting the accused would violate the principles of fundamental justice. The accused may be at fault for voluntarily becoming intoxicated, but that fault cannot be directly linked to the offence.

Even though the Supreme Court of Canada warned that this defence could only be used in the rarest of cases, a public outcry followed the decision. Some people were afraid that the ruling invited offenders to get extremely drunk and then sexually assault their victims. Parliament quickly amended the *Criminal Code* to make self-induced intoxication an invalid defence to general intent offences that interfered with "the bodily integrity of another person." This meant that the defence could no longer be used against a charge of assault or sexual assault.

R. v. Lemky, [1996] 1 S.C.R. 757

CASE

Lemky fatally shot his companion with a rifle during a domestic argument and was convicted of second-degree murder. He maintained at trial that the gun went off by accident. Evidence was conflicting regarding his state of intoxication at the time. The police noted several physical characteristics of drunkenness, and a Breathalyzer taken shortly after his arrest registered .130. Lemky's appeal to the British Columbia Court of Appeal was dismissed. He then appealed to the Supreme Court of Canada, no longer saying that the gun had gone off by accident. Instead, he argued that the trial judge should have instructed the jury on the separate defence of intoxication. He said he did not have the necessary legal intention to kill his companion because he was too intoxicated to appreciate the consequences of his acts. If the jury had accepted this defence, the result would have been a conviction for manslaughter rather than second-degree murder.

In its decision, the Supreme Court stated that the standard for deciding when a jury must be directed on drunkenness relating to intent is when the evidence of drunkenness is sufficient to allow the jury to reasonably infer that the accused may not have foreseen the consequences of his actions. The Court ruled that in Lemky's case the evidence fell far short of supporting such an inference. His blood alcohol level just after the shooting was only slightly over the legal limit for driving an automobile. He carried on purposeful actions both before and after the shooting, actions that ranged from ordering drinks at a dance to calling his mother and the police immediately after the shooting. Viewed in the context of Lemky's intentional and purposeful conduct before and after the act of pulling the trigger, the notion that he was too drunk to understand the consequences of firing the gun was unconvincing. The Court dismissed Lemky's appeal and affirmed his conviction.

1. How would the defendant have benefited if the jury had ruled he was too drunk to form the specific intent to kill his companion?
2. What standard did the Supreme Court use to decide whether the accused had been able to form the intent?
3. What evidence did the Supreme Court use to come to its conclusion? Do you agree with this conclusion? Explain.

Building Your Understanding

1. What is the meaning of the term "balance of probabilities" found in s. 16(2) of the *Criminal Code*? How does this standard of proof differ from "beyond a reasonable doubt"?
2. Explain two requirements, one of which must be met for the defence of mental disorder to succeed.
3. List the three choices available to the judge or Criminal Code Review Board in dealing with an accused person who has successfully raised the defence of mental disorder.
4. When is the defence of automatism used? Give two examples of situations where it might apply.
5. What is the difference between insane and non-insane automatism?
6. Ralph was found unable to form the specific intent to commit murder because he was intoxicated at the time. Can he still be charged with an offence? Explain.
7. Can a person accused of sexual assault be acquitted by proving extreme intoxication at the time the offence was committed? Why or why not?

JUSTIFICATIONS

In some situations, an accused is exonerated from committing an apparently criminal act because the circumstances justified or excused his or her conduct. One of these situations is self-defence, which includes defending oneself or others as well as one's property. The law also excuses certain actions that occur out of necessity and compulsion, or duress. Another defence—the defence of provocation—can be used to reduce a charge of murder to manslaughter but cannot be used to win an acquittal. Note, too, that in some cases if an Aboriginal person is charged with a *Criminal Code* or regulatory offence, the accused can argue that an Aboriginal or "treaty right" justifies the act in question.

Self-Defence

Self-defence is set forth in s. 34 of the *Criminal Code*. Section 34(1) states that a person may use force to defend against an unprovoked assault where there is no intent to kill or to cause serious bodily harm to the attacker.

> 34. (1) Every one who is unlawfully assaulted without having provoked the assault is justified in repelling force by force if the force he uses is not intended to cause death or grievous bodily harm and is no more than is necessary to enable him to defend himself.

A person who is assaulted, without provocation, may only use the amount of force necessary to defend against the attack. This is called "reasonable force." What constitutes reasonable force depends on the circumstances of each situation. Suppose Tom is going home late one night after a party. Unexpectedly, he is approached by Dan, who grabs him by the collar and threatens to beat him up. Tom is allowed to use reasonable force to defend himself.

However, suppose the circumstances are slightly different. Dan threatens to stab Tom with a knife he is holding. In this case, Tom may seriously injure or kill Dan if he believes that he will suffer serious injury or death and cannot save himself in any other way. Such reasonable apprehension of death or harm is explicitly stated in s. 34(2).

> 34. (2) Every one who is unlawfully assaulted and who causes death or grievous bodily harm in repelling the assault is justified if
> (a) he causes it under reasonable apprehension of death or grievous bodily harm from the violence with which the assault was originally made or with which the assailant pursues his purposes; and
> (b) he believes, on reasonable grounds, that he cannot otherwise preserve himself from death or grievous bodily harm.

Battered Woman Syndrome

Violence against women has became an issue of great concern in Canadian society. The courts have tried a number of cases in which women in abusive relationships reacted by killing their spouses. *R. v. Lavallee,* [1990] marked the first time that battered woman syndrome—the effects of prolonged spousal abuse—was used to advance the justification of self-defence.

---

self-defence: the use of reasonable force to defend against an attack

Law in Your Life
In most cases, you would not be able to claim self-defence if you beat up someone much smaller and weaker than yourself.

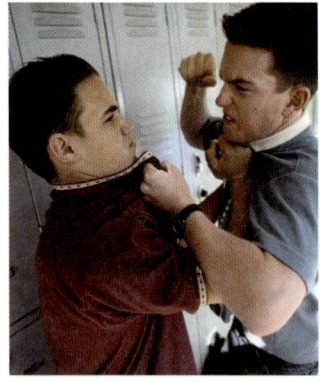

Figure 10.3 What amount of force can be used to defend against an attack like this?

Lavallee shot her common-law husband in the back of the head with a rifle as he left her room late one night after a violent argument. Testimony showed that over the course of their relationship the couple often argued violently. As a result, Lavallee had been treated in hospital for several serious injuries. On the night of the shooting, her husband slapped her on the face and told her he would come back later to kill her. A psychiatrist called by the defence testified that Lavallee was terrorized by her husband, that she found herself unable to escape the relationship despite the ongoing violence, and that the continued pattern of violence had put her life in danger. He characterized the shooting as the final, desperate act of a woman who sincerely believed she would be killed that night.

The jury acquitted Lavallee, but the Manitoba Court of Appeal overturned the acquittal. Lavallee appealed to the Supreme Court of Canada, which restored her acquittal. In its decision, the Supreme Court stated that in cases involving battered woman syndrome, the jury should be instructed on the following three elements:

- why an abused woman might remain in an abusive relationship,
- the nature and extent of the violence that may exist in a battering relationship, and
- the defendant's ability to perceive danger from her abuser.

Since *R. v. Lavallee,* the Supreme Court of Canada has taken pains to note that battered woman's syndrome is not, strictly speaking, a defence in itself. Rather, it is a psychiatric explanation of an abused woman's state of mind that can be used to help advance the justification of self-defence. In other words, merely establishing that a woman suffers from battered woman syndrome does not necessarily justify an act of violence against the abuser.

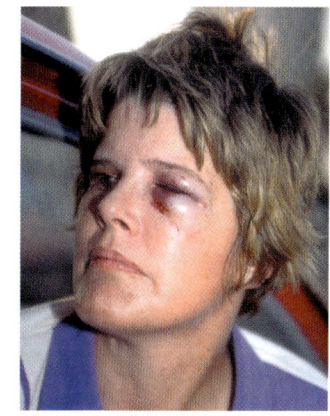

Figure 10.4 Statistics Canada reports that from 1979 to 1998, spousal homicide accounted for 15 percent of all homicides in Canada. Three times as many wives were killed by their husbands as husbands by their wives.

Legal Link WWW
For on-line access to Statistics Canada research on criminal justice matters, visit **www.pearsoned.ca/law**.

Defence of a Dwelling

Sections 40 and 41 of the *Criminal Code* extend the rules for self-defence to the defence of a "dwelling house". Section 2 of the Code defines a **dwelling house** as the whole or any part of a building or structure that is occupied on a permanent or temporary basis. A person is allowed to defend his or her dwelling from any unlawful entry and to remove a trespasser if he or she has entered. The force used to defend one's dwelling must be reasonable under the circumstances. If a trespasser resists the owner's attempts to protect the dwelling, the trespasser is considered under law to be committing an assault. The self-defence provisions in the Code would then apply, allowing the owner to use whatever force might be necessary.

dwelling house: any building or other structure that is occupied on a permanent or temporary basis

Necessity

The defence of **necessity** means that the accused had no reasonable alternative to committing an illegal act. For example, Luke severs his finger with the band saw. Zenobia puts the finger on ice and drives Luke to the hospital, running a red light on the way. After Luke is taken into emergency, a police officer hands Zenobia a summons for dangerous operation of a motor vehicle.

necessity: a defence stating that the accused had no reasonable alternative to committing an illegal act

| CASE | **R. v. *Cardinal*** (2001), Alta. P.C. 92 |

1. What defence did the accused advance to justify pushing a police officer?
2. Why was permission from MacKenzie insufficient to justify the police's entry?
3. Do you think Dick's fears for the safety of his partner should have outweighed the defendant's right to privacy? Why or why not?

MacKenzie had been assaulted by another woman during a social gathering at her home. In an interview on the way to the hospital, MacKenzie gave police constables Dick and McCormack permission to enter her apartment to arrest the suspect. She believed the woman was still in her apartment but might try to escape out the back door when the police arrived.

At the apartment, the officers split up. McCormack entered by the patio door without announcing himself and was immediately challenged by a group of six people, one of whom told him to get out. Dick knocked on the front door, which was opened by Cardinal, MacKenzie's roommate. Dick identified himself and told Cardinal he was looking for the person who had assaulted MacKenzie and that he had her permission to enter the apartment. Cardinal stood in the doorway, refusing to let him enter without a warrant. When Dick saw that his partner was involved in a fight, he stepped into the apartment, and Cardinal pushed him on the chest with both hands. Dick wrestled her to the ground, handcuffed her, and placed her under arrest. She was charged with assaulting a police officer in the execution of his duty.

The trial judge noted that when McCormack entered through the back of the apartment without identifying himself, he became a trespasser in Cardinal's home. The judge ruled that Cardinal was within her legal rights to ask Dick for a warrant. Cardinal's right to privacy outweighed the right of the police to enter her home. When Dick entered the apartment after being refused permission by its owner, he likewise became a trespasser, and, under s. 41(1) of the *Criminal Code*, Cardinal was justified in using "reasonable force" to try and remove him. Cardinal was acquitted.

Consider This

Could a person driving a woman in labour to the hospital be allowed to use the defence of necessity for exceeding the speed limit? Explain.

compulsion or duress: a defence in which the accused person is forced by the threat of violence to commit a criminal act against his or her will

Zenobia could use the defence of necessity because she believed her conduct was absolutely necessary to keep Luke from losing his finger.

For the defence of necessity to succeed, all of the following conditions must be met:

- The accused must show that the act was done to avoid a greater harm.
- There was no reasonable opportunity for an alternative course of action that did not involve a breach of the law.
- The harm inflicted must be less than the harm avoided.

Compulsion or Duress

Section 17 of the *Criminal Code* says that a person will be excused from having committed an offence if the accused did so under **compulsion,** which means that the person was forced by threats of death or bodily harm. **Duress** (almost synonymous with the term "compulsion") is also used in case law, but it offers a slightly broader defence, as explained in *R. v. Ruzic*.

R. v. Ruzic, [2001] 1 S.C.R. 687

BACKGROUND Ruzic, 21, lived in an apartment with her mother in Belgrade, Yugoslavia. One day, a man approached her while she was walking her dog. Over time, a series of encounters took place whenever she went out to walk her dog. Each time he approached, he seemed to know more about her, although she told him nothing. He said he knew her every move, and his behaviour became more and more intimidating. Once he burned her arm with a cigarette lighter; another time he used a syringe to inject her with a substance she thought was heroin. These assaults were coupled with sexual harassment and threats against her mother.

In April 1994, the man phoned Ruzic and ordered her to meet him at a Belgrade hotel. When she arrived, he strapped three packages of heroin to her body and told her to deliver them to a restaurant in Toronto. He gave her a false passport and money to buy an airline ticket. He warned that if she failed to obey him, he would harm her mother. On arriving at Pearson Airport in Toronto, Ruzic was searched and the heroin was found. She was charged with using a false passport, possesssion, and unlawful importation of narcotics.

At trial, Ruzic sought a declaration that s. 17 of the *Criminal Code* violated her right to security of person guaranteed in s. 7 of the *Canadian Charter of Rights and Freedoms*. The trial judge granted the declaration, struck down s. 17, and charged the jury on the common-law defence of duress, which is broader than the statutory defence of compulsion for the following reasons: the threatener does not have to be present; the threat may be of future, not immediate harm; and the threat can be directed at someone other than the accused. For the defence of duress to apply, the accused must be able to show that no "safe avenue of escape" was available. Ruzic was acquitted. The Crown's appeal to the Ontario Court of Appeal was dismissed. The Crown then appealed to the Supreme Court of Canada.

LEGAL QUESTION Section 17 of the *Criminal Code* restricts the defence of compulsion to cases in which the threatener is present when the offence is committed and the threat is "immediate." Do these

Belgrade, Yugoslavia

restrictions place s. 17 in conflict with a defendant's Charter rights?

DECISION The Supreme Court of Canada dismissed the Crown's appeal, affirming Ruzic's acquittal. The Court stated that a basic principle of fundamental justice guarantees that only voluntary conduct can be penalized by criminal law. The Court found, therefore, that "s. 17 of the Code breaches s. 7 of the Charter because it allows individuals who acted involuntarily to be declared criminally liable."

LEGAL SIGNIFICANCE By declaring that s. 17 of the *Criminal Code* is unconstitutional, the Supreme Court of Canada has placed the burden on Parliament to amend that section of the Code so that it no longer violates s. 7 of the Charter.

ANALYSIS

1. Why did the defendant in this case want s. 17 of the *Criminal Code* to be declared unconstitutional?
2. Explain the difference between statutory law and case or common law. Why is the case-law defence of duress considered "broader" than the statutory defence of compulsion?
3. Is s. 17 still in effect? Why or why not?

Section 17 of the *Criminal Code* states the following:

> 17. A person who commits an offence under compulsion by threats of immediate death or bodily harm from a person who is present when the offence is committed is excused for committing the offence if the person believes that the threats will be carried out....

Consider This
Some people believe that the defence of compulsion or duress should be available for all offences. Discuss whether you agree with this position.

Suppose a taxi driver is forced at gunpoint to drive someone who has just robbed a bank to a certain location in the city. The driver is charged with being an accessory after the fact but pleads not guilty by reason of compulsion and is acquitted. Compulsion, however, is not a defence in violent crimes such as murder, sexual assault, robbery, and assault with a weapon.

Two provisions of s. 17 are highly controversial: the threatener has to be physically present when the offence is committed, and the threat has to be "immediate," that is, on the point of being carried out. In the appeal of *R. v. Carker*, the accused raised the defence of compulsion to a charge of wilful damage to the plumbing of his prison cell. Several inmates had threatened to knife Carker, kick him in the head, and break his arm if he did not destroy the plumbing. The Supreme Court of Canada dismissed Carker's appeal, stating that although the threats were made just before the offence was committed, the threateners were all locked in their respective cells, so the threats were not "immediate" and the persons making them were not "present."

In 2001, in its decision in *R. v. Ruzic*, the Supreme Court of Canada declared the immediacy and presence provisions of s. 17 unconstitutional. Once a section of the *Criminal Code* has been declared unconstitutional, the usual next step is for Parliament to amend that section. At the time this book was published, Parliament had not yet acted to amend s. 17.

Provocation

provocation: words or actions that are insulting enough to cause an ordinary person to lose self-control

Provocation is any act or insult that causes a reasonable person to lose self-control. The defence of provocation applies only to the crime of murder. Once the court is convinced beyond a reasonable doubt that the accused has committed murder, provocation may be considered as a partial defence to reduce the conviction from murder to manslaughter. For the defence of provocation to succeed, defence counsel must prove *all* four elements listed below. If any of these elements cannot be proven, then provocation cannot be used as a defence.

- A wrongful act or insult occurred.
- This act or insult was sufficient to deprive an ordinary person of the power of self-control.
- The person responded suddenly.
- The person responded before there was time for passion to cool.

"Moreover, the successful use of the defence of provocation in a number of well-publicized cases has raised public concern, especially about whether the law is in fact condoning violence."

— Federal/Provincial/Territorial Ministers Responsible for Justice, Working Group on Provocation, 1997

R. v. Stone, [1999] 2 S.C.R. 290

CASE

Stone was driving with his wife, who was verbally abusing him. She said his former wife had been unfaithful and that his sons were not his but the result of adulterous liaisons. She told him that she felt sick every time he touched her and she would never have sex with him again. She said she had told the police he was physically abusing her, that he would be arrested, and that she would get a court order forcing him to leave their home and pay her alimony and child support.

Stone pulled off the highway and parked the truck in a vacant lot. As he sat with his head down, listening to his wife berating him, he felt a "whooshing" sensation wash over him. The next thing he remembered was seeing his wife slumped over on the front seat and feeling something in his hand. He was holding a hunting knife and his wife was dead, stabbed 47 times.

In his defence, Stone claimed insane automatism, non-insane automatism, lack of intent, and provocation. The judge instructed the jury on insane automatism, on intention regarding second-degree murder, and on provocation in relation to manslaughter. Stone was found guilty of manslaughter and sentenced to seven years in prison. His appeal to the British Columbia Court of Appeal was dismissed. He then appealed to the Supreme Court of Canada, arguing that the trial judge should have allowed the defence of non-insane automatism. This appeal was also dismissed.

1. Did this case meet the four requirements for provocation? Explain.
2. Why did the jury convict Stone of manslaughter instead of second-degree murder?
3. Do you agree with the statement that "mere words" are not enough to push a normal person into a state of automatism? Discuss, using examples of your own.

Aboriginal or Treaty Rights

There are times when Aboriginal peoples may argue that they have an Aboriginal or treaty right to act in a way that would be illegal for anyone else. Most cases that use this justification deal with hunting and fishing rights. Section 35 of the *Constitution Act, 1982*, guarantees to Aboriginal peoples all their existing Aboriginal and treaty rights plus any rights that currently exist or will be acquired through land-claim agreements. One of the purposes of s. 35 is to recognize that Aboriginal peoples occupied Canada before the arrival of European settlers and that this prior occupation grants them certain rights.

In all of its decisions on the question of Aboriginal rights, the Supreme Court of Canada has to balance those rights with the sovereignty of the Crown. The Supreme Court has stated that s. 35 of the *Constitution Act* should be interpreted in a liberal manner. When any doubt or ambiguity exists in applying s. 35 to a particular case, the case should be resolved in favour of Aboriginal peoples.

Through a number of decisions, the Supreme Court of Canada has set out tests that can be used to establish whether an Aboriginal right exists in a particular case and whether the government can infringe on or restrict that right under certain circumstances. For example, in *R. v. Sparrow*, [1990], Sparrow

Legal Link
The Aboriginal Justice Learning Network (AJLN) is a group of volunteers from the criminal justice system and Aboriginal communities. The AJLN is sponsored by the federal Department of Justice and works for change in justice services for Aboriginal peoples. To learn more about this organization, visit **www.pearsoned.ca/law**.

was accused of fishing with a net that was longer than allowed under the federal *Fisheries Act*. He admitted the facts, but he argued that he had an "Aboriginal right" to fish for food. In its decision, the Supreme Court stated that anyone claiming an Aboriginal right must prove that the right exists, that he or she was acting according to that right, and that this right has been infringed by government action. If all of these points can be proven, and the government still wants to argue the case, then it must show that infringing on this Aboriginal right is somehow justified. For example, the Court recognized that conservation of Canada's fisheries *could* be a valid reason to justify infringing on an Aboriginal right. However, in Sparrow's case, the Court overturned his conviction and ordered a new trial. The new trial never took place because the Crown withdrew the charges.

CASE

R. v. *Van der Peet,* [1996] 2 S.C.R. 507

1. Why was Van der Peet charged with a criminal offence?
2. Explain how Van der Peet's claim to an Aboriginal right differed from Sparrow's.
3. If Van der Peet had traded the fish for clothing, would she have been found guilty? Explain.

Van der Peet, a member of the Sto:lo nation, was charged under the *British Columbia Fishery Regulations* with selling salmon that had been caught under an Aboriginal fishing licence that allowed fishing for food. She argued that she had an Aboriginal right to sell the fish and that the *Fishery Regulations* infringed on this right. The trial judge convicted her, the provincial Supreme Court overturned the conviction, and the British Columbia Court of Appeal restored her conviction. Van der Peet then appealed to the Supreme Court of Canada.

The Supreme Court recognized that in *R. v. Sparrow* it had not fully addressed the way an Aboriginal right should be defined. In that case, the definition of an Aboriginal right had never been in dispute. In this case, the majority of the Court stated that in order for an Aboriginal right to be established, it must meet *all* of the following criteria:

- The right must involve an activity that was a "practice, tradition, or custom [that] was a central and significant part of the [Aboriginal] society's distinctive culture."
- The activity must have existed prior to contact with European settlers.
- The activity, even if evolved into modern forms, must be one that continued to exist after 1982, when the *Constitution Act* was passed.

In its decision, the Supreme Court of Canada stated that Van der Peet claimed "an Aboriginal right to exchange fish for money or for other goods." The Court could find no evidence that selling fish was an integral and defining feature of Sto:lo society. As a result, the Court confirmed Van der Peet's conviction under the *Fishery Regulations*.

Figure 10.5 According to their treaty rights, Aboriginal peoples have the right to make a living trapping lobster in Atlantic waters. How might the conservation of Canada's fisheries be used as way to justify infringing on that right?

Building Your Understanding

1. A person who is assaulted and causes grievous bodily harm or even death to the aggressor in repelling the attack is justified if two conditions are met. List these conditions.
2. How much force may be used to defend one's dwelling?
3. Explain why battered woman syndrome is not in itself a defence to a murder charge.
4. What conditions must be met to succeed with the defence of necessity?
5. Answer the following questions by referring to s. 17 of the *Criminal Code*:
    a) What kind of threats will excuse a crime?
    b) What must the threatened person believe?
    c) What offences are *not* covered in s. 17 of the *Criminal Code*?
6. Can the defence of provocation be used against a charge of aggravated assault? Why or why not?
7. Explain in your own words the purpose behind s. 35 of the *Constitution Act, 1982*.
8. How does an Aboriginal person establish that an Aboriginal right exists in a particular case?

OTHER DEFENCES

There are several other defences available that do not qualify either as mental states or justifications. Some of the most common include officially induced error, mistake of fact, double jeopardy, alibi, and entrapment.

Mistakes of Law and Fact

A **mistake of law** is simply ignorance of the law. As stated in s. 19 of the *Criminal Code,* an accused person may not claim his or her own mistake of law as a defence for committing a criminal act.

mistake of law: ignorance of the law

officially induced error: a defence that the accused relied on erroneous legal advice from an official responsible for enforcing a particular law

"Some say that the principle that ignorance or mistake of law is not an excuse should be revised to take into account the experience of Aboriginal and new Canadians, whose value system may be different from that of the mainstream."
— Communication and Consultation Branch, Department of Justice, Canada

mistake of fact: a defence that the accused made an honest mistake that led to the breaking of the law

double jeopardy: the legal doctrine that an accused person cannot be tried twice for the same offence

Traditionally, this approach has been justified on the basis that criminal law represents the common, fundamental values and laws that all people should know. However, an important exception to this principle is referred to as "officially induced error." An **officially induced error** refers to a situation in which the accused relied on the erroneous legal advice of an official responsible for enforcing a particular law. This defence can be used against an alleged violation of a regulatory law. As we saw in Chapter 6, regulatory laws do not appear in the *Criminal Code;* their main purpose is to protect the health, safety, and welfare of the public.

Consider the following example. Anu was inside her husband's car, which was parked in a no-parking zone while he was at an appointment in a nearby medical building. A police officer approached and told Anu that if the vehicle was not moved immediately it would be towed. In the course of their discussion, the officer found out that Anu's driver's licence was suspended. Anu believed that the officer was giving her permission to drive her husband's car to the medical building's parking lot a block away. On her way to the lot, Anu was spotted by another police officer who knew that her licence was suspended. This officer stopped Anu and charged her with driving a motor vehicle while using a suspended licence. In this situation, the court may acquit Anu if she can prove that she honestly thought the first officer was advising her to drive the car from the no-parking zone to the building's parking lot.

A person whose behaviour would otherwise be criminal may have a defence if he or she made a **mistake of fac**t—an honest mistake that led to the criminal offence. In this case, the accused would not have had the *mens rea* or guilty mind required to commit the offence. For example, Sharon leaves her bicycle in a bike stand at her school, returns later, and by mistake rides off with a similar bike. The mistaken belief in this example would constitute a defence as long as the mistake was an honest one and, if the facts were as the accused believed them to be, no criminal offence would have occurred. In other words, as long as Sharon believed she was taking her own bike, she could argue mistake of fact as her defence.

Double Jeopardy

Generally, a person who has been tried for an offence cannot be tried again or "placed in jeopardy" for the same offence. This defence, called **double jeopardy,** holds true whether the person has been acquitted or convicted of the offence in question. For example, if Paolo was acquitted on a robbery charge, the police cannot bring the same charge against him two years later simply because they have more evidence pertaining to the robbery. In the same way, if Paolo was convicted of the charge and served a prison sentence, he cannot be tried again on the same charge after his release from prison. The *Canadian Charter of Rights and Freedoms* has guaranteed this right in s. 11(h) (see page 520). Note, however, that the Crown does have the right to appeal an acquittal or a sentence if the Crown thinks the court has made a mistake of law. If the Court of Appeal upholds the Crown's appeal, it may order that the accused be tried again on the same charge.

Identical Duffel Bag a Decoy

Woman says she took luggage with marijuana by mistake

An innocent traveller from Jamaica caught up in a nightmarish drug smuggling allegation? Or a cunning marijuana courier using two identical duffel bags to provide an instant alibi if caught?

That's the issue facing a Peel Region jury at the trial of a 50-year-old North York woman arrested two years ago at Pearson International Airport for having 22 kilograms of marijuana in an unmarked duffel bag. When a Canadian Customs officer unzipped the bag to disclose four blocks of packed marijuana worth up to $440 000, Herma Friginette … immediately declared the bag was not hers, her trial has been told.

An identical bag with her bright red luggage ticket on it, accompanied by an orange neon "heavy caution" tag, was still on the luggage carousel. Federal prosecutor Adam Boni charged that Friginette was using that bag "as a decoy, a convenient excuse if you were caught with the marijuana." He and defence lawyer Paul Layefsky will present their closing arguments to the jury next week.

Unknown to her, because she had been given a secretly coded card, Friginette had been sent for a secondary customs inspection because of the jewellery she was wearing and because she looked away from the inspector at the primary booth, the trial has been told.

On her way to secondary inspection, a courteous stranger had lifted her suitcase and what she thought was her duffel bag from the carousel and had put them on an airport cart for her, Friginette testified yesterday in Ontario court, general division. She never noticed the duffel bag she ended up with didn't have the distinctive tags, she told the jury under Madam Justice Moira Caswell.

"I wasn't looking for the tags," she said. "I thought I was taking my own bag."

A customs inspector testified about noticing Friginette drag a heavy, dark duffel bag off the plane and struggle to put it on a collapsible cart she had been carrying. Friginette denied that. She said she had helped an older woman by carrying the woman's smaller and lighter brown suitcase from the plane for her, putting it on the cart, then returning it to her at the primary inspection lineup at customs.

She denied Boni's suggestion that a drug importer bought the $566 return airline ticket for her and that

she would have been paid between $2000 and $5000 to smuggle in the marijuana. A man's handwritten name found in her purse was that of a passenger on the plane to Jamaica who asked her to look him up if she was in Montego Bay, she testified.

Friginette, who has been living on welfare since quitting her bookkeeping job at Metro Catholic Children's Aid Society in 1994, said she paid for the ticket herself. She also denied Boni's allegation that she didn't report she was bringing in fruit and vegetables from Jamaica because that would have surely meant her bags would have been inspected.

SOURCE: Farrell Crook, "Identical duffel bag a 'decoy,' drug trial told; woman says she took luggage with marijuana by mistake," *The Toronto Star*, August 7, 1997, A24.

1. Identify the claims made by the customs inspector and the counter-claims of the accused.
2. Does the accused's defence in this case satisfy the two requirements for having committed a mistake of fact? Why or why not?
3. Imagine you are on the jury that must determine the defendant's guilt or innocence in this case. What additional considerations would you apply to help you decide? What would your decision be? Explain.

Alibi

alibi: a defence raised by the accused claiming that he or she was somewhere else when the offence was committed

A defendant who advances the defence of **alibi** simply claims that he or she was not present at the time the offence was committed. Evidence by witnesses supporting the defendant's claim strengthens the alibi defence. In a jury trial, the judge must instruct the jury that the burden is on the Crown, not the defendant. If the Crown cannot prove that the accused was present when the offence was committed, then the accused must be acquitted.

Entrapment

Most police work consists of reacting to crimes that have already been committed or interrupting crimes in progress. Sometimes, however, police officers pretend to be criminals in order to conduct legal undercover operations. In doing so, they are permitted to present a suspect with the opportunity to commit a crime, but they may not harass, bribe, or induce the person to break the law. The term **entrapment** refers to police conduct that illegally induces criminal behaviour. For example, William was a reformed drug addict who was persuaded to sell drugs to an undercover police officer. William resisted the officer's repeated demands until the officer stated that she urgently needed the drugs because she was sick. When the officer burst into tears, William finally agreed to the transaction and was arrested as he delivered the drugs. At trial he raised the defence of entrapment and was acquitted.

entrapment: a defence against police conduct that illegally induces the defendant to commit a criminal act

The burden is on the accused to prove entrapment, which is considered an abuse of power on the part of the state. It will help the defendant's case to show the lack of any criminal involvement before being approached by the police. Also, the accused should be able to prove that the police went beyond merely offering a chance to commit a crime to actively inducing the accused to break the law.

Consider This

Entrapment involving police misconduct is a question to be decided by the trial judge, and the proper remedy is a stay of proceedings. Should the issue of entrapment be decided by the jury instead of the judge? Discuss.

Figure 10.6 Sometimes a police officer may conduct an undercover operation, presenting suspects with an opportunity to commit a crime. What would a defendant have to show to prove entrapment?

If the judge agrees with the defence that there has been an abuse of power, the judge will "stay" the proceedings, or stop the trial, which is not the same as acquitting the accused of the charges. Staying the proceedings does not mean the accused has been found innocent; but it does reflect on the conduct of the police or the Crown, suggesting that their behaviour violates the standards of a just society.

R. v. Matthiessen (1999), Alta. C.A. 31

CASE

Matthiessen, a suspected drug trafficker, was worried about Revenue Canada enquiries about the source of some of his money. Undercover police operatives offered Matthiessen the services of a fictitious company they had created to launder funds. Matthiessen had to pay an up-front fee of $6300. After that, any money he gave to the company was returned to him later minus a 5 percent processing fee. The company deposited a total of almost $100 000 into a bank account in Canada on Matthiessen's behalf.

In the end, the police arrested Matthiessen and charged him with possession of the proceeds of crime, trafficking in a narcotic, money laundering, and possession of cocaine for the purposes of trafficking. The trial judge held that the conduct of the police was illegal because they had unlawfully laundered drug money. She found, however, that the police acted in good faith and, accordingly, their illegal act did not constitute entrapment or an abuse of process. Matthiessen appealed his conviction to the Alberta Court of Appeal.

The Court of Appeal found that there is no absolute rule against the involvement of the state in illegal conduct. In this case, the police did not manufacture crime, nor did they lure ordinary citizens for the purpose of testing their virtue. The exorbitant commission and servicing rates of the fictitious company ensured that the scheme was unlikely to entrap people who were not already involved in crime. The police deliberately targeted identified drug traffickers, and their conduct did not offend the basic values of the community. Although the investigative techniques went beyond acceptable limits, allowing the accused's conviction to stand would not amount to an abuse of judicial process by the state. Therefore, the Court dismissed Matthiessen's appeal.

1. The trial judge found that the police "acted in good faith." What does this mean?
2. Why did the Court dismiss Matthiessen's appeal?
3. Matthiessen was sentenced to prison, but the police were neither charged nor reprimanded. Do different consequences represent the standards of a just society or an abuse of power? To help you decide, consider Rule of Law, the need to obtain admissible evidence, and police conduct.

Building Your Understanding

1. What is the difference between a mistake of law and a mistake of fact?
2. Provide an example, other than the one in this chapter, of when an officially induced error could be used as a defence to a criminal act.
3. What must be proven for the mistake of fact defence to succeed?
4. Who has the burden of proof regarding the defence of an alibi, the Crown or the accused?
5. Using your own example, explain the meaning of double jeopardy.
6. What two elements must the accused prove to succeed in the defence of entrapment?
7. Why is entrapment considered an abuse of power?

LOOKING BACK

Reviewing Your Vocabulary

alibi *p. 268*
automatism *p. 255*
compulsion or duress *p. 260*
defence *p. 251*
double jeopardy *p. 266*
dwelling house *p. 259*
entrapment *p. 268*
insane automatism *p. 255*
intoxication *p. 256*
mistake of fact *p. 266*
mistake of law *p. 265*
mental disorder *p. 251*
necessity *p. 259*
non-insane automatism *p. 256*
officially induced error *p. 266*
provocation *p. 262*
self-defence *p. 258*

Quick Quiz

1. Choose the appropriate term from the vocabulary list above to complete the following statements:
   a) ____ refers to police conduct that induces criminal behaviour.
   b) A(n) ____ offers an excuse for apparently criminal behaviour and may result in an acquittal or reduction of a charge brought against an accused person.
   c) ____ is usually a defence only in crimes of specific intent.
   d) ____ is a form of automatism caused by an external factor such as sleepwalking.
   e) ____ is a defence if the accused relied on the erroneous legal advice of an official who was responsible for the enforcement of that particular law.
   f) ____ is a defence if the accused made an honest mistake regarding a situation that led to the breaking of the law.
   g) ____ is defined in the *Criminal Code* as a "disease of the mind."
   h) ____ is a condition in which a person acts without being aware of what he or she is doing.
   i) ____ is a form of automatism caused by a mental disorder.
   j) ____ is the legal doctrine that maintains a person cannot be tried twice for the same offence.
   k) ____ is a defence raised by an accused who argues that he or she was somewhere else when the alleged offence was committed.
   l) ____ is a defence that may reduce a murder charge to one of manslaughter.
   m) ____ refers to a situation in which a person has no reasonable alternative to committing an illegal act.
   n) In ____ the victim of an unprovoked attack may use reasonable force to defend against the attack.
   o) ____ is a defence by which the accused person claims to have been forced to commit a criminal act by the threat of violence.

Checking Your Knowledge

2. How is the defence of mental disorder different from the defence of automatism?
3. Suppose a person is stunned by a blow to the head and unconsciously strikes out and hits someone. Has this person committed a criminal offence? Explain.
4. Under what two circumstances can intoxication be used as a defence?
5. List and briefly explain the four elements that must be proven for the defence of provocation to succeed.

6. In deciding whether the police have practised entrapment, does the court have to consider the *mens rea* of the accused? Explain.

Developing Your Thinking and Inquiry Skills

7. "An accused must be deemed mentally fit to stand trial." Relate this statement to the principles of fundamental justice.

8. Conduct a survey of at least 10 students who have not taken a course in law. Explain to them the meaning of a criminal defence and ask them if they can list any defences they know of based on their reading or on watching movies or television. Rank the defences in order from the most mentioned to the least mentioned. Then compare your rankings with those of your classmates. Are they similar or dissimilar? If they are dissimilar, can you think of reasons to explain the differences?

9. Put yourself in the position of a judge. What do you think would be the appropriate verdict in the following case? In making this decision, consider the following: a) evidence of mental disorder and b) ability of the accused to understand the nature of the act and its consequences. Provide reasons for your decision.

> Patricia, an 81-year-old woman, was eating dinner in her home when Lars broke in and stabbed her to death. He claimed he was acting in self-defence because he feared for his life. He believed Patricia was following him all over town and plotting with others to murder him. In reality, Patricia barely knew Lars and had no designs on his life.
>
> At trial, the defence called a noted psychiatrist, who testified that Lars had been suffering from paranoid schizophrenia for the past 14 years. During that period, he had been in and out of various psychiatric facilities, and five years ago he had stabbed his father and was convicted of aggravated assault. On his release, he was prescribed a medication that seemed to improve his condition dramatically. Recently, however, he had stopped taking the medication, and his mental condition had deteriorated.

Communicating Your Ideas

10. Visit your local court house and attend a criminal trial. Complete a report using the following guide:
    a) Briefly describe the facts of the case.
    b) Name the defence that was advanced.
    c) Provide reasons to explain why the defence was successful or unsuccessful.
    d) If you had defended the accused in this case, what would you have done differently to support your defence?

11. In small groups, collect six newspaper articles about criminal trials in which the name of the defence is stated. For each article complete the following activities:
    a) Underline the defence used in the article.
    b) In your notebook:
       • write the source and headline
       • summarize the article
       • list and define the defence used
    c) Present your findings to the class by using visual aids such as handouts, overheads, and charts.
    d) After your presentation, place your articles on a bulletin board under the appropriate defence headings, such as mental disorder, alibi, etc.

Putting It All Together

12. List five defences you have studied in this chapter that you think should be amended. For each defence provide the following:
    a) the name of the defence
    b) the meaning of the defence
    c) an amendment you would make to one of the defences
    d) the reasons for the amendment, which may be based on one or more of these concerns:
       • defence lacks a clear definition
       • defence applies to too many or too few offences
       • conditions for applying the defence are unreasonable or outdated

CASES

R. v. Hibbert, [1995] 2 S.C.R. 973

Hibbert watched while Bailey, a drug dealer, shot Cohen, a friend of Hibbert. The victim survived, and Hibbert, as a party to the offence, was charged with attempted murder. At trial, Hibbert advanced the defence of duress. He said that on the night of the shooting he ran into Bailey, who had a handgun and ordered Hibbert to take him to Cohen's apartment. Hibbert refused, and Bailey punched him in the face several times. Hibbert feared for his life and believed that Bailey would shoot him if he did not co-operate. At Cohen's apartment building, Hibbert told him through the intercom to come down to the lobby. When Cohen arrived, Bailey shot him four times.

Hibbert testified that he pleaded with Bailey not to kill Cohen, but Cohen stated that the accused made no attempt to intervene. After the shooting, Bailey drove Hibbert away and threatened to kill him if he told the police. The next day, Hibbert turned himself in to the police.

The jurors clearly believed that Hibbert acted under duress, but they were concerned whether he could have used a safe avenue of escape. They acquitted Hibbert of attempted murder, but convicted him of aggravated assault. The Ontario Court of Appeal upheld the conviction, but the Supreme Court of Canada ruled that the trial judge had erred in his charge to the jury and ordered a new trial.

1. What evidence did Hibbert show to advance the defence of duress?
2. Discuss whether Hibbert had a safe avenue of escape. How does this issue impact on the defence of duress?
3. Put yourself in the place of a jury member. Would you have convicted Hibbert or accepted his defence of duress? Support your decision.

R. v. Elaschuk (2000), Alta. P.C. 139

Elaschuk was charged with theft for shoplifting items from a Save-On Foods store. She testified that she worked as a nurse on the night shift and had not slept at all the night before the offence. When she entered the Save-On store she felt stressed and was overwhelmed by its size.

Elaschuk viewed herself as a failure and as an incompetent parent. Her own mother had constantly criticized her and had often used Elaschuk as an accomplice on shoplifting expeditions. Elaschuk had participated willingly because she craved her mother's love. Even after leaving home, she felt an urge to steal things on entering a store because she knew this was one thing she did well.

Elaschuk's lawyer put her under the care of a psychiatrist who testified that she suffered from kleptomania (an uncontrollable urge to steal), depression, and an anxiety disorder. He said that at the time of the offence, she had "abandoned [the use of] cognitive logic." Elaschuk pleaded not guilty by reason of mental disorder according to s. 16 of the *Criminal Code*. The trial judge acquitted her.

1. According to s. 16, who had the burden of proof to show that the defendant was suffering from a mental disorder?
2. The judge accepted that the defendant's mental disorder was severe enough to negate her *mens rea* for theft. Explain why you agree or disagree with this decision.

CASES

R. v. Proulx (1998), B.C.C.A. CA023334

BACKGROUND In 1994 Proulx sold his ranch near Kamloops, British Columbia, to Frolek. Proulx had the option to re-purchase the ranch until the year 2000. He was allowed to live on the ranch until then as long as he looked after irrigation and other chores.

Frolek moved into a trailer on the ranch. For the next 18 months, there was conflict between Frolek and Proulx, and Frolek tried unsuccessfully to have Proulx evicted. Witnesses testified to Frolek's aggressive nature and his antagonism toward Proulx. Proulx, however, was not known to be violent and had a reputation for honesty and integrity. Proulx said Frolek had threatened several times to kill or mutilate him.

On September 3, 1995, Frolek confronted Proulx twice while he was working on the ranch. Eyewitnesses described the first encounter, but Proulx was alone when Frolek approached him the second time. Frolek approached Proulx and threatened to kill him. Proulx tried to reason with Frolek, but Frolek kept coming at him with an "ugly" expression on his face. Proulx reached into his truck and grabbed his revolver. He shot Frolek three times, hitting him twice. As Frolek ran toward a nearby gate, Proulx pursued and shot him twice more in the back of the head. An autopsy revealed that Frolek had been drinking and had consumed the equivalent of at least six bottles of beer.

Proulx was charged with first-degree murder for shooting Frolek. At trial, Proulx said he was acting in self-defence and raised the alternate defence of provocation. The jury did not convict him of first- or second-degree murder but did find him guilty of manslaughter. Proulx appealed to the British Columbia Court of Appeal, arguing that the trial judge had failed to instruct the jury on the importance of his state of mind as it related to self-defence in s. 34(2) of the *Criminal Code*.

LEGAL QUESTION The three elements of self-defence in s. 34(2) are

1) the existence of an unlawful assault;
2) a reasonable belief in the risk of death or grievous bodily harm; and
3) a reasonable belief that it is not possible to preserve oneself from harm except by killing the adversary.

Should the judge have instructed the jury that this defence was available to Proulx even if Proulx's belief in the existence of any of these elements was mistaken?

DECISION The Court of Appeal ruled that self-defence still applies under s. 34(2) even if the accused is mistaken about any of these elements as long as the mistaken belief was reasonable in the circumstances. The Court set aside Proulx's conviction and ordered a new trial.

LEGAL SIGNIFICANCE The decision affirmed that the accused person's state of mind has to be considered when applying self-defence as a defence for the accused.

ANALYSIS

1. Analyze the evidence that showed that Proulx may have had reason to fear that Frolek meant to kill him. Is it convincing enough to excuse Proulx for killing Frolek?
2. Do you think the jury accepted Proulx's alternate defence of provocation? Explain your answer.
3. The jury rejected Proulx's claim of self-defence. Considering the evidence presented, what factors might have influenced the jury to reject this defence? Explain why you agree or disagree with the jury's verdict.

11 Sentencing and the Correctional System

CHAPTER OUTLINE

Goals of Sentencing

Sentencing Procedures

Types of Traditional Sentences

Restorative Justice Programs

The Correctional System

Paroles and Pardons

FOCUS YOUR LEARNING

What are the main principles of sentencing?

How do sentencing options differ?

What is involved in restorative justice programs?

What is the role of the correctional system in Canada?

When do offenders qualify for paroles and pardons?

Guilty Teen Out on Bail

A 15-year-old boy was walking his dog in a park when he was attacked by two youths aged 16 and 17 years. They kicked him in the head repeatedly with their steel-toed boots. As a result of the attack, the boy was in a coma for three months. He suffered major neurological injuries and was left disabled.

His attackers were charged with attempted murder and released on bail shortly after the attack. They were later found guilty of aggravated assault. The youths were sentenced to 12 months behind bars and 12 months' probation. One was already in jail in an unrelated case when sentence was pronounced. The other youth, however, was granted bail less than 24 hours after being sentenced to await a decision on a request for appeal.

The media frequently report cases resulting in controversial sentences. Sometimes people find sentences far too lenient in relation to the crime. Others argue about decisions to grant bail to sentenced offenders.

WHAT DO YOU THINK?

- What impressions do you get from the media about crime and sentencing in Canada?
- Should an offender be released on bail while waiting a decision on a request for appeal? Explain your position.

Try to recall a movie or television show in which a guilty person was sentenced by a judge. Think about the courtroom drama. Perhaps the lawyers argue about how long the sentence should be, or maybe heated discussion ensues about the offender's behaviour or the seriousness of the offence. Then the judge slams down a gavel, shouting at the criminal, "I sentence you to 10 years for armed robbery!" The spectators gasp, someone weeps or shouts, and the offender is whisked away in handcuffs to serve the prison sentence.

If these are the kinds of images you have when you think of sentencing criminals, you will be in for a surprise. In reality, the sentencing process involves many people and careful consideration of a variety of factors. This chapter will help you understand the goals, processes, people, and institutions involved in sentencing offenders.

GOALS OF SENTENCING

Once a person has been found guilty of committing a crime, the judge imposes a **sentence**, or punishment. Sentencing has many goals: protection of the public, retribution, deterrence, rehabilitation, restitution, and denunciation. The reasons for sentencing have been established over many years by court decisions. These reasons are now summarized in s. 718 of the *Criminal Code*. All of Part XXIII of the *Criminal Code* is devoted to sentencing matters.

sentence: punishment imposed on a person convicted of committing a crime

Protection of the Public

In society, the main goal of sentencing is to protect the public. This includes protection of their person, their property, and their individual rights and freedoms. When someone commits an offence, that individual harms not only the victim but *everyone* in society. People feel threatened until the offender is apprehended and public protection is restored.

"When the public is demanding stiff penalties, I always turn it around. What if they become the accused? Then they might look at the system a bit differently."
— Ontario Court Justice Charles Vaillancourt

Figure 11.1 Every citizen has the responsibility to obey the laws of the land. Failure to do so carries consequences. What would happen if there were no consequences for criminal behaviour?

Retribution

retribution: punishment to avenge a crime, ensuring that offenders suffer the consequences of their actions

When one person harms another, society wants that person to "pay" for the offence. **Retribution** is punishing an offender to avenge a crime or to satisfy the public that the offender has paid for the crime. Historically, retribution stems from the idea of taking "an eye for an eye," a concept you may recall reading about in Chapter 1.

Deterrence

specific deterrence: punishment to discourage criminals from re-offending

general deterrence: punishment to discourage people in general from offending

Many people believe that punishing offenders sends a message that anyone caught breaking the law will be punished accordingly. They believe that imposing a penalty will deter, or discourage, people from committing crimes. The term **specific deterrence** refers to punishment as a way of discouraging criminals from re-offending. **General deterrence** refers to punishment as a way of discouraging other members of society from committing similar crimes.

Rehabilitation

rehabilitation: punishment combined with treatment and training to help offenders function in society

Another important goal of sentencing is to help offenders become law-abiding citizens. **Rehabilitation** involves treating problems that interfere with an offender's ability to function in society. Services and programs, such as psychiatric and medical treatment for drug and alcohol dependency, help bring about changes in behaviour. Educational programs are also designed to teach offenders skills that will prepare them for reintegration into the community. For instance, suppose Christopher turns to theft because he has no employment skills and cannot find a job. It would be foolish to think that two years in jail without treatment would change anything; Christopher will be just as unemployable when he leaves jail as when he entered. If, however, during that two-year period he enrolled in a prison employment program, he may have a better chance of finding a job when he leaves jail. This job may also decrease the likelihood that Christopher will re-offend.

> **Fast Fact**
> Research indicates that offenders who participate in treatment programs are less likely to re-offend.

recidivism: returning to crime after release from prison

Recidivism occurs when an offender returns to crime after release from prison. Programs that match the treatment to the offender's needs have been shown, on average, to reduce recidivism rates by 50 percent; in other words, offenders are 50 percent less likely to commit new crimes or break any of the conditions attached to their release.

> **Consider This**
> Should inmates be required to participate in rehabilitation programs as part of the sentence? Explain.

Restitution

restitution: punishment that requires the offender to pay society back for the harm or loss suffered

Another reason for punishment is **restitution**, which requires offenders to pay society back for the injury, loss, and suffering they caused. For example, when sentenced to perform community service, an offender returns some good to the community to compensate for the harm done. Actual payment for damages is a more obvious form of restitution.

Denunciation

Sometimes rehabilitation, deterrence, and protection of the public are not relevant as punishment goals. In such instances, the goal of punishment is denunciation, or condemnation of the offender's action. **Denunciation** sends a message that the offender's conduct has violated society's basic code of values and that such conduct will be punished.

In passing sentence, a judge may try to achieve more than one goal. For instance, sentencing an offender to a prison term may accomplish the goals of protecting the public, deterring the individual from re-offending, and denunciating criminal conduct. The judge must weigh the facts of each case to decide which sentencing goals are most important to achieve.

denunciation: punishment designed to show condemnation of the offender's conduct

A Controversial Sentence

On July 30, 1994, 18-year-old Kevin Hollinsky killed two of his best friends when he lost control of his car. The car hit two concrete lampposts and bounced off a tree. Kevin had been drinking.

At trial, Kevin pleaded guilty to two counts of dangerous driving causing death. In a sentence that shocked the community, the trial judge placed Kevin on three years' probation and ordered him to perform 750 hours of community service. Part of the community service included making 14 one-hour presentations to high school students.

In the spring of 1995, Kevin spoke at every high school in the Windsor area. On each occasion, the car he had driven was towed to the school, with the keys still in the ignition. Kevin always began with these words:

> Last year I was in a single-car accident, in which two of my best friends were killed, which I am responsible for. I'm responsible for devastating two families ... whose sons are dead because of me. No one else forced me to get behind that wheel. No one else forced me to drink. It was all my decision. It was the stupidest decision of my life.

In the summer of 1995, in the Windsor area, not a single student was involved in a fatal or serious automobile collision.

Initially, the police officer who accompanied Kevin to each school had been critical of the sentence. Later, however, he had this to say:

> You could send him to jail for five years and you wouldn't have punished him like you punished him by doing what happened here. This man was forced to live with the consequences of his irresponsibility, day after day after day. Every day he went out to speak, he relived it. He touched many young people in this city in a way we could not. It's hard to reach teenagers. He did. Kevin showed them they are not invulnerable.

The Crown appealed the case, insisting that a prison sentence should be mandatory in alcohol-related traffic deaths to act as a deterrent to others. In November 1995, the appeal was denied.

LAW IN ACTION

1. Which sentencing goals do you think the trial judge was considering when he passed sentence?
2. Explain how each goal was achieved.
3. Do you agree with the judge's decision? Why or why not?

Kevin Hollinsky

Building Your Understanding

1. In your own words, define the goals of sentencing.
2. Using examples, distinguish between specific and general deterrence.
3. Indicate which sentencing goal is addressed in each of the following situations. Justify your answers and indicate whether any sentence meets more than one goal.
   a) a court order requires an offender to take part in an anger management program
   b) an offender receives a fine for littering
   c) a person convicted of stealing a CD is required to spend a day in the music store to learn how theft affects the business
   d) a violent repeat offender is sentenced to 10 years in prison
   e) an offender is required to reimburse a store for stolen merchandise

SENTENCING PROCEDURES

After a defendant is convicted in a criminal trial, the sentencing process begins. For summary or minor offences, sentencing usually takes place immediately. For indictable or more serious offences, sentencing is more complex and is often delayed to allow time for the judge to make an informed decision.

Perspectives to Consider

Three perspectives must be considered in the sentencing process: the offender, the victim, and society.

Considering the Offender

pre-sentence report: background information about the convicted offender, prepared for the judge prior to sentencing

A judge may order a **pre-sentence report** for the purpose of gathering information about the offender. This report, prepared by a probation officer, includes information about the offender's background, family, education, employment history, physical and mental health, social activities, potential ability, motivation, and friends. The report must be objective in order to provide "a picture of the accused as a person in society."

psychiatric assessment: a report describing the mental history of the offender

A **psychiatric assessment** may also be ordered. This report, prepared by a qualified psychiatrist, describes the mental history of the offender and may include results from psychiatric tests. The psychiatric assessment is often an important factor in helping the judge determine an appropriate sentence.

Considering the Victim

victim impact statement: a statement prepared by a crime victim or the victim's family describing the harm done or the loss suffered as a result of the offence

To assist the judge in determining the sentence, s. 722 of the *Criminal Code* requires the court to consider any statement prepared by the victim of an offence. This **victim impact statement** describes the harm or loss experienced by the victim or the victim's family. It may be read before the offender or presented in any other manner the court considers appropriate. Being allowed to confront the offender can be particularly significant for victims who have suffered physical and emotional damage.

CASE

R. v. Hovind, [2000] (Sask. Q.B. QB00257), on-line: CanLII

On the nights of April 28 and 29, Jerod Hovind and two of his friends went to two Saskatchewan farms and broke into several buildings. They stole numerous power tools and vandalized the fuel tanks. At one farm they drove a truck, a tractor, and another vehicle around the farm, damaging a tree and the vehicles. They were subsequently charged and convicted of two counts of theft and break and enter.

After reading the statements contained in the pre-sentence reports of the two co-offenders, the judge had this to say about Hovind:

> Having read these reports ... I think I want to send your client [Hovind] to jail. Because of him, there are two other people here who have a criminal record who would not have otherwise had a criminal record. They were with him. They were in his car. He was driving. He took them there. It was his idea. He was leading and if anybody here should go to jail so that this kind of thing stops happening, it should be him.

The judge passed sentence, relying on the statements contained in the co-offenders' pre-sentence reports.

1. Discuss why the judge wanted to give Hovind a jail sentence.
2. Should the pre-sentence reports of the co-offenders be used as the basis for sentencing Hovind? Explain.

Considering Society

The Crown, representing society, presents evidence at trial to support the criminal charges, evidence that is meant to convince the judge or jury of the defendant's guilt beyond a reasonable doubt. Once the accused has been found guilty, the Crown has the right to recommend an appropriate sentence. The Crown may, for instance, introduce the offender's previous criminal record in arguing for a substantial prison term. It is the Crown's role to ensure that society's interests are protected when the offender is sentenced.

"We don't always sentence according to public opinion. Sometimes we have to go against the grain."
— Ontario Court Justice David Cole

The Sentencing Hearing

At a **sentencing hearing** the judge considers all the facts about the crime, the offender, and the victim in order to determine the appropriate sentence. Both defence counsel and the Crown present their recommendations to the judge. The judge must examine the following factors:

- criminal record of the accused
- pre-sentence report findings
- nature and severity of the crime
- offender's background
- circumstances leading to and surrounding the offence
- offender's family and employment situation
- offender's attitude toward his/her own conduct

sentencing hearing: the judge's opportunity to listen to recommendations and to consider all the facts before passing sentence

CASE

R. v. *Bates* (2000), Ont. C.A. C32619, on-line: CanLII

1. What did the Crown mean by suggesting that "the decision did not reflect the principles of denunciation and general and specific deterrence."
2. Compare the trial judge's sentence with the sentence imposed by the Ontario Court of Appeal.
3. What effect do you think the victim's impact statement had in the sentencing decision of the Court of Appeal? Explain.

In September 1998, during an intense argument, Dwayne Bates slapped Kristen Emmett across the face, knocking her to the floor. He then threw her against a cupboard where she struck her head and suffered visible bruising to her body. After this incident, Emmett ended the relationship, but Bates repeatedly harassed her, eventually forcing her to request police protection.

A number of subsequent incidents occurred, and Bates was charged with eleven offences, including one count of criminal harassment, one count of uttering a death threat, three counts of assault, and six counts of failing to comply with the terms of various judicial orders. Bates pleaded guilty to all but the death threat, for which he was found guilty. Taking into account the seven months that Bates had served in pre-trial custody, the trial judge imposed a suspended sentence and three years' probation, with the provision that he not associate with Emmett and some of her friends.

The Crown appealed the sentence, submitting that it did not reflect the principles of denunciation and general and specific deterrence, nor did it consider the seriousness of the crimes. The victim had suffered continuous and unpredictable abuse and had experienced perpetual fear of the offender. This was made clear at trial in Emmett's victim impact statement, in which she stated that she lived in such fear of Bates that she had, at one point, taken a drug overdose. She also expressed ongoing fear for her future safety:

> I'm trying to get on with my life, but I can't help but feel leery about every corner I go around and sets of eyes that stare back a little longer than usual.... I will never let my guard down again, whether or not Dwayne is behind closed doors. It is so easy for people to say, "Get over it" and "Get on," but I will always be cautious.

The Ontario Court of Appeal agreed that the trial judge should have imposed a penitentiary sentence. The Court increased the sentence to sixteen months, which credited the pre-trial custody, followed by the three years' probation with the conditions ordered by the trial judge. In addition, Bates was required to undertake counselling in anger management.

aggravating factors: circumstances that increase the severity of the sentence

mitigating factors: circumstances that decrease the severity of the sentence

Judges are not free to impose sentences outside certain guidelines. Their sentencing decisions are restricted to some extent by the maximum and minimum limits specified in statute laws. They must also consider precedents for similar crimes as well as aggravating and mitigating factors. **Aggravating factors** *increase* the severity of the sentence because they suggest that rehabilitation is unlikely or that a strong deterrent is necessary. An example of an aggravating factor would be an ongoing pattern of assault against the same person. **Mitigating factors** tend to *decrease* the severity of the sentence,

Figure 11.2 **Factors that influence sentencing decisions**

Concerning the Offender	
Aggravating Factors	**Mitigating Factors**
• premeditation • previous criminal record • large profits from the offence • involving others in the offence • ring leader of the group • continuing offence over time	• impulsive act • young or first offender • guilty plea • co-operating with police • mental or physical disability • short life expectancy

Concerning the Offence	
Aggravating Factors	**Mitigating Factors**
• violent offence • number of victims • need for deterrent	• minor offence • time spent in custody • delay in trial

suggesting that an offender can be rehabilitated, does not pose a threat to society, or does not need strong deterrent measures. A first-time offence and evidence of remorse are examples of mitigating factors. Suppose a young woman charged with impaired driving shows remorse for her behaviour and voluntarily enters a treatment program for alcoholism. In considering her sentence, the judge might regard the offender's remorse and her desire to overcome her drinking problem as mitigating factors.

Building Your Understanding

1. Discuss the people a judge must consider when deciding on a sentence.
2. How might a pre-sentence report help in determining a fair sentence?
3. Do you think Jerod Hovind's sentence should be more severe than the sentences of the two co-accused? Explain.
4. Distinguish between aggravating and mitigating factors and provide three examples of each.
5. Collect two newspaper articles about criminals sentenced for offences committed in Canada. Analyze the information in each article to determine which factors might have influenced the judge's sentencing decision. Organize your findings on a chart.

TYPES OF TRADITIONAL SENTENCES

When sentencing offenders, a judge must keep in mind the goals of sentencing. Is this offender a candidate for rehabilitation? Is he or she a threat to society? Should this offender be compelled to make restitution? To accomplish these goals, a judge has a variety of sentencing options.

"Society fails when it can see no further than the prison gates."
— Doug McNally, Retired Chief of Police, City of Edmonton

Discharges

The most lenient sentence is a discharge, or release. A discharge may be granted for a minor or first-time offence that does not carry a minimum sentence and for which the penalty is less than 14 years. There are two types of discharges—absolute and conditional. An **absolute discharge** means that even though the accused is found guilty, the judge sets that person free. After one year, the offender's criminal record is destroyed.

For minor offences, a judge may also grant a **conditional discharge**—a release with terms attached, such as avoiding contact with certain people and observing a set curfew. If these terms are obeyed, after a specified period the discharge will become absolute. With this type of discharge, the criminal record is kept for three years from the date of the conviction and then destroyed. If the terms of the discharge are violated, the discharge is revoked and a more severe sentence is imposed.

Probation

The word *probation* comes from the Latin word *probatio*, which means "proof." **Probation** is a sentence that allows a convicted offender to prove that he or she is able to live in the community without committing another offence. Any offender on probation is under close supervision and subject to certain restrictions. Note that a probation order may be given either in addition to or in place of a prison term.

A parole officer supervises an offender on probation and is responsible for monitoring the offender's behaviour. During probation, the offender must comply with a specific set of conditions in order to prove to the court that he or she will not re-offend. Failure to comply with these conditions can lead to facing additional terms. Or, the order may be revoked, and the offender will be sentenced on the original conviction. Sentencing could mean imprisonment, fines, or both. The offender can also be charged with breach of probation.

Every probation order has three compulsory conditions. The offender must keep the peace and demonstrate good behaviour; appear in court when required; and notify the court or probation officer of any change of name, address, or employment. A probation order may also include optional conditions, such as

- reporting regularly to a probation officer;
- not associating with known criminals;
- staying away from particular locations;
- attending counselling sessions;
- paying for damages resulting from the offence; and
- refraining from alcohol and illegal drug use.

---

absolute discharge: releasing a convicted offender and erasing the criminal record after one year

conditional discharge: releasing a convicted offender under certain terms, and erasing the criminal record after three years if the terms are met

probation: a sentence that allows a person to live in the community under the supervision of a parole officer

Law in Your Life
If you aquire a criminal record, you may be
- unable to travel outside Canada
- deported if you are a landed immigrant
- denied employment in certain industries
- prevented from obtaining a professional licence
- refused a firearms acquisition certificate

Fast Fact
From 1998 to 1999, 42% of convicted offenders received a term of probation, 40% received fines, and 35% were incarcerated.

Suspended Sentence

A **suspended sentence** is a judgment that is passed but not carried out as long as the offender meets certain requirements set out by the judge. Suspended sentences can only be imposed for offences that have no minimum punishment required by the *Criminal Code*. They are usually provided for first-time or minor offences and are given in situations where the judge feels that just the knowledge of the sentence is sufficient to keep the offender in line. The offender would still have a criminal record and could be placed on probation.

suspended sentence: a judgment that is not carried out, provided certain requirements are met

Intermittent Sentence

An **intermittent sentence** is a prison sentence of less than 90 days that can be served on weekends and at night, so the offender can serve the time in intervals instead of all at once. Intermittent sentences are usually given to offenders who are not violent, have steady employment, and whose families depend on their ability to continue working. The court always indicates when the offender must report to jail. When not in jail, the offender is subject to a probation order.

intermittent sentence: a sentence served on weekends and at night

Conditional Sentence

A **conditional sentence** is a prison term of less than two years that is allowed to be served in the community rather than in prison. A judge can impose a conditional sentence if the offence does not carry a minimum prison sentence. The terms for a conditional sentence are stricter than they are for probation or a suspended sentence. Examples include performing community service or seeking treatment for drug addiction.

conditional sentence: a prison sentence that can be served in the community, with strict terms attached

Electronic Monitoring

Electronic monitoring (EM) began as a way to track and supervise offenders on probation. As prison populations and costs increased in the 1980s and 1990s, authorities considered electronic monitoring as an alternative to incarceration. Electronic monitoring is now used to supervise offenders in the community as long as they stay in their homes. Exceptions are allowed for some offenders who have jobs outside the home or who wish to attend devotional services.

The offender wears an electronic bracelet that emits a signal to a computer at a remote location. This signal indicates the offender's whereabouts. Should the offender leave the home base, an alarm sounds to alert the authorities. Other EM systems include random telephone dialling by computer to the offender's home to confirm that the offender is on the premises, a video camera near the telephone to verify the offender's presence, and breath testing from a remote location for detecting violations of alcohol restrictions.

electronic monitoring: allowing an offender to serve a sentence at home under electronic supervision from a remote location

Fast Fact

Electronic monitoring began in Canada as a pilot program in Vancouver in 1987. This program led to the use of EM in British Columbia, Saskatchewan, Newfoundland, and Ontario.

Figure 11.3 This electronic monitoring device is worn around the ankle. The cost effectiveness of such devices is a controversial issue. Investigate the costs involved.

Restitution

An offender may be ordered to make restitution in the form of financial compensation to pay the victim for property loss or personal injury. In some cases, an offender might be ordered to do some work for the victim to make up for the damage caused. For example, a teen who snatched the purse of a 70-year-old widow may be required to shovel her driveway, cut her lawn, and do her weekly grocery shopping for a limited period.

Restitution often takes the form of community service, which can be more meaningful, more effective, and less costly to taxpayers than a jail sentence. After considering the offender's abilities, a judge may issue a **community service order** requiring the offender to perform certain services for a set number of hours. Services could include working at a food bank, coaching a little league ball team, or working in a drop-in clinic.

community service order: a sentence to perform certain services in the community for a specified period

LAW IN ACTION

Rapist Sentenced to Electronic Monitoring

1. What mitigating factors did Justice Dyson consider?
2. Why might this sentence be controversial?

On March 20, 2001, Ontario Court Justice Norman Dyson imposed a sentence of electronic monitoring while under house arrest on 21-year-old Nadeem Khokhar. It is believed to be the first time in Ontario that electronic monitoring will be used in a conditional sentence.

A jury convicted Khokhar of sexual assault, extortion, and forcible confinement of his ex-girlfriend. The terms of his sentence specify that he must wear an electronic bracelet for the first three months, remain under house arrest for the first eight months, remain at home between 9 p.m. and 6 a.m. for the next ten months, and then complete one year of probation.

In considering the sentence, Justice Dyson took into account the pre-sentence report, which indicated that Khokhar is a first-time offender and does not pose any threat or risk to the public.

R. v. Hovind, [2000] (Sask. Q.B. QB00257), on-line: CanLII

CASE

Remember Jerod Hovind, the man charged with two counts of theft and break and enter in Saskatchewan? The trial judge sentenced him to six months' imprisonment on both charges to be served concurrently. In addition, he was placed on probation for 18 months and ordered to pay restitution in the amounts of $809.28 and $373.93. The two co-offenders were each given suspended sentences and placed on probation for 18 months. They were required to pay restitution in the amount of $1182.22. Hovind appealed his sentence.

The Saskatchewan Court of Appeal found that in sentencing Hovind, the trial judge clearly made an error by relying on the pre-sentence reports of the co-offenders. It was the view of the appeals court judge that Hovind should receive a sentence similar to that imposed on the two co-offenders. However, Hovind's pre-sentence record showed that he had a) one prior conviction for mischief for which he was sentenced to a conditional discharge and probation for eight months; b) one fine of $55 for failing to attend court; and c) one driving conviction for which he was fined $385. These circumstances meant that Hovind's probation should be subjected to more stringent conditions than those imposed on the co-offenders.

The appeals court judge suspended the six months' sentence and placed Hovind on probation for 18 months subject to the following terms of the probation order:

- Keep the peace and demonstrate good behaviour.
- Appear before the court when required to do so.
- Notify the court or the probation officer of any change of name, address, or employment.
- Abstain from the use of alcohol or drugs not medically prescribed.
- Participate in any alcohol/drug assessment and treatment program arranged by the probation officer, which may include staying in a residential treatment facility.
- Make restitution in the amounts of $809.28 and $373.93.

1. Why did the appeals court judge find that Hovind's probation required more stringent conditions than the probation of the co-offenders?

2. In view of the offences and Hovind's history, suggest another condition that might be added to the probation order. Explain why.

Binding-Over, Deportation, and Fines

Binding-over is a court order to keep the peace, commonly known as a "peace bond." It may be imposed on someone who threatens another person or that person's family or property. Technically, a binding-over is not actually a sentence, since no crime has been committed. The person who feels threatened presents the details to the court. The complainant and the defendant appear before a judge, who then orders the defendant to keep the peace and demonstrate good behaviour for up to 12 months. No criminal offence occurs unless the peace bond is violated or the defendant refuses to be bound. A restraining order is also a court order, but it is issued immediately to stop

binding-over: a sentence ordering the defendant to keep the peace and demonstrate good behaviour for up to 12 months

deportation: a sentence of expulsion from the country

fines: specific amounts of money paid as penalties for offences

someone from taking any harmful action. A restraining order is temporary, intended to last only until a hearing can be held.

Anyone who is not a Canadian citizen and commits an indictable offence in Canada can be deported. **Deportation** involves expelling an offender from the country, usually sending the offender back to his or her native land.

Fines are specific amounts of money that offenders are required to pay the court as punishment. For summary conviction offences, a maximum fine of $2000 can be imposed. Fines are optional for indictable offences that have a minimum sentence of imprisonment and a maximum prison term of less than five years. Before imposing a fine, the judge considers the offender's ability to pay. An offender who fails to pay a fine may face a prison term.

Suspension of Privileges

suspension of privilege: a sentence that withholds a privilege for a specified period or a lifetime

Some offences are best dealt with through a **suspension of privilege,** such as withholding a driver's licence or a licence to own a firearm. Usually a suspension is in effect for a specified period, but under certain circumstances it can last a lifetime. For example, as shown in Figure 11.4, impaired driving carries the possibility of a lifetime suspension.

Figure 11.4 Penalties for impaired driving offences

	Penalties under the *Highway Traffic Act* (Ontario)	**Minimum Penalty under the *Criminal Code* (Federal)**
First offence	1-year suspension* Remedial measures requirement Minimum 1-year ignition interlock condition upon reinstatement**	1-year driving prohibition $600 fine
Second offence	3-year suspension* Remedial measures requirement Minimum 3-year ignition interlock condition upon reinstatement**	2-year driving prohibition 14-day jail sentence
Third offence	Lifetime licence suspension* (reducible to 10 years if certain conditions are met) Ignition interlock condition for life if suspension is reduced**	3-year driving prohibition 90-day jail sentence
Fourth and subsequent offence	Lifetime licence suspension*	Same as third offence

* Drivers who are caught driving while their licence is suspended for a *Criminal Code* conviction will have the vehicle they are driving impounded for a minimum of 45 days and will face fines from $5000 to $25 000 for the first conviction and $10 000 to $50 000 for subsequent convictions.

**As of December 23, 2001, any driver who commits and is convicted of a drinking and driving offence will, upon reinstatement, have a mandatory ignition interlock condition placed on his or her licence. If this person wishes to drive, it must be in a vehicle that is equipped with an approved ignition interlock device.

SOURCE: Ontario Ministry of Transportation

Plea Bargaining

The majority of people charged with criminal offences never go to trial. Instead, the Crown and the defence counsel negotiate an agreement called a **plea bargain.** Behind closed doors, they consider the range of punishment for the offence and strike a bargain for a lighter sentence, possibly even a suspended sentence. Sometimes, in return for a lighter sentence, the accused exchanges information or pleads guilty to a lesser charge. For instance, someone accused of first-degree murder may agree to plead guilty to second-degree murder. Instead of receiving a life sentence with no eligibility for parole for 25 years, the offender will be eligible for parole after 10 years. Once the bargain is struck, it is presented to the judge, who usually accepts the agreement.

Possibly the most controversial plea bargain in Canadian legal history was the agreement between the Crown and Karla Homolka in May 1993. In exchange for her sworn statements against her estranged husband, Paul Bernardo, she was charged with two counts of manslaughter in relation to the homicides of Leslie Mahaffy and Kristen French. She received two 12-year sentences to be served concurrently (at the same time).

plea bargain: a negotiated deal whereby the accused pleads guilty in exchange for a lighter sentence

"If every case were to go through to a trial, no country could afford them."
— Ontario Chief Justice Roy McMurtry

Incarceration

In Canada, authorities cannot just lock someone up and throw away the key, which is why **incarceration** is defined as imprisonment for a *specified length of time*. Each criminal offence has a maximum sentence. For example, the maximum for robbery or manslaughter is imprisonment for life; the maximum for aggravated sexual assault is 25 years. Such maximum sentences are rarely imposed because of their severity. In fact, some legal experts maintain that certain maximums may be outdated or too broad to be useful. Instead, judges use a range of punishments in determining appropriate sentences. For instance,

incarceration: imprisonment for a specified period

An Impaired Driver Plea Bargains

LAW IN ACTION

When police cruisers finally stopped the motorist after a high-speed chase, he had torn through three red lights at speeds twice the limit. He was also so drunk he could barely get out of the car; when tested, his blood-alcohol level was nearly three times the legal limit. This was the 26-year-old's first offence.

In a plea bargain, he pleaded guilty to impaired driving. Two charges were dropped: high alcohol levels in his blood and fleeing the police. Jointly, the prosecutor and the defence recommended a $600 fine and a one-year suspension.

The judge regarded this sentence as a gift. However, there were mitigating factors involved. It was the offender's first offence, and no one had been injured. The offender had apologized, and he had a steady job. The judge suspended the offender's licence for a year and gave him a sentence of 30 days, which he was allowed to serve at home under the terms of a conditional sentence.

1. Which two charges did the Crown drop? Why?
2. List the mitigating factors in this case.
3. In your opinion, what were the judge's sentencing goals?
4. How do you think the general public would react to the outcome of this plea bargain? Explain.

Figure 11.5 This federal penitentiary for women is located in Joliette, Quebec. One of its most infamous inmates in the 1990s was Karla Homolka. Imagine the restrictions on your life if this prison was your home.

"For a guy who never saw jail before, 30 days could be enough to teach him a lesson."
— Paul Culver, chief Crown attorney

if the maximum penalty for a first non-violent offence is less than five years in prison, the judge is not bound to give any prison sentence at all and may opt for an alternative form of punishment.

Some serious offences carry a mandatory minimum sentence. For example, according to s. 745(c) of the *Criminal Code*, second-degree murder carries a ten-year minimum term of imprisonment.

> 745. (c) in respect of a person who has been convicted of second-degree murder, that the person be sentenced to imprisonment for life without eligibility for parole until the person has served at least ten years of the sentence.

Length of Imprisonment

The length of a prison sentence depends on several factors—the penalty attached to the offence in the *Criminal Code*, details regarding the crime and the offender, and whether multiple sentences should be served. Sentences of less than two years are served in provincial facilities, while those of two years or more are served in federal institutions.

dangerous offender: someone who constitutes a threat to the life, safety, or well-being of others

indeterminate sentence: a sentence for an indefinite period

In rare cases, the court may consider someone a **dangerous offender**—someone who constitutes a threat to the life, safety, or physical and mental well-being of other persons. In such cases, s. 753(4) of the *Criminal Code* requires the judge to impose an **indeterminate sentence,** which means that the offender may be held for an indefinite period in a federal prison. A dangerous offender may apply for parole but will remain in prison until a parole board believes that he or she can be released safely into the community.

concurrent sentences: sentences served at the same time

consecutive sentences: sentences served one after another

When criminals are convicted of more than one offence at a time, they must serve more than one sentence. **Concurrent sentences** are served at the same time, which means that two sentences of four years each would result in a four-year prison term. **Consecutive sentences** are served one after another; two sentences of four years each would result in an eight-year prison term. In Canada, consecutive sentences are rare.

CASE

R. v. Latimer, [2001] 1 S.C.R. 3

BACKGROUND Twelve-year-old Tracy Latimer had a severe form of cerebral palsy caused by neurological damage at birth. As a quadriplegic, she was totally dependent on others for her care. Tracy suffered five to six seizures daily and was thought to be in constant pain; she was not terminally ill.

Tracy was scheduled to undergo surgery on November 19, 1993, to repair a dislocated hip. Her parents, Laura and Robert Latimer, were told that this surgery would cause pain and that further surgery would be required to relieve this pain.

Robert Latimer decided to end his daughter's life. On October 24, 1993, Latimer put Tracy in the cab of his pickup, connected a hose to the exhaust pipe, and inserted the other end into the cab. Tracy died from carbon monoxide poisoning.

At trial, a jury convicted Robert Latimer of second-degree murder. That conviction was successfully appealed on the grounds that the prosecutor had interfered with the jury selection process. At his second trial, Latimer was again convicted of second-degree murder.

After the guilty verdict was delivered, the judge explained to the jury that second-degree murder carries a mandatory minimum jail sentence of 10 years. Nonetheless, jury members recommended that Latimer only serve one year before parole eligibility. The judge then granted a constitutional exemption from the mandatory minimum sentence. He sentenced Latimer to one year of imprisonment and one year on probation, to be spent confined to his farm. When the Crown appealed, the Saskatchewan Court of Appeal overturned the one-year sentence and reinstated the mandatory minimum sentence of 10 years in prison without eligibility of parole. Latimer appealed his sentence to the Supreme Court of Canada.

LEGAL QUESTION In this particular case, would imposing the mandatory minimum sentence for second-degree murder constitute cruel and unusual punishment, contrary to s. 12 of the Charter?

DECISION The Supreme Court of Canada dismissed Latimer's appeal. The trial judge was not correct in finding that (in this specific case) the mandatory minimum sentence prescribed by the *Criminal Code* would be cruel and unusual punishment in violation of s. 12. The Court found that the minimum mandatory sentence was *not* disproportionate in this case. In the absence of any violation of s. 12 of the *Canadian Charter of Rights and Freedoms*, there was no basis for granting a constitutional exemption. The Court also pointed out that it is up to Parliament to decide on the use of minimum sentences, not the courts.

SOCIAL SIGNIFICANCE Human rights advocates applaud the Supreme Court's decision as an affirmation of their cause. They claim it sends a message that people with disabilities have the same right to life as other Canadians. But those who support Latimer are angry and disappointed with the decision. They have organized candlelight vigils, worn ribbons, and signed petitions asking the federal government for a grant of mercy.

ANALYSIS

1. Do you agree with the Supreme Court of Canada that the mandatory minimum sentence does not violate Latimer's Charter rights? Explain.
2. Should the *Criminal Code* be changed to allow for some exceptions that give the courts the flexibility not to impose mandatory sentences for crimes like second-degree murder? Why or why not?

Robert Latimer

Building Your Understanding

1. Identify and define two types of discharges.
2. a) Distinguish between a suspended and a conditional sentence.
   b) What is the difference between an absolute discharge and a suspended sentence?
3. What advantages does electronic monitoring provide?
4. Give two examples of how an offender could make restitution.
5. Why is binding-over not technically considered a sentence?
6. What is meant by "suspension of privilege"? Provide an example of your own.
7. Why might defence counsel advise the accused to enter a plea bargain?
8. For each of the following scenarios, impose a sentence on the offender. Remember that a sentence can include a combination of options.

   a) After Hélène ended her relationship with Nick, he began harassing her. It started with annoying calls on her cellphone and escalated to threatening calls. Hélène reported Nick to police, and he was charged with criminal harassment. This was Nick's first offence.
   b) Warren got into a fight on a basketball court and was charged with assault. He had received a prior conviction for assault as a teenager.
   c) Gina is 20 years old. As she was leaving a clothing boutique, she was stopped and searched by police. Beneath her clothes, Gina had hidden merchandise from the store valued at $800. Police also found two marijuana cigarettes in her purse. Gina has a good job that pays well. This is her first offence.
   d) A 35-year-old woman is charged with abducting her three children in violation of a custody order. The mother has a history of drug and alcohol abuse.

RESTORATIVE JUSTICE PROGRAMS

Restorative justice (also known as alternative justice) differs from traditional approaches because it focuses on using joint problem solving to deal with the harmful effects of crime. The restorative process unites victims, offenders, and the community in the effort to have offenders assume accountability for their crimes and to give them the opportunity to make amends.

The goals of restorative justice are to restore, or rebuild, the offender's self-respect, to empower the offender and the victim to address their conflict, and to facilitate reconciliation between the offender and the victim within the community. The restorative process serves practical purposes as well, by easing the burden of backlog in the courts and by lowering court and prison costs. These programs also keep offenders away from the negative influence of incarcerated criminals.

Section 717 of the *Criminal Code* defines specific situations where alternative measures may be used. For instance, the court must determine that these measures do not conflict with the protection of society. In all cases, the offender must accept responsibility for the offence and enter the restorative program voluntarily. Victim-offender mediation, family group conferencing, and victim-offender panels are three types of restorative programs that may be used as alternatives to incarceration. See Figure 11.6 for a comparison of traditional court procedures and the process of restorative justice.

In the Courts	In Restorative Justice Programs
• Crime is defined as a violation of rules and as harm to the state. • Victim has limited opportunity to speak about his/her injury, loss, and needs during the trial. • Offender, victim, and community remain passive and have little responsibility for a resolution. • Community's role is limited. • Restitution is rare. • Process is controlled and operated by the state and by professionals who may seem remote. • Offender is blamed, stigmatized, and punished. • Repentance and forgiveness are rarely considered. • Process assumes win-loss outcomes.	• Crime is seen as harm done to victims and communities. • Victim is central to the process of defining the harm and how it might be repaired. • Offender, victim, and community actively participate in the resolution that results from the restorative forum. • Community is actively involved in holding offenders accountable, supporting victims, and providing opportunities for offenders to make amends. • Restitution is normal. • Process is overseen by the state, but is usually driven by communities. • Offender is reintegrated into the community, and his/her dignity is preserved. • Repentance and forgiveness are encouraged. • Process makes win-win outcomes possible.

Figure 11.6 Which offences do you think could be handled most effectively by a restorative justice program?

SOURCE: Based on an adaption from the work of Howard Zehr, "Changing lenses: A new focus for crime and justice," reported in the *Waterloo Herald Press*, 1990.

Victim-Offender Mediation

Victim-offender mediation involves four stages: 1) case referral and acceptance, 2) preparation, 3) the mediation itself, and 4) follow-up. Often the first stage takes place after a conviction or a formal admission of guilt, but on occasion, case referral occurs prior to conviction in an attempt to avoid prosecution altogether. Studies indicate that this form of mediation has benefited both offenders and victims by decreasing the incidence of criminal behaviour and by reducing feelings of fear and anxiety among the victims.

In the mediation itself, the offender and the victim meet with a trained mediator. Both parties present their version of the events and express their feelings regarding the offence. In the victim's case, such feelings may include a sense of helplessness and personal loss. The offender may express remorse and may explain the circumstances surrounding his or her behaviour. The mediator's role is to facilitate this interaction. During the process, the participants

victim-offender mediation: an alternative measures program designed to determine restitution; involves the victim, the offender, and a mediator

LAW IN ACTION

Mediation to Make Amends

1. Describe the agreement reached between the victim and the offender.
2. How effective do you think this mediation will be in rehabilitating the offender? Explain.
3. Describe how this incident might be dealt with in a court of law.

After two hours of dialogue and tears, the mediator felt that the victim and the offender had little more to say. They had reached an agreement.

The 19-year-old offender had been baby-sitting for the victim when she stole a $200 necklace from the victim's bedroom. She sold the necklace before the victim discovered the theft. The victim described how much the necklace meant to her because it had belonged to her grandmother. The offender apologized several times before and during the mediation, explaining that she had stolen the necklace because she needed money to fill an expensive prescription for her mother. She agreed to reimburse the victim for the $200 necklace on a payment schedule arranged by the mediator. The offender also agreed to help in the daycare centre (attended by the victim's son) for three hours a day for six months.

The victim stated that she felt less angry after realizing that the offender was sincerely sorry and on learning why she had taken the necklace.

---

agree to appropriate restitution for the offence, which may include payment and/or services. These terms are then recorded and monitored.

Family Group Conferencing

family group conferencing: an alternative measures program in which the victim and the offender meet with family members and other concerned parties to determine restitution

Like victim-offender mediation, **family group conferencing** brings together the victim and the offender. The difference is that family group conferencing also involves family members, community support groups, police officers, social welfare officials, and lawyers. This program is used only when an offender admits guilt.

Before the conference begins, the offender is reminded that he or she has the right to end the conference at any time and proceed to court instead. Throughout the conference, a trained co-ordinator monitors the process so that the offender becomes aware that it is his or her *conduct* that is being denounced, not the offender as a *person*. The offender also learns that support to reintegrate into society will come from the community.

Family group conferencing involves three stages: preparation, the conference itself, and post-conference. The offender begins the conference with an explanation of events. Then the victim tells what happened. They may question one another and be questioned by members of their respective families. Restitution is discussed privately by the offender and his or her family before it is presented as an offer. Negotiations continue until a consensus is reached. After the conference, the co-ordinator monitors the terms of the agreement for successful completion. If the agreement is violated, the case is returned to the courts for action.

Victim-Offender Panels

When victims and offenders are unable or unwilling to meet each other, **victim-offender panels** provide an opportunity for closure. A panel of victims and offenders linked by a common crime (but not the *same* crime) express their feelings about the offence. A moderator issues guidelines and monitors the panel.

Another type of victim panel has been organized by Mothers Against Drunk Driving (MADD). This panel, called a **victim impact panel,** enables victims and victims' families to share the impact drunk driving has had on their lives and to allow offenders to express their remorse.

victim-offender panels: moderated discussions that allow victims and offenders, linked by a common crime, to express their feelings about the offence

victim impact panel: a panel that allows victims and drunk driving offenders to express their views and feelings

Aboriginal Sentencing Circles

Over the years there has been a disproportionate number of Aboriginal people incarcerated in Canadian prisons, which was one reason the federal government proposed changes to the *Criminal Code* to accommodate alternative measures. Sentencing circles qualify as one of these measures. They cannot, however, be used for offences demanding sentences of more than two years in prison.

A **sentencing circle** comprises the offender, the offender's family, the victim, the victim's family, the elders and other members of the offender's Aboriginal community, police officers, and a trial judge. The process involves separating the *person* from the *criminal act* the person committed. All the participants in the circle do their best to convey to the offender that there are people who care for his or her well-being. Because balance and consensus are important traditional values, everyone participates by offering an opinion. For this reason, reaching a consensus requires patience, thought, deliberation, and oratory skill.

"From the perspective of a non-Native judge, sentencing circles can, if used in appropriate cases, be an effective tool in sentencing."
— New Brunswick Provincial Court Judge Jackson

sentencing circle: an alternative measures program that involves a process of healing for both the victim and the offender

Figure 11.7 The Aboriginal sentencing circle embodies the concept of healing so that the offender can become a contributing member of the community. Do you think sentencing circles would work for non-Aboriginal offenders? Why or why not?

Building Your Understanding

1. What are the main goals of restorative justice?
2. Which program do you think would be more effective for the victim—victim-offender mediation or victim-offender panels? For the offender? Explain why.
3. In what ways are family group conferencing and sentencing circles similar? How do they differ?
4. On a PMI (Plus, Minus, and Interesting) chart, categorize information about each of the alternative measures described in this section.

THE CORRECTIONAL SYSTEM

"Most people come out of jail eventually. So you have to consider what's going to be the effect of jail on this person, on the community, when he or she gets out."

— Madam Justice Mary Hogan

Fast Fact

Women represent 9% of the inmate population in provincial prisons and 4% in federal prisons

Prison is the toughest and most expensive penalty we have for offenders in Canada. The adult federal and provincial correctional system costs about $2 billion annually. The cost of keeping an offender in a federal penitentiary is about $55 000 per year. This compares with approximately $26 500 for a halfway house and $12 000 to supervise an inmate on parole. Locking up offenders is an expensive proposition.

Prison may be the right place for some criminals, but it is also the wrong place for others. As the bar graph in Figure 11.8 shows, in Canada there are about 120 prisoners for every 100 000 adults. Although Canada's incarceration rate is less than one-quarter of that in the United States, it is higher than the rate in most western European countries. Yet, there is no real evidence

Figure 11.8 An international comparison of incarceration rates, 1997–1998. Incarceration rates do not necessarily reflect crime rates, but simply indicate the extent to which prison is used as a form of punishment.

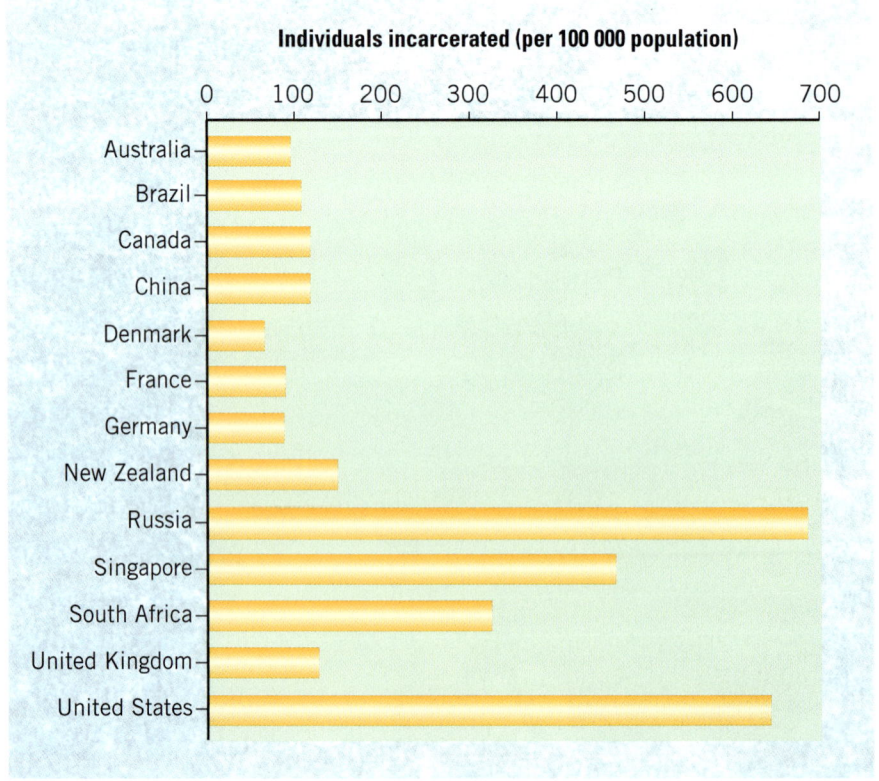

to show that locking people up has a deterrent effect, that it reduces crime, or that it even reduces the rate of recidivism. Canada has adopted an approach that gets tough with violent, high-risk offenders but also finds alternatives to incarceration for non-violent, low-risk offenders.

The Provincial Correctional System

People in the provincial correctional system are either awaiting trial or serving sentences of less than two years. Facilities in this system have various levels of security. **Closed custody** is reserved for dangerous offenders and escape risks. Some of these prisoners require psychological care and are placed in **protective custody,** separated from the rest of the prison population for their own protection. **Open custody** is less secure and more appropriate for prisoners convicted of non-violent crimes; these prisoners are neither escape risks nor dangerous to others. A halfway house would be an example of an open custody facility.

closed custody: secured facilities for dangerous offenders

protective custody: separation of offenders from the rest of the prison population

open custody: less secure facilities for non-violent offenders

The Federal Correctional System

Sentences of more than two years' imprisonment are served in federal institutions. These institutions are classified as maximum, medium, and minimum security. Dangerous offenders are sent to **maximum-security institutions.** Guarded by armed correctional officers, these penitentiaries are secured buildings with high walls, razor-wire fences, and bars on all doors and windows. Those who prove themselves over time can be transferred from a maximum- to a medium-security prison. **Medium-security institutions** have fewer physical barriers and not as many guards. Prisoners are allowed more freedom and more contact with other inmates. **Minimum-security institutions** have no external barriers like fences or walls. They also have more employment and educational programs to assist inmates nearing the end of their sentences in making the transition back to society as law-abiding citizens.

maximum-security institution: a highly secured correctional facility

medium-security institution: a correctional facility with few barriers and some freedom of movement

minimum-security institution: a correctional facility without exterior barriers

Figure 11.9 Almost none of the furniture is movable in the cells of this closed-custody provincial facility in Penetanguishene, Ontario.

Legal Link
To explore a variety of prison topics, visit
www.pearsoned.ca/law.

Fast Fact
Approximately 63% of new offenders in correctional institutions test at or below a Grade 8 level in mathematics and language.

Correctional Programs

The Correctional Service of Canada (CSC) is responsible for the care and well-being of inmates incarcerated in federal penitentiaries. In addition to providing food, clothing, housing, and health care, CSC helps people deal with issues relating to their criminal behaviour. CSC's goal is to contribute to public safety by reducing the chances of prisoners re-offending upon release.

To this end, every prisoner has a correctional plan that outlines his or her needs and priorities. The plan and the progress of the individual are reviewed regularly to determine whether goals are being met and to monitor the level of risk the offender poses. All inmates are required to attend school or work as part of their correctional plan. CSC offers programs in the following areas:

- living skills
- cognitive skills training
- substance abuse intervention
- sex offender treatment
- family violence intervention
- literacy
- work experience

(a)

(b)

Figure 11.10 Compare the tight, secured cells of Kingston's Prison for Women in photograph (a) with the private, comfortable cottages of the Grand Valley Institution for Women in photograph (b).

Building Your Understanding

1. What is the main difference between the provincial and federal correctional systems?
2. Describe the three levels of custody in provincial correctional facilities.
3. Explain the differences among maximum-, medium-, and minimum-security facilities.
4. Investigate one of the correctional programs identified in this section. Prepare a brief report, explaining the program's objectives, length, content, and effectiveness.

PAROLES AND PARDONS

Parole is the inmate's conditional release into the community before the full sentence is served. Except for persons convicted of first-degree murder, prisoners must be reviewed for parole after one-third of the full sentence has been served, or after seven years, whichever is less. This review, however, does not always result in parole. Inmates must meet certain conditions to qualify for parole, providing an incentive for prisoners to demonstrate good behaviour while serving their sentences. Parole also lessens the negative effects of incarceration and gives the parolee the opportunity to return to society with help and supervision.

parole: release of an inmate, on a promise of good behaviour, into the community before the full sentence is served

Parole Decisions

The National Parole Board (NPB), which has regional offices across the country, decides who can be paroled. The protection of society is the most important factor in any decision to release an offender. The parole board will grant parole only if the members believe that the offender will not pose a risk to society and will return to the community as a law-abiding citizen.

The board members review the following information about the offender to make an assessment of the risks involved in granting parole:

- the offence
- criminal history
- social problems, such as drug use or family violence
- mental status, especially if it affects the likelihood of future crime
- performance on earlier releases, if any
- relationships and employment opportunities
- psychological or psychiatric reports
- opinions from professionals, such as police officers and social workers
- the victim impact statement

Once the risk assessment is completed, the board looks at specific information about the inmate, such as

- behaviour while incarcerated
- evidence that behaviour has changed
- benefit from correctional programs
- treatment for any disorder diagnosed by a professional

Fast Fact

After serving one-sixth of a sentence, an inmate can apply for day parole to attend certain events such as funerals and religious holidays.

Victims Win Right to Address Hearings

Priscilla de Villiers scored another victory yesterday when crime victims won the right to address their attackers face-to-face at parole-board hearings. Ironically the breakthrough came the day after de Villiers announced she would be closing the office in Burlington of her group CAVEAT [Canadians Against Violence Everywhere Advocating Its Termination] and winding up her career as Canada's leading victims' rights activist.

The right to speak at parole-board hearings was the latest development in a crusade that started nine years ago when de Villiers and other activists began clamouring for more openness in the federal parole system. At the time, parole hearings were held in secret and crime victims weren't allowed to participate. Eventually, they gained the right to present written statements that the prisoner could review in advance. They weren't allowed to read the material, however.

Federal Solicitor-General Lawrence MacAuley announced yesterday crime victims would be allowed to read impact statements at parole hearings by July. The policy change was prompted by recommendations in a report by the standing committee on justice and human rights, which de Villiers and other victims' rights activists have addressed on a number of occasions.

"I'm not surprised," de Villiers said yesterday. We've continued to beat on that drum for a long time."

SOURCE: Paul Legall, "Victims win right to address hearings," *The Toronto Star*, May 12, 2001, A29, with permission from *The Hamilton Spectator*.

1. Describe the victory for victims' rights groups as reported in this article.
2. Why is this victory so important?

Conditional Release

conditional release: serving part of the sentence in the community under supervision

unescorted temporary absence: brief release from custody for community service or personal reasons

work release: conditional absence from custody to perform paid or voluntary work under supervision

day parole: conditional absence from custody during the day only

full parole: conditional release from custody after serving one-third to one-half of a sentence

statutory release: release, by law, after serving two-thirds of a sentence

A **conditional release** does not shorten the sentence; it simply allows part of the sentence to be served in the community under supervision. The eligibility for each type of conditional release is shown in Figure 11.11.

Unescorted temporary absence, a brief release from custody, is granted for personal reasons such as medical or administrative issues, community service, and family contact. An escorted or unescorted **work release** is given to do paid or voluntary work in the community under supervision. Low-risk offenders are eligible for **day parole** after serving one-sixth of the sentence. These inmates are required to return to the institution or a halfway house each night. Most offenders are normally eligible for **full parole** after serving one-third to one-half of their sentence. By law, most offenders are entitled to **statutory release** after serving two-thirds of their sentence. This law does not apply to offenders serving life or indeterminate sentences.

Offenders convicted of first-degree murder are eligible for full parole after serving 25 years of their sentence, but they can apply for early parole after serving 15 years. This is known as the "faint hope" provision because it is so seldom granted. Parole eligibility for those convicted of second-degree murder may occur after serving between 10 and 25 years. The period is determined by the trial judge and is specified at sentencing.

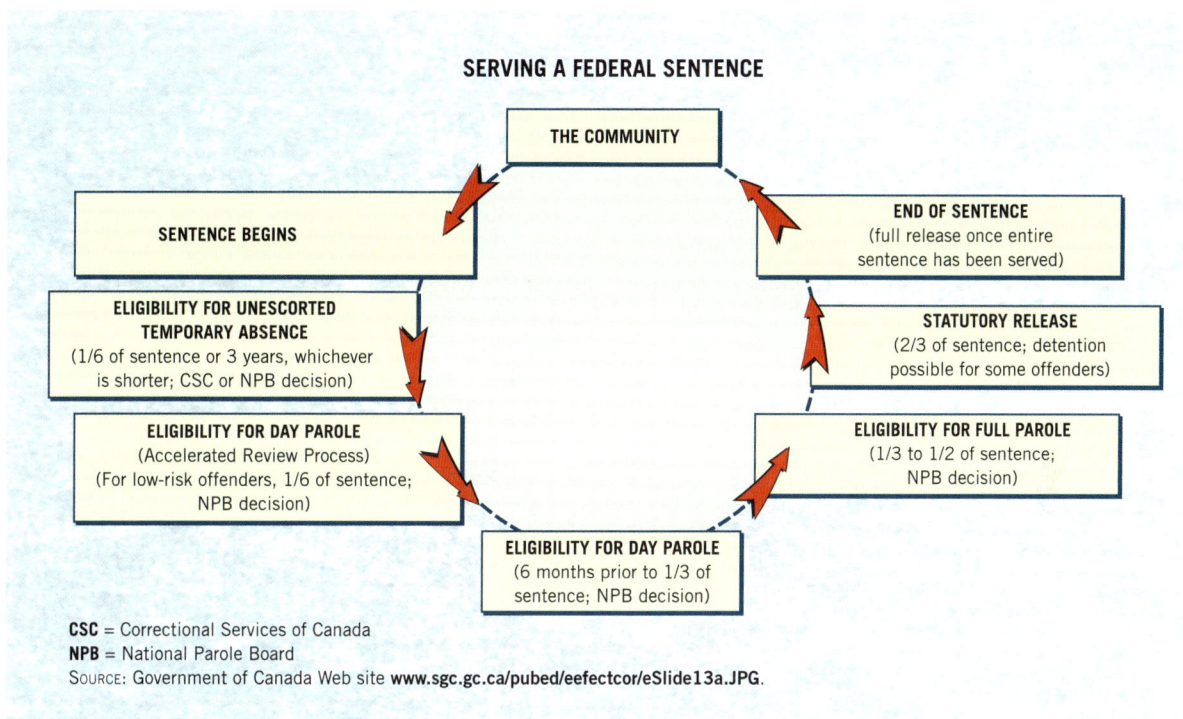

Figure 11.11 Eligibility for different types of conditional release or parole

Conditions for Release

Any offender released on parole or statutory release must agree to *all* of the following conditions. The offender must

- travel directly on release to the place of residence indicated on the release certificate, report to a parole supervisor immediately, and continue to report to the parole supervisor as instructed;
- provide the parole supervisor with an address for place of residence and immediately report any changes in address, occupation, educational training, volunteer work, family, domestic or financial situation, and any other change that might reasonably affect the offender's ability to keep the conditions of the parole;
- remain in Canada at all times and within established boundaries;
- obey the law and keep the peace;
- inform the parole supervisor if arrested or questioned by the police;
- always carry the release certificate and identity card provided by the releasing authority and be ready to produce them on request;
- report to the police as instructed by the parole supervisor;
- not own, possess, or have any control over any weapon as defined in the *Criminal Code* except as allowed by the parole supervisor; and
- if on day parole, to return to the penitentiary at the date and time set out on the release certificate.

law in the extreme

Police Petition Parliament to End "Club Fed"

Picture this—lovely oceanside accommodations on Vancouver Island with fishing and golfing facilities. Sound like a resort? That's exactly why some Canadians call William Head Institution, a minimum-security prison, "Club Fed." Yet this is where Clinton Suzack, who was convicted of first-degree murder in the death of a Sudbury police constable, was sent to begin serving his sentence.

Or, imagine receiving the morning paper and seeing a photo of inmate Karla Homolka, dressed in sexy evening attire, celebrating at a birthday party in Quebec's Joliette Institution.

Incidents like these have many Canadians questioning the policies of a correctional system that they believe is too lenient with first-degree murderers and high-risk offenders.

When two parolees, being stopped for a routine traffic check in Manitoba, shot and killed Dennis Stronquill, an RCMP Constable, in December 2001, Canadian police officers decided it was time to act. In February 2002, the Canadian Police Association (CPA), with the support of 275 provincial and municipal police associations across Canada, initiated a petition to be signed by Canadians, calling for harsher prison terms. The associations want a) an appeal of the "faint hope" clause and b) first-degree murderers to spend at least 25 years in maximum-security prison with no parole eligibility. They are also recommending that victims should have input into sentencing and parole decisions.

The associations are campaigning for a major overhaul of the federal corrections, sentencing, and parole systems through a public inquiry. At a press conference, David Griffin, executive officer, voiced the CPA's concerns: "Canada's police officers have lost all confidence in our nation's prison system. The inmates are running the asylum."

Correctional Service of Canada disagrees. Although this organization has agreed to look at the CPA's concerns, a spokesperson pointed out that freedom *is* taken away—inmates are told what to do and their activities are monitored.

Opposition to the CPA assessment of the system also comes from the John Howard Society, an association dedicated to helping those released from prison readjust to society. According to Duncan Gillespie, an executive director with the society,

> Inmates need to be treated like human beings, rather than warehoused like animals, because they will one day be back in society.... The system we have protects you better than one that says lock them up ... and then release them into the community cold turkey.

When Gillespie says "the system we have," he is referring to prisons like Joliette Institution that has semi-detached bungalow units, where inmates cook their own food in a shared kitchen, do their own laundry, and have separate rooms. Institutions like Joliette are designed to rehabilitate inmates and prepare them to re-enter society.

Many Canadians believe that rehabilitation should be the focus of sentencing, and it is only through rehabilitation that the public will be safe when high-risk offenders return to society. For many other Canadians, the concept of sentencing means punishment, and those convicted of violent offences deserve to be punished for those crimes.

SOURCE: Based on "Police petition demands feds get tough on crime," *Canadian Press*, February 11, 2002; "Policy lobby calls for stiffer laws, harsher prison terms," *Torstar News Service*, February 12, 2002.

Analysis Questions

1. In addition to a public inquiry, what changes is the CPA demanding in its petition to the federal government?
2. What is the "faint hope" clause?
3. Keeping in mind the goals of sentencing that you learned about at the beginning of this chapter, which side of this argument do you agree with? Explain your position.
4. What suggestions would you make to change Canada's sentencing rules and correction policies?

Pardons

Once a **pardon** is granted, a person's record of conviction is set aside. Any federal agency that has records of convictions must keep those records separate. The information may not be disclosed without permission from the Solicitor General of Canada. A pardon can be very important to people who want the opportunities and privileges that other Canadians enjoy. However, some foreign governments may not recognize a pardon; nor will a pardon guarantee entry or visa privileges to another country. A pardon does not erase the fact that a person was convicted of an offence.

pardon: the setting aside of a person's record of conviction

An offender convicted of a summary offence can apply for a pardon three years after completing the sentence. A person convicted of an indictable offence can apply five years after serving the sentence. The offender must demonstrate that he or she is now a law-abiding citizen. In 1998 to 1999, the National Parole Board granted 5476 pardons and denied 52.

Legal Link
For answers to frequently asked questions about pardons, visit **www.pearsoned.ca/law**.

A pardon automatically has no effect if a person is later convicted of an indictable offence. The National Parole Board can also rescind a pardon for any of the following reasons:

- a conviction for a summary offence
- unacceptable conduct
- false information at the time of application

In special cases, on the advice of her ministers, the Queen can extend a **Royal Prerogative of Mercy** under the authority of an Act of Parliament to a person who is sentenced to imprisonment. Mercy usually takes the form of clemency (release) or having the sentence commuted (reduced). For example, in *R. v. Latimer,* [2001], the Supreme Court of Canada indicated that the Royal Prerogative of Mercy is the only potential remedy for persons who have exhausted their rights of appeal and are unable to show that their sentences conflict with the Charter.

Royal Prerogative of Mercy: a release or sentence reduction granted by the Queen under the authority of an Act of Parliament

Consider This
Should Robert Latimer receive a Royal Prerogative of Mercy? Why or why not?

Building Your Understanding

1. What information must the parole board consider before making its decision?
2. Why is parole called a conditional release?
3. Explain the difference between full parole and statutory release.
4. List four conditions the parolee must agree to.
5. Briefly describe the difference between probation and parole.

LOOKING BACK

Reviewing Your Vocabulary

absolute discharge *p. 282*
aggravating factors *p. 280*
binding-over *p. 285*
closed custody *p. 295*
community service order *p. 284*
concurrent sentences *p. 288*
conditional discharge *p. 282*
conditional release *p. 298*
conditional sentence *p. 283*
consecutive sentences *p. 288*
dangerous offender *p. 288*
day parole *p. 298*
denunciation *p. 277*
deportation *p. 286*
electronic monitoring *p. 283*
family group conferencing *p. 292*
fines *p. 286*
full parole *p. 298*
general deterrence *p. 276*
incarceration *p. 287*
indeterminate sentence *p. 288*
intermittent sentence *p. 283*
maximum-security institution *p. 295*
medium-security institution *p. 295*
minimum-security institution *p. 295*
mitigating factors *p. 280*
open custody *p. 295*
pardon *p. 301*
parole *p. 297*
plea bargain *p. 287*
pre-sentence report *p. 278*
probation *p. 282*
protective custody *p. 295*
psychiatric assessment *p. 278*
recidivism *p. 276*
rehabilitation *p. 276*
restitution *p. 276*
retribution *p. 276*
Royal Prerogative of Mercy *p. 301*
sentence *p. 275*
sentencing circle *p. 293*
sentencing hearing *p. 279*
specific deterrence *p. 276*
statutory release *p. 298*
suspended sentence *p. 283*
suspension of privilege *p. 286*
unescorted temporary absence *p. 298*
victim impact panel *p. 293*
victim impact statement *p. 278*
victim-offender mediation *p. 291*
victim-offender panels *p. 293*
work release *p. 298*

Quick Quiz

1. Match the vocabulary terms above with these clues:
    a) separating an offender from the rest of the prison population
    b) one way to keep track of an offender under house arrest
    c) punishment based on "an eye for an eye"
    d) a sentence for an indefinite period of time
    e) circumstances that increase the severity of a sentence
    f) an alternative measures program that involves a threesome
    g) a document reviewed by a judge prior to sentencing
    h) a sentence that involves expulsion from the country
    i) an agreement negotiated between the Crown and defence counsel
    j) a sentence served on weekends or at night
    k) the most lenient sentence anyone can receive
    l) a court order to keep the peace

Checking Your Knowledge

2. Describe how the offender, the victim, and society are taken into consideration during the sentencing process.
3. Compare three types of sentences: suspended, intermittent, and conditional.
4. In Canada, why would someone be deported?
5. Distinguish between victim-offender mediation and victim-offender panels.
6. When is an offender eligible for day parole? Full parole? Statutory release?

Developing Your Thinking and Inquiry Skills

7. Create a survey that ranks the goals of sentencing on a five-point scale, with one being the most important and five being the least important goal.
    a) Survey family members, friends, and people in your community. Try to include men and women of different ages.
    b) Tally your results.
    c) Write up a brief description of your findings. Consider these questions:
        - Did responses vary according to gender?
        - Did the responses reveal any patterns with respect to age?
        - What is the majority view?
8. As a member of the parole board, you must decide whether to grant or deny parole to the offender in the case below.
    a) Indicate your reasons for granting or denying parole. If you grant parole, indicate what type of conditional release you recommend.
    b) Justify your decision on the basis of risk assessment factors.

    > Joe grew up in a dysfunctional home, where alcoholism and physical and emotional abuse were common. As an adult, Joe had difficulty dealing with his problems and often got into trouble. He was arrested several times for stealing cars and driving recklessly.
    >
    > One night, Joe took a friend's car out for a joyride. His driver's licence was under suspension at the time. During a police chase, Joe hit a pedestrian, who died on the scene. Joe was charged and convicted of dangerous operation of a motor vehicle, an indictable offence. He was sent to prison for four years.
    >
    > While in prison, Joe has been attending a substance abuse program as part of his sentence. He has also been seeing a psychologist to help him work through his childhood problems. His uncle has offered him future employment in his radiator repair shop. Joe has already served 18 months of his sentence.

9. Choose a newspaper story about a crime. Assume the role of the victim or a family member and write a one-page victim impact statement, using details from the article.

Communicating Your Ideas

10. Prepare an oral presentation to agree or disagree with *one* of the following statements. Provide evidence to support your position.
    - Sentences for impaired driving are too lenient to act as a general deterrent.
    - Offenders deserve more severe sentences than they are currently receiving.
    - Discharges and suspended sentences let people know they can break the law and get away with it.
11. Work in groups and research *two* of the following topics. Defending your position on the issues, write an essay on one topic and stage a formal debate on the other.
    - Canada should have a three-strike rule—no chance of parole after three convictions.
    - An offender should serve the entire sentence in prison.
    - Halfway houses should not be allowed in residential communities.

Putting It All Together

12. Working in small groups, prepare and present a mock sentencing of an offender.
    a) Use one of two sentencing approaches: traditional sentencing or a restorative justice program.
    b) Determine the various roles for members of your group (the victim, the Crown attorney, defence counsel, the offender, and the judge) and prepare a script.
    c) Prepare a pre-sentence report and include the aggravating and mitigating factors concerning the crime and the offender.
    d) Present the mock sentencing in front of the class.

CASES

R. v. *Owens* (2001), B.C.C.A. 0465

Eighteen-year-old Owens and a companion robbed a gas station. They wore balaclavas to disguise themselves and carried starter pistols. The station was closed, and the young attendant was waiting for his mother to pick him up. They took several hundred packages of cigarettes, $200 to $300 in cash, the attendant's wallet, and his identification. Owens' companion struck the attendant on the head with the pistol, opening a wound.

Owens pleaded guilty just before trial, and the judge sentenced him to 18 months' incarceration. Owens appealed, asking for a conditional sentence to be served in the community. The sentencing judge had considered that option, noting that the case met the three conditions established by precedent for a conditional sentence:

- the offender must be convicted of a crime that is not punishable by a minimum prison term;
- the court must impose a term of imprisonment of less than two years; and
- the public safety must not be endangered by the offender serving a sentence in the community.

Nevertheless, the judge found that the principle of general deterrence outweighed these considerations and decided that the sentence should be served in custody. At the time of the offence, Owens had been on probation for two other crimes, and he had a record of six youth-court offences, two for theft.

In his appeal, Owens argued that the trial judge had put too much emphasis on deterrence and denunciation and too little on rehabilitation. Since the time of the offence, Owens stopped drinking and became reconciled with his family. When the appeal was heard, he was on day parole and working as a baby-sitter and landscaper. He had also registered for a college course. The appeals court found these efforts commendable but agreed with the sentencing judge. Owens' appeal was dismissed.

1. List three mitigating and three aggravating factors in this case.
2. Do you agree with the decision to deny Owens a conditional sentence? Explain.

R. v. *Germain* (2001), B.C.C.A. 463

Germain, who had a long criminal record, committed two bank robberies in Vancouver. During a struggle in the second bank, he lost his cellphone, which enabled the police to locate and arrest him. Germain pleaded guilty and was sentenced by the judge to concurrent prison terms of 12 months each and a probation of 12 months. Defence counsel had suggested a term of 24 to 28 months' imprisonment, while the Crown had sought a sentence of four to six years. In discussion with Germain, the judge said that sending offenders to prison did not do any good and that the 12-month sentence she was imposing was not a light one.

The Crown appealed the sentence, saying the judge had not adequately considered the principles of denunciation, deterrence, and the general protection of the public, and had overemphasized rehabilitation. The Crown cited precedents indicating that the appropriate term for one robbery ranged from three to several years, and Germain had committed two robberies. The Crown argued for a term of four years.

At the time of the appeal, Germain had served six months of his sentence and was doing well in the provincial system. Increasing the sentence to four years would result in Germain having to transfer into the federal system and adapt to new surroundings. The appeal was allowed, and the sentence was increased to two years less a day, plus the two years' probation already ordered.

1. On what basis did the Crown appeal the judge's sentence?
2. Explain what "precedent" is and how it was used in this case.
3. Why was the sentence increased to only two years less a day?
4. Do you agree or disagree with this increased sentence? Why?

R. v. *Joseyounen* (1995), 6 W.W.R. 38 (Sask. Prov. Ct.)

BACKGROUND One night the accused, Robert Joseyounen, got drunk and started a fight with his brother, Napoleon Joseyounen. The victim's injuries were so severe that he suffered brain damage. Robert pleaded guilty to a charge of aggravated assault that endangered the life of his brother. He also applied for an order to hold a sentencing circle.

LEGAL QUESTION Is this case an appropriate opportunity for the Court to seek the guidance of a sentencing circle?

DECISION In determining whether a sentencing circle would be appropriate, Provincial Court Judge C. Fafard established the following seven criteria for assessing such requests and then applied them to this case:

1) The accused must agree to be referred to the sentencing circle.
2) The accused must have deep roots in the community in which the sentencing circle is held and from which the participants are drawn.
3) Elders or respected, non-political community leaders will participate.
4) The victim is willing to participate, without being subjected to coercion or pressure.
5) Although not applicable to this case, the following criterion was added to cover future possibilities: The court should try to determine beforehand whether the victim suffers from battered woman's syndrome. If she does, then she should receive counselling and be accompanied in the circle by a support team.
6) Disputed facts have been resolved in advance.
7) The case is one in which a court would be willing to take a calculated risk and depart from the usual range of sentencing.

In this case, the fourth criterion could not be satisfied. The victim no longer had sufficient mental capacity to express his wishes regarding this matter. Nonetheless, the most important criterion was the seventh. According to Judge Fafard:

> ... properly applied, it is the one [criterion] which guarantees the maintenance of public confidence in the administration of justice.
>
> It is not so much a question of specific or general deterrence. People who get drunk and commit an offence seldom address their minds to the consequence before committing the offence. In practice, deterrence should be aimed at drunkenness. Incarceration here is seen as a necessary measure to afford the accused the opportunity to reflect on the style of life which led him to do this terrible thing to his brother, and to deliberate on changing his attitude.

The judge imposed a sentence of imprisonment. However, he did grant the family's request and authorized a "healing" circle, rather than a sentencing circle.

HISTORICAL SIGNIFICANCE This case established the criteria for determining whether a sentencing circle should be granted.

ANALYSIS

1. Other than the battered woman's syndrome, which criterion could not be met? Why?
2. Why did the judge consider the seventh criterion to be the most important?
3. Explain the judge's views on deterrence in cases like this one.
4. Why do you think the judge granted the family's request for a healing circle even though he had imposed a prison sentence?

12 Criminal Law and Young People

CHAPTER OUTLINE

Youth and Crime

Legal Rights of Young People

Youth Criminal Justice System

Sentencing Options

FOCUS YOUR LEARNING

Why does the legal system treat young people differently from adults who commit the same crimes?

Why was it necessary to reform legislation governing young offenders?

What are the rights of a youth accused of a criminal offence?

What is the legal process for a young person going through the youth criminal justice system?

Figure 12.1 Divers search for the body of Reena Virk.

On a November evening in 1997, 14-year-old Reena Virk was severely beaten by a group of female teens. Later in the evening, two other teens killed her. A 16-year-old boy and a 15-year-old girl were charged with her murder. Because the murder trial made front-page news, many people were convinced that violent offences committed by young people were on the rise. But is this really true?

WHAT DO YOU THINK?

- Do you think the number of violent crimes committed by young people is increasing?

- Are there any advantages in knowing the identity of those charged with Reena Virk's murder? Any disadvantages?

The way Canadian laws deal with young people who commit criminal acts has often led to controversy. Some people believe that Canada's laws have been too lenient on young people, particularly those youths who commit violent crimes. Others feel that a "get tough" policy is not the most effective way to address youth and crime. They maintain that society should concentrate on preventing crime and devoting more resources to the rehabilitation of young people who break the law.

In this chapter, you will examine the issue of youth and crime as well as the legislation that governs youths accused of criminal offences. You will see how changing attitudes are reflected in changes to Canada's laws related to young people. You will also learn about the youth justice system and about sentencing options for those found guilty of criminal offences.

> "A young person once stigmatized as a lawbreaker may, unless given help and redirection, render the stigma a self-fulfilling prophecy."
> — Justice W. Ian C. Binnie, Supreme Court of Canada

YOUTH AND CRIME

The brutal murder of a youth by other youths is a shocking event, one that often causes people to question the safety of their communities. During the past decade, a number of particularly violent crimes committed by young people have made headlines across Canada. Do such incidents mean that violent crime among youth has increased? Many Canadians believe this is so, and they are losing confidence in the ability of the legal system to protect them.

However, serious violent crime, such as murder or aggravated sexual assault, represents a small fraction of reported crimes committed by youths. Some critics argue that it is people's *fear* of young people rather than an actual increase in violent offences that has contributed to the perception that violent crime among youth is on the rise. These critics claim that popular entertainment that glorifies violence as well as mass media that exaggerate changing social behaviour among young people may intimidate an older population that grew up under more clearly defined rules of social conduct.

Court statistics show that between 1984 and 1991 reported crime among Canadian youths rose dramatically, peaking in 1991. Some criminologists argue, however, that the increase in statistics for violent crime reflects the increase in reported incidents under the "zero tolerance" policy adopted by many schools during the past decade. Under this policy, even students involved in pushing and shoving can be charged with minor offences.

American youth commit homicide six to ten times more frequently than Canadian youth, reflecting differences in values and attitudes as well as easier access to firearms in the United States. However, the Canadian youth homicide rate is higher than that of many other countries. Figure 12.2 shows the percentage of criminal charges in Canada that involved youth from 1996 to 2000.

At some point during adolescence, many young people break the law. Lack of self-confidence, troubles at home and at school, and peer pressure to

Fast Fact
Females between the ages of 12 and 17 represent one of the fastest-growing areas of youth crime in Canada.

Law in Your Life
An increase in police involvement in school incidents of violence has led some critics to claim that "zero tolerance" is criminalizing youth. Others claim "zero tolerance" deters youth from violent activity. Which of these two positions do you support? Explain why.

Figure 12.2 In Canada from 1996 to 2000, young people were charged with 16 percent of violent crimes and almost 30 percent of property offences.

Year	Percentage of Violent Crimes Involving Youth	Percentage of Property Crimes Involving Youth
1996	16.1	29.0
1998	16.4	27.7
2000	16.2	27.1

SOURCE: Adapted from Statistics Canada, CANSIM II, table 252–0002 and Catalogue No. 85–205–XIE.

participate in certain activities can all contribute to high-risk behaviour among adolescents. Many adolescents simply make mistakes. Does this mean that *all* young people are destined to become criminals? Certainly not. Most young people go on to become productive, law-abiding citizens. Some, however, become serious or repeat offenders.

Creating a profile of young people who break the law can be difficult. In some cases, for example, brutal acts have been committed by youths with no previous records of violence. However, research does show that certain factors can lead to criminal behaviour among adolescents. For instance, adolescents who were abused or neglected as children tend to be prone to violent behaviour. Spousal abuse or a high level of conflict between parents can influence a young person's behaviour. In addition, parents who abuse drugs or alcohol or are involved in criminal activity can have a negative impact on a youth's respect for the law. Youths who leave home and live on the streets may also be more inclined to break the law.

In many cases, the victims of violent crimes by youths are other youths. Sometimes these crimes are carried out by gangs—adolescents who, on their own, may not engage in violent activity. If a gang is responsible for a violent or criminal act, members of the gang can be charged as "parties to the offence." When deciding on an appropriate sentence, judges try to identify the "ring leader" of the group.

Fast Fact
Winnipeg police have a street gang unit that works with the RCMP to monitor the activities of 1900 street gang members identified in that city.

Legislative Reform and Young People

At one time in Canada, children seven years of age and over who committed criminal offences were tried as adults. If convicted, they could have faced the same kinds of punishment that adults did, such as imprisonment, flogging, or even hanging. Many reformers argued that children need to be treated differently from adults because they lack the maturity and judgment to bear full responsibility for their actions. With proper guidance, these reformers argued, children could be rehabilitated more easily than adults.

In 1908, Parliament enacted the *Juvenile Delinquents Act*. This legislation described children who committed crimes as **juvenile delinquents,** young people whose antisocial or deviant behaviour was attributed to a lack of proper guidance. Delinquents included children who ran away from home,

juvenile delinquents: children between the ages of 7 and 16 to 18 (depending on the province) who committed crimes or were considered "unmanageable" or "sexually immoral"

skipped school, committed crimes, or were considered "unmanageable" or "sexually immoral." These provisions were often applied in a discriminatory fashion, for example, against young females who were sexually active. In theory, delinquent youths were not to be treated as criminals but as misdirected children who needed encouragement and help in turning their lives around. Although the "welfare of the child" was considered to be the guiding principle of the Act, many juveniles were sent to training schools for relatively minor offences. **Training schools** were custody facilities where children received disciplinary and vocational instruction.

> **training schools:** custody facilities that provided disciplinary and vocational instruction to juvenile offenders

By the 1970s, however, many Canadians were becoming critical of the *Juvenile Delinquents Act,* arguing that the "welfare" approach was not working. Critics claimed that instead of being rehabilitated in training schools, many juvenile delinquents were re-offending upon release, threatening public safety. The Act was also criticized because it gave judges and police broad powers in determining what was in the "best interests" of the child. Consequently, treatment of juveniles often depended on the particular judge or police officer dealing with the case, not on what the young person had actually done. In addition, the upper age limit of a delinquent was 16 to 18 years of age, depending on the province. A 17-year-old charged with stealing a car could be treated as an adult offender in one province and a juvenile delinquent in another. Finally, the Act failed to recognize the legal rights of youths, a factor that became more significant with the entrenchment of the *Charter of Rights and Freedoms* in 1982.

> **Fast Fact**
> In some cases, juveniles were subjected to abusive treatment by training-school staff.

Young Offenders Act

In 1984, Parliament replaced the *Juvenile Delinquents Act* with the **Young Offenders Act.** This Act shifted the youth justice system from a welfare-oriented approach to a criminal approach. A young person who committed a crime was officially identified as a **young offender.** The minimum age of a young offender was raised from 7 to 12 years and was extended to the youth's 18th birthday in all provinces. In addition, under the *Young Offenders Act,* young persons were to be held accountable for their crimes but at a lower level of accountability than adult offenders. The Act also recognized both the legal rights of young people as set out in the *Charter of Rights and Freedoms* and additional rights for youths because of their age and vulnerability.

> **Young Offenders Act:** federal legislation that replaced the *Juvenile Delinquents Act* in 1984
>
> **young offender:** under the *Young Offenders Act,* a person, at least 12 years of age and under 18, who breaks the criminal law

By the early 1990s, the number of reported crimes by young people in Canada had increased, and many citizens and critics were calling on the government to take a much tougher approach to youth crime, particularly for violent and repeat offenders. In response to such criticism, the federal government amended the *Young Offenders Act.* While the Act had always allowed young people facing serious charges to be transferred to adult court, amendments to the Act increased the maximum sentence a youth court could impose for murder from 3 years to 10 years.

law in the extreme

Treating Adolescents as Adults

Fourteen-year-old Steven Truscott and twelve-year-old Lynn Harper lived on the military base in Clinton, Ontario. One evening in June 1959, Steven gave Lynn a ride on his bicycle. According to Truscott, he and Harper rode past an area called Farmer Lawson's Bush and then over a bridge. On the other side of the bridge, he dropped Harper off. Truscott claimed that he rode back to the bridge where he stood and watched other children playing near the water.

Two days later, Lynn Harper's body was found in the bushes near the bridge. Harper had been raped and strangled.

The next day, police picked up Truscott and questioned him for seven hours. He told police that after dropping Harper off and returning to the bridge, he noticed a car stop and turn on the highway near the area where he had just left Harper. The police did not believe that Truscott would have been able to see the car at such a distance.

Steven Truscott was charged with Lynn Harper's murder and was transferred to adult court where he was tried by a jury.

At the trial, the prosecution argued that Truscott never rode over the bridge with Harper but dragged her through a barbed-wire fence into the woods at Farmer Lawson's Bush, where he raped and strangled her. Yet, when he returned home, Truscott had no noticeable scratches on his arms or any blood on his clothing.

Truscott maintained his innocence, but he never testified at his trial.

Truscott was found guilty of murder and sentenced to hang. His sentence was commuted to life in prison with eligibility for parole after 10 years. Truscott appealed to the Supreme Court of Canada where his conviction was upheld.

Did Steven Truscott receive a fair trial? Critics of the decision believe that in an attempt to solve the murder quickly, the police failed to conduct an adequate investigation. No one else from the surrounding area was considered as a possible suspect, even though one man with a history of sexual offences had followed three girls on a nearby country road just a few weeks before Harper was murdered.

The coroner concluded that Harper had died between 7:15 and 7:45 p.m. Yet, experts today say it would be difficult to pinpoint death to a specific half-hour period even with today's technology. The time of death was important because Truscott was seen back at the military base around 8:00 p.m.

A "model" prisoner, Steven Truscott was released on parole in 1969. He moved to Guelph, Ontario, where he eventually married and had a family. He lived under an assumed name until 2001 when he filed a request to the federal minister of justice to have his case reviewed and his name cleared.

Steven Truscott in 1959

Steven Truscott in 2001

Analysis Questions

1. Steven Truscott was questioned for several hours without having a lawyer present. Why was this not an issue in 1959?

2. Discuss the inconsistency between the goal of sentencing under the *Juvenile Delinquents Act* and the sentence Truscott received.

R. v. R.S.S., [1999] Alta. C.A. 80

CASE

In July 1997, R.S.S. and two friends, K. and D.L., entered an abandoned commercial garage in Calgary. They found a four-litre can of a substance later identified as toluene. Toluene is a highly flammable solvent. The can of toluene was marked with warning labels. As a prank, D.L. apparently agreed to allow the others to pour toluene into his shoes and light them. Once started, the fire spread quickly from D.L.'s shoes to his pants. He tried unsuccessfully to put the fire out. Later, K. testified that R.S.S. threw more toluene on D.L.'s chest and stomach. D.L. later died from shock and burns to over 90 percent of his body. R.S.S. was charged with second-degree murder. He was 15 years old at the time of the incident.

The Crown argued that the defendant should be transferred to adult court where, if found guilty of second-degree murder, he would face life imprisonment with eligibility for parole in five to seven years. If tried in youth court and convicted of second-degree murder, he would face four years in custody and three years under community supervision.

The youth court judge rejected the Crown's argument. The judge believed that although the defendant was immature, he did not have a propensity for violence and did not have the necessary intent for murder. The Crown appealed the decision, arguing that the youth court judge had erred in minimizing the seriousness of this crime and that a long-term sentence was necessary to protect the public.

The Alberta Court of Appeal dismissed the Crown's appeal, finding that the "goals of protecting the public and rehabilitating the young person" could be achieved by trying R.S.S. in youth court.

1. What was the significance of having R.S.S. tried in a youth court rather than an adult court?
2. Explain how the goals of protecting the public and rehabilitating the defendant could be met by trying R.S.S. in a youth court.

For many Canadians, the amendments to the *Young Offenders Act* did not go far enough in addressing the problem of youth crime, and by the mid-1990s many organizations and provincial politicians were lobbying the federal government for tougher legislation. Some politicians wanted drastic changes, such as lowering the minimum age of youth court jurisdiction to 10 years and requiring all 16-year-olds to be treated as adults. The province of Quebec, however, took the position that drastic changes were not required. Quebec maintained that federal and provincial governments needed to focus more on understanding the problems of youth crime instead of imposing harsh sentences that placed too many youths in expensive facilities.

After several years of consultation with provincial governments and numerous organizations, Parliament passed new youth justice legislation in 2002. This legislation, called the **Youth Criminal Justice Act,** replaced the *Young Offenders Act* and came into effect in 2003.

Fast Fact
In 2000, Canada had one of the highest rates of youth custody in the world.

Youth Criminal Justice Act: federal legislation that replaced the *Young Offenders Act*

Victims' Rights Advocate Enters Politics

NORTH VANCOUVER, B.C. — Chuck Cadman, a leading Canadian voice for crime victims, is challenging a Reform MP for her seat so he can run in the upcoming federal election.

Some in Canada's victims' rights movement are cheering on the critic of the *Young Offenders Act,* suggesting their cause needs a Parliamentary agent seared by the agony of losing a loved one to violence.

"I strongly support Chuck," said Gary Rosenfeldt, whose 16-year-old son was among 11 B.C. children murdered by Clifford Olson....

Cadman, an electrical technician [was] drawn into activism by the 1992 stabbing death of his teenage son.... On October 18, 1992, Jesse Cadman was walking home in Surrey from a party when he and some friends were attacked by six other teens. One of the attackers, Isaac Deas, stabbed Cadman in the back, killing him.

At the time, Deas, then 17, was facing various charges and was out on bail. Hours before the confrontation, Deas was flashing a "Rambo-type" knife and telling friends he was itching for a fight, his trial was told.

Deas was convicted of second-degree murder and sentenced to life in prison, eligible to apply for parole in 10 years.

The night of the killing, Cadman and his family made a pledge. "We sat down—my wife, daughter and myself—and made a conscious decision we were going to do something," he said.

SOURCE: "Victims' rights advocate entering politics; others may follow," Southam Newspapers, 1997, www.southam.com/national/fed97/970319justice_victims.html

1. Chuck Cadman won both the 1997 and 2000 elections and was justice critic for the Canadian Alliance Party in the hearings leading up to the enactment of the *Youth Criminal Justice Act.* As the parent of a murdered youth, what kinds of changes do you think Cadman would want to see in the youth justice system?
2. If Cadman wants to help prevent future violence, what should he focus on— changes in the law or changes in the way society treats troubled teens? Explain.

Consider This

The RCMP work with youth to develop initiatives to help young people overcome delinquent behaviour. What insights do you think youth advisers might give RCMP officers to help them with their initiatives?

Youth Criminal Justice Act

According to the Declaration of Principle in the *Youth Criminal Justice Act,* the purpose of the Act is the long-term protection of society. The Act sets out ways to promote this protection, such as addressing the circumstances underlying a young person's behaviour and focusing on measures that will impact the youth's rehabilitation. One way of ensuring that measures are meaningful and effective is to make the sentence match the crime. Most offences committed by young people are minor, yet Canada has a high rate of custody among young people. Under the *Youth Criminal Justice Act,* police are required to consider measures other than custody for young people who commit minor offences. The Act also makes provisions for members of the youth's family, the victim, youth workers, and other members of the community to be more involved in different stages of the process.

Figure 12.3 How might the new Act help to reduce the number of young offenders behind bars?

Youths no longer have to be transferred to adult court in order to receive an adult sentence for a serious or presumptive offence. **Presumptive offences** are first- and second-degree murder, attempted murder, manslaughter, aggravated sexual assault, and repeat "serious violent offences." Judges in youth justice courts are now empowered to impose adult sentences for these offences. In addition, the identity of a young person who receives an adult sentence may be known to the public, but only after the youth has been sentenced.

presumptive offences: murder, attempted murder, manslaughter, aggravated sexual assault, and third serious violent offences

Incapacity of Children

The law assumes that a child under the age of 12 is incapable of appreciating the nature and consequences of a criminal act and is, therefore, not criminally responsible. This assumption is called the **incapacity of children.** In Canada, children under the age of 12 who commit illegal acts, even serious crimes, are to be dealt with by their parents or according to the social welfare and mental health laws of each province or territory. Under such laws, for example, the police can apprehend a child and place the child in a temporary care facility. Children may be removed from their parents' homes on a permanent basis and placed in foster or group homes. Violent children or those with serious behavioural problems can also be sent for treatment in a secure mental-health facility.

incapacity of children: the legal presumption that a child under the age of 12 cannot form the necessary *mens rea* to be convicted of a crime

Figure 12.4 What values and attitudes of society does each piece of legislation reflect?

Legislation	Characteristics of each piece of legislation
Juvenile Delinquents Act (1908)	• age of youths covered: 7–16 or 7–18, depending on province • child-welfare approach • informal procedures • lack of recognition of legal rights • incidents of institutional abuse • significant judicial discretion
Young Offenders Act (1984)	• age of youths covered: 12–18th birthday • shift from welfare to criminal legislation • more emphasis on youth taking responsibility for actions • more emphasis on society's right to be protected • rights under the Charter and special rights for youth
Amendments to *Young Offenders Act* (1992 and 1995)	• maximum sentence in youth court increased to 10 years for murder • easier transfers to adult court for 16- and 17-year-olds charged with serious offences
Youth Criminal Justice Act (2002)	• age of youths covered: 12–18th birthday • limited use of custody • seriousness of offence to be reflected by the sentence • measures other than court proceedings to be used for non-violent offences • need to transfer youths to adult court eliminated by allowing adult sentences for presumptive offences if youth sentences are insufficient to hold young offenders accountable • publication of youth's identity if adult sentence imposed, but only after sentencing

SOURCE: Based on *Youth Justice Legislation: A Chronology,* Justice Department at http://canada.justice.gc.ca/en/news/nr/1998/yoachron.html

Building Your Understanding

1. In your own words, explain the purpose of the *Juvenile Delinquents Act.*
2. Why did the *Juvenile Delinquents Act* come under greater criticism during the 1960s?
3. What was the significance of raising the minimum age of a young person covered under the *Young Offenders Act* from 7 to 12 years of age?
4. Describe Quebec's point of view regarding the 1995 amendments to the *Young Offenders Act.* Do you agree with this position? Explain.
5. a) Identify the main purpose of the *Youth Criminal Justice Act.*
   b) List four changes introduced by this Act.
6. a) Why does the law assume that children under 12 are not criminally responsible for their actions?
   b) What is this assumption called?

LEGAL RIGHTS OF YOUNG PEOPLE

If a young person is questioned by the police or charged with a criminal offence, that person's rights as set out in the *Charter of Rights and Freedoms* cannot be violated. Furthermore, the *Youth Criminal Justice Act* provides additional rights aimed at protecting young people who may fail to exercise their Charter rights through ignorance or fear. These additional rights also protect youths from being pressured into making false confessions.

If a youth is arrested, he or she has the right to a lawyer during questioning. In addition, under the Act, the youth has the right to consult a parent. The presence of a parent during questioning not only helps ensure that the legal rights of the youth are protected but also allows the parent to play a supportive role in the youth's case. If a parent is not available, the police may notify a legal guardian or other adult known to the youth.

Searches

Under s. 495(1) of the *Criminal Code,* the police are permitted to search youths without a warrant if they have reasonable grounds to believe the search will uncover evidence that might otherwise be lost. For example, in *R. v. D.M.F.* (1999), a woman allowed police officers to search her son's room for evidence, without her son's permission. The police seized a pair of underwear as evidence that the youth had committed two sexual assaults. The Alberta Court of Appeal dismissed the youth's appeal and held that the seizure of the underwear was lawful because the mother had consented to the search.

In contrast, in *R. v. W (J.P.)* (1993), a father in British Columbia gave a police officer the right to search his son's room without a search warrant. At no time did the youth give the police officer permission to search his room. During the search, the officer found stolen goods. When the youth returned home, he was arrested. At trial the youth was acquitted, even though he was in possession of stolen goods. The judge ruled that the father could not waive his son's rights to privacy under s. 8 of the Charter. As you can see, different judges have different views about how to apply the *Charter of Rights and Freedoms.*

> **Consider This**
> With a partner, discuss what elements the judges might have considered to arrive at different interpretations of s. 8 of the Charter in *R. v. D.M.F.* and *R. v. W. (J.P.).*

Rights Regarding Evidence

All young suspects questioned by police or appearing in court are entitled to a lawyer. The youth must be informed that he or she has the right to consult with a parent and a lawyer before answering questions and to have a parent and lawyer present when making a statement. The youth must also be informed in language he or she understands that any statement regarding the alleged offence is voluntary. These rights are intended to prevent young people from giving statements without having the opportunity to obtain proper legal advice. Some youths may be intimidated into making false confessions if parents or lawyers are not present.

Although many young people who are questioned by police waive their rights and make statements without consulting a lawyer, it is rarely to a young

> **Law in Your Life**
> What reasons might a young person have for waiving his or her right to parental or legal representation?

CASE

R. v. M. (M.R.), [1998] 3 S.C.R. 393

BACKGROUND A vice-principal in a high school in Nova Scotia received information from students that M., also a student, was going to sell drugs at a school dance. The vice-principal notified the police and told them of his intention to search the student for drugs. The vice-principal approached M. and asked him to come to the office, where he informed him that he would be searched for drugs. A plainclothes RCMP officer was present and introduced himself but said nothing while the vice-principal searched M. The vice-principal found a cellophane bag of marijuana stuffed into one of M.'s socks and gave it to the officer, who told M. that he was under arrest for possession of a narcotic. The officer then advised M. of his right to counsel and of his right to contact a parent or other adult. M. tried to reach his mother by telephone. When he could not reach her, he said that he did not wish to contact anyone else.

The trial judge concluded that the vice-principal was acting as an agent of the police and held that the search violated M.'s rights under s. 8 of the *Charter of Rights and Freedoms*. As an agent of the police, the vice-principal was obligated to inform M. of his constitutional rights.

The charge was dismissed. The Crown appealed to the Nova Scotia Court of Appeal, which ordered a new trial. M. then appealed to the Supreme Court of Canada.

LEGAL QUESTION Did the search by the vice-principal violate M.'s rights under s. 8 of the *Charter of Rights and Freedoms*?

DECISION The Supreme Court of Canada found that the vice-principal was not acting as an agent of the police and, therefore, was not obligated to inform M. of his constitutional rights. The Court dismissed M.'s appeal. The Court noted that even though there was no express authority for a physical search of the students under the *Nova Scotia Education Act*, such a power could be inferred from the broad discretionary powers the Act gives to school officials to maintain discipline and safety in schools.

LEGAL SIGNIFICANCE With this decision, the Supreme Court established that a warrant is not es-

Figure 12.5 The Supreme Court of Canada ruled that school officials have the right to search students without a warrant. Do you agree with this ruling? Explain.

sential when a school authority searches a student. However, the school authority must have reasonable grounds to believe that there has been a breach of the school regulations, and the search must be "reasonable." For instance, it may be reasonable to conduct an intrusive search for weapons, but it may not be reasonable for a male teacher to search an adolescent female student while looking for drugs.

ANALYSIS

1. Briefly explain why the Supreme Court of Canada decided to allow school officials to search students without first obtaining a warrant.
2. What considerations did the Supreme Court have to weigh in order to arrive at a balanced decision in this case?
3. Do you agree that high school students should be treated differently from other suspects? Why or why not?

person's advantage to do so. Even if the youth has committed the act and thinks that the situation is hopeless, the youth will almost always benefit from the advice and presence of a lawyer before being questioned and while making a statement.

In 1990, the Supreme Court of Canada ruled that evidence could not be used in court against a young accused if the young person's rights had been violated during the gathering of evidence, even if the violation was a relatively minor infraction of the rules about cautioning a youth. For some people, the Supreme Court's decision meant that a young defendant could "get off" on a technicality. However, under the *Youth Criminal Justice Act*, if the officer questioning a youth does not fully comply with the conditions for taking a statement, the evidence may be admitted if the judge finds that only a "technical irregularity" occurred. Also, this irregularity must not violate the youth's rights or procedural protections. Note the following excerpt from s. 146:

> 146. (2) No oral or written statement made by a young person who is less than eighteen years old ... is admissible against the young person unless
>
>   (a) the statement was voluntary;

Consider This

In 1999, a male high school teacher and a vice-principal looked for stolen money by conducting a strip search of a group of male students. The money was not found. Discuss whether the teacher and vice-principal could be charged. If so, what offence would they be charged with? Explain.

R. v. J. (J.T.), [1990] 2 S.C.R. 755

CASE

On September 13, 1985, a three-year-old girl was sexually assaulted and hit over the head with a cinder block. She died instantly.

The next day, the police took 17-year-old J. (J.T.), a youth who lived nearby, down to the station for questioning. Hair similar to J.'s had been found on the body of the victim; fibres were also found similar to those in the clothing J. was wearing.

The police questioned J. for several hours, and he finally confessed to the crime. J. was then charged with murder and was informed that he had the right to retain a lawyer. J. called a lawyer, but prior to her arrival, the police seized J.'s clothing and took hair samples and nail clippings. The youth then spoke to his lawyer, who advised him to say nothing further. After the lawyer left, the police asked the youth if he wanted to make a statement; he responded that his lawyer had told him not to. The police informed the youth that they had some evidence that appeared to implicate him in the crime. They asked him additional questions, which he answered.

J. was transferred to adult court and convicted of first-degree murder. He appealed the decision to the Supreme Court of Canada. The Supreme Court held that J.'s statements were inadmissible because he was not informed of his right to counsel *before* he made his statements, and an adult or lawyer was not present *while* he made his statements. The conviction for murder was set aside, though there was sufficient evidence besides the statements to uphold a conviction for manslaughter.

1. How did the police fail to provide J. with his rights under the *Young Offenders Act*?
2. If you were arrested, would you want a parent or other adult present while the police questioned you? What role would you expect this person to play? Would a parent assume the same role as a lawyer? Explain.

(b) the person to whom the statement was made had, before the statement was made, clearly explained to the young person, in language appropriate to his or her age and understanding, that

  (i) the young person is under no obligation to make a statement,

  (ii) any statement made by the young person may be used as evidence in proceedings against him or her,

  (iii) the young person has the right to consult counsel and a parent or other person …

  (iv) any statement made by the young person is required to be made in the presence of counsel and any other person consulted … unless the young person desires otherwise;

Publication of Identities

The media can report on youth trials, but in most cases they cannot publish the name or other identifying information about the accused or any other youth involved in the trial (such as a witness). Protecting the privacy of a youth is important because many people believe that knowing a young defendant's identity could prejudice teachers, classmates, or community members against the youth and his or her family. This negative publicity could also stigmatize the youth and become a hindrance to rehabilitation. Under s. 110 of the *Youth Criminal Justice Act,* the identity of a youth who receives an adult sentence can be published but only after conviction. In addition, the identity of a young person who is given a youth sentence for a presumptive offence may also be published, unless the judge decides that such publication would hinder the youth's rehabilitation.

Building Your Understanding

1. Under the *Youth Criminal Justice Act,* why are youths provided certain rights in addition to those in the Charter?

2. The search, questioning, detention, and arrest of a young suspect must be conducted in a specific manner. Explain.

3. Identify the most important additional rights youths have with respect to questioning by police. Why are these rights provided?

4. Why do you think the identities of young suspects and witnesses are protected from publication in the media?

YOUTH CRIMINAL JUSTICE SYSTEM

In Chapter 7, you learned about the criminal court system—its structure and jurisdiction, the rules of evidence, and the various stages of a criminal trial. The youth criminal justice system also has its own structure and procedures, as illustrated by the flow chart in Figure 12.6. This chart traces the youth court process from police investigation to sentencing.

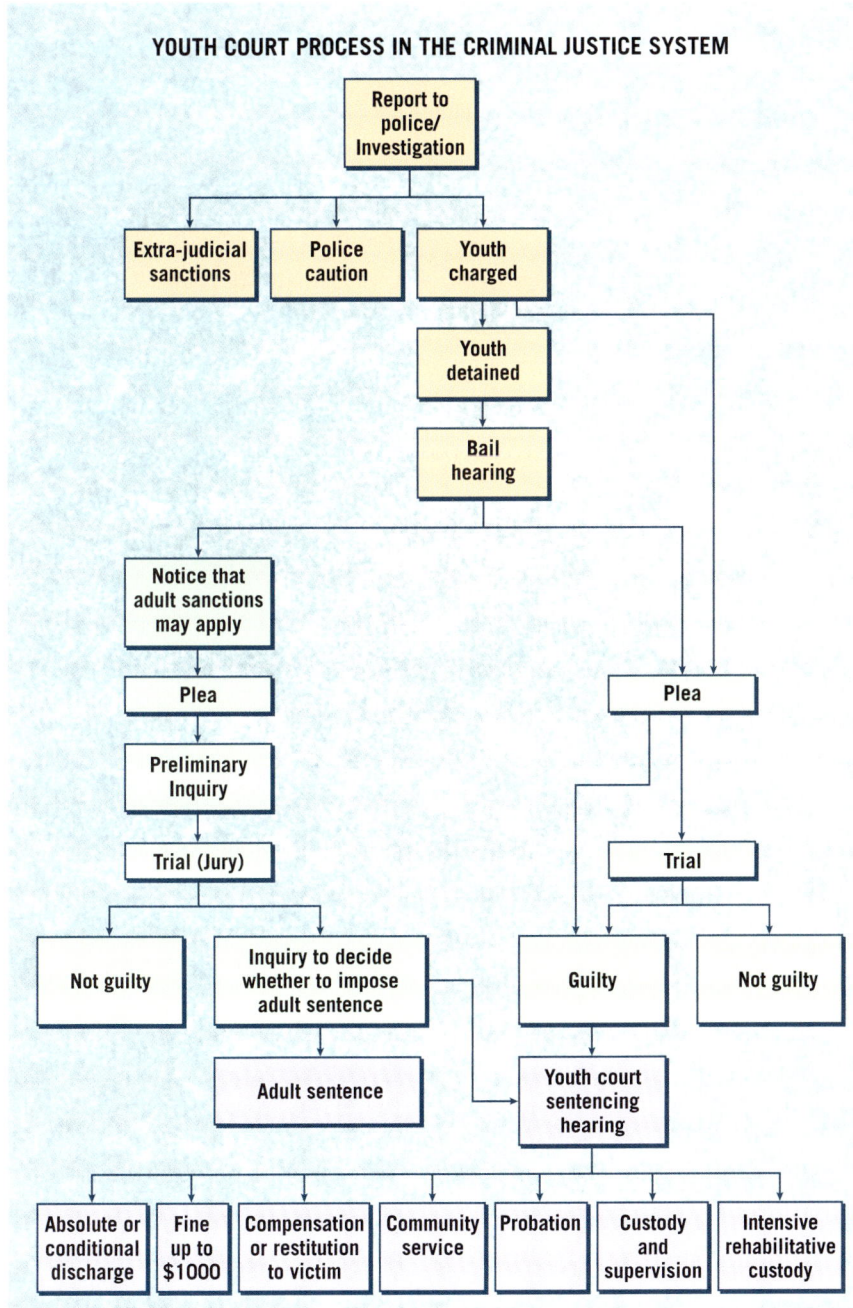

Figure 12.6 This flow chart shows the stages of the criminal court process under the *Youth Criminal Justice Act*.

SOURCE: Adapted from Nicholas Bala, *Canadian Youth Justice Law*, Irwin Law, 2002.

The process begins when a young person commits an offence, and a police officer arrives at the scene. Immediately, the officer has a number of options. For example, suppose the manager of the local music store catches Emily stealing CDs and calls the police. If this is Emily's first offence, the police officer could choose to discuss the problem with Emily, have her return the stolen CDs, and inform her parents of her actions. The officer may then

Figure 12.7 These police officers are questioning the parent of a first-time offender. Do you agree that police officers should be more lenient with first-time offenders than they are with repeat offenders? Explain.

give Emily a warning about the consequences of her actions if she is caught shoplifting a second time. However, if the officer feels that a warning is not a sufficient response to Emily's offence, the officer may consider other options that would keep Emily from going to court but still serve as a meaningful consequence of her wrongdoing. Such options may include the community-based measures discussed below.

Community-based Measures

Under the *Youth Criminal Justice Act,* a police officer's first option in dealing with a first-time offender of a non-violent crime is to consider using an extra-judicial sanction. **Extra-judicial sanctions** are usually community-based programs aimed at having a youth take responsibility for his or her actions. Instead of laying charges in court, the police officer may direct the youth to participate in an extra-judicial sanctions program. In this type of program, the youth may be required to apologize to the victim, replace or repair damaged property, return stolen goods, meet with the victim to find out how the crime affected him or her, or perform some kind of community service for a certain period.

Community programs are often related to the type of crime the youth committed. For example, if René is found guilty of vandalizing a community park, he may be ordered to plant flowers and rake leaves in a public park for a certain number of hours a week. Many professionals who work with youths feel that extra-judicial sanctions help reduce the rate of recidivism, a clear benefit to society in the long run.

extra-judicial sanctions: participating in community-based programs instead of going to court

Fast Fact
Under the *Young Offenders Act,* extra-judicial sanctions were called alternative measures.

Figure 12.8 Provisions under the *Youth Criminal Justice Act* allow for greater participation of the youth's family, the victim, and other members of the community. How would you compare this type of community-based program to an Aboriginal sentencing circle?

An extra-judicial sanction can be used only if

- the Crown prosecutor or police officer is satisfied that such a program would be appropriate;
- the young person agrees to participate in the program;
- the young person has been advised of his or her right to consult a lawyer regarding the program;
- the young person accepts responsibility for his or her actions; and
- there is sufficient evidence to convict should the youth appear in court.

The young person's parents must be informed of the program. The victim also has the right to know the kind of program the youth is participating in. In fact, many programs try to involve the victims in some way, often inviting the victim to meet the offender. Any record of participation in an extra-judicial sanction must be destroyed if the youth does not commit any further offences for two years.

Youth Justice Court

If an offence is serious, and the police have reasonable grounds to believe a certain young person committed the offence, that person can be questioned, charged, and given notice to appear in youth justice court. **Youth justice court** is a special court for young people between the ages of 12 and 18 who have been charged with a criminal offence.

If detained, a young person is entitled to a bail hearing (see Figure 12.6). In deciding whether a youth should remain in detention, the judge takes into consideration the seriousness of the crime and the likelihood that the youth will appear in court if released. If the judge decides to release the youth, the release often comes with certain conditions, such as a curfew or supervision by a parent or other adult. If the judge has reason to believe that the youth will commit another crime before the trial or will not appear in court, the judge may order the youth to remain in detention.

youth justice court: a court for young people between the ages of 12 and 18 who have been charged with a criminal offence

Fast Fact

If a person spends time in detention and is subsequently found guilty, the judge should consider the time in detention as part of that person's sentence.

Detention can be very disruptive for a young person. It could prevent the youth from going to school or being with family members. And not all detention facilities are appropriate. For example, in *R. v. M. (T.)* (1991), the judge found that conditions in a Toronto detention centre constituted "cruel and unusual" treatment because the cells were hot, dirty, and overcrowded. Many staff members had no training in working with youths, and no activities were planned for those detained. This particular detention centre has since improved, but conditions in other centres remain a concern.

A young person who has passed his or her 18th birthday can be tried in youth justice court if that person committed the alleged offence before turning 18. For example, if Stan committed a sexual assault on a younger child when he was 16, but the assault was not reported by the child until Stan was 18 years old, Stan would still be tried under the *Youth Criminal Justice Act*. He would also appear in youth justice court, although he might be required to serve the sentence in an adult correctional facility.

Building Your Understanding

1. What are extra-judicial sanctions? Why are these sanctions the primary consideration in sentencing first-time offenders?
2. What conditions have to be met before extra-judicial sanctions can be used?
3. What factors does a judge take into consideration in a bail hearing?
4. Describe a situation in which a 19-year-old can be tried under the *Youth Criminal Justice Act*.

SENTENCING OPTIONS

Fast Fact

Under the *Young Offenders Act*, a sentence was called a disposition, and a pre-sentence report was called a pre-disposition report.

Section 38 of the *Youth Criminal Justice Act* sets out the principles that must be considered when young people are sentenced. These principles are meant to guide judges (and others involved in the youth justice system) in how to interpret the Act. The main principle under the Act is to hold a young person accountable for his or her actions by imposing a sentence that is fair, meaningful, and helpful in the process of rehabilitation. The sentence is to be proportionate to the crime and cannot be greater than the punishment an adult would receive for the same crime.

Before deciding on a sentence the judge considers many factors:

- the extent to which the youth participated in the offence
- the harm done to the victim and the community
- any reparation that the youth has made to the victim
- the amount of time the youth has already spent in detention
- other crimes the youth may have committed
- the content of the victim impact statement

The judge will also examine the pre-sentence report. A pre-sentence report is usually written by a youth court worker (or a probation officer) to provide the judge with background information about the offender, including school attendance, performance records, employment records, and the relationship the youth has with his or her parents. A psychological or medical assessment may also be undertaken to help the judge understand the situation and determine an appropriate sentence.

The judge must consider all community-based sentencing options other than custody, particularly when sentencing young Aboriginal offenders. This requirement is aimed at reducing the high rate of custody among Aboriginal youth. Many Aboriginal leaders believe that alternatives to custody give Aboriginal communities more control over the rehabilitation and treatment of young people within their communities.

"Our people are over-represented in the prison populations ... we are far more likely to be denied bail, be unrepresented, spend more time in pre-trial detention than non-Aboriginal people, and plead guilty simply because our people are intimidated and alienated."
— Matthew Coon Come, national chief, Assembly of First Nations

Youth Sentences

If a youth is convicted of an offence, there are a number of options the court can consider when handing down a youth sentence. A **youth sentence** takes into consideration the sentencing goals of the *Youth Criminal Justice Act*. For instance, a youth could be discharged on condition that he or she fulfills certain requirements, such as performing community service, paying a fine, or compensating the victim for any damage or loss caused by the offence (see Figure 12.6).

Another option available to the court is to place a youth on probation for a specific period. Once on probation, the youth must comply with the conditions imposed by the court, such as meeting regularly with a probation officer. Generally, probation allows young persons to live at home, but they must meet a number of requirements such as complying with a curfew, attending school regularly, getting professional counselling, appearing in court if required, remaining within a designated area, or performing work in the community.

For more serious crimes, a youth sentence will place the young person in custody. **Custody** for a youth usually means assignment to a group home, participation in a wilderness camp, or incarceration in a youth correctional facility. The conditions of custody are specified by a court order called a **custody and supervision order,** which requires the youth to serve two-thirds of the sentence in a controlled facility away from home and the last third in the community. The opportunity to move into the community under supervision could be suspended if the youth is likely to re-offend or commit a violent crime. There is also the possibility of release under community supervision before the completion of two-thirds of the sentence.

When young persons are ordered to stay in a group home or participate in a wilderness camp, the sentence is usually referred to as **open custody.** Young people in open custody live under certain restrictions. For instance, youths in a group home must obey all house rules such as a complying with a curfew, attending meals on time, and performing household chores. While in open custody, youths can continue to attend school in the community where the group home is located.

youth sentence: punishment imposed on a young person that takes into consideration the principles involved in sentencing people under the age of 18

custody: a sentence entailing confinement within a controlled facility; usually imposed on a young person who commits a serious crime

custody and supervision order: an order from the court that sets out terms and conditions, requiring the youth to spend two-thirds of the sentence in custody and the last third in the community under supervision

open custody: a sentence directing the youth to stay in a group home or participate in a wilderness camp for a certain period

secure custody: a sentence that incarcerates a young criminal in a special youth facility

Secure custody involves removing the young person from the community and incarcerating the individual in a secure facility. Facilities for secure custody vary greatly, depending on the community and province where the facility is located. A secure custody facility could comprise a section of an adult prison or a special youth facility. Most facilities offer educational opportunities, counselling, and recreation; however, the availability of counselling and programming varies widely. The *Youth Criminal Justice Act* restricts the use of custody to serious or repeat offenders only.

youth worker: a person appointed to monitor the youth's progress in the community

A **youth worker** is someone appointed by the government to supervise the young person. The youth worker makes sure that the person released from custody follows the conditions of supervision as specified in the sentence, such as attending school or an educational training program on a regular basis, finding employment, or participating in a treatment program for alcohol or drug abuse.

Post-custody supervision in the community is aimed at helping the youth reintegrate into society. In most instances, probation, custody, and supervision cannot exceed a period of two years. For serious offences, a youth might receive a sentence of three years' custody and supervision. Further, if a young person is convicted of first-degree murder, the sentence imposed by a youth justice court can be up to ten years. For second-degree murder, the maximum youth sentence is seven years.

Figure 12.9 Boot camps, also known as strict-discipline facilities, are controversial because they are modelled on military camps. Youths are made to follow demanding physical routines, and supervision is tightly controlled. Do you think boot camps are an effective alternative to custody? Explain.

R. v. P. (T.M.), [1996] B.C.C.A.

CASE

In 1993 when T. was 13 years old, he broke into a friend's house and stole a Sega video game and some cash. T.'s parents had T. apologize to the family and give his own Super Nintendo machine to the family in restitution. It was not until 1995, however, that T. appeared in youth court on a charge of theft. At the time of his appearance, T. was on probation for another theft committed in 1994. He had also become a regular user of marijuana and had confessed to subsequent break-ins and car thefts since the first offence.

In deciding T.'s sentence for the first charge, the youth court judge took into consideration T.'s behaviour during the two-year interval, and she made a probation order that included, among other conditions, attendance at a wilderness program for nine weekends and participation in a drug and alcohol treatment program.

T. appealed the attendance at a wilderness camp and participation in mandatory drug and alcohol counselling. T.'s lawyer argued that the judge in youth court should not have taken into account the criminal acts committed by T. after the first theft to which he pleaded guilty.

The British Columbia Court of Appeal dismissed T.'s appeal, and the original conditions of the disposition were maintained. In reaching its decision, the Court stated that the emphasis on rehabilitation in the *Young Offenders Act* obligated a judge to consider the conduct of the young person and all relevant background in order to decide on an effective disposition.

1. Why would T.'s lawyer *not* want the youth court judge to take into account T.'s behaviour after the first theft?
2. Do you think the youth court judge's decision to have T. attend a wilderness camp and participate in drug counselling sessions were aimed at protecting society or rehabilitating T., or both? Explain.

Conferences

At any stage in the youth sentencing process, a court may refer the case to a conference in order to determine the most appropriate action. The referral might be made by a judge or, at an earlier stage in the proceedings, by a police officer or Crown prosecutor. Typically, the youth, the parents, and the victim will meet with a facilitator, concerned professionals, and members of the community. The police officer, the youth worker, and a teacher might also attend to discuss the situation and reach a consensus about the best response to the offence. A conference can be held to determine if an extra-judicial sanction would be more appropriate than a court-imposed sentence or to advise the judge about the kind of sentence the youth should receive. Conferences are one way of involving the community, the parents, and the victim in a youth's rehabilitation and treatment.

Fast Fact
Under the *Youth Criminal Justice Act,* if a sentenced youth breaches any conditions of release while under supervision in the community, the youth can be brought back into custody and required to serve the rest of the second period in custody rather than under supervision in the community.

Adult Sentences

In some cases, youths can be found guilty of such serious offences that sentencing under youth legislation would not be adequate to hold a youth accountable for his or her actions. In these cases, the Crown will seek an adult sentence instead of a youth sentence. If the Crown is seeking an adult sentence,

Figure 12.10 This young person (centre), who cannot be identified, pleaded guilty to first-degree murder and two counts of attempted murder. Do you agree that a youth who receives an adult sentence for murder should be eligible for parole earlier than an adult would be for the same crime? Why or why not?

Fast Fact

If a person is 20 years old when sentenced in youth court, he or she will serve custody in an adult facility, not a youth facility.

it must notify the youth of its intentions prior to the trial. If such notice is given, the youth has the right to a preliminary inquiry and a trial by jury. As you learned in Chapter 7, a preliminary inquiry is a pre-trial hearing at which the Crown must present sufficient evidence to establish that the accused should be put on trial. Preliminary inquiries are reserved for the most serious crimes.

Adult sentences are most likely to be sought for presumptive offences. The *Youth Criminal Justice Act* provides that an adult sentence can be considered only for youths who were 14 years old or older on the date of the offence. If the Crown is seeking an adult sentence for a presumptive offence, the onus will be on the defence to satisfy the court that a youth sentence would be sufficient to make the youth accountable for his or her actions.

In deciding if a young person should receive an adult sentence, the court considers a number of factors, such as the youth's background, the seriousness of the offence, and the age, maturity and character of the accused. If the court feels that a youth sentence would not provide a sufficient response to the young person's actions, then it will impose an adult sentence, a portion of which may be served in a youth custody facility. An offender under 18 years of age at the time of sentencing will usually be placed in a youth custody facility until the age of 18. A youth over the age of 18 at the time of sentencing will generally serve the sentence in an adult facility. Note that a young person who receives an adult sentence for murder could be eligible for parole earlier than an adult would be for the same crime.

Records

Youth court records kept in the local police or RCMP databases are usually destroyed after a certain period. The records of a young person involved in an extra-judicial measures program are destroyed after two years, provided the youth completed the program and did not commit any further offences.

Certain individuals have access to a youth's record, including the youth, parents, police, and people involved in the administration of an extra-judicial measure. Teachers and the school board can also be informed of a student's record if this information is necessary to ensure compliance with bail or probation requirements, or to promote the safety of teachers and other students. Victims may also have access to some information about youths who have committed offences against them.

R. v. Glowatski, [1999] B.C.J. No. 1278

CASE

On the night of November 14, 1997, 14-year-old Reena Virk and several other youths gathered at a high school near Victoria, British Columbia. Later in the evening, an argument broke out between Virk and another girl. Warren Glowatski, a 16-year-old youth was at the scene of the attack. He had never met Virk, but after the girls had beaten her, he and an acquaintance, Kelly Ellard, severely beat her again. They then dragged her over to the gorge where Ellard held Virk under water until she drowned. A week later, police found Virk's body. They arrested Glowatski, charging him with second-degree murder.

Because of the seriousness of the offence, Glowatski was transferred and tried in an adult court. During the trial, he admitted that he had helped drag Virk but stated that he had stopped at one point and, on three occasions, had asked Ellard to stop dragging Virk.

The judge found Glowatski's testimony inconsistent, "conveniently incomplete and improbable." In his decision, the judge stated that he was satisfied beyond a reasonable doubt that Glowatski had acted as a co-perpetrator in the second-degree murder of Reena Virk and that he knew his actions would likely result in her death. He found Warren Glowatski guilty of second-degree murder. Glowatski was given a life sentence with no chance of parole for seven years.

1. If the accused was 16 at the time of the crime, why was he tried in adult court?
2. Conduct research about this case. How do you think both the sentencing option and the public's reaction would have been affected if Glowatski had received a youth sentence under the *Youth Criminal Justice Act*?

Building Your Understanding

1. What is the main principle under the *Youth Criminal Justice Act* that guides judges in their consideration of youth sentences?
2. List the factors a judge will consider in deciding each specific youth sentence.
3. Identify three options the courts may consider in handing down a youth sentence for a less serious crime.
4. Explain the custody arrangements available under youth sentencing.
5. What role do conferences play as set out under the youth criminal justice system?
6. What factors does the court consider in deciding if a youth should receive an adult sentence?
7. Who may have access to a youth's record? Why is access permitted?

LOOKING BACK

Reviewing Your Vocabulary

custody *p. 323*
custody and supervision order *p. 323*
extra-judicial sanctions *p. 320*
incapacity of children *p. 313*
juvenile delinquents *p. 308*
open custody *p. 323*
presumptive offences *p. 313*
secure custody *p. 324*
training schools *p. 309*
Youth Criminal Justice Act p. 311
youth justice court *p. 321*
young offender *p. 309*
Young Offenders Act p. 309
youth sentence *p. 323*
youth worker *p. 324*

Quick Quiz

1. Choose the appropriate term from the vocabulary list above to complete the following statements:
   a) ____ includes offences such as murder and manslaughter.
   b) ____ are considered by a police officer rather than sending the youth to court.
   c) ____ assumes a child under the age of 12 cannot form the necessary *mens rea* in criminal law.
   d) ____ replaced the *Young Offenders Act*.
   e) ____ is the name of the court that deals with young people.
   f) If a youth is placed in ____, he or she is sent to a youth facility or prison.
   g) A ____ requires the youth to serve two-thirds of the sentence in custody and the last third in the community under supervision.
   h) Participation in a wilderness camp or group home are examples of two types of ____.
   i) Under the *Youth Criminal Justice Act*, a youth accused of a criminal act is no longer referred to as a ____.
   j) A ____ is usually a probation officer.
   k) Under the *Juvenile Delinquents Act*, ____ were often sent to ____.

Checking Your Knowledge

2. Why were some people critical of the *Juvenile Delinquents Act* in the 1970s?

3. a) At what stage in the youth court process are extra-judicial measures considered?
   b) Identify the steps shown in Figure 12.6, describing what stages a youth goes through from the time of detention to the sentence hearing if the Crown is not seeking an adult sentence. How does the process differ if the Crown is seeking an adult sentence?

4. Identify and explain the seven sentencing options in youth justice court.

5. Under the *Youth Criminal Justice Act*, what legal rights do youths have if they are being questioned or charged by police?

6. Do you think that extra-judicial sanctions are effective? Explain.

7. Distinguish between open custody and secure custody.

8. What rules of gathering evidence apply to a young person's case but not to an adult's?

9. What happens to the criminal record of a young person?

Developing Your Thinking and Inquiry Skills

10. Research the program of a boot camp or wilderness camp. Write a one-page description of the duration of the program, the controls and restrictions in place, and the activities provided. Comment on any strengths or weaknesses of the program.

11. Some aspects of *the Youth Criminal Justice Act* are controversial. Research the controversy around the following issues related to the Act:
    - the age at which a young person can receive an adult sentence
    - publication of the identity of a youth who receives an adult or youth sentence for a presumptive offence
    - the role of victims in the youth justice system

Communicating Your Ideas

12. In wilderness camp, young people learn how to live outdoors, work with others, and survive on their own. Such programs are designed to teach young people how to co-operate and become self-reliant. Discuss the advantages and disadvantages to this type of program.

13. Consider the following quote: "In the non-Indian community, committing a crime seems to mean that the individual is a bad person and therefore must be punished … the Indian communities view a wrongdoing as a misbehaviour which requires teaching, or an illness that requires healing." Research how some Aboriginal communities are dealing with young criminals in their communities. Write a one-page summary of the various measures taken, explaining why measures in some Aboriginal communities differ from those in non-Aboriginal communities.

14. Debate the following statement: For committing violent crimes such as first- or second-degree murder, any child who is 12 years old or younger should face the same penalties an adult would face for the same crime.

15. In small groups, collect five newspaper or Internet articles about trials pertaining to young people charged with criminal offences. For each article
    a) write the source and heading of the article
    b) list the offences committed
    c) summarize the article

    Write the extra-judicial sanction or sentence you would impose in each case. Explain your choice, with reference to the principles of sentencing.

16. A local group has taken out an advertisement in the newspaper, calling on federal legislation that would make parents financially responsible for the offences of their children. The advertisement asks for your opinion. In a one-page letter, state your position on this issue and give reasons for your arguments.

Putting It All Together

17. Your class has been asked to create brochures that highlight certain aspects of the *Youth Criminal Justice Act*. Working in small groups, choose one of the following themes for your brochure:
    - how the Act promotes responsibility for one's actions (crime prevention)
    - how the punishment must match the crime (sense of justice)
    - provisions regarding rehabilitation (reintegration)
    - roles of victims and the community (restitution)

    Present your brochure to the class.

CASES

P. v. R., [2000] P.E.S.C.T.D. 22

In February 2000, P. was spending the night at C.'s place. After C.'s parents went to bed, P. and C. got on P.'s four-wheeler bike and went to C.'s uncle's place where they took the uncle's truck and went on to pick up a friend. The three youths then drove to a used-truck lot where they hot-wired a Ford truck. During the course of the night, they drove and abandoned four more vehicles, including the original Ford truck. P. was eventually charged with possession of stolen property, and he pleaded guilty to six charges of joyriding.

P. was an "A" student. He was captain of the Bantam hockey team and was described by one of his teachers as a "perfect" student. Prior to his appearance in court, P. delivered letters of apology to the owners of the vehicles. His pre-disposition (pre-sentencing) report was very positive.

P. was sentenced to 45 days' open custody for each charge to be served concurrently. Under the *Young Offenders Act,* open custody was to be served away from home in a residential centre, group home, or wilderness camp. Upon release from custody, he would be on probation for 22 months. During probation, P. was to perform 120 hours of community service and take counselling and treatment as prescribed.

P. appealed the 45 days of open custody. His lawyer argued that under the *Young Offenders Act,* rehabilitation was the primary consideration in deciding measures against a young offender and that incarceration in this case would be counter-productive to rehabilitation.

The Supreme Court of Prince Edward Island agreed that the custodial provision of the sentence was too tough, so this particular provision of P.'s sentence was deleted.

1. Which factors would be most effective in convincing a judge that P. did not deserve such a severe sentence?
2. As P.'s lawyer, explain why incarceration would be counter-productive to rehabilitation.

R. v. S. (J.), [2001] Ont. C.A.

In December 1998, the appellant went to a Marilyn Manson concert with some friends. He had $30 worth of marijuana, which he intended to smoke at the concert. While standing outside a restaurant, he was approached by two undercover officers who were dressed as audience members, wearing white make-up and black wigs. One of the officers asked the appellant if he knew anybody who would sell him some marijuana. The officer said he only wanted to buy "a dime" ($10 worth). The officer continued to press the appellant to sell some marijuana, and the appellant eventually met the undercover officers in the washroom of the restaurant where he sold him $10 worth of marijuana. The appellant was then arrested for drug trafficking.

At trial the appellant was found guilty as charged and given a conditional discharge. He appealed the decision. The Ontario Court of Appeal allowed the appeal and stayed the proceedings as an abuse of process. The Court of Appeal concluded that the officers had "entrapped" the youth. The Court found that the youth would not have sold the marijuana if the officer had not approached him and pressured him into making the sale. Furthermore, the appellant was hesitant to make the deal and did not earn a profit from the transaction.

1. Describe how the officers entrapped the youth.
2. Why do you think the police officers provided an opportunity for the appellant to commit the offence of trafficking when they could have charged him with possession of a controlled substance?
3. Why did the Court of Appeal stay the proceedings? Explain whether you agree or disagree with this decision.

R. v. *Stillman*, [1997] 1 S.C.R. 607

BACKGROUND On April 12, 1991, a group of teenagers gathered in a wooded area to drink and take drugs. Sometime later, 17-year-old William Stillman and 14-year-old Pamela Bischoff left the group. When Stillman arrived home that night his pants were muddy and damp from the thighs down. He also had a cut over one eye.

Six days later, Bischoff's body was found in a river close to where she had last been seen with the group. She had died from a wound to the head. Semen was found in her vagina and there was a human bite mark on her abdomen.

Stillman was arrested the next day. In a letter to the police, his lawyer stated that Stillman had been advised not to provide a statement or any bodily samples to police.

After the lawyer left, Stillman was questioned for several hours by police. A hair sample was taken from his head and Plasticine teeth impressions were taken without his permission. When Stillman used a tissue to blow his nose, the police also kept the tissue for DNA testing.

Stillman was eventually released for lack of evidence. Several months later, following the arrival of the DNA results linking him to the victim, he was again arrested. More hair samples, a saliva sample, and another dental impression were taken without his consent.

LEGAL QUESTION Did the gathering of evidence by the police violate the rights of the accused under s. 8 of the *Charter of Rights and Freedoms*?

DECISION At a *voir dire,* the trial judge found that although the hair and saliva samples and teeth impressions were taken in a manner that violated the accused's rights under s. 8 of the Charter, the evidence could be admitted pursuant to s. 24 of the Charter. Section 24 allows evidence taken in violation of the Charter to be admitted in a trial as long as the admission of the evidence does not bring the administration of justice into disrepute. William Stillman was found guilty of first-degree murder.

Stillman appealed his conviction, and the Court of Appeal of New Brunswick dismissed the appeal. The case went to the Supreme Court of Canada, which allowed the appeal, ruling that the evidence would be inadmissible in a new trial. The Supreme Court found that the manner in which the samples were taken was a Charter violation of a "very serious nature."

The Supreme Court found that the police had acted with "blatant disregard" for the fundamental rights of the accused. Even though the accused had refused to provide bodily samples or give a statement, the police waited until his lawyer had left and proceeded through the use of force, threats, and coercion, to take his bodily samples and to interrogate him in an effort to obtain a statement. The police were also aware that the accused was a youth at the time and that he was entitled to the special protection provided by the *Young Offenders Act.*

The Supreme Court of Canada concluded that the police rode roughshod over a young person's refusal to provide bodily samples and that this fact would certainly "shock the conscience of all fair-minded members of the community." To allow such evidence would "bring the administration of justice into disrepute."

HISTORICAL SIGNIFICANCE As a result of this case, the *Criminal Code* was amended to allow DNA samples to be taken from a suspect. However, in order to take DNA samples, the police must obtain a warrant.

ANALYSIS

1. Why did the Supreme Court of Canada allow the appeal?
2. Identify the rights under s. 8 of the Charter that were violated in this case. Explain how the police violated these rights.
3. Why do you think police will need a warrant to take DNA samples?

issue

The Problem of Bullying

WHAT IS A BULLY?

At some point in your life, you have probably encountered a bully—someone who intimidated you through the threat of violence or actual physical harm. Bullying can have serious consequences. Youths who have been bullied may live perpetually in fear of further incidents. In a few cases, young victims of bullies have died after being physically attacked. In other cases, youths have taken their own lives after experiencing verbal abuse or threats from their classmates or peers. In 2000, for example, Hamed Nastoh, a British Columbia student, jumped off a bridge and killed himself. In a note to his parents, he stated that students had been taunting him and calling him names. His parents knew nothing about the incidents. For most youths, the reaction to bullying is not as extreme, but they still suffer physical injuries or emotional trauma.

Who are the victims? Bullies usually pick on someone more vulnerable than they are. Their victims may be a member of a minority group within the school, or they may be different in appearance from most other children (e.g., smaller or heavier). Victims sometimes have a speech impediment or an accent.

Who are the bullies? Bullies often tend to exhibit aggressive and disruptive behaviour; in fact, they may be victims of bullying in their own homes where punishment by parents can be excessive and physical. Males who bully tend to be less successful in school than other male students and are more likely to get into trouble with the law later in life. Their bullying is usually physical. Females can also be bullies. They tend to use indirect tactics such as gossip or verbal abuse, but female bullies can also resort to threats or violence. Bullying sometimes involves theft of property or extortion of money. Many victims feel reluctant to inform teachers, parents, or the police for fear of being perceived as a "rat" or because they are afraid they will not be protected.

What effect does such abuse have on the victims? They often become withdrawn, sullen, and depressed. Some youths fear going to school or going out socially. Many suffer from low self-esteem. Because some bullies send mixed messages of friendliness and aggression, their victims may experience a sense of fear as well as vulnerability. Some victims of bullying may explode in anger, triggering tragic incidents of school violence.

DEALING WITH BULLIES

How society should deal with youths who bully others is an emotional and controversial issue. In many instances, parents and teachers have attempted to deal with the problem through counselling, disciplinary measures, or discussion with those involved. In 2002, the police in British Columbia took the unusual step of charging a student under the *Criminal Code* with criminal harassment. A 15-year-old student was found guilty of criminal harassment after she repeatedly harassed and threatened another student, 14-year-old Dawn-Marie Wesley. This student had accused Wesley of spreading false rumours about her. Shortly after receiving further threats over the phone, Wesley committed suicide.

In discussions leading up to the enactment of the *Youth Criminal Justice Act,* many organizations and individuals argued for harsher sentences for youths who bully others. While the Act does not deal specifically with bullying, s. 38(2) encourages judges to consider "the harm done to victims and the community" when sentencing a youth. Under this guiding principle, judges may regard bullying as a crime that has broad implications because it harms the community as well as the individual victim. Consequently, judges may treat such crimes more harshly.

ANOTHER APPROACH

For some people, however, the answer to bullying is not tougher laws that put more youths behind bars but rather a more comprehensive strategy that involves teachers, parents, legislators, and the community (in many cases, bullies and their victims go to the same school or live in

At her home in Mission, British Columbia, Cindy Wesley holds a photograph of her daughter Dawn-Marie. Dawn-Marie Wesley killed herself after two of her friends threatened to beat her up. One of the teens was found guilty of criminal harassment.

LOOKING AHEAD

In the past, the justice system has often emphasized separating bullies from victims. Bullies were suspended from school or ordered to stay away from their victims as a condition of bail release or probation. Under the *Youth Criminal Justice Act,* however, extra-judicial sanctions could be used by a trained mediator to bring the two sides together. A teacher, a police officer, and the parents of both the victim and the offender might attend. Bullies can be required to meet with their victims, listen to how their actions have affected them, take responsibility for their behaviour, and then apologize and provide some form of restitution. In serious or repeat instances of bullying, the police and the court may be needed to protect the victim or remove the offender from the community. But in most cases, victims and offenders are likely to remain in contact since repairing the relationship may be more valuable than imposing a punishment.

Go to the Pearson Web site at **www.pearsoned.ca/law** and follow the links to discover what action is being taken against bullying in your province.

the same neighbourhood). Some schools are starting to implement policies to deal with bullying. These policies usually concentrate on increasing student and teacher awareness about the problem; encouraging youths to discuss their feelings of anger or aggression; and involving parents, teachers and community members in a strategy to deal with bullying.

Counselling, rehabilitation, discipline, and restitution should be the tools used to treat bullies. As one activist put it, "The answer is firmness and education, not vengeance."

LOOKING AT THE ISSUE

1. Identify some of the characteristics of bullies and victims of bullying.
2. What would you do if you became a victim of bullying?
3. Develop a policy for dealing with bullies in your school. Working in small groups, devise a strategy that identifies acts of bullying, sets out ways of raising awareness of the problem, establishes penalties, and identifies who should be involved in the process. Present your policy to the class.

Career Connections

In this Unit, you read about a variety of cases in criminal law. Whether you choose to be a police officer, a forensic scientist, or a courtroom sketch artist, a career in criminal law offers opportunities for challenge and excitement.

Before choosing a career in this field, it is advisable to talk to your guidance counsellor or someone who works in the area you wish to explore. You should do your own research as well. Visit **www.pearsoned.ca/law** to access Web sites for interesting careers in law. Following the steps on the site, select three criminal-law careers of particular interest to you. Be sure to choose careers that are different from the ones you investigated after Units 1 and 2.

MAKING CONNECTIONS

1. Use the following questions to compare your career choices:
   a) What are the tasks performed by someone in this position?
   b) What education, training, and qualifications are required?
   c) What are the job prospects in this field, and why are these prospects good, fair, or poor?
   d) What else should you know about the career you selected? Why?

2. Once you have gathered all the information you require, analyze your information to determine which career you think would be most suitable for you. In a report, identify your choice and explain why you chose this career over all the others you investigated. Include any follow-up questions you might have that were not addressed in your research.

Civil Law and Dispute Resolution

UNIT 4

In this last unit of *Law in Action*, you will explore the principles and process of private law in Canada, discovering that not all disputes need to be resolved in a court of law. You will also revisit three areas of private law that were introduced in Chapter 2.

The first of these areas is tort law. Every day, people are harmed and property is damaged, often through the negligence of others. Sometimes these injuries are the result of deliberate acts. In the tort chapters, you will learn to identify different types of torts and the defences available to those who are sued for liability.

In the family law chapters, you will discover the legal requirements for entering and dissolving a marriage as well as the rights, obligations, and responsibilities of partners in a relationship. You will also learn how the law protects children regarding issues such as support and custody.

The third area of private law is contract law. You will probably be surprised to find out that contracts play an important role in your life. In these chapters, you will discover the elements that must be present before a contract can exist. You will also learn how a contract can be rendered null and void. These concepts can be important for a person like you, who enters contractual agreements every day.

LOOKING AHEAD

Chapter 13 Understanding Civil Procedures

Chapter 14 Negligence and Unintentional Torts

Chapter 15 Intentional Torts

Chapter 16 Marriage: A Changing Tradition

Chapter 17 Family Matters

Chapter 18 Forming a Contract

Chapter 19 Contract Remedies and Consumer Protection

13 Understanding Civil Procedures

CHAPTER OUTLINE

Private Law Procedures

Civil Courts

Civil Remedies

Alternative Dispute Resolution

FOCUS YOUR LEARNING

What are the stages involved in a civil action?

How do civil courts differ?

What remedies are available to litigants?

How does alternative dispute resolution differ from litigation?

Sara and Shelley went to SuperSonic, an electronics store, to purchase a DVD player. As they were leaving the store, Shelley tripped on the corner of a carpet that had not been properly secured, and she fractured her ankle. Because Shelley was unable to work as a snowboard instructor during peak season, she lost income for six weeks.

❖

Mr. and Mrs. Graham are divorced. Mr. Graham has custody of their three children. Because his job requires that he stay out of town overnight during the week, he has had to hire a live-in caretaker. Mrs. Graham had agreed to share this expense as part of her support payments. Mrs. Graham has since stopped making her support payments to Mr. Graham.

❖

Mandy had contracted with Big Top Roofers to replace the roof on her 30-year-old house. After she paid for the job, she discovered that the quality of the shingles used was inferior to the quality specified in the contract.

WHAT DO YOU THINK?

- These three situations involve disputes between individuals. What do these disputes have in common?
- How can these disputes be resolved?

Situations like those described on the previous page fall under the category of private or civil law, which is part of everyday life. If you have a part-time job, you and your employer are subject to the labour laws of your province. When you buy a new pair of jeans, you are entering into a contract with the retailer. If you plan to marry or adopt children, you will be subject to family law. If you are injured in an accident caused by someone else's negligence, you may find yourself dealing with tort law.

In this chapter, you will learn the difference between public and private law, and you will discover how civil disputes can be resolved.

PRIVATE LAW PROCEDURES

As you learned in Chapter 2, public law (administrative, constitutional, and criminal) deals with the relationship between the state and individuals or organizations. Administrative law refers to the boards and tribunals that regulate how people and government agencies interact. Constitutional law manages the relationship between different levels of government and between government, individuals, and corporations. Criminal law, as discussed in Unit 3, governs the relationship between the accused and the state.

Private law deals with disputes between persons and between individuals and companies, although individuals can also sue the state for matters of a private nature. For example, a government employee may sue the government for a breach of employment law; an individual can sue the government in tort law if he or she suffers personal injury while visiting government-owned premises; and an individual who has a business relationship with the government can sue in contract law when a dispute arises. To settle such disputes, the state provides forums such as courts and tribunals.

Private law, also known as civil law, has several branches. In this unit, we will examine three branches: tort law, family law, and contract law.

Figure 13.1 Categories of Law

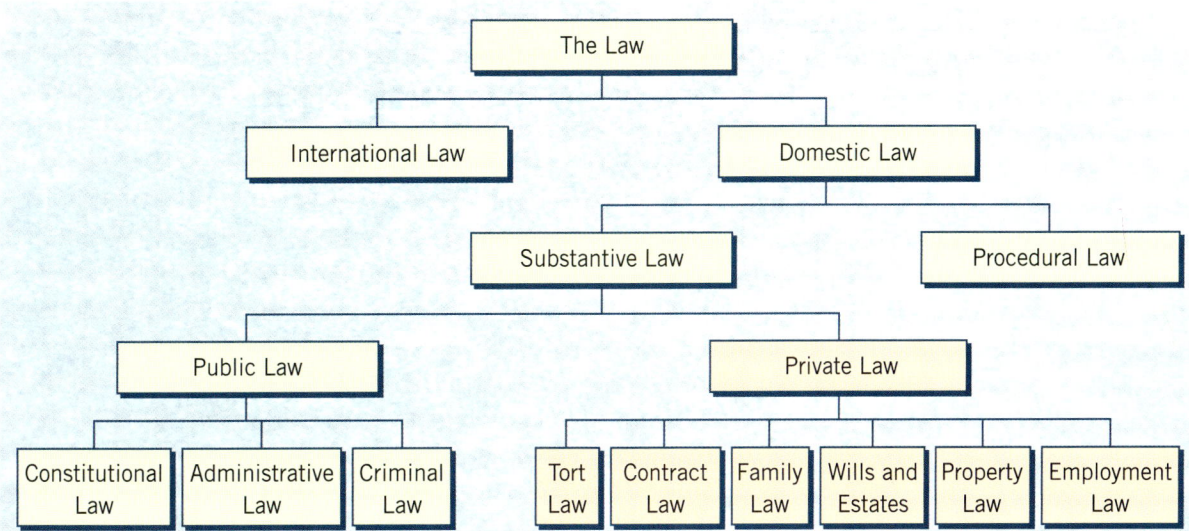

Parties Involved in Civil Actions

litigants: the parties involved in a civil action

The citation (or name and location) of a civil case distinguishes it from a criminal case. Citations for civil cases bear the names of the **litigants,** the parties involved in a civil action. In the case, *Button* v. *Jones,* for example, Button is suing Jones. If an individual sues a government in a civil action, the citation will name the person or government being sued, such as *Rodriguez* v. *British Columbia (Attorney General).*

plaintiff: the party initiating a legal action

defendant: the party being sued in a civil action

litigation: legal action to resolve a civil dispute

damages: compensation for a wrong suffered

The party that initiates the legal action is known as the **plaintiff,** and the litigant against whom the action is taken is known as the **defendant.** In *Button* v. *Jones,* Button is the plaintiff and Jones is the defendant. Button has initiated **litigation,** usually called an action, against Jones. He is suing Jones to receive **damages,** or compensation (usually money), for a wrong suffered.

You will recall that in a criminal case the state must prove beyond a reasonable doubt that the accused committed the offence. If the judge or the jurors deciding the case are not convinced, they must acquit the accused. In a civil case, the standard of proof is not as high—the onus is on the plaintiff to prove the case on a **balance of probabilities.** This means that if the plaintiff can prove that his or her version of the facts is the more likely or the more truthful version, the plaintiff may win. Similarly, if a defence is raised, the onus is on the defendant to prove the facts that may tip the scale in favour of the defendant.

balance of probabilities: the weighing of evidence to decide whether it is the plaintiff's or the defendant's version of the events that is more convincing or likely to be correct

Minors and Parties with Disabilities

Persons under the age of majority, 18 or 19 years old depending on the province, are known in law as minors and cannot sue or be sued in their own name. This law protects minors and ensures that adults represent their interests in court. A minor who wishes to sue must be represented by an adult, known as a **next friend.**

next friend: an adult who represents a child or a person under a disability who initiates a civil lawsuit

A person "under a disability" is someone who cannot pursue an activity due to a physical or mental impairment. Such a person must sue through a representative. If he or she is being sued, a litigation guardian must be court appointed.

A minor who is being sued must also be represented by an adult. The court will appoint an adult to act as the minor's representative. This per-

Figure 13.2 Why would children injured at a playground need adult representation in a legal action if they have a lawyer to represent them?

son is known in law as a **guardian ad litem** (litigation guardian), literally meaning "a guardian for the suit or for the purposes of the suit." In some jurisdictions, the terms "next friend" and "guardian ad litem" mean the same and serve generally the same function.

guardian ad litem: the person appointed to act on behalf of a minor or person under a disability who is being sued

Tsaoussis (guardian ad litem) v. Baetz (1998), Ont. C.A. C27319

CASE

In April 1990, three-year-old Lorrie Tsaoussis was struck by a car driven by Juanita Baetz. Lorrie was hospitalized for three days with follow-up visits to her family doctor and pediatrician. Lorrie's mother, Carol Metcalf, sued Baetz on Lorrie's behalf. After negotiations between the lawyer for Lorrie and the defendant's insurer, a settlement was reached. Because the settlement was for a minor plaintiff, it had to be approved by the Court. The settlement was approved in 1992. The amount of the settlement was based on the information provided by Lorrie's doctor, who stated that Lorrie's injuries were not permanent and that she would fully recover. Mrs. Metcalf agreed with the medical testimony and accepted the settlement on Lorrie's behalf. After the funds were paid, counsel for Ms. Baetz wrote to Lorrie's counsel, confirming that this "resolves all claims arising out of this accident."

However, Lorrie did not fully recover and continued to have numerous ongoing medical and developmental problems. In 1996, Lorrie's doctors gave the opinion that "her problems are attributable to the motor vehicle accident." They also felt that the full extent of her problems would not be determined for another year or two.

A new action was filed by Lorrie's mother in 1994, claiming that Ms. Baetz's negligence had caused injuries to Lorrie resulting in damage of $2.2 million. The defence argued that the claim had been settled by the 1992 judgment. The lawyer for Lorrie applied to set aside the earlier judgment. This application was granted, effectively allowing Lorrie to sue again for the same reasons she had sued initially.

Ms. Baetz appealed. The issue in the appeals court was whether an approved settlement on behalf of a minor could be set aside if it turned out that the minor may have been significantly undercompensated by the terms of the settlement. The Court of Appeal held that in this case, the original judgment should stand. It dismissed the 1994 action brought on Lorrie's behalf.

1. What legal role did Lorrie's mother play?
2. Why did the Court of Appeal uphold the original settlement? What problems, if any, do you foresee with the precedent set in this case?
3. Do you think approved settlements should be set aside under circumstances like Lorrie's? Would your arguments be different if the plaintiff were an adult? Explain.

Civil Action

Complex civil actions or those involving a significant amount of money are brought before a Superior Court. For less serious matters, all provinces have what are known as Small Claims Courts. In either case, launching a civil action can be complicated and stressful, depending on the dispute; moreover, there is no guarantee that it will be successful. Before undertaking litigation, it is always wise to consider alternatives, which will be discussed later in this chapter.

pleadings: documents stating formal allegations by the parties regarding their claims and defences

Figure 13.3 outlines the stages involved in a civil action. These stages, which occur in the higher courts, involve lawyers and numerous documents. All of these documents—statement of claim, statement of defence, counter-claims, third-party claims, and cross-claims—are called **pleadings,** documents that go back and forth between the parties. Pleadings help the judge define the issues and understand the details of a case.

Figure 13.3 Stages in a Civil Action

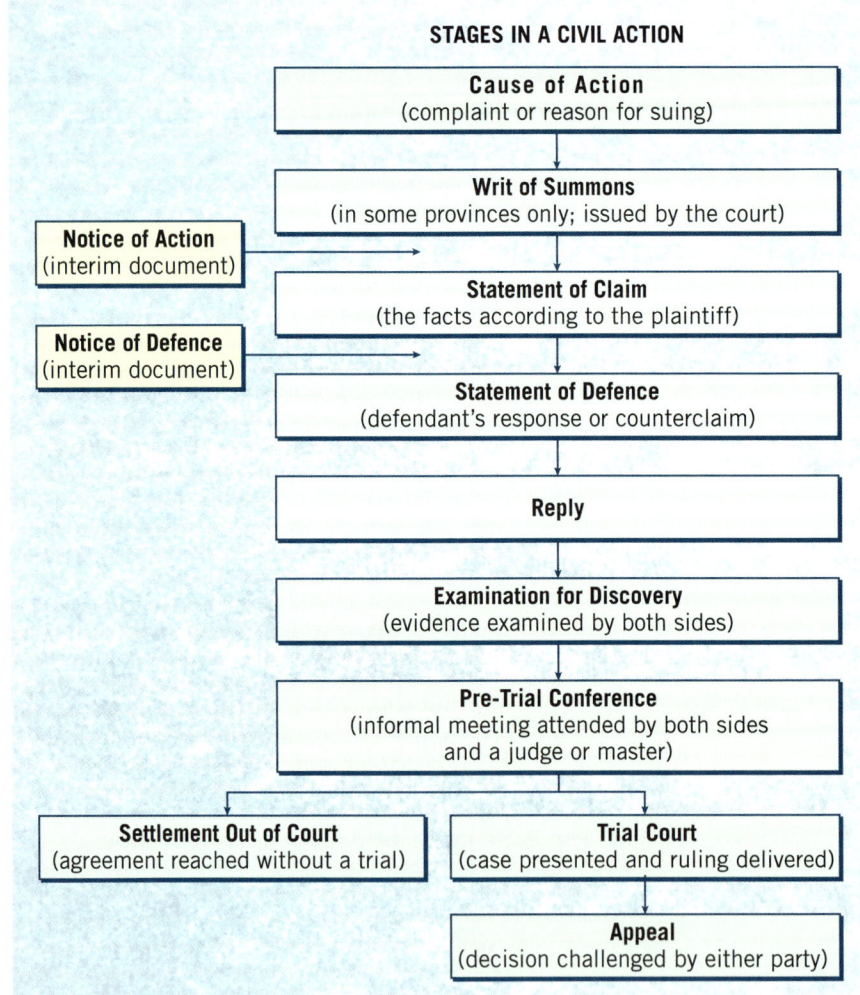

Fast Fact
In some parts of Canada, procedural tasks in civil cases are handled by masters—judicial officers appointed provincially to carry out a limited range of judicial functions.

Starting an Action

Each province makes its own rules about how actions are started and carried out. Although these rules are not exactly the same in each province, starting a civil action in a Superior Court usually begins with issuing an originating document. In some provinces, the process of a civil suit begins with a **writ of summons.** This document issued by the court informs the defendant of the claim and orders the defendant to respond.

writ of summons: a legal document that commences civil actions in some provinces

In most provinces, however, the civil suit starts with a document known as a statement of claim. In some circumstances, the plaintiff may issue a notice of action and file the statement of claim later within a specified time, according to the relevant provincial rules of civil procedure. The **statement of claim** is a court document that explains the nature of the plaintiff's claim and the relief sought, often referred to as the **remedy**—what the plaintiff wants to see happen. Depending on the circumstances of the claim, the plaintiff may request monetary compensation for damages or an apology for a perceived wrong.

statement of claim: a document outlining the facts supporting a civil action and the remedy desired

remedy: the relief sought by the plaintiff

The statement of claim is a concise account of the material facts of the plaintiff's case. It must provide enough detail to allow the defendant to know the nature of the case and make a full defence. It should not include personal opinion, exaggerations, or evidence. If information is lacking, the defendant can ask for **particulars**—more information that allows the defendant to prepare a defence. The purpose of particulars is to provide notice of what to expect at trial.

particulars: specific details of a claim in a civil action

When a summons and statement of claim are received, the defendant has a number of options. The defendant may

- ignore the summons and statement of claim completely, which would result in a **default judgment;** in this case, a judgment could be awarded against the defendant
- file a statement of defence
- accept liability and settle out of court

default judgment: a judgment against a party who has failed to defend a claim

Statement of Defence

A **statement of defence,** as the term implies, sets out the defendant's version of the facts. The defendant may deny any liability whatsoever. If there is insufficient time to file a statement of defence, the defendant may issue a notice of defence and file a statement within a specified period.

statement of defence: the response to the plaintiff's complaint, denying the allegations in part or in whole

In addition to the statement of defence, the defendant may decide to file a **counterclaim.** This means that not only is the defendant denying any liability for the plaintiff's claim, but the defendant believes the plaintiff is either partially or completely at fault. In a counterclaim, the defendant states an independent cause of action against the plaintiff. The amount of the counterclaim may equal or exceed the plaintiff's claim. Generally, the counterclaim has to be attached to the statement of defence, and the whole document is known as a statement of defence and counterclaim.

counterclaim: an action brought in response to the plaintiff's claim aimed at diminishing or removing the defendant's liability

Suppose Ricardo is suing Fran for injuries suffered when his head hit the windshield while he was a passenger in Fran's car. In his pleadings, Ricardo states that because Fran was exceeding the speed limit, she was unable to stop when the dog ran in front of her vehicle. In her statement of defence, Fran might deny she was speeding. She might also file a counterclaim stating that Ricardo's failure to wear his seat belt resulted in his head hitting the windshield when she had to brake suddenly to avoid the dog. In other words, it was Ricardo's fault he was injured.

Third-Party Claim

The defendant may also respond to the claim by adding a new party and by issuing a **third-party claim.** In this situation, the defendant denies liability, either completely or partially, and blames another party for the plaintiff's loss. This claim alleges that a third party (someone not named in the original lawsuit) may be **liable** for all or part of the damages that the plaintiff is seeking from the defendant.

If a plaintiff identifies more than one defendant in a statement of claim, the defendants can make claims against one another through a **cross-claim.** In other words, suppose Jason initiates litigation against Marianna and Elynor. If Marianna feels that Elynor was the one at fault, she might make a cross-claim against Elynor to that effect.

> **third-party claim:** a complaint filed by the defendant claiming that another party is at fault
>
> **liable:** legally responsible for a wrongful action
>
> **cross-claim:** a claim made between parties on the same side of the litigation

Reply

The plaintiff has an opportunity to reply to the statement of defence if the defendant intends to rely on a different version of the facts that might take the plaintiff by surprise or raise a new issue.

Examination for Discovery

Trials you see on television or in movies bear little resemblance to a real trial. Surprise witnesses or shocking, new evidence are generally not permitted. The court does not allow trial by ambush. Before a civil trial, the parties are entitled to question each other in an **examination for discovery** in which each side conducts its own examination of the evidence.

Generally, counsel has the right to question any party with an adverse interest in the case. Most information is acquired through oral examination and is recorded. During the examination, there are fewer restrictions on the types of questions that can be asked than there might be during the trial. Lawyers may ask witnesses not only about their actual knowledge of events, but also about any other information or beliefs they may have. The information provided may be used at trial and read into the trial record. It may also be used to contradict testimony if a party tells a different story at the trial. If one of the litigants is a corporation, usually an officer or director of the corporation is examined. This person has an obligation to be informed about the case and may even have specific personal knowledge about it.

Examination for discovery prevents the element of surprise at trial and provides both sides with the opportunity to assess each other's strengths and weaknesses. It also allows each side to obtain admissions and to identify issues or points they agree about; this reduces court time, saves money, and may even encourage the parties to settle before going to court.

> **examination for discovery:** examination of evidence by both sides before a civil trial
>
> *"Law school taught me one thing: how to take two situations that are exactly the same and show how they are different"*
> — Hart Pomerantz, Canadian lawyer

Examination of Documents

Each side is also entitled to examine all relevant documents that the other parties have in their possession, power, or control. To ensure that this happens, the parties are required to prepare an **affidavit of documents.** If a document is not listed on the affidavit, it usually cannot be used at trial. The obliga-

> **affidavit of documents:** a list of documents relevant to the case that will be used at trial

tion to disclose relevant documents continues right up to the trial itself. **Privileged documents,** such as communications between lawyer and client, do not have to be produced. Also excluded are any comments made by the parties when they negotiate to settle the case. Either party can challenge these claims of privilege or ask the court to force the other side to produce relevant documents it has failed to provide.

privileged documents: records and information that can be excluded from examination by the other side in a civil action

Pre-trial Conference

In most provinces, the rules of civil procedure allow a pre-trial conference. Such a meeting provides the litigants with the opportunity to meet informally with their respective lawyers and a judge (or a master in British Columbia) to try and reach a settlement before going to trial. The judge assists both parties in resolving as many unsettled issues as possible and gives the litigants an unbiased opinion on the possible outcome if they decide to take the case to trial. If the parties fail to reach a settlement and are intent on going to trial, a different judge will be appointed to hear the case.

Fast Fact
In 1997 former prime minister Brian Mulroney and the federal government reached an out-of-court settlement of $1 million and a public apology. Claiming the RCMP had smeared his name by accusing him of wrongdoing, Mulroney had sued for $50 million.

Settlement Out of Court

There are a number of ways civil suits can be resolved before going to court. If a defence is not delivered within the legally prescribed time limits, a default judgment can be made against the defendant. Or, the courts may consider the case trivial or frivolous and strike out the plaintiff's action. Sometimes the parties agree to **settle out of court,** and either party may make an offer to settle. The court encourages settlements, so if a person refuses to accept a settlement offer that turns out to be as good as or better than the result that the refusing party obtains at trial, the refusing party is usually penalized by having to pay the costs of the other party. For example, suppose you are suing for $10 000 and the defendant offers to settle for $8000. You refuse the offer, win at trial, and are awarded only $7000. By refusing to settle, you wasted everyone's time; you could have had $8000 without a trial. The court will likely require you to pay the defendant's costs from the time you refused the offer.

settle out of court: all parties agree to resolve the dispute instead of going to court

Figure 13.4 What are the benefits of settling out of court?

Trial Court

Sometimes it is not possible to resolve the dispute without going to trial. Civil court procedures are similar to those in a criminal trial. Although the plaintiff or the defendant can request a jury trial, it is up to the discretion of the court to grant such a request. Most civil trials are heard by a judge alone. If the trial is by jury, the judge instructs the jury on how to apply the law to the facts of the case.

If there is no jury, the judge decides whether the plaintiff or defendant should succeed and the amount of damages that should be awarded. Quantifying damages, especially in cases involving serious personal injury, is probably the most difficult part of the case.

In all provinces, the court can order plaintiffs to provide security for a defendant's legal costs in certain situations. Plaintiffs are required to post security to ensure that court costs will be covered or to deter frivolous lawsuits; only plaintiffs who feel they have good grounds for launching the lawsuit and a good chance of winning are prepared to provide security. Security is usually ordered when the plaintiff does not live or own property in the province. The plaintiff may be asked to provide cash, a letter of credit, or a surety bond. Security is held by the court until the end of the action and the court determines what costs will be paid and by whom.

The litigant who loses a case in civil court is responsible for the damages awarded by the court. He or she may also be required to pay part or all of the legal costs of the other litigant. Costs are usually based on a fee schedule published by the court and can vary from province to province. For many, the cost of going to court is so prohibitive that it may act as a deterrent.

Appeals

Occasionally, a plaintiff or a defendant challenges the decision of the trial court by appealing the decision to a higher court. As in criminal law, the party that appeals becomes the appellant, and the other party becomes the respondent. In some cases, litigants have an automatic right to appeal, while in other cases, they have to ask for "leave" to appeal, which means getting permission to appeal the decision. When they appeal or ask for leave to appeal, they have to explain their reasons to the court. Grounds of appeal are based on a question of law or a question of fact—the judge made a mistake about either the facts, the law, or how the law applied to the facts. In some cases, appeals can only be granted on a question of law, which may include such matters as whether the judge interpreted the law correctly or properly explained the law to the jury. As we discovered in Chapter 7, leave is usually required to appeal to the Supreme Court of Canada and will only be granted if the case raises an issue of national concern.

Class Action Lawsuits

A **class action suit** is a lawsuit filed by one or more individuals on behalf of a group. The purpose of a class action lawsuit is to enable average citizens with a common complaint to challenge large corporations or private individuals who can afford the best and most expensive legal services.

In 2001, Ontario, British Columbia, and Quebec were the only provinces with class action legislation in place. In all three provinces, it must first be established that a class action procedure is the best way to resolve the issue. Also, the claims or defences of class members must raise common issues and meet certain conditions to be certified as a class action.

Consider This
Under a contingency fee system, a lawyer only receives payment (a percentage of the judgment) if the lawsuit is successful. With a partner, generate supporting and opposing arguments for this type of system.

Fast Fact
The defendant in a divorce action is also called a respondent.

class action suit: a lawsuit initiated by a group of people over a complaint common to all

The number of class action lawsuits in Canada is still small, but it is growing. Because legal costs can be prohibitive in such actions, the three provinces permit contingency fee arrangements in class actions.

The Early Ones

Mr. Justice Arthur Gans had encouraging words last week for the women before him, even as he dashed their immediate hopes.

They and dozens like them had retired as University of Toronto professors and librarians before 1991, the first year that pay-equity legislation required the institution to pay men and women equally for similar work. While many still on staff had their salaries adjusted, those who had retired were out of luck. This year, a few of those women [88 retired faculty members and 20 retired librarians] asked the Ontario Superior Court to let them sue the university as a group to recover what systemic sexual discrimination had cost them: a difference they estimate at 20 percent, a loss that reduced the pensions on which they now must live.

Judge Gans said the cases differed too much to permit a class action. But he said they had a legitimate argument to make if they each sued individually, and rejected the suggestion that they could have made it a couple of decades ago: "I dare say that any complaint by one without tenure might at the time have been tantamount to academic suicide."

These are not young women. The judge worried many might die before having their day in court. It would be impressive if they persevered. It would be more impressive if the university itself found a quick way to address their case for retroactive justice.

Source: "The Early Ones," *The Globe and Mail*, November 13, 2001, A20.

Figure 13.5 **Professors Ursula Franklin (centre front left) and Blanche Van Ginkel (right) were two of the plaintiffs who sought certification for a class action against the University of Toronto.**

1. Why would these women have chosen to participate in a class action suit?
2. Explain what these women were seeking compensation for in their suit.
3. Why do you think Justice Gans rejected this application for a class action suit?

Building Your Understanding

1. Choose one of the scenarios described at the beginning of the chapter on page 336. Describe the situation as a civil action:
   a) Identify the plaintiff and the defendant by name.
   b) Who has the burden of proof in this civil action, and what standard of proof is required?
   c) Suppose the trial decision is challenged. Identify which party won at trial and who is appealing. Use legal terms to describe the parties involved in the appeal.
2. Distinguish between a "next friend" and a "guardian ad litem."
3. Why would a defendant require particulars?
4. Instead of making a statement of defence, the accused has a number of additional options. Identify and explain two of these options.
5. Discuss the procedure and purpose of an examination for discovery.
6. Can a party ever refuse to produce certain documents for discovery? Explain.
7. When litigants lose a civil case, what are they responsible for?
8. In some cases, to be successful an appeal must be based on a point or question of law. What does this mean?
9. Describe a situation where a class action suit might be appropriate.

> **Consider This**
> Statutes in each province limit the time during which a civil action can be brought. Do you think there should be time restrictions? Explain.

CIVIL COURTS

Who decides which cases are heard in which court? Jurisdiction determines whether a court has the right or power to hear a particular case. Different courts have different powers, sometimes defined by common law. Jurisdiction is also defined by a specific statute; in such cases, the court has only those powers allowed by the statute. So, for a case to be heard, it must be brought in the right court. For example, you cannot sue the dry cleaner in the Supreme Court of Canada for ruining your coat. Similarly, you cannot bring before Small Claims Court a complex personal injury suit for $5 million.

Canadian courts are based on an adversarial system that assumes a win-lose outcome. The system works this way because the judiciary believes that the best way to learn the truth is to have each party argue its case and point out weaknesses in the other party's argument. In a civil case, the losing litigant generally has to pay the costs of the successful litigant. If the case is appealed to a higher court, the costs increase. Among the various courts described in the following sections, the least expensive court in which to bring a civil action is Small Claims Court.

Small Claims Courts

All provinces and territories have Small Claims Courts or small claims divisions specifically designed to offer an informal, faster, and less expensive way to settle disputes that are not too complex and do not involve a great deal of money. For example, at the small claims level, there is no examination for discovery. Parties can represent themselves and, in most provinces, are allowed to bring a lawyer, a law student, or an agent to assist or speak on their behalf. Small Claims Courts also limit the kinds of cases that are brought and the amount of money that can be claimed. In most provinces, the financial limit is up to $10 000.

Small Claims Courts hear cases involving money owed for unpaid loans or rents, services performed, goods bought on credit or with bad cheques, property damage, return of shoddy goods, personal injury, and unreturned personal property. Remember Mandy, the woman mentioned at the beginning of the chapter, whose roof was replaced with shingles of a lower quality than those specified in her contract? The difference in value between the shingles used and those she paid for was probably minimal. Mandy's best option would be to make a claim through Small Claims Court for the difference in value between the shingles she paid for and the shingles that were used.

Although suing someone in Small Claims Court is less complicated than in the higher courts, to be successful the plaintiff should be prepared. The plaintiff must provide evidence such as testimony, documents, invoices, receipts, or any other information that will help prove the case. For example, Mandy will need to show that her contract provided for a certain type of shingle and that the contractor used one of lesser value. Also, both the defendant and the judge can ask Mandy questions. If she proves her case on a balance of probabilities, she will succeed, and the judge will order an appropriate remedy. Small Claims Courts generally award only a small amount for costs.

Legal Link
Find out the limit of a claim in the Small Claims Court in your province by visiting **www.pearsoned.ca/law**.

Superior Courts of the Provinces and Territories

If you wish to sue for a larger sum than the limit of the Small Claims Court, or for a matter that is not within its jurisdiction, you must take your case to the Superior Court of the province. Some provinces refer to their Superior Court as the Supreme Court of the province or the Court of Queen's Bench. The chart in Chapter 7 on page 165 shows how this court is identified in various provinces and territories. The Superior Court may have other divisions such as a Small Claims Court or Family Court. All provinces also have a Court of Appeal, which may be a separate, higher court or simply the appellate division of the Superior Court. The Court of Appeal is the highest court in each province or territory, and it hears both criminal and civil cases.

Disputes heard at this level are generally more complex than those heard in Small Claims Court and always require the assistance of a lawyer. Examples of such matters include serious motor vehicle accidents, class action lawsuits, contract disagreements, and serious personal injury cases. Most civil trials are heard by a judge alone, although cases involving torts such as defamation or false imprisonment are usually heard by a judge and jury. You will learn more about these torts in Chapter 15.

Fast Fact
In most provinces, a civil jury consists of only six members.

Provincial and Territorial Courts of Appeal

Canada has ten provincial and three territorial Courts of Appeal. Each Court hears appeals from the Superior Courts or Provincial Courts of their respective provinces or territories. Provincial and territorial Courts of Appeal have

binding: final and enforceable in the courts

dissenting opinion: a minority opinion that disagrees with the majority on a point of law

Consider This

Only three women have been appointed to the Supreme Court of Canada. Discuss whether ethnic and gender diversity should be considered in appointments to the Supreme Court.

no authority to overturn the decision of a jury; they are only empowered to order a new trial in the case. The decisions made in the Court of Appeal are **binding** in the province or territory in which they are made, unless they are appealed to the Supreme Court of Canada.

Generally, a panel of three judges hears appeals, and their decision may be unanimous or split. If the Court is split, there will be majority and minority judgments. Reasons for the decision are released to the public and include the rationale of the **dissenting opinion,** the opinion of the judge who disagreed with the majority.

Supreme Court of Canada

As you learned in Chapter 7, the Supreme Court of Canada is the last and highest Court of Appeal for both criminal and civil cases. Decisions made by the Supreme Court of Canada are binding across the country and in all jurisdictions, which means that all the lower courts in Canada must follow these decisions. As in the provincial Courts of Appeal, Supreme Court decisions can be unanimous or split. When split decisions are recorded, one justice is selected from each side to write majority and minority opinions. Decisions in the Supreme Court of Canada provide case law as precedent for the lower courts.

Generally, as discussed earlier, cases may be appealed to the Supreme Court if a party gets leave to appeal. Only the Supreme Court of Canada and (in certain circumstances) provincial Courts of Appeal have the power to grant leave.

Figure 13.6 This photo shows the interior of the Supreme Court of Canada. Although the nine justices do not hear every case that comes before the Court, all nine do sit for cases of national importance. What would you consider a case of national importance?

348   UNIT 4 ◆ Civil Law and Dispute Resolution

Federal Court of Canada

The Federal Court of Canada, like the Supreme Court, is based in Ottawa; indeed, they occupy the same building. The Federal Court has a trial as well as an appeal division. In general, the Federal Court has jurisdiction over matters involving the Crown or issues that are specifically within federal jurisdiction. Civil cases heard here include intellectual property proceedings (copyright and trademark claims), citizenship appeals, civil cases involving the federal government, and appeals under certain federal statutes. The Federal Court may also hear disputes about employment insurance and federal income tax, and it may share jurisdiction with provincial Superior Courts with respect to claims by and against the Crown.

Fast Fact

The Federal Court of Canada was created in 1970 to replace the Exchequer Court of Canada. The Federal Court will sit in any place in Canada to suit the convenience of the parties.

Pink Panther Beauty Corp. v. *United Artists Corp.* (1998), F.C.J. No. 441 (F.C.A.)

CASE

In 1986, Pink Panther Beauty Corporation applied to register the trademark "Pink Panther" to use in association with hair care and beauty products. This application was opposed by United Artists, the distributor of *The Pink Panther* comedy films in which Peter Sellers starred as Inspector Clousseau. The United Artists' famous trademark, "The Pink Panther," had been registered in Canada for over 30 years. The trial judge found in favour of United Artists, holding that the registration should not be allowed. It stated that United Artists' well-known trademark was "worthy of a wide ambit of protection" and that "the differences in nature of the wares and of the trades [between the two companies] were less significant than they might otherwise be in determining the likelihood of confusion [in the minds of members of the public]." Pink Panther Beauty Corporation appealed that decision.

The majority of the Court held that the appeal should be allowed. The majority found that the trial judge had considered the proper factors, but that he had erred in the way he weighed them and in the conclusion he reached. The issue to be decided was not how famous the trademark was, but whether it was likely that the average consumer would confuse the two trademarks with respect to the goods and services of the parties involved. It was the majority opinion that the trial judge did not give sufficient weight to the fact that not only were the wares completely different, but there was no connection between them at all.

In a dissenting opinion, Mr. Justice McDonald indicated that the trial judge had not erred in weighing the relevant factors to be considered under subsection 6(5) of the *Trademarks Act*. He felt that the name "Pink Panther" had been chosen precisely because of the goodwill associated with United Artists' trade name, and that the appellant had sought to profit financially from that association.

1. Identify the appellant and the respondent in this case. Who was successful?
2. Do you agree with the majority or the minority opinion? Explain your position.

Building Your Understanding

1. Describe three dispute situations that could lead to a claim in Small Claims Court.
2. Identify two advantages and two disadvantages in taking a case to Small Claims Court instead of moving to a higher court.
3. Why are the decisions made by the Supreme Court of Canada so important?
4. Explain why appeal cases are heard by an odd number of justices.
5. What kinds of cases come before the Federal Court of Canada?
6. Design a poster that charts the various levels in the civil court structure and the kinds of cases that might be heard in each court.

CIVIL REMEDIES

Usually a civil action is brought to allow plaintiffs to receive money, or damages, for the losses or injuries they have suffered. In some situations, such as a breach of contract (failure to meet the obligations in a written agreement), the courts may try to return the parties to the same position they were in before the contract was breached. In other situations, the court may try to give the hurt party what it bargained for, or damages for *not* getting what it bargained for. For example, Big Top Roofers might agree to replace Mandy's roof with the shingles specified in the contract; or, they might compensate Mandy for the difference in quality or for the cost of doing the work again.

In cases of property damage, it is usually a simple matter to give the aggrieved party enough money to repair or replace the property. But in cases of serious personal injury, it is often impossible to do anything but attempt to adequately compensate victims and their families for their losses and to make sure they have enough money for future care. In these cases, the court may award both special damages and general damages, which may be either pecuniary or non-pecuniary. Damages may also be awarded in circumstances that are out of the ordinary. The three most common types are aggravated, punitive, and nominal damages. All of these remedies will be explained in the following sections.

General Damages
Pecuniary

pecuniary damages: monetary compensation for losses that can be calculated

The word *pecuniary* simply means "money." **Pecuniary damages** are awards for losses that can be easily calculated by determining how much money the plaintiff lost. Examples include the loss of future earnings or the cost of future care. In determining pecuniary loss, the judge must consider the plaintiff's future earning capacity. For instance, if a highly paid actor or athlete were severely injured, the courts would likely assess potential earnings at a higher rate than the earnings of a junior store clerk. Although it may seem particularly callous, the court may also take into consideration the plaintiff's life expectancy. If the plaintiff is severely injured at a very young age, then it may be necessary to grant a higher award to ensure adequate future care.

It is especially difficult to calculate pecuniary loss for young people. If a plaintiff already has an established career or had definite plans for a specific profession, it is relatively easy to calculate possible future earnings by looking at the average income for individuals in that field. However, if the plaintiff is too young to have started planning a career or to even think about one, assessing damages is much more difficult. Were the plaintiff's marks high enough for admission to university or college? Did he or she demonstrate athletic or artistic ability? Had plans for a future career been discussed with anyone who could testify to such a conversation at trial?

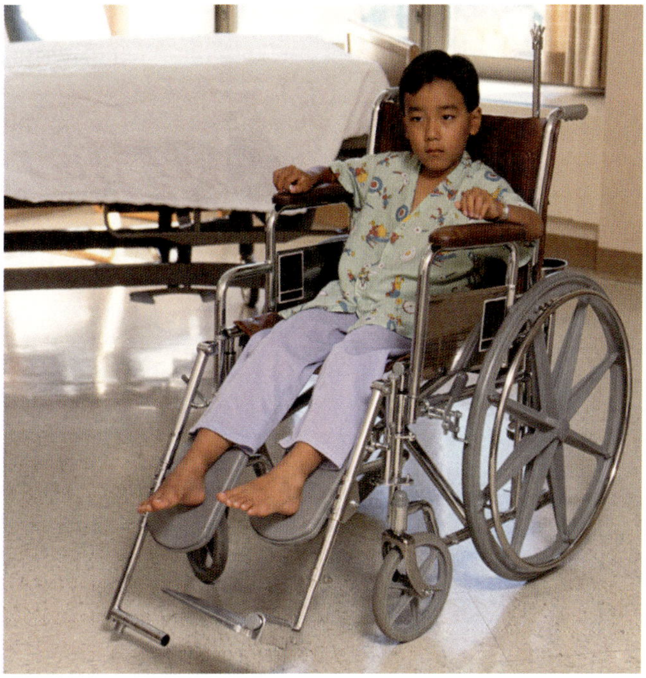

Pecuniary losses for future care can amount to millions of dollars. Plaintiffs may need special facilities, professional help, and expensive equipment to assist them with everyday tasks. Also, keep in mind that if the plaintiff loses a case in civil court, the only available access to these services is the coverage provided by provincial health care or a compensation plan. Even if the plaintiff is successful in court, collecting all the money awarded may not be possible if the defendant has no insurance or assets to cover the amount. Furthermore, when a civil action arises from a criminal situation, the defendant may be serving time in prison and have no source of income.

Figure 13.7 It is difficult to estimate compensation for a young person who must go through life with a disability caused by the negligence of others. List the factors you would need to consider if you had to award damages to the child in this photo.

Non-pecuniary

One of the most difficult things for a judge or jury to decide is how to compensate someone for a terrible personal loss. How can you assign a dollar value to pain and suffering, the loss of a beloved family member, mental anguish, or the inability to enjoy a normal life? In civil law, compensation for losses you cannot put a price on is referred to as **non-pecuniary damages**.

If your car is damaged in an accident, the $1000 repair bill is a pecuniary loss. But if you break your leg, the pain and suffering you endure is not a loss of money—it is a non-pecuniary loss. Assessing these kinds of damages is the responsibility of a judge or civil jury. Would a student with a good prospect of having a professional athletic career suffer a greater loss because of the loss of a leg than a student who does not have that prospect? Should someone who can tolerate a great deal of pain receive less money than someone who is highly sensitive to pain? Because these questions are often difficult to answer, Canadian courts tend to award similar amounts for similar non-pecuniary losses.

non-pecuniary damages: compensation for losses that do not involve an actual loss of money and are difficult to quantify

"Everyone in Canada, wherever he may reside, is entitled to a more or less equal measure of compensation for similar non-pecuniary loss."

— Mr. Justice Dickson, Supreme Court of Canada

In 1978, the Supreme Court of Canada set an upper limit of $100 000 as the maximum compensation that could be awarded (see Law in Action below). The Court has allowed this figure to be adjusted to compensate for inflation. Today, the maximum amount awarded for a non-pecuniary loss is approximately $280 000. This is far less than the large sums awarded in the United States, which according to the Supreme Court "have soared to dramatically high levels."

LAW IN ACTION

The "Trilogy"

1. Explain the Supreme Court's position regarding the purpose of non-pecuniary damages.

2. If the Supreme Court had not placed a ceiling on non-pecuniary damages, what consequences might have resulted in liability cases as devastating as the "Trilogy"?

In 1978, the Supreme Court of Canada established an upper limit on non-pecuniary damages when it delivered decisions in three cases:

- *Andrews v. Grand & Toy Alberta Ltd.*, [1978] 2 S.C.R. 229
- *Thorton v. Board of School Trustees of School District No. 57 (Prince George)*, [1978] 2 S.C.R. 267
- *Teno v. Arnold*, [1978] 2 S.C.R. 287

On the date of the accident, Andrews was a twenty-one-year-old apprentice employed by the Canadian National Railways. He was injured in a traffic accident involving a vehicle driven by a Grand & Toy employee. Fifteen-year-old Gary Thorton was participating in a gymnastics class at his high school when he fractured his spinal cord while using the springboard and box horse. Diane Teno was struck by an oncoming car when she ran across the street to meet the ice-cream truck. She was only four and a half years old.

In these cases, the plaintiffs had incurred such severe injuries that they were left with little more than life itself. All three plaintiffs suffered quadriplegia.

In the "Trilogy" cases, the Supreme Court set a clear upper limit to the amount that can be awarded for non-pecuniary damages. In his opinion in *Andrews v. Grand & Toy Alberta Ltd.*, Mr. Justice Dickson said:

> I would adopt as the appropriate award in the case of a young adult quadriplegic like Andrews the amount of $100 000. Save in exceptional circumstances, this should be regarded as an upper limit of non-pecuniary loss in cases of this nature.

This upper limit was based on the grounds that damage awards should serve a useful function; neither high compensation for pain and suffering nor punitive awards help the plaintiff, but they do unfairly burden the defendant. In *Teno v. Arnold*, the Court said:

> The real difficulty is that an award of non-pecuniary damages cannot be "compensation." There is simply no equation between paralyzed limbs and/or injured brain and dollars. The award is not reparative: there can be no restoration of the lost function.

Another type of non-pecuniary damage is called an aggravated damage. Usually, **aggravated damages** compensate the plaintiff for feelings of humiliation or mental distress. For example, if your employer falsely accused you of theft in front of other employees and then fired you on the spot, you might have a good case for aggravated damages.

aggravated damages: compensation for intangible losses such as humiliation or distress

Special Damages

Special damages are awarded to help pay for out-of-pocket expenses such as drugs, therapy, ambulance services, or vehicle repairs. They may also help cover lost income or any loss that the plaintiff can prove was a result of the defendant's action. To sue for special damages in civil court, the plaintiff must provide all receipts and maintain a record of expenses.

special damages: compensation for out-of-pocket expenses

Miller v. Devenz (2001), O.J. 4084 (Ont. Sup. Ct.)

CASE

While walking her dog, 52-year-old Mavis Miller was pushed to the ground by a large dog running free. The dog was owned by Patricia and Bruce Devenz. Ms. Miller sustained a serious knee injury. The defendants were found liable for damages, and this trial was to assess those damages.

Prior to the attack, Miller had regularly walked six to ten kilometres a day, played golf with her son, and cared for two of her five grandchildren. She travelled annually, frequented flea markets, and kept up her home, both inside and outside. Since the accident, her participation in these activities was severely limited.

When she was knocked over by the dog, Miller sustained a fracture to her left leg from which she never fully recovered. She was hospitalized for five days and subsequently entered a physiotherapy program. She also underwent two knee-joint arthroscopies. She now experiences chronic pain of varying degrees, walks with a distinct limp, and uses a cane. Miller's knee will never improve, and it is expected that she will require knee replacement surgery.

Miller had worked all her life. Although she planned to retire at age 60, at the time of the incident she was about to join a new company. She has since been unable to seek any type of employment. The family has lost the benefit of her financial contribution and will incur costs for future care.

The Ontario Superior Court found for the plaintiff and awarded her $90 000 in non-pecuniary general damages for pain, suffering, and loss of enjoyment of life. In consideration of special damages, the Court reviewed the calculations of an independent assessment company. The company estimated Miller's income and potential earnings based on the salary she would have received from her new position, taking into consideration her intention to retire at age 60. The Court awarded special damages in the amount of $252 140.

1. Describe the factors the Court took into consideration in determining the amount for special damages.
2. Do you think the Court's assessment of general damages was appropriate? Explain.

Punitive Damages

punitive (or exemplary) damages: damages imposed to punish the defendant for reprehensible conduct

Unlike general damages intended to compensate the plaintiff, **punitive (or exemplary) damages** are awarded to punish the defendant. These damages are awarded in cases where the defendant's conduct has been so poor that the courts describe it as "reprehensible" or "malicious." For instance, if the landlord wanted to force you out of your store and wrongfully took possession or prevented customers from gaining access, you might be awarded punitive damages.

Situations where punitive damages are common include cases of false imprisonment or arrest, assault, battery, libel, and slander. You will read more about these torts in Chapter 15.

Fast Fact
In civil lawsuits large businesses such as tobacco companies have been ordered to pay punitive damages because of their actions.

Nominal Damages

nominal damages: minimal compensation to acknowledge a moral victory

Some plaintiffs may not have suffered any significant monetary loss but are seeking **nominal damages**—minimal compensation to show that that the court recognizes the legitimacy of their complaints. For example, Yves decided to sue his local transit authority over a price increase. He had purchased tickets at a certain price. Later, when fares were increased by 10 cents, he was informed that he would have to include an additional 10 cents with each ticket. Yves argued that when he purchased the tickets he had entered into a contract with the transit authority, so they could not, at a later date, change the terms of the contract on their own. Yves won and was permitted to exchange his tickets for tokens without paying the extra 10 cents per fare. A nominal, but moral, victory!

Specific Performance

specific performance: a court order requiring someone to fulfill the terms of a contract

Sometimes in cases of breach of contract, monetary compensation is insufficient. Quite simply, you want what you bargained for. In such cases, the court may order **specific performance,** a court order compelling someone to fulfill the terms of a contract. For example, suppose you use your savings to purchase a puppy from a breeder and patiently wait until the puppy is weaned. When you go to pick up your puppy, the breeder informs you that she has changed her mind and has decided to sell the dog. She offers to return your deposit, but you do not want your money back. You want your dog! The courts may very well conclude that the breeder must honour the terms of the sale and sell you the puppy as specified. You will learn more about specific performance in Chapter 19.

Consider This
Brainstorm civil situations in which the courts may order the defendant to comply with the terms of the contract rather than award damages to the plaintiff.

Injunctions

injunction: a court order requiring or prohibiting an action

An **injunction** is a court order requiring someone to do or *not* to do something. If it requires a person to do something, it is a mandatory injunction. If it forbids a person from doing something, it is a prohibitory injunction. An injunction may be permanent or interlocutory (temporary). Courts grant injunctions to stop activities such as applying dangerous chemicals or using

McDonald's Restaurant of Canada Ltd. v. West Edmonton Mall Ltd. (1994), (A.B.Q.B.) A.J. 634

CASE

McDonald's signed a lease in 1983 with its landlord, West Edmonton Mall. The lease contained a "restrictive covenant," a term in the contract that precluded the landlord from leasing to another tenant in the mall that "primarily engaged in the sale of hamburgers and/or chicken product." In 1993, the defendant leased space near McDonald's Fantasyland to Johnny Rockets, a restaurant that specialized in hamburgers. This location planned to open in April, and the company started renovations on the leased space. The plaintiff sought a permanent injunction to restrain the defendant from operating the restaurant in the mall, claiming a breach of the restrictive covenant. The trial court granted a permanent injunction prohibiting the defendant from breaching its contract.

1. Describe the economic consequences of this decision for Johnny Rockets.
2. What options would Johnny Rockets have to recover its expenses for renovating the space in the mall?

---

copyrighted trademarks or materials. Employers have asked the courts to grant injunctions to force striking workers to return to work. Failure to comply with a court-ordered injunction could result in a charge for contempt of court. Conviction could mean a fine or imprisonment.

Enforcing a Judgment

Now for the bad news! Once a settlement has been awarded, it is up to the plaintiff to collect the money. At the end of a trial, the court does not simply provide a cheque for the amount recovered; the cheque must come from the defendant, who is usually called the "judgment debtor." But what happens if the defendant does not have the money or does not want to pay? Fortunately, a few legal remedies are available to help the plaintiff obtain payment.

Examination of a Judgment Debtor

If the defendant refuses to pay, the defendant may be examined as a judgment debtor, which involves being questioned under oath to find out about the debtor's assets. Does this person own a car, boat, or motorcycle? What about bank accounts or stocks? Who owes the debtor money? Where does the debtor work and how much does he or she earn?

Garnishment

If there are still problems collecting on a court-ordered settlement, the plaintiff may ask the court for the remedy of **garnishment.** This means that the courts can order that a percentage of the wages earned by the judgment debtor can be deducted and paid into the court on the plaintiff's behalf until the amount is paid. Bank accounts, money due on contracts, or money owed by a third party to the defendant can also be garnisheed. Most provinces impose a time limit, but if the settlement is still not paid, it is possible to renew the order to garnishee.

Figure 13.8 Under what circumstances might a court grant an injunction against striking workers?

garnishment: a court order requiring a third party to pay the plaintiff money owed to the defendant

Execution or Seizure

As a last resort, the assets of the debtor can be seized by a sheriff or bailiff and then sold to settle the judgment. Usually a writ of execution is filed with the sheriff who arranges for seizure and notifies the debtor that if the settlement is not paid within a certain period, the assets will be sold in payment. Sometimes the assets are sold at public auction; after deducting the costs for the sale, the rest of the money is paid to settle the judgment. This is not as easy as it sounds. Certain assets cannot be sold, such as clothing, furniture, and the tools a worker needs to earn a living. It may also be difficult to prove that the goods actually belong to the debtor.

> "I was never ruined but twice: once when I lost a lawsuit and once when I won one."
> — Voltaire (1694–1778), French philosopher

Alternative Sources of Compensation

In Canada, several alternative sources of compensation are available, depending on the circumstances. The regulations for these various programs differ by province and territory. Some of these programs are described in general terms below.

Motor Vehicle Liability Insurance

In the case of personal injuries suffered in motor vehicle accidents, it may be possible to receive compensation from sources other than the defendant. The injured party may be able to recover money from the insurer of the defendant's vehicle. Although all car owners in Canada are legally required to purchase liability insurance, some people do not. To address these situations, the provinces have set up special funds, called uninsured driver funds, to compensate people who suffer losses at the hands of uninsured drivers.

No-fault Insurance

It may take many years to bring a civil action to court and then to prove fault. In the meantime, the victim may not have access to financial resources. To address this problem, a no-fault insurance system, available across Canada, provides immediate funds without evidence of fault. If someone is injured and suffers a loss beyond the coverage provided in a no-fault settlement, the victim may still bring an action for damages. If the victim's suit is successful, any earlier settlement is deducted from the eventual award.

Workers' Compensation

Workers who are injured on the job have another source of compensation through their provincial Workers' Compensation Fund. This coverage is not available in all workplaces, so workers are advised to check with their employers regarding coverage. In workplaces that are covered, the employer, not the employee, pays into the fund. Payments are based on the size and type of business operation.

An employee covered under the *Workers' Compensation Act* can still receive compensation even if he or she was at fault for the accident. Claims are usually settled quickly, and benefits are paid immediately. If the settlement is

Fast Fact
If an employer refuses to pay damages to a worker who is not covered by Workers' Compensation, the worker can seek compensation in civil court.

insufficient to cover medical costs, the worker can ask for the case to be reopened and the payments reviewed. If the employee is fatally injured, the employee's dependents will receive compensation.

Workers' Compensation will not award money for pain and suffering or loss of enjoyment of life, so the amount of money paid to an injured worker under the plan may be considerably less than the amount an uncovered worker might be awarded in a lawsuit. To receive awards under the *Workers' Compensation Act,* employees must apply to the Workers' Compensation Board. The Board decides who will receive benefits, and how much and for how long they will be paid. Medical expenses will usually be covered, but awards for lost wages are limited to a maximum percentage of the worker's average salary before the injuries occurred.

Criminal Injuries Compensation

Victims of violent crime will find that the main obstacle to receiving compensation is actually recovering from the assailant any damages the court may award in a civil suit. The assailant may not have any assets, and criminals are rarely insured. To overcome this obstacle, criminal injuries compensation boards have been created to compensate innocent victims. Most provinces have some form of assistance for victims of violent crime, though many plans, including those of British Columbia and Ontario, have specific eligibility criteria. For example, the victim must be a completely innocent party who has not instigated or participated in the violent act in any way. In addition, there are limits to the amount of money that can be awarded.

Figure 13.9 This worker was injured after his crane overturned into the pit of a construction site. Why do you think workers are not compensated for their pain and suffering by the Workers' Compensation Fund?

Building Your Understanding

1. a) Use two examples to distinguish between pecuniary and non-pecuniary losses in reference to general damages awarded in a civil lawsuit.
   b) Determine whether each scenario at the beginning of the chapter on page 336 involves pecuniary or non-pecuniary losses.
2. What are the differences between general and special damages?
3. What is the purpose of punitive damages? Provide two examples.
4. Why would anyone choose to sue for nominal damages?
5. a) Describe two methods the plaintiff can use to collect a court-awarded settlement from the judgment debtor.
   b) Explain the potential difficulties associated with each method.
6. Use a chart to summarize four alternative sources for compensation. Identify each source and indicate the advantages and disadvantages of each.

ALTERNATIVE DISPUTE RESOLUTION

If you have a complaint of a civil nature, litigation should be your last resort. You are probably already familiar with other ways to resolve disputes. Many schools have initiated programs of conflict resolution, peer mediation, or arbitration to settle disputes before they escalate into violence or require intervention by a principal or superintendent.

Alternative dispute resolution (ADR) is a way of resolving a variety of conflicts from child custody battles, to arguments between neighbours, to disputes over liability for injuries. Some situations are so complex and serious that court is the only valid option, but many cases can be resolved using ADR. During a pre-trial conference, the judge or master may suggest that the parties involved in the dispute consider ADR to resolve their differences. The three methods of ADR most commonly used are negotiation, mediation, and arbitration.

alternative dispute resolution (ADR): a way to settle disagreements other than by litigation

Negotiation

Negotiation involves discussion for the purpose of reaching an agreement that benefits both parties. Solving disputes through negotiation is part of everyday life. The key to successful negotiation is communication. For example, you may negotiate with a teacher to change an assignment due date, or with your parents to extend your curfew. Negotiation is the simplest way of coming to an agreement. No third party is necessary if the parties can reach a mutually acceptable decision. Once an agreement is reached, it may be written down more formally in a contract.

negotiation: a process whereby both parties communicate to reach a mutually acceptable agreement

Mediation

Mediation is a process in which a neutral third party intervenes to bring two opposing parties to an agreement. It is probably the most widely used alternative method for resolving disputes. Participation in mediation is not always voluntary. In certain cases, the court will order that the parties meet with a mediator before a trial is scheduled. Voluntary or not, the mediator cannot force the parties to settle the dispute or accept a solution they do not want. The purpose of a mediator is to facilitate the process by keeping the negotiations on track. A mediator may also assess the likely outcome of civil litigation if the parties cannot resolve the conflict, or simply act as a facilitator to encourage the parties to communicate freely so they can resolve the dispute themselves.

mediation: a process in which a neutral third party intervenes to bring opposing parties to an agreement

The benefits of mediation are many. Both parties in the dispute decide what is important and what needs to be resolved. The fact that the eventual solution is "shared" and not imposed by the courts may mean that the solution will be more satisfying and long lasting. The presence of a neutral third party creates a sense of fairness, and in some cases the mediator can introduce new ideas and help the parties work out a solution. Finally, the mediation process is confidential and private, unlike the court process.

Legal Link WWW
To share your point of view on conflict resolution, go to **www.pearsoned.ca/law** and click on the Youth page of the Peacebuilder Web site.

Figure 13.10 People engaged in mediation to solve a dispute share the task of putting a solution package together that will satisfy both parties. Brainstorm a list of disputes that might be resolved through mediation.

Arbitration

In **arbitration,** a neutral third party hears both sides of the dispute and then makes a binding decision. This method is more formal than mediation, and the arbitrator has a greater role in the process. Arbitration can be legislated, as it often is in labour disputes. Both parties in the dispute usually agree on the choice of arbitrator and share the cost for the service. Arbitrators are usually experts in a specific area of the law or in a particular industry. They hear and consider the merits of the dispute based on the facts and the applicable laws. In some situations, the parties may decide in advance that a court can review the decision, but usually the arbitrator's decision is final and binding. Arbitration may be less expensive and less time-consuming than taking the case to court, but the one characteristic it shares with the court process is that someone wins and someone loses.

While a number of disputes over Aboriginal rights and title begin in the courts, many are resolved through ADR. For example, Aboriginal land claims and self-government agreements generally call for the establishment of an arbitration board to resolve disputes over the interpretation or implementation of those agreements. For instance, s. 18 of the Inuvialuit Final Agreement, signed in 1984, establishes a quasi-judicial body known as the Arbitration Board. When a dispute arises involving a matter relevant to the Agreement, a panel of the Arbitration Board is set up to hear the dispute. Its decision is binding on the parties, subject to review by the Federal Court of Appeal.

arbitration: a process in which a neutral third party hears both sides of the dispute and makes a binding decision

LAW IN ACTION

Canada Fails to Give Proper Notice

1. How did the Board arrive at its decision? Was this decision binding? Explain.
2. Why was Canada ordered to pay nominal damages?

In 1994, the Inuvialuit Regional and Land Corporations alleged that the federal government (Ministers of Defence and Indian and Northern Affairs) breached s. 16(8) of the Inuvialuit Final Agreement by failing to provide the Inuvialuit with notice of a series of contracts to clean up dew-line sites in the ISR (Inuvialuit Settlement Region). They alleged that the contracts should have been awarded to them in light of provisions contained in the Agreement. The Board held that the purpose of s. 16(8) is to "provide fair and reasonable opportunity to the Inuvialuit to benefit from the economic activity being undertaken by Canada in the ISR and the Western Arctic." Furthermore, Canada must give proper notice to the Inuvialuit so that they may participate in the contracting process. However, the Board found that the contracts were not improperly awarded because it was unlikely that the Inuvialuit would have received the contracts even if proper notice had been given, since its bid was much higher than that of the firm awarded the contracts. As a result, the Board ordered Canada to pay nominal damages for breaching the terms of the Agreement by failing to provide notice.

Advantages and Disadvantages of ADR

The most obvious advantage of ADR is that it saves time and money. It is also very effective, having a success rate in Canada of 80 to 85 percent. Other advantages include the informality, privacy, and control it affords the parties in the dispute.

There are some situations where ADR is not appropriate. For instance, disputes involving violence are not usually suitable for mediation. Also, the confidentiality of ADR that some parties favour can be seen as a disadvantage to those who want to publicize the outcome as an example for people involved in similar disputes. Finally, where there is a need to establish legal precedent, or where the outcome of the case could affect a large group, the court is probably the more appropriate forum.

Building Your Understanding

1. Identify and distinguish the three main types of ADR.
2. What do you think are the main advantages of ADR?
3. On a scale of one to five, with one being the most likely, rate the likelihood of a successful ADR for each of the scenarios at the beginning of the chapter (page 336). Use the following considerations when rating their likelihood of success:
   - total losses involved compared with court costs
   - desire of both parties for confidentiality
   - evidence of breakdown in prior agreements

   Explain your rationale.

LOOKING BACK

Reviewing Your Vocabulary

affidavit of documents *p. 342*
aggravated damages *p. 353*
alternative dispute resolution (ADR) *p. 358*
arbitration *p. 359*
balance of probabilities *p. 338*
binding *p. 348*
class action suit *p. 344*
counterclaim *p. 341*
cross-claim *p. 342*
damages *p. 338*
default judgment *p. 341*
defendant *p. 338*
dissenting opinion *p. 348*
examination for discovery *p. 342*

garnishment *p. 355*
guardian ad litem *p. 339*
injunction *p. 354*
liable *p. 342*
litigants *p. 338*
litigation *p. 338*
mediation *p. 358*
negotiation *p. 358*
next friend *p. 338*
nominal damages *p. 354*
non-pecuniary damages *p. 351*
particulars *p. 341*
pecuniary damages *p. 350*
plaintiff *p. 338*
pleadings *p. 340*

privileged documents *p. 343*
punitive (or exemplary) damages *p. 354*
remedy *p. 341*
settle out of court *p. 343*
special damages *p. 353*
specific performance *p. 354*
statement of claim *p. 341*
statement of defence *p. 341*
third-party claim *p. 342*
writ of summons *p. 340*

Quick Quiz

1. Referring to the vocabulary list above, create a crossword puzzle, using as many terms as possible. Your crossword definitions should be clear, accurate, and concise; they should identify key features of the concept; and they should range in degree of difficulty or challenge.

Checking Your Knowledge

2. What are the key differences between civil law and criminal law?
3. List the main branches of civil law.
4. Summarize the steps taken in a civil action after a statement has been issued and before a trial takes place.
5. Why is it so difficult for courts to decide on the amount of non-pecuniary damages that should be awarded?
6. Why is it more difficult to assess damages for a child's future income than for an adult's?
7. Why is it not always feasible for a victim to sue in civil court? What other options are available?

Developing Your Thinking and Inquiry Skills

8. Choose one of the cases in this chapter (see also the cases that follow) and create the pleadings for the plaintiff's statement of claim. Exchange documents with a partner and write a statement of defence in response to your partner's statement of claim. Ask for particulars, if necessary.

9. In which civil court would each of the following actions be heard?
   a) Larry and Star are suing Steve for damages resulting from trespassing on their property—an isolated ice-fishing hut on Tobin Lake in Saskatchewan.
   b) Kelly is appealing the trial decision in her case against Fox Run Pet Supplies, a Prince Edward Island retailer.
   c) Ted is involved in a dispute with the federal government over his income tax return for last year.
   d) Kari, a self-employed bookkeeper, is suing a client for non-payment of her invoices totalling $5389.56.

10. Create a situation that would give rise to a civil action. Using appropriate legal terminology, prepare a statement of claim to recover a variety of damages (general and special) from a defendant. Be sure to specify amounts and justify your claim.

11. Choose a criminal case described in Chapter 9 or Chapter 12 that could lead to a civil action. Use a chart to compare criminal and civil aspects of the case. Identify the parties involved, the burden of proof required, the type of court in which the case would be heard, and possible punishment or damages.

12. Do you think the courts should set a monetary limit on an award for non-pecuniary damages such as pain and suffering? Apply the following considerations to your decision:
    - differences in pain threshold or psychological sensitivities
    - consequences such as case load and cost of legal representation

    Apply additional considerations in your decision and write a letter to the editor, defending your point of view. Use specific examples.

Communicating Your Ideas

13. Choose a position and prepare the arguments you would use to debate the following topic. Resolved: Damage awards should be reduced if victims refuse to participate in medical treatment that might mitigate their injuries.

14. Form groups of three, representing a mediator and the parties in dispute. To role-play a mediation process, choose one of the situations described at the beginning of the chapter (see page 336). The parties in dispute should formulate their positions on the issues and submit them to the mediator for analysis. The mediator's role is to ensure that both sides understand the dispute by identifying any assumptions that are based on opinion rather than fact. The mediator should then attempt to find some common ground between the parties as a starting point toward resolution. As you role-play the mediation process, attempt to resolve the dispute.

Putting It All Together

15. In groups of five, representing the parties in the dispute, their legal representation, and the trial judge, follow the stages in a civil action outlined in Figure 13.3 to resolve the small claims case described below. Then stage a mock trial.

    ### Graham v. Sullivan Travel Agency
    Yvette Graham was going on the vacation of her dreams—an exclusive Caribbean cruise on a luxury liner sailing out of Miami. Sullivan Travel Agency had made all the arrangements, including a flight from Halifax. Yvette specifically told the agency not to book a small cabin in the lower decks. Unfortunately, when Yvette arrived on the cruise ship, she was shown to a tiny cabin on the lowest deck. Thinking there was some mistake, Yvette checked with the cruise line but was told that this was the cabin the agency had booked. All other cabins on the ship were occupied.

    Yvette is claustrophobic and knew she could not sleep in the cabin. She got off the ship and flew back to Halifax. Because she had paid $3500 for the cruise, she is suing Sullivan Travel Agency for the $3500, plus $575 for her flight home, and $2500 for inconvenience and personal suffering.

    Sullivan Agency claims that Yvette could have continued on the cruise, but it was her choice to get off the ship and forgo the holiday. The agency would have reimbursed her for the cost of the cabin, even though Yvette had not mentioned her claustrophobia at the time of the booking. The defendant also claims that Yvette's request for a larger cabin on the upper deck was impractical since most of the cabins were small and below deck.

CASES

Button v. Jones (2001), O.J. No. 1976
(Ont. Sup. Ct.)

In 1995, Dick Jones sold his dental practice to Richard Button for $150 000. This figure included $84 260 for goodwill, patients, charts, x-rays, models, and records. Jones and Button then practised in association until this arrangement was terminated on December 31, 2000. In the association agreement, Jones had agreed not to practise in Kitchener-Waterloo for four years following the termination of their association. In early January 2001, Jones began practising dentistry with Dr. Herbert Pfeiffer at the Belmont Medical Centre in Kitchener. Button sued Jones for specific performance and damages.

At trial, Jones admitted that he intended to serve 1400 of the 1900 patients from his former practice. The Court granted an interlocutory injunction restraining the defendant from carrying on or associating in a dental practice in Kitchener or Waterloo.

1. Why did the plaintiff seek specific performance?
2. Explain why the court would grant an interlocutory injunction rather than a permanent injunction.
3. If you were the trial judge, what type of damages would you award and in what amount?

Petersen (guardian ad litem) v. Surrey School District No. 36
(1991), 89 D.L.R. (4th) 517 (B.C.S.C.)

Sixteen-year-old Todd Petersen was an excellent grade-eleven student and a good athlete. He was playing a game of rag ball in the school gym when a bat flew out of a teammate's hands and hit Todd in the face. The bat had a damaged grip and no safety grip. It was the first time Todd had played the game, and he had obeyed the teacher's instructions about where to stand when he was the batter on deck. None of the students had been instructed about the dangers of the game or warned not to lose control of the bat. Todd suffered serious facial injuries that left him with permanent double vision and delayed him from obtaining his university degree by about two years. In his name, Todd's parents sued the school. Expert reports considered at trial estimated that Todd would suffer a loss of $124 422 in future earning capacity due to the two-year delay in his university education. The Court found this amount too high and awarded him $75 000 for loss of future wages and an additional $75 000 in non-pecuniary general damages.

1. Why was a guardian ad litem required?
2. What will the non-pecuniary damages cover?
3. Do you think it was appropriate for the judge to award pecuniary damages that were lower than the amount experts estimated for future loss of income? Explain.

Trizec Equity v. Gallant
(January 1994), WCB Tribunal

Ms. Gallant worked in an Eaton's cafeteria in a mall owned by the defendant. Although she had to be at work at 10:30 a.m., she usually arrived at 9:15 a.m. After setting up tables in the cafeteria, she would do some personal shopping in the mall. Her employer was aware of her routine and did not question it. Just after 9:00 one morning, Ms. Gallant was injured when she slipped on a wet floor approximately 15 metres away from the Eaton's employee entrance. She sued the owner of the mall.

Trizec Equity brought this action before the Tribunal, arguing that Gallant was injured during the course of her employment. Trizec based its claim on the fact that Gallant was on her way to work when she fell and was using an entrance primarily reserved for Eaton's employees. Trizec claimed that Gallant had no suit because her injuries would be covered under Eaton's worker compensation plan.

1. Was this a workplace injury covered under workers' compensation, or is Trizec liable for Ms. Gallant's injuries?
2. What factors would you consider in making your decision?

CASES

Martin v. Mineral Springs Hospital (2001), A.B.Q.B. 58

BACKGROUND Cindy and Stephen Martin's daughter, Kelsey Lee, was delivered stillborn at the Mineral Springs Hospital in Banff, Alberta. Dr. Lynn Marriott admitted that her negligence caused Kelsey Lee's death. The Martins sued Dr. Marriott and the hospital for non-pecuniary general damages to compensate them for their pain and suffering, and the emotional loss of their child. The plaintiffs also claimed that Cindy Martin was entitled to damages for the loss of a body part—her fetus—resulting from the defendant's negligence.

LEGAL QUESTION Should the Martins receive non-pecuniary damages for bereavement and pain and suffering?

DECISION In common law there is no cause of action against a negligent person who causes the death of a family member, and there can be no claim for damages for bereavement. Such claims only arise under statutes such as the Alberta's *Fatal Accidents Act*. Under the Act, if Kelsey had been born alive and then died due to negligence, Cindy and Stephen Martin would have been entitled to $43 000 for bereavement. Also, they would have been able to recover any provable pecuniary loss. However, the Court maintained that such pecuniary losses are difficult to prove because parents generally pay far more to raise a child than they ever receive back from the child later in life.

There could be no award for the death of the child under the *Fatal Accidents Act* because that act applies to a "person," and a fetus is not a "person" as the Act defines the word. The claim that the fetus was part of the mother's body, like a limb, had no merit. The Court awarded Cindy Martin $60 000 for the nervous shock she suffered resulting in ongoing psychological problems, the prolonged labour and delivery, and two subsequent caesarian operations necessitated by the doctor's negligence.

LEGAL SIGNIFICANCE This case illustrates the fine distinctions in the law. Had the child been born alive and then died, the Martins would have been entitled to $43 000 for bereavement and pecuniary damages under the *Fatal Accidents Act*. Since this statute covers persons, and a fetus is not a person under the Act, the Act did not apply.

Cindy and Stephen Martin

ANALYSIS

1. What type of damages were awarded in this case? Do you agree with the amount awarded? Why or why not?
2. What was the Court's opinion about proving pecuniary losses? Do you agree or disagree with this view? Discuss.
3. a) How might the plaintiff argue her claim that the loss of the fetus is similar to the loss of a body part?
   b) How might the defendant counter the claim?
4. Should Alberta change the *Fatal Accidents Act* to allow recovery for the loss of a fetus? Explain.

Negligence and Unintentional Torts

14

CHAPTER OUTLINE

Negligence

Special Types of Liability

Defences to Negligence

FOCUS YOUR LEARNING

When can a person sue for the negligent actions of others?

What are the different types of liability?

What defences can be offered in a lawsuit for negligence?

Weird Tort Claims

Bill Smith has filed a lawsuit against the estate of Elvis Presley charging that the estate has been "perpetrating a fraud" that Elvis died in 1977. He said the fraud interferes with his attempts to sell his books on Elvis's current whereabouts.

Prison inmates Paul Goist and Craig Anthony filed a lawsuit against General Foods, claiming their coffee was addictive and gave them headaches and insomnia.

David Mattatall was awarded $632 in medical expenses. He sued his mother for closing her car door on the paw of his cat Daisy. His mother lost her safe driver discount. Unfortunately, poor Daisy didn't receive anything because she was later run over by another car.

Ernesto Mota suffered brain damage from swallowing a bag of cocaine in a police station so that it could not be used against him as evidence. He is suing the police department for $7 million, claiming that the police should have stopped him.

WHAT DO YOU THINK?

- Do any of these claims have merit?
- What kind of injury did the plaintiffs suffer?
- How should they be compensated for their loss or injury?

While some of the claims on the previous page may seem bizarre, individuals often face the possibility that they may be injured by someone's negligence, or, in a moment of carelessness, that they may injure someone else. What happens to people who are injured through no fault of their own? People usually assume they will be able to sue and get compensated for their injuries, loss of wages, or damage to their property.

Damage to property or a personal injury caused by another person is a civil wrong called a **tort.** As you learned in Chapter 2, the branch of law that holds persons, private organizations, and governments responsible for damages and injuries is known as tort law. In this chapter, you will learn about **unintentional torts**—injuries that are the result of an accident or an action that was not intended to cause harm. You will also learn about the various defences that a person being sued can offer.

tort: harm caused to a person or property for which the law provides a civil remedy

unintentional torts: injuries caused by an accident or an action that was not intended to cause harm

Fast Fact
The word *tort* originally comes from the Latin words *tortum* meaning "wrong" and *torquere* meaning "to twist."

NEGLIGENCE

negligence: careless conduct that causes forseeable harm to another person

The most common unintentional tort is **negligence.** You are negligent when you unintentionally cause injury to someone in a situation where you should have known your action could cause harm. Suppose you decide to push your friend into a swimming pool for fun. Your friend resists and in the scuffle, you accidentally push someone else who falls and hits his head on the side of the pool. He suffers a concussion and misses two weeks of work. Your actions were negligent. You did not intend to give anyone a concussion, but you should have foreseen that your actions, especially in a crowded area such as a swimming pool, could cause injury to someone else.

Every day we hear about different claims for negligence. A woman sues a manufacturer because the bindings on her skis broke during a downhill race, causing her to fall and break her arm. A bar is sued because the bartender served drinks to a person who subsequently killed someone in a car accident. Parents sue a hospital because a nurse gave their child the wrong medication resulting in brain damage. In each of these cases, people sued for what they perceived as the careless or negligent conduct of others. In order for a defendant to be found negligent, each of the factors shown in Figure 14.1 must be proven by the plaintiff.

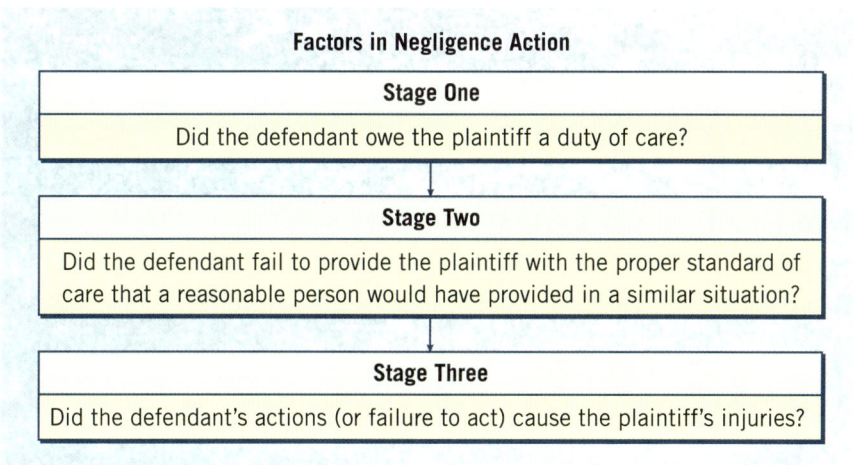

Figure 14.1 If the answer to the question is "no" at any stage of the process, the action will not succeed.

Fast Fact
Statutory duty of care also exists. Under s. 215(1) of the *Criminal Code*, for example, a person has a legal duty to provide the necessaries of life (e.g., food, clothing, etc.) to anyone under his or her charge if that person is unable to provide such necessaries because of age, illness, or mental disorder.

Stage One: Duty of Care

In a negligence case, the plaintiff must prove that the defendant owed the plaintiff a **duty of care**—the obligation to avoid careless actions that could cause harm to one or more persons. For example, if Caroline were hitting golf balls, she *should* foresee that her actions might harm Stewart, who is walking by; she would owe Stewart a duty of care. At one time, Caroline would only owe Stewart a duty of care if she had a contract or a special relationship with him. If such a relationship could be proven, then Caroline had a legal duty to look out for Stewart's safety. Without a contract, Stewart could not sue for negligence. This need for a contract changed as a result of a landmark decision in Scotland in *Donoghue v. Stevenson*, [1932].

The **neighbour principle** is significant because it means that in law everyone owes a duty of care not to harm his or her neighbour by being careless or negligent. According to *Donoghue v. Stevenson*, your neighbour is anyone who you can reasonably foresee being injured by your actions. If you leave your bike on the sidewalk, someone might trip over it and break a leg. That person might sue you, claiming that in law anyone using the sidewalk is your neighbour and that you owe such persons a duty of care. A court would probably decide that when you left your bike on the sidewalk, you should have foreseen that someone walking by could trip over it; therefore, anyone

duty of care: the obligation to foresee and avoid careless actions that might cause harm to others

neighbour principle: the legal responsibility to owe a duty of care not to harm one's neighbour by being careless or negligent

CASE

Donoghue v. Stevenson, [1932] A.C. 562 (H.L.)

1. In your own words, define the neighbour principle, using an example from your personal experience.
2. Do you agree with the House of Lord's ruling to retry the case? Why or why not?

One day Mrs. Donoghue and a friend stopped at a café for a drink. The friend purchased a bottle of ginger beer for Mrs. Donoghue. After drinking some of the ginger beer, Mrs. Donoghue found the remains of a decomposed snail in the bottle, and she became physically ill. She sued the beer manufacturer for being negligent by not having a proper system for inspecting the bottles.

The manufacturer of the ginger beer argued that it did not owe Mrs. Donoghue a duty of care because it did not have a contract with her; she had not purchased the ginger beer. The manufacturer agreed that it had a contract with the friend who had purchased the ginger beer, but the friend did not drink the ginger beer and did not get sick. Based on the existing legal principle that the manufacturer was responsible only to those with whom it had a contract, the trial judge dismissed the case. Donoghue appealed. The House of Lords reversed the decision and ordered the case to be tried. In the majority decision, Lord Atkin wrote the following:

> A person who engages in the manufacture of articles of food and drink intended for consumption by the public has a duty of care to those whom he intends to consume his products.... The rule that you are to love your neighbour becomes in law, you must not injure your neighbour.... Who, then, is my neighbour? The answer seems to be persons who are so closely and directly affected by my act that I ought reasonably to have them in contemplation as being so affected when I am directing my mind to the acts or omissions which are called in question.

The parties settled the action out of court, but a legal principle known as the neighbour principle was formulated.

---

foreseeability: the ability of a reasonable person to anticipate the consequence of an action

Fast Fact
People who own houses or commercial establishments have a duty to keep their sidewalks safe for passers by.

who might use the sidewalk would be your neighbour. Being aware that your actions could cause injury to someone is known as **foreseeability**—an important principle in determining duty of care in tort law.

In some situations you cannot possibly foresee that your actions could injure another person. In other words, your neighbour is not the world at large. Suppose you are running to catch a bus just as its doors are closing. You bang on the door. The driver opens the door to let you in, and in doing so knocks the bag of groceries out of your hand. A large bottle of pop you are carrying smashes on the ground, seriously injuring the little boy standing behind you. His family sues the bus driver for negligence. The courts would probably find that the defendant (the bus driver) could not have foreseen how the action of opening the door for you could have injured the little boy standing behind you.

Family Sues Over Fatal Crash

LAW IN ACTION

In November 2000, 14-year-old Amanda Peat and Robert Fulbrook were killed when the all-terrain vehicle they were driving slammed into a tractor-trailer at the John Deere Plant in Welland, Ontario. The students were participating in a popular job-shadowing program. Although a coroner's inquest ruled that the students' deaths were accidental, the family of one of the students filed a lawsuit alleging negligence against the manufacturer, John Deere, and the two organizations that sponsored the program. The Peat family claimed that the defendants failed to ensure that the students were not placed in a dangerous situation. The family also alleged that the defendants should have known that Amanda had had no experience or training and that she and Robert were not supervised while they were on the vehicle.

1. Who were the defendants in this case?
2. What three factors will the Peat family have to prove?
3. How would you apply the principle of foreseeability in this case?

Stage Two: Standard of Care

If a court decides that the defendant owed the plaintiff a duty of care, it must then decide *how much* care the defendant owed the plaintiff. Under common law, the courts came up with a standard for measuring the amount of care or caution someone should exercise to avoid harming others. In determining this **standard of care,** the courts decided to look at what a reasonable person would have done under similar circumstances. A **reasonable person** is regarded as an ordinary person of normal intelligence. A court will compare the defendant's actions with what a careful person of ordinary intelligence would do in a similar situation. For example, a reasonable person would know that driving 120 kilometres per hour on an icy road could cause an accident. If the courts decide that the defendant failed to meet the standard of caution that a reasonable person would have used, the defendant is said to have breached (failed to provide) the standard of care he or she owed the plaintiff.

standard of care: the degree of caution or level of conduct expected of a reasonable person

reasonable person: an ordinary person of normal intelligence

Consider This
In the early 1980s, tainted blood and blood products supplied by the Canadian Red Cross infected thousands of Canadians with HIV. What was the standard of care owed to people who received blood? Could the agency have reasonably foreseen the consequences of its collection methods?

Professional Liability

Individuals with special skills, expertise, and training, such as engineers, or lawyers, have a higher standard of care toward others than that of the reasonable person. This standard is called a specialized standard of care. The test for a **specialized standard of care** is what a "reasonable person with the same specialized training" would have done in that situation. For example, a doctor would be considered negligent if he or she did not provide the same level of care as other doctors in the same area of practice. Also, a heart specialist must meet a higher standard of care than a general practitioner.

specialized standard of care: the degree of caution or level of conduct considered necessary by a reasonable person with the same specialized training

Medical Negligence

In most situations, a medical practitioner cannot touch a patient, perform an operation, or administer treatment unless the patient has given consent.

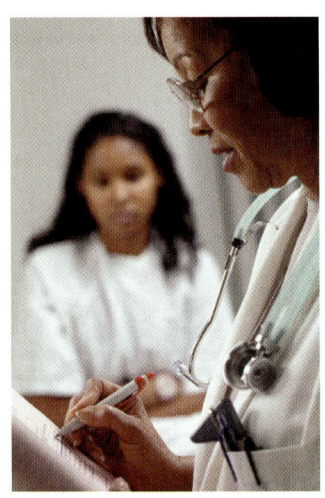

Figure 14.2 What must a doctor disclose to a patient?

Consent must be voluntary—the patient cannot be pressured. The patient's consent must also be informed, which means that the doctor has a duty to explain the medical procedure the patient is going to receive, any significant or unusual risks involved, length of recovery, potential side effects, and any alternatives to the procedure. Serious risks must be disclosed, even if their chances of occurrence are slight. If the doctor fails to share any of this information with the patient, duty of care toward the patient will be breached, and the doctor may be liable for the consequences. Should damage occur, the plaintiff must prove that it was caused by the doctor's failure to adequately inform the patient of the risk. To do this, the patient must prove that he or she would not have had the treatment if this risk had been disclosed.

Suppose David suffers from severe back pain. His doctor informs him that he needs surgery to repair a ruptured disc. The doctor explains the procedure and tells David the surgery is serious but no more than any operation. She does not mention that there is a 1 percent risk of paralysis. David agrees to the operation and subsequently suffers paralysis as a result of the operation. David's doctor could be liable for negligence.

CASE

Thibault v. Fewer, [2001] M.B.Q.B. 231

1. What did the plaintiff have to prove for the neurosurgeon to be liable?
2. Why did the trial judge dismiss the case? Do you agree with his decision?
3. If you were the plaintiff, would you appeal? Explain.

In 1992, Norma Thibault was suffering from a painful illness that affected the muscles in her face. She was on a high dose of an anti-convulsive drug that helped her control the pain. She also underwent root-canal work, had several teeth removed, and even had her dentist anaesthetize the right side of her face so that she could go out socially. The pain continued, and she confided in her doctor that she was considering suicide. Her doctor arranged to send her to a neurosurgeon, Dr. Fewer, who suggested a procedure that could block the pain.

Rather than using an outdated (and dangerous) procedure to permanently block the pain, the neurosurgeon suggested an injection that would kill the pain fibres, while still maintaining the patient's sense of touch. The neurosurgeon wrote that this procedure "has very little in the way of side effects...." After the procedure, Mrs. Thibault began experiencing reduced vision in her right eye and soon permanently lost most of her vision in that eye. She complained that she was never informed of the possible effect the procedure could have on her eyesight. She sued the neurosurgeon.

During the trial, the Court learned that only 1 out of 110 of the defendant's patients had suffered complications from this procedure, and that there was no evidence the procedure had caused the problem.

The Queen's Bench of Manitoba dismissed the plaintiff's action. The Court determined that the less than 1 percent risk of complication was not a material or unusual risk that the defendant should have disclosed to the plaintiff. The Court also decided that because the plaintiff would have had the procedure anyway, the plaintiff's failure to disclose the risk was not the cause of the damage.

Children

Children have a special status under the law. While they can be held responsible for damages they cause, the court recognizes that children may not have the experience and wisdom to foresee how something they do could cause injury. Therefore, the court places a different standard of care on children than it does on adults. Very young children, usually under the age of six, are rarely found liable for their actions because they are too young to understand the notion of danger or how one action can cause another. If a child over the age of six does something that injures someone, the courts will consider the child's age, intelligence, life experience, and what a child of similar age and intelligence would have done under similar circumstances.

However, if a child performs an "adult" activity, such as driving a motorboat, this child is expected to meet the same standard of care in that activity that an adult would have to meet. Suppose that 14-year-old Carmen drives the family powerboat, fails to pay attention, and crashes into someone's dock. A court will likely apply the same standard of care to Carmen that it would to her parents because she has the same obligation to drive carefully, regardless of her age.

Parental Responsibility

Although parents are not automatically liable for damages caused by their children, they can be held liable for negligence if they fail to train their children or supervise their activities. If an unsupervised child starts playing with matches and sets the neighbour's garage on fire, a court would likely find the parents liable for damages because they failed to properly supervise their child. The main reason plaintiffs sue parents is that the children cannot pay damages if they are found liable. Parents generally have the ability to pay and often have **liability insurance** that covers the damages.

Ontario and Manitoba have enacted legislation that holds parents responsible for torts committed by their children. A child is defined as someone under the age of 18. Under the *Manitoba Parental Responsibility Act,* the plaintiff can recover damages up to $7500 from the parents of a child who commits a tort. If parents can demonstrate that they exercised reasonable supervision over the child or that the damage was not caused intentionally, they may not be held liable for the child's actions. (You will learn about intentional torts in Chapter 15.) Provinces that do not have parental responsibility legislation decide such cases under common law, on a case-by-case basis.

If children are injured because of their parents' negligence, they can sue their parents. For example, if a father fails to put a seat belt on his daughter and she is injured in a car accident, the child may sue her father for negligence. As explained in Chapter 13, the child must be represented in court by an adult. Parents usually have liability insurance that would cover some or all of the medical expenses that would have to be paid due to the child's injuries. In cases involving motor vehicle accidents, usually the insurance company, not the parent, pays the damages.

Figure 14.3 Young children do not understand how dangerous guns can be. If this child injures a playmate, it is quite likely that she would not be liable for damages.

liability insurance: insurance that covers part or all of the damages awarded in a tort case

Fast Fact
Under s. 2(1) of Ontario's *Parental Responsibility Act, 2000,* a person who has property destroyed or damaged may bring an action against the parent of the child in Small Claims Court up to the maximum allowed by that court.

CASE

Dobson v. Dobson, [1999] 2 S.C.R. 753

BACKGROUND On March 4, 1993, Cynthia Dobson, who was 27 weeks pregnant, was on her way to Moncton in a snowstorm when she lost control of her car and hit an oncoming vehicle. In the accident her fetus was injured, and later that day the baby was delivered prematurely by caesarian section. As a result of the premature birth, the child, Ryan Dobson, suffers permanent mental and physical impairment, including cerebral palsy. Acting on the child's behalf, Ryan's grandfather sued Ryan's mother for negligence.

LEGAL QUESTION Does a woman owe a duty of care to her fetus?

DECISION A New Brunswick court found that at the time of the injuries, the infant did not exist as a "person" in law. Therefore, Ryan Dobson could not sue his mother for damages. Ryan Dobson (through his grandfather) appealed the decision. The New Brunswick Court of Appeal held that Cynthia Dobson had a duty of care to the fetus and that Ryan's injuries were the result of her negligent driving while she was pregnant.

This decision was appealed to the Supreme Court of Canada. The Court held that a fetus cannot sue its mother for injuries that result from her negligence, stating that "the imposition of a legal duty of care upon a pregnant woman towards her fetus ... constitutes a severe intrusion into the lives of pregnant women." Cynthia Dobson was found not liable for Ryan's injuries.

LEGAL SIGNIFICANCE This case raised important issues about the relationship between a pregnant woman and her fetus. The Supreme Court recognized that although a pregnant woman usually does everything possible to protect the health of the fetus, she is an individual whose rights need to be protected.

Six-year-old Ryan Dobson

ANALYSIS

1. What is the legal term for Ryan's grandfather in his role as the child's representative in court?
2. Keeping in mind the three stages of a tort action, why is a person not able to sue his or her mother for injuries caused before birth?
3. If a duty had been owed to Ryan before his birth, what standard of care would his mother have had to meet? Did she, in fact, have two standards to meet? Explain.

Consider This

If you knew that you could be sued for negligence, would you stop to help at the scene of an accident? Explain.

Rescuers

In most cases, you do not have a duty of care to help others in need. However, because society believes that people should be encouraged to be Good Samaritans—people who help others in need of assistance—the courts are more lenient in cases where someone steps in to help another person but actually causes that person harm. The standard of care required of a rescuer, particularly in an emergency, is quite low.

Figure 14.4 Quebec has a *Good Samaritan Act* that imposes a duty to assist others by making it illegal to fail to assist someone in need of help. Does your province have a *Good Samaritan Act*? If not, do you think it should? Explain.

To further protect rescuers, the courts have held that the person who was negligent owes a duty of care to both the injured person and the rescuer. The court takes the view that you should have foreseen not only that your actions could cause injury, but that someone else might try to save the injured party and be harmed as well. Suppose Igor pretends to push his friend Josh into a deep lake and accidentally knocks three-year-old Ricky into the water instead. Ricky's mother jumps in to save her son, but she can't swim. In the panic, both Ricky and his mother drown. The court would likely find that Igor owed a duty of care to Ricky because he should have foreseen how his actions could have caused injury. He also owed Ricky's mother a duty of care because he should have foreseen that she would try to rescue her son.

Stage Three: Causation

The third factor a plaintiff must prove in a case of negligence is that the actions of the defendant actually caused the plaintiff's injuries. In this third stage, there are two aspects to prove: cause-in-fact and remoteness of damage.

Cause-in-Fact

Cause-in-fact is usually determined by the "but for" test. If an injury would not have happened "but for" the defendant's actions, then those actions were a cause-in-fact of the injury. Suppose a teacher took a group of students on a canoe trip and failed to supply life jackets. In a storm the canoe capsized, tossing a student into the lake. If the student drowned, a court would likely say that she would not have drowned "but for" the teacher's failure to provide a life jacket. Therefore, this negligence was the cause-in-fact of the injury.

Suppose the student fell in the water because another person accidentally pushed her, and she only drowned after a careless boat driver hit her, knocking her unconscious. "But for" not having a life jacket, she would not have drowned. However, "but for" being pushed in, she would not have drowned. She might have been saved "but for" the boat driver who hit her, causing her to

cause-in-fact: the factual "cause and effect" connection between one person's actions and another person's injuries

lose consciousness. What was the cause-in-fact of the student drowning? Who should be liable for the drowning—the teacher, the person who pushed the student into the water, or the boat driver? Should they all be liable?

To deal with the difficult issue of who should be liable in such cases, all provinces have statutes that allow the court to hold each of the negligent parties liable to a certain degree. The concept of dividing up the fault among a number of wrongdoers is known as **apportionment.**

apportionment: the division of fault among different wrongdoers

Remoteness of Damage

Even if the plaintiff can prove that the defendant's actions were a cause-in-fact of the injury, the plaintiff also has to show a *direct connection* between the wrong and the injury. In some cases, the court may decide that the defendant's actions were too far removed from the plaintiff's loss for the defendant to be held liable. If the defendant could not have *foreseen* that his or her actions could cause the type of injury that resulted, then the defendant would not be held liable. This principle is referred to as **remoteness of damage.**

remoteness of damage: harm that could not have been foreseen by the defendant due to the lack of a close connection between the wrong and the injury

Imagine that Meena is speeding on a country road. She swerves to avoid hitting a dog, goes off the road, and hits a barbed wire fence. Staples holding the wire to the fence posts pop off the posts. Later, cows grazing in the field accidentally eat the staples; as a result, some cows get sick and die. The owner of the cows sues Meena for the loss. Is Meena liable? The court would probably find that Meena's speeding was a cause-in-fact of the damage. But for her speeding, there would have been no accident, no loose staples for the cows to eat, and the cows would not have died. But was the loss of the cows a foreseeable result of Meena's speeding? Should Meena be liable for the loss of the cows, or was such a loss too *remote*? Should she be liable for the damage to the fence? Should the dog owner be liable for the loss of the cows because he let his dog run loose, and the dog caused Meena to go off the road?

The actions of the defendant can also be seen as too remote from the plaintiff's injuries if, in the chain of events leading up to the injury, some unforeseeable event occurs that becomes the legal cause of the injury. This new act is known as an **intervening act.** In the earlier example of the student who drowned on the canoe trip, the question was raised: Would the teacher be liable if a negligent boat driver hit the student, and the student drowned as a result? The teacher's failure to provide life jackets was certainly a cause-in-fact of the drowning, but was the act of the boat driver an intervening act? Should the teacher have foreseen that such a thing could happen? It could be argued that the act of the boat driver was an intervening act, and only the boat driver should be liable for the drowning.

intervening act: an unforeseeable event that interrupts the chain of events started by the defendant

In certain cases, a defendant may be liable for an injury that under normal circumstances would be too remote from the defendant's actions. This principle is called the **thin-skull rule.** Under this rule, a defendant can be found liable for *all* damages a plaintiff suffers, even if the plaintiff had a pre-existing condition that makes the injury worse than it would have been without this condition. Suppose Aldo leaves his bike on the sidewalk, and Kathryn trips over

thin-skull rule: the principle that a defendant is liable for all damages caused by negligence despite any pre-existing condition that makes the plaintiff more prone to injury

it. Instead of bruising her arm, Kathryn breaks several bones because she suffers from osteoporosis. In law, Aldo must "take his victim as he finds her," which means that he will be responsible for all the injuries suffered by the plaintiff through his neglect.

The thin-skull rule can be harsh on the defendant. In *Smith v. Leech Brain & Co. Ltd.*, [1962], an employee at work suffered a burn on his lip. The wound became malignant and the employee died of cancer. His family sued the employer for negligence. Because the plaintiff was predisposed to cancer, the burn had a more serious effect than it would have had on someone who did not have this predisposition. The court applied the thin-skull rule and found the employer liable.

Building Your Understanding

1. What is an unintentional tort?
2. Describe the three factors that must be proven in an action for negligence.
3. In law, who is considered your neighbour? How was this principle established?
4. Define the principle of foreseeability, and explain why it is so important in determining duty of care.
5. Distinguish between duty of care and standard of care, and provide an example of each.
6. How does the law define a "reasonable person"?
7. What must a plaintiff prove to be successful in a suit for medical negligence?
8. Explain the principles of cause-in-fact and remoteness of damage, providing your own examples of each.
9. In tort law, what is an intervening act?
10. Identify the name of the process used to divide fault among several negligent parties.
11. Define the thin-skull rule. Does this rule increase or decrease the standard of care? Explain.

SPECIAL TYPES OF LIABILITY

Under the law of negligence, there are several special types of liability. For instance, each of the following groups are subject to slightly different rules: manufacturers, property owners (or those who occupy property), people who serve alcohol, car and pet owners, and those who work with materials that could pollute the environment. These groups may have a higher standard of care or be subject to a wider duty of care than the average person.

Product Liability

Since the 1932 decision in *Donoghue v. Stevenson,* manufacturers have had to meet a high standard of care in order to prevent injury to consumers who use their products. To meet that standard, manufacturers have to make sure that

- the design of the product is free from harmful defects;
- the product is properly manufactured;
- the consumer is informed about how to use the product safely; and
- the consumer is warned of risks associated with using the product.

Consider This

An Ontario court ordered Bacardi to pay $80 000 in damages to a woman who was seriously injured when the bottle of Bacardi liquor she dropped on a cement floor exploded and a piece of glass flew into her eye. Why do you think the judge found the company liable for damages?

© By permission of Johnny Hart and Creators Syndicate, Inc.

product liability: the area of law that deals with negligence on the part of manufacturers

Consumers can sue manufacturers who fail to meet this standard. The area of law that deals with negligence on the part of manufacturers is called **product liability.** Consider the case of *Lambert* v. *Lastoplex,* [1972] S.C.R. 569, which illustrates how high the standard of care owed by a manufacturer can be. Lambert used a highly flammable sealer on his floor while working close to a pilot light. The open flame caused the sealer to explode and Lambert was burned. The product was not defective, and the label contained a warning not to use the product close to an open flame. Even so, the Supreme Court of Canada found the company liable because the warning did not direct the user to extinguish all flames when using the product.

Occupiers' Liability

People who own or occupy property have a duty to maintain their property so that no one entering the premises is injured. This legal responsibility is called **occupiers' liability.** Renters are considered occupiers and they, too, owe a duty of care to people entering their premises.

occupiers' liability: the responsibility of owners or renters to ensure that no one entering their premises is injured

invitee: a person invited onto a property for a business purpose

licensee: a person with express or implied permission to pay a social visit

trespasser: a person who enters another's property without permission or legal right

The courts make a distinction between the purpose of someone's presence on your property and the standard of care you owe that person. There are three kinds of visitors you can have on your property. An **invitee** is a person who has been invited onto the premises for a business purpose. For example, the person who delivers new furniture is an invitee; under common law, you owe this person the highest standard of care. A **licensee** is someone, such as a friend, who may or may not have been invited to your home for a particular occasion but has your express or implied permission to visit socially. A **trespasser** is someone who has no legal right or permission to be on your property. Burglars, stalkers, and vandals are examples of trespassers.

The courts often have difficulty distinguishing among these categories, especially invitees and licensees. Consequently, many provinces, including Prince Edward Island, Nova Scotia, Ontario, Manitoba, Alberta, and British Columbia, have simplified the law by enacting occupiers' liability legislation. Under such legislation, the standard of care owed an invitee and a licensee is

Figure 14.5 Swimming pools are popular allurements. Do you think that marking the shallow end of a pool is a form of protection or enticement? Why? What precautions could be taken at a pool to protect children from harm?

the same: the occupier has a duty to see that such visitors are reasonably safe and are warned of danger or possible dangers that could cause injury. No standard of care is owed to trespassers; however, occupiers cannot purposely injure someone who trespasses onto their property.

Children Who Trespass

The law treats children who trespass differently from adults who trespass. The courts acknowledge that children are easily attracted to sites such as swimming pools or playgrounds. Any item or site that might entice a child is known as an **allurement.** Occupiers must take all reasonable precautions to protect children who could be lured to their premises. Owners of swimming pools, for example, must surround their pools with high fences.

Hosts

People who serve alcohol to their guests are legally known as **hosts.** They may be commercial hosts, such as owners of bars or restaurants, or social hosts, who serve alcohol to guests in their home. Commercial hosts have a statutory duty of care to their patrons and to anyone who may be injured by their patrons' negligent driving. For example, if a bar owner serves alcohol to a patron whose negligence causes an accident while driving home, the bar owner may be liable for the injuries suffered by the patron as well as those suffered by other victims of the accident.

In Canada, the law with respect to social hosts is still developing. As of 2001, no social hosts had been found liable for the negligence of their intoxicated guests. However, this controversial and unsettled question might eventually engage the attention of the Supreme Court of Canada in *Prevost v. Vetter.*

Law in Your Life
List the people who have come to your home during the last week and classify them using these legal terms: invitee, licensee, and trespasser.

allurement: a site or an object that might attract children and result in causing them harm

host: someone who serves alcohol to guests or paying customers

CASE

Prevost v. Vetter (2001), B.C.C.A. 202

1. Why did the Vetters believe that the case should be dismissed?
2. Why did the British Columbia Supreme Court rule that the Vetters owed a duty to Adam Prevost?
3. Explain why causation would have to be established before the existence of a duty of care and the appropriate standard of care could be determined.

Eighteen-year-old Desiree Vetter arrived with several friends at the home of her aunt and uncle, Gregory and Shari Vetter. On past occasions, the Vetters had supervised gatherings, discouraged the use of alcohol by minors, and looked after anyone who appeared to be intoxicated. On the night in question, the Vetters went to sleep before Desiree arrived. The Vetters' 17-year-old son, Scott, was present with some friends.

Desiree and her friends brought their own alcohol, which they consumed on the Vetters' property. After a complaint about noise that led to a visit from the police, Scott woke his mother and told her the police wanted everybody to leave. His mother asked if he needed help. He said he could handle it, and his mother went back to sleep.

Adam Prevost and six other teenage passengers left with Desiree in her car. Desiree was intoxicated and, while driving, lost control of the car. Adam suffered severe injuries and sued Desiree and the Vetters.

The Vetters applied to have the claim against them dismissed without a trial on the basis that it did not raise a cause of action known to Canadian law. They argued that as social hosts, they did not owe the plaintiff a duty of care to prevent him from coming to harm.

The British Columbia Supreme Court refused to dismiss the case without a trial. It found that minors often brought alcohol to the Vetters' property and consumed it there. The court found that the Vetters' past actions had "established a 'paternalistic relationship' with intoxicated teenagers," and they had "created a dangerous situation by permitting minors to drink at their home and drive from it." Further, "the Vetters recognized they had a duty to prevent minors from the potential danger of driving under the influence of alcohol and to protect those who might drive with them." Consequently, the Vetters owed a duty of care to Adam Prevost. According to the Court, they had a duty to exercise control, and it was foreseeable that harm could result from their failure to do so. Because Shari Vetter did not exercise any control after she was woken, she breached that duty. The Vetters appealed.

The Court of Appeal found that it was not possible for the summary trial judge to determine the existence of a duty of care, the appropriate standard of care, or breach of the standard of care without first establishing facts important to the issue of causation, i.e., the issue of impairment. Establishing these facts was beyond his jurisdiction. The appeal was allowed, and a new trial was ordered.

Vicarious Liability

vicarious liability: legal responsibility for the negligence of another person

There are times when the courts will find one person liable for damages in tort law even though that person did not cause the plaintiff's injury. This kind of liability is known as **vicarious liability.** It usually applies in the workplace where employers can be held responsible for the actions of their employees.

F.S.M. v. Clarke, [1999] B.C.J. No. 1973 (B.C.S.C.)

CASE

When he was eight years old, F.S.M. was sent to St. George's Indian Residential School in British Columbia. The federal government funded the school, while members of the Anglican Church instructed the students in various subjects. Residence at the school was mandatory for children from Aboriginal communities. Prior to F.S.M.'s entry to the school, his mother signed a form that gave the government guardianship of F.S.M. until his return.

Between 1970 and 1973, a dormitory supervisor, Derek Clarke, sexually assaulted several students repeatedly, including F.S.M. In 1973, word of Clarke's activities reached the principal of the school. F.S.M. was summoned to the principal's office and asked about Clarke's behaviour. F.S.M. hinted at sexual assaults, but was too frightened to give details. The principal subsequently informed Clarke that he could either resign or "the police would call." The government (Department of Indian Affairs) was informed of Clarke's resignation, but it was not informed about Clarke's sexual misconduct.

Eventually, Clarke was charged with sexual assault; he pleaded guilty and was imprisoned. In 1998, F.S.M. sued the Anglican Church and the Canadian government for negligence. The British Columbia Supreme Court held that both the Canadian government and the Anglican Church were Clarke's employers, and both were vicariously liable for his actions. The Court ruled that the government and the Church owed F.S.M. a duty of care because they assumed a parental role in caring for F.S.M. while he was in their charge. The Court found both the government and the Church in breach of this duty of care because they put Clarke in a position where he could commit sexual assaults; then they failed to adequately supervise him to ensure that these assaults did not occur.

1. Why did the government and the Church owe F.S.M. a duty of care?
2. What standard of care did the defendants have to meet? What could they have done to meet that standard?

For example, if a mechanic fails to properly repair the brakes on a car, and the car is subsequently involved in an accident because of its faulty brakes, the mechanic is responsible for damages. The mechanic's employer could also be held liable because the employer has a responsibility to third parties for the negligence of employees acting within the normal course of their duties.

Automobile Negligence

Many tort actions result from car accidents, and many branches of law may be involved in a single accident. For instance, the driver responsible may be charged with a criminal act, fined for an infraction of provincial motor-vehicle legislation, and then sued in civil court.

Every province and territory has legislation that sets out numerous regulations for owners of motor vehicles. This legislation imposes vicarious liability in that the owner is liable for damages that result from the negligent behaviour of anyone who drives the owner's car. As you learned in Chapter 13, vehicle owners are required to carry substantial liability insurance; a defendant may still have to pay for any damages that exceed this insurance coverage. Driving without insurance is a provincial offence that carries hefty penalties. In Ontario, a first offence could bring a fine of up to $25 000. In addition, uninsured owners or drivers could be liable for large damage awards.

Strict Liability

Certain activities or situations are so dangerous that in the case of injury, the plaintiff does not have to prove the defendant was negligent; the defendant is automatically liable. This principle is called **strict liability.** In common law, strict liability pertains to fires or vicious animals that might cause harm. It also applies in cases involving leaking toxic waste or the escape of dangerous fumes. Strict liability is built into specific legislation. Environmental protection acts, for example, often impose strict liability on the part of persons or municipalities whose actions result in pollution or damage to the natural environment.

Several provinces have introduced legislation that attempts to impose strict liability on dog owners. In some cases, owners may be liable even if their dogs have never bitten anyone before. In fact, the plaintiff may not have to prove that the defendant owed him or her a duty of care. On the other hand, under some statutes, being strictly liable for a dog's behaviour does not mean that the owner will be found 100 percent liable. Dog owners may be able to argue certain defences; for example, the plaintiff could have been teasing the dog, or the dog may have been protecting the owner's property. Having a credible defence could lessen the owner's liability.

strict liability: the defendant is automatically liable for an injury caused by a dangerous substance or activity even if the defendant was not negligent

Figure 14.6 Do you think the principle of strict liability should apply to companies that destroy buildings with dynamite? If so, why? Who could be endangered by this activity?

Building Your Understanding

1. Use an example to explain the concept of product liability.
2. Why have many provinces introduced occupiers' liability legislation? Under such legislation, what standard of care do occupiers owe trespassers?
3. Why are children who trespass treated differently by law from adult trespassers?
4. When might an employer or a car owner become vicariously liable for damages in the event of an accident?
5. What is strict liability? Provide two examples of situations in which strict liability would apply.

DEFENCES TO NEGLIGENCE

In most cases, if you are being sued for negligence, the plaintiff must prove that you owed a duty, breached the standard of care, and caused the injuries. In your defence, you can provide evidence to show you did not owe a duty, you met the standard of care, or your acts did not cause the damage. In addition, you may be able to prove that the plaintiff contributed to the cause of injury, knowingly accepted the risk of harm, or waited too long to sue you.

Contributory Negligence

The defence known as **contributory negligence** states that the plaintiff contributed to the injury by displaying unreasonable conduct. Contributory negligence is a partial defence, which means that the defendant will still bear a portion of the blame. Suppose while skiing, you stop to rest just under a rise on the hill. Another skier sees you at the last minute and is unable to stop. The skier crashes into you, breaking your leg and ruining your skis. You sue the skier for damages. The court may apportion the liability between you and the defendant because it determined that by stopping where it was difficult for other skiers to see you, you failed to act safely. Therefore, your actions contributed to the accident. The court could decide that you were 25 percent responsible for the accident and the defendant was 75 percent responsible for skiing too fast in an area with limited visibility.

contributory negligence: negligent acts by the plaintiff that helped cause the plaintiff's injuries

Law in Your Life
Suppose you are not wearing a seat belt when you are injured in an automobile accident caused by the negligence of the other driver. If you sustain injuries that you would not have suffered if you had been wearing a seat belt, the court may find you partly liable for your injuries and lower the amount of damages you can recover.

Voluntary Assumption of Risk

Another defence to negligence, called **voluntary assumption of risk (or *volenti non fit injuria*)**, claims that the plaintiff knowingly and willingly assumed the potential risks normally associated with a particular activity. Activities such as bungee jumping or paragliding, or contact sports such as football or boxing carry a certain level of risk. For example, as willing participants, hockey players cannot sue other players for causing harm because they have already accepted the risk that during the game they may be injured. Voluntary assumption of risk is a complete defence, which means that even though the defendant may have been negligent, the plaintiff will not be awarded anything if the defence is successful.

voluntary assumption of risk (or *volenti non fit injuria*): the defence that no liability exists because the plaintiff agreed to accept the risk normally associated with the activity

Figure 14.7 Rides like the "Giant Swing" are common in amusement parks. If someone falls, who will be liable? What will the plaintiff have to prove? What defence could the defendant use?

waiver: a document signed by the plaintiff, releasing the defendant from liability in the event of an injury

A person can also assume risk if he or she signs a waiver before the activity begins. A **waiver** is a contract that exempts or frees the defendant from liability in the case of injury. Having someone sign a waiver, however, does not automatically release a defendant from liability, as you will learn in the case of *Crocker v. Sundance Northwest Resorts Ltd.* (page 388).

CASE

Laws v. Wright, [2000] A.B.Q.B. 49

1. What claims did Laws use in trying to prove negligence?
2. Why did the judge dismiss the case?
3. How would you decide this case? Why?

Jane Laws boarded her horse, Snort, at Trakehner Glen Stables. Snort was put in a stable beside Salish, a very nervous and temperamental horse owned by Linda Howard. Linda told Jane not to feed Salish because the horse had once bitten her and was too unpredictable. Jane ignored this advice and fed Salish carrots. On February 24, 1998, Salish bit Jane, causing the loss of the tip of Jane's right thumb. Jane sued the stables for negligence in failing to protect the users of the barn from Salish and for failing to warn her of the potential and real danger Salish posed.

The defendants claimed that the plaintiff had been warned not to feed Salish and to stay away from the horse because sometimes it behaved aggressively. They also pointed out that the stables had large warning signs: "Caution … Be advised that all equine activities involve inherent risks—proceed at your own risk."

The judge dismissed the case on a number of grounds, one of which was the defence of *volenti non fit injuria*. He found that Jane Laws was very experienced when it came to dealing with horses. She was aware that horses sometimes behaved unpredictably, and she had been warned not to feed this particular horse. By continuing to do so, the plaintiff had "knowingly assumed the risk" of injury.

Other Defences

There are three other defences in negligence actions that are closely related: inevitable accident, act of God, and explanation. Because the circumstances that support these defences rarely occur, the courts are often suspicious of such claims.

An **inevitable accident** is caused by something the plaintiff had no control over and could not have prevented by any amount of reasonable care. Suppose Jessica is driving along a country road when a bee flies through the open window and stings her. She loses control and hits an oncoming car. If Jessica is sued for negligence, she could argue that the accident was the inevitable result of being stung by the bee. An **act of God** is similar to an inevitable accident, but the event that caused the accident must be a natural event that is both extraordinary and unexpected, such as violent windstorms or torrential rains.

If the accident was not caused by an uncontrollable event, Jessica may still have a defence if the accident happened even though she took every precaution. In other words, there might be a valid **explanation** for the accident other than an event or any carelessness on her part. Suppose Jessica is driving slowly on a snow-covered road because she knows there may be ice under the snow. She sees a stop sign ahead and gently starts to brake well in advance. Nevertheless, she hits some black ice under the snow and goes off the road, damaging someone's fence. She might be able to explain that the accident occurred even though she took as much care as she possibly could.

inevitable accident: a defence that claims an accident was unavoidable due to an uncontrollable event

act of God: a defence that claims an accident was caused by an extraordinary, unexpected natural event

explanation: a defence that claims the accident occurred for a valid reason even though the defendant took every precaution

Statute of Limitations

People are expected to sue for damages within a reasonable time. After all, memories fade and witnesses may move or die. Every province has a law, known as a **statute of limitations,** specifying the period in which a person must sue for damages. Expiry of that time period is another defence in tort law. The plaintiff's failure to bring an action to court in time may mean the case is dismissed and the plaintiff receives no compensation, even if the plaintiff suffered serious injuries or would likely have won the case.

Some legislation includes the limitation period within the act itself as in the following example from the *Highway Traffic Act* of Ontario:

statute of limitations: a law that specifies the time within which legal action must be taken

> 206(1) No proceeding shall be brought against a person for the recovery of damages occasioned by a motor vehicle after the expiration of two years from the time when damages were sustained.

This section means that anyone who intends to sue the operator or owner of a motor vehicle for damages must commence a court action within two years of the accident.

Limitation periods differ depending on the law of the province and on the type of defendant. To sue certain defendants such as doctors, dentists, or municipal corporations, the law requires a court action to be commenced within a fairly short period of time or the plaintiff loses the opportunity to sue.

CASE: *Smith v. McGillivary,* [2001] N.S.S.C. 17

1. Why did the Court dismiss Smith's case?
2. If the case had gone to court, what defences would you have used?

In August 1989, Richard Smith went to his dentist, Dr. Ron McGillivary, who removed two gold inlays (a type of crown). Later, Smith developed severe tooth decay in the same two teeth. Eventually, he had to have the two teeth extracted. In July 1998, Smith served notice that he was suing his dentist for negligence. The Supreme Court of Nova Scotia found that under the *Limitations of Actions Act,* a plaintiff had two years to begin legal action. Because Smith had not commenced his action within the two-year period, the Court dismissed the case.

Building Your Understanding

1. What is meant by contributory negligence? Use an example to illustrate your answer.
2. Identify three defences, other than contributory negligence, that a defendant may use in a tort action.
3. Kurt Jones was seriously injured in a professional hockey game when Tom Harris gave Jones a particularly hard check. Do you think Jones would be successful if he sued Harris for damages? Why or why not?
4. In which of the following situations do you think the defence of voluntary assumption of risk would apply? Explain your choice.
   a) A passenger who refused to wear a seat belt is injured in an accident.
   b) Dmitri accepts a ride even thought he knows that the driver is intoxicated. He is injured in a car accident.
   c) Kirsten, who has peanut allergies, falls ill after eating a candy bar. No warning about peanuts appeared on the wrapper.
   d) Nurul has never watched or played football. He is just beginning to learn English and did not understand the rules of the game. The first time he is on the field he is seriously injured.
5. Distinguish between an inevitable accident and an act of God, and provide an example of each.

LOOKING BACK

Reviewing Your Vocabulary

act of God *p. 383*
allurement *p. 377*
apportionment *p. 374*
cause-in-fact *p. 373*
contributory negligence *p. 381*
duty of care *p. 367*
explanation *p. 383*
foreseeability *p. 368*
hosts *p. 377*
inevitable accident *p. 383*
intervening act *p. 374*
invitee *p. 376*

liability insurance *p. 371*
licensee *p. 376*
neighbour principle *p. 367*
negligence *p. 366*
occupiers' liability *p. 376*
product liability *p. 376*
reasonable person *p. 369*
remoteness of damage *p. 374*
specialized standard of care *p. 369*
standard of care *p. 369*

statute of limitations *p. 383*
strict liability *p. 380*
thin-skull rule *p. 374*
tort *p. 366*
trespasser *p. 376*
unintentional torts *p. 366*
vicarious liability *p. 378*
voluntary assumption of risk or *volenti non fit injuria p. 381*
waiver *p. 382*

Quick Quiz

1. Match the vocabulary terms above with these clues:
   a) the plaintiff participated in the activity knowing it was dangerous
   b) the actions of the plaintiff helped cause his or her injuries
   c) a playground, park, or swimming pool that may attract children
   d) waiting too long to sue your doctor may prevent you from suing at all
   e) although one person caused the injuries, someone else is liable for the damages
   f) the manufacturer is liable if its product harms anyone
   g) the responsibility to avoid injuring someone
   h) the injury suffered by the plaintiff was the result of the defendant's actions
   i) the principle that you must take your victim as you find him or her
   j) the ability of a reasonable person to anticipate the consequences of an action
   k) a civil wrong
   l) harming another person through carelessness

Checking Your Knowledge

2. Why are some individuals held to a higher standard of care than others?
3. What standard of care is generally required of rescuers? Why?
4. Describe the two aspects of causation that must be proven to show that the defendant's actions caused the plaintiff's injuries. Provide an example to illustrate each aspect.
5. What steps do manufacturers have to take to ensure their products are safe for consumers?
6. Give an example of an invitee, a licensee, and a trespasser.
7. Create two imaginary cases that involve unintentional torts. For one case, use the defence of negligence that a duty was not owed, the defendant met the standard of care, *or* the defendant's action was not the cause of the injury. For the other case, use the defence of inevitable accident, act of God, *or* explanation to argue the case.

Developing Your Thinking and Inquiry Skills

8. List three situations in your home or school that could lead to a tort liability. Identify the tort by name and describe how the risk of injury could be avoided.

9. Alex wanted to try bungee jumping, so he went to a company that operated bungee-jumping equipment at the local exhibition centre. Alex was warned that the activity was dangerous, so he signed a waiver acknowledging the risk. However, unknown to Alex, the operator that day was a new employee who did not know that the jump had to be adjusted for someone of Alex's weight. The bungee cord ripped apart. Alex fell and suffered severe injuries.

    a) You are Alex's lawyer. List the important facts of this case. What are the grounds for Alex's case against the defendant?
    b) What defence would the company likely use in this case?

10. At lunchtime Rafay was lifting weights in the school weight room. Rafay asked the teacher on duty to "spot" him while he tried to increase his normal lifting level. The teacher came over and was standing near Rafay when the fire alarm went off. The teacher immediately moved away to get the rest of the students out of the building. The noise startled Rafay, and he dropped the weight on his chest causing serious injuries. Rafay sued the teacher and the school board.

    a) What kind of tort would this be?
    b) Apply the three tests of negligence to this case and explain whether you believe Rafay would be successful in his lawsuit.

Communicating Your Ideas

11. Work in groups of three and, using examples and information from this chapter, create a storyboard for a television program involving a case of negligence. The storyboard should include an incident, people involved in the incident, and damages or injuries suffered. It should conclude with the judge's decision and reasons for the decision. Present your storyboard to the class.

12. Prepare and present a class debate on the following statement: Tobacco companies knowingly manufacture a dangerous product and sell it to an unsuspecting public. Therefore, these companies are negligent.

Putting It All Together

13. Watch a movie or TV program dealing with tort law. Your teacher will give you some suggestions based on real cases. Prepare an analysis of the case using the following outline:
    - Background
    - Legal question
    - Decision
    - Legal, social, historical, or political significance
    - Analysis

    Use the case of *Crocker* v. *Sundance Northwest Resorts* as a guide (see page 388).

14. Select a recent and controversial Supreme Court decision dealing with the tort of negligence. Divide into three groups with each group representing one of the following: the appellant, the respondent, and the justices of the court. The groups representing the appellant and the respondent will present written briefs and oral arguments to the court. The group representing the court will prepare questions after reviewing the written briefs. The court will then use the oral argument session to probe for weaknesses in each side's case. Justices may also ask the litigants questions from the bench. To find out more about cases from the Supreme Court of Canada, visit **www.pearsoned.ca/law**.

CASES

Cempel v. Harrison Hot Springs Hotel Ltd., [1998] 6 W.W.R. 233 (B.C.C.A.)

One night in May 1993, 16-year-old Cassandra Cempel and her friends went camping at Harrison Hot Springs, near Chilliwack, British Columbia. It was late when they arrived, but they decided to go to the hot pool. Instead, by mistake they went to the source pool, which contained scalding hot water. The pool was obviously closed, but Cassandra started to climb over a fence that surrounded the pool. As she was climbing the fence, part of it gave way and bent over. Cassandra fell into the water, which was 60°C. She was badly burned and spent 51 days in hospital. Cassandra sued Harrison Hot Springs Hotel Ltd. for damages.

The trial court found that the fencing around the source pool was inadequate, and the hotel was in breach of its duty to take care that persons on the premises were reasonably safe. It also found the plaintiff's actions "foolhardy and imprudent," and that she was "primarily the author of her own misfortune." The court apportioned fault 75 percent to the plaintiff and 25 percent to the hotel. The plaintiff appealed on the basis that she could not have anticipated the kind of damage she suffered and that the trial court had attributed too much fault to the plaintiff and too little to the defendant.

The British Columbia Court of Appeal agreed with the trial judge as to the law, but altered the apportionment of damages. In the opinion of the Court, apportionment should be assessed on the extent of departure from the respective standards of care. The court apportioned 60 percent to the defendant and 40 percent to the plaintiff.

1. Was Cempel an invitee or a trespasser? Should this determination have any bearing on the duty of care owed and the damages awarded? Explain.
2. Do you agree that both plaintiff and defendant should share liability? Support your view.
3. Explain the significance of the altered apportionment regarding the "the extent of departure from the respective standards of care."

Empire Co. v. Sheppard, [2001] N.F.C.A. 10

Joan Sheppard was shopping in a mall in Corner Brook, Newfoundland. At one point she stepped on the escalator, placing her left hand on the rail. As she turned to speak to her husband, her coat hooked onto the seam of the escalator wall. The snagging of her coat caused her head to jerk back suddenly. The woman behind her reacted quickly and managed to free Joan's coat, preventing a more serious injury. As a result of the accident, Joan suffered back and neck injuries. She sued the mall.

The trial judge found that because Joan was an invitee of the mall, the mall owner owed her a duty to use reasonable care to prevent injury. He further found that the mall owner failed to meet the standard of care required and was liable for Joan's injuries. The Newfoundland Court of Appeal reversed this decision. It found that because the owner of the mall had the elevators examined regularly by professionals, and because a security person had examined the escalator the day of the accident, the mall owner had used reasonable care in maintaining its escalator. It had met the standard of care required and was not liable for Joan's injuries.

1. What was the cause of Joan's injury?
2. Identify the appellant and the respondent in this appeal.
3. Do you think the Court of Appeal would have rendered the same decision if Joan had suffered a more serious injury? Explain.

CASES

Crocker v. Sundance Northwest Resorts, [1988] 1. S.C.R. 1186

BACKGROUND As a promotion for its ski resort, Sundance Northwest Resorts hosted a competition in which a two-person team raced down a steep hill in an inner tube. The prize was $200. Mr. Crocker paid the $15 entrance fee and signed the entry form, without reading it. Consequently, he did not know the form contained a waiver clause.

Crocker was visibly drunk at the beginning of the first race. At the start of the second race, the owner of Sundance asked Crocker if he was in any condition to compete but did nothing to stop him. The resort manager also suggested that he not continue but took no further steps to restrict him when he insisted on competing. During the second race, Crocker suffered a serious neck injury and was rendered quadriplegic.

Crocker sued the ski resort for negligence. At trial, he was successful in his suit, but the Court applied the defence of contributory negligence. Crocker was awarded 75 percent of his damages. He appealed. The Ontario Court of Appeal overturned the trial judge's decision and found that the resort was not liable at all. Crocker appealed this decision to the Supreme Court of Canada.

LEGAL QUESTION: Did Sundance owe a duty of care to Mr. Crocker? If a duty existed, what standard of care was required and was the standard met?

DECISION The Supreme Court found that the plaintiff's injuries were "clearly foreseeable in this case," and the resort failed to take reasonable steps to prevent Mr. Crocker from competing in the race that caused his injuries. By allowing Crocker to participate in the event, the resort breached the duty of care it owed him and was therefore liable for damages that resulted from its negligence. However, the Court did uphold the finding that Crocker was 25 percent liable due to contributory negligence.

LEGAL SIGNIFICANCE The Court ruled that when a resort organizes an event to enhance its profits, it has a duty of care to prevent a visibly intoxicated person from competing in a dangerous competition. Crocker's signing of the entry form containing the waiver did not release the resort from its duty of care because Crocker's attention had not been drawn to the waiver; in fact, he had not read it and had no idea it existed.

Figure 14.8 Should resorts be allowed to hold competitions that may be dangerous? Explain.

ANALYSIS

1. What did Mr. Crocker have to show in order to prove the resort was negligent?
2. What are three possible defences Sundance could argue in this case?
3. Why do you think Crocker appealed the trial judge's decision? How did the trial judge's decision differ from that of the Supreme Court of Canada?
4. If Crocker's intoxication had not been evident, would Sundance Resorts still have been liable for his injuries? Explain.

Intentional Torts

15

CHAPTER OUTLINE

Intentional Torts

Intentional Interference with the Person

Intentional Interference with Property

Defences to Intentional Interference

Defamation of Character

FOCUS YOUR LEARNING

What is an intentional tort and how does it differ from a crime?

What are intentional interferences with the person and with property?

What are the defences to intentional torts?

How does someone damage another person's character?

Zits

WHAT DO YOU THINK?

- Explain what happens in this cartoon.
- From what you have learned about torts, has a tort been committed in this situation? Explain.

389

intentional torts: actions intended to cause injury to others

People are often harmed by the deliberate actions of others. The injury may result from a physical attack, a false rumour, or a stroll through a stranger's property. In this chapter, you will learn about **intentional torts**—actions intended to cause injury to others by interfering with their personal safety, health, or enjoyment of property. You will also learn about the defences that are available to persons being sued for intentional torts.

INTENTIONAL TORTS

When someone intentionally injures a person or interferes with a person's property, an intentional tort has been committed. Intentional torts such as assault (the threat of bodily harm), battery (harmful physical contact), trespass, and defamation (damaging someone's reputation) are wrongs that have been recognized in common law for centuries. The law of intentional torts is based on the principle that individuals, in the course of their daily lives, should be free from interference or injury from others.

intent: the desire to commit an act for a specific purpose

How does an intentional tort differ from an unintentional tort? The difference is the element of **intent.** As shown by his or her actions, the perpetrator of an intentional tort must desire to bring about a specific result or consequence, or be substantially certain that those actions will have that result or consequence. If Sam swings a stick at Joe, hits him in the head and gives him a concussion, an intentional tort has occurred. Sam may have intended to *scare* Joe, not actually hit him and give him a concussion. However, Sam's motive for swinging the stick is not important. He intended to carry out an action that could have a specific consequence. If Sam swings a stick intending to hit Joe but misses and hits Andrea, an intentional tort has still occurred. It does not matter that Sam made a mistake in the second case and hit someone he did not intend to hit. In a battery action, once the plaintiff establishes that the defendant hit him or her, the plaintiff must prove that the contact was intentional and not negligent.

Figure 15.1 Someone who commits an intentional tort must intend, by his or her actions, to bring about a specific consequence. What consequences might result from this action?

An intentional tort also has to cause an injury to someone. If your neighbour spreads a false rumour that you are using your basement as headquarters for drug dealing, and as a result you are asked to resign from your coaching position on the local basketball team, your reputation has been damaged and an injury has taken place. If your neighbour tells someone that you were charged with illegal possession of marijuana, and you actually were, her comments have not damaged your reputation because she is telling the truth. In this case, any injury to your reputation was caused by your illegal acts.

Intentional Torts and Criminal Acts

Many events that involve a criminal act might lead to legal action as an intentional tort. Often the same event can result in two distinct legal consequences: one in criminal law and one in civil law. The purpose of criminal court is to bring the accused to justice and protect society from further offences. The purpose of civil court is to compensate victims for loss or injury. If an accused is found guilty in criminal court for vandalizing your property, the court may order the accused to pay you some compensation as part of the sentence. However, to receive complete compensation, generally you must sue the defendant in civil court.

Another significant difference between a tort and a crime relates to the burden of proof that must be met in order to win the case. As you learned in Chapter 7, in criminal law the burden of proof must be beyond a reasonable doubt. In civil law, proof is based on a balance of probabilities, as explained in Chapter 13.

Figure 15.2 This chart lists actions that are both torts and crimes.

Torts and Crimes		
If one person	**it is the crime of**	**and also the tort of**
• hits another	• assault	• battery
• holds another against his/her will	• forcible confinement	• false imprisonment
• breaks into another's house [with the intent to steal]	• break and enter	• trespass to land
• take's another's belongings	• theft	• conversion, or trespass to goods
• kills another	• homicide	• wrongful death

SOURCE: Margaret Kerr, JoAnn Kurtz, and Laurence M. Olivo, *Canadian Tort Law in a Nutshell* (Toronto: Carswell, 1997) 5.

Building Your Understanding

1. What is an intentional tort? How does it differ from an unintentional tort?
2. Name two differences between an intentional tort and a criminal act.
3. Explain how the same event can lead to both a criminal action and a civil action.
4. Reread *R.* v. *Quinlan* in Chapter 9 on page 224. Explain how this case might lead to a civil action. Identify the tort, the plaintiff, and the defendant in such an action.

INTENTIONAL INTERFERENCE WITH THE PERSON

One of the largest categories of intentional torts is known as "intentional interference with the person" and it includes such offences as assault, battery, medical battery, false imprisonment, malicious prosecution, intentional infliction of mental suffering, and invasion of privacy. Many forms of intentional interference with the person evolved out of the law of "trespass to the person." Today, however, trespass is popularly thought of as wrongful entry onto someone's land. Trespass will be discussed later in the section on Intentional Interference with Property.

Assault

assault: offensive conduct that causes a reasonable apprehension of imminent harm

When we hear the word *assault,* we tend to think of a harmful physical act. In tort law, however, assault has a different meaning. In the case of **assault,** the plaintiff must simply prove that the defendant threatened imminent harm, the plaintiff believed the threat was genuine, and the defendant could have carried out the threat. Suppose Teresa and Elena share a ski lift. Elena's skis accidentally touch Teresa. Teresa yells angrily to Elena, "Do that again and I'll push you off the lift." Would this be an assault? Perhaps. The courts would have to decide whether Elena actually believed Teresa's threat, whether Teresa was capable of carrying out the threat, and if Elena actually feared she would be harmed because of the threat. If Teresa were a tiny woman and Elena a physically imposing woman, it would be hard to believe that Elena feared imminent harm. But the harm does not have to be physical. Assault is one of the few torts that permit a plaintiff to recover damages even if no physical injury occurs. "Assault" as one judge said, "lies in the apprehension of a danger in the mind of the intended victim." In other words, a victim merely has to *believe* that the threat can be carried out. A person who points a gun at someone or threatens to unleash a growling dog could be liable for assault.

Battery

battery: intentional, unauthorized physical contact that the victim considers harmful or offensive

If Teresa carries out her threat and pushes Elena off the ski lift, Elena may sue for **battery.** A person can also be liable for battery for intentionally touching someone without his or her consent. "Touching" does not have to *injure* anyone, but it has to *offend* the person in some way. Defendants have been liable for battery for actions as seemingly harmless as a hug or a kiss simply because such an action was considered offensive by the plaintiff. Generally, the court looks at whether a reasonable person would find the contact unacceptable or offensive. Assault and battery are often tried together because in most cases the assault occurs first and is quickly followed by the battery.

Figure 15.3 Every day people are touched or pushed by others in crowded places such as subways or busy streets. Why, in most cases, are these actions not considered battery?

Does this mean you can sue every time someone bumps into you in the school hallway? Not likely. The courts recognize that every day we are subjected to all kinds of minor jostling in crowded areas. Unless the bump was deliberate and caused you injury, it would not likely constitute a case of battery.

Dunne v. *Gauthier* (2000), B.C.S.C. 1603

CASE

On November 21, 1996, Mr. Dunne, a bus driver, picked up the four Gauthier children for school. They informed Dunne that they would not be returning home on the bus that afternoon. However, at the end of the day, three of the four children boarded the bus. Nothing was said about the absence of the fourth child.

Meanwhile, Mr. Gauthier received a phone message from his son, upset at being left behind at school. When the school bus arrived at the Gauthier home that afternoon, Gauthier entered the bus, yelling at Dunne and threatening him. When Dunne tried to phone the bus garage, Gauthier grabbed the phone from Dunne, tore it from its mount, and threw it out of the bus. He then grabbed Dunne by the neck and forced him to the ground. When Gauthier finally let go, he told Dunne that if he ever saw him on the road he would "take him and the bus out." Dunne believed Gauthier's threat because Gauthier drove a large tractor-trailer unit. Dunne suffered a number of physical injuries and psychological problems as a result of the incident. He was unable to return to work.

Gauthier was convicted in criminal court for his actions against Dunne. Dunne then sued in civil court for the losses associated with the assault and battery. Gauthier was ordered to pay Dunne $20 025 in damages.

1. Which of the actions in this case would be an assault? A battery?
2. How does the court determine whether a threat constitutes an assault in tort law? Do you think Gauthier's threats would be considered an assault? Why or why not?

Sexual Assault

A growing number of survivors of sexual assault, spousal abuse, or incest are seeking compensation for their injuries in the civil courts. While these people may seek financial compensation for their injuries, many also want to have their assailants publicly exposed for their wrongdoing.

Many cases of this nature involve people who were sexually abused while in the care of residential facilities such as group homes, camps, long-term care hospitals, boarding schools, and residential schools for Aboriginal children, which were established by religious groups and by the federal government.

LAW IN ACTION

Justice Delayed

1. Why would the government prefer to settle these claims out of court?
2. Do you think mediation is an appropriate method for resolving this kind of dispute? Explain.

In October 2001, the federal government announced that if victims of abuse at residential schools settle out of court, it will pay 70 percent of compensation claims. The government and individual victims are to negotiate settlements through arbitration and other forms of dispute resolution.

More than 8500 plaintiffs have brought tort claims against the offenders, the government, and religious organizations. But some former students of residential schools are reluctant to accept the government's offer because they feel the process takes too long, and it could be years before they receive compensation.

"They should speed it up … we've waited too long," said Flora Northwest, a 56-year-old who spent nine years in the 1950s and 1960s in a residential school in Alberta.

Medical Battery

As you learned in Chapter 14, a doctor must obtain a patient's consent before carrying out a medical procedure. If a doctor does not explain the procedure to the patient properly, performs a different procedure from what was proposed, or obtains consent through fraud or misrepresentation, then the doctor is liable for **medical battery.** For example, in the case of *Gerula* v. *Flores,* the doctor had consent to operate on a disc in the patient's back. Unfortunately, he operated on the wrong disc. This was a battery. The doctor later operated on the correct disc. Although he obtained the patient's permission for the second operation, he did not inform his patient of the original mistake. Therefore, the consent to the second operation was not a valid consent, and the doctor was liable for a second battery.

medical battery: performing the wrong medical procedure or performing a procedure without the patient's consent

Sometimes it may not be possible to get the patient's consent. For instance, if a patient is unconscious, a doctor is permitted to administer treatment but cannot provide any treatment that goes beyond what is necessary to save the patient's life or preserve the patient's health. If an unconscious patient is at risk of dying but carries a card stating that because of religious beliefs certain measures are not to be taken even in life-threatening circumstances, the doctor may face a moral dilemma. Should the doctor respect the wishes of the patient, even if it means the patient could die? What if the patient has had

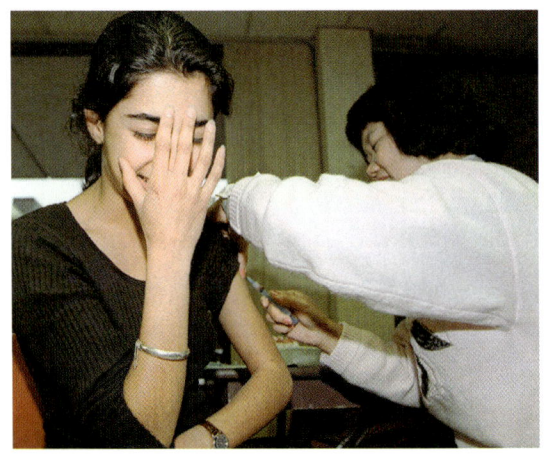

Figure 15.4 Is extending your arm for an injection a form of consent? Explain.

a change of mind since signing the card? What if the card was signed under duress?

In *Malette* v. *Shulman* (1990), a doctor was found liable for medical battery when he gave an unconscious woman a blood transfusion. He knew that the patient carried a card in her purse indicating she was a Jehovah's Witness and would not accept blood because of her religious beliefs, even in an emergency. The doctor acted on the belief that the woman would have died without the transfusion.

> **Fast Fact**
> Patients in hospitals must sign consent forms before undergoing surgery or other kinds of treatment.

False Imprisonment

If someone confines you without legal justification and against your will, and you cannot escape, the tort of **false imprisonment** has occurred. Once the plaintiff shows that the defendant restrained the plaintiff's liberty, the defendant must show that the restraint was legally justified in order to avoid liability. The word *false* in this instance means "wrongful." You do not have to be held in a jail to be falsely imprisoned. You could be held against your will in someone's car, in an office, or in a room—wherever a situation is so intimidating that you feel you have no option but to stay.

While most cases of false imprisonment involve plaintiffs being held against their will, there are situations where plaintiffs "consent" to the arrest or imprisonment to avoid embarrassment. For example, if a store detective arrested you at your local mall, you might "consent" to go with the detective to avoid an embarrassing scene that could damage your reputation. The courts have determined that such consent is not voluntary and, therefore, cannot prevent you from suing if the arrest was unlawful.

false imprisonment: detention of a person without consent and without legal authority

> **Law in Your Life**
> Suppose you were trying on jeans in a dressing room, and the retailer negligently closed the store, locking you inside. Could you sue the retailer for false imprisonment? Explain.

Malicious Prosecution

How many times have you seen a television program or a movie in which a person is charged and tried for a crime he or she did not commit? Such scenes are not only found in fiction, they can also happen in real life. Suppose Ly is arrested and charged with murder even though the police have little evidence connecting her to the crime. Ly's case goes to court, but the judge dismisses the case due to lack of evidence. Should Ly be compensated for the mistake made by the police and the Crown? What about the mental anguish she suffered, the loss of wages she incurred, and the damage to her reputation?

If the police and the Crown acted in good faith, and they had reasonable grounds to believe that Ly was guilty, then she will probably not receive compensation for their mistake. However, if the criminal proceedings against her were unjustified, she may be able to claim malicious prosecution. **Malicious prosecution** is a tort that occurs when individuals abuse the process of the courts by allowing proceedings to be brought or continued even though they know that the prosecution is wrong. To constitute malicious prosecution several conditions usually occur:

malicious prosecution: wrongful prosecution of a person without reasonable and probable cause

- Someone has to be charged with a crime when there are no reasonable grounds for the charge.

- The individual instigating or continuing the proceedings must be motivated by malice (the desire to harm another).
- The proceedings against the defendant must be resolved in the defendant's favour.
- The defendant suffers damages as a result of the wrongful proceedings.

CASE

Oniel v. Marks (2001), Ont. C.A. C30682

1. What factors must exist for a tort of malicious prosecution? Were these factors present in this case?
2. What evidence did Oniel have to support his claim?
3. On what basis did Oniel appeal the jury's decision?

On April 10, 1985, Mr. Cantero told the police that he had been robbed of $40 while in a local bookstore and assaulted later that day in a cinema. Mr. Cantero identified Mr. Oniel as the person who had committed the crimes. The police arrested Oniel and charged him with theft. Oniel protested his innocence. He asked the police to interview two potential witnesses: his hairdresser who could confirm that at the time of the robbery his hair was long, not short as described by Cantero; and the employee at the bookstore where the alleged robbery took place. The police did not follow up on either of these requests.

Oniel was charged solely on the identification of Cantero. Prior to the trial, Oniel's lawyer sent a letter to the senior Crown attorney that pointed out several major inconsistencies in Cantero's statement. The letter also informed the Crown attorney that the bookstore employee had given a statement claiming that it was highly unlikely that the robbery took place in the store. Despite this information, no significant further investigation took place, and the trial went ahead.

At his trial, Oniel was acquitted. He then filed suit in civil court against the two police officers for malicious prosecution. His case was dismissed by a jury. Oniel appealed the decision because the judge failed to explain to the jury that even though the police had grounds for charging Oniel, they continued with the prosecution after they discovered that no reasonable grounds existed. In January 2001, the Court of Appeal found that the police officers "lacked reasonable and probable cause to continue the prosecution" and awarded Oniel $75 000 in damages.

Nervous Shock and Mental Suffering

Every day people are shocked or frightened by unpleasant news or experiences, and most of these incidents never result in a court case. However, if someone deliberately shocks another person or acts in a way that causes a person mental anguish resulting in emotional stress and illness, the perpetrator could be liable for **intentional infliction of nervous shock or mental suffering.** The defendant's conduct must be extreme and intentional, and the victim must be able to prove that he or she suffered mental or physical harm as a result of the defendant's conduct.

A precedent recognizing liability for intentional infliction of nervous shock was set in England in 1897. In *Wilkinson v. Downton,* Mr. Downton told Mrs.

intentional infliction of nervous shock or mental suffering: deliberately shocking someone, causing the victim to suffer mental or physical harm

Figure 15.5 Street musician Michael McTaggart, also known as Subway Elvis, won his case against Halton police for wrongful prosecution. The judge decided that McTaggart had not received a fair trial on bank robbery charges because a police officer failed to inform the Crown attorney that another suspect had been identified. How would the police officer's actions constitute malicious prosecution?

Wilkinson that her husband had been in a serious accident and had broken his legs. The story was a prank, but Mrs. Wilkinson believed it to be true. She suffered emotional shock and was physically ill for several weeks. Mr. Wilkinson sued Mr. Downton for damages. The courts found the defendant liable because his intentional shock to the plaintiff resulted in injury.

Invasion of Privacy

As more personal data is monitored and stored electronically, people have become concerned about the legal protection of their privacy. For example, should police officers have access to your personal medical records if you are under investigation for a crime? Should a government be allowed to compile a data bank on your health and financial records? Should businesses be allowed to monitor their employees' e-mail? Should newspapers be allowed to print someone's photograph without permission, or expose details about a person's private life?

Traditionally, governments have been reluctant to establish invasion of privacy legislation for fear of interfering with certain freedoms such as freedom of the press or freedom of expression. What is the correct balance between an individual's right to privacy and the public's legitimate interest in information? Invasion of privacy may be considered an evolving tort because provinces deal with it differently. Some provinces, such as Alberta and Ontario, do not have legislation that identifies invasion of privacy as a tort, but they have introduced laws to protect personal information held by other people. For example, the Ontario *Personal Health Information Privacy Act* is designed to protect the privacy of citizens regarding information about their personal health. Other provinces such as British Columbia, Manitoba, Newfoundland

Law in Your Life
Suppose you are at the Ski and Snowboard show and you fill out entry forms at the various booths to win equipment or lift tickets. Sometimes these companies give your name and phone number to telemarketing companies. Is this an invasion of privacy? Do you think you could successfully sue a company that gives away your personal information? Explain.

and Labrador, and Saskatchewan have brought in legislation that recognizes invasion of privacy as a tort. Note the *Privacy Act* of British Columbia:

> *Privacy Act,* R.S.B.C. 1996, c. 373
> Violation of privacy actionable
> 1. (1) It is a tort, actionable without proof of damage, for a person, willfully and without a claim of right, to violate the privacy of another.
> (2) The nature and degree of privacy to which a person is entitled in a situation or in relation to a matter is that which is reasonable in the circumstances, giving due regard to the lawful interests of others.
> (3) In determining whether the act or conduct of a person is a violation of another's privacy, regard must be given to the nature, incident and occasion of the act or conduct and to any domestic or other relationship between the parties.
> (4) Without limiting subsections (1) to (3), privacy may be violated by eavesdropping or surveillance, whether or not accomplished by trespass.

CASE

Malcolm v. Fleming, [2000] B.C.J. No. 2400

In 1994 Sherry Malcolm rented a room from Perry and Carol Fleming. One day, Perry and Carol's son, Ken, pointed out a scratch on the mirror in Sherry's bathroom. A few months later, Sherry and her boyfriend examined the mirror more closely and discovered wires in the ceiling that looked like computer or cable wires. Upon further investigation, they discovered a hidden cupboard. When they forced open the cupboard, they found a VCR, a video screen, and several videotapes.

Sherry viewed seven of the tapes and, to her horror, discovered that she had been videotaped in the "privacy" of her bathroom and bedroom. She found the tapes humiliating and embarrassing and, as a result, suffered emotional and psychological stress. She sued the Flemings for invasion of privacy.

The judge agreed that such actions constituted a repeated and protracted invasion of privacy and awarded Sherry a total of $50 000 in damages.

1. As Sherry's lawyer, what section(s) of the *Privacy Act* would you use to prove your case of invasion of privacy?
2. Was it necessary for Sherry to prove the damages she suffered in her case? Explain.

Building Your Understanding

1. List five torts in the category of intentional interference with the person.
2. Use examples to explain the difference between assault and battery.
3. When would a doctor be liable for medical battery?
4. Distinguish between false imprisonment and malicious prosecution.
5. What factors must the plaintiff prove to successfully sue for the infliction of mental suffering?
6. Why are legislators reluctant to pass laws protecting an individual's privacy?

INTENTIONAL INTERFERENCE WITH PROPERTY

You should be able to enjoy your property and possessions without interruption or disturbance. Interference with enjoyment of property occurs if people enter your premises without permission, play loud music, create constant noise, or use items that belong to you. For example, suppose your favourite magazine is delivered to your neighbour's house by mistake. Your neighbour reads it and then takes it to work to show an article to a colleague before delivering it to your house. Your neighbour's actions have interfered with your enjoyment of property, in this case, your magazine. People can cause interference with property in three main ways: trespassing, causing a nuisance, and using your property as if it were their own.

Figure 15.6 Signs warn trespassers that property is private.

Trespass to Land

In most cases, anyone who intentionally enters your property without permission or legal authority is committing the tort of **trespass.** This tort does not require damage to your property, nor does the person need to be aware that the property is private. In this case, "intent" means intent "to go on the land." An "innocent" trespass is still a trespass. Simply by being there, without your permission, a person could be liable for trespass.

If someone you invited onto your property refuses to leave when asked to do so, that person becomes a trespasser. In this situation, you can use reasonable force to remove this person from your property. However, you may have to prove that the defendant refused to leave voluntarily, and the courts will determine what constitutes reasonable force. As discussed later in the chapter, some people have the right to enter your property to carry out certain jobs, such as reading a gas meter or repairing lines.

trespass: an unlawful interference with the person, property, or rights of another

Consider This
Even if you did not know that the property you were walking on was private, you could still be sued for trespassing. Why?

Nuisance

Loud noises, noxious fumes, and barking dogs are just some of the annoyances that may prevent you from enjoying your property. A cause of action for nuisance may also arise if an activity on your neighbour's property physically damages yours, or if the vibration from nearby construction causes damage to the foundation of your house. In law, such annoyances may be considered **private nuisances** and are a form of trespass, even though no one has actually entered your property.

Neighbours also have the right to enjoy their property. In determining whether certain acts are nuisances, the court looks at many factors such as the character of the neighbourhood and the purpose of the activity in question. Suppose your neighbour had a party and played loud music all night long. Could you sue your neighbour for private nuisance? To argue successfully that an activity should be considered a nuisance, you must prove that it was unreasonable and that you suffered some damage. The courts might find that noise from one party, while it may have been excessive, was not unreasonable.

private nuisance: unreasonable and substantial interference with someone's right to enjoyment of property

Figure 15.7 Residents of this subdivision have complained about a nearby slaughterhouse that has been in operation for 70 years. How would this slaughterhouse constitute a nuisance?

However, if the party turns into a nightly event that interferes with your sleep, the court may decide that this activity has become a private nuisance.

In general, all neighbourhoods are expected to put up with some noise and pollution from the people or businesses that share the community. However, in an effort to protect communities, all cities have zoning bylaws that prevent industries from being set up in residential areas. Of course, residents who live in a downtown apartment in a large city cannot expect the same degree of quiet that may be available in a suburb. Also, in law, everyday activities such as traffic are not normally considered a nuisance. Certain noises or activities are even permitted because they benefit the public. For instance, police and ambulance sirens are not considered nuisances because they provide a service to the public.

When a nuisance interferes with the public interest in areas of safety, health, comfort, convenience, or morality, it is called a **public nuisance.** Generally, public nuisances affect a greater number of people than private nuisances. Examples include oil spills that damage coastlines or the accidental pollution of a town's drinking water. Usually, in these situations, a government or provincial attorney must sue on behalf of the public. In rare cases where the nuisance harms not only the general public but also an individual or group of people in a special or unique way, the plaintiff or plaintiffs themselves may bring an action for public nuisance.

public nuisance: unreasonable and substantial interference with interests that affect the community at large, such as public health and safety

Trespass to Chattels

Most people own clothes, jewellery, cars, bikes, furniture, art, and CDs. In tort law, this type of movable property is known as **chattel.** If people intentionally and directly interfere with someone's chattels, they have committed a

chattel: movable personal property

400 UNIT 4 ◆ Civil Law and Dispute Resolution

trespass. To be sued, trespassers do not have to damage the chattel, but in most cases there would be little point in suing if no damage occurred. However, suppose someone harassed you by constantly committing a trespass to your chattel; in this case, an action might be warranted even in the absence of damage.

"No man can set his foot upon my ground without my licence, but he is liable to an action though the damage be nothing."
— *Entick v. Carrington* (1765)

Conversion

In criminal law, if someone takes your property with the intention of depriving you of it, even temporarily, it is considered theft. The civil law equivalent of theft is **conversion.** The defendant simply has to "convert" your property (or property you hold for someone else) to his or her own use. For instance, if your sister goes on holiday and leaves her bike with you to use, and someone takes it, you have an action for conversion against the taker. The neighbour who took your magazine to work for a few days did not steal the magazine, but she deliberately interfered with your property and treated it as though it were her own. Suppose a letter carrier mistakenly delivered theatre tickets to Sima's house. Instead of returning the tickets to their rightful owner, Sima decides to use the tickets herself. In this case, she could probably be successfully sued for converting her neighbour's tickets to her own use. These actions are all examples of conversion. In the last example, Sima would likely be guilty of theft as well.

conversion: unauthorized and substantial interference with another's property, which deprives the owner of its use

Merely possessing property that belongs to someone else would not necessarily make you liable for conversion. If you find a wallet on the street, it might be reasonable for you to keep it until the rightful owner can be found. But if you make no effort to find the owner, you could be liable for conversion and theft. Conversion is a substantial interference. Taking a friend's bicycle without asking and using it for five minutes might only constitute a trespass; taking it on a three-day bike trip would be considered conversion.

Building Your Understanding

1. Describe two types of interference with property.
2. Distinguish between private and public nuisance.
3. How do chattels differ from real estate?
4. Explain the tort of conversion, using an example of your own.

DEFENCES TO INTENTIONAL INTERFERENCE

In most cases, if someone is sued for interference with the person or property, it is up to the plaintiff to prove that the defendant intentionally committed the tort that caused suffering, an injury, or a wrong. Anyone sued for intentional interference can raise a variety of defences.

Defences to Interference with the Person

Consent

We often agree to physical contact that without consent would be considered a tort. We consent to haircuts, hugs, or eye examinations. All of these activities are perfectly legitimate if we agree to them. A person's **consent** must be given *voluntarily* and to a *specific* act. The onus of proving consent is on the defendant.

Suppose Jeremy consents to participate in a pie-throwing event to raise money for charity. Charlene, who is upset at Jeremy for breaking up with her, sees this as an opportunity for a little sweet revenge and laces her pie with pepper. The pepper burns Jeremy's eyes. Jeremy did consent to one form of battery—having pies thrown at him—so he cannot complain if he gets bruised by the impact of the pie. But he did not consent to having his eyes burned by the pepper that was added to the pie, so Charlene would be liable for battery.

consent: permission granted voluntarily for a specific act

Law in Your Life
When you consent to having a haircut, you allow someone to engage in an activity that without your permission could be battery. What recourse would you have if you did not like the haircut?

Self-Defence

People are allowed to defend themselves in the event of either a physical attack or a threat of violence. Using reasonable force to protect oneself against injury is known as **self-defence.** Defendants must prove that they were in immediate danger of actual or threatened harm, that the use of force was necessary to prevent personal injury, and that the force used was not excessive. A threat of physical violence must be real in the eyes of the defendant. For example, if John is a spectator at a soccer match and yells that he is going to come over and beat some sense into Gadi, a fan on the other side of the field, Gadi could not run across the field and attack John. However, if John suddenly appeared beside Gadi with his fists clenched, ready for a fight, Gadi might be justified in defending himself. If Gadi saw John later at a party, however, he could not punch John and claim that he felt threatened by the earlier remarks.

Self-defence often escalates the confrontation, and the "innocent" party can end up being liable for battery along with the original aggressor. Once the need for defence has passed, any further force is a battery. For instance, if you have fought off your attacker and he is lying on the ground, you cannot continue to kick him. If a person about your size attacks you with his or her fists, it is considered excessive to then beat that person with a baseball bat.

self-defence: the legal right to use reasonable force to protect oneself against injury from another

Defence of a Third Party

People are also allowed to use force in the **defence of a third party** if they believed at the time that someone else was in immediate danger. For example, suppose you are on the bus when a passenger starts to threaten the bus driver. The passenger then approaches the driver in a menacing manner. To protect the driver, you grab the passenger and wrestle him to the ground. If the passenger is injured and sues for battery, you might be successful in arguing defence of a third party. Even if you were mistaken in your belief that the driver was being attacked, the court may still accept

defence of a third party: the legal right to use reasonable force to protect someone from being injured by another

Herman v. Graves, [1998] Alta. Q.B. 471

CASE

On a January evening in 1994, 17-year-old Jesse Herman was driving his 15-year-old brother, Christopher, home in his mother's car. Jesse was proceeding east when he passed a half-ton truck that was driven by Ms. Jackson. Mr. Graves, the owner of the truck, was a passenger. After passing the truck, Jesse and Chris noticed that the lights on the truck were on high beam. Jesse tapped the brakes to signal to the driver to dim her lights. The lights were dimmed momentarily and then put back on high beam. The truck driver then began tailgating. Jesse increased his speed and the truck driver chased after him. His car was eventually bumped from behind and forced off the road.

Jesse claimed that when he got out of the car to check for damages, Graves came toward him and started swearing, saying he was going to teach him a lesson. According to Jesse, Graves struck him in the face. Jesse fell, and Graves kicked him repeatedly. Once Graves left, the boys went home, and their parents took Jesse to the hospital where he was treated for lacerations and severe bruising. Graves was eventually arrested; he pleaded guilty to assault causing bodily harm and mischief (a form of interference).

In a subsequent civil action, Graves agreed that he struck Jesse, but said it was in self-defence because Jesse had struck him first. The Court of the Queen's Bench of Alberta rejected the claim of self-defence, finding that the beating Graves gave Jesse "far exceeded any justifiable self-defence."

1. What tort did Graves commit when he put on the high beams and chased Jessie?
2. If Jessie had knocked Graves down when he was attacked and then kept kicking him, could Jessie claim self-defence to a battery action by Graves? Explain.

this defence because, under the circumstances, it was reasonable for you to believe that the driver was in immediate danger. The force you use, however, must be reasonable; if it is excessive, you could be liable for battery.

Legal Authority

In some cases a person may have the right, or the **legal authority,** to perform an action that would be a tort if someone else were to perform that same action. For example, police officers can arrest and detain someone if they have reasonable grounds to believe that person may be guilty of a crime. Without such authority, this action would be considered battery and false imprisonment. Parents and teachers have legal authority to discipline their children or students as long as the force used is not excessive. Firefighters, paramedics, and other medical personnel may also be given authority to restrain someone or use force to protect themselves or others.

legal authority: the right given by law to engage in conduct that would otherwise be a tort

Defences to Interference with Property

Consent

Like interference with the person, consent is a defence used in the tort of "trespass to property." For instance, if someone gave you permission to be on his property, he could not argue that you were trespassing unless you damaged the property or abused the purpose for which you were allowed to enter the premises. If your neighbour hires you to cut her grass, she has consented to your being on her property. She has not consented to your wandering around her basement looking for items you could buy at her next garage sale.

Defence of Property

defence of property: a defence stating that a person can use reasonable force to protect one's property

Individuals can use reasonable force to eject trespassers from their property. This defence is known as **defence of property.** However, if the person being ejected was originally on the property lawfully or is a trespasser who entered the land or premises peacefully, this person must be asked to leave and given a chance to do so before any force is used.

Legal Authority

As discussed earlier, some people do have the legal authority to trespass on your property. For instance, police officers can legally search your property if they have a search warrant. Other public officials can also enter your property for a range of activities, such as determining the value of your land for tax purposes or checking to ensure that your house complies with building codes.

Statutory Authority

statutory authority: legislation that grants someone authority to perform an act that could create a nuisance

The main defence to actions for nuisance is **statutory authority.** This means that a statute authorizes the activity being complained about, and the nuisance created is the inevitable result of carrying out the activity. For instance, if the government authorizes the building of an airport, it is fairly obvious that there will be a lot of noise that cannot be avoided.

Building Your Understanding

1. Define the term "consent" in law. Provide an example to illustrate your answer.
2. Explain self-defence as a defence in a tort action for assault or battery.
3. Under what circumstances might someone use the defence of a third-party in an action for battery?
4. Why can certain individuals or groups use the defence of legal authority?
5. Provide an example, other than the one given in the text, when the defence of statutory authority might be used.

DEFAMATION OF CHARACTER

defamation: injury to a person's reputation or good name by slander or libel

You may have seen headlines that sensationalize celebrities on the covers of tabloids, or perhaps you have watched investigative television programs that make damaging statements about ordinary citizens. If the accusations are unfounded and cause injury to a person's fame, reputation, or character, these media may be sued for **defamation.** Even calling someone a liar in the hall at school could make you liable for defamation.

When a person is defamed, that person's good name and status in the community is damaged. Defamation can be committed in various ways, but it is generally divided into two categories—slander and libel. Some provinces have passed laws doing away with this distinction, treating all damaging statements as defamation.

> **Fast Fact**
> The word *defame* comes from the Latin word *diffamare*, meaning "to spread evil reports."

Slander

Slander is an oral statement or a gesture that damages a person's reputation. For a slander suit to be successful, the plaintiff must establish that the statements were made to someone other than the plaintiff, that these statements referred to the plaintiff, and that they would lower the plaintiff's reputation in the eyes of a "reasonable person." Almost any critical comment can be considered defamatory.

slander: a defaming oral statement or gesture

Suppose you are running for student council, and Lisa, another student, makes a nasty comment to you about your leadership ability. While your pride and self-esteem may be hurt, Lisa's statement is not defamatory because no "publication" occurred—you were the only one who heard her comments. However, if one other person overheard Lisa's comments, the statement would be considered "published," and you might have a cause of action. But even if you establish that Lisa made a defamatory comment, to establish slander you usually have to show special or actual damages such as loss of income. Such damage may be difficult to prove. Mere loss of friendship is not considered grounds for action.

Libel

Libel is defamation in a permanent form—statements that are written, printed, recorded, or filmed. Libel may also include drawings, cartoons, and carvings. Civil courts consider libel far more serious than slander; damage is usually greater because publication is more widespread. As a result, the court presumes that your reputation has been injured as long as the libel is proven. You do not have to prove any special or actual damages.

libel: defamation in a permanent form, such as written or recorded statements

Suppose Lisa writes an article in the student paper accusing you of plagiarizing your last assignment in law class. The article might cause some teachers and students to question your honesty, which could lead to your losing the election for president of the student council. You might consider suing Lisa for libel. If the libelous information is repeated in other publications, such as community newspapers, they, too, could be sued for libel. However, if a newspaper is simply reporting on the original action, it is not liable.

> *"Whatever a man publishes, he publishes at his peril."*
> — Lord Mansfield, 1774

Although defamation is an intentional tort, it is possible that the defendant in a defamation action did not *intend* to defame the plaintiff. Nevertheless, that person is still responsible for any damage caused. What if Lisa believes that her article is true and considers it her responsibility to inform the student body about election candidates? If the article is actually false, the fact that Lisa *thought* she was performing a public service is irrelevant. She could still be liable for defamation.

> **Fast Fact**
> The first step in starting a libel action is to issue a libel notice.

Defences to Defamation

As with other torts, plaintiffs in defamation cases must prove that the defamatory remarks lowered their reputations in the eyes of the public and that they have suffered damage as a result of those remarks. Defendants also have a variety of defences that can be argued in defamation cases under common law. These defences include truth, fair comment, absolute privilege, and qualified privilege.

Truth

truth: the defence that the comments alleged to be defamatory are verified and established facts

The strongest defence to slander or libel is **truth.** A plaintiff who sues for defamation will not succeed if the defendant can prove that the statements are true. For example, if Lisa presents a previously published article identical to your law assignment, she has proof of your plagiarism and proof that her article is true. In the face of this evidence, your suit for libel will fail.

In defamation cases, the court must balance the right to freedom of speech with a person's right to have his or her reputation protected. Even true statements can be very damaging. Suppose a newspaper finds out that a famous person who has devoted his whole life to public service was convicted of selling drugs when he was a teenager. Should the paper be allowed to tarnish the person's reputation by publishing this information years later?

Fair Comment

fair comment: a defence to defamation that the comments were honest and made without malice

If someone expresses a comment or personal opinion based on fact regarding a matter of public interest, this person is protected by the defence of **fair comment.** For instance, if a music critic negatively reviews a concert, the musicians are not likely to sue this person for defamation, even if the comments affect ticket sales. The critic is simply making an honest assessment. Ordinary citizens are also entitled to give their opinions on the quality of restaurant food, the entertainment value of a play, the performance of a sports figure, or on countless other topics. Regardless of who makes the comments, they must be fair and made without **malice.** They must reflect an honestly held opinion, not one that is motivated by spite, ill will, a desire to harm, or any other improper purpose.

malice: any improper or ulterior motive for publishing a defamatory statement

Absolute Privilege

absolute privilege: protection from liability for statements made in Parliament, in a legislature or a courtroom, at a military hearing, or before a tribunal

State officers performing their duties, politicians speaking in Parliament or provincial legislatures, and persons participating in courts or tribunals cannot be held liable for statements about others as long as these statements are made during legislative or court proceedings. This defence, called **absolute privilege,** allows them to speak openly about others without fear of legal action. Individuals making the same remarks outside the legislature or courtroom could be sued for slander unless they can prove the statements are true. This protection ensures that the best interests of society are served. In fact, freedom of speech is considered so important in these situations that even malicious statements are protected.

CASE

Ross v. Beutel, [2001] N.B.C.A. 62

BACKGROUND In 1993, the New Brunswick Teachers' Association held workshops on Jewish history and culture. The Association invited the political cartoonist Josh Beutel to make a presentation. In his presentation, called "An Editorial Cartoonist Confronts Holocaust Issues," Beutel displayed political cartoons dealing with racism and stereotypes. He also discussed freedom of the press versus hate literature. A number of Beutel's cartoons depicted Malcolm Ross, a former teacher in New Brunswick who was known for his anti-Semitic and racist opinions. Ross's books and articles alleged that an international Jewish conspiracy existed to take over the Christian world. Because of his publications, Ross was removed from his teaching position, although he remained a member of the Association.

Malcolm Ross

Ross attended Beutel's presentation. One cartoon Beutel showed was of Ross holding two of his books. To the left of Ross was the name "Goebbels," a German Nazi leader who was Hitler's minister of propaganda. The setting of the cartoon was a concentration camp showing a group of German soldiers with someone who looked like Hitler. The word *Conspiracy* was prominently displayed, and the caption asked, "What's the difference between the views of … Josef Goebbels and Malcolm Ross?" Beutel also read a passage from one of Ross's books about the theory of a Jewish conspiracy. Ross sued Beutel for defamation.

LEGAL QUESTION Was Beutel's cartoon fair comment about Ross?

DECISION The Court of Queen's Bench of New Brunswick found that Beutel had defamed Ross in the cartoon. The judge found that a reasonable listener and viewer of the commentary and cartoon would regard Ross as a Nazi who advocated the extermination of the Jewish people. Ross was awarded $7500 in damages. Beutel appealed the decision.

The New Brunswick Court of Appeal accepted Beutel's defence of fair comment and allowed the appeal. The Court of Appeals found that Beutel's cartoon was based on his opinion that Ross and Goebbels had similar beliefs about a Jewish conspiracy and that a reasonable person would not take the cartoon to mean that Ross was a Nazi who advocated the extermination of Jewish people. While the cartoon was still defamatory, it was a fair comment in that Beutel's opinion was honest, not malicious. According to the Court, "… [cartoons] by their very nature, contain statements of opinion rather than statements of fact. Relying, as they do, on the devices of allegory, caricature and analogy, cartoons contain subjective expressions of opinion."

LEGAL SIGNIFICANCE This decision became a precedent for subsequent defamation cases involving cartoon depiction.

ANALYSIS

1. In the defence of fair comment, does the comment have to be true? Explain.
2. The "right of fair comment is one of the essential elements which go to make up our freedom of speech." Explain the meaning of this statement. How would you relate it to this case?

Figure 15.8 In 2000, Stockwell Day was sued for defamation by an Alberta lawyer. Day, who used the defence of qualified privilege, lost the suit.

Qualified Privilege

People who make statements in certain situations are protected as long as the statements are made without malice. This protection, called **qualified privilege,** applies when someone has a duty to make the statement or an interest to protect, and the person receiving the statement has a duty or an interest in receiving it. For example, employers and teachers are often asked to write letters of reference for former employees and students. Qualified privilege makes it possible for them to be honest and forthright in their assessment of an individual without concern that they will later be sued. Employers may even be sued for negligence if they do *not* tell the truth when supplying references. In such cases, the court favours freedom of speech over protection of a person's reputation because of the importance of allowing people to be open and frank in certain situations.

qualified privilege: protection from liability for statements made in certain situations as long as the statements are made without malice

Building Your Understanding

1. Define defamation of character.
2. Use examples to explain the difference between slander and libel.
3. What does the plaintiff need to prove in a slander suit?
4. Why is libel considered more serious than slander?
5. What is the strongest defence to a defamation suit? Why?
6. Explain what is meant by "fair comment."
7. Distinguish between absolute privilege and qualified privilege. Why are certain groups entitled to such defences?

LOOKING BACK

Reviewing Your Vocabulary

absolute privilege *p. 406*
assault *p. 392*
battery *p. 392*
chattel *p. 400*
consent *p. 402*
conversion *p. 401*
defamation *p. 404*
defence of a third party *p. 402*
defence of property *p. 404*
fair comment *p. 406*
false imprisonment *p. 395*
intent *p. 390*
intentional infliction of nervous shock or mental suffering *p. 396*
intentional torts *p. 390*
legal authority *p. 403*
libel *p. 405*
malice *p. 406*
malicious prosecution *p. 395*
medical battery *p. 394*
private nuisance *p. 399*
public nuisance *p. 400*
qualified privilege *p. 408*
self-defence *p. 402*
slander *p. 405*
statutory authority *p. 404*
trespass *p. 399*
truth *p. 406*

Quiz

1. Refer to the vocabulary terms above to identify the intentional tort and/or defence in the following statements:
   a) "You may say you're not guilty—the whole world may say you're not guilty—but I will prosecute you to the ends of the earth and put you behind bars for the rest of your life."
   b) "Well, if you will build your house next to a pig farm, you'd expect to get an unpleasant whiff now and then."
   c) "It's not as if I stole your boat; it was just sitting there, and I decided it was a nice day to go for a little ride. I only had it for a week."
   d) "No one else ever complained about a little peck on the cheek. I was just being affectionate."

Checking Your Knowledge

2. a) What factors must be present for an action to be considered an intentional tort?
   b) What are the two main categories of intentional torts?
3. How can medical practitioners protect themselves from medical battery?
4. Why have lawmakers been reluctant to bring in legislation on invasion of privacy?
5. Explain the concept of nuisance in law. What is the difference between nuisance and trespass?
6. Name four defences against intentional interference with the person.
7. What are two ways a person can defame another person's character?
8. In the defence of fair comment, what factors have to be present in order for a comment to be considered fair?

Developing Your Thinking and Inquiry skills

9. Determine which of the following situations would describe an intentional or an unintentional tort. Identify the specific tort involved in each scenario. Indicate which legal defence, if any, could be used in each case.
   a) Ms. Johnston was carrying an expensive vase she had just bought as a wedding present. A strong gust of wind pushed Mr. Bristow into Ms. Johnston, causing her to drop the vase, which smashed to the ground.

b) Michael hadn't paid the rent. His landlord banged at his door and yelled, "If you don't pay up, I'm going to break both your legs."

c) Colin was in a serious snowmobile accident and lay unconscious in the snow, which caused frostbite to his leg. When he got to the hospital, he told the doctor that no matter what, he did not want his leg amputated. The doctor agreed. Unfortunately, when the doctor began the operation, he realized he could not save Colin's leg. He called the orthopedic surgeon who agreed that the leg had to be removed or Colin would die. The doctor amputated the leg.

d) Don was walking through a store with his friend James. Unknown to Don, James shoplifted a CD. The store security guard stopped both of them and ordered them to wait at the back of the store for the police. Don had a job interview and asked to leave. The security guard told him not to leave until the police arrived. Don did not get the job.

10. Read the following situations and indicate whether you think the defendants would be successful in their defence of fair comment. Give reasons for your decisions.

a) A restaurant critic working for a local newspaper never wrote favourable reviews. A group of restaurant owners decided to sue the newspaper for defamation. The critic argued that her reviews were fair because they reflected a personal and honest belief that the restaurants failed to live up to their advertisements claiming world-class status.

b) Two friends met in a coffee shop after seeing a play. One friend said to the other that the performance of a particular actor was the worst she had ever s reen. Unknown to her, at the next table, were the actor's agent and a film producer discussing the possibility of hiring the actor for a new movie. The actor did not get the job, so the agent sued.

11. In 2000, Lorne Goddard, an Alberta lawyer, sued Stockwell Day, a member of the Alberta legislature, for defamation of character. Research this case and report your findings, using the following headings: Background, Legal Question, Decision, and Legal Significance.

Communicating Your Ideas

12. Your provincial government is drafting a new invasion of privacy bill and has asked for input from a variety of organizations. Working in small groups, draft a 200-word presentation to the government that

a) defines "invasion of privacy" in your own words;

b) explains why your group supports or opposes such legislation; and

c) lists specific examples of how you feel your privacy has been or is being invaded.

Putting It All Together

13. Research print sources to find examples of five different intentional torts. In a report, identify each intentional tort and explain the circumstances surrounding the incident. Report on any legal action that might have been taken. Identify the plaintiff and defendant in each tort, and suggest an appropriate defence for each of the defendants.

CASES

Brushett v. Cowan, [1990] N.J. No. 145 (Nfld. C.A.)

In 1984, Sheila Brushett underwent a bone scan and an x-ray because of a persistent pain in her right leg. The specialist, Dr. Cowan, noticed a lump on her right thigh and advised her to undergo a muscle biopsy, a procedure that involved removing a sample of muscle to determine whether she had a malignant tumor. Prior to the operation, she signed a consent form, agreeing to the procedure and to "further or alternative measures as may be found to be necessary during the course of the operation …"

During the operation, Cowan noticed that an area around the bone appeared abnormal, so he took a portion of the bone for biopsy. Brushett was released from the hospital that day. She was not told that she should use crutches, nor was she offered any. Two days later she returned to Cowan's office, and he gave her a pair of crutches. According to Brushett, the doctor did not tell her about the second biopsy, nor did he tell her not to put weight on her leg. Several days later she broke her right leg. According to Brushett, it was only when she was having her broken leg attended to that she discovered that the doctor had performed a biopsy on her bone as well as her muscle. She sued Cowan and the General Hospital for battery for performing the second biopsy, and for negligence for failing to inform her that she should not put pressure on her right leg.

The trial judge found the doctor liable for battery and negligence. Cowan appealed the decision. The Newfoundland Court of Appeal found that the biopsy Cowan performed on Brushett "did not go beyond the consent given by her to him"; therefore, battery did not occur. However, the Court found Cowan partially liable for negligence because he failed to adequately inform Brushett of the consequences of putting weight on her right leg after the operation.

1. What torts did the trial judge find the doctor liable for?
2. What factors did Brushett have to prove to satisfy the balance of probabilities?
3. Identify the appellant and the respondent in the appeal case. Explain the appeals court decision. Which party was successful? Why?

Runcer v. Gould, [2000] Alta. Q.B. 25

Eighteen-year-old Ryan Runcer stole two recreational vehicles from Mr. Gould while working on Gould's property. When Runcer showed up for work two days later, Gould and his business partner, Mr. Hunley, asked him about the whereabouts of the two vehicles. When Ryan claimed he did not know, Gould and Hunley allegedly got angry, threw him to the ground, duct-taped his arms and legs, and forced him into a helicopter. While in the air, they opened the helicopter door and threatened to throw Runcer out. Runcer agreed to take Gould and Hunley to the bush area where he had concealed one of the missing vehicles.

Ryan Runcer was charged with theft, and he pleaded guilty to the charge. Runcer sued Gould and Hunley for several torts including assault, battery, and false imprisonment. Gould and Hunley were held liable for assault, battery, trespass to the person, false imprisonment, detention, intimidation, and intentional infliction of mental stress.

1. What did the plaintiff have to prove to win his actions for assault and battery?
2. Explain why Gould and Hunley were liable for the torts of false imprisonment and intentional infliction of mental stress.

CASES

Nelles v. Ontario, [1989] 2 S.C.R. 170

BACKGROUND Susan Nelles, a nurse at the Hospital for Sick Children in Toronto, was charged with the murder of four infants. It was alleged that the infants had been deliberately given a fatal overdose of heart medication. Although the police had almost no evidence against Nelles, she was arrested and jailed for five days.

At a preliminary inquiry, the judge dismissed the case, saying there was insufficient evidence to bring Nelles to trial. The judge publicly criticized the Crown for bringing a totally unsupported charge of murder against Nelles. Although she was free to go, the effect of the murder charges on Nelles and her family was considerable. The Nelles family incurred extensive legal fees in fighting the charges. Dr. Nelles, Susan's father, died during the legal battle, and there was speculation that his death was partly due to the stress of the case.

In 1985, Susan Nelles sued for malicious prosecution. In her suit, Nelles named the Crown, the Attorney General of Ontario, and certain police officers who had investigated her case. She claimed financial compensation for the pain, humiliation, and mental anguish she had suffered as a result of the charges.

LEGAL QUESTION Do the Attorney General and Crown attorneys have absolute immunity against suits for malicious prosecution?

DECISION At trial, the judge dismissed the action against the Crown and the Attorney General, but not against the police. Susan Nelles appealed, and the Ontario Court of Appeal heard the case. It dismissed her appeal, stating that the Attorney General and Crown attorneys have absolute immunity from charges of malicious prosecution.

Nelles appealed to the Supreme Court of Canada, and the Court allowed her appeal. The Supreme Court said that granting the offices of the Crown and the Attorney General absolute immunity from being sued for malicious prosecution would threaten the individual rights of those who have been wrongfully prosecuted.

Figure 15.9 Susan Nelles speaks at a commission of inquiry more than three years after she was charged with the murder of four infants.

HISTORICAL SIGNICANCE The Supreme Court decision set a precedent whereby Crown attorneys and the Attorney General are no longer immune from charges of malicious prosecution.

ANALYSIS

1. What did Susan Nelles have to prove to be successful in her malicious prosecution action? Why might this be a difficult tort to prove?
2. Do you believe that police and prosecutors should be immune from civil liability? Explain.
3. Do you think this precedent established in a civil case will affect the way future criminal investigations are conducted? Why or why not?

Marriage: A Changing Tradition

16

CHAPTER OUTLINE

Entering a Marriage

Families Today

Ending a Marriage

FOCUS YOUR LEARNING

What are the legal requirements for entering a marriage?

How are different types of families structured?

How is a marriage legally dissolved?

WHAT DO YOU THINK?

- If you were to plan a wedding, what traditional features would you include? What innovations would you add?
- Why are some wedding traditions changing?

On their wedding day, most couples are usually too excited or nervous to think seriously about the gravity of getting married. However, the ceremony itself is a reminder that marriage is a contract, which recognizes certain rights and obligations on the part of each partner. By taking vows and saying "I do," a couple becomes a family, assuming responsibility for any children they may have. All of these issues come under the category of family law.

In this chapter, you will learn about the requirements for a valid marriage, the obligations spouses owe each other, and the procedure for dissolving a marriage. You will also learn how lawmakers try to keep pace with changes in the traditional family structure.

ENTERING A MARRIAGE

In most cultures, weddings are important ceremonies because they mark the beginning of a new relationship. A marriage formalizes the intimacy between two individuals and the change in status from single person to spouse. People marry for different reasons, but most people marry because they want a lasting, intimate relationship that is legally binding. To ensure that a marriage is legal, certain requirements must be met.

Both the federal and the provincial and territorial governments have jurisdiction over marriage and family matters. Section 91(26) of the *Constitution Act, 1867*, gives the federal government jurisdiction over the **essential requirements** for a valid marriage—laws that deal with an individual's legal and personal capacity to marry. These requirements apply to all Canadians, regardless of where they live. In order to clarify these essential requirements, provinces and territories have enacted their own marriage laws under s. 92(12) of the *Constitution Act, 1867*, which gives the provincial and territorial governments jurisdiction over certain bureaucratic aspects of marriage. Under these laws, provinces and territories have set out **formal requirements**—additional rules regarding the **solemnization of marriage** (the wedding ceremony).

essential requirements: federal laws that determine a person's ability to marry

formal requirements: provincial and territorial laws regarding the solemnization of marriage

solemnization of marriage: the marriage ceremony

Essential Requirements for Marriage

The federal government has enacted very little legislation that deals explicitly with the essential requirements for marriage. In the absence of statute law, the requirements for a valid marriage follow principles established under English common law. According to the federal government, the essential requirements of a valid marriage include the following:

- mental capacity
- valid consent
- minimum age or parental consent
- absence of a prohibited relationship
- termination of prior marriages
- sexual capacity

If a marriage does not meet the essential requirements, it can be declared **void *ab initio*,** which means that in the eyes of the law the marriage never existed (*ab initio* is a Latin term meaning "from the beginning"). The judge issues a decree of nullity, a legal document that states that the marriage never took place.

void *ab initio*: a legal process that declares a marriage null and void

Mental Capacity to Marry

In order to legally marry, both parties must have the mental **capacity,** or ability to understand, both the nature of the marriage contract and the responsibilities and duties involved in marriage. If a person is not mentally capable due to illness, alcohol, or drugs, that person cannot legally marry. For a marriage to be valid, mental capacity must exist at the time the marriage took place; if a problem arises after the marriage ceremony, the marriage remains valid.

capacity: one's ability to understand the nature of one's actions and to voluntarily enter into a contract

Barrett Estate v. Dexter, [2000] Alta. Q.B. 530

CASE

In 1993, 93-year-old Dwight Barrett met Arlene Sharon-Dexter, aged 54. Arlene rented a room in Dwight's house for $100 a month plus cooking and cleaning chores. Withdrawals from Dwight's bank account increased dramatically, and Dwight's sons, John and Daryl, became concerned about Arlene's influence over their father. John arranged to have his father examined by a geriatric specialist who found that Dwight was unable to make reasonable decisions about legal and financial matters. When the doctor certified Dwight as mentally incapable of making sound judgments, John became the legal guardian, or executor, or his father's estate.

The following month, Arlene and Dwight were married. Two months later, Dwight drew up a new will that made Arlene the executor of his estate. In the new will, Dwight left the house, the furniture, and most of his estate, which was valued at approximately $1 million, to his wife. A few months later, Dwight broke his hip and died of complications.

After his father's death, John sought to have his father's marriage declared null and void, citing the report of the geriatric specialist. The Court of Queen's Bench of Alberta found in favour of the plaintiff, declaring that Dwight Barrett had lacked the legal capacity to enter a marriage contract. The marriage was declared null and void.

1. What does it mean to have a marriage declared null and void?
2. Why did the Court declare this marriage void?
3. If the marriage had taken place before Barrett was examined by the specialist, do you think the Court would have made the same decision? Explain?

Freedom of Consent

When the bride and groom answer, "I do," they have just given their consent to be lawfully married. Couples entering into marriage must do so of their own free will—they must **consent** willingly. Consent cannot be given **under duress,** which means that the parties are afraid of the consequences if they do not marry, that their fear is reasonable, and that their fear is caused by someone else. Suppose Anna's father tells her she must marry David, even

consent: agree to enter a marriage willingly

under duress: being forced into marriage through fear

though she has no interest in doing so. If she refuses, her father will disown her and never allow her to visit the family home again. Should Anna agree to the marriage, she would likely be able to show that she married under duress, and the marriage would be declared void.

If Anna does choose to marry someone, there must be no **mistake** about the identity of that person or the purpose of the ceremony. For example, if Anna marries someone and discovers after the ceremony that she has married that person's identical twin, then there has been a mistake in identity, and the marriage can be declared invalid. However, if she marries someone thinking he is a millionaire and finds out after the ceremony that he is not, the marriage is still valid in the eyes of the law.

mistake: confusion or error about the identity of the person someone is marrying or about the purpose of the ceremony

Age of Consent

In order to be legally married in Canada, both parties must be of a certain age. Historically, case law established the minimum ages of 14 for a boy and 12 for a girl. In time, many Canadians felt that these ages were too low, so each province and territory set a higher minimum age. These age requirements must be met for a marriage to be legal. Young people who wish to marry but have not reached the minimum age must get written permission from their parents before a marriage licence can be issued. If parents refuse to give their consent, then the couple may apply to the courts to dispense with parental consent. Parental consent may be waived if the judge finds no valid reason for the parents to deny their consent to the marriage.

Fast Fact

In all provinces, the minimum age requirement for marriage with parental consent is 16; it is 15 in the three territories. The minimum age without parental consent varies. In Alberta, Manitoba, Ontario, Prince Edward Island, Quebec, and Saskatchewan it is age 18. In the rest of Canada, it is 19.

Absence of a Prohibited Relationship

People who intend to marry cannot be too closely related to each other by blood. Under the federal *Marriage (Prohibited Degrees) Act*, the rules for **consanguinity** (blood relationships) prohibit close relatives from marrying each other in order to prevent mental or physical disorders in offspring. For example, a woman cannot marry her father, grandfather, son, brother, adopted brother, or grandson. A man cannot marry his mother, grandmother, daughter, sister, adopted sister, or granddaughter.

consanguinity: relationship by blood

Prior to 1991, the Act also included a list of prohibited relations based on **affinity** (close relationships through marriage), but those laws were repealed. The following prohibitions remain as indicated by s. 2 of the Act:

affinity: relationship through marriage

Al-smadi (father and next friend of Emman Al-smadi), [1994] M.J. No. 13

CASE

In 1991 Emman Al-smadi met Ra' A Ahmed Said at an Islamic cultural event. Emman was from Winnipeg, and Ra was from the Middle East, in Canada on a student visa. Emman and Ra became friends and eventually fell in love. In 1992, with her father's consent, Emman married Ra in an Islamic religious ceremony. She was 14 years old and Ra was 26. The following year they had a child. In 1993 Emman applied to have her marriage to Ra legally recognized. Her application included the fact that in the Islamic faith a girl who has reached puberty may marry if she wishes, provided she has the consent of her father. The judge dismissed the application, claiming that such a marriage was "contrary to general public interest …" The judge was unaware that Emman and Ra had a child.

In 1994 Emman applied again to have her marriage legally approved. During the application process, the judge learned that Ra had completed a master's degree in Canada and was enrolled in a Ph.D. program in electrical engineering in Manitoba. He planned to return to the Middle East upon obtaining his degree. Emman completed her grade 9 in 1993. She was taking her grade 10 by correspondence and planned to complete her grade 12 and go to university. Emman was recognized by her teachers as a mature and responsible person.

In considering the application, the judge concluded that Emman and Ra's marriage was not one of convenience in order to facilitate Ra's immigration to Canada. The judge was also convinced that Emman had willingly consented to the marriage, that adequate consideration had been given to her future education, that her father approved of the marriage, and that Ra offered Emman reasonable financial stability. The judge granted consent to the application.

1. In what way did the first judge's decision reflect a bias?
2. Why did Emman require court approval for her marriage when she already had her parent's approval?
3. Why did the Court grant approval to Emman's application after rejecting it just one year earlier?

---

2. (2) No person shall marry another person if they are related
   (a) lineally by consanguinity or adoption;
   (b) as brother and sister by consanguinity, whether by the whole blood or by the half-blood; or
   (c) as brother and sister by adoption.

Prior Marriages

In Canada, a person can be legally married to only one spouse at a time, a practice called **monogamy.** Being married to two spouses at the same time is called **bigamy,** which is a criminal offence in Canada punishable by up to five years in prison. If someone is guilty of bigamy, the second marriage is considered illegal and void.

Before anyone can enter into a marriage, all previous marriages must be ended by annulment, divorce, or death of one spouse. An annulment is a

Fast Fact
Some religions identify additional prohibited relationships.

monogamy: the state of being married to one person

bigamy: the state of being married to two people at the same time

annulment: declaration by the court that a marriage never existed

legal declaration by the courts that a marriage is void and has never existed. An **annulment** is granted when one of the essential requirements for a marriage was missing at the time the marriage took place. Couples may also seek an annulment if their religion does not allow divorce.

In the event that a spouse disappears and cannot be found, an application may be made to the court for a "presumption of death" certificate. In Ontario, for example, if a spouse has been continuously absent for at least seven years and there is no reason to believe that this person is still alive, a judge can declare the missing spouse deceased. In unusual circumstances, such as an accident, the courts may not require the full seven-year waiting period. For instance, if a spouse were lost in a shipwreck or plane crash and many of the bodies were not recovered, it would be reasonable to assume that anyone not found had died. Under these circumstances, the surviving spouse would be able to marry legally without waiting the seven years. If a spouse, legally presumed dead, is actually alive and returns after the surviving spouse has remarried, the second marriage would be declared void.

CASE

Stevenson v. Stevenson, [1997] B.C.J. No. 1154

1. On what basis did Tom and Carol believe their first marriage was not valid?
2. Why did the British Columbia Supreme Court determine that Tom's marriage to Jenny was void?

Orren Tomas Stevenson and Carol Ann Costanzo were married in California in 1974. Three years later they separated. When they filed for divorce, the law office dealing with their case informed them that it could not find their marriage licence. Consequently, a separation agreement was drawn up and signed by both parties, stating that they had attempted to file for divorce but that a marriage licence could not be found. As a result, they were under the assumption that they were never legally married.

In 1978, Tom married Jenny Arntzen in Kaslo, British Columbia. They obtained a marriage licence, and a British Columbia Certificate of Marriage was issued. In 1980, however, Tom consulted a lawyer and decided to petition Carol for divorce. This first marriage was formally dissolved on June 1, 1981.

Tom and Jenny's marriage ended in 1995. In January 1997, Tom brought an action before the Court to have the marriage to Jenny declared null and void. The Supreme Court of British Columbia determined that because Tom was still married to Carol at the time of his marriage to Jenny, the marriage between Tom and Jenny was void.

Sexual Capacity

Traditionally, the primary purpose of marriage was to have children. Therefore, the ability to consummate the marriage became an essential requirement. **Consummation** of the marriage occurs as soon as the couple has sexual intercourse after the wedding ceremony.

consummation: legally validating a marriage through sexual intercourse between husband and wife

Since consummation is an essential requirement, both parties must have sexual capacity. If either spouse is unable to consummate the marriage, the

For Better Or For Worse

© Lynn Johnston Productions, Inc./Distributed by United Feature Syndicate, Inc.

marriage may be annulled. The inability to have sexual intercourse must result from a physical or psychological problem; the simple refusal by one of the parties to participate in sexual intercourse is not enough to have a marriage declared void. Also, absence of sexual capacity must exist prior to consummation. For example, suppose a man is injured after the wedding and is rendered impotent. Sexual capacity could not be a reason for annulment if the marriage had already been consummated.

Consider This
Discuss whether a person infected with the HIV virus would have sexual capacity to enter a marriage.

Formal Requirements for Marriage

As mentioned previously, each province passes its own legislation in the form of marriage acts to clarify and fill in any gaps regarding marriage under common law. These formal requirements can vary from province to province.

Marriage Licence or Publication of Banns

Most provinces and territories require a couple to purchase a marriage licence prior to the marriage ceremony. A **marriage licence** is a legal document authorizing the marriage of the applicants. It can be purchased wherever its sale is authorized by the province's marriage act. In Saskatchewan, for example, licences can be purchased at jewellery stores or from town administrators, while in Ontario licences are sold at municipal government offices.

In some provinces, instead of obtaining a marriage licence, a couple may have **banns of marriage** proclaimed at a religious ceremony, where a member of the clergy announces to the congregation the couple's intention to marry. (Such proclamations are available only for those who have not been previously married.) The banns are proclaimed, or read, on the regular day of worship at the church the couple usually attends. The number of times the banns are read depends on the practice of individual churches. The couple may marry five days following the last reading of the banns.

marriage licence: a legal document proving that two people are married to each other

banns of marriage: a public declaration in a church announcing a couple's intention to marry

Legal Link
To find out if your province allows banns of marriage, visit the Pearson Web site at **www.pearsoned.ca/law** and follow the links to provincial statutes.

Legal Link

There is no legal requirement for a woman to change her surname when she marries. Go to **www.pearsoned.ca/law** and find the procedure a woman must follow if she chooses to take her husband's surname.

Marriage Ceremony

Marriage ceremonies can be elaborate or simple, depending on the wishes of the couple. Sometimes people write their own vows or create their own rituals. All marriage ceremonies, however, have to fulfill certain requirements. The marriage must be witnessed by at least two people 18 years of age or older, and the ceremony has to be conducted by someone who is authorized by law to do so. This person can be a member of a religious organization in the case of a religious ceremony, or a judge, justice of the peace, or marriage commissioner in the case of a civil marriage. Each party must declare that he or she is not aware of any impediment to the marriage. Also, the couple being married must take each other as his or her "lawfully wedded"

With this doughnut I thee wed

WATERLOO — The bride wore jeans and running shoes. The groom wore shorts and a tank top. Their rings were honey crullers, which they promptly ate after the five-minute ceremony at a Waterloo Tim Hortons.

Their parents are "still in shock."

But newlyweds Nick Skalkos and Sarah LeRiche of Kitchener, who had what the officiating minister called "the weirdest wedding I've ever done," are ecstatic after getting married in a spur-of-the-moment decision and subsequent ceremony Saturday night.

"We basically skipped all the formalities," said LeRiche, 22.

The rings were two honey crullers, which the newlyweds wolfed down after the ceremony, washing them down with double-double coffees bought by Rev. Frank Joseph Quinto, who charged them nothing for the service.

SOURCE: Eugene McCarthy, "With this doughnut I thee wed," *The Toronto Star*, August 20, 2001, A20.

Figure 16.1 Nick Skalkos and Sarah LeRiche display their honey-doughnut wedding rings. The ceremony had to be repeated the next day by another minister because the couple had failed to obtain a proper marriage licence, and the minister who had married them was not recognized by the Province of Ontario.

husband or wife. Finally, the person performing the ceremony must pronounce the couple "husband and wife."

The Marriage Act, 1995 (Saskatchewan)
31. Marriage may be solemnized by a marriage commissioner and contracted in his or her office or any other place he or she selects, but only in the following form and manner:
(a) the marriage must be contracted in the presence of the witnesses mentioned in s. 37, and with open doors;
(b) in the presence of the marriage commissioner and witnesses, each of the parties shall declare: "I do solemnly declare that I do not know of any lawful impediment why I, A.B., may not be joined in matrimony to C.D.," and each of the parties shall say to the other: "I call upon these persons here present to witness that I, A.B., do take you, C.D., to be my lawful wedded wife (or husband)"; and after which the marriage commissioner shall say: "I, E.F., a marriage commissioner, by virtue of the powers vested in me by *The Marriage Act, 1995,* do hereby pronounce you A.B. and C.D. to be husband and wife."

CASE

Debora v. Debora, [1999] Ont. C.A. C28709

In 1987, Miriam and David Debora were married in a religious ceremony. At the time, David was receiving a widower's pension. He suggested to Miriam that they not get a marriage licence or register their marriage with the government because to do so would terminate his pension. Miriam agreed. By 1994, David had acquired substantial assets, so they decided to get married in a civil ceremony. This time they obtained a licence.

A few years later David and Miriam separated, and a disagreement ensued over what marriage date should be used for the division of property. David believed the marriage date should be 1994, and Miriam felt it should be 1987. Miriam knew that the 1987 ceremony had not been conducted in accordance with the *Ontario Marriage Act,* but she claimed that David had assured her that the marriage would be considered legal. David denied making this statement. Miriam took the case to court, but her action was dismissed. She appealed the decision to the Court of Appeal. The Court upheld the lower court's ruling that under the *Ontario Marriage Act,* Miriam was not entitled to the same rights as a "spouse" until the marriage of 1994.

1. Explain why neither court regarded Miriam as a "spouse" from 1987 to 1994.
2. As Miriam's lawyer, what arguments would you use to show that the couple had been "married" since 1987? Why was determining the marriage date so important?

Aboriginal Customs

Federal and provincial laws relating to marriage and divorce apply to Aboriginal peoples. In addition, courts recognize **custom marriages,** Aboriginal ceremonies that follow established cultural practices. Divorces based on Aboriginal customs have also been recognized by the courts.

custom marriages: marriage ceremonies between Aboriginal spouses that follow traditional practices

In the case of *Noah Estate* (1961), a judge had to determine whether the marriage between two Inuit people, Noah and Igah, was valid. Noah and Igah were married according to Inuit custom, and after Noah's death, Igah and her daughter sought recognition as the legal heirs. A representative of the Department of Indian and Northern Affairs argued that Igah was not Noah's legal wife because Noah was aware of the territorial laws relating to marriage but had chosen not to follow them.

After reviewing the evidence, the judge dismissed the representative's arguments as "pure fantasy." He held that the marriage was valid under the laws of the Northwest Territories because Noah and Igah's marriage met all the requirements of an Inuit marriage, and everyone in their community recognized their marriage. According to Inuit custom, a valid marriage required the woman's consent to the man's proposal as well as the agreement of both sets of parents.

Figure 16.2 Gilbert and Winnie Chingee celebrate their wedding day in October 2000 near Prince George, British Columbia. The couple participated in the first traditional wedding ceremony held at that site since 1866.

CASE

Connolly v. Woolrich (1867), 17 R.J.R.Q. (Q.S.C.) aff'd (1869), 17 R.J.R.Q. 266 (Q.Q.B.)

1. What did the Court mean when it said that the common law did not "abrogate or derogate from the uses, laws and customs of the aborigines"?
2. Explain why the plaintiff was entitled to a share in Connolly's estate.
3. What was the status of Connolly's second marriage? Why?

William Connolly moved to Hudson's Bay Territory (Northwest Territories) and married Susanne Pas-de-nom, a Cree. They were married according to Cree custom. Due to the absence of priests or ministers, the marriage was not solemnized by the Church. They lived together for 28 years and had six children. The couple was "known, acknowledged, and reputed to be married persons during the whole period of the cohabitation." The couple moved to Lower Canada, but after a short time, Connolly obtained a dispensation from the Bishop and married another woman in a Catholic ceremony. Connolly died some time later leaving his assets to his second wife and children. A son from the first marriage contested the will, arguing that he was a legitimate heir because his parents had been married.

The Quebec Superior Court held that the common law did not "abrogate or derogate [abolish or detract] from the uses, laws and customs of the aborigines." Such customs included marriage ceremonies and divorce. The Court held that William Connolly and Susanne Pas-de-nom's marriage was valid under Cree customary law and that the divorce Connolly sought once he returned to Lower Canada was not valid because he could only be divorced according to Cree custom. The Court's decision meant that the plaintiff (William and Susanne's son) would inherit a share in the estate.

Building Your Understanding

1. List the six essential requirements for a valid marriage. What is the legal status of a marriage if any one of these requirements is not met?
2. Identify two situations in which genuine consent to marriage is absent.
3. How might drugs or alcohol affect a person's mental capacity to legally marry?
4. What conditions must exist to prove consent under duress?
5. What are the legal implications of bigamy?
6. What are the age requirements for marriage? Why did the provinces and territories raise the minimum age in their marriage acts?
7. Identify two restrictions or limits associated with employing the banns of marriage.
8. List the formal requirements for marriage.
9. Go to **www.pearsoned.ca/law** and access a copy of your province's marriage act. What are the specific phrases that must be used during the ceremony? Why would the government include these phrases in a marriage ceremony?
10. Identify four requirements all marriage ceremonies must fulfill.
11. According to Inuit custom, what two requirements must be met for a marriage to be considered valid?

FAMILIES TODAY

Trends in family life have changed in the past 40 or 50 years. During the 1950s, the traditional family usually had a stay-at-home mother who took care of the children and a father who worked outside the home as the sole income earner or "breadwinner." Most couples who lived together were married, and people married in order to have a family. Today, many women with children have their own careers and work outside the home. Some men are the primary caregivers and stay at home to raise their children. Many people choose to live as common-law partners rather than married couples, and some couples are choosing not to have children. Also, same-sex couples are more open about their living arrangements.

The structure of families is also changing. Increasingly, a single parent—usually a woman—heads the family. Blended families, or families made up of more than one family unit, are also more common as divorced or separated parents with children find new partners, and children from both former relationships live in one home. Extended families comprising different generations may also live together as a family unit.

Even though the definition of family has evolved over many years, the majority of Canadians still prefer to have their relationships legally recognized through marriage. However, as Figure 16.3 indicates, the number of Canadians who do choose marriage is decreasing.

Consider This

According to Statistics Canada, the average age for first marriages in 1962 was 25.2 for men and 22.5 for women. By 1997 it had increased to 29.5 for men and 27.4 for women. What factors may have contributed to an increase in the average age?

Law in Your Life

You are a statistic. Which family structure applies to your family? Is this different from the family structure of your grandparents?

Year	Percentage Married	Percentage Common-Law	Percentage Single-Parent Families
1981	83.1	5.6	11.3
1991	77.2	9.9	13.0
1996	73.7	11.7	14.6

SOURCE: Statistics Canada, Census, 1991. Statistics Canada, 1996.

Figure 16.3 Family Structure in Canada, 1981–1996

CASES

Pettkus v. Becker, [1980] 19 R.F.L. (2d) 165 (S.C.C.)

BACKGROUND Rosa Becker met Lothar Pettkus in Montreal in 1955. Soon they started living together. Rosa suggested they get married, but Lothar said they should wait until they knew each other better. They never married. For the next five years, Rosa paid the rent and looked after household expenses while Lothar saved his money for future investment in a bee-keeping farm. All savings were kept in Lothar's name.

In 1961 the couple decided to buy a farm. Money for the farm came from Lothar's account, and the farm was registered in his name. The couple eventually established a bee-keeping business, which they both ran for the next 14 years. Their business expanded, and by 1973 they had made a net profit of $30 000.

During the early 1970s, however, the relationship began to deteriorate. Rosa left Lothar, alleging that she had been beaten and abused. She then brought an action seeking one-half interest in the estate, which was worth $300 000.

LEGAL QUESTION How should assets and property of a common-law partnership be divided when the relationship terminates?

DECISION The trial judge awarded Rosa 40 beehives, without the bees, and $1500.

Rosa appealed the decision, and the Ontario Court of Appeal awarded her one-half interest in the property and the business. The appeals court judge determined that Rosa and Lothar had lived together as husband and wife for almost 20 years even though they never married. Lothar was able to purchase property because Rosa supported them both during the "lean years," and she worked side by side with him for 14 years "building up the bee-keeping operation which was their main source of livelihood."

Lothar was granted leave to appeal this decision to the Supreme Court of Canada. In a precedent-setting ruling, the Supreme Court upheld the Ontario Court of Appeal ruling that Rosa be awarded a one-half interest in the assets accumulated during her relationship with Lothar.

Figure 16.4 Rosa Becker never received her share of the estate because Lothar refused to accept the Court's decision. In 1986 Rosa committed suicide.

SOCIAL SIGNIFICANCE The Supreme Court of Canada recognized that Rosa had made a valuable contribution toward increasing the value of the assets accumulated by Lothar. To award everything to him would have been unfair to Rosa.

ANALYSIS

1. The legal term that applies to the Pettkus/Becker relationship of nearly 20 years is "cohabitation." Explain why.
2. Why did the Court of Appeal award Rosa one-half interest in the property and the business?
3. Explain why you agree or disagree with this statement: There should be some legal mechanism to force Pettkus to comply with the Supreme Court's decision.

Figure 16.5 The structure of families varies according to culture, tradition, and changes in society.

Cohabitation

Today many couples in Canada live together in what is often called a common-law relationship. A **common-law relationship** refers to an intimate relationship between two people who are not legally married. The term "common-law" is somewhat misleading because there are no rights or obligations in common law to protect a couple living together. A more accurate term is **cohabitation,** which is the term used in most legal documents to describe any couple who live together in an intimate relationship, whether the partners are married or not.

For many years, unmarried partners did not have a legal responsibility to financially support each other. Similarly, there existed no obligation to divide assets or property equitably if the relationship ended. This situation often left one partner, usually the woman, with no right to property or home if the relationship terminated.

Lawmakers in Canada have tried to keep pace with social attitudes and practices regarding unmarried couples who cohabitate, so all provinces and territories have enacted family legislation that recognizes cohabiters as "spouses" under certain circumstances. Being recognized as a spouse is important because a spouse has certain rights and obligations under federal and provincial law. For example, if a relationship ends, one spouse has an obligation to financially support the other if such support is deemed necessary. For instance, in Ontario, a couple who have lived together for at least three years are regarded as spouses for the purpose of support obligations. But if they have a child, it does not matter how long they have been together—one spouse has the obligation to support the other if financial assistance is required. Both parents are legally responsible for supporting the child, even if the relationship between the parents is casual and they have never lived together.

common-law relationship: an intimate relationship between two individuals who are not legally married

cohabitation: the legal description of two people involved in a common-law relationship

Fast Fact

In 1996, one in six Canadians aged 25–29 were cohabiters.

CHAPTER 16 ◆ Marriage: A Changing Tradition 425

While cohabitating partners have gained many of the benefits that married couples receive automatically, under current legislation their legal status is not the same as that of married spouses. Only through a legal contract can cohabiters acquire such rights and obligations.

Domestic Contracts

It is now possible for cohabitating couples to set out their rights and obligations in a domestic contract. A **domestic contract** is a general term for a legal agreement that partners or spouses make regarding certain aspects of their relationship. A **cohabitation agreement** is one type of domestic contract; depending on the agreement, it can give unmarried partners the same rights and obligations that married partners have. A cohabitation agreement deals with issues that may arise during the relationship, after separation, or in the event of death. However, partners cannot contract out of an obligation to support their children.

Some married couples draw up **marriage contracts**, another type of domestic contract that deals specifically with certain conditions of the relationship and the division of property in the event of a divorce, separation, or death of a spouse. The idea of a marriage contract is a relatively new concept. Traditionally, when people married they became one legal unit or person, which meant that they could not sign an agreement since a valid contract must include at least two persons. Because attitudes and laws have changed, all provinces and territories now recognize partners in a marriage as two separate, legal identities.

Same-Sex Relationships

Same-sex marriages are not legally recognized in Canada. The common-law interpretation of marriage has always been a union between a man and a woman. Provincial marriage acts define spouses as married persons of the opposite sex, and most provincial family-law acts define "spouse" as a man or a woman. However, legislation is changing. The *Family Relations Act* of British Columbia, for example, defines the word *spouse* as a "person." In the precedent-setting case of *M. v. H.* in 1999, the Supreme Court of Canada ruled that the definition of "spouse" as a man or woman in Ontario's *Family Law Act* violated s. 15(1) of the Charter. The case of *M. v. H.* is examined in depth at the end of this chapter.

Since the early 1990s, a number of reforms have been made to federal and provincial legislation regarding same-sex partners. Depending on the province in which they live, same-sex partners share many of the same rights as opposite-sex partners, including adoption, pension benefits, spousal support, and workers' compensation benefits.

While many gay and lesbian couples prefer to have a non-legal religious or social ceremony to celebrate their union, others want the right to be legally married. Some couples have challenged existing law in an attempt to have gay marriages legally recognized. In 1992, two gay men, Todd Layland and Pierre Beaulne, applied for a marriage licence and were refused. Layland and Beaulne

---

domestic contract: a legal agreement that defines rights and obligations of married or cohabitating partners

cohabitation agreement: a type of domestic contract that sets out the rights and obligations of both partners

marriage contract: a domestic contract that deals with specific aspects of the marriage, including the division of property in the event of a divorce, separation, or death

Fast Fact

On April 1, 2001, The Netherlands became the first country in the world to allow gay and lesbian couples to enter into civil marriage and enjoy the same rights as heterosexual couples.

Figure 16.6 Kevin Bourassa (left) and his partner Joe Varnell exchange vows. They hope to have their marriage legally recognized in Canada.

"Parliament cannot choose sides in the religious debate by enforcing one religious view of marriage on all. Otherwise, we are on the path to state religion, a concept that is currently unconstitutional and morally repugnant."

— Senator Lois Wilson, speaking out in favour of legalizing same-sex marriage

Quebec Considers Same-Sex Unions

QUEBEC— Quebec has taken a step towards extending marital rights and obligations to same-sex couples.

Yesterday, Justice Minister Paul Begin tabled a draft bill that would change Quebec's *Civil Code* to create a new status of partners, allowing same-sex couples to enter into a civil union with rights similar to those of married couples, but with no right to adopt children.

"What we are aiming for is to eliminate discrimination that exists in our laws and make it so that same-sex couples have the same rights as heterosexuals," Mr. Begin said. If passed, Quebec would become the second province, after Nova Scotia, to create a civil union for same-sex partners.

Under the Quebec proposal, same-sex couples would be permitted to enter into a civil union before a justice of the peace or in a religious ceremony and be governed by the same rules that apply in marriage contracts. When civil unions split up, the law would treat the parties the same as divorce laws do when it comes to dividing up homes and possessions.

The draft bill does not recognize the right of same-sex couples to adopt children. A homosexual or lesbian in Quebec who is single can legally adopt a child, but same-sex couples cannot.

SOURCE: Adapted from an article by Rhéal Séguin, *The Globe and Mail*, December 8, 2001, A12.

1. What is the difference between a marriage and a civil union?
2. Why do you think Quebec law allows single homosexuals or lesbians to adopt children, but does not extend the same right to same-sex couples? Do you agree with this law? Why or why not?

challenged this decision in court, but the judge found that under common law "persons of the same sex do not have the capacity to marry." Capacity to marry was also the issue when several same-sex couples applied to the Director of Vital Statistics in British Columbia in 2001 for marriage licences. Their requests were refused on the grounds that the capacity to marry fell under federal jurisdiction, so only the federal government could enact legislation to change the rules regarding capacity.

The province of Nova Scotia became the first jurisdiction in Canada to formally recognize same-sex partnerships. In a recently adopted law, same-sex couples in Nova Scotia can register a "domestic partnership" with the province's Office of Vital Statistics. This registration, however, is not the equivalent of a marriage, and it does not give same-sex couples the same rights and privileges married couples have.

Building Your Understanding

1. Referring to the chart in Figure 16.3 (page 423), explain how the percentage of people who marry has changed from 1981 to 1996. Describe the trends for common-law relationships and single-parent families for the same period.
2. What is the significance of having an unmarried person legally recognized as a "spouse"?
3. What is a cohabitation agreement? Explain why some partners enter into such an agreement.
4. Todd Layland and Pierre Beaulne challenged the Ontario government's refusal to issue them a marriage licence. According to the judge, what was the legal issue in their case?
5. Identify three rights and obligations that apply to both opposite-sex partners and same-sex partners.

ENDING A MARRIAGE

Not all marriages last a lifetime. Some couples get divorced, while others decide, for religious or personal reasons, to obtain an annulment. Married couples may also choose to live apart but remain legally married.

separation agreement: a domestic contract that sets out the terms and conditions of the separation, dealing with issues such as support payments and division of assets and property

Many couples sign a **separation agreement,** which is a domestic contract that sets out the terms and conditions of the separation, such as division of assets and property, support payments, and other matters the couple may want to include. Each party usually consults a separate lawyer. The lawyers then draw up the separation agreement, and each party signs it. The courts would not normally become involved unless a dispute arose. For example, if one spouse is denied the other access to the children as previously agreed, then the courts could order compliance with the agreement. Those who separate with the intention of obtaining a divorce should also sign a separation agreement that sets out their obligations and rights until they receive a divorce.

Fast Fact
The divorce rate peaked at 50% in 1987 and has been declining since then.

Divorce

divorce: the legal termination of a marriage

Divorce is the legal ending of a valid marriage. A divorce is initiated when one spouse files a petition for divorce. The **petition for divorce** will include reasons for the divorce and requests or arrangements regarding support payments and child custody. The person seeking the divorce is called the **petitioner;** the spouse being sued for the divorce is the **respondent.**

Divorce cases are decided by a judge of the Superior Court of Justice. However, the majority of divorce cases are finalized on the basis of sworn documents without a trial and without the parties seeing a judge. If one party contests (disagrees) in court, it is usually about economic or child-related issues, not the granting of the divorce itself.

A judge cannot grant a divorce without being satisfied that "reasonable arrangements" have been made to support the children. If the divorce is granted, it takes effect on the thirty-first day after the decision was handed down. The waiting period provides a dissatisfied party with the opportunity to appeal and also allows for the possibility of reconciliation. When the final **certificate of divorce** is issued, the marriage is formally dissolved. At this point both spouses are free to remarry.

The procedures for divorce were not always as straightforward as they are today. Prior to 1968, a divorce was difficult to obtain. The *Divorce Act* did not exist, and grounds for divorce varied from province to province. Grounds included **adultery** (voluntary sexual intercourse with someone other than one's spouse) cruelty, and abandonment. In cases where adultery had not occurred but divorce was desired, one party might claim to have committed adultery in order to obtain a divorce. In 1968 the federal government passed the *Divorce Act,* which unified the grounds and procedures for divorce throughout the country.

However, the 1968 legislation still made granting a divorce a complicated procedure. In 1985, the federal government brought in a new divorce act that simplified the process considerably. For example, prior to the *Divorce Act, 1985,* the petitioner had to establish a cause for the divorce. Determining who was at fault tended to make an already stressful situation even more difficult. Today, courts are not concerned with who is at fault in the breakdown of a marriage; their task is to determine *if* the marriage has broken down, not *why.*

Marriage Breakdown

Under the *Divorce Act, 1985,* the only grounds for divorce is **marriage breakdown.** Breakdown of the marriage is established if spouses live apart for one year, if one spouse commits adultery, or if one spouse has been physically or mentally cruel to the other.

Living Separate and Apart

A one-year separation period has become the most common way couples demonstrate marriage breakdown to the courts. Under the old legislation, a couple had to wait three years before they could file for divorce. The 1985 Act reduced the period of separation to one year. One of the spouses may begin divorce proceedings as soon as the separation begins, but the divorce will not be granted until they have lived "separate and apart" for at least one year.

---

petition for divorce: a document providing reasons for the divorce and arrangements for support payments and child custody

petitioner: the person seeking a divorce

respondent: the person being sued for divorce

certificate of divorce: a legal document that terminates a marriage

adultery: sexual intercourse by a married person with someone other than his or her spouse

Fast Fact
Divorce was not allowed in Newfoundland or Quebec prior to the federal *Divorce Act* of 1968.

marriage breakdown: grounds for divorce under the *Divorce Act, 1985*

Consider This
Since the introduction of the *Divorce Act, 1985,* almost 90% of divorces are uncontested (the parties do not disagree about the facts and issues of the case). What are the advantages of an uncontested divorce?

Although this usually involves living in different homes, couples can still live separate and apart while under the same roof. They may have to demonstrate however, that they have little or no contact with each other, living as though they are "separate and apart."

Adultery and Cruelty

The one-year separation period is not required if the breakdown of the marriage is the result of adultery or cruelty. Adultery can be established by reasonable proof to the court or by the spouse admitting to the adulterous relationship.

cruelty: the mental or physical behaviour of one spouse causing harm to the other, making staying together intolerable

Cruelty can be either physical or mental. Physical cruelty is usually proven through statements by witnesses, medical or police reports, or photographs. Mental cruelty is more difficult to establish in court due to the lack of visible signs. However, court rulings have established that chronic alcoholism, constant criticism, and mental disorders are among the actions that constitute mental cruelty. In a case of physical or mental cruelty, the petitioner must prove that he or she was the object of cruel treatment, that the cruelty was the result of the respondent's behaviour, and that because of the cruel treatment, remaining together would be intolerable.

Today, we often refer to physical and mental cruelty as spousal abuse. Although the vast majority of reported cases concern men attacking women, husband abuse does occur. Spousal abuse is an attempt to control or intimidate the other partner. It may involve physical or psychological cruelty, but it can also include sexual or financial abuse (often a person may experience more than one kind of abuse). In situations where there is serious risk of physical harm, provincial laws provide protection through a peace bond or a restraining order against the abuser.

Fast Fact

A 1999 Statistics Canada survey showed that about 8% of women and 7% of men who were living together experienced some type of violence from their partners on at least one occasion. Although men reported a significant amount of violence, the survey showed that the nature and consequences of spousal violence were more severe for women.

Figure 16.7 Cities across Canada have shelters like this one where abused women can seek refuge with their children.

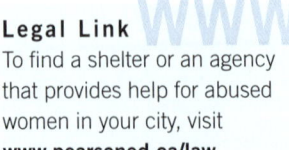

Legal Link
To find a shelter or an agency that provides help for abused women in your city, visit www.pearsoned.ca/law.

In Canada, the following forms of spousal abuse are considered crimes:

- physical abuse—punching, slapping, burning, cutting, stabbing, and shooting (crimes known as assault)
- psychological abuse—stalking, damaging property, and making threats
- financial abuse—taking a partner's paycheque and withholding money for food or medical treatment
- sexual abuse—sexual activity or touching without consent

Collusion, Condonation, and Connivance

Situations that involve deception for the purpose of obtaining a divorce can prevent a divorce from being granted. Collusion, condonation, and connivance are three legal barriers to divorce.

Collusion means that the couple has deliberately lied or deceived the court in some manner in order to obtain a divorce. For example, the couple may lie about an adulterous relationship in order to avoid having to wait for the one-year separation period. Such an action constitutes a fraud and is an absolute bar to divorce.

Condonation involves one spouse forgiving the other for an act that is being used as grounds for divorce. Suppose a spouse petitions for a divorce on

collusion: an agreement between the spouses to deliberately lie or deceive the court in order to obtain a divorce

condonation: one spouse forgives the other for an act that is being used as grounds for divorce

CASE

Spurr v. Brown, [1990] N.S.J. No. 441

In 1987, Kelly Lynn Spurr married Dana Floyd Brown. In 1989, Spurr changed jobs, and the couple moved to Tupperville, Nova Scotia. After the move, Brown was unable to find a new job, and the marriage began to deteriorate. Spurr alleged that after working 12- to 16-hour days, she came home to a dirty house because her husband alleged that doing housework made him feel like a "slave."

Spurr wanted to have children, but she believed that her husband did not. However, for Christmas, Brown gave Spurr a hand-carved baby cradle. In February 1990, Spurr became pregnant, but she claimed that her husband showed no interest in the pregnancy. In May, Brown admitted to his parents that he felt "tied down." In June, he left the matrimonial home. Two weeks later, he broke into the house and took a number of furnishings. He then wrote letters to the neighbours giving reasons for his departure, but he did not send a letter to his wife. In September, he told his wife that he did not want to be a father.

Spurr was distraught after the break up. She suffered insomnia but was unable to take sedatives because of her pregnancy. She was also upset that her husband made no inquiries about her or the baby. In November 1990, she petitioned for a divorce on the grounds of cruelty. Her petition was granted. The judge found that "the cumulative effect of [the respondent's] behaviour" constituted cruelty.

1. What did Spurr have to prove for the Court to accept the grounds of cruelty?
2. Which of Brown's actions constituted cruelty?

the grounds of adultery. The couple is then reconciled and all is forgiven. At this stage, the wronged spouse cannot seek a divorce on the grounds of adultery. However, if the couple agreed to separate, then the divorce could be granted after a one-year period of living separate and apart.

Connivance may arise when one spouse encourages the other to commit an act that would constitute grounds for divorce. For example, if one spouse asked the other to commit adultery in order to obtain a divorce, the courts would consider this act connivance and would not grant the divorce.

connivance: one spouse encourages the other to commit an act that would constitute grounds for divorce

LAW IN ACTION

Mediation in Family Law

1. What are the benefits of mediation?
2. Do you agree that it should be mandatory for couples to attend a seminar before their first appearance in the courtroom? Explain your view.

Emotions run high during divorce proceedings, and sometimes even the smallest detail can lead to arguments between the two parties. Such confrontation was common prior to the *Divorce Act, 1985* when one party was blamed for the breakdown of the marriage. The Act attempted to lessen the confrontational aspect of divorce in two ways. It dropped the requirement that one party must be found guilty or responsible for the marriage breakdown, and it introduced a section on mediation.

Mediation is a non-confrontational process designed to resolve differences between spouses over the many contentious issues that can arise in a divorce settlement. This process can reduce the time and expense of a court proceeding, allowing the couple to meet with a third party trained in mediation, psychology, or sociology. To be successful, mediation requires the co-operation of both parties since they must be willing to make a serious effort at resolving their differences. Divorce lawyers are obliged to make their clients aware of these services but are not required to be present during mediation.

The success of mediation can be seen in recent developments surrounding family law proceedings. Some provinces, such as Alberta and British Columbia, have introduced mandatory seminars that deal with the impact of divorce on children, child support guidelines, and dispute resolution options. In many instances, couples must attend these seminars before they make their first appearance in court.

Building Your Understanding

1. List three ways a marriage can be dissolved.
2. Use examples to distinguish between divorce and annulment.
3. What is a separation agreement? Describe the issues that might be included in such an agreement.
4. Identify the parties involved in a divorce proceeding and outline their roles.
5. Explain the term "marriage breakdown." Briefly describe three ways marriage breakdown can be established.
6. Why is there a 31-day waiting period in a divorce case between the date of a decision and the date the decision takes effect?

LOOKING BACK

Reviewing Your Vocabulary

adultery *p. 429*
affinity *p. 416*
annulment *p. 418*
banns of marriage *p. 419*
bigamy *p. 417*
capacity *p. 415*
certificate of divorce *p. 429*
cohabitation *p. 425*
cohabitation agreement *p. 426*
collusion *p. 431*
common-law relationship *p. 425*
condonation *p. 431*
connivance *p. 432*
consanguinity *p. 416*
consent *p. 415*
consummation *p. 418*
cruelty *p. 430*
custom marriages *p. 421*
divorce *p. 428*
domestic contract *p. 426*
essential requirements *p. 414*
formal requirements *p. 414*
marriage breakdown *p. 429*
marriage contract *p. 426*
marriage licence *p. 419*
mistake *p. 416*
monogamy *p. 417*
petition for divorce *p. 429*
petitioner *p. 429*
respondent *p. 429*
separation agreement *p. 428*
solemnization of marriage *p. 414*
under duress *p. 415*
void *ab initio* *p. 415*

Quick Quiz

1. Choose the appropriate term from the vocabulary list above to complete the following statements:
   a) The dissolution of a marriage by the courts is called ____.
   b) In some provinces, instead of purchasing a marriage licence, couples may have ____ proclaimed at their place of worship.
   c) It is the federal government that establishes the ____ of marriage.
   d) Under the *Constitution Act, 1867*, the provinces have authority over the ____ of marriage.
   e) When couples agree to marry, they cannot give their consent while ____.
   f) The spouse filing for divorce is referred to as the ____, while the other spouse is called the ____.
   g) People who are too closely related by ____ are not permitted to marry.
   h) Under the *Divorce Act, 1985*, the only basis for divorce is ____.
   i) If a spouse were unable to consummate a marriage because of a physical condition that existed at the time of the marriage, the courts would declare the marriage ____ and grant a(n) ____.
   j) An attempt by a couple to deceive the court in order to obtain a divorce is referred to as ____ and is a bar to divorce.
   k) The courts have recognized the ____ of Aboriginal peoples as legal marriages.

Checking Your Knowledge

2. Using your knowledge of the essential and formal requirements of marriage in Canada, indicate which of the following marriages would be valid. Explain your reasoning.
   a) Toshi and Barry plan to be married in an evening ceremony. On the afternoon of the wedding, friends take Barry out to a bar to celebrate. Barry consumes a great deal of alcohol and arrives at the ceremony intoxicated.
   b) Nandana is the youngest of six children. All of her siblings agreed to arranged marriages, but Nandana wants to marry someone of her own choice. Her parents have been pressuring her to marry a man whose family has paid them

a large dowry. Nandana finally gives in and reluctantly goes through with the wedding ceremony.

c) Rick and Simone began dating almost two years ago. Rick is now 19 and Simone is 17. Simone becomes pregnant, and the two decide to elope. Simone lacks parental consent but asks a friend to sign her mother's name on the marriage-licence application.

d) Sandi has been secretly dating Harold since the two were in grade 10. They are now both 20 years old and have decided to get married. Sandi's parents object because they do not approve of Harold. They insist that the marriage is invalid.

e) Maude and Travis are married in a religious ceremony in June and in a civil ceremony in July. Travis is diagnosed with Alzheimer's disease in November of that year.

3. Why would someone apply to the courts for an annulment rather than a divorce?

4. What are the minimum ages for marriage in your province *with* and *without* parental consent? Do you agree with these age requirements? Explain your position.

Developing Your Thinking and Inquiry Skills

5. Your province is debating a bill that would raise the minimum age for marriage (with parental consent) to 18. The proposed bill is based on the belief that people under 18 years of age lack the maturity to make such an important commitment. Write a 300-word presentation to the government outlining your opinion of the proposed bill.

6. With a partner, prepare a domestic contract that includes 10 to 15 terms. Consider aspects of the relationship and issues that might arise during the relationship—everything from sharing daily responsibilities to dividing property in the event of separation. Once you have agreed on the terms, draw up your contract.

7. Research the *Criminal Code* to identify the type of offence and the minimum and maximum penalties for two forms of spousal abuse.

Communicating Your Ideas

8. One of the objectives of the mediation section in the *Divorce Act, 1985,* is to make divorce less confrontational. Write a job description for a mediator, including responsibilities and qualifications required.

9. The Netherlands is the first country to legalize same-sex marriage. With a partner, research the Netherlands' same-sex marriage law. Write a report that compares this law with Canada's law for heterosexual marriage. Include a comparison of the essential and formal requirements of each. Present your findings to the class.

10. Debate the following statement: Easier access to divorce in Canada has resulted in many couples opting to get a divorce rather than working out their differences. A more rigid divorce act would result in fewer marriage breakdowns.

Putting It All Together

11. Your class has been asked to make a presentation on the requirements for marriage and divorce. Working in groups, prepare two pamphlets, one dealing with the requirements for a valid marriage, the other dealing with the steps involved in a divorce. Include any necessary legal agreements. Make sure that your pamphlets are easy to read and visually appealing. Include pictures, charts, and graphics.

CASES

Felton v. Felton, [1999] B.C.S.C. F970476

Robert Felton married Christine in 1978. They adopted a child, born in 1979. The couple separated in 1983 and entered a separation agreement that was filed in a Winnipeg court. Robert Felton testified that he had consulted a lawyer in Winnipeg, asked her how much the divorce would cost, and then paid her that amount. Christine Felton moved to British Columbia with their daughter later in 1983.

In 1985 Robert began cohabitating with Claire, and in 1988 the couple moved to Hudson Hope, British Columbia. Claire began to call herself "Claire Felton" even though they were not married until December 1989.

In the early 1990s, Robert resumed contact with Christine and his daughter. Christine mentioned that they should get a divorce. Robert was surprised when he learned that Christine had not obtained a divorce. He viewed himself as a criminal and felt frightened.

Meanwhile, Claire and Robert's relationship was deteriorating, and in 1995 Robert moved out of their home. In March 1996, they signed a separation agreement that laid out the division of assets. Robert began a divorce action in December 1996. After receiving legal advice, Robert revised his claim and sought to have his marriage to Claire and the separation agreement declared void. Claire testified that she was unaware that Robert had never divorced Christine until February 1998 when she received notice of his motion declaring their own marriage void. Claire counter-claimed that she had lost the opportunity to marry and suffered shock and anxiety "as a result of the plaintiff's bigamy."

The Court declared Robert's marriage to Claire void *ab initio* because the marriage between Christine and Robert had never been dissolved. The Court also found that the separation agreement between Robert and Claire was fair and valid. Claire's counter-claim for bigamy was dismissed.

1. Explain how the Court could declare the marriage between Robert and Claire void while finding their separation agreement valid.
2. As the judge, how would you have decided this case? What facts would you use to support your decision?

Feiner v. Demkowicz, [1974] 2 O.R. (2d) 121

Miss Demkowicz was Mr. Feiner's aunt. Demkowicz had tried to emigrate from Poland twice, but was refused permission. In 1969 Feiner decided to leave Poland because of the political system. He knew that it would be possible for a wife to leave with him, so he and his aunt decided to get married in order to leave the country. They went through the formal requirements of marriage, but the marriage was never consummated.

They left Poland, went to Rome, and eventually came to Canada. Demkowicz decided to return to Rome while Feiner remained in Canada. He found work and eventually met someone he wished to marry. He then took steps to have his marriage to the defendant annulled.

An Ontario judge found that because a marriage between a man and his mother's sister is void in Ontario, the marriage between the plaintiff and the defendant was void.

1. What is the Latin term that applies to the finding of the Ontario judge?
2. On what grounds did the judge find this marriage void? According to the case, on what other grounds might the marriage be considered void?

CASES

M. v. H, [1999] 2 S.C.R.3

BACKGROUND In 1980 M. and H., two women from Toronto, began living together in a same-sex relationship. They started their own advertising business, and purchased business and vacation property. In 1992, the relationship started to deteriorate, and M. eventually left the common home. The end of the relationship left M. financially disadvantaged, and she filed an application for support payments from her former partner under the Ontario *Family Law Act*. M. knew that her claim would not be successful because, according to the Act, a "spouse" could only be someone of the opposite sex. However, M. intended to challenge this definition under the *Canadian Charter of Rights and Freedoms.*

LEGAL QUESTION Did the words *a man and woman* in the definition of "spouse" in the Ontario *Family Law Act* discriminate against cohabitating partners of the same sex?

DECISION The judge ruled that the definition of "spouse" in the *Family Law Act* was discriminatory. She declared that the words *a man and woman* in the definition were to be changed to *two persons.*

H. appealed. The Ontario Court of Appeal upheld the lower court's decision. The Attorney General for Ontario was then granted leave to appeal the decision to the Supreme Court of Canada. The Supreme Court of Canada found that limiting the definition of "spouse" to heterosexual couples violated the equality provisions set out in s. 15 of the Charter. Justice Peter Cory wrote the following in the majority decision:

> Section 29 of the *Family Law Act* established differential treatment on the basis of a personal characteristic, namely sexual orientation. This discriminates in a substantive sense by violating the human dignity of individuals in a same-sex relationship.

The Supreme Court of Canada also noted that the purpose of the *Family Law Act* was to provide support for spouses upon the breakdown of a relationship and that excluding same-sex couples was contrary to the purpose of the law.

Figure 16.8 Same-sex couples who cohabitate believe that the law discriminates against them. If they fulfill the same obligations as married heterosexual couples, should they be denied the same rights?

LEGAL SIGNIFICANCE This decision set a precedent regarding the legal definition of "spouse" in Ontario. It recognized same-sex relationships in a way they had not been legally recognized before. The Court gave the government of Ontario six months to change the definition in the *Family Law Act.*

ANALYSIS

1. Explain how the definition of "spouse" in the Ontario *Family Law Act* was discriminatory.
2. What do you think the long-term implications of this ruling are?

Family Matters

17

CHAPTER OUTLINE

Issues in Ending a Marriage

Other Family Issues

Spousal Support

Family Assets

FOCUS YOUR LEARNING

How do laws regarding custody, support, and property division reflect changing attitudes and societal values?

What are the important factors in determining child custody?

What financial responsibilities do partners have to one another when their relationship ends?

How are a couple's property and possessions divided when a relationship ends?

Four-year-old Elijah Van de Perre was the subject of a bitter, mixed-race custody battle that went all the way to the Supreme Court of Canada. His mother is Kimberly Van de Perre, a 27-year-old woman who never completed high school and has had difficulty finding employment. His father is millionaire Theodore (Blue) Edwards, a well-known basketball player who is married with two children. The case gained media attention when the issue of race was raised as a consideration in deciding what was best for the child. You will read about the details of this case at the end of the chapter.

WHAT DO YOU THINK?

- What factors would you consider important in deciding which parent should have custody of a child?

- Explain your reasons for each of the factors you listed.

When a couple end their relationship, whether through divorce or separation, a number of important issues must be resolved: Who will have custody of the children, and how will they be supported financially? Will one spouse be obligated to provide financial support to the other and if so, for how long? How should property and assets be divided between the two spouses?

What happens when someone's partner dies, particularly if there is no will? In this situation questions always arise regarding property rights, pensions, and benefits.

The legislation dealing with custody, support payments, and the division of family property falls into the area of family law. In this chapter, you will examine these issues and learn how this branch of law continues to evolve in order to reflect changing social attitudes.

ISSUES IN ENDING A MARRIAGE

Fast Fact

Spouses who agree on the divorce and on support and custody arrangements can save money by purchasing a kit sold in bookstores that will allow them to divorce without the services of a lawyer.

As you learned in Chapter 16, a marriage is legally dissolved through the *Divorce Act, 1985*. The Act also allows for settling issues involving custody of children, child support, and spousal support. In some cases, spouses reach agreement on their own, so there is no need to use the Act for any purpose other than dissolving the marriage, as long as the agreement complies with the Act. However, when spouses are unable to reach an agreement on custody or support, they can turn to the provisions in the *Divorce Act,* and a judge will decide these matters for them. Only partners who are married have the right to apply for spousal support, child support, and custody under the provisions of Canada's *Divorce Act*. Unmarried partners must file for custody and/or support under provincial family laws.

The *Divorce Act* does not cover the division of family property. Consequently, every province and territory has enacted legislation regarding the division of family property upon the termination of a marriage. When a divorce goes to court, the judge considers the following factors:

- Is child or spousal support a factor in the divorce?
- Is there a domestic contract concerning the division of assets?
- Is there a separation agreement on the custody and support of the children?
- What are the family assets and where are they?

After reviewing these factors, the judge must then take into account the particulars of each case.

Child Custody

custody: care of a child awarded to a parent by a court when the relationship ends

custodial parent: the parent with childcare responsibilities

access: the non-custodial parent's right to visit the child

When a couple with a child (or children) decide to dissolve their relationship, **custody** must be determined to decide which parent the child will live with. If the parents cannot agree on who has custody, a judge will make this decision. The parent who cares for the child is called the **custodial parent.** The other parent, known as the non-custodial parent, is usually given **access** to the child, which means he or she has the right to spend time with the child.

A judge's primary concern in determining which parent will have custody is what arrangement would be in "the best interests of the child." The divorce or separation of a child's parents can be a very emotional and difficult adjustment for the family, so in deciding who the custodial parent should be, a judge tries to minimize any disruption for the child—physical, emotional, and social. A judge must consider a number of factors: Was the child abused by either parent? Does the child prefer living with one parent? Can one parent provide a more stable home environment? Would living with one parent interfere with the child's schooling or social life?

At one time, custody of young children was usually awarded to mothers. This practice, known as the **tender years doctrine,** was based on the assumption that women were more nurturing and caring than men. In recent years, however, the traditional roles of men and women have changed. Many men have become actively involved in the raising of their children, and more frequently, men are being awarded custody. Nonetheless, up to the age of five or six, the tender years doctrine can still be a factor in determining custody.

tender years doctrine: the belief that young children should be in the custody of their mothers

Figure 17.1 What difficulties might a custodial parent encounter caring for children as a single parent?

Fast Fact

Other considerations being equal, if the courts have to choose between a parent who will care for the child and a parent who will leave the child with a stranger or a daycare facility, the court will lean toward awarding custody to the care-giving parent.

Types of Custody

sole custody: only one parent has care of the child

There are four main types of custody arrangements. **Sole custody** refers to an arrangement that awards the responsibility of childcare to one parent. In this arrangement, the custodial parent makes all major decisions about the child's well-being, including health, education, and extra-curricular activities. **Joint custody** is a co-operative agreement that involves both parents in making decisions about the child's welfare. In a joint custody arrangement, the child lives primarily with one parent but spends a generous amount of time with the non-custodial parent. In a **shared custody** arrangement, the child spends at least 40 percent of the time with each parent. In this situation, parents share the major decisions affecting the child's upbringing. **Split custody** occurs when there is more than one child, and custody of the children is divided between the parents (e.g., one child lives with the mother, and the other child lives with the father). Although the courts try not to separate siblings, there are certain situations where doing so is in the best interest of the children.

joint custody: one parent has primary care of the child, but both parents make decisions concerning the child's upbringing

shared custody: both parents spend "equal time" with the child and make decisions involving the child's upbringing

split custody: siblings are separated, and their care is divided between parents

Access

The non-custodial parent is usually granted access to the child, which means that this parent can spend a certain amount of time with the child in order to maintain their relationship. There are three main forms of access: reasonable, defined, and supervised. **Reasonable access** allows the parents to arrange flexible visiting times that are not subject to a fixed schedule. This kind of access only works if the parents are not hostile toward each other and can make arrangements without the help of a judge. In situations where the parents cannot agree on visiting rights, the courts will impose a schedule that lists the days and times when the non-custodial parent has access to the child. This kind of access is called **defined access.**

reasonable access: an agreement between parents regarding the non-custodial parent's right to visit the child

defined access: visitation terms for the non-custodial parent that are defined by the court

CASE

Purdy v. Purdy, [2001] A.B.Q.B. 134

1. What factors did the judge consider to determine the "best interests" of the children?
2. Why do you think the judge rejected a shared custody or split custody arrangement?

Monique and Scott Purdy were married in 1993. They have two children. Because of Scott's addiction to gambling, the couple separated in 1998. The addiction had reached the point where Scott was gambling away his entire paycheque, causing considerable financial difficulty for the family.

Following the separation, Scott moved from Edmonton to Calgary and had little contact with the children. Eventually his child support payments were $5428 in arrears. Monique applied for sole custody; Scott sought joint custody.

The Court gave Monique sole custody of the children. In his ruling, the judge noted that joint custody involves both parents making decisions about the welfare and upbringing of the children. In examining the evidence regarding the parents' maturity, self-control, and relationship with the children, he concluded that joint custody was not in the children's best interests.

Normally, access is not denied unless being with the parent is likely to cause harm to the child, emotionally or physically. Sometimes the parent is granted **supervised access,** which means that he or she can only visit the child in the presence of a third party, usually a social worker, a childcare worker, or, in some cases, a responsible family member.

What happens if a custodial parent refuses to let the non-custodial parent see the child, even though that parent has access? When such conflicts over access arise, the courts often try to have the parents meet with a mediator or another third party who can help the parents resolve their differences. If an agreement cannot be reached, the non-custodial parent can seek a court order for access; but enforcing such orders can be a difficult task. The custodial parent could be charged with contempt of court, which can carry the penalty of a jail sentence. The courts are usually reluctant to impose such a sentence on a custodial parent.

In some cases, a parent denied access might resort to the extreme measure of kidnapping the child. The abduction of one's child is a criminal offence, and a parent guilty of such a crime could face up to 10 years in prison.

Grandparents

Parents are not the only family members who wish to maintain their relationship with children after a divorce or separation; many grandparents also long for regular access to their grandchildren. In most cases, parents agree that maintaining such family ties is important for the child. If a custodial parent refuses a grandparent access to his or her grandchild, the grandparent can apply to the courts. Generally, the courts regard continuing contact with grandparents to be in the best interests of the child and will favour such access. However, where contact with a grandparent would not be in the best interests of the child, access may be denied.

supervised access: visits with the child by the non-custodial parent that are supervised by a third party

Fast Fact
Parental abduction of children tends to occur during weekends and summer or winter holidays. The majority of children are between 3 and 7 years of age, and the parents who abduct them range in age from 28 to 40.

Figure 17.2 In what circumstances might the courts deny grandparents access to their grandchildren?

law in the extreme

A Question of Access

In 1999, John Schneeberger, a well-respected doctor in Saskatchewan, was found guilty and sentenced to six years in prison for drugging and sexual assaulting two women. One of the women was Schneeberger's 17-year-old stepdaughter whom he had sexually assaulted twice between 1994 and 1995.

In prison Dr. Schneeberger applied to the courts to be allowed to visit with his two biological daughters, aged five and six. Saskatchewan's Court of Queen's Bench accepted Scheeberger's application, finding that it was in the best interests of the children to visit their father once a month in Bowden penitentiary. The girls' mother, Lisa Dillman, was upset by the court order, believing that Schneeberger had lost his right to have access to his children when he sexually assaulted her teenage daughter from a previous marriage. Nevertheless, Dillman complied with the order, and in May 2001, she took her children to Bowden Institution to visit their father. When Dillman and the girls arrived at the prison, however, a social worker and several other people had gathered to protest the Court's decision, and they prevented the girls from visiting their father.

Schneeberger's lawyer made a statement that all Schneeberger wanted was to have contact with his children. "He has a strong hope that one day Ms. Dillman will be able to view that there is some benefit to his having access to the children and will actively facilitate that," his lawyer said.

The two girls were not told why their father is in prison. They have only been told that he "hurt their mother."

The main issue in this case is whether children of a sex offender should have to obey a court order to visit that parent. Is access in this situation in the best interests of the children?

An opposition MP called on the federal minister of justice to create a law that would prevent children from having to visit parents who are sex offenders. The federal minister responded that this was a family dispute. "It is between a mother and father.... It is about who has custody and who has access and ... the court makes that determination based on what is in the best interest of the child or children."

Dr. John Schneeberger

Analysis Questions
1. What reasoning did the Court give for imposing defined access in this case?
2. What reasoning did Lisa Dillman provide for opposing defined access?
3. Should there be a law that would prevent children from having to visit parents who are sex offenders, or should the criteria of "best interest of the child" be applied on a case-by-case basis? Defend your position.

Parental Mobility

It is not uncommon for divorced or separated parents to move from their original location to remarry or start a new job. A move by the custodial parent can severely disrupt the social and emotional ties the child has to the community. It can also drastically change the access the non-custodial parent has to his or her child. Suppose, for example, that Bryan has custody of his daughter, Fiona, and that his former wife, Jasmine, has generous visiting rights. One day Bryan decides to accept a promotion in his job, which will mean moving from Winnipeg to the head office in Toronto. Should he be allowed to take Fiona with him? Is it in Fiona's best interest to move away from her friends and her school and to see her mother less frequently? Should Jasmine be allowed to prevent Bryan from taking Fiona to Toronto?

In the case of *Gordon v. Goertz*, [1996], the Supreme Court of Canada faced such a decision when Robin Goertz tried to prevent his former wife, Janet Gordon, from moving to Australia with their daughter in order to study orthodontics. Janet had custody of their daughter while Robin had generous access. The Supreme Court dismissed Robin's appeal to have Janet and his daughter remain in Canada, finding that the interests of the child, not those of the custodial or access parent, were paramount in any new situation. In this particular case, the Supreme Court decided that staying with her mother was in the child's best interests even though it meant moving to Australia.

> "It is not for the court to enter into an inquiry as to the reason why the custodial parent wishes to move unless it is relevant to that parent's ability to meet the needs of the child."
>
> — Madam Justice Beverley McLachlin, in *Gordon* v. *Goertz*

Child Support

All parents have a legal obligation to provide for the needs of their unmarried children until these children reach the age of majority in the province or territory in which they live. Parents also have a financial obligation to children over the age of majority who are enrolled in post-secondary education or who, because of a disability or an illness, are unable to provide for themselves. Divorce or separation does not change a parent's obligation to support any unmarried children from that relationship. When parents separate, either they or a judge determine how much money each parent must contribute to the care of the children. The amount of money the non-custodial parent pays to support his or her child is called **child support.**

Fast Fact

The *Criminal Code of Canada* requires all parents to provide their children under the age of 16 with the necessities of life.

child support: payment one parent makes to the other to financially meet the needs of their child (or children)

Calculating Support Payments

At one time, the judge in a custody case made the calculations for support payments. This method gave judges a great deal of discretion; consequently, child support payments often varied from case to case and province to province.

In 1997, in an effort to guarantee consistency and fairness throughout the country, the federal government amended the *Divorce Act* to include new regulations on how to calculate child support payments These regulations, called the *Federal Child Support Guidelines,* provide specific tables and rules for calculating support payments based on the paying parent's income, the number of children, and the income tax rates for each province. The Guidelines apply to all parents, whether they were married at the time of separation or in a common-law relationship.

Legal Link
To find out the federal child support amounts for your province or territory, visit **www.pearsoned.ca/law**.

Another objective of the Guidelines is to ensure that children are included in any additional financial benefits that parents may enjoy after their separation. For example, if the financial situation of the parent making the payments changes, the custodial parent can apply to have an existing child support order changed. However, the applicant must demonstrate to the court that the financial change in the paying parent's income is substantial enough to warrant changing the support order.

Other Reforms

Changes to Canada's *Income Tax Act* were also part of the federal government's reforms to child support. At one time, a parent receiving child custody payments could be subject to tax on those payments. Parents who paid child support, however, could deduct these payments from their taxable income. In 1994, Suzanne Thibaudeau, a single parent in Quebec, challenged this practice under s. 15 of the Charter regarding equality rights, claiming that taxing these payments discriminated against custodial parents, who are almost always women. Thibaudeau won her case when the Supreme Court of Canada ruled in *Thibaudeau v. Canada*, [1995] that the *Income Tax Act* did discriminate against the custodial parent. The Act has since been amended.

CASE

Francis v. Baker, [1999] 3 S.C.R. 250

1. In order for Monica Francis to succeed in her application to vary support payments, what must she demonstrate?

2. Should the guidelines for determining child support payments be based primarily on the parents' income, or should factors other than the expenses of the child be taken into account? Explain.

In 1979, Thomas Baker, a lawyer, married Monica Francis, a high school teacher. Their first child was born in 1983, and a second child was born in 1985. Five days after the birth of the second child, Thomas left the family home. When the youngest child was four months old, Monica returned to teaching. In 1987, Thomas and Monica were divorced. Monica had custody of the children and received $30 000 per year in child support payments.

In 1988, Monica applied for an increase in child support. The trial over support payments did not take place until 1997. During the trial, Monica amended her application to include payments under the new *Federal Child Support Guidelines*. At that time, Monica was earning $63 000 annually; Thomas was earning $945 538 annually and was worth an estimated $78 million.

The trial judge found that under the Guidelines, the focus of determining payment was on the non-custodial parent's income, not the expenses of the child. The judge decided that considering Thomas's income, the payments should be increased to $10 034 per month. Thomas appealed the decision.

The Ontario Court of Appeal upheld the decision that the support payments should be increased. Thomas was given leave to appeal the decision to the Supreme Court of Canada. The Supreme Court of Canada ruled that the appellant failed to prove that the trial judge erred in the original decision. The appeal was dismissed, and the monthly support payments remained at $10 034.

Girls Sue Grandparents

TORONTO — In the first ruling of its kind, a Toronto judge has decided that two girls can sue their wealthy grandparents for stopping their financial support after the children's parents split up.

Shari Lynn Fein, 37, is suing businessman H. Lawrence Fein, and his wife, Beverley, on behalf of herself, and her five- and nine-year-old daughters, for allegedly turning off the financial tap when Ms. Fein's marriage to their son, Eric, ended last year.

"What [Ms. Fein] has said is the grandparents created a dependency on the income they supplied, arranged for the father to lose his job when things started going sour between the mother and father, assisted him in becoming judgment proof, and after the separation, cut off all the support they had formerly been providing to her and the children. Further, they continued to support [their son] in his former comfortable lifestyle."

Ms. Fein alleges the senior Feins underwrote, directly and indirectly, all aspects of the junior Feins' affluent lifestyle during their marriage. This included groceries, gas, clothing, a $715 000 house in an upscale area of Toronto, vacations in Palm Springs, Florida, a trust for the children, and a $300 weekly allowance for Ms. Fein, who quit work as a medical assistant to become a full-time homemaker.

SOURCE: Cristin Schmitz, "Girls can sue grandparents for cutting off money flow," *National Post,* December 10, 2001.

1. What is meant by the saying "assisted him in becoming judgment proof?"
2. When this case goes to trial, what will Ms. Fein and her daughters have to prove for their suit to be successful?
3. Should grandparents generally have a legal obligation to support their grandchildren? Why or why not?

Building Your Understanding

1. What aspect of a divorce does the *Divorce Act* not cover?
2. List the factors that the courts use in determining child custody.
3. Distinguish between joint and shared custody.
4. What is a major contributing factor in a split custody arrangement?
5. Distinguish between reasonable access and defined access.
6. What must occur before one spouse can apply to have the amount of child support changed?
7. What are the main objectives of the *Federal Child Support Guidelines*?

OTHER FAMILY ISSUES

Crucial family issues sometimes arise regardless of whether parents are married, separated, or divorced. Two important matters to consider are protecting children from abuse and giving children up for adoption.

Protection of Children

Parental responsibility goes beyond financial support. Parents must also care for their children and protect them from harm. Governments used to be reluctant to interfere in the way parents raised their children, but as issues involving child abuse have become more public, Canadian society has called upon governments to do more to ensure the protection of children both inside and outside the home.

Under the *Criminal Code*, it is an offence to abuse a child, physically or sexually. All provinces and territories have also enacted laws to protect children from neglect and abuse. Under these laws, everyone has the responsibility to report suspected cases of child abuse, which includes physical abuse, sexual abuse, failure to meet the child's medical needs, neglect, or abandonment.

A number of agencies, such as the Children's Aid Society, have been established to help ensure the protection of children. The main task of the Children's Aid Society is to investigate allegations of abuse against children under a certain age (usually 16), to protect children who are in need of protection, and to provide counselling and other services to parents and children. The Society tries to resolve problems without removing the children from the home, but if counselling and other measures fail, the children may be removed. As with the issue of custody, the family court judge takes into consideration the best interests of the children, which may include returning the children to their parents or temporarily removing the children from the home. In extreme cases, the judge may find that the natural parents should no longer have the right to care for their children. In this situation, the judge will issue a **Crown wardship order,** removing the children permanently from their parents' home. The children will then be placed in a foster home or put up for adoption.

Fast Fact

The *Criminal Code* allows children who testify against abusers to do so from behind a screen or by video to protect them from having to see their abusers.

Crown wardship order: a family judge's order to make the state (government) the guardian of a child

Figure 17.3 Each province has special child protection laws that allow the social services or health ministries to remove a child from a dangerous home situation to a safe, nurturing environment.

Matthew Vaudreuil's Legacy

LAW IN ACTION

Although agencies exist to protect children from abuse, sometimes these agencies fail to provide adequate protection. One example is Matthew Vaudreuil, a British Columbia boy who was severely abused by his mother. Matthew died at the age of five when his mother asphyxiated him while trying to force him to stop crying.

Details of Matthew's death were so shocking that the provincial government established an inquiry to investigate the situation. The inquiry into the case concluded that "serious inadequacies in the ministry's child protection system ... contributed to Matthew's suffering and death." Research showed that by the time Matthew died, the British Columbia Ministry of Children and Family Development had received at least 60 reports about his safety and well-being. Twenty-one ministry social workers had been involved in his case, and he had been to a doctor 75 times.

The Gove Inquiry, named after the judge appointed to head the inquiry, made numerous recommendations for improved child protection. Some of Judge Gove's recommendations included the following:

- the establishment of a government ministry dedicated to children and youth
- more extensive training for doctors, social workers, and child welfare supervisors in diagnosing, investigating, and assessing child abuse
- access to a computerized database containing information about previous investigations
- a co-ordinated, multidisciplinary team of doctors, nurses, psychologists, family support workers, and financial assistance counsellors to handle each case
- an independent children's commissioner to oversee death and injury reviews

1. List three of Judge Gove's recommendations. How would these changes have made a difference in Matthew Vaudreuil's case?

2. The Gove Inquiry that the government be proactive rather than reactive in dealing with child abuse. Do you think that taking preventative measures is the best way to deal with child abuse? Explain your position.

Adoption

Adoption is the process whereby a couple (or a single person) becomes the legal parents of a child. To be eligible for adoption, a child must be under the age of 18. At one time, only people who were legally married were allowed to adopt a child. However, legislation has changed, and now single people may adopt children. In some provinces, same-sex couples are also permitted to adopt.

If a child has been removed from an abusive situation through a Crown wardship order, permission for the adoption from the natural parents is not needed. In fact, in such cases, the natural parents may be denied the right to visit their child. If, however, the child is put up for adoption for other reasons, the child's natural parents must give consent for an adoption to take place. In the case of infants, most provinces have established a waiting period of be-

adoption: a legal process by which a couple (or a single person) becomes the legal parents of a child

CHAPTER 17 ◆ Family Matters

Consider This

Do you think an adopted child should have the right to know the identity of his or her biological parents? Be prepared to share your opinion in an oral presentation.

tween seven and fourteen days after the birth before a child can be placed for adoption. There is a further period of three to four weeks before the child is placed with the adoptive parents in case the natural parents change their minds. Older children who are being adopted must give their consent.

Once the adoption process is complete, the child becomes the legal child of the adopting parents, and they assume all responsibility for the child. In the event of a marriage breakup, the adopted child is treated in the same manner as a biological child.

Adoption and Aboriginal Children

[T]he child will perhaps be much better off in the way of education, comfortable surroundings and the material things of life….or will this little girl as she grows up feel she is treated differently, is discriminated against?

— Justice Morrow
Re: Adoption of Kakfwi, 1970

Laws in many provinces or territories require adoptive parents to consider an Aboriginal child's heritage and traditions while raising the child. In many adoption cases, the Indian band to which the child belongs must be given notice of the intention to put that child up for adoption. The band can request to have the child placed with or adopted by Aboriginal parents.

Many lower courts, in recognizing the importance of a child's Aboriginal heritage, have favoured Aboriginal adoptive parents over non-Aboriginal applicants. However, in two cases involving the adoption of an Aboriginal child by non-Aboriginal parents (*Natural Parents* v. *Superintendent of Child Welfare*, [1976] and *Racine* v. *Woods*, [1983]), the Supreme Court of Canada decided in favour of the non-Aboriginal parents. This decision was made despite the protests of the natural parents and their efforts to either gain custody of their children or to have their children placed with an Aboriginal family. The Supreme Court also held that a child who is registered under the *Indian Act* will not lose his or her status as an Indian when adopted by non-Aboriginal parents.

Building Your Understanding

1. Under the *Criminal Code*, what actions constitute child abuse?
2. What is a "Crown wardship order" and when is it issued?
3. When is permission from the natural parents not required for the children to be adopted? Explain.
4. Why is there a waiting period before infants are placed with their adoptive parents?
5. What issues should be considered when Aboriginal children are being put up for adoption? Why are these issues important?

SPOUSAL SUPPORT

During their marriage, partners are obligated to financially support each other, and in certain situations, that financial obligation continues after the marriage ends. Such obligations are particularly common in situations where one spouse has stayed at home to raise the children. When a spouse is a full-time homemaker, he or she becomes financially dependent, and this dependency may continue after a separation or divorce.

Suppose, for example, that Anita and Sean decide to get married and raise a family. Anita quits her training in physiotherapy and raises their three children. She remains out of the workforce for 10 years. During this period, Sean continues to work and support the family. If the couple goes through a divorce, Anita is at a disadvantage financially because she interrupted her education and has not had any training since she left school. Even if she returns to school and is successful in finding a position as a physiotherapist, she may never reach the income or professional level she would have attained if she had worked continuously for the preceding 10 years. Anita can apply for spousal and child support under the *Divorce Act* if she files for divorce, or under provincial legislation if she does not seek a divorce.

The money one spouse pays the other following their separation is called **spousal support,** and it is intended to relieve the economic hardship one spouse suffers as a result of the breakdown of the marriage. Support payments are meant to help the disadvantaged spouse become financially self-sufficient within a reasonable period. When deciding on spousal support, a divorce court examines the need of the spouse applying for support and the ability of the respondent spouse to pay. In applying this test, the court takes into consideration how long the spouses have lived together, the role each person played in the relationship, the ability of one spouse to support the other, and whether there are any existing agreements relating to the financial support of one or the other. Traditionally, men have paid spousal support because they usually earn more money than their spouses, who often stay at home to care for their children. However, as more women enter the workforce, and as their salaries increase, spousal support for men may become more common.

In the case of a common-law relationship, the partners have a legal obligation to support each other only if they have an agreement that specifies support payments, or if they are regarded as "spouses" under the family law act of their province. While the legal definition of spouse can vary from province to province, most family law acts specify a required period (usually three years) that two people must live together in an intimate relationship

> *"Marriage, while it may not prove to be 'till death do us part,' is a serious commitment not to be undertaken lightly. It involves the potential for lifelong obligation."*
> — Madame Justice Beverley McLachlin

spousal support: money that one spouse pays the financially dependent spouse once the marriage or relationship has terminated

Hagar the Horrible

before they are defined as "spouses." If the partners meet the criteria of "spouses" under the family law act, then to determine support payments a judge applies the same criteria to common-law partners that are applied to married spouses.

Self-Sufficiency

While many spouses who seek support payments eventually become economically self-sufficient, what happens when the dependent spouse is not able to achieve this goal? For example, in the case of Anita and Sean, suppose Anita had remained at home for 30 years and, at the age of 55, was unable to take retraining courses or could only find a part-time job that did not pay her enough to become financially independent. What should Sean's obligation to his former spouse be? In this situation, a court may require Sean to pay spousal support for an indefinite period, a decision Sean may resent. After all, once divorced, shouldn't individuals feel free to remarry and start a new life?

In the mid-1980s, the Supreme Court of Canada was faced with such a decision in three similar cases, *Pelech* v. *Pelech*, [1987], *Richardson* v. *Richardson*, [1987], and *Caron* v. *Caron*, [1987]. The cases are often referred to as the "Pelech Triology" because the Supreme Court of Canada released the decisions at the same time, and the decisions in all three cases were similar.

In the case of *Pelech* v. *Pelech*, [1987], Shirley Pelech agreed to a lump-sum payment when she and her husband were divorced in 1969. Shirley and John Pelech had been married for 15 years. John had a contracting business, and Shirley had worked in the office for many years. After the divorce, Shirley suffered severe psychological and physical problems, was unable to work, and eventually started living on welfare. In contrast, John remarried and became financially successful.

In 1982, Shirley sought to have the original support agreement changed. The case went all the way to the Supreme Court of Canada, where it was dismissed in 1987. The Supreme Court chose not to interfere with the original divorce settlement because it believed that it was unfair to force John to pay his former wife support for so many years after the marriage ended.

Five years later, however, in *Moge* v. *Moge*, [1992], the Supreme Court of Canada recognized that the goal of self-sufficiency could not always be achieved by the dependent spouse. In this case, spousal support for an indefinite period remained an obligation.

Enforcing Support Payments

Failure to pay child or spousal support can cause serious financial hardship. In recent years, the provinces have established enforcement agencies that

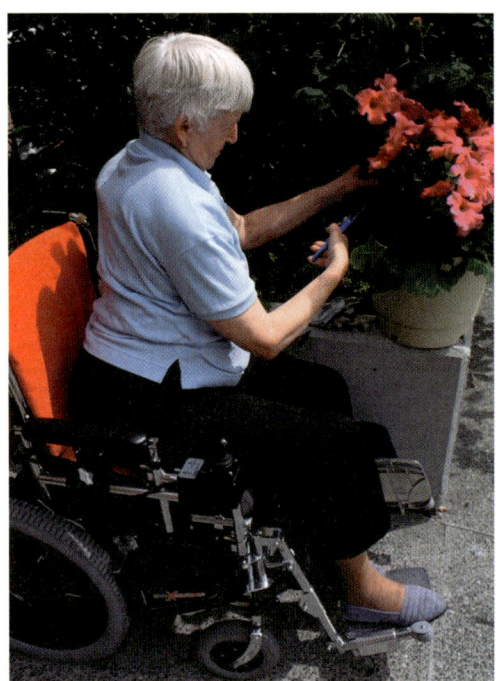

Figure 17.4 In a divorce, when one spouse is financially dependent, the other spouse may be obligated to pay support indefinitely. How does a court balance this obligation with the spouses' desire to start a new life?

"I believe that the courts must recognize the right of the individual to end a relationship as well as to begin one and should not ...treat the financial responsibility as continuing indefinitely into the future."
— Justice Wilson
in the *Pelech* v. *Pelech* decision

Moge v. Moge, [1992] 3 S.C.R. 813

CASE

Andrzej and Zofia Moge were married in Poland and moved to Canada in 1960. They separated in 1973 and were divorced in 1980. During most of the marriage, Zofia stayed home to raise their three children. The household chores were also her responsibility. She had little formal education and did not speak English well. Zofia had a part-time job cleaning offices in the evenings, and Andrzej had a full-time job as a welder.

Zofia was awarded custody of the children and $150 a month in spousal and child support. After the separation, she continued cleaning offices. At the time, she was making approximately $800 per month; Andrzej was earning approximately $2200 per month. However, in 1987, Zofia lost her job, so she had her support payments increased to $400 a month.

In 1989, Andrzej was successful in having the support payments terminated. The judge who granted the application determined that Zofia had had enough time to become financially independent. However, the Manitoba Court of Appeal reinstated the support payments and ordered Andrzej Moge to pay $150 per month in spousal support for an indefinite period. Andrzej was given leave to appeal this decision to the Supreme Court of Canada.

The Supreme Court dismissed the appeal and found that Andrze was obligated to continue paying spousal support indefinitely. The Court acknowledged that while spouses have an obligation to support themselves after the breakdown of a marriage, in situations where the dependent spouse is unable to escape his or her dependency, the other spouse is obligated to continue to financially support the dependent spouse.

1. Is there a relevant difference between the support agreements established in *Moge* v. *Moge* and *Pelech* v. *Pelech*?
2. Do you agree with the Supreme Court's decision in *Moge* v. *Moge*? Why or why not?
3. What important precedent did this case establish?

help collect child and spousal support. For example, in British Columbia, the agency is called the Family Maintenance Enforcement Program; in Ontario, it is called the Family Responsibility Office.

These agencies collect the money from one parent and pass it on to the custodial parent. If the payments stop, the agencies have a number of options at their disposal. One option is garnishing wages, whereby the court orders an employer to deduct the money owed from the employee's paycheque and remit it directly to the enforcement agency. Other actions can also be taken. In Ontario, for example, a parent who defaults on support payments may have his or her driving licence suspended.

The person paying support can apply to have the amount of support payments adjusted should his or her financial situation change due to illness, unemployment, or retirement. In the following case of *Boston* v. *Boston*, [2001], the Supreme Court of Canada ruled that a retired man could reduce his support payments because he was living on a pension.

Consider This

Discuss whether a parent who refuses to pay child support should be put in jail.

CASE

Boston v. Boston, [2001] 2 S.C.R. 413

1. Identify the main issue in this case.
2. "This ruling may result in more elderly, single women living in poverty." Do you agree or disagree with this statement? Support your position.

Shirley and Willis Boston were married for 36 years. Willis worked in public education, and Shirley took care of the home and their children. When the couple separated in 1994, Shirley received $3200 per month in spousal support. Willis's pension was included as part of the family assets.

When Willis retired in 1996, he asked the Court to reduce the amount of support he paid his former wife because he was now living on a reduced income. He argued that she had already benefited from the inclusion of his pension as part of the assets, and if he now had to use money from his pension to pay spousal support, Shirley would be "double dipping," that is, receiving funds twice.

The trial judge agreed with Willis and lowered the support payments to $950 a month. Shirley appealed, and the Ontario Court of Appeal increased the support payment to $2000. Willis was given leave to appeal this decision to the Supreme Court of Canada. The Supreme Court allowed the appeal, and Willis was permitted to reduce his monthly support payments. The Court's decision was based on the fact that a spouse should not have access to a pension that has already been considered in determining the divorce settlement.

Building Your Understanding

1. What is the purpose of spousal support?
2. Explain the principle of self-sufficiency.
3. Under what circumstances might the courts vary a support order?
4. What happens when a spouse disobeys a court order to make support payments?

FAMILY ASSETS

family assets: property owned by either spouse (or both) and normally used for family purposes

The end of a relationship usually involves the division of assets—ownership of items, investments, and property. While the definition can vary depending on the jurisdiction, **family assets** are usually those items or kinds of property the couple have acquired during the marriage, such as the family house, vacation property, vehicles, furniture, appliances, and savings. In British Columbia, Alberta, Saskatchewan, Manitoba, and Ontario, business interests acquired during the marriage are also considered family assets, as are pension plans and registered retirement savings plans.

Equal Division of Property

At one time, Canadian laws governing divorce and division of property resulted in many spouses (usually women) receiving little of the family property when the couple divorced. Before the 1980s, when a court considered the spouses' individual contribution to family assets, only monetary contributions were included; raising children and working in the home were not seen as contributions to family assets. Women who stayed at home to raise their children often had little or no property in their own name because they did not earn an income. The family home and other investments were usually in the husband's name.

A case in point was *Murdoch* v. *Murdoch,* [1975]. The Murdochs had been married for 25 years. During their marriage, they worked hard and acquired several cattle ranches. All property was registered in the husband's name. Mr. Murdoch also worked outside the ranches and was often away for long periods. During her husband's absence, Mrs. Murdoch continued to work the ranches and maintain the home. When they divorced, she asked for a half share of the property. Her claim was denied in both the lower court and in the Supreme Court of Alberta. She was given leave to appeal the decision to the Supreme Court of Canada, where her appeal was dismissed. The Supreme Court of Canada ruled that she was not a partner in the ranches because she had not contributed financially, and her work comprised what any farm wife would have done. Without a formal agreement that held land in trust for her, and without proof of financial contribution, the courts had to rely on existing legislation, which only recognized financial contributions to family property.

The Supreme Court's decision shocked and angered many Canadians and became a major factor in bringing about much needed reform to family law. Current family laws are based on the principle that marriage is a partnership between two people and that both partners contribute to the family wealth in different but equal ways. One partner, for example, may work outside the home for a salary, while the other works in the home, raising children and performing tasks for which he or she is not paid.

> **Fast Fact**
> Under the old common law system, once they were married, a man and woman were regarded as a single entity. Only the husband was allowed to make financial transactions and asset purchases, and he owned all of the matrimonial property.

Dividing the Assets

The first step in dividing family assets is to add up the value of each party's assets. Once the value of the family assets has been determined, any outstanding debt by each spouse is deducted from their total value. What is left is called the **net family property,** and it is this property (or the value of this property) that is divided between the spouses. In cases where the property cannot be equally divided, one spouse may have to pay the other spouse cash, or the equivalent, in order to make the division of assets more equitable. This payment by one spouse to another is called an **equalization payment.** Each spouse is also allowed to keep assets that were his or hers at the time of the marriage. In some provinces, any increase in assets during the marriage is considered a family asset.

Inheritances and gifts received during marriage are not included in the net family property. Suppose Ricardo and Janet divide their assets after 10 years of marriage. Janet is entitled to the antique dining set, the bedroom set, and the small appliances she had at the time of the marriage. Ricardo is entitled

net family property: the value of a couple's assets, less any debts, at the date the relationship ends

equalization payment: what the spouse with the higher value of assets pays to the other spouse to make the division of total assets more equitable

CASE

Marinangeli v. Marinangeli, [1997] 54 O.R. (3d) 179

1. How was the concept of "equal division of family assets" applied in this case?
2. What did the judge base his ruling on? Explain whether you agree with the judge's decision.

Daniel and Jennifer Marinangeli were divorced in 1997. At the time of the final divorce settlement, Daniel was to pay his ex-wife $8600 per month in spousal support plus child support. The day after signing the final divorce papers, Daniel cashed in stock options worth $1 million. Jennifer then brought an action against her ex-husband for an increase in support because his finances had dramatically changed immediately after their marriage ended. Daniel argued that he had cashed in the stock options to help pay for the divorce settlement.

The Court decided in Jennifer's favour and ordered Daniel to pay approximately $300 000 in retroactive child and spousal support, which would cover payments she should have received since the final divorce proceedings. The judge also ordered that spousal support payments be increased to $10 500 per month and child support payments to $5841 per month. The judge made his ruling based on the fact that Daniel had failed to fulfill his obligation to tell his ex-wife about a "material change" in his financial circumstances, which resulted from exercising his stock options.

---

to the stereo system, the other bedroom set, and the stainless steel pots and pans he had when the marriage took place. Anything that was acquired after the marriage is equally divided. But what about the rare print they bought together after they were married? Since Janet likes the print, she keeps it and pays Ricardo one-half of its value.

The Matrimonial Home

matrimonial home: the principal residence where spouses resided before their separation

The family home, referred to in family law as the **matrimonial home,** is the main residence where the couple lived at the time of the separation. The matrimonial home—often the biggest and most important family asset—is automatically considered part of family property regardless of when and how it was acquired. Each spouse has an equal right of possession, which means that neither spouse can force the other one to leave. However, a judge may decide that in the interests of the children, one spouse may have exclusive possession of the family home—the right to live in the house for a certain period, perhaps until the children grow up and move away. Once the children have moved out, the house can be sold and the money split between the spouses. A spouse's right to the matrimonial home can be altered, but only with the consent of both spouses.

Unequal Division of Property

Although every attempt is made to ensure that the value of the assets is divided equally, such equality might actually prove unfair to the spouse who contributed more to the marriage financially. In this instance, the court may

Figure 17.5 For most couples, the value of the matrimonial home is more than financial. As the centre of family life, the home can also create strong emotional bonds. In what way can emotional factors affect how the value of the matrimonial home is measured?

make an **order of unconscionability,** an order stating that an equalization of the parties' net family property would be unreasonable or unfair. In this case, the court would divide the assets *unequally*; in other words, some of the assets that one spouse brought to the marriage would be excluded from the net family property and would not be subject to division. The following case, *Mari* v. *Mari*, [2001], provides a good example of unequal division of the matrimonial home.

order of unconscionability: an order requiring a division of property that recognizes the unequal contribution of the spouses

Mari v. Mari, [2001] S.C.B.C.

CASE

William and Kathryn Mari were married in 1983. They separated in 1999, and a divorce hearing was completed in January 2001. Both parties agreed on the issues regarding child custody, support payments, and division of family assets.

The only issue in dispute was division of the matrimonial home. William wanted an *equal* division of the matrimonial home because it was his higher income that had allowed them to purchase such an expensive house. Kathryn wanted an *unequal* division of the home because the couple's purchase of their first home was made possible by her cash payment of $24 823. In addition, Kathryn's parents had loaned her and William $57 000 for the purchase of their current home, valued at $440 000.

The Supreme Court of British Columbia ruled in Kathryn's favour. Kathryn was awarded a 60 percent share in the matrimonial home and William a 40 percent share.

1. Why did the trial judge award Kathryn a greater share of the matrimonial home?
2. Should the matrimonial home always be divided on a 50/50 basis, regardless of the source of the money used to buy the home? Explain.

Division of Property on Reserve Lands

Married couples who live on reserve lands are subject to different laws regarding the division of matrimonial property because they cannot buy the land. Reserve land is owned by the Crown for the use and benefit of Aboriginal people who live on the reserves. A person living on a reserve can apply to the federal government for the right to possess a piece of land. However, if a person is granted the right to possess reserve property, he or she can transfer this right only to another member of the band or to the band itself. As illustrated by *Derrickson* v. *Derrickson,* [1986] the division of reserve property was challenged.

Division of Property in a Common-law Relationship

Fast Fact
To benefit from a life insurance policy, a common-law partner must be identified as the beneficiary. The *Canada Pension Act,* however, allows a common-law spouse to claim survivor benefits if the couple have lived together for the one-year period immediately preceding the death.

As you learned in Chapter 16, couples in a common-law relationship can draw up domestic contracts that give them the same rights and obligations that married spouses have, depending on what the contract includes and whether it complies with family law acts. However, not all common-law couples have such contracts, and should their relationships end, they do not have the rights and privileges that married spouses automatically have.

In matters involving the division of property, each common-law spouse is entitled to what he or she brought into the relationship. Where one spouse has contributed to family assets in a non-financial way, such as staying home and raising children or working in a family business without receiving a salary, the courts take into consideration the nature of the contribution of each spouse. *Pettkus* v. *Becker,* [1980] (see Chapter 16) was an important case because it recognized that in a common-law relationship one spouse should not benefit or be "enriched" unjustly by the contribution of the other spouse.

Division of Property on Death

will: written instructions for the distribution of property and possessions after death

A **will** is a legal document that states how a person's property and possessions are to be divided upon his or her death. Most people do not think about drawing up a will until they earn a salary or have a family. However, it is important for anyone who has assets to make a will.

Most spouses bequeath their property and possessions to the surviving spouse. If the surviving spouse has not been provided for in the will, he or she can apply to the province for division of matrimonial property within six months of the death. This application gives the surviving spouse the same rights he or she would have had if the couple had separated one day before the spouse's death.

intestate: the state of dying without a will

succession: the legal right to inherit property

When a person dies without a will, he or she dies **intestate.** In this situation, **succession,** or the legal right to inherit property, is determined under provincial and territorial legislation. Should a married person die intestate, provincial and territorial laws provide that the surviving spouse is entitled to a share of the property. However, there is no legal protection for a common-law spouse whose partner dies without a will.

CASE

Derrickson v. Derrickson, [1986] 1 S.C.R. 285

BACKGROUND Rose and William Derrickson are members of the Westbank First Nation in British Columbia. Rose sought a divorce from William. In her petition for divorce, she applied under the British Columbia *Family Relations Act* for one-half of the interest in the properties that William had been granted under s. 20 of the *Indian Act*. Rose was prepared to accept compensation in lieu of the property.

The Supreme Court of British Columbia dismissed Rose's application, saying that the British Columbia Court had no jurisdiction because the federal *Indian Act* supersedes the provincial *Family Relations Act*. On appeal, the Court of Appeal held that Rose was not entitled to an interest in the reserve lands, but it recognized that she should be compensated financially when family assets were divided between the spouses. Rose was given leave to appeal the decision to the Supreme Court of Canada.

LEGAL QUESTION Do the provisions dealing with division of family assets in the British Columbia *Family Relations Act* apply to reserve lands held by an Aboriginal person?

DECISION The Supreme Court of Canada held that the right to possess reserve lands is a federal matter and that provisions of the provincial *Family Relations Act* dealing with the division of family assets did not apply to reserve lands. The Court awarded Rose compensation for her interest in the reserve lands, but it could not award her the equal division she would have had under the provincial legislation.

SOCIAL SIGNIFICANCE The Supreme Court's decision was intended to ensure that reserve lands continue to be set apart for the use and benefit of Indian bands. However, many people argue that the decision leaves Aboriginal women without recourse in the courts because the majority of the holders of Certificates of Possession are Aboriginal men. Furthermore, many critics of the decision point out that awarding Rose compensation was not a practical form of assistance because in order to obtain compensation in lieu of division of lands, she would have to return to the Supreme Court of British Columbia—an expensive step. Furthermore, her husband would have to own sufficient liquid assets to comply with any order.

ANALYSIS

1. Explain why the Court could not award Rose one-half interest in the reserve property.
2. Would the decision have been different if the property had not been reserve land? Explain.
3. What arguments have been raised by critics of the Supreme Court of Canada decision? Explain why you agree or disagree with this decision.

Building Your Understanding

1. Define "family assets," and explain why they become an issue when a marriage dissolves.
2. How have statutes on family matters changed since the 1980s? Explain the reason for these reforms.
3. What is an equalization payment? Give an example of your own.
4. Why is the matrimonial home given special consideration under family law?
5. How does the division of family assets differ for people living on Indian reserve lands?
6. What precautions should common-law partners take to protect their shared assets in the event that the relationship ends?
7. Why is it important to have a will? Use the words *intestate* and *succession* in your explanation.

LOOKING BACK

Reviewing Your Vocabulary

access *p. 438*
adoption *p. 447*
child support *p. 443*
Crown wardship order *p. 446*
custodial parent *p. 438*
custody *p. 438*
defined access *p. 440*
equalization payment *p. 453*
family assets *p. 452*
intestate *p. 456*
joint custody *p. 440*
matrimonial home *p. 454*
net family property *p. 453*
order of unconscionability *p. 455*
reasonable access *p. 440*
shared custody *p. 440*
sole custody *p. 440*
split custody *p. 440*
spousal support *p. 449*
succession *p. 456*
supervised access *p. 441*
tender years doctrine *p. 439*
will *p. 456*

Quick Quiz

1. Check your knowledge of the vocabulary terms above by completing the following exercise:

    Form small groups. Each member of the group selects five terms from the list above and writes each term and its definition on an index card. All the cards are placed in a pile and shuffled. Each player selects one of the cards, reads the definition, and asks another member of the group to identify the term. Alternatively, each player reads the term and asks for the definition. Complete this process until all of the cards have been used.

Checking Your Knowledge

2. Name four issues that must be resolved when a marriage ends.
3. Define the "tender years doctrine" and explain how it was originally used. Why has its application changed in recent years?
4. What factors does the court use to determine spousal support?
5. When would the courts order an unequal division of family property? Provide an example of your own to illustrate this principle.
6. Calculate the equalization payment for each of the following examples:

    a) Titiana and Richard were married for 15 years. Richard had $30 000 in assets when they married and Titiana had $45 000. They bought (and paid for) a home valued at $280 000. Richard has a pension that is currently worth $70 000, and Titiana has RRSPs valued at $30 000. They also own a family vacation home worth $170 000 with a $120 000 mortgage.

    b) When Josh and Mala got married, each had assets worth $25 000. During their 17-year marriage, Josh built a successful business valued at $250 000, bringing his total worth to $275 000. All personal assets the couple acquired had a value of $50 000 and were placed in Mala's name, bringing her total worth to $75 000.

Developing Your Thinking and Inquiry Skills

7. Use your library resource centre or the Internet to access the *Federal Child Support Guidelines*. Compare the support-payment requirements of your province with those of another province. Now compare how the two provinces enforce payment. Suggest reasons for any differences or similarities.

8. In many instances, parents disobey court orders to pay child support. As a social worker, you have been asked to develop a system of enforcement that is effective and reasonably inexpensive to implement.

9. Examine the following case:

> James and Michelle McBride were married in 1974. At the start of the marriage, James was the major wage earner. However, by 1996 Michelle's gross income was substantially larger than that of her husband.
>
> In 1998 they separated, and James applied for interim spousal support of $10 500 per month. The Court estimated Michelle's income that year to be about $173 200. The couple also owned a matrimonial home in Vancouver and a recreational property in Whistler.
>
> The Court awarded James interim support of $3000 per month, stating that he had suffered some financial disadvantages from the separation, "as he no longer had his wife's large income available to him."

a) Identify three considerations the Court would apply to making a decision on spousal support. Which consideration is most relevant to this case?

b) Is the Court decision consistent with the primary purpose of spousal support? Explain.

Communicating Your Ideas

10. Write a letter to your Member of Parliament in which you express your views on how child custody should be determined.

11. Thousands of Canadian children live in poverty because non-custodial parents do not pay child support. Use the your library resource centre to research the following: How many children are affected? How many parents fail to pay support? Why do they refuse to pay? What can be done to solve this problem? When you have completed your research, present your findings in a poster-board display. Include photos, charts, and graphs to communicate your ideas.

12. Use the Internet to select a case dealing with one of the issues covered in this chapter. Choose an issue that has been decided by a court or court of appeal in your province. Write a brief summary of the case under the following headings: Background, Facts, Issues, Decision, Significance, and Analysis. Present your summary to the class, using visual aids.

Putting It All Together

13. Working with a partner, choose one of the family relationships described below and develop a separation agreement to resolve issues such as custody, access, child support, spousal support, and division of family assets.

a) Sara and Jake met in 1987 when Sara applied for a position in Jake's hairdressing salon. After a whirlwind courtship, they were married in 1988. As a wedding gift, Jake gave Sara a 50 percent partnership in the business, which was valued at $100 000. They worked together in the salon for 10 years, until Sara gave birth to their only child, Hedy. Sara stayed at home caring for Hedy, working one day a week. Sara and Jake have decided to separate. The estimated worth of their business is $1 950 000. They own a house and a cottage by the lake valued at $250 000 and $125 000, respectively.

b) Zachary and Shauna have been in a common-law relationship for five years, and they have two-year-old twins. The boys adore their father, even though he is a harsh disciplinarian; in fact, Zachary's abusive child-rearing methods are at the root of the couple's separation. The family home, which Shauna's father purchased for her before she met Zachary, is valued at $175 000. Shauna operates a daycare facility from the home and earns an annual salary of $33 200. They have one vehicle that Zachary uses to get to and from his job as a construction worker. Zachary's last tax return showed a gross income of $68 500.

CASES

Bracklow v. Bracklow, [1999] 1 S.C.R. 420

Marie Bracklow began living with Frank Bracklow in 1985. Four years later, they got married in Coquitlam, British Columbia. Both parties had been previously married. Marie had two children, and Frank assumed the role of their father. During the first two years of their marriage, Marie contributed more than Frank because at the time she was making more money than he was. Soon Marie began experiencing health difficulties. However, in late 1990 she obtained a new position with a company, where she worked from November 1990 to October 1991.

In October 1991, Marie was admitted to the hospital, suffering from psychiatric problems. She was unable to return to work. In 1992, she was diagnosed with fibromyalgia, a painful, debilitating muscle condition. That same year, Frank left the relationship, and the couple was divorced in February 1995. Prior to the divorce, Marie obtained an order for spousal support of $275 per month, which increased to $400 per month in May 1994. The trial judge found that "no economic hardship befell [Marie Bracklow] as a consequence of the marriage or its breakdown," and he concluded that Marie was not entitled to support from her husband. However, he did order the $400 monthly payments to continue, but only until September 1, 1996.

Marie appealed the decision, and the appeals court agreed with the original judge's decision. Marie was then given leave to appeal to the Supreme Court of Canada. The appeal was allowed. The Supreme Court found that divorce did, in fact, render the appellant in a state of economic hardship. It concluded that she was legally eligible for post-marital support based on the length of time she and Frank had lived together, the hardship the marriage breakdown imposed on her, her need, and Frank's ability to pay.

1. What evidence indicates that Marie Bracklow contributed significantly to the marriage?
2. What factors did the Supreme Court of Canada consider to determine the amount of support for Marie? Which factor is most difficult to calculate? Why?
3. Do you agree with the decision in this case? Why or why not?

Miglin v. Miglin, [2001] 53 O.R. (3d) 641

Eric and Linda Miglin were married on February 17, 1979. The couple jointly owned and operated a resort called Killarney Lodge. Linda was the primary caregiver for their four children.

In 1993 the couple separated, and in 1994 they signed separation, custody, and child support agreements. Both parents shared the responsibility of raising the children, although Linda had custody. Eric agreed to pay $60 000 a year in child support. The couple also signed an agreement that instead of spousal support, Linda would receive an annual consulting fee of $15 000 from Killarney Lodge.

Following their divorce, Eric's attitude toward his ex-wife changed dramatically. He was no longer friendly in his dealings with her and became quite aggressive with Linda and the children. Linda's consulting agreement for $15 000 was not renewed. In June 1998, Linda applied to the Court for sole custody of the children and for both child and spousal support.

In February 2000, the trial judge awarded Linda spousal support of $4400 per month for five years and monthly child support of $3000. The couple agreed to joint custody. Eric appealed the order for spousal support and child custody. The Ontario Court of Appeal dismissed Eric's appeal. The Court recognized that the original agreement to pay Linda a consulting fee was intended as a form of spousal support; termination of the consulting agreement meant that Linda no longer received this form of support.

1. Using your knowledge of previous court decisions on changes to divorce settlements, how would you have decided this case? Justify your decision.
2. This controversial decision by the Ontario Court of Appeal made headlines in newspapers across the country. Research public reaction to this case. Why was this decision so controversial? What reasons did people have for either supporting or opposing the decision?

CASES

Van de Perre v. Edwards (2001), S.C.C. 60

BACKGROUND In 1996, Kimberly Van de Perre met Theodore Edwards, a professional basketball player, who was married with two children. Theodore and Kimberly had a sexual relationship, and Kimberly became pregnant. Before the birth of the baby, Theodore and his wife, Valerie, returned to North Carolina. In 1997, Theodore returned to Vancouver for the basketball season, and his relationship with Kimberly resumed. When their son, Elijah, was three months old, Kimberly began court proceedings for custody and child support. The trial judge awarded Kimberly sole custody of Elijah, and Theodore was granted access for four weeks each year.

Theodore appealed the decision. In the appeal, Theodore's lawyer argued that the trial judge had failed to consider Theodore's parenting skills and the fact that Theodore and his wife were better able to provide Elijah with a stable home than Kimberley was. The lawyer argued that Kimberly was a "24-year-old single parent with poor employment qualifications and a spotty employment record" who had dropped out of high school and depended on her parents for financial support. Theodore's lawyer also argued that the trial judge had ignored the "race issue" and had not considered the interracial problems Elijah might experience because his mother is Caucasian and his father is African-American.

The Court of Appeal for British Columbia, deciding that the trial judge had erred, reversed the original decision. The Court of Appeal granted Theodore and his wife, Valerie, custody of the child; Kimberly was granted generous access. Kimberly was given leave to appeal to the Supreme Court of Canada.

Theodore (Blue) Edwards

LEGAL QUESTION Did the trial judge err in determining the best interests of the child when he awarded Kimberly custody of Elijah?

DECISION The Supreme Court of Canada allowed the appeal, and Kimberly was awarded custody of Elijah. In reaching its decision, the Supreme Court found that the parenting skills and attributes of both parents had been taken into consideration in the trial judge's decision. In fact, the Supreme Court agreed with the trial judge's opinion that because of the nature of his job, Theodore travelled extensively and was away from home for long periods. Consequently, Valerie was responsible for all of the childcare activities. Also, Theodore had had numerous extra-marital affairs, and the Court was not convinced that this pattern would change.

On the question of race, the Court was of the opinion that "there was absolutely no evidence indicating that race was an important consideration."

SOCIAL SIGNIFICANCE The Supreme Court's decision illustrated that in this case, the parenting skills of the biological parents overrode considerations regarding the race of the parents in determining the best interests of the child.

ANALYSIS

1. What arguments did Theodore's lawyer use to win custody for Theodore and Valerie?
2. Why do you think Kimberly was granted leave to appeal to the Supreme Court of Canada?
3. What factors did the Supreme Court of Canada take into account in deciding this case?
4. If you were placing a value on the factors involved in determining the "best interests of the child," where would you place racial identity? Explain why.

18 Forming a Contract

CHAPTER OUTLINE

Classifying Contracts

Elements of a Contract

Invalidating Factors

FOCUS YOUR LEARNING

What are the various types of contracts?

What are the essential elements of a contract?

How does contract law protect individuals?

WHAT DO YOU THINK?

- The photographs above show people engaged in activities involving contracts. How do these situations influence your perception of contracts?
- In a group, brainstorm how these contracts might work and consider your rights and responsibilities under the law.

Items dealing with contract issues are regularly in the news. Public service employees, professional athletes, and other workers seem to be constantly in the midst of contract disputes or settlements. These news stories may leave you with the impression that contracts only involve people who work full-time. However, you will learn in this chapter that contract law is part of your life every day.

Contracts help people exchange goods and services in the marketplace. They are about promises that people make to perform certain actions; but they differ from ordinary promises in that contracts can be enforced in court.

This chapter describes various types of contracts, the elements that are necessary to form a contract, and what happens if the parties fail to live up to their agreement. As you learn about contracts, keep in mind how this branch of law affects you. Is the law different for minors? Can *you* enter into a contract?

CLASSIFYING CONTRACTS

A **contract** is an agreement between two or more competent parties that can be enforced in court; in other words, it is a legally binding bargain. Contracts are often thought of as promises, but there are no legal consequences for breaking a simple promise. Across Canada, under both common law and the *Quebec Civil Code,* people are free to enter into contracts and to have them enforced by the courts.

contract: an agreement between two or more competent parties that can be enforced in court

Contracts allow people to count on certain promises made by others. If you work, you expect to get paid on payday. Or, if you take a cab ride, the driver expects to be paid by you at the end of the ride.

Most contracts are **bilateral contracts;** that is, both parties to the contract promise to do something for each other. Suppose your friend offers to sell you a used CD for $10. If you accept her offer, you have entered into a bilateral contract—she has agreed to give you a CD, and you have agreed to give her $10. Unilateral contracts will be discussed later in the chapter.

bilateral contract: a contract formed when both parties promise to do something for each other

Contracts can contain numerous promises by each party. In addition to promises to *do* something, contracts can involve promises *not* to do something. For example, a dentist selling her practice might agree *not* to set up a new practice in the same neighbourhood for 10 years.

Contracts can be made in different ways—orally or in writing. Some written contracts are long, complex documents that are signed and sealed. While the law requires that certain contracts be in writing, for many contracts this is not necessary. Contracts may also be "express" or "implied," involving simple transactions performed without either party speaking a word.

Oral Contracts and Written Contracts

An **oral contract** is an agreement entered into verbally by the parties involved. Suppose you verbally accept a friend's offer to sell you his computer for $400. You have entered into an oral contract. What if your friend decides, before any money changes hands, that he wants $550 for the computer? You could probably sue to have the contract enforced because once a contract

oral contract: a verbal agreement between two or more parties

Figure 18.1 An oral contract can be accepted by a simple handshake. What are the pitfalls of oral contracts?

is properly formed, neither party can change the terms of the contract on their own. However, without witnesses, oral contracts are difficult to enforce because they lack hard evidence to prove the terms or that a contract was even made. Oral contracts break the golden rule for contracts in general: get it in writing.

In a **written contract,** the terms of the agreement are recorded on paper. The parties involved usually date and sign the contract as an indication of their intent to fulfill it. The advantage of a written contract is that it usually provides clear evidence of what the parties agreed to, making it easier for the courts to enforce.

written contract: an agreement between two or more parties in which the terms are set out on paper

Implied Contracts and Express Contracts

implied contract: an agreement in which the parties indicate concensus through their conduct

In an **implied contract,** the conduct of the parties indicates their intention to enter into a valid contract. Suppose you get on a bus, drop your money into the fare box, and then take your seat. Although no words are spoken, your actions indicate your intention to enter into a contract—placing money in the fare box in exchange for a ride. The driver fulfills the bus company's part of the contract by giving you a ride. No words need be spoken, but a contract has been formed—a service was exchanged for money.

express contract: an agreement in which the terms have been discussed and agreed upon in advance

An **express contract** is one in which the parties have discussed in advance what each of them will do. Suppose your cousin offers to sell you her CD player. You discuss the equipment and set a price. Once you have agreed on the things each of you will do, you have made an express contract. You will give your cousin a certain amount of money; she will give you the items you agreed upon.

Contracts Under Seal

A **contract under seal** is a specialty contract, which is also called a deed. It is simply a written contract that has a seal on it. In earlier times, the seal was made of wax that carried an impression of the family's crest. Today, it may be a red sticker or handwritten dot placed beside the signature, or even the word *seal* added after the signatures. In some provinces, certain contracts, such as the sale or mortgage of land, must still be under seal to be enforceable by the court.

contract under seal: a written agreement bearing a red sticker, handwritten dot, or the word *seal*

Building Your Understanding

1. Define "contract" in your own words. Bring in newspaper articles or recount situations that represent contracts and analyze them to identify the features contained in the definition.
2. Identify the type of contract each of the following situations represents:
   a) Ali enters a restaurant and points to an item on the menu.
   b) Reese stops at a garage sale and finds a used lawn mower. The owner says, "I'll sell it for $75," and Reese says, "I'll take it."
   c) Bryan and Grace sign a mortgage agreement with Connie, their banker.
   d) Mohindar hails a cab to get to work.
   e) Richard signs a repair order at his car dealership.
   f) Carlos signs an agreement with Athens Lawn Care to look after his lawn this summer.
3. Outline the disadvantages of an oral contract. Why do the courts prefer to have contracts in writing?

ELEMENTS OF A CONTRACT

A contract is formed only if the parties intend to be legally bound by their promises and have clearly agreed on what those promises are. The promises are known as the terms of the contract. Although this may sound simple, the courts are often called upon to determine whether a contract has actually been formed.

If your neighbour offers to sell you her computer and you agree, has a contract been formed? The answer is probably no, because you have not set a price or discussed what you are getting. What if you think the sale includes the monitor and keyboard, but your neighbour thinks that it does not? Have you agreed on a price?

The essential terms of the contract must be certain or else no contract can be formed. The court will not make up a contract for the parties; they have to do that for themselves. For a contract to be valid, there must be a **meeting of the minds** (in Latin, *consensus ad idem*), which indicates that the parties have thought about and agreed to the essential terms of the contract.

The court will look for certain elements to determine whether a valid contract has been made. The essential elements that must be present in a contract are offer, acceptance, and consideration. Although there are other elements, which will be examined later in the chapter, these three form the foundation of a contract.

Fast Fact
A life insurance policy is a contract between the person being insured and the insurance company. Upon the death of the insured person, the beneficiary named in the policy is entitled to receive the amount of money specified.

meeting of the minds: a clear understanding between the parties of the terms of the contract and the willingness to abide by them

Offer

offer: a proposal to another party to enter into an agreement on certain terms

offeror: a person who makes an offer

offeree: a person who receives an offer

An **offer** is a clear proposal to another party to enter into an agreement on certain terms. It is the first element necessary to form a contract. The person who makes the offer is called the **offeror.** In the case of your neighbour who wants to sell her computer, she is the offeror. The person who receives the offer, in this case you, is called the **offeree.**

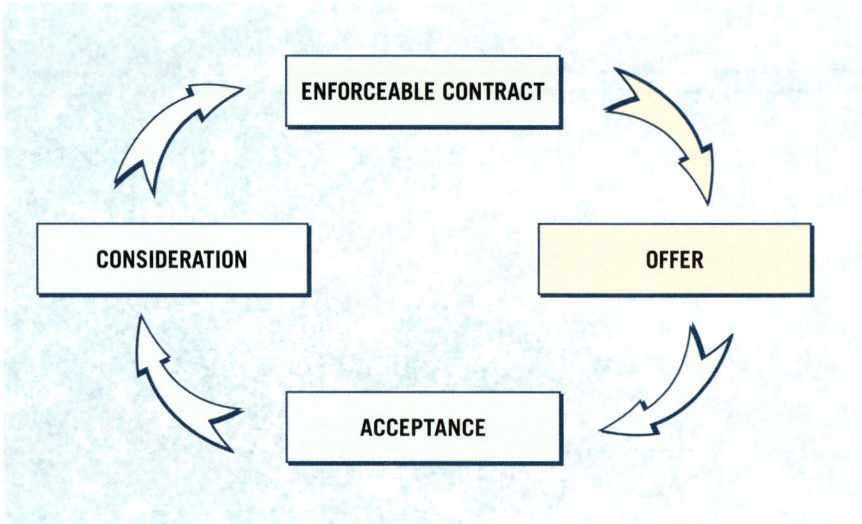

Figure 18.2 Essential Elements of a Contract. The first step in forming a contract is the offer.

Making a Valid Offer

For an offer to be valid, it must be intended seriously and its terms must be certain. If Samantha offers to sell her goalie skates to Jesse for $50, it is possible that she has made a serious offer. But if the skates are actually worth $400, it is likely that Samantha does not really intend to sell the skates.

An offer made as a joke or in anger or frustration is not valid. Suppose Dan comes off the golf course after having his worst game in years, throws his bag of clubs on the ground, and says to John, "These are worthless! Give me $10 and they're yours." Even if John answers, "It's a deal!" a contract has probably not been formed. Dan made the offer because he was frustrated with his game, not because he seriously intended to sell the clubs.

Invitation to Treat

invitation to treat: a communication intended to elicit offers from the persons who receive it

Placing a "For Sale" sign on an item or advertising goods in the newspaper is almost never considered an offer. This type of communication is usually called an **invitation to treat;** in other words, it is an invitation to the general public to make an offer to the advertiser along the terms set out in the advertisement. The advertiser will then treat, or consider, the offer made by the customer.

A sign advertising a "2-for-1 shirt sale" is an invitation for people to look at the shirts and consider buying them. Anyone who chooses to purchase the product can pick out the shirts and take them to the sales counter. The consumer is then making an offer to purchase the shirts, which can be accepted or rejected by the sales clerk.

Whether a communication is an offer or an invitation to treat depends on the *intent* of the sender of the communication. The intent is determined by the language used and the surrounding circumstances. If an advertisement is viewed as a serious offer by someone who reads it, the advertiser may have to live up to the terms of the advertisement, even if in his own mind he did not think he was making an offer. *Carlill v. Carbolic Smoke Ball Company*, [1893] was a precedent-setting case that highlighted the difference between an offer and an invitation to treat.

Communicating an Offer

An offer is not an offer until it has been communicated to the party for whom it is intended. Offers may be communicated in many ways, including by mail, courier, fax, and e-mail, as well as in person. In cases such as *Carlill v. Carbolic Smoke Ball Company*, [1893] the offer may be communicated through an advertisement. In contract law, it is important to know *when* the offeree became aware of the offer or *if*, in fact, the offeree was even aware of the offer.

Fast Fact
Clicking on the "I accept" or "I confirm" buttons on an electronic commerce Web site indicates that you are agreeing to the contractual terms being offered.

Consider This
The *Carlill* case became the basis of a play by Rosemary Rowe—called *Carlill v. The Carbolic Smoke Company*—that links the story to modern advertising. Discuss your own experiences involving issues related to advertisements.

Carlill v. Carbolic Smoke Ball Company, [1893] 1 Q.B. 256 (C.A.)

The Carbolic Smoke Ball Company sold a medical remedy called a "smoke ball" that consisted of a ball with a nozzle on top from which the user could inhale vapours. The company claimed that using its product three times a day would prevent the flu. To back up this claim, the company placed advertisements in a newspaper, offering to pay £100 to anyone who contracted the flu despite using the ball and informing the public that £1000 had been deposited in the bank for that purpose.

Mrs. Carlill purchased a smoke ball and used it as directed; nevertheless she caught the flu. When she tried to claim the money, the company refused to pay. Carbolic Smoke Ball Company asserted that the advertisement was an invitation to treat and did not constitute an offer.

Mrs. Carlill sued Carbolic Smoke Ball for breach of contract and was successful. The Court ruled that the company had made a serious offer, not an invitation to treat. By going so far as to place the money in the bank, the company had indicated that it intended to create a unilateral contract with users of the smoke ball. This case set a precedent that is still followed today: serious promises that are intended to be binding and that are made in advertisements must be kept.

CASE

1. With whom was the company making a contract in its advertisement?
2. Why did the Court rule in Mrs. Carlill's favour?
3. Outline the arguments that each side might have made in court, using the following terms: contract, parties, legally binding, offer, offeror, offeree, acceptance, valid, and invitation to treat.

Ending an Offer

It is not realistic for an offer to remain open for acceptance indefinitely. An offer comes to an end and can no longer be accepted under a number of circumstances.

lapse: to be terminated or cease to exist

An offer **lapses** if it is not accepted before the date set out in the offer. If no date is specified, the offer comes to an end after a reasonable time, which depends on the situation. An offer also lapses if the offeror dies, becomes mentally incompetent, or goes into bankruptcy.

revoke: to withdraw or take back

In most cases, an offer can also be withdrawn or **revoked** by the offeror before it has been accepted by the offeree. The offeree must know that the offer has been revoked, but there is no rule about how this withdrawal of the offer should be communicated or by whom.

CASE

Dickinson v. *Dodds*, [1876] 2 Ch.D. 463 (C.A.)

1. At what date and time did Dodds's offer to Dickinson end? At what date and time was Dickinson's acceptance communicated?
2. When and how should Dodds have revoked the offer?
3. Explain the significance of this court decision with regards to the element of "acceptance" in contract law.

On Wednesday, June 10, 1874, John Dodds signed and delivered to George Dickinson a document stating the following:

> I hereby agree to sell to Mr. George Dickinson the whole of the dwelling-houses, garden ground, stabling, and outbuildings thereto belonging, situated at Croft, belonging to me, for the sum of 800 pounds. As witness my hand this tenth day of June, 1874.
>
> 800 pounds [signed] John Dodds.
>
> P.S.—This offer to be left over until Friday, 9 o'clock a.m. J.D. (the twelfth), 12th June, 1874.
>
> [signed] J. Dodds.

On Thursday, June 11, Dodds sold his property to Thomas Allan, a third party. He sent a Mr. Berry to inform Dickinson that the property had been sold. Nevertheless, Dickinson delivered a formal acceptance to purchase the property to Dodds's mother-in-law, as Dodds was staying at her house. He explained what the document contained and asked her to give it to Dodds. She forgot to do so.

On Friday morning at 7:00, Dickinson delivered a duplicate of his acceptance to Dodds. Dodds replied that it was too late; he had already sold the property to another party the previous day. Dickinson took Dodds to court, alleging that the property should rightfully have been sold to him.

At the trial, the judge ruled in favour of Dickinson, but on appeal the property was awarded to Allan. The Court held that since Dickinson had been informed that the property had been sold, he knew that the offer was no longer open for acceptance. Dodds was under no obligation to keep the property unsold for Dickinson, just as Dickinson was under no obligation to accept Dodds's offer.

If Samantha offers to sell her goalie skates to Jesse for $50, and Jesse says, "Sure, I'll take them for $50," Samantha and Jesse have made a contract. However, if Jesse replies, "I'll give you $40," there has been no acceptance, and Samantha and Jesse have not formed a contract. In fact, Jesse has made a **counteroffer,** which ends Samantha's offer and becomes the new offer. In effect, Jesse is now the offeror and Samantha the offeree. A counteroffer usually renders the original offer void.

counteroffer: an offer made in response to an existing offer

Acceptance

Acceptance means that the offeree agrees to make a contract on the offeror's terms. There cannot be a contract unless the offeree has accepted an offer.

Sometimes the offer states *how* acceptance must be made, and a contract can be formed only if acceptance is made as specified. In most cases, however, acceptance is made orally, in writing, or by conduct, as long as it is clear that the offeree is accepting the offer. Suppose you enter a store, pick up a newspaper, and offer money to the proprietor. If you offered enough money, the proprietor may just nod in acceptance or say thank you. If you offered less than the price of the newspaper, she would indicate that she did not accept your offer to buy the paper for the amount you offered, and no contract would be formed. She might then offer to sell you the paper at a different price, and you would accept by handing over the required amount.

acceptance: a clear indication by the offeree to enter into a contract on the terms set out by the offeror

Communication of Acceptance

Generally speaking, the acceptance of an agreement takes effect once the acceptance is communicated to the offeror. Suppose a contractor offers to paint your house and provides you with a quote indicating what will be done and how much it will cost. If the offer says nothing about *how* to accept it, you can simply call the contractor and accept by phone.

Law in Your Life
You enter contracts every day. Keep a record of your contract activity for one day. Identify the offeror, offeree, and the terms of the contract for each activity.

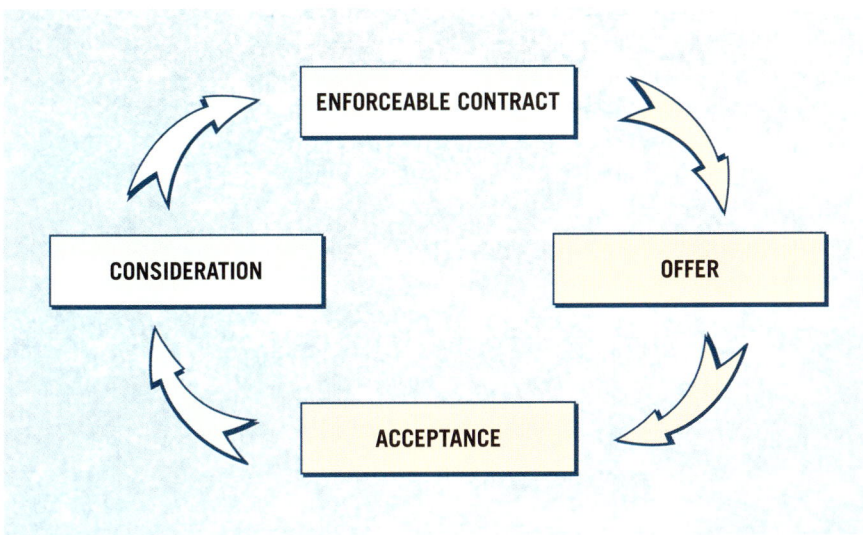

Figure 18.3 Essential Elements of a Contract. The second step in forming a contract is acceptance.

"It's a deal, but just to be on the safe side let's have our lawyers look at this handshake."

© 2002 Robert Mankoff from cartoonbank.com. All rights reserved.

Controversy may arise as to what actually constitutes acceptance and communication of that acceptance to the offeror. The following rules govern how acceptance can be made and communicated.

1. **Acceptance of an offer is usually required to be active.** This means that inaction or silence cannot be taken as acceptance. This rule removes uncertainty about whether the offeree has accepted. It also prevents what is called "foisting," which occurs when someone tries to form a contract with an offeree without that person's acceptance or consent. Suppose a company sends a product to your home and encloses a letter offering to sell you the goods, stating that if the goods are not returned within 10 days, you will have purchased them. A contract cannot be formed in this manner, so you have no contractual liability to pay for the goods.

Fast Fact

Legislation in many provinces protects consumers from being liable for unsolicited products. In Ontario, a person who receives unsolicited goods is not liable to pay for them even if the goods are used, misused, lost, damaged, or stolen.

Consider This

If an offeror living in British Columbia makes a contract over the telephone with an offeree who lives in Nova Scotia, British Columbia law applies to the transaction. This is because the verbal acceptance by the offeree is received in British Columbia, so that is where the contract is formed. What are the implications of such situations for those dealing in cross-Canada trade?

2. **The contract is formed when the offeror receives notice of acceptance from the offeree.** If two friends are negotiating orally over the sale of a snowmobile, the contract is formed when the purchaser (offeree) calls the seller (offeror) to say that he or she accepts the offer.

3. **Acceptance must be made in a reasonable manner, or in the form required by the offeror.** Generally, acceptance is communicated in the same way that the offer was communicated; oral offers are usually accepted orally, and written offers are usually accepted in writing. If the offeror does not stipulate the manner of communicating the acceptance, it must be done by a reasonable and appropriate method. Offerors may indicate that acceptance must be made in a certain way, such as by mail, phone, fax, or other means of communication. If the offeree fails to accept by using the method specified, no contract will be formed.

4. **When the offeror has expressly required acceptance by mail, or it is clear that the mail may be used, acceptance is completed as soon as the letter is mailed, even if the offeror never receives the letter.** The proof of the time at which the offer was accepted is the postmark that is placed on the stamp at the post office. The contract is formed in the place where the letter is posted because that is where the acceptance occurs. The "postal acceptance" rule puts the risk of losing the letter on the offeror. If the offeree's letter of acceptance is delayed or lost in the mail, the offeror is still bound by a contract, even though he or she may be unaware of it.

5. **An offer cannot be accepted if the offeree knows it has been revoked by the offeror.** For example, Simon cannot accept Naomi's offer to sell him her SUV if he already knows that Naomi sold it last week.

In a **unilateral contract,** communication of acceptance is not required. In such a contract, acceptance of the offer comes from performance of some act specified in the offer (or in some cases, by *refraining* from some act). This differs from the bilateral contracts discussed earlier, where each party made promises prior to the formation of the contract. With unilateral contracts, the offeror does not expect any communication of acceptance; all the offeree must do is perform the act requested. *Carlill v. Carbolic Smoke Ball Company,* [1893] is the classic example of such a contract. Mrs. Carlill accepted the company's offer simply by using the smoke ball. She was not required to tell the company she had done so.

Suppose your neighbour offers a $50 reward in the local newspaper for the return of his lost dog, Buddy. Anyone who knows about the offer can create a unilateral contract with your neighbour by finding and returning Buddy to him. However, remember that a contract is made only if an offer is accepted with the intent to create a binding contract. Someone who found Buddy wandering in the park and brought him to his owner without knowing about the newspaper notice would not be able to compel your neighbour to pay the reward. Being unaware of the reward offer, this person could have no intention to accept your neighbour's offer and form a contract.

unilateral contract: a contract formed when the offeree accepts an offer by performing an act requested by the offeror

Consideration

An agreement can be an enforceable contract only if the parties exchange benefits. When you enter a store and buy a magazine, you receive the magazine (*your* benefit) and the owners receive your money (*their* benefit). The exchange of benefits, which is necessary for the existence of a contract, is called **consideration.** Consideration is the thing of value that each party to the contract receives from the other. In *Dickinson v. Dodds,* [1876], Dickinson would probably have won his case if he had given consideration to

Law in Your Life
Record three contracts you have entered where the consideration was something other than money. Identify the consideration for the offeror and offeree in each situation.

consideration: something of value that either benefits the party that receives it or is a loss or inconvenience to the party that provides it

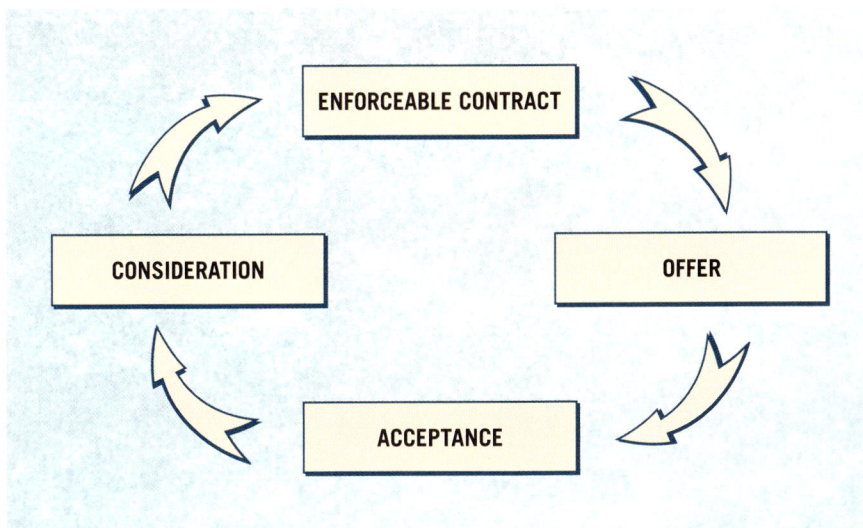

Figure 18.4 Essential Elements of a Contract. The third step involved in forming a contract is consideration, or the exchange of benefits.

Dodds for keeping the offer open until Friday. Consideration is not necessary for contracts of a specialty nature, such as contracts under seal.

We generally think of consideration as being in the form of money, typically in exchange for a product or service. But consideration can be anything that has value, as long as the courts are able to put a dollar figure on that value. For example, Rachel may agree to mow your lawn if you agree to use your season's tickets to take her to the opera. The consideration Rachel gives is mowing the lawn; the consideration you give is taking her to the opera.

Consideration can also come from refraining from something you usually do. Suppose your sister attends a hockey game every Friday. Your parents will only let you go to an out-of-town rock concert on Friday night, *if* your sister drives you to the concert. She agrees to forgo Friday's game and you agree to buy her a ticket to the concert. Agreeing *not* to go to the game would constitute adequate consideration.

Gratuitous Promises

gratuitous promise: an offer that gives a benefit to the offeree only

One reason the law requires consideration is to distinguish enforceable contracts from gratuitous promises. A **gratuitous promise** is an offer that gives a benefit to the offeree only. It is a promise made for free since the offeror (or, in this case, the promisor) receives no consideration. Acceptance by the offeree generally does not create a contract enforceable by the court.

It has long been argued that gratuitous promises should be enforceable. Suppose your neighbour goes away on vacation. She says she needs someone to check on her house daily in her absence, and you offer to do it for her. But you decide to go away for a few days and do not check the house. You return to find that her toilet tank broke, and water has been running on the floor for several days. Because you made a gratuitous promise, you would not be liable. On the other hand, if your neighbour had agreed to pay you for checking the house, a contract would have been formed, and you would probably be liable.

Law in Your Life
Describe a gratuitous promise that you have engaged in. Did you receive or give the consideration?

In the case of charitable donations, the person making a pledge to donate funds does not receive any consideration for making the pledge, so it is normally not enforceable in court. However, there are exceptions. Suppose Eli makes a generous pledge to a hospital's building fund, and the hospital begins renovations based on the pledge. If Eli then refuses to honour his pledge, the hospital can ask the court to enforce it. In this case, because the hospital took on an obligation to pay for the renovations and would lose money itself if Eli did not pay, the pledge would constitute consideration.

Valid Consideration

present consideration: consideration that is exchanged at the time a contract is formed

Not all forms of consideration are sufficient to create a contract. The most common forms of valid consideration are present consideration and future consideration. In a contract of sale, **present consideration** may occur when the contract is formed if money is exchanged for goods right at that moment.

CASE

The Copy Cats v. Rosney and Rosney (B.D.) Corp. (1989), 62 Man. R. (2d) 308 (Q.B.)

BACKGROUND The defendant, Mr. Rosney, and a partner ran a company called Concept 2000 Management that did business with Copy Cats to which it owed $551.05. When Concept 2000 Management went out of business, the plaintiff received a letter from Mr. Rosney that stated the following:

> ...thank you for your patience and understanding ... regarding Concept 2000 Management Incorporated's account.... I was forced to restart under the B.D. Rosney Corporation.... The enclosed cheque for $551.05, although written on a B.D. Rosney Corporation cheque, is to clear the Concept 2000 account.... Thank you for your patience and rest assured, as my company's growth continues, your operation will benefit from your trust and patience.

One or two days later, Rosney telephoned the plaintiff and asked that the cheque not be cashed yet because there were insufficient funds to cover it. Copy Cats complied with Rosney's request, but when they finally did try to cash the cheque, there were still insufficient funds in the Rosney Corp. account.

The plaintiff wrote to Rosney, asking for a new cheque. Rosney replied that the debt was owed by Concept 2000 and neither he personally nor his new company were liable for it.

The plaintiff sued, and a hearing officer gave judgment to the plaintiff against both Rosney and his new company. They appealed to the Court of Queen's Bench.

LEGAL QUESTION Did the plaintiff give any consideration to Rosney or his new company for the agreement to be liable for the debt of Concept 2000?

DECISION The Court held that Rosney was not personally liable since it was his company, Rosney (B.D.) Corp., that issued the cheque. However, the new company could be found liable for paying the debt of Concept 2000 if the plaintiff had given some consideration to Rosney (B.D.) Corp. The Court determined that the plaintiff's agreement to delay cashing the cheque when asked to do so constituted that consideration. The Court also found that the new company received valid consideration in the form of the plaintiff's "trust, confidence, and goodwill" when it issued a cheque to pay the debt. Since there was valid consideration, Rosney (B.D.) Corp. was liable for the debt.

LEGAL SIGNIFICANCE The Court reaffirmed that consideration could come from one of the parties by an "act of forbearance," which, in this case, was to refrain from cashing the cheque. The Court further affirmed that it is not particularly concerned about the adequacy of the consideration given.

ANALYSIS

1. Explain why the fact that the plaintiff had rendered services to Concept 2000 was not consideration for the new company's promise to pay the $551.05.
2. Do you think the $551.05 was worth the trust, confidence, and goodwill Rosney hoped to obtain from the plaintiff? How might the plaintiff have affected the success of Rosney's new business had Rosney refused to pay the bill of his old company?
3. Discuss the judgment, identifying the timing of the contract and the consideration. Might the judge have been mistaken? Explain.

future consideration: consideration that is exchanged after a contract is formed

Future consideration occurs when one (or both) of the parties promises to perform some part of the contract in the future. If you order shingles for your roof, the lumberyard agrees to deliver them, and you agree to pay for them on delivery, the consideration passes in the future when the contract is performed.

Generally, the courts are not concerned with whether the consideration given by each party is adequate or equal. Usually, individuals are free to enter into contracts as they wish, and if someone agrees to sell something at a very low price, the contract may still be valid. For example, if Rob agreed to sell Brad his Jaguar for $15 000 even if it is really worth $25 000, the courts might enforce the contract and not release Rob from a bad deal. As you will see later, in some cases, an exceptionally bad deal is a sign that the contract should not be upheld for other reasons, such as fraud or duress.

Invalid Consideration

past consideration: a benefit conferred before a contract is alleged to have been formed

Past consideration arises when an act has already been performed. Such an act cannot be used to create a contract because it was not done in exchange for consideration from the other party. Suppose Angelo is moving and Larry shows up to help. After the move, Angelo tells Larry that he will give him $100 for helping, but Angelo fails to pay the money. No contract exists that Larry can enforce because no exchange of consideration was necessary to form a contract. Had Angelo offered the money before Larry helped, a contract could have been formed.

Building Your Understanding

1. Create a contract situation and use at least five of the terms you learned in this section to describe the transaction.
2. Explain the various ways an offer can come to an end, using examples for each.
3. For each of the following, describe what requirements must be met for valid acceptance of an offer to occur.
   a) the reaction of the offeree to the offer
   b) the form of communication used by the offeree
   c) the date the offeror receives the acceptance
4. Discuss the following cases in terms of valid acceptance. For each case, answer the following questions: What must be done for acceptance to occur? When did acceptance occur? Is acceptance possible?
   a) Paulo sends a letter to Bill offering to sell him his fishing boat. The same day, Frank sends a letter to Paulo telling him that he would like to buy the boat.
   b) Rafaela puts 50¢ into a newspaper box.
   c) Rick says to Shainaz, "I'll sell you my skis for $100." Shainaz replies, "I'll take them for $75."
   d) After reading an advertisement in a newspaper, Brandon phones and expresses his interest in buying a used guitar from Sylvie.
   e) Craig sees a sales flyer for a house on the next street. He goes to the house and tells the owner that he will pay the asking price.
5. Distinguish between past, present, and future consideration. How does a gratuitous promise differ from these types of consideration?
6. Why do you think the courts are concerned only with the fact that consideration has been exchanged rather than with the adequacy of the consideration?

INVALIDATING FACTORS

If someone makes an offer on certain terms, another person accepts that offer, and both parties have given valid consideration, an enforceable contract seems to exist. Why then, do people often end up in court disputing their contracts? Usually it is because things are not always as clear as they first appear.

Many factors can cause the court to rule that a contract either does not exist, or exists but is unenforceable. Such factors include incapacity, illegality, public policy, mistake, misrepresentation, duress, undue influence, and unconscionability. In this section, you will learn how each of these factors invalidates a contract.

Incapacity to Contract

A contract can be made only when the parties have a meeting of the minds and consent to be bound by their promises. A contract cannot be formed if one of the parties does not have the **capacity** to understand what they are getting into and the ability to perform the contract.

capacity: the ability to enter into a legally binding contract

Generally, adults are free to enter into any contract they wish. However, the law offers special protection to vulnerable members of society. The law assumes that certain people lack the experience or ability to make informed choices and, therefore, cannot enter into binding contracts. People under the age of majority (minors) and adults with impaired mental ability receive special treatment under contract law.

Minors

People who have not yet reached the age of majority can make contracts, but most adults will not contract with a minor because the contracts are usually unenforceable in court. Over the years, the courts have developed a set of rules to determine whether a contract with a minor is enforceable by either the minor or the other party. These rules apply in most provinces; however, British Columbia has passed specific legislation dealing with the contracts of minors.

> **Consider This**
> A minor who lies about his or her age when making a contract is protected under the law. How might this fact affect how merchants deal with minors? Could the minor be liable for fraud or the tort of negligent misrepresentation?

Enforceable Contracts Minors are bound by contracts for the purchase of **necessaries.** Necessaries are such items as food, clothing, shelter, and medical and dental services. A minor who enters into a contract for necessaries is only obligated to pay a fair and reasonable price for the goods or services. The courts will not require a minor to pay an exorbitant amount under such a contract.

necessaries: basic items a person requires to function in society, such as food, clothing, shelter, and medical and dental care

Employment contracts or apprenticeships are usually considered necessaries for minors. Once again, however, these contracts must be in the best interests of the minor and cannot be a disadvantage to the young person.

Voidable Contracts A **voidable contract** is simply one that can be avoided. A contract exists, but it may not have to be carried out in certain circumstances. A voidable contract for a minor means that the minor can get out

voidable contract: a contract that can be avoided or not carried out

Law in Your Life
What item might be a necessary for one minor but not for another?

of the contract if he or she wishes. Until the minor decides whether to carry out the contract, the adult who entered into the agreement is bound by it and does not have the option of avoiding the contract if the minor wants to fulfill it. Some types of contracts are voidable because minors fail to ratify them; others are voidable because minors repudiate them. Such situations are discussed below.

Minors are usually not bound by a contract (except for necessaries or an employment contract that substantially benefits them) unless they take steps to show that they intend to be bound by the agreement shortly after reaching the age of majority. This is known as **ratification,** and it can be done in writing or by implication. Suppose Leslie, a minor, purchases a motorcycle for $1500, making monthly payments of $100. As long as she is a minor, she can stop making payments and return the motorcycle at any time. However, if Leslie reaches the age of majority and continues to make the monthly payments, she has ratified the contract, and it is now binding.

ratification: an indication of willingness to be bound by a contract

Certain kinds of contracts are binding *unless* the minor repudiates them upon reaching the age of majority. Contracts for partnership agreements, holding shares in a company, or interests in land through lease agreements fall into this category. **Repudiation** means that the minor makes it known that he or she does not intend to be bound by the terms of the contract.

repudiation: an indication that one does not intend to be bound by a contract

Void Contracts
The courts want to ensure that minors are not taken advantage of in business dealings. If a contract is prejudicial to a minor, then it is absolutely void; it is as if no contract was ever made. Such **void contracts** cannot be ratified by a minor. For example, if a youth, unaware of the true value of a collector's card, sold it to an adult who knew that it was very valuable, the courts would probably declare the contract void. The card would then be returned to the youth.

void contracts: agreements without legal force

Parental Liability
Parents are not liable if their children fail to pay for goods that are not considered necessaries. For this reason, most merchants will not make deals with minors unless a parent or guardian is willing to co-sign the contract. Co-signing means that the parent or guardian agrees to fulfill the minor's obligation to pay if the minor does not.

Incapacitated Persons
People who are incapacitated because of mental incompetence do not have the capacity to contract. The law assumes that such individuals cannot understand the terms of a contract, so there can be no meeting of the minds and no consent. As with a minor, a contract for necessaries with a mentally incompetent person is enforceable, but only a reasonable price can be charged. A contract involving non-necessaries is voidable by the incapacitated party if the other party knew about the incapacity.

Fast Fact
A person under hypnosis or the influence of drugs is considered incapacitated.

Contracts made by intoxicated persons are voidable if such persons can prove that they were so impaired that they did not comprehend what was taking place and that the other party was aware of this. The person who claims impairment must make an effort to avoid the contract within a reasonable period

Kootenay Ice Hockey Club Ltd. v. Slovak Ice Hockey Association, [2001] B.C.S.C. 51

CASE

Marek Svatos, a Slovakian hockey player, signed a contract to play for the Kosice Hockey Club in Slovakia. He was given assurances that he would be released from this contract if he were drafted by a Canadian Hockey League (CHL) club at some later date.

When Svatos was drafted by the Kootenay Club in July 2000, Kosice refused to provide him with the necessary release, and the CHL would not let him play without it. Kosice later provided a temporary release, and Svatos moved to Canada and played 11 games with the Kootenay team. The Kosice Club then demanded US$10 000 for a full release. The CHL rules prohibit payment for a release.

The Court granted an interlocutory injunction, allowing Svatos to play the balance of the season for Kootenay. Svatos was 17 years old when he signed the Kosice contract; he did not have the benefit of legal advice, and no guardian signed on his behalf. The contract was for three years with virtually no remuneration. The Court concluded that under Slovak law this contract was probably void. The validity of Svatos's contract with Kosice could be litigated at a later date.

1. Would Svatos's contract with the Kosice Hockey Club be considered enforceable if it had been made with a Canadian team? Explain.
2. What factors do you think the Court considered in deciding whether to grant an interlocutory injunction in favour of Svatos?

---

of time after the effects of the impairment have subsided. Anyone who does not do so will be deemed to have ratified the contract.

Illegality

An enforceable contract must be formed for a **legal purpose,** and the consideration given must also be legal. Contracts for an illegal purpose or for illegal consideration are void. It is not possible, for example, to enter into a valid contract to purchase narcotics because both the sale and purchase of narcotics are crimes. Any such contract would be illegal. If you agreed to wash a friend's car in exchange for drugs, the consideration given by your friend would be illegal. A contract is also illegal if it requires performance of an act that is not criminal but is barred by a specific statute.

Contracts to commit torts are also illegal. Suppose your friend does not like his neighbour. The neighbour works nights, so your friend hires you to make noise all day outside his neighbour's home so the neighbour cannot sleep. If you perform your end of the bargain but do not get paid, you could not have the court enforce the contract.

Usually if a contract is void, the courts will help the parties return to their original positions as if the contract had never existed. This is known as **rescission.** In a contract of sale, the merchandise or property would be returned, as would any money that had been paid. However, in the case of an illegal contract, the courts will simply declare the contract void and refuse to have any further dealings with the parties. The courts will help only if one of the parties acted innocently and was unaware that an illegal act was involved.

legal purpose: a purpose not forbidden by law

rescission: restoring the parties to the positions they would have occupied had there been no contract

Crime doesn't rule out claim

Lawyer says insurance companies must pay for death, even of bomber

A Montreal widow should receive the proceeds for her husband's insurance policy because he was killed by accident while trying to blow up a car at Dorval airport and was not deliberately trying to collect on his insurance, lawyers for the woman told Canada's top court yesterday.

"We are not here to condemn, reprimand or dissuade the perpetration of criminal acts," said Jean Blaquiere, lawyer for Danielle Goulet."

It is the role of criminal law, not of the insurance law, to do that. The insurance law is not here to punish anyone."

Moreover, anyone could be killed while inadvertently committing a criminal act, such as drunk driving or driving negligently....

The case centres on the death of Roger Arbic, a man who had more than his share of run-ins with Canada's criminal-justice system. Arbic was killed in January 1994 while trying to plant a bomb in a car parked at Dorval airport....

When Arbic's widow, Danielle Goulet, applied to the Transamerica Life Insurance Company to collect on her husband's $50 000 insurance policy, the company rejected her claim on the ground he died while committing a crime and it would be contrary to public order to honour the claim ...

Speaking later to reporters, Goulet said she is confident she will win the case at the Supreme Court, just as she has won in two lower courts.....

SOURCE: Elizabeth Thompson, "Crime doesn't rule out claim," *The Gazette* (Montreal), November 9, 2001, p. A9

1. On what grounds is the company refusing to pay the insurance to Arbic's wife?
2. Is there a relevant difference between a death related to drunk driving and a death connected to blowing up a car? Explain.
3. In your opinion, was the contract between Arbic and Transamerica created for a legal purpose or is it contrary to public policy? Explain.

Contrary to Public Policy

contrary to public policy: against the morals and ethics of a community

Agreements that are **contrary to public policy** are not necessarily crimes, but they are seen to be immoral or not in the best interests of society. Over many years, the courts have identified certain types of contracts as being against public policy (see Figure 18.5).

If the court feels that an agreement is against public policy, then the contract will be declared void. The parties involved will usually be able to recover any money that has been paid and have property returned. However, if the nature of the contract is offensive, the courts will treat it as they do illegal contracts and not help the parties recover any goods or money.

Mistake

mistake: an error about an important term of a contract

As you have learned, a contract can be formed only if the parties have a meeting of the minds, which is impossible if one or both parties make a **mistake**, or error, about an important aspect of the contract. The courts have established rules about the effect a mistake will have on a contract. If a party wants to get out of a contract because of a mistake, the mistake must be about an im-

Figure 18.5 Examples of contracts contrary to public policy

Contracts Contrary to Public Policy	Example
Contracts interfering with the administration of justice	• paying a witness to testify
Contracts that unduly restrain trade	• making it a condition of sale of a business that the purchaser never open a similar business anywhere
Contracts that restrict competition	• agreements among merchants to sell a product at a certain price • mergers among companies that would reduce competition
Contracts that are bets or wagers	• gambling and betting activities that take place outside provincially licensed facilities (however, gambling debts incurred in a place where gambling is legal may be enforceable)
Contracts injurious to the state	• paying a member of the provincial Legislature to vote for or against a bill

portant part of the agreement itself and not about the parties' motives for making the agreement. Often the courts say the mistake must go to the root of the contract or concern a material or fundamental term. For example, if Mr. and Mrs. Yee bought a piece of land, thinking that a new mall was going to open nearby, and it turned out that this assumption was incorrect, the court would not declare the contract void. Because the Yees' mistake was not about an important term of the contract, such as the location or size of the property, it would not be grounds for setting aside the contract.

The courts have recognized several types of contractual mistakes. Mistakes are classified as **common mistake** (both parties make the same mistake); **mutual mistake** (both parties are mistaken but they make different mistakes); and **unilateral mistake** (one party is mistaken and the other party knows it). Consider how these types of mistakes might apply if Connie agreed to sell her extensive record collection for $10 000 to the owner of Yesterday's Sounds, a vintage-record store.

- Connie's record collection is destroyed in a fire while she and the store owner are making a deal. The contract would be void because a common mistake had occurred—both parties thought that Connie still had a record collection to sell.
- Or, suppose the records are 78s, and Connie thinks the store sells 78s; the store owner thinks the records are LPs, and his store sells only LPs. This would constitute a mutual mistake—Connie believes the owner wants to buy her 78s, and the owner believes Connie is selling LPs.
- Connie tells the store owner that she is selling everything but her Elvis Presley collection. The owner comes to Connie's house to inspect her

Fast Fact
If a person signs a document without paying attention to what it actually says, the doctrine of mistake cannot be used to set aside the contract.

common mistake: an error made by both parties to a contract about the same thing

mutual mistake: an error made by both parties to a contract about different things

unilateral mistake: an error made by one party to a contract, of which the other party is aware

collection. In one of the boxes is a rare Elvis Presley recording on the Sun Records label. The owner recognizes that the value of the Elvis record alone is at least $10 000. He does not think that Connie meant to include it, but says nothing. Connie later notices the record is missing, but the owner refuses to return it saying, "A bargain is a bargain." This is a unilateral mistake on Connie's part and, as the owner knew about it, the court probably would not allow him to keep the Elvis record.

Suppose a **clerical mistake** were made when the parties had the contract drawn up, and the selling price was incorrectly recorded as $20 000. Connie notices the error but says nothing, and the owner of Yesterday's Sounds signs the contract. This would be a unilateral mistake on his part, and Connie would not be able to force him to pay $20 000 instead of the $10 000 they had agreed upon.

If Connie declared that she did not understand the nature of the contract when the time came to hand over the records, she might plead ***non est factum***, Latin for "it is not my deed." This defence was more common when fewer people were able to read but is now restricted to occurrences of fraud or misrepresentation by the other party. Usually, this defence is not accepted by the courts if someone simply neglects to read a contract prior to signing it.

Misrepresentation

Misrepresentation means that one party has made a false or inaccurate statement of fact that causes the other party to enter into a contract. Suppose Asif knows that a mall is going to be built on the vacant land across the street from his house when he puts it up for sale. According to the maxim ***caveat emptor*** (Latin for "let the buyer beware"), he is under no obligation to volunteer this information to a prospective buyer. However, if he deliberately

clerical mistake: an error made in recording the details of a contract

non est factum: Latin for "it is not my deed," which can be used as a defence to void a contract

misrepresentation: a false or inaccurate statement of fact that causes the other party to enter into a contract

caveat emptor: Latin for "let the buyer beware," implying that a purchase is made at the buyer's risk

Consider This
In Canadian law, it is up to the buyers to find out information regarding real estate deals they are entering. Do you think this is just? Explain your position.

"He never said that! I saw your lips move."

MacLean v. Hafford Motors Ltd. (2000), N.B.R. (2d)

CASE

MacLean purchased a 1989 automobile on the assurance of Knox, a salesman at Hafford Motors, that an older lady had previously owned the vehicle and it "seemed to be well kept up." To MacLean, this constituted an express warranty, which implied that the vehicle was well maintained and sound. At the time of the sale, MacLean received a one-month 50/50 warranty on internal parts of the motor and transmission.

The following day, having noticed a "clunking noise," MacLean returned the car, and Hafford Motors arranged to have the front struts and the transmission replaced. This was done free of charge despite the 50/50 warranty agreement.

After the warranty period elapsed, the car needed further repairs adding up to approximately $900. When the second transmission also failed, MacLean took Hafford Motors to court asking that the contract for the sale of the car be rescinded. He demanded that the purchase price and the expenses he had incurred be returned.

The judge concluded that Knox's comments were "in the nature of mere sales talk ... so vague and so obviously statements of opinion ... it would be unreasonable for a buyer to rely on them." The contract was upheld.

1. Do you think any misrepresentation occurred, or do you agree with the judge's conclusion? Discuss.
2. Did Hafford Motors meet its obligations regarding the future consideration in the contract? Explain.
3. What types of considerations, other than the one mentioned in question 2, would the judge apply to this decision?

lied and told the buyer that houses were going to be built on the vacant land, this would be considered a misrepresentation. It would also be misrepresentation if he were asked if he knew *what* was to be built on the vacant lot but said he did not. A buyer who relied on the misrepresentation could go to court and ask that the contract be declared void on the grounds that no genuine consent actually existed since the buyer was misled about an important part of the contract.

Misrepresentation can take place in two forms: innocent and fraudulent. The process for dealing with each of these is somewhat different.

Innocent Misrepresentation

Innocent misrepresentation occurs when someone makes a false statement of fact but honestly believes that it is true. In situations of innocent misrepresentation, the contract may be voidable at the victim's option, but that depends on whether the terms of the contract have been executed (carried out). If not, then the court is more willing to set the contract aside. If the contract has been executed, it will be set aside only if what was received is so different from what was *supposed* to be received that it amounts to a failure of consideration.

Suppose an inexperienced clerk tells Jake that his new lawn mower will never need to have its blades sharpened; however, this statement is not true. If Jake has not yet paid for the mower, he may be able to have the contract set aside. If he has paid, the contract is complete, and it is unlikely he could have the contract set aside. But he could get damages.

innocent misrepresentation: a false statement that is believed to be true by the party making it

Fraudulent Misrepresentation

When one party to a contract deliberately makes a false statement in order to induce the other party into agreeing to the contract, and the other party acts on the false statement, a **fraudulent misrepresentation** has occurred. For example, a salesperson wanting to make a sale might knowingly sell Mark a used car that had been in an accident and then repaired, even though Mark had specifically said he wanted a car that had *not* been in an accident. In such cases, the victim can seek rescission of the contract and also sue for damages.

fraudulent misrepresentation: a statement of fact that the maker knows is false, made with the intent to cause another person to act on the statement

Duress

If unlawful force or pressure is used to convince a person to enter into a contract, the contract is voidable because of **duress.** If someone acts under duress or pressure, that person does not truly consent to entering into a contract. Under Canadian law, duress can arise in numerous ways. The most obvious form is threats of physical harm to a person or a person's family. However, duress can also arise from threats to someone's property, threats of imprisonment, financial threats, or threats to reveal information that would be embarrassing or scandalous to the individual.

duress: the use of unlawful threats or pressure to force someone into a contract

Undue Influence

Undue influence occurs when there is a special relationship between the parties that creates a power imbalance, making it impossible for the subordinate or less powerful party to freely give consent. For the contract to be set aside, the party challenging it must demonstrate to the court that the subordinate party was coerced into agreeing to the contract. Sometimes it is difficult to determine when undue influence is present, but generally it involves an unequal bargaining position between the parties to the contract.

undue influence: pressure arising from a special relationship with an individual that is used to convince him or her to enter into a contract

Suppose a nephew was his elderly aunt's caregiver, and he completely dominated her actions. If he induced her to sell him all of her property at a very low price, it is likely the contract would be set aside for undue influence.

The courts have established some guidelines whereby undue influence is assumed to be present. Such situations include

- a lawyer contracting with a client
- a doctor contracting with a patient
- a parent contracting with a minor child
- an adult contracting with a senile parent
- a religious adviser contracting with a follower

"There. Now it's all on paper. Feel better?"

The New Yorker Collection 1999 Charles Barsotti from cartoonbank.com. All rights reserved.

Undue influence generally does not apply to parents contracting with adult children and spouses contracting with each other. However, if it can be shown that the special relationship was actually used to unduly pressure the other party into the contract, the contract is voidable at the option of the injured party.

The difference between undue influence and duress is the nature of the pressure involved.

Unconscionability

While the courts are reluctant to interfere with a contract on the basis that the bargain is unfair, they will do so in extreme cases. Generally, the courts will intervene in cases of **unconscionability,** that is, where the contract involves a weak party and a strong party, and both the behaviour of the stronger party and the bargain made are so poor that unreasonable advantage is taken of the weaker party.

unconscionability: unreasonable advantage taken of one of the parties to a contract

Suppose Larry is trying to sell his snowmobile in mid-July because he needs $1100 to make his mortgage payment. The snowmobile should sell for approximately $3500, but people are not generally interested in such a purchase during the summer. Bonnie, knowing that Larry needs the money for the mortgage, offers him $1100 for the snowmobile. The courts might consider this a case of unconscionability.

Building Your Understanding

1. Explain how the terms "ratify" and "repudiate" relate to minors and contracts.
2. Define "void contract," using an example.
3. Why will the courts not help parties who enter into an illegal contract?
4. Explain how a contract might be against public policy. Provide an example.
5. Why is a contract not formed when there is a mistake about an important term of the contract?
6. What are the remedies available for a common, mutual, and unilateral mistake?
7. Define and explain the concepts of *caveat emptor* and *non est factum*.
8. Distinguish between fraudulent and innocent misrepresentation, using examples. What remedies are available in each situation?
9. Why is a valid contract not formed when duress, undue influence, or unconscionability are present?
10. For each of the following situations, indicate whether the contract is valid and explain why or why not.
    a) Orly is 17 and just got her driver's licence. On her way home from school, she stops at a car dealership and a high-pressure salesperson sells her a new car.
    b) A pizzeria is losing money, so the owner hires a friend to set the building on fire in order to collect the insurance.
    c) Gaelen and his friends are celebrating the end of university. After drinking for several hours, they take a cab to a restaurant. Obviously intoxicated, Gaelen tells the waiter, "All drinks are on me."
    d) Simon is 15. He goes into a restaurant and orders a meal.

LOOKING BACK

Reviewing Your Vocabulary

acceptance *p. 469*
bilateral contract *p. 463*
capacity *p. 475*
caveat emptor p. 480
clerical mistake *p. 480*
common mistake *p. 479*
consideration *p. 471*
contract *p. 463*
contract under seal *p. 465*
contrary to public policy *p. 478*
counteroffer *p. 469*
duress *p. 482*
express contract *p. 464*
fraudulent misrepresentation *p. 482*
future consideration *p. 474*
gratuitous promise *p. 472*
implied contract *p. 464*
innocent misrepresentation *p. 481*
invitation to treat *p. 466*
lapse *p. 468*
legal purpose *p. 477*
meeting of the minds *p. 465*
misrepresentation *p. 480*
mistake *p. 478*
mutual mistake *p. 479*
necessaries *p. 475*
non est factum p. 480
offer *p. 466*
offeree *p. 466*
offeror *p. 466*
oral contract *p. 463*
past consideration *p. 474*
present consideration *p. 472*
ratification *p. 476*
repudiation *p. 476*
rescission *p. 477*
revoke *p. 468*
unconscionability *p. 483*
undue influence *p. 482*
unilateral contract *p. 471*
unilateral mistake *p. 479*
void contracts *p. 476*
voidable contract *p. 475*
written contact *p. 464*

Quick Quiz

1. Choose the appropriate term from the vocabulary list above to complete the following statements:
   a) A legal agreement that is enforceable in court is a _____.
   b) The ability to enter into a contract is called _____.
   c) _____ occurs when the goods have been delivered and the money has been paid.
   d) Using threats of physical force to induce someone to enter into a contract is called _____.
   e) A contract with a minor for non-necessaries is _____, which means that the minor may get out of the contract if he or she wishes.
   f) Signing your name to a sales contract is an example of _____ of a contract.
   g) The person offering the goods or services for sale is referred to as the _____ while the person to whom the offer is made is called the _____.
   h) If both parties to a contract make the same mistake about a fundamental element of the contract then a _____ mistake has occurred.
   i) _____ means that the parties are returned to their original positions as if the contract never existed.
   j) If a person deliberately misleads a prospective buyer then a _____ has occurred.

Checking Your Knowledge

2. Distinguish between an implied and an express contract, using examples.
3. How does an invitation to treat differ from an offer? What is the legal effect of the differences between the two?
4. What is the "postal acceptance" rule? What is its significance in contract law?
5. Explain the relationship between misrepresentation and *caveat emptor*.

Developing Your Thinking and Inquiry Skills

6. Work in a group to create a situation in which there might be confusion or disagreement about the existence of an offer. Describe your scenario to your classmates and invite them to identify the points of contract law involved.

7. Use an Internet search engine to locate cases involving contract issues. Begin by keying in the name of a province or territory followed by the word *courts*. Be prepared to share research tips and resources with your classmates. When you have found a case that interests you, write a two-page summary outlining the arguments put forward by both sides and the reasons for the judgment. Present your summary to your classmates and invite them to speculate on the outcome of the case. Then, read and discuss the actual judgment together.

8. Using the essential elements of a legal contract, explain how a marriage might be viewed as a contract.

Communicating Your Ideas

9. Work with a group to role-play a mediation based on one of the following situations. Invite your audience to assess your use of the principles of contract law to support your position.
   a) Chris and Alexis travel to work together every day for a year. Chris always uses his car for the trip, but Alexis has not contributed any money toward the gas. At the end of the year, Chris gives Alexis a bill for half the gas expenses. Alexis refuses to pay.
   b) Boris's elderly father owns a large piece of lakefront property. Boris and a partner come up with a plan to develop the property and build cottages to sell. Boris discusses the plan with his father and convinces him to sell the land at current market value. Boris's sister urges her father to renege on the deal, claiming he was unduly influenced.
   c) Raoul sends Pierre a letter offering to sell him his boat for $3500. Pierre receives the letter and sends a reply, by mail, that he will take the boat for the $3500. Before receiving the acceptance letter, Raoul changes his mind and phones Pierre to tell him that he is no longer interested in selling the boat at that price; now he wants $4800. Pierre insists that Raoul abide by the original bargain.

10. Write an editorial of about 300 words outlining your position on one of the following issues in contract law:
    - Some minors should be bound by contracts in the same way adults are.
    - The "postal acceptance" rule should be extended to e-mail.
    - Silence should be considered a form of misrepresentation.
    - All contracts should be in writing so that the terms are certain.

Putting It All Together

11. Commerce is increasingly conducted electronically, and, as a result, a whole new set of online contract laws have been developed. The "postal acceptance" rule, for example, has been extended to telegrams, but the courts have been reluctant to extend it to faxes. Other technological developments such as the widespread use of e-mail are going to lead to new decisions by the courts and new laws by government.

    Use your resources to research the *Uniform Electronic Commerce Act* and outline its main provisions. What impact will it have on contract law? Prepare a presentation for the class in which you outline the current laws and future trends of how the law will deal with these new technologies. Sources for your research should include law magazines such as *LawNow*, Internet sources regarding on-line contract law and electronic commerce, and business and technology magazines.

CASES

Harry v. Kreutziger (1978), 9 B.C.L.R. 166 (B.C.C.A.)

The plaintiff, Mr. Harry, was illiterate. He sold a boat and a fishing licence to the defendant, Mr. Kreutziger. The defendant knew that the plaintiff was in financial difficulties and offered a price that was adequate and reasonable for the boat but was far below the market value of the licence. The defendant's real interest was the licence because without the licence, he could not embark on a fishing enterprise.

The plaintiff changed his mind and asked the Court to rescind the contract. His request to do so was based on the fact that unfair advantage had been taken of him. He was unsuccessful and appealed. The British Columbia Court of Appeal allowed the appeal and the transaction was rescinded. The Court concluded:

> ... where a claim is made that a bargain is unconscionable, it must be shown for success that there was inequality in the position of the parties due to the ignorance, need, or distress of the weaker, which would leave him in the power of the stronger, coupled with proof of substantial unfairness in the bargain.

1. If you were the plaintiff's lawyer, what arguments would you put forward in terms of unconscionability, legal capacity, and consideration?
2. If legal capacity is present, the courts are generally not concerned with consideration being fair to both parties. Should a concern for fairness be applied regularly or should both parties simply accept the risks involved?

Dream Weavers Wedding Consultants v. Astley (2000), P.E.I. S.C.T.D 32, on-line: CanLII

Dream Weavers hired Susan Astley in March 1998. Both parties signed a contract, which read in part:

> ... [the employee] shall not during the term of this contract or for a period of two years thereafter, directly or indirectly ... create or be part of directly or indirectly any business or venture that is the same as or similar to or competes with that of Dream Weavers.

In October 1999, the parties signed a new contract that did not contain similar restrictions. Astley was dismissed in January 2000, and soon after started her own business in a line of work similar to Dream Weavers.

Dream Weavers applied for an injunction to stop Astley and submitted to the Court that the restrictive covenant of the 1998 contract should survive the termination of the agreement itself.

The Court found in favour of Astley saying that there was rescission of the March 1998 agreement when the October 1999 agreement was signed. In addition, the restraint of trade clause was vague and, therefore, unenforceable.

1. Why does the principle of rescission apply to the original contract?
2. Rewrite the original contract in a form that would have made it enforceable.

CASES

Dale v. Government of Manitoba (1997), 147 D.L.R. (4th) 605 (Man. C.A.)

BACKGROUND The province and the University of Manitoba created a four-year program called ACCESS. This program enabled members of disadvantaged groups to obtain post-secondary education, which would not have otherwise been accessible due to social, economic, cultural, or linguistic barriers, or lack of a formal education. The four plaintiffs, who were disadvantaged persons, accepted positions in the program on the understanding that the Government of Manitoba would pay them living expenses of $144 biweekly; that it would pay all costs of obtaining the education; and that, if required, the student would be guaranteed an opportunity to obtain a $3000 Canada Student Loan. This funding arrangement was put in writing, and no possibility of a future change in funding was mentioned to the students.

In 1994, the third year of the program, the Manitoba government changed the level and character of the funding. As a result, the students would, on graduation, have larger student loans to repay than the amounts they contemplated when they first registered in the program.

LEGAL QUESTION Was the agreement between the students and the government a binding contract?

DECISION The province argued that it had not intended to offer a contract to the students; therefore, it could not be held to the original funding terms. The students argued that the province had entered a binding agreement with them regarding the funding of the program. They gave consideration for the contract by altering their lifestyles, and the province derived indirect benefits from them as taxpayers once they obtained an education. The students succeeded in their claims.

LEGAL SIGNIFICANCE A contract can only arise if all the parties intend to form a contract. However, the Court found that in this case, although the province may not have realized it was contracting with the plaintiffs, it objectively intended to contract with them by signing an agreement committing itself to pay their expenses. The province knew that it was dealing with disadvantaged students, and it

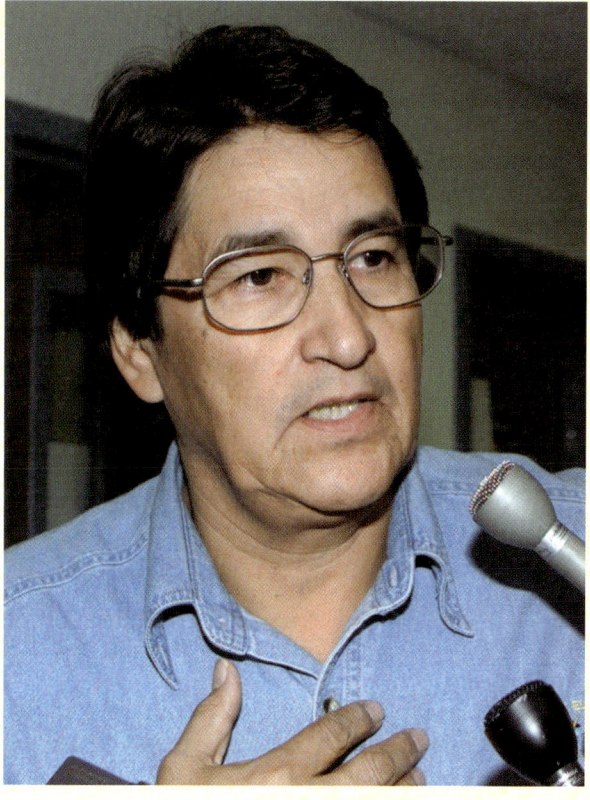

Figure 18.6 Ovide Mercredi, former grand chief of the Assembly of First Nations, graduated from the University of Manitoba under the ACCESS program.

owed them a duty to disclose the possibility that the funding might change.

ANALYSIS

1. Identify the offeror, offeree, and consideration in this case.
2. What factors would a judge have to consider in deciding this case?
3. Recall the discussion that preceded the *Carlill* v. *Carbolic Smoke Ball Company*, [1893] case earlier in the chapter. Why do you think the Court found there was a contract in *Dale* v. *Government of Manitoba* when the province said it did not intend to enter into a contract?
4. What do you think the Court might have ordered the province to do as a result of this ruling?

issue

Electronic Copyright Protection

Have you ever borrowed software from a friend and loaded it onto your computer or burned a CD off the Internet? If you have, then you have infringed the *Copyright Act.* If you burn CDs on a regular basis and sell them to your friends, you could be charged with a criminal offence.

COPYRIGHT LEGISLATION

Both Canada and the United States have legislation regarding copyright, or ownership, of books, newspaper and magazine articles, musical compositions, sculptures, films, CD-ROMs, and software programs. In Canada, these laws exist in the *Copyright Act,* which is a federal statute enacted in 1924 and amended most recently in 1997.

The word *copyright* literally means "the right to copy." Legislation gives the owner of the work the exclusive right to reproduce, publish, or perform that work. To use someone's material, you must get permission from the copyright owner. For example, the publisher had to obtain permission and pay fees to include the newspaper articles that appear in this textbook. If the publisher had reproduced the articles without permission, it could have been charged with a criminal offence because the sale of this work generates a profit. Copyright holders, such as *The Globe and Mail,* could also sue the publisher for damages in civil court. Copyright infringement can be a serious matter.

However, some provisions in the *Copyright Act* do allow certain uses of copyrighted material without obtaining permission or paying compensation or royalties. These limitations on the rights of copyright owners fall under the term "fair dealing." Fair dealing covers the use of short quotes or small passages and includes "fair" purposes such as book reviewing, news reporting, research, criticism, and private study. Of course, when the Act was passed, technology like photocopiers, computers, and scanners had not been invented; all copying was done by hand.

Generally, copyright expires 50 years (at the calendar year-end) after the author's death. The work is then said to be in the "public domain" and may be copied freely and without permission. Copyright holders can, by choice, allow others to use their work without permission or payment.

TECHNOLOGY VERSUS COPYRIGHT

If you have Internet access and are interested in music, the name Napster is probably familiar to you. Nineteen-year-old Shawn Fanning, a co-founder of Napster, created software that would allow fans to exchange MP3 music files. By using Napster's free service to download their favourite music, consumers were able to bypass the retailer and avoid purchasing CDs. Naturally, the music industry considered this practice a major threat to its profits. In 2001, it successfully sued Napster for violation of copyright laws, and an injunction was placed on Napster's activities.

In spite of the injunction, other shareware sites quickly filled the void, providing free music to those who chose to download it. Shareware is

copyrighted software that is distributed free of charge. Users are usually requested to submit a fee if they continue to use the software. Shareware supporters disregard copyright laws; they consider the Internet a free source of information for all.

As advances in technology continue to escalate, an interesting question arises: Should copyright protection take precedent over technological innovation?

SUPPORTING COPYRIGHT PROTECTION

Traditionally, the music industry operated by contracting musicians and making recordings, and consumers purchased records, tapes, or CDs. Copyright laws have always ensured that the owners were paid. In Canada, under s. 19(3) of the *Copyright Act,* royalties are split 50-50 between the performer and the maker of the recording.

The advent of shareware sites has resulted in a 15 percent decline in sales. According to the president of the Canadian Alliance Against Software Theft (CAAST), the recording industry has lost $475 million in sales to shareware sites. The Recording Industry Association of America estimates losses at more than US$1 million a day in the United States alone. The industry, a high-risk business at the best of times, claims that it costs between $300 000 and $500 000 to produce a recording. It maintains that a decline in profits for investors and compensation for artists is destroying the industry and leading to job losses in related fields such as retail, advertising, packaging, and the manufacturing of recordings.

In short, the Internet has threatened the traditional economics of the music industry, and the industry wants more protection through forceful legislation.

SUPPORTING TECHNOLOGICAL FREEDOM

Entrepreneurs who operate shareware sites have been called "pirates" and "pickpockets." They consider copyright legislation out of date. In their view, the Internet opened up an age of global freedom that should not be hampered by copyright protection. The global sharing of music and information provides a wider distribution of alternative views and music, which benefits everyone.

In response to claims that shareware is destroying the recording industry, those who champion shareware point out that the industry survived the bootlegging of recordings in the past. They suggest that the industry must change its thinking and develop new techniques for *utilizing* the phenomenon of sharing instead of *resisting* it. They need to find inventive ways to finance music, such as using shareware sites to promote public appearances and live concert tours. In other words, they need to cultivate fans. With a strong following and superior sound quality on CDs and DVDs, music will continue to sell. The difference will be in *how* it is sold.

LOOKING AHEAD

It is unlikely that with Internet access and rapid technological evolution, corporations and governments will be able to control the free flow of information, music, or ideas. Moreover, file sharing on broadband networks, which is now considered leading edge, will one day be as commonplace as a telephone call. Then new leading-edge technology will offer its own challenges, some of which may also disregard existing copyright protection. Is there a solution to this dilemma?

LOOKING AT THE ISSUE

1. Survey 20 people from different age groups. Ask, "Should people be required to pay a fee for any material they download from the Internet?" Compile the data and calculate the results of your survey. With the class, discuss the implications of your results.

2. With a partner, assume the roles of an interviewer and a performing artist. As the interviewer, prepare a list of questions about shareware and the issue of copyright infringement. Show your list to the performing artist to allow him or her to prepare responses. Present your interview to the class either as a taped or live role play, or as a magazine article with a question-and-answer format.

3. How would you resolve this copyright dilemma? Working in a group, create a copyright policy to address this issue. Share your findings with the rest of the class.

4. Create a mind map to illustrate the far-reaching effects of electronic copyright infringement.

19 Contract Remedies and Consumer Protection

CHAPTER OUTLINE

Rights and Obligations

Discharging a Contract

The Sale of Goods

Protection for Consumers

FOCUS YOUR LEARNING

What rights and obligations does a contract create?

How is a contract discharged?

What constitutes breach of contract?

What remedies are available for breach of contract?

What laws have been put in place to protect consumers?

WHAT DO YOU THINK?

- In the situation shown in this cartoon, do the legal requirements of a contract exist with respect to definite terms, valid consideration, and capacity?

- Assuming a valid contract does exist in this situation, would it be reasonable to end the contract because of frustration or impossibility of performance?

A friend promises to meet you for a movie. You wait outside the theatre while everyone goes in. The movie has begun, and still your friend has not arrived. Are you annoyed, hurt, or perhaps even angry? What recourse do you have? Not much, in the case of a broken date. But if a friend fails to pay for a bike you sold him, your rights would be protected by the law. In this case, a contract was formed because of the parties'—your and your friend's—intention to be legally bound.

The proper performance of contracts is key to the economic functioning of our society. All contracts have to come to a close or, in legal terms, be "discharged." But what happens when one, or both, of the parties to a contract fail to live up to their end of the bargain? Just as society has developed laws to deal with those who break the criminal law, society has also developed laws to deal with those who break the civil law by failing to live up to their contractual obligations.

The courts can impose **remedies** ranging from an order that the offending party live up to the contract, to an award for monetary damages. In addition, most provinces have enacted legislation dealing with consumer purchases in an effort to clarify the parties' rights.

remedies: methods of enforcing rights and preventing or compensating violations

RIGHTS AND OBLIGATIONS

Privity of Contract

When a contract is formed, it creates rights and obligations, but only for the parties to the contract. This principle is called **privity of contract.** The parties to the contract cannot place obligations on people who are third parties, that is, people who are not parties to the contract. Only the parties privy to the contract may sue if the other party breaches it.

The idea of privity of contract has a long history in British law. The case that established the rule of privity was *Tweddle* v. *Atkinson* (1861). At a wedding celebration, the father of the groom promised the father of the bride that he would give the newlyweds £100 as a gift. The father of the bride, in turn, promised to give them £200. The bride's father died before the £200 was paid, so the groom, Tweddle, sued the estate for the money. Tweddle's father could not sue, because he, too, had died.

Tweddle lost because the court ruled that "no stranger to the consideration can take advantage of a contract, although made for his benefit. Consideration must move from the person entitled to sue upon the contract." This precedent meant that persons could not sue for breach of contract unless they were a party to the original agreement. The rule applied even if the contract was made for the benefit of a third party.

privity of contract: only the parties to the contract can enforce the rights and obligations created by the contract

Law in Your Life
Suppose your aunt buys you a Walkman, which is defective. According to the principle of privity, if the company refuses to refund the purchase price, you could not sue the company.

Fast Fact
When an individual makes a contract in the name of a company, the company has privity of contract, not the individual employee who worked out the deal.

Exceptions to Privity

Exceptions to the rule of privity came about because, on occasion, the rule led to unfairness. For example, in the *Tweddle* v. *Atkinson* (1861) case, there was no reason that the bride's father should not have had to honour his agreement with the groom's father. There are a number of exceptions, but two of the most common occur in cases involving insurance contracts and trusts.

In the case of a life insurance policy, the contract is between the insurance company (the insurer) and the individual purchasing the policy (the insured). However, the insurer's obligation to pay only arises upon the death of the insured, at which time the company must pay the value of the policy to the beneficiary. If the rule of privity were strictly followed, then the beneficiary, as a stranger to the contract, would not be able to sue the insurance company if it failed to pay out the policy. However, provincial laws allow beneficiaries to sue life insurance companies for non-payment. Similar provisions exist in the case of automobile insurance.

A **trust** is an arrangement whereby a person gives property or money to another person (the trustee) who must look after it for a third party (the beneficiary). For example, a person who has young children may put a clause in his or her will that sets up a trust to care for the children. Usually, trusts require the trustee to turn over the money or property to the children when they reach a specified age. If the trustee fails to do so, or mismanages the trust before the children reach the specified age, the children can sue to have the trust enforced. If the children are minors, an adult, called a "next friend," can sue on their behalf.

trust: an arrangement whereby one person gives property or money to another person (the trustee) who must look after it for a third party

Assignment of Contracts

When **assignment** of a contract occurs, the rights and obligations of the contract are transferred to someone other than one of the original parties to the agreement. In professional sports, for example, when a player is traded from one team to another, the new team usually assumes the player's existing contract with respect to salary, benefits, and so on. The contract has been assigned, or transferred, to the new team.

assignment: the transfer of the rights and obligations of a contract to another party

Suppose that Tara had a contract with Mr. Prall to cut his grass for the summer and he now owes her $150. Tara owes Rick's Bike Repair $150, so she assigns Mr. Prall's debt to the repair shop. This means that Mr. Prall now owes Rick's Bike Repair the $150. Tara might do this provided

- the assignment is absolute and unconditional, which means that Tara must assign the entire amount owed—$150—not just part of it;
- the assignment is in writing and identifies the parties and the amount of money involved. The **assignor,** in this case, Tara, must sign it; and
- the person who owes the debt, in this case Mr. Prall, is given written notice outlining the details of the assignment.

assignor: the person who transfers his or her contractual obligations to someone else

assignee: the person to whom contractual obligations are transferred

If the debtor, Mr. Prall, fails to pay the **assignee,** Rick's Bike Repair, then Rick's can sue Mr. Prall. However, an assignee takes the assignment "subject to the equities." This means that if Tara had failed to cut the lawn as often as required by the contract, Mr. Prall may not have to pay the entire $150 to Rick's. In addition, only the debt was assigned, not the contract itself; so if Mr. Prall wanted to sue for damage to his property, he would have to sue Tara, not Rick's Bike Repair.

Vicarious or Substituted Performance

In some businesses, the assignment of a portion of a contract may be a normal way of operating. For example, in the construction industry, a general contractor will take on a building job and then subcontract tasks such as plumbing, electrical work, bricklaying, and painting. When a third party performs a contractual obligation, this arrangement is referred to as **vicarious or substituted performance.**

vicarious or substituted performance: a situation whereby some of the contractual obligations are performed by a third party

Figure 19.1 Who do you think is liable if a subcontractor fails to do a proper job?

Groom v. MacFarlane (2000), P.E.I. S.C.T.D. 61, on-line: CanLII

CASE

Freddie Martin, a friend of the defendant, MacFarlane, told him about a warehouse that was "cleaning out" year-old television sets at a very low price. The plaintiffs heard about the deal and asked MacFarlane to obtain bargain televisions for them as well.

The plaintiffs gave MacFarlane down payments ranging from $630 to $730. MacFarlane refused to provide them with receipts. Two of the plaintiffs admitted that MacFarlane explained that he was passing the money along to a third party who would obtain the television sets.

In the end, none of the plaintiffs received their television sets. Their money went to a third party who was eventually convicted of fraud and sent to prison. The plaintiffs sued MacFarlane to get their money back, alleging that he had contracted with them to obtain television sets and failed to do so.

The Court found that the evidence supported MacFarlane's claim that he was merely acting as agent or "middle-man" and that he had carried out these duties "with reasonable diligence." The plaintiffs' case was dismissed. The Court, however, did not order the plaintiffs to pay MacFarlane's costs.

1. If a contract existed in this case, who would be privy to it?
2. What would have to occur for assignment of a contract to be possible in this case?
3. What lessons can be learned about privity of contract and assignment of a contract from the experience of the plaintiffs?

Building Your Understanding

1. Re-examine the definition of a contract. Why is it important for a contract to be "legally enforceable"?
2. For each of the cases below, answer the questions that follow, applying principles of contract law.
   a) Jerzy buys Tomas a new fishing reel for his birthday. When Tomas tries to put the new reel on his fishing pole, he discovers that the rewinding mechanism does not work. Based on what you have learned so far, could Tomas sue the maker of the fishing reel? Why or why not?
   b) Terry's father purchased a life insurance policy and named Terry as the beneficiary. After his father's death, the insurance company wanted to pay Terry only one-half the value of the policy. Can Terry take action against the company? Why or why not?

DISCHARGING A CONTRACT

When a contract is discharged, or brought to an end, it means that the parties are no longer bound by any obligations within it. Contracts can be discharged in four ways: by performance, mutual agreement, frustration (or impossibility of performance), and breach of contract. The manner in which the contract is discharged will determine whether the courts become involved and what remedies are available if the contract has been breached.

Discharge by Performance

performance: completion of the obligations under the contract

A contract can be discharged when the parties involved complete their parts of the bargain satisfactorily. This is called **performance.** If Jake contracts with Matthew to build a deck, the contract is discharged by performance when Matthew has completed the deck and Jake pays him.

If one of the parties refuses to perform their part of the contract, the other party is usually not obligated to complete their part of the bargain. If Matthew does not build the deck, for example, Jake is not required to pay.

Historically, some unfairness resulted when a contract called for a lump sum payment "upon completion" of a service; no money was paid unless the contract was fully completed. If Matthew had built most, but not all, of Jake's deck, he would not have been entitled to *any* money. This rule was clearly not fair, so exceptions have been applied over the years.

Substantial Performance

substantial performance: carrying out the essential elements of a contract

Fulfilling the essential elements of what was required by a contract is called **substantial performance.** When substantial performance has occurred, the courts may treat the contract as if it is discharged, even though some minor details have not been fulfilled. Suppose Lafleur contracts with Jones for 500 cases of oil, but Jones delivers only 499. The contract has likely been substantially performed, but it depends on the circumstances. Suppose Jones needed exactly 500 cases of oil to run a certain machine, and being one case short meant he could not run the machine at all. In this instance, the court might find that the contract had not been substantially performed.

Epp v. Town Cobbler (2000), P.E.I. S.C.T.D. 57, on-line: CanLII

CASE

The plaintiff, Garth Epp, sold his business, known as The Town Cobblers, to the defendant, Scott Murray. The defendant gave a promissory note to the plaintiff in the amount of $8000 at 9 percent interest. The defendant made monthly payments for five months, and then stopped payment on the remaining post-dated cheques. The defendant claimed that the plaintiff misrepresented what was included in the sale of the business, specifically, a harness stitcher and a glass-fronted display cabinet.

In the Agreement of Sale that the parties executed, neither the harness stitcher nor the glass-fronted display case was listed. The plaintiff claimed that he had explained to the defendant that the stitcher was rented from the Craft Council and the glass-fronted display case belonged to the landlord. The defendant denied that this information was conveyed to him (even though he had an opportunity to review the sales agreement before he signed it).

The Court ruled that the plaintiff was to receive the amount owed him by the defendant. In reference to the other items, the Court stated,

> ... it is incumbent upon him [the defendant], if he thought another item should be on the list of equipment, to inquire at that time or to have it added. There is no evidence that he did so.

1. At what point do you think the contract between Epp and Murray would be considered discharged?
2. Why did the Court rule in favour of Epp?
3. How does this case illustrate the difficulties in coming to a judgment based solely on the testimony of the parties involved?

Some contracts cannot be discharged by substantial performance. If the contract is to drill a water-producing well, the contract is not discharged by substantial performance unless a usable well is successfully drilled. A dry hole 30 metres deep is of no use. The key to substantial performance is whether the party got more or less what it bargained for, even though the agreement has been breached.

Discharge by Agreement

At times, the parties to a contract may wish to end the contract even if all of its terms have not been completed. This is called "discharge by agreement" and could take place in a variety of ways. For example, the parties might cancel or terminate the contract, which means that they agree to discontinue performance of the terms of the contract. Or, both parties might agree to substitute a new contract to replace an existing one. Suppose a logging company had a contract with a pulp and paper mill to deliver a certain amount of lumber each month. If the mill asked the logging company to increase the amount of a lumber it supplied and the logging company agreed, the parties would then draw up a new agreement to replace the existing one. The replacement of an old agreement with a new one is called **novation**.

Still another way to discharge a contract by agreement is to have the contract state that the parties are relieved of their obligations under certain

novation: agreement of the parties to substitute a new contract for an existing one; the old agreement is thereby cancelled

circumstances. For example, Yoana and Cam might offer to purchase a house, subject to a satisfactory home inspection. If the home inspector's report is positive, Yoana and Cam will fulfill the contract by purchasing the house. However, if the inspector discovers termites and recommends that Yoana and Cam not go through with the purchase, then they do not have to buy the house, and the contract is discharged.

Discharge by Frustration

frustration: an event that makes performance of the contract impossible

The principle of **frustration,** or impossibility of performance, recognizes that sometimes the parties to a contract may not be able to carry out the terms of the agreement because events beyond the parties' control prevent them from doing so. For example, if a band has signed a contract to perform

Trucking contractor died, but not the contract

Bidulock Oilfield Service Ltd. operates out of Hairy Hill, 100 miles [160 km] northeast of Edmonton. In March 1985, it contracted with Wayne and Kevin Dobush, who operated W-K Trucking, to broker W-K's oil field services in return for 15 percent of W-K's earnings. [This means that Bidulock would find customers and sign contracts with them. W-K would do the actual trucking, but Bidulock would get a 15 percent commission.] Under the agreement and for three years after its termination, W-K was prohibited from trucking within 100 miles [160 km] of Hairy Hill "any water or crude oil" intended for petroleum exploration except under contract for Bidulock. When Kevin Dobush passed away in 1986, Wayne continued the agreement with Bidulock. But in February 1998, Wayne ended his agreement with Bidulock and took approximately 50 percent of its customers with him. Bidulock then asked the Court of Queen's Bench in Edmonton for an injunction enforcing the restraint-of-trade agreement.

On November 20, Justice Philip Clarke rejected W-K.'s argument that the contract's restrictions died with Kevin Dobush. The judge noted, "Wayne Dobush reaffirmed the agreement by his continued acceptance of hauling contracts under the agreement." Because Bidulock "lost more than 50 percent of its customers when W-K purported to terminate the agreement and has lost more since," Mr. Justice Clarke ruled the service company would indeed suffer irreparable harm if the injunction were not granted.

SOURCE: Philip Hope, "Trucking contractor died, but not the contract," *Alberta Report*, December 21, 1998, p. 20.

1. Why do you think W-K Trucking entered into the original contract with Bidulock? Why might Wayne Dobush have decided to end the contract?
2. Outline possible arguments for each side both for and against granting an injunction.
3. Do you agree with the judge's ruling? Explain. If you do not agree, state what your ruling would have been.

Figure 19.2 Consider other ways frustration might apply to the obligations of a band to put on a performance.

an outdoor concert, and a violent storm erupts on the night of the show making performance impossible, the contract would be frustrated. In this situation, the band might be relieved of its contractual obligation because it would be impossible to carry out its part of the agreement.

Frustration may also occur because property is destroyed, one of the parties becomes ill or dies, or a change in the law makes the contract illegal. When frustration exists, the parties to the contract cannot sue for breach of contract.

A party cannot intentionally make performance impossible and then rely on the principle of frustration. Bill cannot contract to sell his car to Min, then sell it to Nur at a higher price and claim that it is impossible to sell the car to Min because he (Bill) no longer owns the car.

Discharge by Breach

Breach of contract occurs when one of the parties fails to live up to the obligations agreed to in the contract. The effect of a breach of contract is not a simple matter; for example, breach does not necessarily terminate a contract. In some cases, the party who has not received what was agreed to under the contract may be released from contractual obligations. But in other cases, the party who has *not* breached the contract may have to continue to perform the obligations agreed to and can sue only for damages that resulted from the breach. In still other cases, such as where a party wants **specific performance,** the party asking for specific performance must be ready and willing to perform his or her part of the contract.

Suppose you have a contract to mow your neighbour's lawn every week for six months. You perform the contract for four months, and then miss one week. How serious is your breach when the contract as a whole is considered?

> **Consider This**
> If a house is found to be infested with termites after a home inspection company has declared it termite-free, the homeowners can sue the home inspection company for damages. How might the damages be calculated?

breach of contract: failure by a party to perform the obligations agreed to in the contract

specific performance: the party breaching the contract is ordered by the court to perform its part of the agreement

Should your neighbour be able to cancel the contract and hire someone else? What if you mowed the lawn consistently week after week but did a poor job? Would your neighbour have to honour the contract and pay you? As you can see, breach of contract is a complex issue.

Breach of Condition

The law distinguishes between terms in a contract that are more important and those that are less important. A very important term is called a **condition.** If a condition is not fulfilled, it amounts to a failure of consideration because one of the parties did not get what he or she bargained for.

If parties breach a condition, they are said to have repudiated the contract. This means that they have either not performed as required or indicated that they do not intend to perform the contract. The innocent party can either accept or reject the **repudiation.**

If Ashmit orders a new truck, but the car dealership provides a van instead, a fundamental term of the contract has not been fulfilled. Ashmit could simply accept the van or reject it. If he had to pay more for the identical truck at another dealer, he could recover damages. The important thing is, the choice is his; the car dealer could not sue him for payment if he rejected the van.

condition: a very important term of a contract

repudiation: words or conduct that indicate one of the parties will not honour its obligations under the contract

Breach of Warranty

If a minor term of the contract is not performed, a breach of **warranty** exists. Suppose Madeline contracts to paint Elissa's dining room. One of the terms of the contract is that paint splatters will be removed from the windows after the painting is done. The job is done beautifully, but the paint splatters are not removed. Elissa is not relieved of her contractual obligation to pay Madeline. However, she can deduct the amount she pays someone else to remove the paint splatters from the money she owes Madeline.

warranty: a minor term of a contract

Figure 19.3 Why would a small sign posted in an out-of-the-way location not constitute a valid exemption clause?

Exemption clauses are terms in contracts stating that one of the parties will not be liable for certain specified things. Parking lot ticket stubs often contain a statement on the reverse saying that the owner of the lot is simply renting space to you and is not responsible for any damage to your vehicle. The owner is trying to limit his or her liability by making it clear that the terms of the contract do not make the owner responsible for your car.

Remedies for Breach of Contract

Since a contract is a legally enforceable agreement, the parties involved are bound by the terms of the contract. If the contract is breached, the courts may become involved and impose a solution, or remedy, to help the injured party. Remedies may be in the form of damages, specific performance, or injunctions.

The court may order the defendant to pay monetary **damages** (an amount of money) to make up for losses that the injured party suffered as a result of a breach of contract. If Madeline agreed to paint Elissa's tool shed and neglected to paint the trim, then Elissa could sue for damages that would amount to the cost of having the job completed. The court would not award Elissa a large sum of money in order to punish Madeline but would only allow Elissa to recover her actual losses.

The injured party must attempt to minimize the loss suffered. This is called **mitigation of damages.** If Nadia and Daryl enter a contract to sell their house to Norbert, and Norbert later refuses to close the deal, a breach of contract has occurred. Nadia and Daryl cannot simply keep their house and sue Norbert for the purchase price. They have a duty to try to sell their house to someone else at the best possible price.

Nadia and Daryl might also decide to sue Norbert for damages. For example, if they sell the house for a lesser amount than what Norbert had agreed to pay, they might sue Norbert for the difference between what he would have paid and what they eventually received for the house. If Nadia and Daryl receive more for the house than what Norbert had agreed to pay, they would not be awarded damages.

In some cases, damages may not be a suitable remedy for a breach of contract. The remedy of specific performance, for instance, is often used in situations involving unique property, art, antiques, and other similar goods. Suppose Jono signed a contract to buy Bart's rare Wayne Gretzky rookie card, but the next day Bart decided not to go through with the deal. This would constitute a breach of contract by Bart, and Jono could sue him. If the card is so rare that Jono cannot buy it elsewhere, he might not want damages. He might want the court to compel Bart to specifically perform his obligation under the contract and sell the card to him.

An **injunction** is another remedy available under contract law. Injunctions can either *require* a party to do something or *bar* a party from doing something. An example can be found in the *Bidulock Oilfield Service Ltd.* case discussed earlier in this chapter. There, the Court granted an injunction against W-K Trucking, barring them from trucking water or crude oil in the area described in the contract.

---

exemption clauses: clauses that release a party from liability

Law in Your Life
If an exemption clause is not posted in clear view or brought to your attention, the court may decide that it is not a term of the contract and is of no effect.

damages: money awarded by the court for actual losses resulting from a breach of contract

mitigation of damages: the obligation on the part of the injured party to attempt to minimize losses suffered

Fast Fact
Two methods of calculating damages:
- the difference between what was contracted for and what was received
- the cost to put the plaintiff in the position he or she would have been in had the defendant performed the contract

injunction: a court order requiring a party to perform, or prohibiting it from performing, a specified act

CASE

Granum v. Northwest Territories [1992] N.W.T.R. 20 (Terr. Ct.)

1. Explain why you think the Court found in favour of the plaintiff.
2. What damages do you think the Court might have ordered as part of its decision?

Ms. Granum accepted employment as a teacher from Mr. Kakfwi in his capacity as minister of personnel for the government of the Northwest Territories. She was to receive remuneration and certain benefits specified in the collective agreement for teachers. By law, the collective agreement could not deal with housing, but Granum was concerned about costs since she had never lived in the North. Consequently, Granum and Kakfwi entered into a verbal agreement regarding housing and utilities, under which Granum was to have a house and utilities for a price not to exceed $600 a month for a period of one year.

When Granum relocated, she was given a document showing rent and utilities at $591 a month. Subsequently, the defendant increased the rent to $725 a month and told the plaintiff she was also responsible for utilities. Granum sued the government for damages and specific performance of the oral contract she had made with Kakfwi. The Court found in favour of Granum.

Building Your Understanding

1. How is a contract discharged through performance?
2. Frustration, or impossibility of performance, is a valid defence against breach of contract. Explain why it would not apply if a party to the contract deliberately did something to make performance impossible.
3. Using examples, explain the difference between a breach of condition and a breach of warranty.
4. Under what conditions are monetary damages awarded?
5. Do you feel that the principle of mitigation of damages is just? Why or why not?
6. Why might the courts order specific performance or grant an injunction rather than award damages for breach of contract?
7. What would be your judgment in the following cases? Support your opinion with principles of contract law.
    a) A tire manufacturer sold tires to a wholesaler on the condition that the tires would only be resold to retailers who agreed to sell them at a certain price. The wholesaler sold them to Bob's Tires, who sold them below the specified price. The tire manufacturer sued Bob's Tires. What problems might arise for the tire manufacturer?
    b) Dave rented a fishing trawler from Trawlers Inc., bringing his fleet to four vessels. The federal minister of fisheries allocated only three fishing licences to Dave. Dave claimed his contract with Trawlers Inc. was frustrated by lack of a licence and wanted to back out of it. Can he do this? Explain.

THE SALE OF GOODS

Contract law concerning the sale of goods (as opposed to the sale of land) was developed by the courts of common law and the courts of equity; that is, through decisions made by the courts. This resulted in a complex set of rules, some governed by the form of the transaction and some governed by what was fair in a particular case. Toward the end of the nineteenth century, however, governments began to pass statutes to regulate the sale of goods. In addition, more recently, consumer protection legislation has been enacted.

The British Parliament took the first steps in codifying the law concerning the sale of goods in 1893 when it passed the *Sale of Goods Act*. This law was the model on which all of the provinces in Canada (except Quebec, which uses the *Civil Code*) enacted legislation dealing with the sale of goods.

These provincial statutes make functioning in the modern economy easier. The legislation sets out clear and concise rules governing contracts in which the seller transfers ownership of goods in return for money. The *Sale of Goods Act*s define "goods" as personal property such as televisions, books, and furniture. The Acts do not cover the sale of land or *services* such as banking, restaurant dining, and automobile repair.

Fast Fact
In the nine provinces and three territories, the sale of goods legislation applies only to written contracts in which goods are exchanged for amounts of at least $30 to $50, depending on the jurisdiction.

Title and Risk

In many cases when people buy goods, they simply hand over money and receive goods in return. Problems arise, however, when someone agrees to buy something and does not immediately take possession of it, or when someone is allowed to take delivery of goods before having paid for them in full. The time at which **title** passes from the seller to the buyer is important, because this usually determines who bears the risk of a loss if the goods are damaged or destroyed. It can also affect the remedies the seller and the buyer have against each other and against third parties.

title: legal ownership

The *Sale of Goods Act*s make a distinction between an actual sale and an agreement to sell. A **sale** refers to a situation whereby the title to the goods is transferred immediately when the contract is made. An **agreement to sell,** on the other hand, means that title to the goods does not pass immediately to the purchaser when the contract is made but will be transferred at some future time. Unfortunately, people often fail to think about the issue of *when* they intend title to pass.

sale: the immediate exchange of title for goods and consideration by two parties

agreement to sell: an agreement whereby title is transferred to the buyer in the future

Figure 19.4 It is important that the parties to a sale are clear on when they intend title to pass from the seller to the buyer.

The basic rule is that title to goods passes when the parties *intend* it to pass. Because people do not always indicate at what point they intend title to pass, the *Sale of Goods Act* created five basic rules. Each rule has an effect on who suffers the loss if the goods are destroyed or damaged, and each affects the remedies available both under the contract and against third parties. Remember, the parties are free to clearly express when the property passes, so they do not have to rely on the rules in the Act.

- **Rule 1** When the item to be purchased is available in the store, title passes to the buyer as soon as the contract is made. Suppose that Mila walks into a store and agrees to purchase the laser printer on display. Nothing remains to be done except for Mila to pay and take delivery. As soon as Mila agrees to buy the printer, title or ownership passes to her. If Mila was planning to pick up the printer the next morning, but it was destroyed in a fire overnight, she would bear the loss since the title had already passed to her. If she had not yet paid, she could be sued for the price. This is called an **unconditional sale of specific goods in a deliverable state.** Remember that Mila could have changed this arrangement by getting the store to agree that it would be responsible for the printer until she picked it up.

- **Rule 2** If the seller has to do something to specific goods to put them in a deliverable state, then title does not pass until the changes have been made and the purchaser is notified. Suppose Pierre bought a new suit at the tailor shop, but the pants had to be hemmed and the jacket needed to be taken in. Pierre does not have title to the suit until the alterations have been made and he has been notified that the suit is now in a deliverable state. If shoplifters stole the suit before it was altered or before Pierre was notified, the tailor would suffer the loss, not Pierre.

- **Rule 3** On certain occasions, title passes only after there has been some type of evaluation of the goods (e.g., weighing, measuring, testing) in order to determine the price. For example, if Sean agreed to purchase a load of grain from Mandy, it would be necessary to first weigh the load of grain in order to calculate the price. Title to the grain would pass only after the weight had been determined, the price calculated, and Sean informed.

- **Rule 4** Sometimes the buyer may take the goods away in order to test them before deciding whether to complete the purchase. For example, a farmer may take home a new plough and try it out before agreeing to finalize the sale. If the farmer notifies the seller of his intention to go through with the contract, then the contract is complete and the title passes. If the farmer keeps the plough beyond the trial period specified in the contract and neglects to inform the seller that he does not wish to keep the plough, then the title will automatically pass to the farmer. Liability for loss or damage remains with the seller until title has passed to the buyer.

- **Rule 5** In some cases, the goods being contracted for have not yet been manufactured or are an unspecified part of a large amount. If, for example,

unconditional sale of specific goods in a deliverable state: the goods being purchased are specifically identified (no changes or alterations are required) and at hand (available to the purchaser)

Fast Fact

A buyer does not take title to goods purchased on an instalment plan until the last payment is made. If the buyer wants to sell the goods to a third party before title is transferred, the buyer requires the permission of the seller and the agreement of the third party to take over any remaining payments.

Ron orders a new car at the dealership and it has not been built yet, there are no specific goods to identify in the contract. Title to the car would pass to Ron once (a) the car had been manufactured, (b) the dealer advised Ron that his car was ready, and (c) Ron agreed to accept the car.

Standardized Terms

Manufacturers have adopted standardized terms to describe responsibilities and delivery arrangements for goods. For instance, when you see the term **c.i.f.** in a contract, it means "cost, insurance, and freight." Although title passes to the buyer at an early stage, the seller accepts responsibility to pay the cost of transporting and insuring the goods (in the buyer's name) to the point of destination.

c.i.f.: cost, insurance, and freight

Some contracts carry the term **f.o.b.**, which stands for "free on board." This means that the parties have agreed that the seller will bear the risk until the goods are placed on board the carrier chosen by the buyer. Once they are "on board," the buyer assumes the risk for delivery.

f.o.b.: free on board

A contractual term that may be more familiar to you is **c.o.d.**, or "cash on delivery." When goods are shipped c.o.d., the seller maintains title and control over the possession of the goods until they are delivered to the buyer's premises and paid for. The risk remains with the seller until this point.

c.o.d.: cash on delivery

Manufacturer's Warranties

Some products such as appliances and audio equipment, are covered by a **manufacturer's warranty.** The warranty is given by the maker of the product and deals with the quality of the product. A "warranty card" outlining the conditions of the warranty comes with the item at the time of purchase.

manufacturer's warranty: a promise from manufacturers to repair their products without cost within a specified period

Under the warranty, the manufacturer is usually responsible for replacing any parts that may be defective, but only for a specified length of time. If there are problems with the product, the purchaser is usually responsible for getting it to and from an authorized repair centre. As with all contracts, you

Figure 19.5 Warranty card for a portable CD player

DICSCO CANADA LIMITED WARRANTY

This apparatus has a warranty against faulty materials and workmanship for the period of one year from the date of purchase subject to the following conditions:

The warranty registration must be completed and mailed within 14 days of purchase.

Any claim arising under this warranty should be made either directly to Dicsco Canada or the authorized dealer from whom the apparatus was purchased.

In the event of service being required from Dicsco Canada, the apparatus must be securely packaged and sent to the nearest Dicsco Canada service depot, prepaid by the owner.

Defective component parts will be replaced free of charge and the apparatus will be returned freight collect.

This warranty expressly excludes: damage caused by incorrect use; loss or damage in transit; contingent and third party liability.

Any service carried out by any person other than an authorized representative of Dicsco Canada or their agents renders this warranty invalid.

No alteration or variation of this warranty will be recognized.

This warranty is not transferable.

Consider This

Should consumers who are stuck with a "lemon" have legal recourse beyond the limitations of a written warranty? Why or why not?

CASE

Miller v. Jaguar Canada Inc. (2000), Man. Q.B. 156, on-line: CanLII

BACKGROUND The plaintiff, Mr. Miller, purchased a 1985 Jaguar from Motor Sales Inc. in Winnipeg. He paid $49 275 for the car, which came with the following warranty:

> Jaguar Company Inc. ... hereby warrants to the original and subsequent owner of a new model Jaguar that it will, through an authorized Jaguar dealer, repair or replace without charge any part that is defective in material or workmanship ...
>
> This warranty is for a 24-month or 60 000 km period, whichever occurs first, and starts on the date the vehicle is delivered to the first retail purchaser ...

A 1997 XK8 Jaguar

It soon became clear that the paint job on the car was defective, and Jaguar agreed to repaint it. However, Miller moved to Victoria before the work could be done. Jaguar refused to authorize another Jaguar dealership in Victoria to do the paint job because they had already contracted Motor Sales to do it. Miller finally agreed to take the car back to Winnipeg. He notified Motor Sales of his intention but made no definite appointment. Motor Sales could not do the job immediately, so Miller returned to Victoria and had the paint job completed there. He claimed for the cost of the paint job and $4400 in expenses for the wasted trip to Winnipeg.

Miller had many further problems with the car, including the alternator, the brakes, a gas smell in the car interior, the leather seats, and water leakage causing problems with numerous electrical components. He also had to replace the engine and argued that this was the result of constant overheating caused by the car having too small a radiator. Some of these problems showed up during the warranty period, others when the warranty had expired.

LEGAL QUESTION Should a company's responsibility for a product extend beyond the warranty period?

DECISION Miller was awarded $20 280.22 to cover repairs to the car due to problems that originated during the warranty period and interest on money he spent on these repairs. Some of these problems were caused by design defects in the car rather than strictly "material or workmanship" as stated in the warranty. Jaguar had spent over $10 000 in warranty repairs and did cover certain items that might be characterized as design defects. The claim of almost $11 000 for replacing the engine was rejected. The evidence did not establish that the problem originated during the warranty period, and the repairs were performed more than four years after the warranty period had expired and the car had been driven many thousands of kilometres.

Only $2000 was allowed for the wasted trip to Winnipeg. And Miller's claim for inconvenience and distress associated with the many breakdowns of the car was not allowed. The Court held that these damages were not covered under Jaguar's warranty.

LEGAL SIGNIFICANCE Generally, a manufacturer is only liable for defects covered by a warranty if the defects occur during the warranty period. If the defect is an inherent one, which is present on delivery, or a continuing one, the manufacturer may be liable for repairs even though the need for them arises outside of the warranty period.

ANALYSIS

1. Describe the factors the Court took into consideration in determining the damages.
2. What legal option could Jaguar have pursued instead of refusing to authorize Mr. Miller's paint job in Victoria?

should read the warranty cards at the time of purchase and not assume any coverage outside what is listed in the contract. In many cases, you must mail a registration card to the manufacturer for the warranty to be enforced.

Implied Conditions and Warranties

The *Sale of Goods Act* lists a number of **implied conditions** concerning the sale of goods (see Figure 19.6). These conditions are "implied" because, although they are not expressly made part of the contract by the parties, they are deemed to be part of the contract by the *Sale of Goods Act*. Unless they are specifically waived by the parties to the contract, the buyer may sue for damages if any of these conditions are breached. The purpose of the conditions is to impose duties on the seller, not the manufacturer, and to protect purchasers.

implied conditions: essential elements of a contract that are not specifically stated in the contract

"*Oops!*"

Fast Fact
Manufacturers can include a disclaimer or exemption clause within the warranty that specifically states that no implied warranties or conditions apply. However, some legislation makes such disclaimers invalid because they are attempts by the manufacturer to avoid statutes passed to protect consumers.

Figure 19.6 **Implied conditions**

Condition	Example
There is an implied condition that the seller has the right to sell the goods.	If the seller does not have the right to sell the goods, the rightful owner can take them back from you.
The goods must be of a merchantable quality.	If you purchase a gas barbecue, it must be in good working order and capable of cooking food. If it will not light, it is not merchantable.
The goods must be fit for a particular purpose.	If you tell a store clerk you need rope for lifting your boat out of the water, the rope sold to you must be strong enough to do the job.
The goods must comply with their description.	If you see a white couch in a store and order it in a different colour, you must receive the identical model in the appropriate colour.
Goods sold by sample must comply with their sample.	If your hockey team purchases uniforms based on a sample provided by the seller, the goods you receive must be of the same quality and materials as the sample.

Fast Fact
Unlike stolen merchandise, if a buyer innocently receives stolen money as part of a business transaction, the money does not have to be returned.

Keep in mind the difference between conditions and warranties discussed earlier in this chapter; the remedies available for a breach of the contract depend on whether it is a warranty or a condition that is breached.

Though not expressly made part of the contract by the parties, implied conditions are deemed to be part of the contract by the *Sale of Goods Act*.

Remedies for Breach of Sale of Goods

Remedies are available for both the buyer and the seller if the other party breaks the terms of a sales contract. Remedies are provided by the *Sale of Goods Act*, but common law remedies may also be available.

Buyers' Remedies

default: to fail to do something required by law

If the seller **defaults** on the contract, then the purchaser can use the appropriate remedy as follows:

Consider This
Businesses are under no legal obligation to accept returned items unless they are defective. However, if a sign regarding exchanges or returns is displayed, it becomes part of the sales contract, and the store is obliged to comply with its own policy. Why do you think most businesses offer refunds or exchanges on merchandise?

- If the seller *misrepresents* the product, the contract may be rescinded. Damages can be awarded if the misrepresentation is negligent or fraudulent.
- If the seller *breaches a condition* of the contract, the contract may be rescinded, or the goods can be rejected by the buyer. Alternatively, the buyer can demand that money paid to the seller be returned.
- If there is a *breach of warranty* by the seller, the buyer can use the breach as a valid reason not to pay all or part of the purchase price. The buyer can sue for damages for breach of warranty if the buyer suffers damages that exceed the price.

Sellers' Remedies

The seller has a number of options available if the buyer breaches the contract. The most common breach is failure to pay for the goods ordered. The remedies available may depend on whether title to the goods has passed to the buyer. In some cases, the location of the goods also affects the seller's remedies.

lien: the right to hold or dispose of another person's property in payment for a debt

stoppage in transit: goods that have been shipped out are returned to the seller before they have been delivered to the buyer

- If the goods *have not been delivered* then the seller may exercise a seller's **lien** against the goods. Even though title to the goods has passed to the purchaser, the seller can refuse to make delivery until payment is received.
- If the goods *are being transported to an insolvent buyer* (a buyer who is unable to pay), then the seller may exercise a right called **stoppage in transit.** If the goods have not been paid for, the seller can halt delivery and have the goods returned. For example, if a company shipped an order to a retailer, and then the retailer declared bankruptcy and could not pay for the goods, the company would want to take the goods back.
- The seller *may resell the goods*. After notifying the buyer and providing adequate time to make payment, the seller may sell the goods to another party. If the goods are perishable, the seller need not delay the sale because the produce may spoil. The right to resell is related to the principle of mitigation of damages. A seller who sues for damages for breach of contract must show that an attempt was made to mitigate the damages. The seller cannot just let the goods rot or sit in a warehouse.

Mann v. Cobra Jeans, [1996] N.B.R. 2d Uned. 3 (Q.B.)

CASE

Leonard Mann purchased a pair of jeans for $39.95 on December 23, 1994, from the Cobra Jeans store as a Christmas gift for Reginald Hickey. Hickey returned the jeans to the store with the receipt because after wearing them on two occasions and washing them twice, a seam was coming undone. The owner advised Hickey that the jeans would not be replaced, nor would the purchase price be refunded.

Mann went to court, seeking damages on the basis that the jeans were of poor quality and should have lasted for a longer period of time. The store owner maintained that the jeans probably ripped due to Hickey's negligence.

The judge, after assessing the credibility of the parties, had this to say about the case:

> I find as a fact that the jeans ... had a latent defect which resulted in the seam coming apart.... A contract for the sale of goods in these circumstances is governed by the *Consumer Product Warranty and Liability Act*.... Section 12(1) states: "In every contract for the sale or supply of a consumer product there is an implied warranty given by the seller to the buyer that the product and any components thereof will be durable for a reasonable period of time."

The judge ruled against the store owner and ordered him to pay $10, which was the cost of repairing the jeans, plus the $35 filing fee that Mann had to pay to bring the case to court. A $1500 counterclaim by Cobra Jeans based on the owner's claim that Mann threatened to slander the store was dismissed because there were no witnesses to the conversation in question and there was no proof of losses suffered by the store.

1. Identify the issues in this case in terms of implied conditions, warranties, and buyer's remedies.
2. Why did Mann sue if the jeans were Hickey's? Why might Hickey be unable to sue?
3. Draft a general clothing warranty that you think would be fair to both the buyer and the seller. What are the difficulties in such a warranty?

Figure 19.7 Suppose this farmer's contract specifies shipment to the buyer's grain elevator c.i.f. What does this mean? When does the buyer take title to the grain?

Building Your Understanding

1. Distinguish between an agreement to sell and an actual sale.
2. Apply the five basic rules of the *Sale of Goods Act* to determine when title would pass in the following situations. If applicable, suggest what the party who suffered a loss might have suggested during the sales transaction.
   a) Gloria paid Fred $1400 for a cedar canoe on February 14 and then agreed to pick it up in the spring. Before she picked it up, the canoe was stolen.
   b) Ted bought a used car from a local dealer on condition that the dealer install new tires and paint the vehicle. The vehicle was painted and the tires installed, but before Ted was notified of this, the car was damaged in a fire.
   c) Javed agrees to buy a load of landscape mulch for $5 per cubic metre. The landscape company delivered the load but does not inform Javed about the volume of mulch in the load.
   d) Gail tries out Jerry's snowboard and then informs Jerry that she intends to buy it. Before she pays him, the snowboard is damaged.
3. What is the difference in the purpose behind a manufacturer's warranty and the conditions of sale implied in the *Sale of Goods Act*?
4. Although a warranty may include a disclaimer that no implied warranties apply, why are such disclaimers invalid in certain jurisdictions?
5. State the implied condition of the *Sale of Goods Act* found in each of the following contracts:
   a) Yosh buys a belly boat from Merick for $285, but on his first fishing trip he discovers it is impossible to keep the boat inflated.
   b) The auto store clerk tells Cindy that the jack she is purchasing to lift her 4 x 4 will be adequate, but Cindy discovers it will not lift her truck.
   c) Alicia contracts with Dave to build a patio from quality-grade, treated cedar but discovers the cedar used to build the patio is untreated.
6. For each of the situations in question 5, state the remedies available to the buyer, the seller, and the rightful owner.

Legal Link
Find your provincial *Sale of Goods Act* at **www.pearsoned.ca/law**. Read this document and prepare a short oral presentation outlining its main consumer protection provisions.

PROTECTION FOR CONSUMERS

The *Sale of Goods Act*s enacted by the provinces deal specifically with transactions that involve the *selling* of goods. In order to provide consumers with wider protection in the marketplace, the federal and provincial governments have passed a series of laws designed to regulate business relationships that fall outside of those contracts. Unique aspects of business dealings between First Nations peoples or Indian bands and companies and persons off the reserves are also discussed below.

Federal Consumer Law

The federal government has passed laws, such as the *Competition Act*, that deal with dishonest business practices and misleading advertising. The various federal laws treat infractions as offences against society as a whole, much like a criminal offence, and the government prosecutes offenders.

The *Competition Act*, for example, makes it illegal to engage in **bait and switch** advertising. Bait and switch means advertising an item at a very low price when there are only a few samples in stock. Customers are lured into

bait and switch: advertising an item at a low price and maintaining a small amount of stock in hopes of luring consumers into the store to purchase higher-priced goods

the store by the low-priced item but find only more expensive goods available. Penalties for such an offence can be a fine or imprisonment, or both. This type of legislation does not offer any form of compensation for the consumer, but the consumer can sue for damages in civil court.

Provincial Consumer Law

Provincial legislation has been enacted to protect consumers from unconscionable business practices and to provide remedies should consumers fall victim to such actions.

Door-to-Door Selling

All the provinces closely regulate the practice of door-to-door sales through legislation such as a *Consumer Protection Act* or a *Direct Sellers Act*. This sales method is closely regulated because legislators recognize that a great deal of pressure may be exerted on the consumer. Door-to-door sales are often worked out before the salesperson leaves the consumer's home, providing the consumer almost no time to reflect on whether he or she really wants, or can afford, the purchase. The following terms are usually included in provincial legislation:

The buyer has a right to cancel the contract for a period of 10 days after receiving the written copy of the contract. The contract is usually given to the buyer at the time the sale is made. This "cooling-off period" allows buyers to consider, without the salesperson present, whether they actually want to purchase the goods or services.

The buyer may cancel the contract within the 10-day period by giving proper notice to the seller. This can be done in person, by mail, or by other means set out in the Act. It is important that the buyer retain proof of cancellation of the contract.

The cancellation has the effect of rescinding the contract. Both parties return to the same situation they were in before the contract existed. The buyer must return any goods, and the seller must return any money paid.

Buying on Credit

Credit buying is another area where provincial legislation has been enacted to protect consumers. When people wish to have a product or service but are unable to pay for it in full, they may decide to buy the product "on credit." This means that the buyer is financing the purchase either by taking out a loan through the seller, a bank, or some other financial institution, or by being allowed to make instalments in return for paying interest charges.

Because many consumers are unaware of all the hidden costs associated with credit buying and might be tempted to make purchases without considering these costs, the provinces have passed laws requiring contracts to set out the annual interest rate charged as well as the cost of borrowing the money.

Law in Your Life
If there are two prices on an item, or one price on the item and another that appears when the item's bar code is scanned at the cash register, you must be charged the lower price. If you are charged the higher price, you can complain to the Competition Bureau listed under Consumer Information in the Government Blue Pages of your phone book.

Consider This
It is considered unethical for a salesperson to put "far too much pressure on the consumer." What kind of behaviour do you think constitutes "far too much pressure"? Is the age or health of the consumer a factor?

credit buying: purchasing goods by paying for them in instalments that include interest or service charges

Fast Fact
Between 1997 and 2002, the average interest rate for credit cards was 13% higher than the cost of borrowing money from the bank.

CASE

Saxton v. Aloha Pools Ltd. (1998), B.C.S.C. A970668

1. Outline the arguments used by Saxton to support her non-payment of the money owing on the contract.
2. Identify three factors the Court considered in making its judgment.
3. What arguments could Aloha Pools use to show the contract with Saxton was valid?

On April 28, 1995, Joan Saxton contacted Aloha Pools Limited and subsequently signed a contract for the company to build a rock wall and repair her swimming pool for $11 000. Work on the project began within a few days. On June 16, 1995, Saxton wrote a letter to Aloha Pools declaring that the contract would not be paid off until the work was completed to her satisfaction. At that point she had paid $8827. In the letter, she stated $11 000 as the total price of the contract.

Saxton later refused to pay the remaining balance because she claimed that the original oral contract between her and Mr. Rizzo, the owner of Aloha Pools, was for $6600, not $11 000. She said that he filled in the $11 000 amount after she signed the contract.

Aloha Pools sued Saxton for the money owed under the contract. Saxton said that Rizzo had taken advantage of her and talked her into a contract she did not want to sign. She also claimed that the contract was a direct sale under British Columbia's *Consumer Protection Act,* which allows consumers 10 days to cancel contracts with door-to-door salespeople. She argued that Rizzo started work so quickly that she had no chance to cancel the contract.

The Court ruled in favour of Aloha Pools. Since Rizzo came to Saxton's home at her request, Aloha Pools was not a direct seller as defined by the *Consumer Protection Act*. In addition, there was no evidence to support Saxton's charges of unsatisfactory work or that the true price for the contract was $6600.

Property Situated on a Reserve

Section 89(1) of the *Indian Act* describes the restriction on mortgage, seizure, etc., of property on a reserve by non-First Nations peoples:

> 89.(1) Subject to this Act, the real and personal property of an Indian or a band situated on a reserve is not subject to charge, pledge, mortgage, attachment, levy, seizure, distress or execution in favour or at the instance of any person other than an Indian or a band.

Therefore, in case of non-payment, a non-First Nations seller cannot seek a lien against property or seize such property. These restrictions can lead to problems. For example, First Nations peoples and Indian bands may have trouble purchasing goods on credit, which makes it difficult to start businesses that could benefit the community. Suppose that Jacques, a First Nations person, wanted to arrange financing with a bank to purchase a restaurant franchise. The bank would require someone in Jacques' position to put up property as collateral for the loan. However, because the bank could not seize Jacques' property if he defaulted on the loan, the bank might be reluctant to give him financing.

Fast Fact

An Aboriginal person who lives off the reserve has the same contractual capacity as any other citizen.

To protect a seller in these circumstances and to ensure that a First Nations person or Indian band can conduct business, s. 89(2) of the *Indian Act* provides that where the seller maintains the right to property or right of possession, the seller may exercise the rights set out in the contract. Therefore, sellers should ensure that the contract of sale provides that title to the goods remains with the seller until he or she is paid, or that the sale takes place on condition that the asset can be repossessed for non-payment.

Building Your Understanding

1. What is the main difference between federal and provincial consumer protection legislation?
2. Why is the government so concerned about regulating door-to-door salespeople? Outline the special protections for consumers that have been built into the legislation.
3. Outline the information that must be included in a contract involving credit buying.
4. For each of the following scenarios, indicate whether a valid contract has been formed according to consumer protection legislation.
    a) A retail furniture store advertises low-priced computer desks but instructs its sales staff to persuade customers to purchase their top-of-the-line desks.
    b) Two weeks after Kelly signed a contract to purchase a vacuum cleaner from a door-to-door salesperson, she personally delivers her cancellation notice to the company.
    c) Avrum purchases a DVD player. He needs to finance the purchase, and the contract indicates only his monthly payment.
5. Why might First Nations peoples and Indian bands have difficulty purchasing goods on credit? What terms can be included in a contract of sale to protect a seller in these circumstances?

LOOKING BACK

Reviewing Your Vocabulary

agreement to sell *p. 501*
assignee *p. 492*
assignment *p. 492*
assignor *p. 492*
bait and switch *p. 508*
breach of contract *p. 497*
c.i.f. *p. 503*
c.o.d. *p. 503*
condition *p. 498*
credit buying *p. 509*
damages *p. 499*
default *p. 506*
exemption clauses *p. 499*
f.o.b. *p. 503*
frustration *p. 496*
implied conditions *p. 505*
injunction *p. 499*
lien *p. 506*
manufacturer's warranty *p. 503*
mitigation of damages *p. 499*
novation *p. 496*
performance *p. 494*
privity of contract *p. 491*
remedies *p. 491*
repudiation *p. 498*
sale *p. 501*
specific performance *p. 497*
stoppage in transit *p. 506*
substantial performance *p. 494*
title *p. 501*
trust *p. 492*
unconditional sale of specific goods in a deliverable state *p. 502*
vicarious or substituted performance *p. 493*
warranty *p. 498*

Quick Quiz

1. Match the vocabulary terms above with these clues:
   a) a court orders a party to a contract to complete its terms
   b) goods sold must meet the expectations of the customer
   c) often called "ownership," this passes to the purchaser when the contract is fulfilled
   d) having a subcontractor perform the contract
   e) a court order prohibiting a party from doing something
   f) completing the contractual obligations
   g) advertising a product at a low price and then encouraging the buyer to purchase a higher-priced product instead
   h) failure to fulfill a minor term of a contract
   i) legislation that applies to transactions with salespeople
   j) transferring contractual obligations to a third party

Checking Your Knowledge

2. What is the importance of the concept of "privity of contract"?
3. Identify and explain four main ways a contract can be discharged.
4. Describe five situations in which it would be necessary for the courts to become involved in the discharge of a contract.
5. What is the purpose of the *Sale of Goods Acts* that the provinces have enacted?

Developing Your Thinking and Inquiry Skills

6. What would be your judgment in the following cases? Support your opinion with principles of contract law.
   a) Reena signed a contract with Filmtime Ltd. to star in a movie. Even before Reena had signed her contract, Filmtime Ltd. had already begun pre-production by employing a director and a set designer, arranging for a location, etc. Then Reena's agent informed Filmtime that because of a scheduling mix-up, Reena could not appear in the film after all. Filmtime cancelled the movie after failing to find a substitute for Reena and sued for the entire amount of money spent on pre-production. Reena's lawyers claimed that

Filmtime was entitled only to money spent after the contract was signed. Who is right? Explain why.

b) Balzac entered into a contract to build a stable on Peterson's land for a lump sum. When the building was partly finished, Balzac informed Peterson that he had run out of money and could not go on with the work. What recourse does Peterson have?

c) A ship was 10 days late delivering a cargo of sugar. At this time, the market price of sugar fell substantially. The company receiving the sugar asked for damages based on the amount it could have sold the sugar for if it had been delivered on time. Should the company win its suit? Provide reasons to support your answer.

7. Obtain copies of federal and provincial consumer protection legislation. Collect examples of sales contracts and warranties from businesses in your community. Compare these with the consumer protection laws. Use this information to write an opinion essay regarding how adequately you think consumers are protected by legislation in your province.

8. Some contracts contain damages clauses that spell out a specific amount of money that must be paid out if one of the parties does not live up to the contract. What would be the advantage of this clause? Describe a situation where such a clause might operate unfairly or penalize one of the parties.

Communicating Your Ideas

9. Work with a small group to locate articles in the *Canadian Periodical Index* or *Canadian NewsDisc* about a recent case involving contract issues. Use the information you gather to re-create the trial based on the legal questions in the case. Present your trial to your class, and invite questions and comments about your use of the principles of contract law.

10. According to an international survey of electronic commerce sites, 75 percent of traders failed to provide crucial contract terms, and one in ten items ordered failed to arrive. Do you think it is safe to give your credit card number over the Internet? Should you be concerned with security when making an on-line transaction? In addition to security issues, there are also concerns about unfair business practices via the Internet. Use your library resource centre to find out more about this topic. For example, does the *Sale of Goods Act* apply to Internet purchases? Are there any special rules or laws governing Internet sales? If you buy a product from a U.S. company, which laws apply, Canadian or American?

When you have completed your research, prepare a one- or two-page "fact sheet" outlining what people need to know about buying goods on the Internet. Present your work to the class for feedback. Make copies of your revised fact sheet to post in places such as your school, supermarket, and local community centre.

Putting It All Together

11. Work in pairs to develop a contract to define the obligations between two parties in one of the following relationships: buyer and seller; employee and employer; landlord and tenant; creditor and debtor. Your contract should concern a specific business transaction between two parties.
    a) Obtain examples of the kind of contract you have written and compare your contract with them. Consider whether you need to make any changes to your contract.
    b) Ask members of another group to make a list of breaches that might take place regarding your contract.
    c) Determine remedies for these breaches. Use your contract, applicable statutes (such as *Residential Tenancy Act*s or *Sale of Goods Act*s), and decided cases.

CASES

Vargek v. Okun (1997), Man. C.A.
AI96-30-02745, on-line: CanLII

Robert and Ann Vargek purchased a motor vehicle from Almey Autobody Ltd., a dealership owned by John Okun. The odometer reading on the used-vehicle purchase agreement was 82 000 km. The couple later discovered that the vehicle had, in fact, been driven 182 000 km at the time of purchase. They brought an action against the dealership, and the court awarded judgment against Almey Autobody Ltd. for $1000.

Okun appealed the decision, claiming he was not a party to the change in the odometer reading. The judge at the Queen's Bench Appeal Court dealt with the case on the basis of liability for innocent misrepresentation. He found that since the vehicle had been retained and driven by the Vargeks for an extended period of time, they were not entitled to restitution. However, he indicated that he would have been inclined to award them damages in the vicinity of $2200.

The Vargeks appealed the judge's decision to the Manitoba Court of Appeal. It was the opinion of this Court that the Queen's Bench judge had erred in approaching the case on the basis of innocent misrepresentation. In the Court's view, the case was a matter of breach of warranty. Section 58(1)(f) of the *Consumer Protection Act* has an express condition that the goods correspond with the description under which they are sold. This description included the odometer reading, which was clearly inaccurate. The Court allowed the appeal and awarded damages of $2200, using the calculations arrived at by the Queen's Bench Appeal Court judge.

1. Explain the concept of innocent misrepresentation.
2. Why did the Queen's Bench Appeal Court deny the Vargeks restitution?
3. How does the *Consumer Protection Act* apply to this case?

Gandy v. Robinson (1990), 108 N.B.R. (2d) 436 (Q.B.)

Ms. Gandy bought a neutered, purebred, registered, golden Labrador retriever from the Robinsons for $325. She later found that the dog had canine hip dysplasia and spent $1400 for an operation correcting this painful condition.

The plaintiff sued to recover her $1400 expenditure or at least her $325 purchase price. Either way, she wished to keep the dog. The defendants offered to refund the purchase price or replace the dog, but only if the dog was returned to them or destroyed. The parties agreed that this oral guarantee was originally made when the dog was sold to Gandy.

The Court ruled that the dog fell under the definition of a "consumer product" in the *Consumer Product Warranty and Liability Act* and that the express warranty in the contract between the parties should be honoured. Therefore, Gandy's claim was dismissed.

1. Compare the express warranty in this case with a manufacturer's warranty for repair or replacement found in this chapter. In whose favour do you think the contract is weighted? Why?
2. Had the parties not made an express warranty, do you think Gandy would have been able to recover damages? Was the dog of merchantable quality? Did it have an inherent defect?
3. In this decision, the judge spoke of the contract between a person and his or her dog in our society, and commented that the $1400 spent on the operation was really part of the contract between the person and the dog. Discuss this comment with respect to privity of contract between Gandy and Robinson.

CASES

Coast Hotels Ltd. v. Royal Doulton Canada Ltd. (2000), B.C.S.C. C956773

BACKGROUND In 1992, Coast Hotels wished to enhance their image and, as part of this business plan, decided to use Jupiter pattern tableware from the prestigious Royal Doulton Company in all their hotels. The deciding factor in purchasing this product was the words "Royal Doulton" printed prominently on the back of the tableware. Samples of the Jupiter pattern were sent to the hotel management.

In 1995, it was noticed that the backstamp on the tableware had been changed so that the word "Capital," referring to the Capital Collection of which Jupiter was part, was much more prominent than the words "Royal Doulton." Coast Hotels were not advised of this change.

The hotel chain decided that the new backstamp changed the product substantially. They subsequently moved all their Royal Doulton tableware into just a few of their hotels and purchased Steelite tableware for the rest of their chain at a higher price than the Royal Doulton.

Coast Hotels claimed that this was a breach of sale by description as provided for in s. 17 of the *Sale of Goods Act*. Section 17 says that in a contract for the sale of goods by description there is an implied condition that the goods must correspond to the description. Coast argued that if samples are provided, the sample may be the best evidence of what the parties intended the contractual description of the goods to be. Royal Doulton admitted that it was a sale by description but argued that the description did not include the words on the backstamp.

Coast Hotels asked for damages amounting to $53 836.59. This represented the difference between the cost of the Steelite and Royal Doulton and the administrative costs of the substitution.

LEGAL QUESTION Was there a breach of the condition that goods must correspond to the description?

DECISION The Court agreed that the new tableware did not correspond to the description of what had been ordered by Coast.

> ... the production of a sample during the course of the negotiations can be relevant to the common intention of the parties ... Any minor deviation from the contractual description of the goods may constitute a breach of the implied condition ... The substitution of prominence of the word "Capital" for "Royal Doulton" altered the kind of goods the plaintiff received ...

In assessing damages, the judge took into consideration the following: Coast Hotels had had the use of the Royal Doulton tableware for a period of time; they had no account of how many table settings were in existence or how many were transferred to other Coast hotels; and they did not know the value of what was transferred. Coast Hotels was awarded $20 000.

LEGAL SIGNIFICANCE This case illustrates the importance that the law places on the intentions of the parties to the contract. Coast Hotels had made it clear throughout their dealings with Royal Doulton that Royal Doulton name recognition was crucial. Royal Doulton also emphasized the importance of its name in its sales pitch. The Court's decision acknowledged that the backstamp was of vital importance in the contract.

ANALYSIS

1. What did Coast Hotels and Royal Doulton disagree about? What is the legal basis for this lawsuit?
2. Was there a breach of condition or a breach of warranty in this case? Based on your determination, what remedies are available to Coast Hotels?
3. What factors did the judge consider in assessing the damages? With the hotel's concern about enhancing its image, would the expectation of mitigation of damages be a relevant factor to consider? Explain.
4. Do you agree with the judgment and the damages? Why or why not?

issue

Protecting Personal Information

When a telemarketer interrupts your dinner, have you ever wondered how the caller knew your name and telephone number? The answer is that you probably supplied it yourself. Not directly, of course. But if you have ever completed a questionnaire in a shopping mall, then you provided personal information that could become part of a data bank.

When consumers use debit cards or company credit cards, they provide personal information, such as their age, gender, and income bracket. They also provide information about their personal spending habits—everything from the brand of gasoline they use to the type of clothing they wear. Marketers, advertisers, and retailers use the information data bank compiled from these types of transactions in order to target you, the consumer.

Should you be concerned that your personal information is so readily available? Government and concerned citizen groups believe you should be. While information is initially collected for legitimate purposes, the technology used to facilitate collection and storage can just as easily be used to divert data into the wrong hands. Your personal and financial information can be used for a variety of fraudulent practices, from obtaining a false passport to making electronic purchases to accessing your bank account. For example, one Ontario woman discovered she owed a finance company $8000 and a bank $17 500 for a loan. She learned that she was also expected to repay a $260 000 mortgage she had supposedly taken out on her house. Not only had she never dealt with these financial institutions, she didn't even own a house!

CONSUMER PROTECTION

Consumer protection advocates suggest that legislation needs to be tightened to protect consumers from marketers who exchange private information without permission, thereby increasing the possibility of personal identity theft. Identity theft is the unauthorized collection and use of your personal information, usually for criminal purposes. In Canada, identity theft is the third-most reported consumer crime. More than 12 000 Canadians are victims of identity theft every year.

Because Canada's *Privacy Act* (1982) only protects individuals in relation to information held by government institutions, the federal government recognized the need for private-sector privacy laws. In 2000, it initiated Bill C-6, which was intended to balance consumers' rights to privacy with business plans to promote electronic commerce. Bill C-6 was given Royal Assent on April 13, 2000. It became law on January 1, 2001, as

Any information you provide, even in a shopping mall survey, can get into the wrong hands. What can you do to protect yourself?

the *Personal Information Protection and Electronic Documents Act*. This legislation establishes rules for the collection, use, and disclosure of personal information in a manner that any "reasonable person" would consider appropriate. A reasonable person would acknowledge that the collection of personal data is a legitimate business practice. On the other hand, a reasonable person would challenge excessive and persistent collection and indiscriminate sharing.

Provincial governments are also considering privacy legislation to address the problem. In Ontario, the onus is currently on the consumer to stop information sharing by contacting companies and asking them not to distribute personal data. The proposed *Protection of Personal Privacy Act* being developed in 2002 would reverse this "negative option" system, placing responsibility on the private sector to ask permission from consumers to collect and share their personal information. This is known as the "opt in" approach.

PRIVATE SECTOR OPPOSITION

The private sector argues that while governments are implementing legislation to control its collection of personal data, those same governments continue to enjoy the benefits of collecting personal information themselves. Governments use census data to determine everything from immigration patterns to how many schools need to be built. Canada's National DNA Data Bank, which is shared with domestic and international police forces, is just one of many databases compiled and stored by the federal government.

Businesses are also concerned that the new laws will hinder the future of e-commerce. The Canadian Marketing Association (CMA) regards Ontario's proposed restrictions to personal information access as damaging to its industry. The Association forecasts a loss of 300 000 direct-response marketing jobs. The CMA claims the "opt in" approach will also cost the provincial economy $17 billion.

Data banks and information sharing have been a tremendous boost to advertisers and marketers. It has allowed them to refine their previous targeting methods so that only potential consumers are identified. For example, companies that manufacture diapers now send coupons for disposable diapers only to new mothers. To make effective use of such advertising techniques, marketers claim they must be able to share information. Forcing them to request permission first would be too time-consuming and costly; this practice would cripple a growing e-commerce industry.

Those opposed to more restrictive laws argue that the responsibility for preventing misuse of information must rest with the individual. They claim that you, the consumer, should ensure that your personal information doesn't fall into the wrong hands. They suggest that the money spent on new laws would be better spent on educating the public on how to protect their personal information.

LOOKING AT THE ISSUE

1. Using the "reasonable person" criterion in the *Personal Information Protection and Electronic Documents Act,* describe two situations—one that would be considered reasonable information collection and one that would not.

2. Under Ontario's proposed legislation, a company in financial difficulty that wanted to sell its database to stay solvent would have to get permission from each consumer on its list for every company it wanted to sell the list to. Should there be concessions built into the new legislation to allow some companies to avoid the "opt in" approach? Explain your position.

3. Consumer protection advocates advise consumers to be vigilant about sharing personal information. Create a list of 10 tips on how consumers can protect themselves from identity theft. Share your list with the class and generate a combined list of Top 10 Tips to be posted in the classroom.

4. Your provincial government has invited you to a focus group to consider the problem of personal information protection. As a class, assume the roles of consumer protection advocates, marketing and advertising lobbyists, and ordinary citizens. Prepare notes that identify your concerns and present your ideas in the focus group.

Career Connections

CORPORATE SECRETARY

We require a person with a minimum of 5 years' experience and with expertise in overseas corporate dealings. The ideal candidate will be detail oriented, computer literate, and bilingual. The successful applicant will participate in contractual discussions and will handle corporate financial transactions in all currencies. Position requires extensive travel.

Legal Assistant

Wanted to assist in office management, document preparation from precedents, research, transcription, and preparation of court documents and representations. Sometimes required to assist in court. The candidate should be computer literate, mature, and pleasant, and should demonstrate personal initiative. Must be well groomed and have a pleasant telephone manner.

Legal Litigation Assistant

Required for mid-sized downtown law firm. Candidates should have 5 years' experience in litigation. Proficiency in MS Word and knowledge of POLAW required. Ability to proceed independently with files is a must.

Law Librarian

The successful candidate will be responsible for the overall leadership, management, and development of electronic initiatives and law library collections and services. Will also assume teaching duties in legal research and related areas. Qualifications include strong management, interpersonal, and communications skills; demonstrated teaching skills; knowledge of legal research; and proven ability to work productively in a team-based environment.

Real Estate Administrator

We are looking for a person with 2 to 6 years' experience in commercial real estate law. Responsibilities include drafting and reviewing lease agreements and tax legislation. This position requires self-sufficiency and the ability to co-ordinate activities in collaboration with legal counsel.

MAKING CONNECTIONS

1. Read the advertisements above and create an organizer, using the following headings:
   - Position Advertised
   - Experience Required
   - Necessary Skills
   - Responsibilities
2. a) What similarities did you notice with regard to the skills required?
   b) How might this information affect your plans for the future?

Canadian Charter of Rights and Freedoms

SCHEDULE B

Constitution Act, 1982 (79)

Enacted as Schedule B to the *Canada Act 1982* (U.K.) 1982, c. 11, which came into force on April 17, 1982.

PART I

Canadian Charter of Rights and Freedoms

Whereas Canada is founded upon principles that recognize the supremacy of God and the rule of law:

Guarantee of Rights and Freedoms

1. The *Canadian Charter of Rights and Freedoms* guarantees the rights and freedoms set out in it subject only to such reasonable limits prescribed by law as can be demonstrably justified in a free and democratic society. — *Rights and freedoms in Canada*

Fundamental Freedoms

2. Everyone has the following fundamental freedoms:
a) freedom of conscience and religion;
b) freedom of thought, belief, opinion and expression, including freedom of the press and other media of communication;
c) freedom of peaceful assembly; and
d) freedom of association.
— *Fundamental freedoms*

Democratic Rights

3. Every citizen of Canada has the right to vote in an election of members of the House of Commons or of a legislative assembly and to be qualified for membership therein. — *Democratic rights of citizens*

4. (1) No House of Commons and no legislative assembly shall continue for longer than five years from the date fixed for the return of the writs of a general election of its members. — *Maximum duration of legislative bodies*

(2) In time of real or apprehended war, invasion or insurrection, a House of Commons may be continued by Parliament and a legislative assembly may be continued by the legislature beyond five years if such continuation is not opposed by the votes of more than one-third of the members of the House of Commons or the legislative assembly, as the case may be. — *Continuation in special circumstances*

5. There shall be a sitting of Parliament and of each legislature at least once every twelve months. — *Annual sitting of legislative bodies*

Mobility Rights

6. (1) Every citizen of Canada has the right to enter, remain in and leave Canada. — *Mobility of citizens*

(2) Every citizen of Canada and every person who has the status of a permanent resident of Canada has the right — *Rights to move and gain livelihood*

a) to move to and take up residence in any province; and

b) to pursue the gaining of a livelihood in any province.

Limitation (3) The rights specified in subsection (2) are subject to

a) any laws or practices of general application in force in a province other than those that discriminate among persons primarily on the basis of province of present or previous residence; and

b) any laws providing for reasonable residency requirements as a qualification for the receipt of publicly provided social services.

Affirmative action programs (4) Subsections (2) and (3) do not preclude any law, program or activity that has as its object the amelioration in a province of conditions of individuals in that province who are socially or economically disadvantaged if the rate of employment in that province is below the rate of employment in Canada.

Legal Rights

Life, liberty and security of person 7. Everyone has the right to life, liberty and security of the person and the right not to be deprived thereof except in accordance with the principles of fundamental justice.

Search or seizure 8. Everyone has the right to be secure against unreasonable search or seizure.

Detention or imprisonment 9. Everyone has the right not to be arbitrarily detained or imprisoned.

Arrest or detention 10. Everyone has the right on arrest or detention

a) to be informed promptly of the reasons therefor;

b) to retain and instruct counsel without delay and to be informed of that right; and

c) to have the validity of the detention determined by way of habeas corpus and to be released if the detention is not lawful.

11. Any person charged with an offence has the right

a) to be informed without unreasonable delay of the specific offence;

b) to be tried within a reasonable time;

c) not to be compelled to be a witness in proceedings against that person in respect of the offence;

d) to be presumed innocent until proven guilty according to law in a fair and public hearing by an independent and impartial tribunal;

e) not to be denied reasonable bail without just cause;

f) except in the case of an offence under military law tried before a military tribunal, to the benefit of trial by jury where the maximum punishment for the offence is imprisonment for five years or a more severe punishment;

g) not to be found guilty on account of any act or omission unless, at the time of the act or omission, it constituted an offence under Canadian or international law or was criminal according to the general principles of law recognized by the community of nations;

h) if finally acquitted of the offence, not to be tried for it again and, if finally found guilty and punished for the offence, not to be tried or punished for it again; and

i) if found guilty of the offence and if the punishment for the offence has been varied between the time of commission and the time of sentencing, to the benefit of the lesser punishment.

Proceedings in criminal and penal matters

12. Everyone has the right not to be subjected to any cruel and unusual treatment or punishment.

Treatment or punishment

13. A witness who testifies in any proceedings has the right not to have any incriminating evidence so given used to incriminate that witness in any other proceedings, except in a prosecution for perjury or for the giving of contradictory evidence.

Self-crimination

Interpreter	**14.** A party or witness in any proceedings who does not understand or speak the language in which the proceedings are conducted or who is deaf has the right to the assistance of an interpreter.

Equality Rights

Equality before and under law and equal protection and benefit of law	**15.** (1) Every individual is equal before and under the law and has the right to the equal protection and equal benefit of the law without discrimination and, in particular, without discrimination based on race, national or ethnic origin, colour, religion, sex, age or mental or physical disability.
Affirmative action programs	(2) Subsection (1) does not preclude any law, program or activity that has as its object the amelioration of conditions of disadvantaged individuals or groups including those that are disadvantaged because of race, national or ethnic origin, colour, religion, sex, age or mental or physical disability.

Official Languages of Canada

Official languages of Canada	**16.** (1) English and French are the official languages of Canada and have equality of status and equal rights and privileges as to their use in all institutions of the Parliament and government of Canada.
Official languages of New Brunswick	(2) English and French are the official languages of New Brunswick and have equality of status and equal rights and privileges as to their use in all institutions of the legislature and government of New Brunswick.
Advancement of status and use	(3) Nothing in this Charter limits the authority of Parliament or a legislature to advance the equality of status or use of English and French.
English and French linguistic communities in New Brunswick	**16.1** (1) The English linguistic community and the French linguistic community in New Brunswick have equality of status and equal rights and privileges, including the right to distinct educational institutions and such distinct cultural institutions as are necessary for the preservation and promotion of those communities.
Role of the legislature and government of New Brunswick	(2) The role of the legislature and government of New Brunswick to preserve and promote the status, rights and privileges referred to in subsection (1) is affirmed.
Proceedings of Parliament	**17.** (1) Everyone has the right to use English or French in any debates and other proceedings of Parliament.
Proceedings of New Brunswick legislature	(2) Everyone has the right to use English or French in any debates and other proceedings of the legislature of New Brunswick.
Parliamentary statutes and records	**18.** (1) The statutes, records and journals of Parliament shall be printed and published in English and French and both language versions are equally authoritative.
New Brunswick statutes and records	(2) The statutes, records and journals of the legislature of New Brunswick shall be printed and published in English and French and both language versions are equally authoritative.
Proceedings in courts established by Parliament	**19.** (1) Either English or French may be used by any person in, or in any pleading in or process issuing from, any court established by Parliament.
Proceedings in New Brunswick courts	(2) Either English or French may be used by any person in, or in any pleading in or process issuing from, any court of New Brunswick.
Communications by public with federal institutions	**20.** (1) Any member of the public in Canada has the right to communicate with, and to receive available services from, any head or central office of an institution of the Parliament or government of Canada in English or French, and has the same right with respect to any other office of any such institution where *a)* there is a significant demand for communications with and services from that office in such language; or *b)* due to the nature of the office, it is reasonable that communications with

Communications by public with New Brunswick institutions

and services from that office be available in both English and French.

(2) Any member of the public in New Brunswick has the right to communicate with, and to receive available services from, any office of an institution of the legislature or government of New Brunswick in English or French.

Continuation of existing constitutional provisions

21. Nothing in sections 16 to 20 abrogates or derogates from any right, privilege or obligation with respect to the English and French languages, or either of them, that exists or is continued by virtue of any other provision of the Constitution of Canada.

Rights and privileges preserved

22. Nothing in sections 16 to 20 abrogates or derogates from any legal or customary right or privilege acquired or enjoyed either before or after the coming into force of this Charter with respect to any language that is not English or French.

Minority Language Educational Rights

Language of instruction

23. (1) Citizens of Canada
   a) whose first language learned and still understood is that of the English or French linguistic minority population of the province in which they reside, or
   b) who have received their primary school instruction in Canada in English or French and reside in a province where the language in which they received that instruction is the language of the English or French linguistic minority population of the province

have the right to have their children receive primary and secondary school instruction in that language in that province.

Continuity of language instruction

(2) Citizens of Canada of whom any child has received or is receiving primary or secondary school instruction in English or French in Canada, have the right to have all their children receive primary and secondary school instruction in the same language.

Application where numbers warrant

(3) The right of citizens of Canada under subsections (1) and (2) to have their children receive primary and secondary school instruction in the language of the English or French linguistic minority population of a province
   a) applies wherever in the province the number of children of citizens who have such a right is sufficient to warrant the provision to them out of public funds of minority language instruction; and
   b) includes, where the number of those children so warrants, the right to have them receive that instruction in minority language educational facilities provided out of public funds.

Enforcement

Enforcement of guaranteed rights and freedoms

24. (1) Anyone whose rights or freedoms, as guaranteed by this Charter, have been infringed or denied may apply to a court of competent jurisdiction to obtain such remedy as the court considers appropriate and just in the circumstances.

Exclusion of evidence bringing administration of justice into disrepute

(2) Where, in proceedings under subsection (1), a court concludes that evidence was obtained in a manner that infringed or denied any rights or freedoms guaranteed by this Charter, the evidence shall be excluded if it is established that, having regard to all the circumstances, the admission of it in the proceedings would bring the administration of justice into disrepute.

General

Aboriginal rights and freedoms not affected by Charter

25. The guarantee in this Charter of certain rights and freedoms shall not be construed so as to abrogate or derogate from any aboriginal, treaty or other rights or freedoms that pertain to the aboriginal peoples of Canada including
   a) any rights or freedoms that have been recognized by the Royal Proclamation of October 7, 1763; and

Other rights and freedoms not affected by Charter

b) any rights or freedoms that now exist by way of land claims agreements or may be so acquired.

26. The guarantee in this Charter of certain rights and freedoms shall not be construed as denying the existence of any other rights or freedoms that exist in Canada.

Multicultural heritage

27. This Charter shall be interpreted in a manner consistent with the preservation and enhancement of the multicultural heritage of Canadians.

Rights guaranteed equally to both sexes

28. Notwithstanding anything in this Charter, the rights and freedoms referred to in it are guaranteed equally to male and female persons.

Rights respecting certain schools preserved

29. Nothing in this Charter abrogates or derogates from any rights or privileges guaranteed by or under the Constitution of Canada in respect of denominational, separate or dissentient schools.

Application to territories and territorial authorities

30. A reference in this Charter to a Province or to the legislative assembly or legislature of a province shall be deemed to include a reference to the Yukon Territory and the Northwest Territories, or to the appropriate legislative authority thereof, as the case may be.

Legislative powers not extended

31. Nothing in this Charter extends the legislative powers of any body or authority.

Application of Charter

Application of Charter

32. (1) This Charter applies
a) to the Parliament and government of Canada in respect of all matters within the authority of Parliament including all matters relating to the Yukon Territory and Northwest Territories; and
b) to the legislature and government of each province in respect of all matters within the authority of the legislature of each province.

Exception

(2) Notwithstanding subsection (1), section 15 shall not have effect until three years after this section comes into force.

Exception where express declaration

33. (1) Parliament or the legislature of a province may expressly declare in an Act of Parliament or of the legislature, as the case may be, that the Act or a provision thereof shall operate notwithstanding a provision included in section 2 or sections 7 to 15 of this Charter.

Operation of exception

(2) An Act or a provision of an Act in respect of which a declaration made under this section is in effect shall have such operation as it would have but for the provision of this Charter referred to in the declaration.

Five-year limitation

(3) A declaration made under subsection (1) shall cease to have effect five years after it comes into force or on such earlier date as may be specified in the declaration.

Re-enactment

(4) Parliament or the legislature of a province may re-enact a declaration made under subsection (1).

Five-year limitation

(5) Subsection (3) applies in respect of a re-enactment made under subsection (4).

Citation

Citation

34. This Part may be cited as the *Canadian Charter of Rights and Freedoms*.

Glossary

abetting the crime of encouraging the perpetrator to commit an offence

abrogate to abolish or annul a law

absolute discharge releasing a convicted offender and erasing his or her criminal record after one year

absolute liability offences offences that do not require *mens rea* and to which the accused can offer no defence

absolute privilege protection from legal action for statements made during legislative or court proceedings

acceptance a clear indication by the offeree to enter into a contract on the terms set out by the offeror

access the non-custodial parent's right to visit the child when the parents separate

accessory after the fact someone who knowingly receives, comforts, or assists a perpetrator in escaping from the police

accommodate to eliminate or adjust requirements or conditions to enable a person to carry out the essential duties of an activity or job

accommodation the place where people live or want to live

accused (or defendant) in criminal court, the person charged with committing a criminal offence

act of God a defence claiming that an accident was caused by an extraordinary, unexpected natural event

actus reus Latin for "the guilty act," which refers to a voluntary action, omission, or state of being that is forbidden by the *Criminal Code*

administrative law a category of public law governing the relationship between people and government departments, boards, and agencies

adoption a legal process by which a couple (or a single person) becomes the legal parents of a child

adultery sexual intercourse by a married person with someone other than his or her spouse

adversarial system the judicial process whereby evidence is presented by two opposing parties to an impartial judge or jury

affidavit of documents a list of all documents that may be used at a trial; each side in the case has the right to examine them

affinity relationship through marriage

affirmative action giving advantages to groups who have been discriminated against in the past

aggravated assault wounding, maiming, disfiguring, or endangering the life of the victim

aggravated damages compensation for intangible losses such as humiliation or distress

aggravated sexual assault the most violent level of sexual assault that involves wounding, maiming, disfiguring, or endangering a victim's life

aggravating factors circumstances that increase the severity of an offender's sentence

agreement to sell an agreement whereby the title is not transferred to the buyer when the contract is made but will be transferred in the future

aiding a criminal offence that involves helping a perpetrator commit a crime

alibi a defence raised by the accused claiming that he or she was somewhere else when the crime was committed

allurement a site or object that might attract children and result in their harm

alternative dispute resolution (ADR) a way to settle disagreements other than by litigation

ameliorate to improve

amending formula the procedure for amending the Constitution that requires the approval of Parliament plus two-thirds of the provinces representing 50 percent of the population

annulment declaration by the court that a marriage never existed

appeal an application to a higher court to review the decision made by a lower court

appearance notice a legal document, usually issued for less serious offences, compelling an accused person to appear in court

appellant the party that files an appeal

apportionment the division of fault among parties in an action

arbitration an ADR process in which a neutral third party hears both sides of the dispute and makes a binding decision

arraignment the first stage of a criminal trial in which the court clerk reads the charges and the defendant enters a plea

arrest legally depriving someone of liberty by seizing or touching the person to indicate that he or she is in custody

arrest warrant a written court order directing the arrest of the suspect

assault threatened or actual physical contact without consent; offensive conduct that causes reasonable apprehension of imminent harm in the mind of the intended victim

assault with a weapon or causing bodily harm injuring a person in a way that has serious consequences for the victim's health or comfort

assignee the person to whom contractual obligations are transferred

assignor the person who transfers his or her contractual obligations to someone else

assizes travelling courts

attempt the intention to commit a crime, even if the crime is not completed

automatism a condition in which a person acts without being aware of what he or she is doing

bail the temporary release of the accused who posts money or some other security to guarantee his or her court appearance

bailiff the court official who assists the sheriff

bait and switch advertising an item at a low price and maintaining a small amount of stock in the hopes of luring consumers into the store to purchase higher-priced goods

balance of probabilities the weighing of evidence to decide whether it is the plaintiff's or the defendant's version of the events that is more convincing or likely to be correct

banns of marriage a public declaration in a church announcing a couple's intention to marry

battery intentional, unauthorized physical contact that the victim considers harmful or offensive

bench warrant an arrest warrant issued directly by the judge when an accused person fails to appear in court

beyond a reasonable doubt a standard of proof whereby a defendant's guilt must be proven to the extent that a reasonable person would have no choice but to conclude that the defendant did indeed commit the offence

bigamy the state of being married to two people at the same time

bilateral contract an agreement wherein both parties promise to do something for one another

bill a proposed law

binding final and enforceable in the courts

binding-over a sentence ordering a defendant to keep the peace and demonstrate good behaviour for up to 12 months

bona fide occupational requirement a qualification that would normally be considered discriminatory but is necessary for proper or efficient job performance

breach of contract failure by a party to perform the obligations agreed to in a contract

breaking and entering breaking into a place without permission in order to commit an indictable offence such as robbery

bugging recording a speaker's oral communication by using an electronic device

burden of proof the Crown's obligation to prove the guilt of the accused beyond a reasonable doubt

bylaws laws that deal with local issues and are passed by municipal governments

c.i.f. cost, insurance, and freight; a contractual term that specifies responsibility and delivery arrangements

Canadian Charter of Rights and Freedoms a section of the *Constitution Act, 1982*, which sets out constitutionally protected rights and freedoms

capacity in criminal law, the ability to understand the nature of one's actions; in civil law, to voluntarily enter into a legally binding contract

capital offence a crime punishable by death, in some jurisdictions

case law a method of deciding cases based on recorded decisions of similar cases

cause-in-fact the "cause and effect" connection between one person's actions and another person's injuries

caveat emptor Latin for "let the buyer beware," implying that a purchase is made at the buyer's risk

centre the immediate area in which the offence was committed

certificate of divorce a legal document that terminates a marriage

chain of custody the witnessed, written record detailing dates, times, and circumstances of evidence handling by all of the people who had control over items of evidence

challenge for cause the right of the Crown or defence to exclude someone from a jury for a particular reason

character evidence evidence used to establish the likelihood that the defendant is the type of person who either would or would not commit a certain offence

charge to the jury the judge's explanation to the jurors of how the law applies to the case before them

chattel personal property that can be moved

child support payment the non-custodial parent makes to the custodial parent to financially meet the needs of their child or children

circuit judges judges of travelling courts

circumstantial evidence indirect evidence that leads to a reasonable inference of the defendant's guilt

citation the reference heading of a legal case

citizen's arrest an arrest without a warrant by any person other than a peace officer

civil law the area of law that deals with legal relationships between individuals and between individuals and organizations; also known as private law

civil liberties basic individual rights protected by law, such as freedom of speech

class action suit a lawsuit initiated by a group of people concerning a complaint common to all of them

class characteristics general attributes of an object such as type, make, model, style, and size

clerical mistake an error made in recording the details of a contract

closed custody highly secured provincial facilities for dangerous offenders

c.o.d. cash on delivery; a contractual term that specifies responsibility and delivery arrangements

Code of Hammurabi one of the earliest-known sets of recorded laws, written by King Hammurabi of Babylon in the eighteenth century BCE

Code of Li'kvei a set of Chinese laws written around 350 BCE

codified arranged and recorded systematically

cohabitation agreement a domestic contract that sets out the rights and obligations of two people living together in a common-law relationship

collusion an agreement between the spouses to deliberately lie or deceive the court in order to obtain a divorce

colour of right the honest belief that a person owns or has permission to use an item

common law law that developed in English courts; relies on case law and is common to all people; also known as English common law

common-law relationship an intimate relationship between two individuals who live together but are not legally married

common mistake an error made by both parties to a contract about the same thing

community service order a sentence to perform certain community services for a specified period

complainant the person making an allegation of discrimination

compulsion or duress a defence in which the accused person is forced by the threat of violence to commit a criminal act against his or her will

conciliation bringing conflicting parties to a resolution of their differences

concurrent sentences sentences served at the same time

condition a very important term in a contract

conditional discharge releasing a convicted offender under certain terms and erasing his or her criminal record after three years, provided the terms have been met

conditional release serving part of a sentence in the community under supervision

conditional sentence a prison sentence of less than two years that can be served in the community, with strict terms attached

condonation one spouse forgiving the other for an act that is being used as grounds for divorce

connivance one spouse encouraging the other to commit an act that would constitute grounds for divorce

consanguinity being closely related by blood

consecutive sentences sentences served one after the other

consent to agree voluntarily to an action; also, permission granted voluntarily for a specific act

consideration something of value that either benefits the party that receives it or is a loss or inconvenience to the party that provides it

conspiracy an agreement between two or more people to carry out an illegal act, even if that act does not actually occur

constitutional law the body of public law set out in the Constitution that deals with the distribution and exercise of the powers of government and establishes paramount legal principles and standards

constructive discrimination employment policies that inadvertently exclude certain individuals, resulting in discrimination

consummation legally validating a marriage through sexual intercourse between husband and wife

contamination the loss, destruction, or alteration of physical evidence

contract an agreement between two or more competent parties that can be enforced in court

contract law the branch of civil law that provides rules regarding agreements between people and businesses when they purchase or provide goods and services

contract under seal a written agreement bearing a red sticker, handwritten dot, or the word *seal*

contrary to public policy against the morals and ethics of a community

contributory negligence negligent actions by the plaintiff that were the partial cause of the plaintiff's own injuries

controlled substance any narcotic or drug listed in Schedules I to V of the *Controlled Drugs and Substance Act*

conversion unauthorized and substantial interference with another's property that deprives the owner of its use

counselling a crime that involves advising, recommending, or persuading another person to commit a criminal offence

counterclaim an action brought by the defendant in response to the plaintiff's claim that is aimed at diminishing or removing the defendant's liability

counteroffer an offer made in response to an existing offer

court clerk the court official who assists the judge in administering oaths and performing other duties

court of appeal a court with the authority to review decisions made by lower courts

court reporter the court official who records everything said in court during a trial

court security officer the court official who maintains security in the courtroom

credit buying purchasing goods by paying for them in instalments that include interest or service charges

crime an act or omission of an act that is prohibited and punishable by federal statute

crime scene the site where the offence took place

criminal law a category of public law that prohibits and punishes behaviour that injures people, property, and society as a whole

criminal negligence wanton or reckless disregard for the lives and safety of others, sometimes causing serious injury or death

cross-claim a claim made between parties on the same side of a litigation

cross-examination the second questioning of a witness to test the accuracy of the testimony; performed by the opposing attorney

Crown attorney (or prosecutor) the lawyer representing the government's interests in prosecuting criminal offenders

Crown wardship order an order by a family judge that permanently removes children from the parents' home and makes the state their guardian

cruelty the mental or physical behaviour of one spouse causing harm to the other, making staying together intolerable

culpable homicide a killing for which the accused can be held legally responsible, such as murder, infanticide, or manslaughter

custodial parent the parent responsible for the child's care when the parents separate

custody and supervision order a court order that sets out terms and conditions, requiring the youth to spend two-thirds of the sentence in custody and the last third in the community under supervision

custody in criminal law, a youth sentence entailing assignment to a group home, participation in a wilderness camp, or incarceration in a youth correctional facility; in family law, care of a child awarded by a court when a couple separates

custom marriage an Aboriginal marriage ceremony that follows traditional practices

damages money awarded by the court in compensation for a loss or wrong suffered

dangerous offender someone who constitutes a threat to the life, safety, or well-being of others

day parole conditional absence from custody during the day only

defamation injury to a person's character or reputation by slander or libel

default failure to do something required by law

default judgment a judgment against a party who failed to defend a claim in court

defence a denial of, or a justification for, an act

defence counsel the lawyer who represents the defendant's interests

defence of a third party the legal right to use reasonable force to protect a person from being injured by another party

defence of property a defence stating that a person can use reasonable force to protect his or her property

defendant the party being sued in a civil action; also the party charged with an offence in a criminal case

defined access visits with the child by the non-custodial parent that are defined by the court

denunciation punishment designed to show the offender that society condemns his or her conduct

deportation a sentence expelling an offender from the country

derogate to take away or detract from

detention legally depriving a person of liberty for the purpose of asking questions, with or without physical restraint

direct discrimination an overt act of discrimination

direct evidence testimony given by a witness to prove an alleged fact

direct examination the first questioning of a witness to determine what he or she observed about the crime

directed verdict a decision by the judge to withdraw the cases from the jury and enter a verdict of not guilty

discrimination making a distinction between people and treating them differently on a basis other than individual merit

disorderly house a place used for the purpose of prostitution, gambling, or betting; also known as a common bawdy house

dissemination spreading ideas widely

dissenting opinion judicial opinion that disagrees with the majority opinion regarding a point of law

distinguishing a case a decision by a judge to reject previous decisions and create a new precedent

divine right the idea that monarchs and their successors derived their power to rule from God and that they were accountable only to God

divorce the legal termination of a marriage

domestic contract a legal agreement defining rights and obligations of married or cohabitating partners

domestic law law that governs activity within a nation's borders

double jeopardy the legal doctrine that an accused person cannot be tried twice for the same offence

due diligence the defence that the accused took every reasonable precaution to avoid committing a particular offence

duress in criminal law, the defence that the accused was forced by the threat of violence to commit a criminal act against his or her will; in contract law, the use of unlawful pressure or threats to force a person to enter into a contract, which invalidates the contract

duty counsel a lawyer on duty in a courtroom or police station to give free legal advice to persons arrested or brought before the court

duty of care the obligation to foresee and avoid careless actions that might cause harm to others

dwelling house the whole or part of a building or structure that is occupied on a permanent or temporary basis

electronic monitoring allowing an offender to serve a sentence at home with electronic supervision from a remote location

electronic surveillance the use of any electronic device to overhear or record communications between two or more people

employment law the branch of civil law that governs employer-employee relations

English common law *see* common law

entrapment a defence against police conduct that illegally induces the defendant to commit a criminal act

entrench to place within for purposes of protection; in constitutional law, to protect or guarantee a right or freedom by ensuring that it can only be changed by an amendment to the Constitution

equalization payment what the spouse with the higher value of assets pays to the other spouse to make the division of the couple's total assets more equitable when they separate

essential requirements federal laws that establish whether a person can marry

estate law the branch of civil law that deals with the division and distribution of property after death

evidence information that tends to prove or disprove the elements of an offence

examination for discovery examination of evidence by both sides before a civil trial

executive branch the administrative branch of government responsible for carrying out the government's plans and policies; consists of the prime minister (or premier), the Cabinet, and the public or civil service

exemption clauses clauses that release a party from liability

explanation a defence claiming that an accident occurred for a valid reason even though the defendant took every precaution

express contract an agreement in which the terms have been discussed and agreed upon in advance

extradition surrendering an accused person to another jurisdiction to stand trial

extra-judicial sanctions participation in community-based programs instead of going to court

facilities areas or buildings designated for public use

fair comment the defence to defamation that the comments made about a person were honest and made without malice

false imprisonment detention of a person without consent and without legal authority

family assets property owned by either spouse (or both) and normally used for family purposes

family group conferencing an alternative measures program in which the victim and the offender meet with family members and other concerned parties to determine restitution

family law the branch of civil law that deals with various aspects of family life

Federal Court of Canada a court that hears cases involving the federal government; consists of a trial and an appeal division

federal system system of government where responsibility for governing is divided between two levels of government: the central government and the provincial government

fines specific amounts of money paid to the court as penalties for offences

fingerprint a patterned mark left on a surface by a fingertip

first-degree murder a killing that is planned and deliberate, is the result of a contract, causes the death of a peace officer, or occurs during the commission of another serious crime

f.o.b. free on board; a contractual term that specifies responsibility and delivery arrangements

forensic science the use of biochemical and other scientific techniques to analyze evidence in a criminal investigation

foreseeability the ability of a reasonable person to anticipate the consequence of an action

formal requirements provincial and territorial laws regarding the solemnization of marriage (the wedding ceremony)

franchise the right to vote

fraud intentionally deceiving someone in order to cause a loss of property, money, or service

fraudulent misrepresentation a statement that the maker knows is false, made with the intent to cause the other person to act on the statement

freedom the right to conduct one's affairs without governmental interference

frustration an event or circumstance that makes the performance of a contract impossible

full parole conditional release from custody after serving one-third to one-half of a sentence

future consideration consideration that is exchanged after a contract is formed

garnishment a court order requiring that money owed by a defendant to a plaintiff be paid out of the defendant's earnings or bank account

general deterrence punishment to discourage people in general from offending

general intent the desire to commit a wrongful act for its own sake, with no ulterior motive or purpose

goods merchandise that can be purchased

government or public bill a bill that is proposed by a Cabinet minister

gratuitous promise an offer that gives benefit to the offeree only

gravamen the most serious part of an accusation

Great Laws of Manu laws compiled in India between 1280 and 880 BCE, previously transferred through oral tradition

guardian ad litem the person appointed to act on behalf of a minor or person under a disability who is being sued

habeas corpus a court order designed to prevent unlawful arrest by ensuring that anyone detained is brought before a court within a reasonable amount of time; Latin for "you must have the body."

harassment persistent annoying or negative behaviour that violates the human rights of the victim

hearsay evidence evidence given by a witness based on information from a third party

homicide the killing of another human being, either directly or indirectly

host someone who serves alcohol to guests or paying customers

human rights the right to receive equal treatment, to be free from prohibited discrimination and harassment, and to have access to places, services, and opportunities

human rights codes legal documents that protect people from prohibited discrimination

hung jury a jury that cannot reach a unanimous verdict and, consequently, is dismissed from the case

hybrid or dual procedure offence an offence that the Crown can try either as a summary or an indictable offence

implied conditions essential elements of a contract that are not specifically stated in the contract

implied contract an agreement in which the parties indicate consensus through their conduct

impressions patterns or marks found on surfaces and caused by various objects such as fingers, gloves, shoes, tires, or tools

inalienable rights entitlements that are guaranteed and cannot be surrendered or transferred to another, for example, equality and liberty

incapacity of children the legal presumption that a child under the age of 12 cannot form the necessary *mens rea* to be convicted of a crime

incarceration imprisonment for a specified period of time

indeterminate sentence a sentence that allows an offender to be held for an indefinite period of time

indictable offence a serious crime that carries a heavier penalty than a summary conviction offence

individual characteristics specific and unique features of an object

inevitable accident a defence claiming that an accident was unavoidable due to an uncontrollable event

infanticide the killing of a newborn infant by the child's mother

information a statement given under oath, informing the court of details of the offence

injunction a court order requiring or prohibiting an action

innocent misrepresentation a false statement that is believed to be true by the party making it

insane automatism a condition, caused by a mental disorder, in which a person acts without being aware of what he or she is doing

intelligence the collecting, evaluating, analyzing, and reporting of information, especially of a military, criminal, or political nature

intent a state of mind in which someone desires to carry out a wrongful action, knows what the results will be, and is reckless regarding the consequences

intentional infliction of nervous shock or mental suffering deliberately shocking someone, causing this person to suffer mental or physical harm

intentional torts actions intended to cause injury to others

intermittent sentence a sentence of less than 90 days that may be served on weekends and at night

international law laws that govern the conduct of independent nations in their relationships with one another

interveners third-party participants in a legal proceeding; also called "friends of the court"

intervening act an unforeseeable event that interrupts the chain of events started by the defendant

intestate not having made a will before death

intoxication the condition of being overpowered by alcohol or drugs to the point of losing self-control

intra vires Latin for "within the power," which means the power a government has to pass laws within its own jurisdiction

invitation to treat a communication intended to elicit offers from the persons who receive it

invitee a person invited onto a property for a business purpose

invoke to put a law into effect

joint custody one parent has primary care of the child, but both parents make decisions concerning the child's upbringing

judge the court official appointed to try cases in a court of law and to sentence convicted persons

judiciary the branch of law made up of justices, or judges, who adjudicate disputes, interpret the law, and decide on punishments in Canada's court system

jurisdiction the political or legal authority to pass and enforce laws; also, the judicial authority to decide a case

jury in a criminal law, a group of 12 people who decide whether the accused is guilty or not guilty; in civil law, a group of 6 people (in most provinces) who decide for the plaintiff or the defendant

jury panel the large group of randomly selected citizens from which jury members are chosen

justice of the peace a court official who has less authority than a judge but can issue warrants and perform other judicial functions

Justinian's Code the clarification and organization of Roman law commissioned by Byzantine Emperor Justinian I (527–565 CE)

juvenile delinquents under the *Juvenile Delinquents Act,* children between 7 and 16 to 18 years of age (depending on the province) who committed crimes or were considered "unmanageable" or "sexually immoral"

knowledge an awareness of certain facts that can be used to establish *mens rea*

lapse to be terminated or cease to exist

latent fingerprint a print formed by natural oils and perspiration on the fingertip that is invisible to the naked eye

leave permission to appeal a case from a lower court to a higher court

legal authority the right given by law for a person to perform an action that would otherwise be considered a tort

legal purpose a purpose not forbidden by law

legislative branch the branch of government that has the powers to make, change, and repeal laws; consists of the House of Commons and Senate at the federal level and the Legislative Assembly at the provincial and territorial level

liability legal responsibility for a wrongful action

liability insurance insurance that covers part or all of the damages awarded in a tort case

libel a written or recorded statement that damages a person's reputation or character

licensee a person with express or implied permission to pay a social visit

lien the right to hold or dispose of another person's property in payment for a debt

line-up a group of people shown to a victim or a witness for the purpose of identifying the perpetrator

litigants the parties involved in a civil action

litigation legal action to resolve a civil dispute

lobby groups organizations that try to influence legislators in favour of their cause

Magna Carta a charter signed by King John of England in 1215 that recognized individual basic rights for people in England

malice an ulterior or improper reason for publishing a negative or defamatory statement about an individual

malicious prosecution wrongful prosecution of a person without reasonable and probable cause

manslaughter any culpable homicide that is not murder or infanticide

manufacturer's warranty a promise from a manufacturer that a product will work for a specific period of time and, if not, the product will be repaired without cost to the purchaser

marriage breakdown grounds for divorce under the *Divorce Act, 1985*

marriage contract a legal agreement between spouses that deals with specific aspects of a marriage, including the division of property in the event of divorce, separation, or death

marriage licence a legal document proving that two people are married to each other

matrimonial home in a divorce, the principal residence where the spouses resided before their separation

maximum-security institution a highly secured federal correction facility

mediation an ADR process in which a neutral third party works with the parties in a dispute to reach a compromise or settlement agreeable to both parties

medical battery performing the wrong medical procedure or performing a procedure without obtaining the valid consent of the patient

medium-security institution a federal correction facility with few barriers and some freedom of movement

meeting of the minds a clear understanding between the parties regarding the terms of a contract and their willingness to abide by them

mens rea Latin for "the guilty mind"; a deliberate intention to commit a wrongful act, with reckless disregard for the consequences

mental disorder defined in the *Criminal Code* as a "disease of the mind"

minimum-security institution a federal correctional facility without exterior barriers

mischief wilfully destroying or damaging property or data, interfering with the lawful use of property or data, or interfering with any person in the lawful use of property or data

misrepresentation a false or inaccurate statement of fact given in contract formation that invalidates the contract

mistake confusion or error about the identity of the person an individual is marrying or about the purpose of the ceremony; an error about an important term of a contract

mistake of fact a defence that the accused made an honest mistake that led to the breaking of the law

mistake of law ignorance of the law

mitigating factors circumstances that may decrease the severity of an offender's sentence

mitigation of damages obligation on the part of the injured party to attempt to minimize their losses

money laundering the practice of transferring cash or other properties to conceal their illegal origin

monogamy the state of being married to one person

Mosaic Law Biblical or Hebrew law found in the Old Testament

motion for dismissal a request by defence counsel that the judge dismiss the charges against the defendant

motive the reason a person commits a crime

murder the intentional killing of another human being

mutual mistake en error made by both parties to a contract about different things

Napoleonic Code a code of law in France commissioned by Napoleon Bonaparte in 1804.

necessaries basic items a person requires to function, such as food, clothing, shelter, and medical and dental care

necessity the defence that the accused had no reasonable alternative to committing an illegal act

negligence careless conduct that causes foreseeable harm to another person

negotiation a process whereby both parties participate in discussion to reach a mutually acceptable agreement

neighbour principle the legal responsibility not to harm one's neighbour through careless or negligent actions

net family property the value of a couple's assets, less any debts, on the date the relationship ends

next friend an adult representing a child or person under a disability, who initiates a civil lawsuit

nominal damages minimal compensation awarded by the court to the plaintiff to acknowledge a moral victory

non est factum Latin for "it is not my deed," which can be used as a defence to void a contract

non-culpable homicide a killing for which a person cannot be held legally responsible, such as one that results from an unforeseeable accident

non-insane automatism a condition caused by an external factor, such as a concussion or medication, in which a person acts without being aware of what he or she is doing

non-pecuniary damages compensation to the plaintiff for losses that do not involve an actual loss of money and are often difficult to quantify

notwithstanding clause Section 33 of the *Canadian Charter of Rights and Freedoms*, which allows federal and provincial governments to pass legislation that is exempt from s. 2 and ss. 7 to 15 of the Charter

novation replacement of an old contract with a new contract

occupiers' liability the responsibility of owners or renters to ensure that no one entering their premises is injured

offer a proposal to another party to enter into an agreement on certain terms

offeree a person who receives an offer to enter into an agreement

offeror a person who makes an **offer** to enter into an agreement.

officially induced error a defence that the accused person relied on erroneous legal advice from an official responsible for enforcing a particular law

open custody a youth sentence directing a youth to stay in a group home or participate in a wilderness camp for a certain period; also, less secure provincial facilities for non-violent offenders

oral contract a verbal agreement between two or more parties

order of unconscionability an order requiring a division of property that recognizes the unequal contribution of the spouses

override to prevail over

pardon the setting aside of a person's record of conviction

parole release of an inmate, on a promise of good behaviour, into the community before the full sentence is served

particulars the specific details of a claim in a civil action

parties to an offence people indirectly involved in committing a crime

party to common intention the shared responsibility among criminals for additional offences that are committed in the course of the crime they originally intended to commit

past consideration a benefit conferred before a contract is alleged to have been formed

patriate to bring legislative power under the authority of the country to which it applies

peace officer a person responsible for preserving the public peace, such as a police officer, a mayor, or a customs officer

pecuniary damages compensation for losses (as assessed by the court) to be paid to the plaintiff

peremptory challenge the right of the Crown or the defence to exclude someone from a jury without providing a reason

performance completion of the obligations under a contract

perimeter the area surrounding the centre of a crime scene, where the offender may have left evidence

perjury the criminal offence of knowingly making false statements in court while giving evidence under oath or affirmation

perpetrator the person who actually commits a crime

petitioner the person who initiates a divorce action

petition for divorce a document providing reasons for the divorce and arrangements for support payments and child custody

physical evidence any object, impression, or body element that can be used to prove or disprove facts relating to an offence

plaintiff the party initiating a legal action

plea bargain a negotiated deal whereby the accused pleads guilty in exchange for a lighter sentence

pleadings documents stating the claims and defences of the parties involved in a civil action

poisoned environment an uncomfortable or disturbing atmosphere created by the negative comments or behaviour of others

police log a written record of what an officer has witnessed

possession the state of having knowledge of and control over something

prejudice a preconceived opinion based on a stereotype or inadequate information

preliminary hearing a judicial inquiry to determine whether there is sufficient evidence to put the accused on trial

present consideration something of value that is exchanged at the time a contract is formed

pre-sentence report background information about the convicted offender prepared for the judge prior to sentencing

presumptive offences serious crimes including murder, attempted murder, manslaughter, aggravated sexual assault, and repeat serious violent offences

prima facie legally sufficient to establish a fact or case unless disproved by contrary evidence

Principle of Equalization Section 36 of the *Constitution Act, 1982*, which includes the principle that essential services such as health care, education, or access to social services should be available equally to residents in all parts of Canada

private law *see* civil law

private member's bill legislation that is proposed by a Member of Parliament (MP) or Member of the Legislative Assembly (MLA) who is not in the Cabinet

private nuisance unreasonable and substantial interference with someone's right to enjoyment of property

privileged documents records and information that can be excluded from examination by the other side in a civil action

privity of contract in a contract, the rights and obligations of the parties to the contract

probation a sentence that allows a convicted offender to live in the community under the supervision of a parole officer

procedural law law that prescribes the methods of enforcing the rights, duties, and responsibilities of substantive law

product liability the area of law that deals with negligence on the part of manufacturers

promise to appear a signed agreement than an accused person will appear in court at the time of the trial

property law the branch of civil law that governs ownership rights in property

prostitution the act of engaging in sexual services for money

protective custody separation of dangerous offenders for their own protection from the rest of the prison population

Provincial Court the lowest level in the hierarchy of Canadian courts

provocation words or actions that could cause a reasonable person to behave irrationally or lose self-control

psychiatric assessment a report prepared by a psychiatrist describing the mental history of the offender

public law a category of substantive law that regulates the relationship between the government and its citizens

public mischief providing false information that causes the police to start or continue an investigation without cause

public nuisance unreasonable and substantial interference with interests that affect the community at large, such as public health and safety

punitive (or exemplary) damages damages imposed to punish the defendant for reprehensible conduct

qualified privilege protection from liability for statements made in certain situations as long as the statements are made without malice

quasi-criminal laws laws covering less serious offences at the provincial or municipal level; most often punishable by fines

Quebec Civil Code the system of law used in Quebec for resolving private matters; based on the *French Civil Code*

ratification an indication of willingness to be bound by a contract

reasonable access an agreement between parents that allows the non-custodial parent flexible visiting times with the child

reasonable grounds information that would lead a reasonable person to conclude that the suspect had committed a criminal offence

reasonable person an ordinary person of normal intelligence

rebut to contradict evidence introduced by the opposing side

recidivism returning to crime after being released from prison

recklessness consciously taking an unjustifiable risk that a reasonable person would not take

recognizance a guarantee that the accused will appear in court when required, under penalty of a fine of up to $500

regulatory laws federal or provincial statutes meant to protect the public welfare

rehabilitation treatment and training programs designed to help jailed offenders function in society

remedy the relief sought by the plaintiff in a civil suit; the method by which a person's rights are enforced or violations of these rights are compensated

remoteness of damage harm that could not have been foreseen by the defendant due to the lack of a close connection between his or her wrong action and the resulting injury

repudiation words or conduct that indicate one of the parties will not honour its obligation under the contract

rescission restoring the parties to the positions they would have occupied had there been no contract between them

residual powers federal responsibility to make laws in areas not specifically assigned to either the federal government or to the provinces

respondent the party that responds to an appeal; also, the person or organization being sued in a legal action, such as a divorce or complaint of discrimination

restitution punishment that requires the offender to pay the victim or society back for the harm or loss caused by the crime

retribution punishing an offender for revenge or to satisfy the public that the offender has paid for the crime

reverse onus shifting the burden of proof to the defence

revoke to withdraw or take back

right an entitlement that citizens can expect from their government, for example, the right to a fair trial

robbery the theft of personal property through violence or the threat of violence

Royal Prerogative of Mercy a release or sentence reduction granted by the Queen under the authority of an Act of Parliament

Rule of Law a three-part principle of justice stating that the law is necessary to regulate society, the law applies equally to everyone, and people are not governed by arbitrary power

rule of precedent applying a previous decision to a case that has similar circumstances

sale the immediate exchange of title for goods when a contract is made

search warrant a court document that gives the police the right to search a specific location

second-degree murder any murder that does not fit into one of the four situations listed in the category of first-degree murder

secure custody a sentence that incarcerates a youth in a special youth facility

self-defence the legal right to use reasonable force to protect oneself against injury from another

sentence punishment imposed on a person convicted of committing a crime

sentencing circle an alternative measures program used in the Aboriginal community that involves a process of healing for both the victim and the offender

sentencing hearing the judge's opportunity to consider all the facts and listen to recommendations before passing sentence

separation agreement a domestic contract that sets out the terms and conditions of the separation, dealing with issues such as support payments and division of assets and property

services ways of meeting consumer needs that do not involve the purchase of tangible goods

settle out of court the parties agree to settle the dispute among themselves instead of going to court to resolve it

sexual assault an assault that violates a victim's sexual integrity; usually involves touching of a sexual nature that is not invited or consensual

sexual assault with a weapon, threats to a third party, or causing bodily harm a form of sexual assault that involves the use of weapons, threats, or physical injury

sexual harassment unwelcome sexual contact, remarks, leering, demands for dates, requests for sexual favours, and displays of sexually offensive pictures or graffiti

shared cost agreements agreement between the federal and provincial governments to share the cost of certain programs such as health care

shared custody both parents spend equal time with the child and make decisions involving the child's upbringing

sheriff the court official responsible for jury management

show-cause hearing a judicial hearing in which the Crown or the accused has to convince the judge either to detain or release the accused before trial

slander an oral statement or gesture that damages a person's reputation or character

sole custody only one parent has care of the child and makes all major decisions about the child's upbringing

solemnization of marriage the wedding ceremony

special damages compensation to the plaintiff for expenses such as drugs or ambulance services, deemed to result from the defendant's actions

specialized standard of care the degree of caution or level of conduct considered necessary by a reasonable person with the same specialized training

specific deterrence punishment to discourage criminals from re-offending

specific intent the desire to commit one wrongful act for the sake of accomplishing another

specific performance a court-ordered remedy that requires the party breaching the contract to perform its part of the agreement

split custody siblings are separated and their care is divided between the parents

spousal support money that one spouse pays the financially dependent spouse once the marriage or relationship has ended

standard of care the degree of caution or level of conduct expected of a reasonable person

stare decisis a Latin phrase meaning to "stand by the decision," i.e., abide by the decisions already made

statement of claim a court document outlining the plaintiff's claim in a civil suit and the remedy desired

statement of defence the response to the plaintiff's complaint setting out the defendant's version of the facts

statute law laws that are passed by the government

statute of limitations a law that specifies the time period within which legal action must be taken

Statute of Westminster an amendment to the *BNA Act* that extended Canada's law-making powers

statutory authority legislation that grants someone the right to perform an act that could create a nuisance

statutory release by law, release from prison after serving two-thirds of a sentence, excluding life or indeterminate sentences

stereotyping having an oversimplified, standardized, or fixed judgment of a group of people

stoppage in transit the returning of goods to a seller before they are delivered to a buyer

strict liability in civil law, the defendant is automatically liable for an injury caused by a dangerous substance or activity even if the defendant was not negligent

strict liability offences in criminal law, offences that do not require *mens rea*; the accused offers the defence of due diligence

subpoena a court order requiring the witness to appear in court on a certain date to give evidence

substantial performance carrying out the essential elements of a contract

substantive law a category of domestic law that defines the rights, duties, and obligations of citizens and government

succession the legal right to inherit property

summary conviction offence a minor offence that carries a relatively light penalty

summons a legal document issued for an indictable offence, ordering an accused person to appear in court

Superior Court of the province the highest criminal and civil court in a province, consisting of a trial division and an appeal division; this court has jurisdiction beyond that of the lower courts

supervised access visits with the child by the non-custodial parent that are supervised by a third party

Supreme Court of Canada the highest court of appeal in Canada; also deals with constitutional questions referred to it by the federal government

surety a person who agrees to make a payment if the accused does not appear at trial

surrebuttal a reply to the opposing side's rebuttal

suspended sentence a judgment that is not carried out, provided certain requirements set out by the judge are met

suspension of privilege a sentence that withholds an offender's privilege for a specified period

telewarrant a search warrant obtained by phone or fax

Ten Commandments laws given to Moses to guide the Hebrew people

tender years doctrine the belief that young children should be in the custody of their mothers

theft taking property permanently or temporarily, without the owner's permission

theft over the indictable offence of stealing goods worth over $5000

theft under the hybrid offence of stealing goods worth under $5000

The Great Binding Law the Constitution of the Iroquois Confederacy that outlined many of the same principles of justice and fairness that are found in modern civil rights documents

thin-skull rule the principle that a defendant is liable for all damages to a plaintiff caused by his or her negligence despite any pre-existing condition that makes the plaintiff more prone to injury

third-party claim a complaint filed by the defendant denying liability and blaming another party for the plaintiff's loss

title legal ownership

tort harm caused to a person or property for which the law provides a civil remedy

tort law the branch of civil law that holds persons or private organizations responsible for damage they cause another person as a result of accidental or deliberate action

trafficking a criminal offence that involves selling, giving, transporting, or distributing a controlled substance

training schools custody facilities that provided disciplinary and vocational instruction to juvenile offenders

transcript a typed record of everything said in court during a trial

trespass an unlawful interference with the person, property, or rights of another

trespasser a person who enters another's property without permission or legal right

trial by combat determining guilt or innocence by having the parties involved in a dispute fight a duel

trial by oath helping requiring friends of the accused to swear on the Bible that he or she is innocent

trial by ordeal requiring the accused to undergo torture to determine guilt or innocence

trust an arrangement whereby one person gives property or money to another person who must look after it for a third party

truth the defence that comments made about a person that are alleged to be defamatory are actually verified and established facts

ultra vires Latin for "beyond the power," which refers to areas that are beyond the power or jurisdiction of a government

unconditional sale of specific goods in a deliverable state the passing of title of a specific good that is on hand to the buyer as soon as the contract is made

unconscionability unreasonable advantage taken of one of the parties to a contract

under duress in family law, to be forced into marriage through fear

undue hardship the result of a change that would affect the economic viability of an enterprise or produce a substantial health and safety risk that outweighs the benefit of accommodating someone

undue influence pressure arising from a special relationship between the parties to convince a person to enter into a contract

unescorted temporary absence brief release from custody for personal reasons or community service

unilateral contract a contract formed when the offeree accepts an offer by performing an act requested by the offeror

unilateral mistake an error made by one party to a contract, of which the other party is unaware

unintentional torts injuries caused by an accident or an action that was not intended to cause harm

unitary system a system of government where power is centralized in one level of government

vicarious liability legal responsibility for the negligence of another person

vicarious or substituted performance a situation whereby part of a contractual obligation is performed by a third party

victim impact panel a panel that allows victims and drunk driving offenders to express their views and feelings

victim impact statement a statement prepared by a crime victim or the victim's family describing the harm done or the loss suffered as a result of the offence

victim-offender mediation an alternative measures program designed to determine restitution; involves the victim, the offender, and a mediator

visible fingerprint a print formed when a fingertip is coated in blood, grease, or some other substance, making it visible to the naked eye

void *ab initio* a legal process that declares a marriage null and void

void contracts agreements without legal force

voidable contract an agreement that can be avoided or not carried out

voir dire a mini-trial that takes place during a trial; jurors are excluded while the judge, the Crown, and the defence discuss the admissibility of evidence

voluntary assumption of risk (or *volenti non fit injuria*) the defence that no liability exists because the plaintiff agreed to accept the risk normally associated with the activity

waiver a document signed by the plaintiff, releasing the defendant from liability in the event of an injury

warranty a minor term of a contract

wilful blindness a deliberate closing of one's mind to the possible consequences of one's actions

will a legal document containing instructions for the distribution of a person's property and possessions after his or her death

wiretapping the interception of telephone communications

witnesses persons who give evidence while under oath in a court of law

work release conditional absence from custody to perform paid or voluntary work under supervision

writ of summons a legal document that begins civil actions in some provinces; it informs the defendant of the claim, ordering him or her to respond

written contract an agreement between two or more parties in which the terms are set down on paper

young offender Under the *Young Offenders Act*, a person between 12 and 18 years of age who breaks the criminal law

Young Offenders Act federal legislation that replaced the *Juvenile Delinquents Act* in 1984

Youth Criminal Justice Act federal legislation that replaced the *Young Offenders Act* in 2003

youth justice court a court for youths between the ages of 12 and 18

youth sentence punishment imposed on a youth that takes into consideration the principles in sentencing people under the age of 18

youth worker a probation officer appointed to monitor a youth's progress in the community

Index

A

abetting, 153
Aboriginal peoples
    adoption, 448
    custom marriages, 421–422
    governing statutes, 37
    law, 28–29
    Maritimes, conflict in, 108–109
    police, 191–192
    property situated on reserves, 456, 457, 510–511
    Royal Commission, 68
    sentencing circles, 168, 293
Aboriginal rights, 101, 108–109, 263–264
abrogation of rights, 101
absolute discharge, 282
absolute liability offences, 150
absolute privilege, 406
acceptance of contract, 469–471
access, 438, 440–443
accessory after the fact, 153
accommodate, duty to, 122
accommodation, 126–127
accused, 169
act of God, 383
actus reus, 143–145, 155, 227
administrative law, 43, 337
adoption, 447–450
adult sentences for young people, 325–326
adultery, 429–430
adversarial system, 26
affidavit of documents, 342–343
affinity, 416–417
affirmative action, 120
aggravated assault, 230
aggravated damages, 353
aggravated sexual assault, 231
aggravating factors, 280

agreement to sell, 501
aiding, 153
alibi, 268
allurement, 377
alternative dispute resolution (ADR), 358–360
ameliorate, 99
amending formula, 60
annulment, 418
anti-terrorist legislation, 113, 134–135
appeal, 164, 182–183, 344
appearance notice, 204
appellant, 182
apportionment of fault, 374
arbitrary detention or imprisonment, 95–96
arbitration, 359
arraignment, 172
arrest and detention
    appearance notice, 204
    arbitrary detention, 95–96
    arrest, definition, 203
    bench warrant, 204
    citizen's arrest, 206
    detention, definition, 203
    interrogation of accused, 202–203
    lawful arrest, 203
    procedures, 203–207
    procedures after, 210–211
    reasonable grounds, 204
    rights while under, 95–96
    searches. *See* search and seizure
    with a warrant, 204–205
    without a warrant, 205
arrest warrant, 205
assault
    aggravated, 230
    definition, 228, 392
    intentional tort, 392
    sexual, 230–232

    with a weapon or causing bodily harm, 228
assembly, freedom of, 88–89
assignee, 492
assignment of contract, 492–493
assignor, 492
assizes, 27
association, freedom of, 88–89
attempt, 155–156
automatism, 255–256
automobile negligence, 379–380

B

bail, 212
bailiff, 170
bait and switch, 508–509
balance of probabilities, 251, 338
banns of marriage, 419
battered woman syndrome, 258–259
battery, 392–393
bawdy house, 239
bench warrant, 204
beyond a reasonable doubt, 168, 174
bigamy, 417
bilateral contract, 463
Bill 101 (Quebec), 81
Bill of Rights, 77
bills, 64–66
binding decisions, 349
binding-over, 285–286
blood samples, 234
blood transfusions, 87
bona fide occupational requirement, 120
Book of Exodus, 19
breach of conditions, 498
breach of contract, 497–499
breach of warranty, 498–499

breaking and entering, 236–237, 391
breath samples, 234
British North America Act, 1867, 53–58
bugging, 178
bullies, 332–333
burden of proof, 174
bylaws, 37

C

Canadian Bill of Rights, 79–80
Canadian Charter of Rights and Freedoms
    Aboriginal rights, 100, 101, 108
    arbitrary detention or imprisonment, 95–96, 192
    cruel and unusual treatment or punishment, 97–98, 289
    democratic rights, 90–91
    DNA data bank and, 218–219
    duration of legislative bodies, 90, 91
    enforcement, 83–84
    entrenchment of, 60, 80–82
    equality rights, 99–100, 113, 426, 436
    freedom of assembly, 88–89
    freedom of association, 88–89, 192
    freedom of conscience, 86
    freedom of expression, 87–88
    freedom of religion, 86
    freedom of thought, 81, 87–88, 89, 107
    fundamental freedoms, 80, 86–89
    guarantee, 84, 93, 106, 108
    interveners, 84
    jurisdiction, 83
    jury trial, right to, 165
    language education rights, 101, 106
    language rights, 100–101
    legal rights, 93–99
    life, liberty and security of the person, 93–94, 95, 98, 192, 218, 261
    mobility rights, 90, 92, 192
    multicultural rights, 99, 100, 102–103
    notwithstanding clause, 80–81
    reasonable limits, 84
    rights when charged with criminal offence, 85, 96–97, 174, 175, 212, 213, 266
    rights while under arrest or detention, 96
    sitting of legislative bodies, 90, 91
    unreasonable search and seizure, 94–95, 192, 207–208, 218, 315, 316
    witnesses' rights in court, 98–99
Canadian Human Rights Act, 112–113
capacity, 415, 475
capital offences, 92
careers in law
    aptitudes and skills, 136
    areas of interest, 136
    education and training, 136
    environmental conditions, 136
    lawyer, 74
    other types of positions, 518
case citations, 4–5
case law, 27
causation, 373–375
cause-in-fact, 373–374
caveat emptor, 480
centre (of crime scene), 193
chain of custody, 200
challenge for cause, 173
character evidence, 178
charge to jury, 180–181
Charlottetown Accord, 61
Charter of Rights and Freedoms. See *Canadian Charter of Rights and Freedoms*
chattels, 400–401
child custody
    access, 438, 440–443
    definition, 438
    tender years doctrine, 439
    types of, 440
child support, 443–445
children
    see also minors
    allurement, 377
    civil actions, 338–339
    custody issues. *See* child custody
    guardian ad litem, 339
    incapacity of, 313
    mens rea, 146
    negligence, 371
    next friend, 338
    protection of, 446
    as trespassers, 377
    youth and crime. *See* young people and crime
c.i.f., 503
circuit judges, 27
circumstantial evidence, 178
citations, 3–6
citizen's arrest, 206
civil actions
    appeals, 344
    class action suit, 344–345
    counterclaim, 341
    cross-claim, 342
    default judgment, 341
    defendant, 338
    disabilities, parties with, 338–339
    examination for discovery, 342
    examination of documents, 342–343
    jurisdiction, 339
    see also civil courts
    minors, 338–339
    parties, 338–339
    plaintiff, 338
    pleadings, 340
    pre-trial conference, 343
    reply, 342
    settlement, 343
    stages, 340
    starting an action, 340–341
    statement of claim, 341
    statement of defence, 341
    third-party claim, 342

trial court, 343–344
civil courts
    Federal Court of Canada, 349
    provincial courts of appeal, 347–348
    Small Claims Courts, 346–347
    Superior Court of the province, 347
    Supreme Court of Canada, 349
    territorial courts of appeal, 347–348
civil law, 44–46
civil liberties, 58
class action suit, 344–345
class characteristics, 196
clerical mistake, 480
closed custody, 295
c.o.d., 503
Code of Hammurabi, 17–18
Code of Li k'vei, 17
codified rules, 17
cohabitation, 425–426
cohabitation agreement, 425
collective bargaining, 89
collusion, 430–431
colour of right, 236
common law, 27, 35
common-law relationship, 425, 456
common mistake, 479
community service order, 284
complainant, 115
compulsion, 260–262
conciliation, 117–118
concurrent sentences, 288
condition, 498
conditional discharge, 282
conditional release, 298–300
conditional sentences, 283
condonation, 430–431
conflict of power, 54–55
connivance, 430–431
consanguinity, 416
conscience, freedom of, 86
consecutive sentences, 288

consent
    age of, to marriage, 416
    as defence to criminal offence, 231
    as defence to intentional interference, 402, 403–404
    definition, 415–416
    vs. duress, 415
    to marriage, 415–416
    sexual assault, 231
consideration, 471–474
conspiracy, 156
the Constitution
    see also *Constitution Act, 1982*
    British North America Act, 1867, 53–56
    and civil liberties, 58
    patriation, 57–61
    Statute of Westminster, 57
Constitution Act, 1982
    Aboriginal rights, 108
    amending formula, 60
    Charter of Rights and Freedoms. See *Canadian Charter of Rights and Freedoms*
    division of powers, 59
    federal government structure, 63
    natural resources, 59
    patriation of Constitution, 58
    Principle of Equalization, 59
    Quebec and, 60–61
constitutional law, 37, 337
constructive discrimination, 120
consumer protection
    federal legislation, 508–509
    personal identity, 516–517
    property situated on reserve, 510–511
    provincial legislation, 509–510
consummation of marriage, 418–419
contamination (of crime scene), 193
contingency fee system, 344
contract
    bilateral, 463

    classification of, 463–465
    defined, 463
    discharge of, 494–499
    elements of, 465–474
    express, 464
    implied, 464
    incapacitated persons, 476–477
    invalidating factors, 475–483
    see also invalid contracts
    legal purpose, 477
    novation, 496
    oral, 463–464
    ratification, 476
    rescission, 477
    rights and obligations. See contract rights and obligations
    under seal, 465
    unilateral, 471
    void, 476
    written, 464
contract law, 45
contract requirements
    acceptance, 469–471
    consideration, 471–474
    meeting of the minds, 465
    offer, 466–469
contract rights and obligations
    assignment of contract, 492–493
    privity of contract, 491–492
    substituted performance, 493
    vicarious performance, 493
contributory negligence, 381
Controlled Drugs and Substances Act, 241–245
controlled substance, 241
conversion, 401
copyright, 484–485
correctional programs, 296
correctional system, 294–296
costs, 344
counselling, 153
counterclaim, 341
counteroffer, 469
court clerk, 170
Court Martial Appeal Court, 167

court reporter, 170
court security officer, 170
courts of appeal, 165, 347–348
crime
    abetting, 153
    absolute liability offences, 150
    accessory after the fact, 153
    actus reus, 143–145
    aiding, 153
    attempt, 155–156
    conspiracy, 156
    counselling, 153
    definition, 139
    elements of, 143–151
    incomplete, 154–156
    involvement in, 152–156
    mens rea, 145–149
    parties to an offence, 152–153
    party to common intention, 154
    perpetrator, 152
    strict liability offences, 150
    vs. tort, 391
    youth. *See* young people and crime
crime scene
    centre, 193
    contamination, 193
    definition, 193
    perimeter, 193
    physical evidence at. *See* physical evidence
    police, role of, 194–195
    protection and preservation of, 193–194
Criminal Code of Canada
    amendments to, 141
    arrest without warrant, 205
    citizen's arrest, 206
    history of, 141–142
    offences under. *See* offences
    provincial jurisdiction, 142
    sex offenders' records, 141
criminal court system
    court personnel, 170
    the defence, 169–170
    judge, 169
    jury, 171
    justice of the peace, 169
    participants, 168–172
    the prosecution, 170
    structure, 163–167
    witnesses, 171
    young people. *See* youth criminal justice system
criminal injuries compensation, 357
criminal law, 43–44, 140, 337
criminal negligence, 148
criminal trial jurisdictions, 222
criminal trial process
    appeal, 182–183
    burden of proof, 174
    charge to jury, 180–181
    Crown's opening statement, 175
    defence's response, 175
    evidence, rules of, 175–176
    evidence, types of, 177–180
    examination of witnesses, 175
    summary of case, 180
    verdict, 182
cross-claim, 342
cross-examination, 175
Crown attorney, 170
cruel and unusual treatment or punishment, 97–98
cruelty, 429–430
culpable homicide, 225
custodial parent, 438
custody, 323
custody and supervision order, 323
custom marriages, 421–422
customs and excise, 189

D

Dakota-Ojibway Police Service, 192
damages
    aggravated, 353
    breach of contract, 499
    definition, 338
    exemplary, 354
    general, 350–353
    mitigation of, 499
    nominal, 354
    non-pecuniary, 351–352
    pecuniary, 350–351
    punitive, 354
    remoteness, 374–375
    special, 353
    upper limit on non-pecuniary, 352
dangerous offender, 288
dangerous operation of a motor vehicle, 233
day parole, 298
death, division of property on, 456
defamation, 404–408
default judgment, 341
defaults, 506
defence counsel, 170
defence of a third party, 402–403
defence of dwelling, 259
defence of property, 404
defences (criminal)
    alibi, 268
    automatism, 255–256
    consent, 231
    definition, 251
    double jeopardy, 266
    due diligence, 150
    entrapment, 268
    intoxication, 256
    justifications. *See* justifications
    mental disorder, 251–253
    mistake of fact, 266
    mistake of law, 265–266
    officially induced error, 266
defences (intentional torts)
    absolute privilege, 406
    consent, 402, 403–404
    defamation, 406–407
    defence of a third party, 402–403
    defence of property, 404
    fair comment, 406
    legal authority, 403, 404
    qualified privilege, 408
    self-defence, 402
    statutory authority, 404
    truth, 406
defences (negligence)
    act of God, 383
    contributory negligence, 381
    explanation, 383

inevitable accident, 383
limitation periods, 383–384
voluntary assumption of risk, 381–382
waiver, 382
defendant, 169, 338
defined access, 440
democratic rights, 90–91
denunciation, 277
deportation, 286
derogation of rights, 101
detention, 203
see also arrest and detention
deterrence, 276
direct discrimination, 121
direct evidence, 177
direct examination, 175
directed verdict, 175
disabilities, parties with, 338–339
discharge of contract
by agreement, 495–496
by breach, 497–499
by frustration, 496–497
by performance, 494–496
discharges, 282
discrimination
accommodate, duty to, 122
accommodation, 126–127
affirmative action, 120
bona fide occupational requirement, 120
constructive, 120
definition, 111
direct, 121
employment, 120–125
exceptions under the law, 120
facilities, 127
grounds of, 120–129
interpretation of, 99
prohibition of, 113
retirement and, 114
special needs, accommodation of, 127
stereotyping, 112
disorderly house, 240
dissenting opinions, 349
distinguishing a case, 35

divine right, 26
division of powers, 54–55, 59
division of property. *See* family assets
divorce
access issues, 440–443
certificate, 428–429
child support, 443–445
custody issues, 438–445
definition, 428
factors considered by court, 438
petition for, 428
property issues. *See* family assets
spousal support, 448–451
DNA data bank, 218–219
DNA testing, 198, 200
documents, examination of, 342–343
domestic contracts, 426
domestic law, 40
double jeopardy, 97, 266
drug enforcement, 189
drug offences
controlled substance, 241
money laundering, 244–245
possession, 241–243
trafficking, 243–244
dual procedure offence, 223
due diligence, 150
duress, 260–262, 415, 482
duty counsel, 169–170
duty of care, 367–368
dwelling house, 259

E

early British law, 24–26
electronic copyright protection, 484–485
electronic monitoring, 283
electronic surveillance, 178–179
employment issues, 120–125
employment law, 46
enforcement
Charter, 83–84

examination of judgment debtor, 355
execution, 356
garnishment, 355
judgments, 355–357
seizure, 356
support payments, 450–451
English common law, 35
entrapment, 268
entrenchment of rights in Charter, 80–82
equality rights, 99–100, 444
equalization payment, 453
essential requirements of marriage, 414–419
estate law, 46
evidence
character, 178
circumstantial, 178
definition, 170
direct, 177
electronic surveillance, 178–179
hearsay, 176
immaterial or irrelevant questions, 176
leading questions, 176
non-response answers, 176
opinion statements, 176
physical. *See* physical evidence
polygraph tests, 179
rules of, 175–176
technical irregularity, 317–318
types of, 177–180
voir dire, 179–180
young people's rights, 315–318
examination for discovery, 342
execution, 356
executive branch, 62–63
exemplary damages, 354
exemption clauses, 499
explanation, 383
express contract, 464
expression, freedom of, 87–88
extra-judicial sanctions, 320–321
extradition, 92

F

facilities, 127
facts of the case, 5–6
failure to stop at scene of accident, 233
fair comment, 406
false imprisonment, 395
families
    adoption, 447–450
    cohabitation, 425–426
    common-law relationship, 425
    definition of, 423
    domestic contracts, 426
    protection of children, 446
    same-sex relationships, 426–427
family assets
    common-law relationship, 456
    defined, 452
    division on death, 456
    equal division of property, 452–454
    equalization payment, 453
    matrimonial home, 454
    net family property, 453
    order of unconscionability, 455
    on reserve lands, 456
    unequal division of property, 454–455
family group conferencing, 292
family law, 45–46
Federal Child Support Guidelines, 443, 444
federal correctional system, 295–296
Federal Court of Canada, 166, 349
federal court system, 165–167
federal government, 36–37
    see also government
federal police, 189–190
federal system, 53
feudal system, 26–27
fines, 286
fingerprints, 196–197
first-degree murder, 226
First Nations Policing Policy, 191–192

fitness to stand trial, 253
f.o.b., 503
forced sterilizations, 82
forensic science, 195
foreseeability, 368
formal requirements of marriage, 414, 419–421
franchise, 78
fraud, 238
fraudulent misrepresentation, 481
freedom(s)
    of assembly, 88–89
    of association, 88–89
    of conscience, 86
    definition, 77
    of expression, 87–88
    fundamental, 86–89
    of religion, 86
    of thought, 87–88
friends of the court, 84
frustration, 496–497
full parole, 298
fundamental freedoms, 86–89
future consideration, 474

G

gambling offences, 239–241
garnishment, 355
general damages, 350–353
general deterrence, 276
general intent, 145
goods, 128
government
    bill, 64
    executive branch, 62–63
    federal, 36–37
    judiciary, 64
    legislative branch, 63
    local, 37
    provincial, 37
grandparents' access, 441
gratuitous promise, 472
gravaman, 115
The Great Binding Law, 28–29
Great Laws of Manu, 17
Greek law, 21

guardian ad litem, 339

H

habeas corpus, 28, 213
harassment, 122–124
hearsay evidence, 176
Hebrew law, 19–20
homicide, 225–226
hosts, 377–378
House of Commons, 63
human rights, 111
human rights codes, 111
Human Rights Commission, 117–118
human rights legislation
    administration of, 115–118
    Canadian Human Rights Act, 112–113
    discrimination. *See* discrimination
    dismissal of complaint, 117
    filing a complaint, 115
    goods and services, access to, 128
    Human Rights Commission, role of, 117–118
    provincial human rights codes, 113
    remedies, 118
hung jury, 182
hybrid offence, 223

I

immaterial or irrelevant questions, 176
impaired driving, 233–234
implied conditions, 505–506
implied contract, 464
impressions, 196
in vitro fertilization, 69
inalienable rights, 77
incapacity of children, 313
incarceration, 287–288
incomplete crimes, 154–156
indeterminate sentences, 288
Indian bands, 37, 113

see also Aboriginal peoples
indictable offences, 165, 211, 221–222
individual characteristics, 196
inevitable accident, 383
infanticide, 227
information, 205
injunctions, 354–355, 499
innocent misrepresentation, 481
insane automatism, 255–256
insanity defence. See mental disorder
intelligence, 190
intent, 145–147, 390
intentional infliction of nervous shock or mental suffering, 396–397
intentional interference with property
    chattels, trespass to, 400–401
    conversion, 401
    defences, 403–404
    land, trespass to, 399
    nuisance, 399–400
intentional interference with the person
    assault, 392
    battery, 392–393
    defences, 402–403
    false imprisonment, 395
    intentional infliction of nervous shock or mental suffering, 396–397
    malicious prosecution, 395–396
    medical battery, 394–395
    privacy, invasion of, 397–398
    sexual assault, 393–394
intentional torts
    and criminal acts, 390–391
    defamation of character, 404–408
    defences. See defences (intentional torts)
    definition, 390
    intentional interference with property, 399–401

intentional interference with the person, 391–398
interest groups, 66–67
intermittent sentences, 283
International Court of Justice, 40
international law, 38–40
interrogation of accused, 202–203
interveners, 84
intervening act, 374
intestate, 456
intoxication, 256
intra vires, 55
Inuvialuit Final Agreement, 360
invalid contracts
    duress, 482
    fraudulent misrepresentation, 481
    illegality, 477
    incapacity to contract, 475
    innocent misrepresentation, 481
    minors, 475–476
    misrepresentation, 480–482
    mistake, 478–480
    non est factum, 480
    parental liability, 476
    public policy, contrary to, 478
    repudiation, 476
    unconscionability, 483
    undue influence, 482–483
    void contract, 476
    voidable, 475–476
    voidable contract, 475–476
investigation, 193–195
invitation to treat, 466–467
invitee, 376
invoke, 80

J

joint custody, 440
judge, 169
judge-made laws. See common law
judgment debtor, 355
judgments, enforcement of, 355–356
judiciary, 64

jurisdiction, 36, 83, 222, 339
jury
    challenge for cause, 173
    charge to, 180–181
    definition, 171
    hung, 182
    panel, 172
    peremptory challenge, 174
    qualifications of juror, 172
    role of, 172–174
    selection, 172–174
    trial by jury, right to, 165
justice, 14–15
justice of the peace, 169
justifications
    Aboriginal rights, 263–264
    battered woman syndrome, 258–259
    compulsion, 260–262
    defence of dwelling, 259
    duress, 260–262
    necessity, 259–260
    provocation, 262
    self-defence, 258
    treaty rights, 263–264
Justinian's Code, 22
juvenile delinquents, 308–309

K

keeping a common bawdy house, 239
knowledge, 147

L

language education rights, 101
language rights, 100–101
lapse of offer, 468
latent fingerprint, 197
law making
    enactment of statute, 64–66
    individuals, role of, 66–67
    interest groups, role of, 66–67
    lobby groups, 67
    Royal Commissions, 68
law(s)
    administrative, 43, 337
    categories of, 38–46
    civil, 44–46

common law, 27, 35
constitutional, 37, 337
criminal, 140, 337
definition, 11–12
domestic, 40
historical roots, 17–23
influences on Canadian law, 29
international, 38–40
and justice, 14–15
and morality, 14
need for, 12–13
private, 44–46
procedural, 42
public, 43–44
quasi-criminal, 142
regulatory, 150
vs. rules, 10
sources, 35–37
statute law, 35–36
substantive, 41
lawyer, 74
leading questions, 176
leave to appeal, 166–167
legal authority, 403, 404
legal purpose, 477
legal reforms, 27–28
legal research, 2
legal rights
arbitrary detention or imprisonment, 95–96
cruel and unusual treatment or punishment, 97–98
life, liberty and security of the person, 93–94
trial within reasonable period of time, 97
unreasonable search and seizure, 94–95
when charged with criminal offence, 96–97
while under arrest or detention, 96
witnesses' rights in court, 98–99
young people, 315–318
legal terms, 2
legislative branch, 63
liability

absolute, 150
definition, 150
dog owners, 380
insurance, 371
occupiers', 376–377
parental, 476
product, 375–376
strict, 150, 380
vicarious, 378–379
libel, 405
licensee, 376
lien, 506
life, liberty and security of the person, 93–94
line-up, 211
litigants, 338
lobby groups, 67
local governments, 37

M

Magna Carta, 28, 77
malice, 406
malicious prosecution, 395–396
manslaughter, 227–228
manufacturer's warranty, 503–505
marijuana, legalization of, 95
marriage
Aboriginal customs, 421–422
age of consent, 416
annulment, 418
banns of, 419
breakdown, 429–431
ceremony, 419–420
consent, freedom of, 415–416
consummation of, 418–419
contract, 426
dissolution of. *See* divorce
essential requirements, 414–419
formal requirements, 414, 419–421
licence, 419
mental capacity to marry, 415
prior, 417–418
prohibited relationship, 416–417
same-sex, 426
sexual capacity, 418–419

solemnization of, 414
void *ab initio,* 415
matrimonial home, 454
maximum-security institutions, 295
mediation
benefits, 358
definition, 117, 358
family law, 432
victim-offender, 291–292
medical battery, 394–395
medical negligence, 369–370
medium-security institutions, 295
Meech Lake Accord, 60–61
meeting of the minds, 465
mens rea
attempt, 156
children and, 146
definition, 145
intent, 145–147
knowledge, 147
manslaughter, 228
negligence, 148
recklessness, 148–149
wilful blindness, 149
mental capacity to marry, 415
mental disorder, 251–253
mental states
automatism, 255–256
fitness to stand trial, 253
intoxication, 256
mental disorder, 251–253
mental suffering, 396–397
minimum-security institutions, 295
minors
see also children
and civil actions, 338–339
and contracts, 475–476
mischief, 238
misrepresentation, 480–482
mistake
clerical, 480
common, 479
defined, 478
of fact, 266
in identity (for marriage), 416
of law, 265–266
mutual, 479

unilateral, 479
mitigating factors, 280–281
mitigation of damages, 499
mobility rights, 90, 92
money laundering, 244–245
monogamy, 417
morality, 14
Mosaic Law, 19–20, 30
motion for dismissal, 175
motive, 147
motor vehicle liability insurance, 356
motor vehicle offences, 233–234
multicultural rights, 102–103
municipal police, 191
murder, 226
mutual mistake, 479

N
Napoleonic Code, 23
National DNA Data Bank, 218–219
National Parole Board (NPB), 297
natural resources, provincial powers over, 59
necessaries, 475
necessity, 259–260
negligence
    act of God, 383
    apportionment of fault, 374
    automobile, 379–380
    causation, 373–375
    cause-in-fact, 373–374
    children, 371
    contributory, 381
    criminal, 148
    defences, 381–383
    definition, 366
    duty of care, 367–368
    explanation, 383
    foreseeability, 368
    hosts, 377–378
    inevitable accident, 383
    medical, 369–370
    mens rea and, 148
    neighbour principle, 367–368
    occupiers' liability, 376–377
    parental responsibility, 371
    product liability, 375–376
    professional liability, 369
    reasonable person, 369
    remoteness of damage, 374–375
    rescuers, 372–373
    special types of liability, 375–380
    standard of care, 369–373
    statute of limitations, 383–384
    thin-skull rule, 374–375
    vicarious liability, 378–379
    voluntary assumption of risk, 381–382
    waiver, 382
negotiation, 358
neighbour principle, 367–368
nervous shock, 396–397
net family property, 453
new reproductive technologies, 69
next friend, 338
Nisga'a Court, 167–168
no-fault insurance, 356
nominal damages, 354
non-culpable homicide, 225–226
non est factum, 480
non-insane automatism, 256
non-pecuniary damages, 351–352
non-response answers, 176
note-taking, 2
notwithstanding clause, 80–81
novation, 496
nuisance, 399–400

O
occupiers' liability, 376–377
offences
    criminal negligence, 148
    disorderly house, 240
    drugs. *See* drug offences
    dual procedure offence, 223
    fraud, 238
    gambling, 239–241
    hybrid offence, 223
    indictable offences, 165, 211, 221–222
    keeping a common bawdy house, 239
    levels of, 221–223
    mischief, 238
    perjury, 171
    against the person. *See* offences against the person
    against property. *See* property offences
    prostitution, 239
    public mischief, 238
    summary conviction offence, 164, 221
offences against the person
    assault, 228–229
    dangerous operation of a motor vehicle, 233
    failure to stop at scene of accident, 233
    homicide, 225–226
    impaired driving causing bodily harm, 233–234
    infanticide, 227
    manslaughter, 227–228
    motor vehicle offences, 233–234
    murder, 226
    sexual assault, 230–232
    suicide, 233
offer, 466–468
offeree, 466
offeror, 466
officially induced error, 266
omissions, 144–145
open custody, 295, 323
opinion statements, 176
oral contract, 463–464
order of unconscionability, 455
override, 80

P
pardon, 301
parental liability, 476
parental mobility, 443
parental responsibility, 371
Parliament, 63
parole, 297–300

parole officer, 282
particulars, 341
parties to an offence, 152–153
party to common intention, 154
past consideration, 474
patriation of Constitution, 57–61
peace officer, 205
pecuniary damages, 350–351
peremptory challenge, 174
performance, 494
perimeter (of crime scene), 193
perjury, 171
perpetrator, 152
personal identity, 516–517
petition for divorce, 428
petitioner, 428
physical evidence
    body elements, 198–199
    chain of custody, 200
    definition, 195
    DNA, 198, 200
    fingerprints, 196–197
    gloves, 197
    impressions, 196
    labelling procedures, 200
    shoe prints, 197–198
    tire tracks, 197–198
    tools, 196
plain-language guidelines, 181
plaintiff, 338
plea bargain, 287
pleadings, 340
poisoned environment, 124–125
police
    Aboriginal, 191–192
    crime scene, role at, 194–195
    criminal identification officer, 194–195
    criminal investigations bureau officer, 195
    federal, 189–190
    investigation. *See* investigation
    log, 193–194
    municipal, 191
    patrol officer, 194
    provincial, 190
    scenes of crime officer, 194

polygraph tests, 179
possession, 241–243
post-custody supervision, 324
pre-sentence report, 278
pre-trial conference, 343
pre-trial release, 212–213
prejudice, 112
preliminary hearings, 164
present consideration, 472
presumptive offences, 313
prima facie, 115
Principle of Equalization, 59
prisons. *See* correctional system
privacy, invasion of, 397–398
privacy issues, 516–517
private home, 210
private law, 44–46
private law procedures. *See* civil actions
private member's bill, 65–66
private nuisance, 399–400
privileged documents, 343
privity of contract, 491–492
probation, 282
procedural law, 42
product liability, 375–376
promise to appear, 212
property, defence of, 404
property law, 46
property offences
    breaking and entering, 236–237
    robbery, 145–147, 236, 256
    theft, 235–236
prosecutor, 170
prostitution, 239
protection of the public, 275
protective custody, 295
provincial correctional system, 295
Provincial Court, 163–164
provincial court system, 163–165
provincial governments, 37
    see also government
provincial human rights codes, 113

provincial police, 190
provocation, 228, 262
psychiatric assessment, 278
public bill, 64
public law, 43–44
public mischief, 238
public nuisance, 400
public policy, 478
publication of young people's identities, 318
punitive damages, 354

Q

qualified privilege, 408
quasi-criminal laws, 142
Quebec, and *Constitution Act, 1982,* 60–61
Quebec Civil Code, 30, 427, 463, 501

R

ratification, 476
reasonable access, 440
reasonable doubt, 168, 174
reasonable grounds, 204
reasonable limits, 84
reasonable person, 369
rebut, 175
recidivism, 276
recklessness, 148–149
recognizance, 212
regulatory laws, 150
rehabilitation, 276
religion, freedom of, 86
remedies
    alternative sources of compensation, 356–357
    apportionment of fault, 374
    breach of contract, 499
    civil actions, 341
    damages. *See* damages
    defined, 491
    enforcement of judgments, 355–356
    human rights complaints, 118
    injunctions, 354–355, 499

lien, 506
  sale of goods, breach of, 506
  specific performance, 354, 497
  stoppage in transit, 506
remoteness of damage, 374–375
repudiation, 476, 498
rescission, 477
rescuers, 372–373
reserve lands, 456, 457, 510–511
residual powers, 54–55
respondent, 117, 182, 428
restitution, 18, 276, 284
restorative justice programs
  family group conferencing, 292
  sentencing circles, 168, 293
  vs. traditional approaches, 290
  victim impact panel, 293
  victim-offender mediation, 291–292
  victim-offender panels, 293
retirement, 114
retribution, 18, 276
reverse onus, 212
revocation of offer, 468
rights
  Aboriginal, 101, 108–109
  Charter. See *Canadian Charter of Rights and Freedoms*
  definition, 77
  democratic, 90–91
  entrenchment in Charter, 80–82
  equality, 99–100
  evolution in Canada, 78–80
  historical documents, 77–78
  inalienable, 77
  language, 100–101
  language education, 101
  legal, 93–99
  mobility, 90, 92
  multicultural, 102–103
  recognition of, 77–82
  when charged with criminal offence, 96–97
  while under arrest or detention, 96
  of witnesses in court, 98–99
robbery, 145–147, 236, 256

Roman law, 21–22
Royal Canadian Mounted Police (RCMP), 189–190
Royal Commissions, 68
Royal Prerogative of Mercy, 301
Rule of Law, 13, 28
rule of precedent, 27
rules versus laws, 10

S
sale, 501
sale of goods
  buyers' remedies, 506
  implied conditions, 505–506
  manufacturer's warranty, 503–505
  remedies for breach, 506
  risk, 501–502
  sellers' remedies, 506
  standardized terms, 503
  title, 501
  unconditional sale of specific goods in a deliverable state, 502
same-sex relationships, 426–427
search and seizure
  Charter protection, 207–208
  person, 208
  place, 208–210
  private home, 210
  telewarrant, 210
  unreasonable, 94–95
  young people, 315
search warrant, 208
second-degree murder, 226
secure custody, 324
seizure, 356
self-defence, 258, 402
self-sufficiency, 450
Senate, 63
sentences
  see also specific offences
  binding-over, 285–286
  community service order, 284
  concurrent, 288
  conditional, 283
  conferences, 325

  consecutive, 288
  dangerous offender, 288
  definition, 275
  deportation, 286
  discharges, 282
  electronic monitoring, 283
  fines, 286
  incarceration, 287–288
  indeterminate, 288
  intermittent, 283
  length of imprisonment, 288
  plea bargain, 287
  probation, 282
  restitution, 284
  restorative justice programs, 290–293
  suspended, 283
  suspension of privilege, 286
  traditional types of, 281–289
  youth, 323–325
sentencing
  aggravating factors, 280
  denunciation, 277
  deterrence, 276
  goals of, 275–277
  hearing, 279–281
  mitigating factors, 280–281
  offender's perspective, 278
  pre-sentence report, 278
  procedures, 278–281
  protection of the public, 275
  psychiatric assessment, 278
  rehabilitation, 276
  restitution, 276
  retribution, 276
  society's perspective, 279
  victim impact statement, 278
sentencing circles, 168, 293
separation agreement, 428
services, 128
settle out of court, 343
sexual assault
  aggravated, 231
  causing bodily harm, 231
  consent as defence, 231
  definition, 230–231
  intentional tort, 393–394
  threats to a third party, 231
  with a weapon, 231

sexual harassment, 122–124
shared cost agreements, 58
shared custody, 440
sheriff, 170
show-cause hearing, 212
slander, 405
Small Claims Courts, 346–347
social hosts, 377–378
sole custody, 440
solemnization of marriage, 414
sources of law, 35–37
special damages, 353
special needs, accommodation of, 127
specialized standard of care, 369
specific deterrence, 276
specific intent, 145
specific performance, 354, 497
split custody, 440
spousal support, 449–451
spouse, definition, 426
standard of care, 369–373
stare decisis, 27, 35
statement of claim, 341
statement of defence, 341
statute citations, 3
statute enactment, 64–66
statute law, 35–36
statute of limitations, 383–384
Statute of Westminster, 57
statutory authority, 404
statutory release, 298
stem cell research, 69
stereotyping, 112
stoppage in transit, 506
strict liability, 380
strict liability offences, 150
studying, 2–3
subpoena, 171
substantial performance, 494–495
substantive law, 41
substituted performance, 493
succession law, 46, 456

suicide, 233
summary conviction offence, 164, 221
summons, 204
Superior Court of the province, 165, 347
supervised access, 441
Supreme Court of Canada
    appeals court, 166–167
    Charter, interpretation of, 84
    civil actions, 349
    described, 166
    legal power of, 103
    role of, 84
surety, 212
surrebuttal, 175
suspended sentences, 283
suspension of privilege, 286

T

Tax Court of Canada, 167
telewarrant, 210
Ten Commandments, 19
tender years doctrine, 439
theft, 235–236, 391
theft over, 236
theft under, 236
thin-skull rule, 374–375
third party, defence of a, 402–403
third-party claim, 342
thought, freedom of, 87–88
title, 501
tort law, 45, 366
torts
    vs. crime, 391
    definition, 366
    intentional. *See* intentional torts
    unintentional, 366
trafficking, 243–244
training schools, 309
transcript, 170
treaty rights, 263–264
trespass
    to chattels, 400–401
    definition, 391, 399

    to land, 399
trespasser, 376
trial by combat, 25–26
trial by oath helping, 25
trial by ordeal, 24–25
trial within reasonable period of time, 97
trust, 492
truth, 406

U

ultra vires, 55
unconditional sale of specific goods in a deliverable state, 502
unconscionability, 483
under duress, 415
undue hardship, 122
undue influence, 482–483
unequal division of property, 454–455
unescorted temporary absence, 298
unilateral contract, 471
unilateral mistake, 479
unintentional torts, 366
    see also negligence
unitary system, 53
United Nations (UN), 40, 77–78
Universal Declaration of Human Rights, 40, 77, 78, 79
unreasonable search and seizure, 94–95

V

vicarious liability, 378–379
vicarious performance, 493
victim impact panel, 293
victim impact statement, 278
victim-offender mediation, 291–292
victim-offender panels, 293
visible fingerprint, 197
void *ab initio,* 415
void contract, 476
voidable contract, 475–476
voir dire, 179–180

volenti non fit injuria, 381–382
voluntary assumption of risk, 381–382

W

waiver, 382
warrants, 205, 208, 210
warranty, 498–499, 503–505
wilful blindness, 149
will, 456
wiretapping, 178
witnesses
    definition, 171
    examination of, 175
    perjury, 171
    rights in court, 98–99
work release, 298
Workers' Compensation, 356–357
workplace issues, 120–125
writ of summons, 340
written contract, 464

Y

young offender, 309
Young Offenders Act, 309–311
young people and crime
    adult sentences, 325–326
    bullies, 332–333
    conferences, 325
    custody, 323–324
    evidence, rights regarding, 315–318
    legal rights, 315–318
    legislative reform, 308–309
    presumptive offences, 313
    publication of identities, 318
    rise in reported crime, 307
    searches, 315
    sentencing options, 322–327
    technical irregularity, 317–318
    waiver of rights, 315–317
    youth court records, 326
    youth sentences, 323–325
Youth Criminal Justice Act, 311, 312–313
youth criminal justice system, 319–321
youth justice court, 321–322
youth sentences, 323–325
youth worker, 324

Credits

The publisher wishes to thank the following sources for photographs, illustrations, and other materials used in this book. Care has been taken to determine and locate ownership of copyright material used in this text. We will gladly receive information enabling us to rectify any errors or omissions in credits.

Photos

p. 9 (left) Antonio Mo/Getty Images/FPG; (right and bottom) Bill Ivy/Ivy Images; **p. 11** Tannis Toohey/*The Toronto Star*; **p. 12** Bill Ivy/Ivy Images; **p. 13** CP Picture Archive; **p. 17** Gianni Dagli Orti/Corbis/Magma; **p. 20** Jeffrey L. Rotman/Corbis/Magma; **p. 21** Liz McAuly/D.K Images; **p. 24** Paul McCusker; **p. 26** Gianni Dagli Orti/Corbis/Magma; **p. 29** BC Archives/pdp00235; **p. 33** Bill Ivy/Ivy Image; **p. 34** (top) Ray Kolly/O.P.P; (bottom left) Bill Ivy/Ivy Images; (bottom right) Jerome Delay/CP Picture Archive; **p. 36** W.J Gibbons; **p. 39** Pool/CP Picture Archive; **p. 40** Tom Hanson/CP Picture Archive; **p. 42** Peter Power/CP Picture Archive; **p. 46** (left) Vanessa Davies/D.K Images; (right) Jeff McIntosh/CP Picture Archive; **p. 49** Fred Chartrand/ CP Picture Archive; **p. 52** National Archives of Canada/ C733; **p. 55** Jacques Boissinot/CP Picture Archive; **p. 56** Mark Tayti/CP Picture Archive; **p. 58** Ron Poling/ CP Picture Archive; **p. 61** Wayne Glowacki/CP Picture Archive; **p. 66** Peter Stigter/Fashiontalk; **p. 67** Allen McInnis/CP Picture Archive; **p. 72** Ottmar Bierwagon/ Ivy Images; **p. 73** Ivy Images; **p. 74** Osgoode Law School/York University; **p. 77** John McConnico/CP Picture Archive; **p. 78** VPL/6231; **p. 79** (top) National Archives of Canada/PA-195432; (bottom) National Archives of Canada/C-024452; **p. 80** CP Picture Archive; **p. 81** Pierre-Paul Poulin/Magma; **p. 82** Walter Tychnowicz/CP Picture Archive; **p. 84** CP Picture Archive; **p. 88** (top) Nick Procaylo/CP Picture Archive; (bottom) Andrew Vaughan/CP Picture Archive; **p. 90** Andrew Stawicki/*The Toronto Star*; **p. 92** Courtesy of Osgoode Law School, York University; **p. 94** Chuck Stoody/CP Picture Archive; **p. 98** Paul McCusker; **p. 102** Tom Hanson/CP Picture Archive; **p. 107** Jeff Mcintosh/CP Picture Archive; **p. 109** Andrew Vaughan/ CP Picture Archive; **p. 111** Bob Wilson//CP Picture Archive; **p. 114** Andrew Stawicki/CP Picture Archive; **p. 117** PhotoDisc; **p. 121** Fred Chartrand/CP Picture Archive; **p. 122** Dick Hemingway Photographs; **p. 123** Myrleen Ferguson Cate/PhotoEdit; **p. 125** Comstock Photofile; **p. 127** Fred Chartrand/CP Picture Archive; **p. 128** *The Toronto Star*; **p. 136** David Young-Wolff/PhotoEdit; **p. 138** First Light; **p. 140** Dan Riedhuber/ CP Picture Archive; **p. 141** Bill Ivy/Ivy Images; **p. 142** National Archives of Canada/C2090; **p. 144** Carlos Serrao/ Getty Images/Stone; **p. 150** Frank Gunn/CP Picture Archive; **p. 151** Andreas Pollok/Getty Images/ FPG; **p. 155** Robert Galbraith/CP Picture Archive; **p. 162** Paul McCusker; **p. 164** Dick Hemingway Photographs; **p. 167** Jonathan Hayward/CP Picture Archive; **p. 173** Paul McCusker; **p. 179** Spencer Grant/ PhotoEdit; **p. 182** Paul McCusker; **p. 188** (left) Stan Behal/Canada Wide; (centre) Mo Doiron/CP Picture Archive; (right) Ken Gigliotti/CP Picture Archive; **p. 189** Ivy Images; **p. 191** Bill Sanford/*The Toronto Star*; **p. 194** (left) Chuck Stoody/CP Picture Archive; (right) CP Picture Archive; **p. 197** Dana White/PhotoEdit; **p. 198** Ray Kolly/O.P.P; **p. 203** Randy Fiedler/CP Picture Archive; **p. 205** Ray Kolly/ O.P.P; **p. 206** Jacques Boissinot/CP Picture Archive; **p. 210** Walter Tychnowicz/CP Picture Archive; **p. 217** Pascale Simard FRL/CP Picture Archive; **p. 219** Canadian Police Services Information Centre; **p. 227** Cal Millar/CP Picture Archive; **p. 229** New Brunswick Telegraph; **p. 230** Rejean Gosselin/CP Picture Archive; **p. 232** Michael Newman/PhotoEdit; **p. 236** Richard Hutchings/PhotoEdit; **p. 239** Taras Kovaliv; **p. 249** Chuck Stoody/CP Picture Archive; **p. 252** Archives of Ontario/RG 15-82-0-1; **p. 254** Rod MacIvor/*Ottawa Citizen*; **p. 255** CP Picture Archive; **p. 258** S.W. Productions/PhotoDisc; **p. 259** Michael Newman/PhotoEdit; **p. 261** Paul Almasy/Corbis/Magma; **p. 265** Jacques Boissinot/CP Picture Archive; **p. 267** Spencer Grant/PhotoEdit; **p. 268** PhotoEdit; **p. 275** Bill Ivy/Ivy Images; **p. 277** *The Windsor Star*; **p. 284** Chuck Stoody/CP Picture Archive; **p. 288** CP Picture Archive; **p. 289** Kevin Frayer/CP Picture Archive; **p. 293** Joe Bryska/CP Picture Archive; **p. 295** Steve Russell/*The Toronto Star*; **p. 296** (left) CP Picture Archive; (right) Rick Eglinton/ CP Picture Archive; **p. 306** Debra Brash/CP Picture Archive; **p. 310** (left) CP Picture Archive; (right) CBC National News; **p. 313** Peter Bregg/CP Picture Archive; **p. 316** David

Young-Wolff/PhotoEdit; **p. 320** Ray Kolly/ O.P.P; **p. 321** PhotoEdit; **p. 324** Doug Crawford/CP Picture Archive; **p. 326** Clayton Grose/CP Picture Archive; **p. 333** John Lehmann/*Globe and Mail*; **p. 334** (top) Paul McCusker; (bottom left) Richard Lam/CP Picture Archive; (bottom right) Richard Lautens/*The Toronto Star*; **p. 338** Eyewire; **p. 343** Romilly Lockyer/ Getty Images/Image Bank; **p. 345** Tannis Toohey/*The Toronto Star*; **p. 348** Philippe Landreville/Supreme Court of Canada; **p. 351** Keith Brofsky/PhotoDisc; **p. 355** Paul Chiasson/CP Picture Archive; **p. 357** Peter Power/CP Picture Archive; **p. 359** Stephen Simpson/ Getty Images/FPG; **p. 364** Carlos Amat/CP Picture Archive; **p. 370** Getty Images/Image Bank; **p. 371** Jim Corwin/Getty Images/Stone; **p. 372** Greg Agnew/CP Picture Archive; **p. 373** John Major/CP Picture Archive; **p. 377** Bill Ivy/Ivy Images; **p. 380** Susan Bradnam/CP Picture Archive; **p. 382** Tom Braid/CP Picture Archive; **p. 388** David Moll/CP Picture Archive; **p. 390** Ryan Remiorz/CP Picture Archive; **p. 392** Dick Hemingway Photographs; **p. 394** Kim Stallknecht/CP Picture Archive; **p. 397** Mike Slaughter/CP Picture Archive; **p. 399** Jeffrey Sylvester/ Getty Images/FPG; **p. 400** Randy Quan/*The Toronto Star*; **p. 407** CP Picture Archive; **p. 408** Dave Olecko/ CP Picture Archive; **p. 412** JLB/CP Picture Archive; **p. 413** (left) Courtesy of Angela and Michael Burrows; (bottom right) Frank Gunn/ CP Picture Archive; (top right) John Kenney/CP Picture Archive; **p. 420** Peter Lee/*The Record* (Kitchener); **p. 421** CP Picture Archive; **p. 423** Dick Hemingway Photographs; **p. 425** Denis Pacquin/CP Picture Archive; **p. 426** Kevin Frayer/CP Picture Archive; **p. 430** Rhonda Sidney/PhotoEdit; **p. 436** Steve Skjold/PhotoEdit; **p. 437** Ward Perrin/*The Vancouver Sun*; **p. 439** Will Hart/PhotoEdit; **p. 441** Courtesy of Mas Kikuta; **p. 442** Roy Antal/CP Picture Archive; **p. 446** Phil Snel/CP Picture Archive; **p. 450** AL Harvey/Slide Farm; **p. 155** Myrleen Ferguson Cate/PhotoEdit; **p. 461** (top) Ward Perrin *The Vancouver Sun*; (bottom) *The Toronto Star*; **pp. 462, 464** Dick Hemingway Photographs; **p. 473** Getty Images/FPG; **p. 487** Jacques Boissinot/CP Picture Archive; **p. 488** Bill Ivy/Ivy Images; **p. 493** Felicia Martinez/PhotoEdit; **p. 497** Bernard Brault/CP Picture Archive; **pp. 498, 501** Dick Hemingway Photographs; **p. 504** CP Picture Archive; **p. 507** Bill Ivy/Ivy Images; **p. 515** Corbis/ Magma; **p. 516** Mark Richards/PhotoEdit.

Cartoons

p. 2 Reprinted with special permission of King Features Syndicate; **p. 76** Reprinted with special permission of King Features Syndicate; **p. 134** Reprinted with permission—The Toronto Star Syndicate; **p. 161** Reprinted with special permission of King Features Syndicate; **p. 196** © Tribune Media Services, Inc. All rights reserved. Reprinted with permission; **p. 211** © The New Yorker Collection 2000 David Sipress from cartoonbank.com. All Rights Reserved; **p. 243** Reprinted with special permission of King Features Syndicate; **p. 389** Reprinted with special permission of King Features Syndicate; **p. 416** Reprinted with special permission of King Features Syndicate; **p. 449** Reprinted with special permission of King Features Syndicate; **p. 480** HERMAN® is reprinted with permission from LaughingStock Licensing Inc., Ottawa, Canada. All rights reserved; **p. 490** Reprinted with special permission of King Features Syndicate.

Literary Credits

Statistics Canada information is used with the permission of the Minister of Industry or Minister responsible for Statistics Canada. Information on the availability of the wide range of data from Statistics Canada can be obtained from Statistics Canada's Regional Offices at **http://www.statcan.ca**. Its toll-free access number is 1-800-263-1136.

p. 16 "MacIsaac discharged for fiddling with pot," as appeared in *The Globe and Mail,* August 23, 2001 © The Canadian Press; **p. 87** "Calgary teen to appeal transfusion ruling" by Charlie Gillis, *National Post Online,* February 22, 2002. Reprinted with permission from *National Post*; **p. 110** "Chief Justice urges students to value Canada's diversity" by Harold Levy, *The Toronto Star,* January 30, 2002. Reprinted with permission—The Toronto Star Syndicate; **p. 114** "Put an end to retirement at 65" by Richard Brennan, *The Toronto Star,* May 18, 2001. Reprinted with permission —The Toronto Star Syndicate; **p. 116** Courtesy of Alberta Human Rights and Citizenship Commission; **p. 141** Used by permission of B.C. Crime Stoppers Advisory Board; **p. 146** "Father jailed in death of son left unsupervised" by Mary Jo Laforest, *The Toronto Star,* May 3, 2001. © Mary Jo Laforest, The Canadian Press; **p. 181** "Judges to receive plain-language guidelines for instructing juries" by Janice Tibbets, *National Post,* August 13, 2001, p. A6. Reprinted with permission from *National Post*/Southam News; **p. 201** "Forensic test dashes hopes of prisoner" by Kirk Makin, *The Globe and Mail,* July 21, 2002, p. A9. Reprinted with permission from *The Globe and Mail*; **p. 220** "Voyeurism laws to get fresh look at meeting" by Daniel LeBlanc, *The Globe and Mail,* September 5, 2001, p. A4. Reprinted with permission from *The Globe and Mail*; **p. 225** (top) from the Statistics Canada Web site at <www.statcan.ca/Daily/English/991007/d991007b.htm>; **p. 225** (bottom) Statistics Canada publication "Canadian Crime Statistics," Catalogue 85-205, 1999; **p. 231** Statistics Canada publication "Juristat," Catalogue 85-002, 1999; **p. 254** "Killer not responsible for Smith's death" by Dave Rogers, *Ottawa Citizen,* April 30, 1997 © Dave Rogers, *Ottawa Citizen,* and "Smith killing avoidable, irate widow insists" by Dave Rogers, *Ottawa Citizen,* May 1, 1997. © Dave Rogers, *Ottawa Citizen*; **p. 267** "Identical duffel bag a 'decoy,' drug trial told," by Farrell, August 7, 1997. Reprinted with permission—The Toronto Star Syndicate; **p. 286** © Queens Printer for Ontario, 2002; **p. 291** Adapted from "Changing Lenses" by Howard Zehr, Herald Press, Scottdale, PA 15683. Used by permission; **p. 294** Adapted from "World Prison Population List," *Research Findings No. 88,* Home Office Research Development and Statistics Development and Statistics Directorate (U.K.) © Crown copyright. Used by permission; **p. 298** Courtesy of *The Hamilton Spectator*; **p. 299** Reproduced with the permission of the Minister of Public Works and Government Services Canada, 2001; **p. 308** "Youths and adults charged in criminal incidents, Criminal Code and federal statutes, by sex." From the Statistics Canada Web site <http://www.statcan.ca/english/Pgdb/State/Justice/legal14.htm>; **p. 312** From "Victims rights advocate entering politics" by Ian Bailey, Canadian Press, March 20,1997. © The Canadian Press; **p. 314** Adapted from "Youth Legislation: A Chronology," Justice Department; **p. 319** Adapted from N. Bala, *Canadian Youth Justice Law* (2002, Irwin Law); **p. 345** "The Early Ones" from "Globe Interactive" Web page, November 13, 2001, p. A20. Reprinted with permission from *The Globe and Mail*; **p. 365** NEWS OF THE WEIRD © by Chuck Shepherd. Reprinted with permission of UNIVERSAL PRESS SYNDICATE. All rights reserved; **p. 391** Reprinted by permission of Carswell, a division of Thomson Canada Limited; **p. 420** "With this doughnut I thee wed" by Eugene McCarthy. Reprinted with permission from *The Record* (Kitchener); **p. 423** From the Statistics Canada Web site <www.statcan.ca/english/census96/oct14/fam.htm>; **p. 427** "Quebec considers same sex unions" by Rheal Seguin, *The Globe and Mail,* December 8, 2001, p. A12. Reprinted with permission from *The Globe and Mail*; **p. 445** Cristin Schmitz, Southam News; **p. 478** "Crime doesn't rule out claim" by Elizabeth Thompson, *The Gazette,* March 9, 2002. Used by permission of *The Gazette* (Montreal); **p. 496** "Trucking contractor died, but not the contracted" by Philip Hope, *Western Report,* December 21, 1998, vol. 13, no. 48, p. 20. Reprinted with permission from Report Newsmagazine; **pp. 519–523** Department of Canadian Heritage. Reproduced with the permission of the Minister of Public Works and Government Services Canada, 2002.

References

Bala, Nicholas. *Young Offenders Law.* Toronto: Irwin Law, 1997.
Bala, Nicholas. *Canadian Youth Justice Law.* Toronto: Irwin Law, 2002.
Fodden, Simon R. *Family Law.* Toronto: Irwin Law, 1999.
Kerr, Margaret, JoAnn Kurtz, and Laurence M. Olivo. *Canadian Tort Law in a Nutshell.* Toronto: Carswell, 1997.
Osborne, Philip H. *The Law of Torts.* Toronto: Irwin Law, 2000.